UNDERSTANDING OUR WORLD
An integral ontology

Each age, it is found, must write its own books;
or rather, each generation for the next succeeding.
The books of an older period will not fit this.

The preamble of thought, the transition through which it
passes from the unconscious to the conscious, is action.
Only so much do I know, as I have lived.

Thinking is the function.
Living is the functionary. ...This is a total act.
Thinking is a partial act.

Ralph Waldo Emerson, *The American Scholar*, 1837

UNDERSTANDING OUR WORLD
An integral ontology

HENDRIK HART

UNIVERSITY
PRESS OF
AMERICA

LANHAM • NEW YORK • LONDON

Copyright © 1984 by

University Press of America,™ Inc.

4720 Boston Way
Lanham, MD 20706

3 Henrietta Street
London WC2E 8LU England

Library of Congress Cataloging in Publications Data

Hart, Hendrik.
   Understanding our world.

   (Christian studies today)
   "Co-published by arrangement with the Institute for
Christian Studies, Ontario, Canada"—T.p. verso
   Bibliography: p.
   1. Ontology. I. Title. II. Series.
BD311.H28 1984   111   84-17238
ISBN 0-8191-4257-3 (alk. paper)
ISBN 0-8191-4258-1 (pbk. : alk. paper)

All University Press of America books are produced on acid-free
paper which exceeds the minimum standards set by the National
Historical Publications and Records Commission.

For
Evan Runner,
besides whom there is no one
to whom this book
could have been dedicated,
in appreciation for
times past

Contents

Acknowledgments

MOST OF THE MATERIAL IN THIS BOOK is the crystallization of fifteen years of course work in systematic philosophy at the Institute for Christian Studies in Toronto. I am aware that more justice can be done to this material than I have done to it in this book. But the development of a philosophical paradigm is a communal effort, and therefore the presentation of the work of one member of a community is at best incomplete. Further, it is clear to me that my conceptualizations continue to develop, so that presentation of them in this form at best represents my views at the moment of writing. That nevertheless I am willing at this stage to make my contribution public is due to the encouragement and support I have received over the years from others in my work community.

This book is literally the fruit of four very formative years at Calvin College in Grand Rapids, Michigan, with H. Evan Runner as a teacher. Whatever I believe to be of significance in the book I somehow learned from him. Hence the dedication.

I am deeply grateful to the Senior Members and Junior Members— my colleagues and students—at the Institute for Christian Studies. They have not only criticized my views, but have also claimed to have benefited from them and have encouraged me to share them in printed form.

Others have also supported me. Peter A. Schouls and Arthur F. Holmes have read through all of an earlier version and have made countless valuable suggestions and criticisms. John Van Dyk and Nicholas P. Wolterstorff have read parts of the manuscript and have also suggested many improvements. The latter has also taught me much as a Christian working in the analytic tradition.

In addition, I owe much to the Institute for Christian Studies. Without its supportive and stimulating environment my sustained effort over fifteen years would have been unthinkable.

I owe a different kind of debt to my wife and children. They are justly persuaded that the writing of books is an academic's normal duty, rather than a legitimate excuse for neglecting one's family. They have tried not only to get me to agree, but also to get me to practice accordingly. In this they have only been partly successful. I do agree, but I'm still learning. For their continuing support and patience while I learn I am deeply grateful.

Finally, I must thank my editors, especially Don Sedgwick, who have helped me to write so that others can read; and various typists, especially Betty Polman who typed almost the entire final version.

Hendrik Hart
Toronto, Autumn 1983

Note on Terms and References

Glossary

As always when an unfamiliar paradigm is introduced, many terms and concepts are at first difficult to grasp. This is especially the case when familiar terms are used to name unfamiliar concepts. The almost irresistable tendency then is to read such terms as meaning what one has always taken them to mean. For that reason I have made a Glossary of most of the important terms I use. I recommend its frequent use for readers who are unfamiliar with the paradigm in which I work.

Literature

When in the text or the notes I refer to other literature, the references are in abbreviated form. Full references are to be found in the Bibliography. When I refer to a work by using a letter symbol (e.g., UPD, 59) the symbol can be found in the Bibliography as the last item of the entry for that work. Where text and Bibliography combined make it clear which author and which work are meant, only a page number will be given for reference.

Introduction

THIS BOOK IS AN ATTEMPT to promote Christian philosophical think-ing. My aim is to contribute to the renewal of systematic philosophy as a discipline whose purpose is to reflect on the unity, totality, and coherence of the world's general structure or, to put it differently, my aim is to construct an integral ontology. Though this work has a strongly religious context, I wish this book to be received as a work of philosophy—philosophical themes treated in a philosophical manner. It is nevertheless true that philosophy, perhaps more directly than other disciplines, draws upon deeper intentions and firmer assump-tions than can be rationally justified. Those intentions and assump-tions which underlie this text arise from my adherence to the Chris-tian tradition. I am aware of this, and at the end I will be explicit about how I affirm the Christian faith and how I understand my beliefs to shape my philosophical work. However, it would be a mistake to view this book as a work of theology.

I accept Stephan Körner's claim that "metaphysics aims at the exhibition of implicitly accepted categorial frameworks," and in keeping with this, the chapters which follow are an attempt to sketch a metaphysic or ontology dependent on a Christian worldview.[1] In a recent volume Arthur F. Holmes has appealingly set forth the main tenets of such a worldview.[2] I intend here to make explicit a general categorial framework, that is, a framework concerning the most general structures of our world, which I believe is consistent with a worldview like that presented by Holmes. If Holmes is right in saying that worldviews are needed to promote integrality in life, to help us clarify our deepest aims and intentions, and to guide us in our think-ing or whatever else we may be doing,[3] then the philosophical ex-plication of a general categorial framework implied in a worldview is needed to integrate scholarship and to relate it integrally to the rest of human culture.

Each in their own way, Thomas Kuhn, Michael Polanyi, and
Jürgen Habermas have done much to promote the idea that the
scholarly construction of theoretical models depends on factors ex-
traneous to scholarship. Another way of saying this may be that
scholarship itself is constitutively more than pure ratiocination and
observation. But it is likely that most academics are not prepared to
accept religious faith as a legitimate constituent of genuine scholarship. I am pursuaded, however, that if Christians are to participate in
the development of scholarship as Christians and to contribute to the
cultural significance of science in an integral manner, the elucidation
of an ontology that is implied in and at the same time guided by a
Christian worldview is a task that needs to be taken up.

I wish, then, to clarify certain elementary concepts that constitute the minimal requirements of a general categorial framework.
None of these concepts can stand in isolation and, consequently, they
are not treated independently. Each concept is explored in the assumed context of the others. The framework itself is a simple one.[4] I
hold that our empirical universe is an ordered world which consists of
individual things exhibiting properties and existing in relation to one
another. These propertied and related things are creatures who have
their origin in a Creator who determines their nature.[5]

To speak of Creator and creatures presents problems. If what I
am trying to do is, as Anthony Quinton characterizes it, "an attempt
to arrive by rational means at a general picture of the world," it may
be objected that one comes to accept the reality of a Creator by faith
and not by argument.[6] One may admit the presence of elements in a
metaphysic which "do not admit of justification by argument," as
Quinton does. But one might then stipulate, as he also does, that these
elements "are justified by universal acceptance."[7] Belief in a Creator
certainly does not enjoy such acceptance. I agree that philosophy
should primarily be argument. But I also submit that faith plays a
crucial role in philosophical argument, even though I accept that this
should not convert philosophy into confession. I have dealt with this
problem in the following manner. I have tried to keep explicit discussion of religious beliefs out of the main body of the text as much as
possible. But in order to be fair to the fact that in my own thought
these beliefs always played a guiding role, I have appended a discussion of them at the end. That discussion is not philosophical and it is
not intended to be. Nor is it theological in the sense of responsible
academic theology. It is, rather, a presentation of beliefs which did in
fact guide my thinking, and so are referred to as prescientific, stated in
such a manner that their relevance to my thought will be apparent.[8]

It is clear that I depend on a concept of rationality that is not generally accepted, certainly not by the dominant schools of thought. And indeed, it is my conviction that one of the more crucial tasks of philosophy today is a radical reorientation in our view of rationality. But this involves another conviction, namely, that rather than leaving reason with the task of telling us what the world is really like, we have the prior task of orienting ourselves in the world in order to become aware of the role played by reason in that world. In philosophy, epistemology needs an ontological framework, more than ontology needs to be epistemically justified.[9] In philosophy after the classical Greek period the primacy of ontology was gradually replaced by the primacy of epistemology. We need to recover from this episte-mological turn in Hellenistic thought between Aristotle and Plotinus. Though partly held in check during the Middle Ages, this turn emerged to become our culture's dominant point of view in the years between Descartes and Kant. Therefore, to undo its damage we need to explore epistemology in the context of ontology, and ontology in the context of the history of our deepest convictions.[10] So I aim here at an ontology in touch with the commitments of philosophers relevant to the world they live in, to the history of their culture, and to the priorities of their time.[11]

Christians in philosophy in North America have recently wit-nessed an upsurge of interest in their task as believers.[12] But I am not aware of any attempt here to offer a model for a general categorial framework which explicitly depends on the Christian tradition.[13] It is important that such an attempt be made, since without such a tool Christian scholars lack the means to integrate their variety of con-cerns in a truly academic manner. Such an attempt is also important for historical reasons. The history of our culture can be seen as the history of emancipation and secularization. Seen in that way, the history of our culture becomes the story of the quest for ultimate human authority and autonomy, the story of the quest for liberation from all subjection. In that story the role of reason has been crucial,[14] since human autonomy has predominantly been viewed as rational autonomy.

Both humanism (the secular religion of human emancipation) and naturalism (the secular religion of nature) have often been characterized as rational or scientifically respectable positions. This is related to the fact that the epistemological turn in philosophy was much more than an isolated philosophical development. It was, rather, the start of Western culture's devotion to reason. It was, in fact, a function of the history of secularization and emancipation.

And neither the worldviews that support this history nor the general categorial frameworks implied in them are compatible with the Christian faith.[15] Therefore, the development of an alternate general conceptual framework is an important demand.

In secular philosophy itself there is now suspicion of a devotion to reason that cannot be rationally justified.[16] But in that philosophy there remains a devotion to reason, even if without rational justification.[17] This devotion is another reason why it is important to develop an ontology in which the legitimate role of rationality, namely, to provide our conceptual grasp of the structure of things, is both recognized and relativized. The development of such an ontology requires abandoning the practice of rational justification which is current in the dominant philosophical paradigms of analytic philosophy.[18] This does not mean abandoning truth in philosophy, but only recognizing that what is true is not the same as what is rationally justified.[19]

The development of a general categorial framework will in part depend on the acceptability of rational conclusions. But it will also depend on the responsibility of personal decisions. No matter which general conceptual scheme we choose, any such scheme will in its most fundamental and general concepts yield logically unacceptable consequences.[20] A decision to maintain the scheme we have chosen as our own incorporates extralogical factors such as one's personal history, one's culture, the scholarly tradition in which one was raised, and so on. Once we have chosen certain fundamental concepts as our own, their incorporation in a general conceptual framework implies that we will be logically compelled to accept certain conclusions and reject others. Some questions which in relation to my ultimate commitment are important for all scholarship are whether or not the world is ordered, whether or not that order has any constancy, and whether or not that order has an origin. But logical argument will not finally or by itself provide answers to these questions. Ultimate, or religious, choices and commitments are unavoidable here.[21]

Even so, no actually articulated general conceptual model should be expected to account adequately for all that it tries to grasp. Apart from the fact that no truth is timeless, certainly no conceptual model can be such a truth. But that limitation need not frighten us from attempting to articulate an inclusive model for contemporary use.[22] The Western worship of reason has long led us to believe that we could clear up the problems of rationality by being more rational. This has led us to the present debacle of a shattered world in scholarship and of a preoccupation with the isolated and trivial in philosophy. But philosophy can, it seems to me, give up the worship of reason and turn again to a concern for totality and coherence in the realm of conceptual experience.

Recognition of the relative usefulness of a general conceptual framework requires an open declaration of the basic orientations to which such a model is relative.[23] My own statement of religious orientation, without which what follows may well be thinkable but without which it has in fact not been thought, can be found at the end in the Appendix. In this Introduction I will only say a few words about the philosophical influences which guided me.

All my formal philosophical training has been oriented to Calvinian Christianity.[24] This Christian tradition is philosophically best known for its rejection of the ultimate autonomy of reason.[25] The most elaborate philosophical statement of this position in modern times is Herman Dooyeweerd's *A New Critique of Theoretical Thought*. That work, the large body of literature it engendered, and the philosophical tradition to which it gave rise have fundamentally shaped my outlook in philosophy.[26]

A second influence has been the work of John Dewey, for which I have deep though critical respect.[27] The catalyst I needed to reconcile these two very different influences I found in Michael Polanyi's *Personal Knowledge*. Finally, though I received most of my formal training in the continental European tradition, I have spent the last fifteen years working in a climate dominated by analytic philosophy. Years of personal dialogue with persons sharing in that tradition have also shaped my thought and resulted in my style of doing philosophy as a curious mixture of continental European and analytic approaches.

In this book I consider the correlated pair of ordered world and world order to be the most fundamental relationship which philosophy needs to treat.[28] This theme has surfaced in Western philosophy in various ways. At times, it has been treated in the context of the problem of necessity and at other times in relation to causality.[29] If world order is seen as essential order and ordered world as concrete existence, then we often see the discussion of this relation surface in talk about universals (essences) and individuals (concrete existents). In keeping with this, I use the traditional problem of universals to introduce my discussion of ordered world and world order. This takes place in the first two chapters.

The problem of universals, however, has also been perceived as the problem of substance and attribute. Therefore, since talk about universals has also been related to talk about predicable attributes, the next two chapters present a framework for dealing with what I believe is the next major problem of philosophy, namely, the problem of the two basic constituents of the empirical world, particulars and their properties, or, as I will refer to them, functors and their functions.

Then follow two chapters which deal with the fact that things in this world are related. I deal especially with the relations of part and whole, of subject and object, and of the structured interrelation of wholes. I also deal with unity and diversity, totality and coherence, and time.

Thus, in the first six chapters I explain an ontological model which may be summarized simply as follows: Our empirical world is ordered and consists of propertied particulars in relationship.

In a concluding chapter I develop some elements of the philosophical anthropology that is part of my overall framework. The reason for its inclusion is that philosophical reflection needs human self-reflection; ontology implies anthropology. How we see the world depends partly on how we see ourselves.

At this point in the book I believe that I have reached the limits to which the methods of academic philosophy can properly take us. Beyond those limits lie the important ultimate convictions which are the roots of the thought developed within those limits. The Appendix deals with these roots and concludes the book.

My intent in this book is not primarily to argue that a particular point of view is more valid than others, nor to address a particular philosophical problem in order to contribute to its solution. Rather, my primary aim is to expound and explain an ontology which may help us to understand our world in relation to central beliefs of Christianity and in a philosophically responsible manner. Consequently, I have not depended on justifying the model with arguments in order to make it acceptable. Rather, I have tried to demonstrate that the model, if it were clear and coherent, is acceptable in the construction of a unifying view of the world in philosophical terms using concepts consistent with a Christian worldview. Whether or not my views can sustain objections from other points of view is not unimportant, but it has not been an explicit concern in this book. Nor have I tried to deal adequately with each theme as though the section dealing with that theme were a separate treatise. Instead I have explored any theme only in so far as it was needed to fit the total picture. That total picture, my philosophical understanding of our world, is what I have tried to clarify.

One device I have used to clarify new concepts needs explanation. Sometimes I have assigned a name to a concept already in use by others for naming another concept. In order to communicate the sense of my concept I have often used synonyms or I have referred to the names other philosophers have used to indicate what I express with my concepts. I hope this occasional use of different names for one and the same concept will help to convey its new sense.

I have written for any serious reader who might be interested in the possibility of a philosophical framework implied by a Christian worldview. In my experience of the last two decades such readers are found not only in the company of professional philosophers, but also among students and teachers sincerely interested in the relevance of their Christian faith for their academic interests. As a result I have tried to make the book accessible for advanced college and university students who have taken some philosophy and who can count on the assistance of an interested teacher. This choice has certainly had an impact on the way I have related to existing philosophical literature, on the examples and illustrations I have used, and on what I thought could or could not be assumed.

Chapter I
The Problem of Universals
and the Nature of Things

1.0 Introduction to the Problem

OUR UNIVERSE, THE EMPIRICAL WORLD of time and space, is populated by little girls, white-tailed deer, yellow lady slippers, planets and many other things. We can attribute what may be called qualities, or functions, or properties to all of these entities in our world and we can say that they relate to each other. Little girls are cute and have mothers. White-tailed deer are fast and eat leaves. Yellow lady slippers have brown spots on their petals and need light. Planets move around the sun. We can record countless situations that always have these three elements: *things* with *attributes* in *relation*. Little girls feeling warm as they are cuddled by their mothers. White-tailed deer standing motionless as they listen to a sound. Yellow lady slippers hanging low as they bend under the weight of unexpectedly late snow. Planets never erring in their path as they revolve in the solar system.

In the history of philosophy there is a long tradition of people talking about our universe in terms of these three: first, what we may call substances, or things, or functors, or entities, or particulars; second, what we may call attributes, or qualities, or functions, or properties; and third, relations.[1] I will follow this tradition and I will refer to these three components in our world as *functors functioning in relationship*. My world hypothesis or ontology, which is and has been the world hypothesis or ontology of many others, is that functors functioning in relationship, or what others have called substances with qualities relating to each other or particulars with properties interrelating, are all that there is in our temporal, empirical world.

Nevertheless, in spite of this agreement among philosophers, there is widespread disagreement over how this hypothesis is to be interpreted and worked out. One of the crucial issues giving rise to much controversy is this. No two people are alike. Prosecutors make much of this fact when they present fingerprints as evidence. Yet at the same time, Ronald Reagan, Lech Walesa, Golda Meir, Eva Peron, and many others are or were very much alike. For they are or were people, all of them; known and followed as leaders, all of them. As people they are or were unique. And as people they are or were alike. Here then is the problem: How can they or anything else be both alike and unlike, similar and dissimilar, the same and different? How is it possible that things in our world are all *one* (unique) of *a kind* (the same)?

Indeed, what I have said is true not only of people, but of all functors. Moreover, it is true of functions and relations as well. No two wines have identical tastes. But all wines have the taste of wine. My wife's and my marriage is uniquely different from the marriages of friends and relatives we know. Yet they and we are all married. Whatever there is in our empirical world is both unique and of some kind.[2] It has the same nature as others of that kind. Functors typically reveal the kind of which they are in the arrangement of their functional complexity and relationships, in the array of their properties or qualities and of their interrelations. Functions are also of kinds. My lips, the stone in my college ring, the brick of our home, and many other things have the same kind of color. Finally, relations too come in kinds, such as friendships, distances, and being indebted.

When we have a word to name a kind, we can use it to refer to whatever is of that kind. I am called human, Maria Callas is called human, John Paul II is called human, and the old woman next door is called human. A concept in which we grasp the nature or structure of a kind can be used to understand whatever is of that kind. If I have a concept of fun I can understand people referring to a circus as fun, a party as fun, and a joke as funny. I will also understand that a gallbladder operation is no fun. And also that my cat is not human, if I have a concept of human.

An old and persistent problem in philosophy is the attempt to deal with things being both unique and similar. How is it possible that in a world of individual and unique particulars, we can say the same thing about many different things? How can we, to put it more technically, predicate one and the same thing of many different things? Some people have said that the only way to account for this is to say that there are more entities than the three I admitted into my world hypothesis. These other entities are universals.[3] One and the same universal can be predicated of many different particulars. The unique phenomena in our universe are alike in so far as they resemble, instantiate, exemplify, or participate in such universals. Others have said that the words or concepts that name or grasp what is similar in the world are enough to account for such similarity.[4] There are those who claim that functors are unique, while functions and relations are the same.[5] There are also those who believe that all three are both the same and unique.[6] There is further disagreement about whether whatever it is that accounts for similarity in this world is a part or dimension of what is unique, or whether the sameness originates in another realm, separate from our empirical world.

The issues that have arisen over this problem are many, varied, complex, and interwoven in different ways. Two of these complexities I will distinguish very clearly in this book. I will deal with the problem of particulars and their attributes (in the third and fourth chapters) as a different problem from that of particulars in relation to something universal (in the first two chapters). The latter problem in my view is the genuine problem of universals and it has to do with essences, kinds, or natures; and with the necessity or possibility they bring about in particular existences, in concrete entities of some kind, in realities having a certain nature. The problem of substances and attributes, of particulars and qualities, is one of particular substances in relation to particular qualities; both of which are, in turn, of some kind.

I hold that much that is irresolvable in these problems depends on one ingredient of dealing with them. That ingredient is every philosopher's taking seriously the question of the existence of universals. Are there universals? Do universals exist? Need we admit universals into our universe in addition to, over and above, or independent of and separate from unique particulars?[7] Besides or in addition to the unique green in Henk Krijger's painting "The Survivors" which hangs in the hallway outside of my office, is there also a property green which is universal? Or even: is a property, also the green in that painting, just a universal? And can such a property be a universal which exists alongside of the unique individual whose property it is?[8] Is there a whole realm of such immutable and eternal universal entities?[9] These questions, I submit, lead us in the wrong direction. No answer I have ever read to this sort of approach to the problem has satisfied me.

Yet there is a real and important problem here. I agree with nominalists that in our empirical world of space and time there are only unique functors with unique functions in unique relations. Neither in this world nor in another are there entities called universals. But I disagree that words or concepts will do to account for what

is similar in functors, functions, and relations. Empirical entities that
are universal kinds, properties and relations will not do. But words or
concepts will not suffice either. Words or concepts refer to something,
they name or grasp something. Perpahs it is a mistake to ask: What
empirical entity do they name or grasp? Yet we still need to ask: What
is their reference?

But why is this problem real and important at all? One answer
could be this. If our experience of sameness were not real, if we could
not account for what makes things similar (i.e., if we had no way of
explaining the nature of structure of things), then science would be
fantasy. But science is no fantasy. And science does not deal with the
particular entities that populate our world. It deals with kinds, properties, relations, and laws, in so far as these are the same in things.
And we should try to account for the obvious success of science,
especially since what science tells us about the nature of things allows
us to deal more successfully with those things. What then is the reality
of the things science deals with?[10]

What is generally referred to as the nature of things may not be
in a separate world of immutable and eternal entities. But the nature
of a thing does seem to have to do with its identity, continuity, and
stability, and with whether or not particular entities are proper instances of their kinds. Knowing the nature of things, scientifically or
otherwise, allows us to evaluate and critically assess many realities of
our experience. Thus, realism in social theory may lead to conservatism, but it may also lead to pertinent criticism. Nominalism in
social theory may promote more flexibility, but it may also lead to
anarchy.[11]

So, though I deny the existence of the Platonic Host of eternal
and immutable properties, kinds, numbers, natures, states, and similar entities, I agree with the realist that something more than the
existence of particulars in our empirical world is needed to account
for the nature of these particulars. And though I deny that our world
is a closed natural system of particulars, I agree with the nominalist
that no existing entities in our empirical world are universals (such as
natures, or kinds, or qualities, and the like). Although I do want to
find a solution to the problem of how one thing can be both unique
and the same in relation to other things, I want to avoid the traditional problem of existing universal entities.

Though I reject existing entities called universals, I nevertheless
also reject accounts of the world in terms of particulars only. Consequently, I will be perceived as siding more with realism than with
nominalism. And indeed, since nominalism is not intended as a

positive account of the nature of things, I do not further explore nominalist views. That I do look into the problem of universals in this chapter is due to the fact that when dealing with that problem the tradition has dealt with a reality which I acknowledge. Those who have dealt with the problem of universals are bound to provide important clues to our understanding of the nature of things.

In this chapter and the next I shall deal with the problem of how to account for the fact that things are both unique and similar to other things. I shall approach that problem as the problem of the order of reality. It has traditionally been treated as the problem of essences, kinds, or natures; often in relation to the problem of necessity. In this first chapter I explore traditional approaches as well as the testimony of nonexperts who refer to what have been called universals. I hope to find some clues there to the approach we may have to take. In the second chapter I formulate a solution to the problem. Then follow two chapters on what are traditionally known as particulars and qualities, which I call functors and functions. And after that come two chapters on relations. The last chapter then deals with special problems related to the place of humankind in our world.

So in the first section of this chapter I explore some traditional problems that have been raised by those who have especially looked into the problem of universals. But I am even more interested in examining the relevant things scholars have said about universals explicitly in contexts not designed to deal with the traditional problem of universals. I expect that exploring this will yield helpful clues for the simple reason that these people do not discuss universals as an isolated issue, but as a real problem in relation to other perplexities they face. So in the second section of this chapter I look at nonexperts commenting on what traditionally are known as universals.

1.1   Initial Explorations

These initial explorations may not only provide clues to a solution of the problem of accounting for both uniqueness and sameness in the world, but they may also help us understand how the traditional approach to the problem of universals leads to unsatisfactory solutions. In these explorations my own view will affect the discussion at every stage, for I will be raising certain problems and giving a certain slant that might not normally be encountered in the context of looking at universals.

It is my view that there exist no universals such as are talked about in the traditional debate. It does make sense to say that bicycles, plants, horses, and paper clips *exist*. In the universe of discourse which it makes sense to talk about the *existence* of these things, one could legitimately raise the question: Do plants exist on Mars? But it is my view that within the same universe of discourse one cannot legitimately ask: Do universals exist? Yet, as I have said, I am not a nominalist, and I do subscribe to the *reality* of properties, predicables, relations, species, standards and social structures. What I call "reality" encompasses more than what I use *existence* to name.

The view which I will develop is that whatever exists in our world exists as creature. And there are no creatures called universals. In the world of really existing creatures there are pears and apples, rabbits and rats, Canadians and Swedes—but no universals. There is no class of things such that universals belong to that class. There is no kind or category of things such that "being a universal" is one such kind, which could then be instantiated in the universal "being a horse." "Being a universal" does not exist; it is nowhere instantiated. However, since I do not agree with the nominalists, the discussion in this section may seem somewhat artificial, for I cannot identify with any existing tradition in the discussion. Yet, in order to establish the relationship between the view of world and world order developed in the next chapter on the one hand, and the tradition concerning universals in the history of philosophy on the other, it will be necessary to try to move from a traditional discussion into one that breaks with the tradition at certain points.[12]

1.1.1   Do universals exist?

What is the tradition talking about? What is meant by a universal? Why not simply talk about universality? Universality is an easily distinguishable trait of certain relationships. It is not difficult to understand the expression "Today the search for a cure for cancer is universal" or the statement "The problem of food and energy is a universal one" or the sentence "Suffrage for women is not yet universally accepted." The meanings of *universal* and *universally* here are familiar: everywhere, all over, in all instances. Now, in relation to these meanings, what can be said about universals? We can say that in the case of all horses in all places and at all times it is true that every horse is a horse. One can truly predicate "being a horse" of any, every, and all horses at any and all times and in any and all places. But is there an entity "being a horse"? Can one even imagine such a thing?

"Being a horse" is one example of what is traditionally meant by a universal.[13] Universals can go by all sorts of names. "Being a horse" could also be called the concept "horse," or the predicate "horse," or the essence of a horse, or the nature of horses, or horseness, or the necessary structure of horses, or the kind "horse," or the general property complex of horses. But whatever a universal is called, the common referent is the subject of the universals debate.

The debate first of all concerns the real existence of predicables, qualities, kinds, properties, categories, relations, essences, necessary natures, exemplars, standards, laws, and the like. These all have the universal extension; that is to say, they apply to all things everywhere that belong to that kind or category or are subject to that standard. Do they exist in space and time? Do they exist apart from things that are of that kind? Do they exist apart from people thinking them? These are the questions. The *existence* of universals is probably more controversial than what they are. The latter may explain why both essences and qualities have been treated as universals and why the confusion has often gone unnoticed.

When philosophers ask whether a certain something exists, what sort of questions are they asking? Unicorns exist. For philosophers, "unicorn" is a concept of an imaginary being whose role is not without importance in the history of philosophy. Unicorns have existence in the imagination and as subjects of philosophical discourse. They do not have existence outside of that context. If, however, in some context unicorns can exist, is there anything that cannot exist? And if there is a sense in which unicorns can exist, couldn't the universal "horse" or "horseness" or "the horse itself" exist just as easily? It probably could. But if we allow unicorn to exist, we must recognize that we are then predicating existence of the imaginary creations of persons. Would that be enough when we discuss the problem of universals? No, it would not, for that would mean that we have accepted a more or less nominalist position. The issue in the realist-nominalist controversy is not whether products of the imagination can exist. It is, rather, whether universals exist apart from people thinking them and apart from things exemplifying them. Do universals exist separately, distinctly, by themselves in space and time?

Not all realists conceive of universals as existing in space and time. While Armstrong does conceive of them in this way, Loux does not. Perhaps all that realists need is to minimally assert that the existence of universals is part and parcel of the same world whose constituents include particulars. Some realists might also say that only the particulars are in space and time. That universals exist apart from and perhaps even independent of particulars is precisely what makes it possible to speak of them as spatial or temporal. Armstrong conceives of universals as existing always and only when they belong to particulars (USR2, 168). Loux, on the other hand, holds that properties exist apart from and independently of particulars. (See, e.g., SA, 96). So at least some realists say that there is such an entity as "being a unicorn" whether there are unicorns or not. Loux even holds that "being a unicorn" exists necessarily, forever, and without change. If this is the sort of thing a realist has in mind when she affirms the existence of universals, one might ask: Where are they? How are they there? Do they have weight? Can they be observed? What is their identity? What kind of independence do they have? Are they temporal or eternal? How are they to be distinguished from other existents? What do they share with all other existents so that they can all be called existents? Is it possible that they exist and that none of these questions are even applicable? If so, could we then even talk about universals?

We should resist the inclination to dismiss these questions as irrelevant and first look at the difference between what one might call easy existence problems and hard existence problems. We can speak of unproblematic existence: the existence of entities capable of independent action is unproblematic. Take a person, a horse, a flower, a planet, or an army as examples. Each exists in such a way that no normal person would have any difficulty with affirming its existence. Neither do we normally have any problem with the real existence of real events such that we can say of such events: "They are real; they really happened." The Battle of the Bulge and eclipses of the sun are real; they are event-like relations among existing things capable of action.

There are entities of a material kind, of a plant-like kind, of an animal-like kind, and of the human kind, and there are also events which occur in active relations among these entities. All of us have seen these, heard these, been involved with them, bought them, and otherwise experienced them. The entities have parts and functions. Human entities have arms which they may wave. Plants have roots with which they suck up liquids. And these entities are related to one another. A human being may reach out to a plant with her hands to pick it up. Entities, functions, parts, and relations are real. They happen; they occur; they exist.

Many of these unproblematic existents can be referred to simply by means of a noun—a woman, an arm, a greeting, a message, an accident. Thus we sometimes get the idea that nouns always refer to separate entities that are real, entities that really exist. But what about an entity like an odor? Does an odor exist? Are there smells? I do believe there are. If I sniff the air around me and the air carries certain minute particles, my nose picks up those particles and I will sense them. If I stand in that air long enough, I might even pick up that odor and take it home with me. But what is the odor? It is not my nose, and it is not the particles. The odor, in fact, never does exist by itself, for it is more like an event. When there is smelling going on, a particular way of perceiving, some particles are referred to as an odor. Odors exist because a person (an independent entity capable of action) uses his nose (a part) to sniff (function) particles (other entities) suspended in the air around him (relation). If a number of persons standing together are fairly normal and have ordinary noses and are sniffing fairly clean air near an orange blossom in bloom, the chances are that most will be able to recognize the odor and will recognize it as the same odor. They will all be able to refer to that event as the smelling of the orange blossom.

Well then, does an odor exist? Of course it does! But an odor is not quite the simple entity we might take it to be if we let the noun fool us. In other words, the odor is not quite as simple as the separate noun that names it. The noun points to a very complex relationship involving entities, parts, functions, and relationships. Odors do exist, but they do not exist in the same way in which people exist—or feet, or coughing. They are not simple entities or functions or parts. Still, they do exist. One can note them, identify them, and name them. It is not possible to paint them green or to tie ribbons around them. They are neither tall nor fat. On the other hand, one can like them, take them home, keep them in bottles, and write poems about them.

Now, could it perhaps be said that "universals" are like odors? Perhaps, for there are indeed things you can do with universals as well. You can conceive of them, name them, write books about them, and worry about their existence. And, like odors, they can be referred to by means of a noun. Then why do some people not object to the existence of odors whereas they do object to the notion that universals exist? What is difference between the smell of an orange blossom and "being the smell of an orange blossom"? One difference is that you can smell the smell of an orange blossom, but not "being the smell of an orange blossom." But if we can indeed do other things with universals, why make a big point of not being able to smell them? Why can't we admit the reality of things with which we can do this and that?

Perhaps the problem is that universals are supposed to have independent existence. This might mean that they must be more independent than odors, which are relationships. Universals might be thought to be more like trees. Trees have a relatively independent existence; at least, they exist quite independently from persons. Persons can relate to trees, and quite often they do. But even though not relating to trees would impoverish our existence, we do not *need* to relate to them—at least, not on many given occasions.[14] And the reverse is even more true: trees do not need people and would probably be better off without our kind of people. Thus trees do exist quite independently from people. Still, if we wish to experience a tree, we can. The existence of trees has never been much in doubt. However, whether we can experience independently existing universals is quite another matter.

But perhaps one can indeed experience universals. Is it possible that we deny such experiences because we conceive of experience too much in reductionistic terms? If experience is nothing more than sensory experience, it would indeed be hard to experience a universal. One can see, smell, hear, and touch horses, but one cannot see, smell, hear, and touch universals. On the other hand, we say we can sense *that* some things are the case about horses. In fact, this is something one can smell—and hear as well. We say: "I can hear that horses are coming near." Couldn't we analyze this sort of strongly sense-oriented experience and draw the conclusion that we can experience something common to all horses? Perhaps, but then is it not the analysis which picks out what is common, rather than the hearing? But what of that? Doesn't analysis also count as experience? Isn't the drawing of a conclusion a real activity?

Scientists draw conclusions about the existence of subatomic particles on the basis of other things that they do see or otherwise experience, even though they never actually see subatomic particles. Can't horses, therefore, be taken as evidence for the existence of "being a horse"? If we see more than one horse, don't we also see that these horses are the same sort of creatures? Don't we *see* a *sort* of thing when we see different horses? And if we do see it, may we then not conclude that "being a horse" must exist? What if we simply allow that universals are noticeable, distinguishable and identifiable, and on this basis conclude that somehow they are there? The objection might be raised that this would only allow the conceptual existence of universals, but this objection does not seem entirely valid. The fact that I have the concept of person in mind does not compel me to conclude that persons are conceptual only. One might even argue that because there is a concept "universal," there must be a universal to which this concept refers. But this would again open the door to the unicorns and the problems that come with them. Their conceptual existence, as has often been noted, does not give them so-called real existence.

There is one more issue that I want to raise in relation to the question whether universals exist in somewhat the same way as un-problematic existents. Realists who affirm such existence always insist that universals are exceptional existents. In some views they are standards or models or ideals for the rest of what exists. Yet they are unlike the copies of them in every possible way. In Michael Loux's view they are ingenerable, incorruptible, necessary beings (SA, 97). In all views, universals are irreducibly different from the particulars that exemplify universals, or that have universals as aspects of them, or that are cases of universals. There are very few things you can do to a horse that you can also do to "being a horse." Can you ride it? Stroke it? Comb it? This even goes for talking about it. One can talk about horses, and also about "being a horse," but the two kinds of conversation are hardly the same. You cannot say about both: "Let's feed it." If you engage in scholarly talk, the chances are that you are talking about the concept, and not about the actual horse.

Thus it appears that we can have the smell of a horse, the hunger of a horse, and the concept of a horse. But why should the concept refer to a very exceptional reality? Something that is apart from our conceiving—and even apart from there being any horse in particular? If this is the kind of reality to which conceiving points, is it then not true after all that what we have here is a very exceptional kind of reality? If universals are held by some to be standards *for* all that *exists* (except for themselves), *do* they then themselves exist? If *existence* in such a view requires a universal as a standard, do universals themselves then also require universals as standards? If not, in what sense then can they be said to *exist*?

From this brief discussion one thing emerges. Whatever it is that realists talk about, it seems just too difficult to accept that what are known as universals point to the existence of entities other than and in addition to little girls, white-tailed deer, yellow lady slippers, and heavenly bodies; entities other than and in addition to the delicate peach pink color of this girl's skin, the lightning speed with which this deer just now ran into that bush, the slight discoloration of the bottom leaf of this lady slipper, the actual temperature of that place on the moon where and at the exact moment when the first people landed; entities other than and in addition to the understanding between this girl and her mother, the relation between this deer's being near death and that snowmobiler's merciless chase of it three hours ago, the relation between this lady slipper's fresh appearance and the rain now coming down after it had been dry for so long, or the connection between our now better understanding Venus and the data sent back by Explorer. I, at least, do not believe that there exists an entity The

Little Girl, or The White-Tailed Deer, or The Yellow Lady Slipper. Nor do I subscribe to the existence of Delicate Peach Pink, Speed, Discoloration, or Temperature. At the same time, when people talk about what they have read in a book on North American mammals under the heading "white-tailed deer" they are right when they think that this heading refers to more than all the white-tailed deer that now exist, that ever did exist, or that ever might exist. And they are also right that this heading points to a *reality* which is more than just a linguistic convention or a widely held concept. What then is that reality?

1.1.2   Can universals be characterized?

I trust that my somewhat impressionistic remarks about the problem of the existence of universals have at least given rise to some idea of what I am talking about. The discussion was far too sketchy to give birth to a clear concept, but some sense of what the issue is should at least be present in the reader's mind at this point. If this is indeed the case, I can momentarily drop the problem of the *existence* of universals and come at the matter at hand from a little different angle by asking: What manner of reality is there to these so-called universals we have been talking about?

It seems entirely legitimate to raise such a question. I might ask a friend: "Do swobbles exist?" My friend might reply by asking: "What do you mean? I don't understand your question. What are they?" I might then say: "They are beings with four legs. In the past they were often used on farms to pull plows and wagons, and now they are used in races with or without carriages. Some people use them for show." My discussion partner would doubtless respond by saying: "Oh, sure, they exist; we call them horses." Thus it appears that we can describe something before deciding whether or not it exists. This still leaves open the possibility, of course, that given a certain description, the item described turns out not to exist—at least, not apart from the imagination of certain people.

To help us get away somewhat from the notion of universals as existing entities, I will focus now on what is meant by the universality of these so-called universals. Why consider whatever we are dealing with as universal? One characteristic that readily comes to the fore, no matter what meaning of the term *universal* is considered, is its peculiar relationship to a state of affairs that one might call *all*-inclusiveness. Universality has to do with *all* things, *every*where, at *all* times, and in *all* places. If there are horses, it seems clear that of every horse, wherever and whenever, we can say that it is a horse. That's true of all horses. Then what relation does universality have to "all"? Is it itself the "all"? Is universal simply the universe-of-all (whatever entities may be included)? Is the universal "horse" simply the universe-of-all horses? Or is the "all" different from what is universal? Do we see a connection here between the problem of universals on the one hand and the problem of the one and the many and the problem of the whole or a totality and its parts on the other hand?

Since I intend to deal with the problems of unity and diversity and of parts and wholes separately (see 6.2, and also 7.1 and 7.2 below), I will simply say at this point that I consider them to be different problems having to do with the unity of a diversity of distinctly different parts, functions, and relationships.[15] The problem of the universality of universals as I see it has to do not with unity in diversity, but with *sameness* in *all* the different entities to which what is called the universal relates. *All* different birds are *the same* in that *all* birds are *bird*. The problem of the one and the many in my view has to do with the fact that *one* and *the same* thing has *many different* parts or functions or aspects or relationships to it. Every bird is one whole, that is, a single entity, but it has many feathers, different body organs, two wings, and many more parts. The problem of how one entity is complex (i.e., is one and many) differs from the problem of how many entities can be similar. Though the two problems are related, they are different. So universality is not the same as either unity or wholeness.

What about the connection of universality with generality? Is universal the same as general? I don't think so. The two should not be confused, even though they are related. To say that people generally display racist attitudes is not the same as saying that they do so universally: there is an important difference. We might conceivably choose to understand the statement that people universally display racist attitudes to mean that people of every race and people in all countries and cultures and civilizations do so. This meaning would not necessarily have to be taken as covering all human beings everywhere and at all times—each and every person whatsoever, under any and every condition. In that case *universal* and *general* would mean the same. But the difference between these two terms shows up when we look at the following two statements: "Universally, people are either male or female" and "Generally, people are either male or female." The former statement has an acceptable meaning, but the latter does not. It is universally the case that well-formed persons are either male or female, but to say that this is generally so would be to misstate the truth.

Wolterstorff speaks of ontology as dealing with "the most general

structure of what there is" (UN, xii) and Quinton states that properties "are general and may apply to many things" (4). It would seem
that what these authors have in mind is universality not generality as
I have characterized it here. If the difference is merely one of terms
there is no problem. But since there are also authors who speak of
statistical laws as general laws and who are aware of the fact that
there are exceptions to such "laws," it can be confusing to refer to
universality as generality.[16] So I prefer to make a choice here. *General*
will mean: in virtually all cases, in almost all circumstances—but not
necessarily in every last one. *Universal* will mean: in all normal instances. Any instance in which it is not the case is therefore not a normal instance. Universality points to a standard for all normal instances, although this standard is not an automatic guarantee of a
good sample. *General* is more of a statistical term, while *universal* is
a term pointing to a standard which allows no exception.

So although universality, unity, wholeness, and generality all
have to do with the many, that is, with diversity, all three have different
relations to diversity. Knowing this helps us point to certain
characteristics which universality does *not* have in its relation to
"all." The "all" are not parts of the universal or functions of the
universal or aspects of the universal. The various horses in existence
are not part of the universal horse. The universal cannot be treated as
the unity of a single entity within which the "all" occurs as a diversity. Furthermore, the sense of "all" is a very strict one; it is very inclusive—completely so. It does not have the more or less character of
generality. Whatever is universally the case can be expected to be the
case in every instance of the "all."

But there is more that needs to become clear. One important
question in connection with the relation between "all" and universality is whether there is a difference between them. This problem surfaces in a comparable manner in the case of the one whole and the
many parts, although it is a different problem in that context. In both
cases, however, I take the view that an understanding of the difference between universality and "all," on the one hand, and between
whole and parts, on the other, is crucial. Every horse, universally and
without exception, is an instance of "being a horse."[17] It is true of each
and every horse that it is a horse. But is what all these horses are the
same as all these horses? Is universality just the class of all instances?
Every member of the class of all horses does exemplify "being a
horse." Is the universal "horse" just a name for or a concept of the
class of all instances? That is nominalism. A realist sees it differently.
I am here exploring what is said about universals by those who accept

them. "Being a horse" is neither itself a horse, nor is it all horses (cf. 2.5.6).

Is there any relation between universality and membership in a class? There could be. If the universal accounts for some things, one kind could have certain members in virtue of the fact that all those members are of the kind in question, that is, in virtue of the fact that they exemplify the same universal. One might then say that universality does not have membership but is a criterion for inclusion in a class or collection. Universality can then be understood in relation to classes and class membership, but not be fully explained in terms of them. The "all" with respect to which a universal is universal would be neither one of those "all" nor the same as those "all." The class of all horses would be a collection of entities whose "being horse" qualifies them for inclusion in this class. Although this class then includes whatever is so qualified, "being horse" is not that collection and does not belong to that collection.

By now we know a little more than we knew before. The "all" are to be distinguished from the universality of what is called a universal. Universality is to be understood in connection with "all," but it must also be viewed as distinct from "all." This would be consistent with the view that universality is something like a qualification, a condition, or a standard, for standards differ from that for which they are standards. Whatever is universal would then differ from "all" the entities with respect to which it is universal. It is a standard for "all" of them, universally so. But what is the relation between the two? How do they differ?

Is it possible that the entities which together make up the "all" which are universally of the same kind are individualizations of that kind? Are the individual or particular instances or examples of the universal kind the individualizations or particularizations of it? The relationship between universal and particular is sometimes portrayed as though there is a hierarchy with one all-inclusive universal at the top and all the individually real things in the world at the bottom. One might then say that there is a sliding scale from universality to individuality: at the one end is pure individuality, and at the other end pure universality. "Being" is what might be the most universal entity, since all that exists has being. And this universal "being" might be differentiated in many universal forms of it, all of which are particulars when materialized. Matter individualizes all universality. As we move from the universal to the individual, things get more and more individualized. An example of such a progression might be: animal, vertebrate, mammal, carnivore, cat-like, lion, Kalahari lion, this particular lion.

When we look more closely, we can see problems with this view. The move from animal to Kalahari lion differs in an important respect from the further move to include this particular lion. Only this particular lion appears to be a genuine, concrete, individual entity; this cannot be said of any other member of the series. The relationship of "this particular lion" to "Kalahari lion" is not the same as the relationship of "carnivore" to "mammal." If we look carefully at all the members in the series, we see that this particular lion is in fact a particular instance of all the previous members, whereas none of the other members are particular instances of any of the others. All the ones that come before this particular lion are universals; not one of them is an individual.

The series may be a genuine one if we leave out this particular lion. But is it then still a series representing progressive individualization? What it seems to represent instead is the progressive *extension* of universality. There are obviously more individuals that are "lion" than are "kalahari lion," and "animal" clearly extends to more individuals than does "lion." One category or kind appears to be more or less extensive than another. Is it then also more or less universal?

"Animal" clearly is universal to all animals, while "lion" is universal to all lions. Each universal is universal to all members of the class of things that are of that universal kind. One universal may be more *extensive* than another, but can it also be more *inclusive*? Are not all universals *all*-inclusive? This is an important point, for it appears that on the one hand the universal is universal with respect to specific individual entities. On the other hand, within its specific area the universality of a specific universal is completely universal and extends to all of its instances. One might say: Universals relate to a *species* of particulars and are therefore understandably *specific*. But specific (Kalahari lion) and individual (this lion) are different categories.

But if whatever has universality may be universal only in a specific area, it appears that this universality is limited. If universality is limited, then, what does this tell us about the connection between particularity and universality? If the universality of whatever it is that is universal is limited to a specific kind, does it make sense to say that only the applicability of the kind to its examples is universal, while the kind itself is not universal? Is it possible to view kinds, even though they are universal in application, as particular kinds or even individual kinds?[18] Could it be that the relationship between universality and "all" is simply that whatever is universal is universal in its relation to some specific "all" only and might itself be a particular?

Similar observations might be made with respect to each member of the "all." Each particular member of the "all" could be said to show some universality. Every particular bird "is a bird." Only a particular bird can "be a bird." A universal can never "be a bird." "Being a bird" is not a bird. Each bird shares with "all" other birds the characteristic that it "is a bird." It appears that although "is a bird" is an example of "being a bird," it is universal in each and every bird.[19] Universality appears to be a dimension of each particular bird. We may refer to the entity "bird" as a particular and to the universal "being a bird" as a universal, but it also appears to be possible to speak of particular universals and of universality in particulars.

One way to overcome this sort of difficulty could be to look upon universality and individuality as a pair of correlates lying outside of one another, not so much as two different entities but as two different relations. We might, for example, recall that of all concretely existing entities in our empirical space-time world we can say two things. One is that each such actual entity is one singular and unique particular. To express this singular uniqueness, we may refer to the particular entity as an individual entity. At the same time each actual entity is never totally and completely and only uniquely singular or singularly unique. Each is a particular of some *kind*. Each particular existent has uniquely individual traits as well as shared universal traits. *This* bird is *a* bird. It is *this* entity which is of such and such a *kind*.

Suppose that each particular entity in our world has both individual and universal traits and that this is a clue to our general problem. We might then say that a realist looks for what explains the fact that entities, their properties, and their relationships are all of some kind, of some sort, of the same nature, or of an identical structure. If so, it could be that what explains or accounts for this fact has a relation to the actual particulars in our empirical world such that it *relates universally* to all the particulars of that kind; while at the same time these particulars *relate uniquely*, singularly, individually to what accounts for the shared or common traits. Then, in view of these relations, the particular entities of our world could be seen to have both universal and individual traits. One might even say that a particular's traits themselves were both universal and individual. The entity itself, the particular, would not be wholly and totally unique, nor would it or anything about it be wholly or totally universal. Rather, it would exhibit both universality and individuality in all of its existence.

This opens up the possibility that what we are dealing with is not so much an entity, the universal, but a relationship; not an entity which is instantiated or exemplified, but a relationship of universality. It may be that what realists call a universal may just be a common name for the common relation that particulars have to attributes, qualities, properties, predicates, general words, concepts, categories, kinds, classes, sets, genera, species, natures, laws, standards, and the like. For in all of these we have something to which particulars relate in such a way that particulars are "all" involved in it in the same way. At the same time these particulars do so each in their own unique way. The particular relates to these individually, while they relate to particulars universally. If we could get closer to what makes all of these relate universally to particulars, while particulars relate individually to them, we may make some progress.

If there is a clue here, a question to ask is this. Instead of wondering what is the entity that all horses have in common, could we ask what is common to all of the concepts used by philosophers to explain what universals are? Wolterstorff, for example, begins by treating properties, actions, assertibles, and relations as examples of universals (UN, 80, 84). He calls them predicable entities. Predication is for him *the* entrance to universals. If something can be truly predicated of many, it is and must be a universal; if not, it must be an individual or particular. But later he expands his analysis and concludes that universals, all of them, are kinds. And of kinds there are more than just the four sorts of predicables he analyzes. Everything in the universe whatsoever is either a kind or an example (UN, 300). But Wolterstorff's primary method of analysis is to get at universals via predication. Now, Armstrong disagrees with this. For him not all true predication leads us to universals, nor is it likely that whatever is universal is predicable. He rejects the position that "predicates stand in a one-one correlation to universals" (USR2, 9). And with this we can go on. What one philosopher finds the most characteristic trait of universals, another regards as a misleading focus for analysis.

The identity of universals has been associated with many things. In addition to the traditional list presented two paragraphs back, universals are also associated with necessity, causality, identity, and continuity. Armstrong, Loux, and Quinton, for example, do this. What I am suggesting here is that, indeed, there is room for all of this. We could look at all that has been presented and ask: What sort of universality is there in all of these? One could let the long list of candidates be and not attempt to reduce all of them to one of them. One could just ask: If universality is part and parcel of all of them, then what is it?

This approach by itself does not solve the problem of the nature or reality or existence of standards, categories, kinds, and similar items. It does, however, give a specification to the concept of universality that will help me to begin exploring the formation of a hypothesis. Such a hypothesis will have various parts. First, it would do justice to nominalist leanings. In our world there are things or entities such as tables, people, macadamia nuts, hydrogen atoms, and many more. These things have characteristics, functions, and traits. They also do things in relationship. We sometimes use such words as *events* and *actions* to refer to the complexity of things (with parts and functions) doing something in relationship. Complex though our world may be, however, the world does not include any things or entities such as universals. What the realist refers to when she speaks of a universal I take to be a hypostatization or absolutization or reification or substantialization of the fact that whatever we meet in our world is of some kind or other.

Secondly, the hypothesis would have a realist element. Whatever there is in our world will, does, or must meet certain qualifications before we can accept it or experience it as being of some kind. Bears do not meet the qualifications for being birds: no bear can be a bird. Things are of their own kind only. This is well established, and the qualifications of each kind apply universally. Things in this world are not just individuals, nor can we say that there are entities such as pure universals in this world. The point is simply that all things that are birds meet the qualifications for being a bird individually, each in its own unique manner. They are, however, not *simply* or only or just individuals. When nominalists speak of individuals, they overstate the fact that all birds are birds individually. Combining the nominalist and realist elements may lead to this hypothesis. Universality and individuality are traits, not entities.

A third element for a hypothesis is that universality as a trait points to something that is not just common to the species and genera of which Boethius spoke or to the properties and relations that moderns discuss. Rather, standards, norms, conditions, laws, sorts, kinds, and the like all display the same characteristics as genera and species, properties, and relations. They relate universally to all things that in turn relate individually to them. What we need to look for is what I have named when I talk about universality, and also for what I have named when I talk about individuality as its correlate.

We might frame a hypothesis as a result of these brief explorations. I think we are looking for a real way to account for the unusual fact that all individual particulars relate in the same way to whatever we call kind, category, property, relation, and many others. All particulars relate to them individually, while they, without exception, relate universally to all particulars in a certain way. And that universal way of relating to particulars allows us to account for these particulars as being of a certain kind, belonging to a certain category, having a certain property, and standing in some relation. Whatever it is that universally accounts for this is what we mean by universality in the universals debate. But whatever it is, it is not a class of entities that are all examples of an entity called the universal. We are looking for whatever will constitute the ground, reason, cause, or explanation for why all birds are bird, all cherries red, and all spouses married.

1.2   Further Explorations

So far I have explored the concept of universality in relation to "all." I did this especially in relation to the traditional problem of universals. Now I want to explore what has been said about universals or what has been recognized as universality in universals in different contexts, namely, in contexts in which they play an important role but are not the express focus of discussion. Two traits manifested by such discussions are helpful for my purposes in this chapter. In the first place, these discussions make it clear that one can profitably talk about universals and universality without concerning oneself with "the classical problem" of universals; in fact, often discussions of universals and universality seem necessary, though they are not obviously dependent on references to the traditional problems. Secondly, it appears that the talk about universals and universality is reducible to talk about other realities, such as conditionality, order, structure, and system. Guided by the light these other realities might be able to shed on my quest for a hypothesis about universality, I will present in this section a summary survey of several of these treatments.

1.2.1   Views about universality

Karl Popper believes that *"all universals are dispositional"* (CR, 118, 277). He means that universal terms indicate that the thing named by the term exhibits "behavior *under certain conditions*" (CR, 118). Popper means to say the same thing by referring to such behavior as "a certain *law-like behavior. . ."* (CR, 278). We need not be concerned here about using the phrases "under certain conditions" and "certain law-like" as synonyms. Popper undoubtedly means that things behave *subject to* laws (which is different from behaving *like* laws). The point is clear enough. The use of a universal term indicates that whenever certain specified conditions obtain, a law seems to hold, and we can expect certain realities to be the case. When Popper talks about universals, he is talking about semantic realities like terms or words. But he leaves no doubt that, at least in the natural sciences (see below), he is assuming the reality of both the conditions and the dispositions to which the terms refer.

Popper also insists that we must distinguish between genuine and nongenuine universals. "All apples in this basket" is not genuinely universal in its reference. It refers to particulars. Genuine universals are words "with an indeterminate extension, though perhaps with a reasonably definite intensional 'meaning' " (CR, 262, 277-78). He means that these universals do not depend on the enumeration of instances. Genuine universals are indeterminate in the sense that they refer to any and all actual, possible, future, and past instances, that is, to the most inclusive "all" (i.e., all possible). Their reference is to "any x must be" rather than to "all (or some) x are such and such." Genuine universals in this sense are indispensable for science (CR, 262, 272-78). Strictly speaking, they are words which do not refer to the entities which are instances or examples of universals but to dispositions in things or to the conditions that must be met by them if we are to have the entities.

Popper restricts these genuine universals to the world investigated by the natural sciences. It is his view that "social phenomena . . . should be analyzed in terms of individuals and their actions and relations" (CR, 341). Just why he makes this distinction is hard to see. If we say that glass has the disposition to break under certain conditions, why wouldn't we also say that people have the disposition to raise families under certain conditions? Why should natural dispositions be more real than social dispositions? Wouldn't social dispositions also be natural in the case of people? Yet, whether Popper restricts his use of "universal" is not as important as what he means by it when he does use it. He stresses two dimensions of universality which are particularly helpful: (1) that it points to states of affairs in conformity with a law or subject to conditions, and (2) that it has to do with more than generality, in the sense that the enumeration of instances is not relevant to genuine universality. Universality admits of no exceptions, and in that sense it is indeterminate.[20]

Popper's view here might be at variance with Norwood Russell Hanson's interpretation of what the latter calls "the logical status" (93) of laws. Hanson concludes: "There is no such thing as *the* law of

inertia, *the* law of force, *the* law of gravitation" (94). This could indicate the opposite of what Popper holds, namely, that the reality of
laws *is* context dependent. In a sense, Hanson's statement is clearly
right. Statements about and formulations or interpretations of a law
may vary. Hanson himself compares talk about *the law* with talk
about *the use* of some object (94). There are many uses of objects.
There is probably also more than one use of the expression "*the* law"
for such-and-such. One of them would be to distinguish between any
number of formulations or functions of the law on the one hand, and
the underlying universality on the other hand.

We might say that, for Popper, *the* law would not be the *statement* but the universal state of affairs to which the statement refers.
The state of affairs might be something like the fact that alcohol,
given a certain pressure, boils at 78.3°C (a Hanson example; see p.
97). Such a fact might be used in many different contexts and in many
different ways. The fact might also be formulated in many different
statements. But the fact that any particular sample of alcohol has
such a disposition, one which alcohol exhibits in all possible instances,
is an undeniable state of affairs which can be interpreted as a law. If
anything is alcohol, it must conform to this law. And there may well
be other states of affairs which are equally law-like. Such states of affairs, in all formulations, would be *the* law.

If scientific terms are to have any univocity of reference in common usage, there needs to be such a thing as *the* meaning of a given
term. Let's take the word *breakable*. A given window might shatter in
any one of a number of different ways when hit by a ball. Any
number of windows may crack in exactly the same place when hit in
the same place. But the specific circumstances, in their specificity, are
irrelevant to the disposition of glass to break under certain conditions.
Glass would have that disposition to break even if there were no
record of any particular piece of glass ever breaking. And that's what
breakable refers to.

Carl G. Hempel does accept such genuine universality. In fact,
he introduces specific terminology to express the difference between
what he calls strict or deterministic universality and probabilistic or
statistical generality (ASE, 89). The latter becomes empirical universality (ASE, 234), while the former is expressed in sentences of law-
like or universal conditional form, provided that law-like sentences
are not limited in their extension (ASE, 339-40). The unlimited
universality of a law-like sentence is referred to by Hempel as *essential generality* (ASE, 340). Hempel quite clearly, like Popper, connects universality in its genuine character with conditionality and
law-conformity. This conformity to law viewed from the standpoint

of law means that the universal is unlimited in its scope; it cannot refer to any given particular object. The law-like sentence has to make use of "purely universal predicates" in its formulations (ASE, 264-70). Hempel likewise reaches these conclusions not through an examination of universals but from a consideration of the nature and necessity of laws in the sciences.

Both Popper and Hempel, then, assert that genuine universality (or essential generality) is neither empirical nor quantifiable. It is not a generalized observation of actual events, nor is it just a matter of all particulars. "Some or all *x* are" is a quantified empirical observation. "Any *x* must be" is a statement of genuine universality. Universality is nonextensional or unlimited in scope. A statement that refers to each and every specimen, that is, to "all" objects within its universe of discourse, may be universal in form, but it states its universality not from the point of view of whatever it is that is universal (e.g., a law), but from the point of view of the objects referred to. Genuine universality is essentially not a trait that refers to specific objects; rather, it refers to any possible object.[21] It refers to conditions, not to what meets the conditions; or to what makes things possible, not to actual things.

Michael Polanyi often discusses universality in ways that at first sight seem entirely contrary to the views of Popper and Hempel. For example, he may speak of comprehension as "a responsible act claiming universal validity" (PK, xiii), giving the possible impression that the action of one specific person becomes a standard for all humanity. However, this is not what he means, as the context makes clear. What he intends to say is that when someone has truly comprehended something, she has acted responsibly, so that anyone else who acts as responsibly in comprehending the same thing will comprehend it similarly. The personal is not simply the same as the universal, but, there is a "correlation between the personal and the universal" (PK, 303) such that the two are distinct but not unrelated.

The relationship between them is demonstrated, for example, in the commitment situation. Within "the framework of commitment . . . the personal and the universal mutually require each other. Here the personal comes into existence by asserting universal intent, and the universal is constituted by being accepted as the impersonal term of this personal commitment" (PK, 308). What Polanyi is emphasizing here seems actually very similar to what Popper and Hempel asserted for the area of the natural sciences, namely, that genuine universality is law-like and is not specific with respect to any objects. Polanyi expresses the latter view with respect to persons as follows: "If I, left alone in the world, and knowing myself to be alone, should believe in a fact, I would still claim universal acceptance for it" (PK, 313).

Where Polanyi differs from Popper is that he discusses universality not just in the context of the physical sciences but also in connection with the world of personal knowledge and human responsibility. He tends to carry over into the human world what he has learned about the physical world in his capacity as a chemist. He does so in a way that leaves the human world fully human. Thus he affirms that universality in the human world is also law-like and without limit in its scope.

Ervin Laszlo writes about universals in a way that supports the findings of Polanyi. Yet he is closer to Hempel and Popper in his natural-scientific spirit. His writings are, in fact, marked by the characteristic rigor so thoroughly criticized by Polanyi. Laszlo does not, however, accept the damage to belief in social universals done by modern sociological relativism of the nominalist variety. In his view, social universality cannot be dismissed quite so easily as it was fashionable to do some time ago. He claims that modern research—even in the human sciences—provides hard evidence for accepting behavioral universality.[22] He notes that earlier in our century "anthropologists came to reject universal values as anthropomorphic schematizations of investigators" (SP, 270) with very little basis in reality, and he re-evaluates this fact. "The contemporary trend is to gather empirical data to locate cross-cultural universals: norms and values shared by all people, everywhere, notwithstanding differences between their particular cultures. These cultural universals are fundamental invariants to be located by theory construction, and inferences to and from the phenomenal findings" (SP, 271).[23]

Thus a number of thinkers reflecting on the nature of scientific knowledge, whether in the area of the natural empirical sciences or in the area of the humanities, insist that science requires a recognition of universality. According to these thinkers we are to view universality in relation to laws and conditions with unlimited scope. These laws and conditions point to requirements which must be met by those entities for which the laws and conditions obtain. Both empirical analysis and inquiry into the logical structure of universality reinforce these conclusions for the thinkers discussed above. At the same time, they believe that this nomic reality should not be confused with any of the empirically existing particulars that must conform to it.

1.2.2   *The concepts of conditionality and law*

The views of Hempel and Popper on universality can best be summarized by speaking of "law-like conditions." It is important that the term *conditions* be qualified by *law-like*. If I telephone a friend to find out the weather conditions in his area at the time of my call, I am asking for a description of prevailing circumstances. However, if I call to inform him that I will come for a visit only if the roads are not icy or only if the roads are bare and dry, I am laying down a condition to be met. There is a great deal of difference between prevailing circumstances and conditions to be met. Conditions as circumstances prevail or occur. Conditions conceived of as terms to be met may not prevail or occur. Nevertheless they obtain whether or not this or that set of specific circumstances ever prevails or occurs. Conditions to be met are law-like or nomic conditions, while conditions as circumstances are simply empirical events or situations.

Often these two very different meanings of the term *condition* are not fully recognized as different in philosophical literature.[24] Rarely is the difference as explicitly formulated as by Körner, who writes: "To discover that somebody or everybody accepts a certain rule is to discover an empirical fact. But no rule, as such, is an empirical proposition. . . . A rule can be accepted and then satisfied, or violated. . . . An empirical . . . proposition cannot" (CT, 5). That any *x* must be *y* might be taken as a rule, whereas the fact that all *x*'s are *y*'s can, by contrast, be taken to describe an empirical given. Conditions to be met are like rules, whereas conditions as prevailing circumstances are like empirical givens. In this section I will use the terms *condition* and *law* as equivalents, so I am dealing with nomic conditions.

Suppose now that universality has to do with law-like conditionality, that is, suppose universality is like a rule. It would then be understandably hard to decide on the question of the existence of entities named universals. Just where would we locate the rule "Ball playing in our back yard is prohibited"? Still, it makes good sense to say: "In the Hart family there is a rule to the effect that ball playing in the back yard is prohibited." We are not likely to disagree strongly with this claim by Stebbing: "Thus the faith of the scientist can be summed up in the statement: *What happens happens in accordance with laws, and these laws are such that we can discover them*" (401). However, if laws can be discovered but do not exist, we are faced with a rare puzzle indeed. If universals are like laws, then if universals did not exist, one would expect that laws could not be discovered.[25] But, like

Popper and Hempel, Stebbing points to the essential role of laws in science. And we are not disturbed by this.

Gerard Radnitzky connects science even more strongly with laws. "In science explanation is concerned with explanation of laws and not with singular events" (168). He claims that in explanation we deal with events as kinds, not with events as empirically individual actualities (173).[26] Indeed, science deals with *the* cell, *the* atom, *the* whatever. In thus connecting explanation with both laws and kinds, Radnitzky raises the possibility of a relation between kinds and nomic relations. Both are important ways in which universality surfaces in science.

As we saw earlier, Hempel views the connection between science and law as fundamental. One can even speak of the heart of science, for "to understand a phenomenon scientifically is to show that it occurs in accordance with general laws or theoretical principles" (ASE, 139). Now, it is important to bear in mind that Hempel distinguished between law understood as "a statement of universal conditional form" (ASE, 231) and law understood as *the concept* to which the statement refers (ASE, 139). The importance of this distinction is that it allows us to understand on the one hand how Hempel makes mutually exclusive statements about laws, and on the other hand how strictly he interprets the universality of laws.

When Hempel says that the laws of nature "are now assumed to have a statistical or probabilistic rather than a strictly universal, deterministic, character" (ASE, 89), we can easily understand this in view of his assertion that "we never have more than a very incomplete knowledge of the laws of nature . . ." (ASE, 89). But how do we then explain his rejection of a "relativized concept of law" (ASE, 265)? Does not a statistical view of law in fact imply a relativized law concept? It does, but when we take into account Hempel's distinction between statements and concepts of law, it is likely that the relativized approach has to do with our present statements, while the underlying concept is applicable to "true statements only" (ASE, 265). And if this distinction is indeed what Hempel has in mind, it also highlights that underneath his relaxed view of our achievements in discovering true laws lies a high view of law as strictly universal.

Genuine law statements for Hempel truly affirm a law (ASE, 42). A nomic statement can be a genuine and true statement of law only if the law is in fact a law and not a probability. A law-like statement must refer to nomic natural connections. Thus it appears possible that Hempel, in spite of his probabilities, turns out to be more than a conceptualist with regard to laws.[27] This does not, however, commit him to "a realm of entities over and above the concrete objects in space and time" (Quine, LPV, 102), although it does imply that the law-like connections are real. Genuine natural connections refer us to true universality and conditionality in a way that is beyond our power to define.[28]

Toulmin does not connect nomic reality with truth the way Hempel does. He distinguishes between the truth of a statement and the holding of a law. Since laws are like rules, they cannot be true or false in the same sense in which statements are true or false. Laws, like other rules, "are not themselves true or false, though statements about their range of application can be" (PS, 79). Toulmin states that the "opposition 'holds'/'does not hold' is as fundamental as the opposition 'true'/'untrue', and cannot be resolved into it" (PS, 80). When Toulmin makes this distinction (PS, 49), is he confirming Hempel's finding as reported above or not? Is he saying anything more than that we must distinguish between law and statements of universal empirical generality?

Toulmin indeed says that laws hold universally (PS, 80), and he distinguishes a law from a statement of it. This might lead one to think that he refers to the same state of affairs that Hempel has in mind when he claims that statements about genuine universality point to something (a concept) that is beyond definition. However, it also appears that Toulmin introduces an element *not* found in Hempel, namely, the idea that laws represent something entirely different from empirical facts. This comes out in his view that statements of law do not assert (truly or falsely) what is in fact the case but assert what holds for whatever may or may not be the case. Nevertheless, for Toulmin, laws are empirical. Statements of law are empirical statements (PS, 82), and laws themselves are empirical as well. They refer to facts in our empirical world.

In addition to speaking of laws and of statements of fact, Toulmin also introduces the principles of science into the discussion. They differ from laws in the sense that although a statement of a law could conceivably be challenged, a statement of a principle is inviolable in a fundamental sense. Toulmin uses the criterion of inviolability or invariance or unfalsifiability to logically stratify the various types of statements that occur in an exact science (PS, 82-85). The various levels of statement (hypothetical generalizations, laws, principles) are all empirical. Each level serves to give meaning to what transpires on the level above it. Statements of law have their foundation in certain principles. If the principle were to be abandoned, the edifice of laws would cave in. Further, if the law were found not to hold, much that was held to be factual would have to be reviewed.

Thus Toulmin speaks of different levels of theoretical statements, that is, hypotheses, laws, and principles. Although they are all empirical, they cannot be referred to as true (or false); rather, they hold (or do not hold). What these levels of theoretical statements refer to is very different from empirical facts. Since they are nevertheless empirical, it is not the criterion of being empirical that distinguishes them from what is factually the case. The difference is rather that law-like statements are not about actual concrete objects but about the nature of things. Merely general statements "summarize the observed behavior" of members of a class, whether all of them or only some of them (PS, 87-88). A law is properly a law of nature and is in that sense empirical. But in being a law it is logically different (as the term is used by Toulmin) from an actual fact. On a certain level, a law of nature is a "principle of natural necessitation" (PS, 91).[29]

Both Hempel and Toulmin appear to interpret conditions, laws, principles, and limits as phenomena that order and regulate nature. One might say that laws as nomic conditions hold nature within limits or patterns of regularity. This is what conditions, laws, principles, and rules have in common. And their relationship to whatever they hold for is universal. Universality here is connected with that which we experience as a law in science. This universality has the character of not being fully explainable in terms of any particular factual-empirical phenomenon.

1.2.3   Order, structure, system

If conditions or laws can be regarded as principles of order, that is, if rules (i.e., *regulae*) bring about regularity and pattern, it will be helpful to look at what some authors have to say about universality in the context of order, structure, and system. We encounter laws and conditions as systems of order. And systems of order, in turn, are what we refer to as structures. Are structures and universality as obviously related as nomic conditions and universality?

There is a classical tradition which regards order and system as predominantly logical in nature. In this tradition we do not use the word *logical* simply to mean "orderly" in a sense quite distinct from what the word *logical* means when it refers to properties of successful inference. Rather, what we have here is a logicistic view of order. An example is the position Stebbing holds. She describes systems in a manner that is typical of this tradition: "A system is an ordered system only if all its constituent elements are related by relations having certain logical properties. These logical properties *define* order" (201). Order is here viewed from a logical standpoint, and the logicality intended is typically found in inference procedures—not in the sense that inference is one example of what is orderly but in the sense that nothing is orderly if it does not have the same properties that inference has. Here order and the orderly way of discovering order (through inference) are being conflated. Thinking produces order in a world of facts that would otherwise lack order, and it relates these facts in certain orderly ways. "Particular facts" are ordered (227). *Orderly* and *logical* are synonymous. The same goes for structure, which Stebbing uses and defines in the same way as order (204-7, 227-30).

Polanyi's views represent an attempt to escape from the logicistic tradition. As thinkers have done throughout the history of Western thought, he connects order with knowledge: "Every kind of human knowing . . . includes an appreciation both of order contrasted to randomness and of the degree of this order" (PK, 38). But for Polanyi this knowledge is not to be taken as primarily or predominantly logical in nature. And there is a significant sense in which human knowledge is not the origin of order. According to Polanyi "standards of orderliness" cannot even be "falsified by" experience (PK, 64). More fundamentally, order presupposes an ordering principle (see note 29 above). Experience is made possible by order, but the order does not originate in the experience of order. Order is available to experience in terms of human insight. But "insights reveal a reality," and that reality is not created by the insights (PK, 359). Thinking may put us in contact with order, but thought itself does not produce the order.

Neither Polanyi nor Stebbing explicitly mentions universality when discussing order. However, they both do relate the treatment of order and system to a correlate of universality, that is, particularity. For Stebbing, as we saw, order comes about by the thoughtful ordering of particulars. Polanyi states that "particulars become meaningless" outside their patterned relationships (PK, 57). Particulars are what they are within a certain order. Order is understood in terms of a correlation with particularity. The relation of order to particulars appears similar to the relation between universality and particularity.

Laszlo makes this connection between order and universality more direct through his explicit connecting of order with law. Like Stebbing and Polanyi, he discusses order in the context of knowledge. It is one of his "primary presuppositions" (SP, 8) that the world is "*intelligibly ordered*." He clarifies this as meaning that it is "*open to rational inquiry*" (SP, 8). Laszlo leaves open the question (which for him is unanswerable) "whether or not nature *is* in fact ordered" (SP, 18), although he does speak of an isomorphism between the empirical world on the one hand and the "laws and principles" on the other (SP, 18). It is this isomorphism that suggests to Laszlo "a fundamental unity of the observables" (SP, 18). In this way he directly connects law with system and order.

The fundamental importance Laszlo attaches to order becomes even more significant when we recognize that he postulates not only specific orders in specific contexts but also a general order of the world as a whole (SP, 8, 18, 55). When we relate this to his view of systems as ordered wholes (SP, 95), we can see that the world is both a whole and a system for Laszlo. In this world scientists go to work with a double-barreled approach. On the one hand, they cannot presuppose that order is a given; rather, it is a rational hypothesis (SP, 55). On the other hand, they hope that this hypothesis is founded on a real order, regardless of whether the real order is capable of being rationally demonstrated. There always remains the correcting influence of the world on the rational mind (SP, 139).[30]

Laszlo, like Polanyi, struggles to come to terms with the inadequacies of a logicist system. At the same time he sees a connection of order with knowledge and analysis. Laszlo attempts to preserve a notion of order transcending experience without making it sterile. He therefore explicitly connects his view of order with progress and dynamics and then asserts that this connection has an inner logic of its own (SP, 288). In making such a move, he seeks support in the writings of Ludwig von Bertalanffy, who holds that the world confronts us with "everlasting orderly processes" (SP, 70). In this context Laszlo uses *structure* as a term to refer to the temporal-spatial evidence of order in the concrete objects of our world. Order becomes evident as structure in the visible patterns and arrangements that are evident in definiteness of shape, for example.

The reality of order in the empirical world presents a special problem. Is there an ontic gap between order and an ordered world? Polanyi's discussion suggests this and the possibility is present also in Laszlo. The issue of universals is specifically bound up with this problem. The following remark by Popper about the rules of logic applies. He says: "Thus a world in which they do not apply would not be an illogical world, but a world peopled by illogical men" (CR, 205). In this way Popper locates the area in which logical principles apply. One might say that they are not principles of world order but principles of inference. They apply more directly to human logical procedures than to the world which is approached by way of those procedures via the concepts we have of the world. However, although such an observation is helpful, it does not make the problem of the applicability of the rules of logic disappear. The question can still be asked: Is it sensible to be logical in this world? Popper realizes this (CR, 213): "Why, we could ask, are we at all successful in speaking about reality? Is it not true that reality must have a definite structure in order that we can speak about it?"

Popper does not give us a clear and definite answer to his question. Hanson does. He claims that our desire to limit and order our world is not subject to any outside order or limit. He makes the nominalistic claim that "we force upon the subject-matter of physics the ordering we choose" (98). Wolfgang Köhler explicitly asserts that the logical point of view for looking at order is itself a limited point of view. Order is not an arbitrary choice but something presenting itself to us; he also believes that "experience itself exhibits an order *which is itself experienced*" (GP, 38). We see that there is no more agreement on the question of the relation of order to reality than on the more abstract question of whether or not universals exist. There is irreconcilable disagreement on the very character of order. Köhler regards logical order as just one type of order, whereas Stebbing simply conceives of order as logical.

1.2.4   Kinds and classes

Of the various issues bound up with the problem of universality, I have thus far dealt only with those connected with whatever it is that is universal, whether this be order, or law, or nomic conditions, or something else. But universality, we have noted, also confronts us as a side of concrete reality, particular objects, and subjective individuals. This dimension surfaces especially when kinds are viewed in terms of classes. I will now briefly consider this side of the problem of universals.

There are indeed treatises on individuality or concrete subjectivity to be found in the Western intellectual tradition, but they are characteristically absent in the traditions that concern themselves with order, system, and rationality in particular.[31] When scholarship focuses so heavily on what is general, reflection on individuality winds up being left in the nonscientific domain of thought. Still, there are philosophical traditions that do make a point of analyzing individuality and subjectivity, for example, existentialism, philosophy of life (*Lebensphilosophie*), and pragmatism. These traditions are often characterized as irrationalist. The reason for such a characterization is the conviction of many thinkers that science and the rational arts cannot deal with what is subjective and uniquely individual.

According to Hempel, rational disciplines or sciences "can give an account of their subject-matter only in terms of general concepts," and none have the ability to "grasp the unique individuality" of things—not even history (ASE, 233). Scientists aim to eliminate from their scientific analysis all subjective factors, even the presence of their own subjectivity (ASE, 146). Subjectivity and individuality are neither welcomed by science nor comprehensible to it.

However, the general concepts and propositions of science itself do concern individuals. What science does can apply to individual objects. As Susanne K. Langer observes, it is true that "general propositions . . . never mention individuals" (112). But when individuals do figure in science, they do not play a role in their individuality but in their relation to universality. They then function as "*a member, or members, of a certain class*" (113).

The role of individuals in a treatment of general propositions seems to indicate at least that the general or universal does not appear in isolation from that which is individual or subjective. Universality is never understood scientifically except in statements relating it to that which is individual. Laszlo refers to this as the isomorphism of laws and empirical reality. It is impossible to treat one side of the isomorphism as a type of the other, but it is also impossible not to treat one in terms of the other in science. Universal statements refer to a state of affairs which is correlated with classes. Indeed, the very reality of the universality of universals is constituted by their universally relating to these individuals.

Because universality is not reducible to individuals, universality as such cannot be quantified. Universality must remain fully indeterminate. However, the correlation of universality with individuality enables us to deal with universality in terms of quantified references. Universality is not the same thing as an aggregate of individuals, nor is individuality just one universal. Collections or aggregates of individuals do not produce universality, nor does only one universal constitute an individual. But, the isomorphism between universality and classes of individuals allows us, in dealing with classes, to deal with universality. This is done in quantifying over predicates, that is, in the expression of universality in terms of "any" or "some" or "all" individuals of a certain kind. These individuals of a certain kind form a class. Perhaps an analysis of classes of individuals can shed some light on the problem of universality.[32]

Nicholas Wolterstorff contrasts kinds of classes or sets as follows:

"All universals . . . are *kinds*—not sets or classes, but kinds" (UN, 7). He examines the fundamental characteristic of universals when treated in a logical or scientific context, namely, that they can be predicated of many particulars. The traditional universals debate deals with what Wolterstorff calls predicable universals. If there are such entities as universals, they will have to be predicable entities. Classes, however, do not fall into this category. "It seems that classes cannot be predicated" (UN, 86). Universals cannot be understood as collections of individuals. The predication relation between individual entities and kinds shows that the two are not reducible.

However, Wolterstorff is not committed to a strict correlation between universality and individuality. Although it will never be possible to predicate individuals either singularly or in collections, it will be possible to have predicates that can never be truly predicated of any individual or that can be predicated only of one. "There is such a kind of shape as: the Square Circle" (UN, 239). There can be kinds of which it is necessarily true that they cannot have examples; it is necessarily impossible that they be exemplified. Thus they cannot have correlates in individual existence.

In his book Wolterstorff does not consider that if the impossibility of being truly predicated entails that something cannot be a universal, the impossibility of being exemplified may likewise show that something cannot be a universal. The fact that there is such an *expression* as "square circle" or the fact that boxing *rings* are *square*, need not commit us to the existence of the square circle as a *kind*. Furthermore, a true statement to the effect that certain "examples" cannot possibly exist might entail the necessary nonexistence of a kind of that sort. Wolterstorff suggests that "a sentence of the form *k's are f*, when interchangeable with one of the form *The K is f* . . . [refers to] what is true of *normal, properly formed k's*" (UN, 245). But is it not so that the sentence "Square circles are necessarily nonexistent" could be taken as interchangeable with "The Square Circle is necessarily nonexistent"?

Would there not be considerable difference between nomic conditions of possibility that were never and perhaps may never be realized (i.e., so-called uninstantiated kinds), and conditions that make for the impossibility of certain realities? Conditions for being square and conditions for being circular (the kind Square and the kind Circle) may be such that squareness and circularity cannot be simultaneously united in one actual spatial configuration. But is this the same as saying that there *is* a kind Square Circle, and that it cannot be exemplified? The notions of nul sets or nul classes may be needed as notions in mathematics and logic. The language of these disciplines may require the use of these terms. But with respect to what they stand for, need one be more than a nominalist?[33]

What this analysis of Wolterstorff shows us is that at least in his mind a correlation such that whenever there is some universal there must be a particular of that sort and whenever there is a particular it will be an example of some universal is not acceptable. If there is a correlation between universality and individuality, it is not a one-to-one correspondence. For Wolterstorff the conclusion seems to be that we must admit of at least universals which have never yet been instantiated and therefore of which no examples have yet existed, though we may still know that there is such a universal. But this seems to commit him to the idea that both unrealized possibilities and necessary impossibilities are really existing entities called universals.

1.3 Concluding Reflections

The problems surveyed do not lead to a solution of the problem of universals. The discussion shows us a problem, and it acquaints us with positions people have taken in dealing with it. Nevertheless, we have touched on realities which are undeniable and which are of significance for a realistic outlook on the question of universals. *One* of these is that no science is possible—whether logic, a natural science, or a humanities discipline—without the use of universal terms and propositions. Those who are in fact dealing with the nature of these terms and propositions in the workshop of science (as distinct from engaging in "merely" philosophical analysis for its own sake) would not understand these terms and propositions as fictions. They are regarded as referring to laws, conditions, and dispositions whose reality is simply taken for granted, even though differences might well emerge when a definition or description of that reality was presented. *Another* reality which has emerged from the discussion is that meta-questions about the nature of universal terms and propositions take us beyond empirically demonstrable or observable particulars. Universality goes beyond particulars. A *third* reality is that science of any kind can be connected with empirical reality only if propositions containing universal terms will also provide for a connection with singular terms. That is, whatever it is that is universal is for all practical purposes connected with what is concretely individual.

Given these realities, in the next chapter I will attempt to construct an ontology of universality. I will do so on the basis of a clue which, throughout the entire discussion, has emerged as a reality in addition to the three already mentioned, namely, that the universality of universals may point to something nomic. It may point to the fact that all the various concepts used in talking about universals (kinds, categories, properties, relations, and many others) have in common that particulars *must* relate to them in a certain way *if* they are to be the particular they are.[34] In fact, a test for the ontology I propose to develop is whether or not that ontology allows us to understand all these concepts used to deal with universals as *nomic universality*. Will the view of universality I develop solve some of the problem encountered in this chapter? It is indeed my claim that once we understand the nature of universality we will be able to deal with the traditional problem of universals in a different and perhaps more fruitful way. Another test, then, for the ontology I shall develop is to see whether it can effectively address and solve the various problems that arose in this chapter.

Five complex concepts will play an important role in the construction of this ontology. They are all related to problems surveyed in this chapter. The *first* is that both universality and individuality must be accepted as real in some sense of the word *real*, even though their reality is radically different in each case. That is, they are real and irreducible. *Secondly*, their reality is correlative. There is no universality apart from individuality, and no individuality apart from universality. *Third* is the concept of the relation between universality on the one hand, and conditions, laws, and orderliness on the other. Though the literature surveyed may have indicated certain disagreements about the nature and origin of order, it also pointed to the possibility that universality is a nomic characteristic of limitation and determination. This concept is therefore clearly related to a *fourth*, namely, that a concretely individual entity exists only in a framework of universality, and to a *fifth*, namely, that an individual entity is knowable only within such a framework.

Chapter II
Order: An Ontology of Universality

MANY WORLDVIEW HYPOTHESES ASSERT that the world is made up of particulars with properties and in relation to each other.[1] By contrast, Ervin Laszlo states that his most general worldview hypothesis is that the world exists and that it is intelligibly ordered.[2] If one takes the first approach, then probably traditional theories of universals and of the nature of substance will dominate one's ontology. If one takes Laszlo's approach, then an analysis of systems will be a preoccupation. By the end of this chapter it will become clear that I merge the two approaches. I think that a fundamental way of stating what the world is like is to say that there are functors functioning in relationships. Nevertheless, I also think that we must make our *primary* distinction between world and world order. It is the world, the empirical world of space and time, which is made up of functors functioning in relationships. All three (functors, functions, and relations) will turn out, on my analysis, to be particulars of our experience. But I will claim that this world is ordered. And I will claim that the order for the world relates universally to the particulars of the world. The universality of "universals" is the universality of order. World order has been hypostatized as universals. The order of functors has been viewed in terms of particularizing universals or substance universals.[3] Functions and relations have been viewed as the universals of predication and attribution, or as properties or qualities. Relations have also been seen as universals.[4]

The nature of things, the system of the universe, or the order of the world is particularly the domain of scientific investigation. Although science has never developed a theory of universals and is quite content to leave that task to philosophers, scientists are at the same time busy investigating properties, necessary connections, laws, species and kinds, concepts and categories, and many other items often called universals by philosophers or seen by them as having universality in their relation to the things of our empirical world. In this chapter I propose to look at what is called the order of the world and to see it as the fundamental reality behind universality. Universality will, on my analysis, turn out to be a feature of an ordered world.

Another way of describing the burden of this chapter is to say that I will examine the problem of universals by looking at what have been called universals, or what has been connected with them (such as causality) from the viewpoint of how science experiences universality.[5] The problems of realism or nominalism need not bother us here. No scientist doubts the reality of certain laws of nature. Rather than saying that these laws exist, the scientist views them as *holding for* certain functors, functions, or relations between them. And for whatever these laws hold, they hold universally. Moreover, the objects of scientific investigation always relate to one another in an orderly, structured, systematic fashion. Science investigates a *system* of universality. This system of universality is an order of conditions, or a conditional order. What I mean here is an order which obtains wherever and whenever an empirical entity or event occurs.

So I propose to look at universality from a scientific point of view and to deal with it in terms of conditionality. Functors, functions, and relations occur in our world as they do because they meet certain conditions. And these conditions must be met universally if functors, functions, and relations are to occur at all.

Laws and standards can be viewed as conditions to be met by functors functioning in their relations with one another. Dispositions can be understood as tendencies in things to behave in certain conditioned ways. Concepts can be viewed as our intellectual grasp of conditions to be met. I propose to make use of the five complex concepts introduced at the end of the previous chapter and to relate them to the discussion of universality as conditionality. This will take the form of looking for the reality of conditions in relation to the conditioned, viewing conditions as correlates of conditioned entities, and developing the view that individual entities exist in a framework of conditions, and so forth.[6]

I will begin by raising the question what conditions are. This inquiry will yield an important distinction, for which I will introduce a provisional nomenclature, thereby providing some initial refinement in the search for the connection between conditions and universality. I will then proceed to discuss the relationship between conditions and existence and also the relationship between conditions and universality. The discussion will lead me to the conclusion that there are different kinds of conditionality. An analysis of these differences will occasion a revised set of terms. At that point, with a number of concepts in hand, I will go back to the various problems uncovered in the previous chapter. I will then inquire into the effectiveness of the new concepts in dealing with the problem of universality. Since the new concepts help me to resolve some key issues in the debate, I will adopt the approach arrived at in this chapter for the rest of this book.

The view of universality for which I shall argue does not allow for entities called universals whose existence or reality can be determined in the same way in which we determine the reality or existence of colors, sea gulls, and racial prejudice. What I will argue for is the reality of regulatory principles which hold universally. My position will turn out to be that universality is a characteristic of law-like realities which hold universally for entities within their scope. An appropriately formed existing entity will have to conform to a rule-like reality. The proper occurrence of individual entities will be correlated with conditions that hold universally, that is, that include all entities of the same kind within their scope of conditionality.

When I speak of the reality of laws, I do not mean to imply that they are empirically observable entities in space and time; for the moment I mean no more than that whatever is referred to by means of such terms as *rule*, *law*, or *condition* cannot be disregarded or ignored with impunity. These realities are not fictions; they are not constructions of the human imagination. Exactly what is real about them is a question to be taken up later.

One approach I shall avoid in inquiring into the reality of these rule-like principles which hold universally is to regard them entirely from a logical point of view. I do not believe that what is or is not proper to conclude is dependent on rules of inference alone. I do not mean, of course, that in talking about universals I ignore the law of noncontradiction. If I were entertaining the hypothesis that the universals I am inquiring into are conceptual or propositional in nature, it might be appropriate to approach their reality primarily from a logical point of view, for concepts and propositions must satisfy logical criteria. At this stage, however, I cannot prejudice the inquiry by committing it to such a direction. I do not hereby mean to say that my inquiry is allowed to be illogical, but only that it should not be taken to be purely logical, or logically demonstrable by formal proofs.[7]

2.1 *What Are Conditions?*

I want to ask what we mean by conditions when we talk about them as making things possible. We use the term *conditions* in this sense when we ask such a question as: Under what conditions are you willing to consider accepting our offer? When the enemy is asked to surrender unconditionally in wartime, what is meant is that the surrender must be without any ifs, ands, or buts. I mean to inquire into conditions in the broadest sense possible—conditions that make anything whatsoever possible. Whatever exists is possible. What is the nature of the conditions that make this existence possible? Thus I am inquiring into the nature of conditions for existence, including the conditions for the knowledge of existence and for the theoretical inquiry into such matters. As this study unfolds, I hope it will become clear that I do not mean this investigation as an inquiry into the origin of or the causes for what exists. Though these questions are related, in my view they are not the same.

Conditions is a term with a rather ambiguous meaning. It can mean the state that something (e.g., my car) or someone (e.g., the team's star player) is in. It can also mean circumstances as they have a bearing on events. We might explain that the conditions were unfavorable when our invasion occurred: enemy reinforcements had just arrived, rain had made the terrain soggy, and one of our best generals was recuperating from a heart attack. Thus conditions can be states or circumstances. We confront a very different meaning when we refer to conditions that must be met. Someone might stipulate: "I will not join the team unless I am guaranteed such-and-such an amount of playing time." The condition obtains regardless of whether the event referred to ever occurs. In fact, some events (joining the team) will not occur unless some other events occur first. The other conditions (states and circumstances) always refer to actually occurring realities, but conditions that are to be met are conditions for possible events, events that become possible *if* certain states or circumstances prevail.

One difference that can be observed between the first two senses of *condition* (states or circumstances) and the third (stipulation or requirement) is that in the case of the latter there are priorities among events and a relation of dependence between some events and others. Certain events will occur only subject to the condition that other events occur as well. Whether or not events of one kind occur will depend on the occurrence (or promised occurrence or expected occurrence) of other events. A person will not get a degree unless certain examinations are passed. The obtaining of the degree depends on the passing of the examinations. The passing must come first. Conditions of this kind imply a relation of dependence. The dependence in question is one of being subjected to something. Something is being demanded; something *must* occur; something is said to *have to* occur, *if* something else is to occur as well.

It should be noted that this dependence relation is not necessarily temporally fixed in the strict sense of the word. The actual event subject to which another event occurs need not occur before the latter—at least, not in any straightforward sense. I can perform an action today subject to the condition that someone else perform another action tomorrow. I can send some money today subject to the condition that it be returned tomorrow. Thus it is not necessary that the stipulated event occur before the event it makes possible. Of course, if the stipulated event does occur after the event it makes possible, there must be some function of the future event which precedes the present event and makes the latter possible.

For example, if I am to send money away now, I must actually believe now that it will be returned tomorrow. Moreover, that belief must be present before I act. Or perhaps someone has made a promise or given a guarantee that some event will take place in the future. Thus we might say that even though the actual condition-event need not take place prior to the event it conditions, some event which "stands in for" the event conditioning the other event must temporally precede the conditioned event. In view of this consideration, it can be said that the dependence relation in the case of a stipulation of conditions is irreversible.

Although the dependence relation is certainly irreversible in some basic sense, it is not irrevocable. In the human environment, especially, there exists the possibility of a great measure of control over conditions. If the player we want on the team will not or cannot meet our conditions, we can always change them. We can even drop all the conditions if we want him badly enough. People can also exercise control over conditions that are not of their own making. Natural conditions determine that crops will grow only if and when exposed to a certain quantity of moisture. In certain arid regions that are too dry for this or that crop, we can institute the conditions which nature insists must be met. If a certain area is too dry for a given crop, we also can try to develop a strain of the crop that will do well in a drier environment.

There is a limit to our ability to revoke or alter conditions, however. There are certain conditions that are, one might say, irrevocable; there are also conditions that are entirely beyond our control. If the political party of our choice will not be in power unless it wins the election by a certain margin, we can try to influence the voters and thereby help the party win the election. This is by no means easy to accomplish, but it is not impossible either. But what if I suddenly find that I must be at a place thirty miles from here in fifteen minutes? If I leave instantly, I will not make it to my destination on time unless I travel at an average speed of 120 miles per hour. This condition is simply beyond my control. Within certain limits I still have room to maneuver. I could wait ten minutes and then set off in a vehicle in which I travel at an average speed of 360 miles per hour. Yet, once the distance is fixed, the ratio between the time and the speed is also fixed beyond anyone's control.

The condition we encounter here is one that we can state as a universal rule: Whenever or wherever anything whatsoever needs to cover a distance of thirty miles in fifteen minutes, it must travel at an average speed of at least 120 miles per hour.[8] *That* anything with this need must fulfill this condition is *not an event* of any kind. It is neither a statement nor a circumstance. What we have here is a condition that must be met by any possible object having this need, a rule-like condition which includes in its scope any and all actual and possible objects of this kind, now, in the past, and in the future. The condition holds universally, irrevocably, and irreversibly. Moreover, the condition is not an event; it calls for an event, but it is not itself an event. The relation of dependence is a necessary one.[9]

We now see that earlier, when a distinction was made between mere states and events on the one hand, and dependence relations on the other, it could have been said that every condition which is a rule or which makes for a dependence is not an event. The dependence has the sense of: Something will have to happen. *That* it will have to happen (even when *what* has to happen is an event) is never an event; rather, it is a condition to be met by events. Thus the earlier distinction between states and circumstances on the one hand, and conditions as rules on the other, can now be recognized as a distinction between conditions that are events and conditions that are not events. The "demanding" of the controlling conditions is not an event.[10]

Of course the term *condition* cannot be used in both senses in one and the same treatise without causing confusion. Even when it is understood that conditions as rules can only take effect in conditions as events, the two senses are so different that confusion remains a danger if the two senses of *condition* are not carefully distinguished terminologically. From now on I will use the term *conditions* only in the sense of rules or dependence relations. I will use the terms *circumstances* and *states* to refer to circumstances and states. And since the term *conditions* can still have the double meaning of dependence that is not an event as well as dependence actualized in events, I will use two different terms to forestall confusion between these separate meanings. In what follows, I will abide by these provisional definitions:

> *conditions-1* will mean conditions as rules that are not events, nomic conditions
>
> *conditions-2* will mean conditions as rules actualized in events
>
> *conditions*   will mean conditions as rules whether or not actualized as events

The following three sentences give examples of the three usages of *conditions*. We have a condition (= condition-1) that we will never eat dinner until all members of the family are home. We are all home, and so the conditions (= conditions-2) for eating dinner are present. The conditions mentioned in the previous two sentences are conditions in the sense of rules.

That events have been referred to by some as conditions-1 is probably due to nominalism. Since in science there can be no serious investigation of reality without nomic conditions, that is, without dependence relations that are irrevocable and irreversible, and if actual events in one's view are the only things that can be so related, then these events must be assigned the role of conditions-1. However, no single, individual event, as such, allows us to state a nomic condition as a universal proposition. As Hume was so keenly aware, events without conditions-1 are not structurally connected; at most they are in touch. Let's take a look at an event viewed as a condition-1.

Suppose that I will accept a certain position only if the salary is above $20,000. In that case, is the handing over of the sum of money in question the condition-1, or is the condition-1 the fact *that* I must have this amount of money? Should it not be said that the sum of money is not the condition-1 but that the handing over of the money is the event in which the condition-1 is met? The depositing of the sum is a condition-2. To say *that* an outing will take place only if the sun shines is to state a condition-1, but to go out *when* the sun shines is to act with respect to a condition-1 that has been met, that is, to act with respect to a condition-2.

What I am getting at here is that nomic conditions can always be phrased in a "that" statement. Things are possible on the condition

that. . . . Conditions can also be expressed in statements to the effect:
"If such-and-such, then such-and-such." We speak of such statements
as conditional statements. The "if . . . then" statement formulates the
condition-1 to be met in a condition-2. An "if . . . then" sequence, as
such, is never a sequence of events. Only a "when . . . then" statement
can be about a genuine event. In "if . . . then" statements we refer to
rule-like or nomic reality, whereas we refer to events in "when . . .
then" statements.

We have no control over conditions-1. We might be able to
change some of them, but as long as they remain in effect they are
beyond our control. During the time they are in effect, our only ac-
cess to them lies in conditions-2, that is, in contingent circumstances
in which conditions-1 have been realized. When conditions-1 obtain,
control is limited to the events that will or will not meet the
conditions-1. If I stop breathing I will die; this is a matter entirely
beyond my control. If I do decide to keep breathing, this does not
alter the *fact* that *if* I should stop, I will die.[11]

Both the "if . . . then" and the "when . . . then" statement state
relationships. The former always states a possibility, whereas the latter always states an actual future occurrence. The former formulates
what may possibly happen, while the latter states what will be or is
the case. The former statement concerns the limits of possibility,
while the latter concerns the extent of actual circumstances. The
former covers many possibilities, while the latter covers just one actuality. All these differences are differences between stating nomic
conditions and describing a future event. The "if" in the "if . . . then"
statement means *whenever*. These differences of statement,
moreover, point to differences of fact. Conditions are to be met by
events, while events must meet conditions if they are to occur. The
conditions limit the possibility of any event of a certain kind, whereas
the event simply realizes one of the possibilities. Events, being subject
to conditions, do not function as rules, whereas conditions as rules,
that is, as conditions-1, do not actually occur. Events do not obtain,
rules do not occur. Conditions are always universal, whereas events
are always concretely individual. Conditions determine, while events
are determined. Conditions condition, while events are conditioned.

But what if our experience suggests to us that only events are conditions? Events depend on one another; they are interdependent. The
actual shining of the sun and the occurrence of the annual picnic are
interdependent. That's indeed how it seems to us, but for the sake of
analysis we must take the trouble to determine what this really adds
up to. When an event occurs, some condition-1 has gone into effect.

The conditional connection is now also bound to take effect. The relation between events, however, is a conditioned or determined one. Only by virtue of the determining conditions-1 can an event possibly be said to function as a condition-2. We do get to know about conditions-1 from conditioned events, but these events are not themselves the conditions-1. The conditions-1 do not even relate to any event in particular; rather, they relate to any possible event of a certain kind.

2.2 *Provisional or Transitional Terminology*

The discussion of conditions above took place in the context of events. This limitation was imposed for the sake of clarity, and also because that was where the confusion lay. But are events the only conditioned realities? The ancient discussion of universals was less closely related to laws, rules, and events than to genera and species, to natural kinds. But might not what we call genus or species be what we understand of the complexity of the conditions that actual objects must meet in the natural world?[12] These objects are all of a particular kind. In order for an object to be an object of the kind that it is, must it not meet certain conditions? Besides events, must not also frogs and dandelions meet certain conditions if they are to come into existence and then continue to exist as frogs and dandelions?[13]

What we need at this point is a set of terms that can generally express the distinction between conditions-1 and empirical reality.[14] Empirical reality is the reality of functors functioning in relation: events, objects, relations, functions of these, parts of these, actions, and so forth. The terminology I will introduce is not meant to be permanent; it is only intended to enable us to carry the discussion forward. Perhaps later discussion will reveal difficulties and subtleties that will encourage a change in terminology. For the moment I want to make clear that the difference between conditions-1 and the empirical world of conditions-2 is not a difference that should be expressed by means of the contrast between reality and nonreality. That there are nomic conditions and dependence relations is simply a matter of experience.

It is too early to say at this point just what nomic conditions are and what the nature of their reality is. That we do know them, however, is a matter of record. And this is no less true even if it should become clear that *reality* is not a term that can be applied equally well to conditions-1 on the one hand and sticks and stones on the other. The typewriter I am using to write this book exists; it really exists. *That* my typewriter exists is the case; it is really the case. The "really" qualifying "exists" and the "really" qualifying "is the case" may be incommensurate, but this does not alter the fact that there appears to be nothing strange or suspect about the propriety of using "really" in both contexts.

For the present I will speak of "subjective existence" in referring to the world of sticks, stones, racial prejudice, headaches, and concepts. This "subjective existence" might be referred to by others (with or without all the items I include) as the empirical world, the world of space-time existence, or the world of observable entities. The terminology I shall use for the present is not meant to prejudice the question whether this world is mental or physical or both. The use of the term *subjective* is proper in that it is intended to indicate a relationship to the other term I introduced earlier—*condition*. Conditions-1 are such that events occur *subject to the condition that* such-and-such take place. Thus *subject* or *subjective* is here used as a term to indicate the relation of whatever goes on in our world to conditions-1. In using the terms *subjective existence* and nomic *condition*, I am not prejudging the issue of the reality of either or the issue of their reality being commensurate; I am only introducing the consideration that whatever exists empirically does exist subject to conditions that must be met.

2.3   Conditions, Universality, and Existence

With the help of the terms introduced above, I will now address the following questions: (1) Will an understanding of conditions help us to understand universality as we meet it in what have been called universals? (2) Will it help us to decide whether whatever it is that has this character of universality exists? I will address these two problems separately, beginning with the second.

2.3.1   The existence of conditions

Suppose a certain event (x) cannot occur unless another event (y) occurs first. What I mean is not that x always comes after y, but that x will occur *only if* y occurs.[15] In other words: x cannot possibly occur unless y has occurred first. The occurrence of y *must* precede x. The occurrence of x *necessarily* comes after y. In this case what we have is a relationship between two events such that one is the consequence of the other. The one event can occur only *subject to the condition that* the other occurs first. Suppose that x is the birth of a calf. Then y can be the impregnation (in whatever manner) of the cow that gave birth to the calf.[16] The relationship between x and y is such that whenever we know x has occurred, we can take it that y has also occurred. The occurrence of y as a certainty is evident in other events and relationships that have occurred. This not only allows us but *forces* us to conclude that there are conditions. The conditional relationship between x and y which I have just explored is even a *necessary* condition. If the condition for x must be met and if the occurrence of x is subject to that condition, then it simply cannot be that there is x apart from y. If x depends on y, then we can say: "If x, then y."

The implantation of a fertilized egg in the womb of a cow is a necessary condition, but it is not a sufficient condition. It is necessary in addition that there be a successful gestation period, that the fetus remain alive, that the calf to be born not be strangled by the umbilical cord, and so forth. Nevertheless, we should not simply accept a Humean argument concerning the relationship between the fertilization of an ovum and the birth of a calf. It is simply not the case that we know nothing more than that these events are always joined and that we do not know how they are related and therefore cannot say anything about the necessity of a relationship between them.[17]

Science could not survive if the necessity of such relationships were actually regarded as fictional, as an unavoidable psychic circumstance, or as human habit. The necessity in question is not *logically* established (i.e., demonstrable by formal argument), of course, for the simple reason that the necessity in question is not a necessary relation between propositions but a relation between fertilization and birth. But this is insufficient reason to deny that we know that there are necessary relations between events.[18]

To use the terminology developed above, we can say that events occur subject to conditions. When we look at those conditions, we see that conditions-2 point to conditions-1. If we are dealing with necessary events and relations, we are naturally inclined to ask: What makes it so? Logic may help us conclude that something is necessary. Yet necessity is not always logical. But what if nomic conditions obtained, and what if they obtained universally? Would that not make things necessary? The question remains: Just what would be the reality of nomic conditions, especially of conditions-1? (There is also a problem with regard to conditions-2, of course, for what is in question is not their status as events but their function as incorporators of conditions-1.)

It seems to me that we need not see anything mysterious here. We do not need to draw the conclusion that there is a special place somewhere or a special time, or perhaps some specific place at some time outside our space or time, where one could meet (hypothetically) or observe conditions-1 by themselves. To wonder about the reality of nomic conditions and to insist that it must be totally unlike all subjective existence (i.e., unlike any functor, function, or relation between them) at least implies we're not looking for anything in space or time. Nor are we searching for something *like* anything in space or time which is not in space or time.[19]

To say that there are conditions-1 is not necessarily to say that they are observable as six feet tall, or that they must have weight or color, or that they must smell good. Neither need they be minds or concepts, or exist as concepts in minds. They could be just what they are, that is, just be themselves. They could be conditions, and as conditions they could be unlike anything else. As far as I know, there is no law stipulating that if there are conditions, they must be like what they condition in some way.[20] But in order not to prejudice the issue needlessly, I will simply state only that we know there are conditions. Knowing this does not invalidate the hypothesis that nomic conditions need not be like subjective existence.[21]

What are conditions? Can they be described? Can they be defined? If the argument concerning events made above can be extrapolated, we could say that conditions are limits within which subjective existence is possible. Nomic conditions could be understood as limits of possibility. No subjective existence is possible, this thesis would imply, unless certain conditions are met. This holds for events, things, and relationships. Every existent is then a subjective existent (in the sense previously defined) simply because it exists subject to nomic conditions and *can* exist only subject to such conditions. In this sense, conditions order subjectivity, that is, existence is subject to limits. Nomic conditions "prescribe" how something must exist or in what way subjective existence is to be.

If this is one way to describe what conditions are, it may shed some light on the question of their existence. If we normally use the term *existents* to refer to phenomena that can only occur subject to conditions, that is, whose existence is their being subject to conditions and whose existence is made possible only by subjection to these conditions, it may turn out not to be possible to say meaningfully that conditions exist.[22] The expression *subjection to conditions* is intended to enable us to distinguish between conditions and that which is subject to them. If *all* that *exists* is subject to conditions and if conditions are to be distinguished from *all* that is subject to them, they cannot themselves be conceived as *existent*. Still, we must conclude that there are conditions, and also that existence is subject to conditions.

Suppose I were to say: Children exist subject to the condition that they have parents. Their parents make them possible. Parents both exist and are distinguished from the children that exist. What, then, is so difficult about saying that conditions exist and also that all that exists exists subject to conditions? Why shouldn't some existent function as condition for some other existent? This is precisely what the problem is all about. When some existent functions as a condition, what is that functioning like? How can it be that I am talking about a relationship that obtains quite apart from any specific children or parents? This relationship can be stated in terms of a universal conditional rule: If anything, no matter what, is to be a child, it will have to have parents. This rule obtains quite apart from any specific people who are either children or parents. The conditions formulated in this conditional statement are conditions-1. The existing parents are conditions-2 with regard to particular children. But our concern here is with the universal conditional, that is, with the rule.

Would it help to look at the existence of conditions solely in terms of statements or sentences?[23] I don't believe so. Nothing is a statement if it does not state something. A statement stating a rule or condition states what the rule or condition is that is being stated. What is it that is being stated? Only if the statement and the rule were the same thing could rules be statements, but this will clearly not do. Just as the term *hat* is not a hat, so the statement "Children must have parents" is not a condition. Statements do no conditioning. Only conditions do.

An example may be helpful to make this clear. Imagine the entire collection of statements of all countries that have traffic moving on the right-hand side of the road. These statements differ from each other, and even if they were all translated into English they would still be different statements. But all of them state a condition in stating what they state. What they provide for is that traffic in the country concerned *must* move on the right-hand side of the road. None of these statements state or imply that all traffic without exception (or, for that matter, even a single vehicle) does move that way or will move that way. The statements only state that traffic in keeping with the existing order, that is, traffic that escapes fines and accidents, must (and probably will) move on the right-hand side of the road, and in any case is allowed (is possible) only on the right-hand side. That's the only possibility for the sensible existence of traffic in these countries under the present rules.

What all these different statements state, then, is not a statement but a rule. They state a nomic condition.[24] They do not state what happens but what *must* happen. And not all conditions are like traffic conditions. Traffic conditions-1 are human inventions and conventions, but the conditions that certain animals must meet in order to be frogs are not human conventions or inventions. Nor did frogs invent them. Frogs have less say about the conditions they must meet than human beings do. But this does not give us a reason to affirm the reality of traffic rules while denying the reality of the conditions frogs must meet. And who would want to deny that in many countries there are rules, regulations, stipulations, and laws pertaining to traffic?

It might appear unreasonable to question the reality of traffic rules even when the term *existence* has perhaps been reserved for things that *meet* conditions-1. But if this is the case, wouldn't it be equally unreasonable to deny the reality of conditions in the natural world? Doesn't the pattern of argument that leads observers in a city to conclude that there must be traffic rules of some kind also lead to the conclusion that there must be conditions for frogs? In both cases, doesn't the regularity along with the continuity of the regularity induce us to conclude that there is indeed some ground for the continuity of those patterns? Why might one not be justified in concluding that there are conditions-1?

This line of argument could be said to ascribe temporality and location to conditions. There are conditions in Canada (location) in the twentieth century (time) which hold for all traffic. No one doubts this. Can this inference also be made in the case of natural nomic conditions? In traffic there are conditions-1 and conditions-2. The former are the decisions (on the books) of competent bodies, while the latter are actual traffic patterns. There are limiting conditions-1 (prescribing where traffic can move legally, and in what direction) as well as subjective existents (actual traffic subjected to the conditions-2). The conditions-1 stipulate *that* traffic must move in a certain direction. What is the significance of the word *that* in the previous sentence?

In philosophy, science, or logic, we deal with "that" statements as statements of fact, that is, as propositions, statements of what is the case. I will take the term *proposition* to refer to the analytic or conceptual referent of statements of fact. The statement of fact refers to what has conceptually been grasped. What has conceptually been grasped, the proposition, is stated. When the statement is taken only for its factual, analytic, conceptual significance, the statement itself is sometimes called a proposition. A proposition is then the content of a statement of fact; in such propositions we then state our conceptual grasp of something. But let me use *proposition* to mean the fact stated, not the statement of the fact.

But if "*that* traffic must move in certain directions" is a condition grasped as well as stated, does this imply that conditions can be identified with propositions? I think not, for the same reason I gave earlier for not accepting the identity of conditions with statements. A proposition is simply the conceptual content of some kind of statement, that is, of a statement made for the significance of its factual content. A proposition is a logical or analytic entity.[25] The logical significance or analytic meaning of a (semantic) statement finds its origin in the fact that the statement arises as a way of stating a conceptual result. The (semantic) statement "Frogs are amphibians" has as part of its conceptual content "are amphibians" or the proposition to the effect *that* frogs are amphibians.

The factual statement or assertion, then, is not itself a proposition (as I use the term) but is a statement of some special kind, referring to a proposition. When the statement is made in order to state a proposition, the statement is intended to state a fact. *Proposition* is a name for the stated fact.[26] But this requires that we find out what the reality called "proposition" calls our attention to. The proposition, in my view, is a conceptually grasped relationship such as that frogs are amphibians. The relationship *as* grasped (conceived) differs from the relationship *that* is grasped. Not only do words and sentences need references, but so do concepts and propositions.[27] Terms and statements name and state concepts and propositions on one level, but these concepts and propositions must in turn refer to something beyond themselves. Analytic, logical, or rational content is conceptual, that is, conceptually grasped; but what is grasped is (generally) not conceptual itself.[28]

What is it that is conceptually grasped? In "Frogs are amphibians," we do not grasp frogs or amphibians; frogs and other amphibians are grasped in nets—not concepts. That which we grasp conceptually is certainly unlike a frog. In this sense, frogs are not analytic or conceptual entities.[29] As subjective existents, however, frogs are entities that exist subject to conditions. There are conditions that hold for all frogs whatever, that is, for any possible frog. Could it be that these conditions are named in the predicate "being a frog"? When it is stated that frogs are amphibians, is the relation of "being a frog" to "being an amphibian" stated as it has been grasped conceptually?

"That traffic must move on the right-hand side" is what the condition is. "That traffic must move on the right-hand side" is also what we typically call a fact. Moving traffic is not what we refer to when we speak of facts. "That it moves" is what we mean by a fact. But does this not suggest that what we conceptually grasp are nomic conditions? Does this not suggest that concepts and propositions are our monadic and polyadic conceivings of conditional frameworks? Might this also not be the explanation for why many philosophers have "solved" the problem of universals by saying that universals do not exist, whereas concepts or words do? How could that "solution" even begin to be a solution unless there were in fact some relation there? If terms name concepts and if concepts are our grasp of universally obtaining nomic conditions, then one might indeed confuse or substitute concepts for nomic conditions. And this is indeed what my analysis leads me to conclude. There are conditions. No one denies that. These conditions are what we know, understand, experience in concepts. And concepts are named in words. In this analysis, conceptual relations are conceived relations among conditions. Multi-conceptual conceivings are propositions. They are linguistically asserted in statements of fact.[30]

The statement of fact (and it is indeed a fact that frogs are amphibians) turns out to be a statement of conditions. If anything is to be a frog, it must be an amphibian, and if anything was a frog, it was an amphibian. "Being an amphibian," like "moving on the right-hand side," is a conditioning state of affairs, and existing frogs must relate to it. They exist in subjection to those conditions. Some frogs are not well formed; they do not fully meet the conditions. It could even be that no frog will ever be well formed in the future. Even so, "being a frog" would still be our reference to what we have grasped of the conditions that would have been met if there were a well-formed frog somewhere.

So conditions-1 are themselves not concepts or propositions, nor statements or assertions; they are neither conceptual nor semantic in kind. However, they can be conceptually grasped and semantically asserted. We make use of conceptual terms and propositional statements for these assertions. Statements of condition are statements of fact, stating what must be the case. The fact or the case is *that* traffic in such-and-such countries moves (must move) on the right-hand side. True statements of fact, or true propositions, refer us to what is in fact the case. And what is the case is either that certain conditions-1 have been met (e.g., that there is a frog) or that certain conditions are to be met (e.g., that frogs are amphibians).

The grasping of conditions is, on this analysis, conceiving a pattern of order. The people who proclaim the order in the case of the traffic patterns also have the power to take steps to extract the desired response. They have issued a law ordering people to behave in certain ways, a law that makes them limit their possible behavior by subjecting themselves to certain limiting conditions. If the responses are not satisfactory, there will—or can—be sanctions. If you drive the wrong way up a one-way street, you might get a ticket, and you might even be involved in an accident. If, as a frog, you are without hind legs, you are liable to get caught and eaten.

In the case of traffic laws, is the law the statement on the books? No, the statement states the law; it articulates a certain relationship to be maintained by the lawgivers and to be met by their subjects. That the relationship is regulated in a certain way is what the law is all about. If a law did in fact obtain but were somehow not on the books, it could still be discovered through an analysis of the behavior of traffic and of law-enforcement officers. As a result of such analysis, one would conclude *that* such-and-such is the case.

Thus, conditions that are fulfilled and then analyzed lead to the discovery and grasping of these conditions. Analysis of conditions-2 leads to the conceptual grasp of conditions-1. Analysis is itself conditioned to grasp conditions. An analytic, conceptual, or logical statement is a statement of conditionality-1. Analytic statements state relationships in the fashion of rules and laws. The rules for analysis, its nomic conditions, if met in the actual analysis of x, are destined to lead to the nomic conditions obtaining for x. Order, structure, conditions, and so forth, are analytically or conceptually stated in terms of propositions, theorems, systems, and the like.

The conclusion I draw is that it is partly a matter of terminology whether or not one refers to conditions-1 as existing. If we always use the term *existence* to mean that which exists in subjection to conditions, that is, the empirical world of observable entities in their relations and activities, then conditions-1 cannot be said to exist.[31] But all that is meant by this is that the term *existence* should not be used with reference to them. I certainly do not mean to say that conditions-1 do not really present themselves to us. And if they do indeed present themselves to us, what are we to say about their reality? Perhaps we should say no more than that they hold or obtain. This is something a tree does not do: no tree obtains. Neither do other objects or events or actions in our world obtain. What, then, is the reference for *hold* or *obtain*? What does it stand for? Is it an action? And in virtue of what does anything hold or obtain? To answer these questions, I must move on from existence to universality.

2.3.2   *Conditions and the universality of order*

In the case of ordered traffic patterns we can clearly accept conditions. Such conditions are discovered in various ways. We may look them up in law books. We may also observe and analyze traffic as behavior subject to conditions and thus as revealing those conditions. In any case, there is something there to be discovered. But the history of philosophy presents us with a legacy of difficulty in attaching the term *existence* to conditions in the sense developed above. Conditions are neither the statements that state them, nor the propositions in which we grasp them conceptually, nor the behavior that conforms to them and is subject to them. Even so, we must accept them. What, then, are we to say about the reality of these items that are not statements, concepts, or subjective existents (such as things, events, or the relations between them), but whose reality we accept by way of concepts, statements, and subjective existents? What is the reality of the laws, in traffic as well as elsewhere, and rules we all know are there?[32]

I am suggesting, then, that we move from the rules and patterns we recognize in the case of traffic to patterns and structures we know to be present in our world. This move involves postulating that there is an analogy between the regularity of traffic patterns and the regularity of the empirical world.[33] Mammals regularly give birth to offspring after having been impregnated and after a specified gestation period. The sun rises regularly. We detect the difference between tree sparrows and chipping sparrows in regularly occurring features. Dividing ten by two regularly yields five. For centuries the scientific world has taught us that these observable regularities can be stated in terms of law-like sentences and can be conceived of as occurring in conformity with conditions that are expressed in those law-like sentences.

What makes the whole empirical world go round in patterns? What makes everything in the world behave in structured, continuous patterns? Why can we successfully recognize individual variety despite these patterns? On what basis can we talk about deviation from these structured patterns? If there did obtain an order of conditionality, a coherent framework of conditions-1, we would be able to explain law-like statements and individual variety and deviation quite well. Observed regularity, especially such regularity as we have come to expect and predict since we experience it as necessary, can be explained by behavior which conforms to conditions. Individual variety is explainable by differences in the conformity to the same conditions. Deviation is explained by behavior which does not conform to conditions. Deviant behavior, of course, would result in chaos in the world just as it would in traffic. Death, destruction, error, disease, and other such phenomena would naturally confront us.

Suppose the analogy is valid. That would also help us understand that such an order is universally extended. Each condition holds invariably for any possible object, event, or relation that the condition in question is intended to condition.[34] One-way streets are conditions-2 holding for all vehicular traffic—not just for foreign-made cars. A traffic condition-1 can even be limited. For example, on some streets travel is permitted only for bicycles, motorcycles, cars, and small trucks. Large trucks over a certain weight are not permitted. The rule prohibiting large trucks holds for any possible large truck.

Likewise, our conceptual grasp of what it is to be a frog refers to a pattern of conditions which we call "being a frog" and which holds for all possible frogs. That pattern would hold whether or not all frogs meet all conditions. Any frog not meeting them would be a variant or abnormal frog. As a limit of possibility for all frogs, they would be a universal order of possibility for frogs. The observation of events and behavior involving frogs shows this. If someone asks whether universals exist, then, I would answer as follows: "Science has discovered that for all reality whatsoever there are limiting conditions. Patterns of order and principles of possibility relate to the entire world of subjective existence in such a way that we can conclude that they hold universally and obtain without exception. And they are not incompatible with either individuality or deviation in existence."[35]

An analysis of what goes on in science also yields the conclusion that the conditions uncovered can be conceptualized and semantically formulated. They are, in fact, uncovered *in* being conceived and articulated. Yet what we conceive of or state is not the concept or statement. In other words, conditions-1 cannot be reduced to the status of semantic or logical-analytical, that is, conceptual, reality. Conditions-1 are simply not the same as the reality they condition. Does this imply that there are universals, that is, object-like entities apart from our world? I don't believe it does. What it implies instead is that certain realities must be talked about in a universe of discourse different from the one in which we talk unequivocally about existents in our empirical world. But we would be going too far if we said that these realities were in *existence somewhere* apart from our world or even apart from our conceptual activity. If the scientific record is at all accurate, these realities *obtain* with respect to our world and are explicitly known only as a result of our conceptual activity.

If the postulate of a coherent pattern of order or of a structure of conditions-1 is useful, how are we to conceive of the origin of such a conditional order? We want to know what we are postulating.[36] How are the limits of possibility made possible? Is there a limit to order? Are these even legitimate questions? Are they meaningful questions? Although it might appear at first glance that they are acceptable questions, it turns out on further reflection that they are at least ambiguous. The questions assume the legitimacy of a series that can be pursued continuously. Some x is made possible by some y, and that y by some z, which is in turn made possible by. . . . But the child who asks such a series of questions with regard to her own bed (which rests on the rug, which rests on the floor, which rests on the foundations, which rests on the earth, which rests . . .) will ultimately have to accept the conclusion that although the earth is quite secure, it does not rest on anything else in the way in which things on earth can be said to rest on other things.

Can we be assured automatically that the series "is made possible by" runs on? I think not. It would seem that the postulation of conditions-1 with respect to subjective existents might be such that the category "is made possible by" could apply only to the relation between conditions-1 and subjective existence. The inquiry into the likelihood that conditions-1 also obtain with respect to conditions-1 rests on the supposition that the conditions-1 in question can in turn be treated as subjective existents, which in turn need conditions-1. But if the reality of conditions holds for subjective existence, is it then legitimate to ask for the conditions behind the conditions? In this context, are not conditions postulated as irreducible to subjective existence? The two would be related. But would they not also be irreducibly different? If subjective existence is conditionally limited, it does not follow that an inquiry can be undertaken into the limits of these limits.

What I am getting at here is that if the very being of an entire world, of all of its objects, their properties, and their relations, depends on that world's being constituted by a nomic order of conditions, then being so conditioned separates the conditioned from the conditions. The problem tackled here has the ambiguity of asking whether a bird cage is contained in any cage. That question treats cages as birds and asks bird-sort questions about cages. Perhaps asking what conditions a condition is that sort of question. Why should conditions be conditioned? Subjective existence might be conditioned. That it is conditioned may be its sort of reality. But why conditions? If to be subject to conditions points to a reality that is not subjective, conditions subject to other conditions would seem contradictory.

But perhaps the questions above were simply phrased in the wrong way. Perhaps by asking about the conditions-1 for conditions-1, we ask: What is the origin of conditions? Is that a proper problem? Or are the conditioning limits of subjective existence *sui generis*? Are they perhaps eternal? In the case of traffic rules, what we have is traffic, a body of regulations, and a competent institution authorized to make regulations. If the postulated analogy is to hold, what is there in the relation between conditions-1 and subjective existence that is comparable to the competent institutional authority?[37]

The postulation of an order of nomic conditionality makes it possible to explain a variety of significant phenomena. I do not claim to be already finished with the analysis of conditionality; in the next section I will have to explore certain problems further. Still, at this point the following conclusion is clearly before us: If science is correct in maintaining that the world is conditioned and that statements ultimately referring to these conditions use genuine universals that do not point to anything objectively present in our observable world of subjective existence, then the postulation of a correlation between two irreducibles, namely, conditionality and subjective existence, is warranted as a justifiable hypothesis. Conditions, though not existing, will nevertheless be real.

This correlation supports the nominalist claim that whatever nomic conditions may be, they are not like anything we know in the empirical world. And if whatever exists, exists only in the mode of subjective existence, existence cannot be said to be characteristic of conditions. Thus, "existence" cannot be a genuine predicate. But the correlation referred to also supports the realist claim that the empirical world does not exhaust all reality. Furthermore, the positing of this correlation helps us to relate concepts and propositional statements to conditions. It also helps us to understand that the problem of the origin of conditions may not be the same as the problem of how conditions make possible what exists in our empirical world. Finally, this correlation gives us an approach to what the universality of universals may be all about.

2.4 *Differences of Conditionality*

Before my postulated hypothesis of a correlation between conditions and subjective existence can be either accepted or rejected, it will have to be considerably refined.[38] What is especially in need of clarification is the ambiguity in the notion of conditionality. Up to this point I have explored the ambiguity to a certain extent. I sought to resolve the apparent problem by using the terms *conditions-1* and *conditions-2* for the two senses of conditions as "conditions to be met," and by using *circumstances* for conditions as prevailing realities. But as I went along I considered that the difference between conditions-1 and subjective existence could be that of an irreducible relation of correlates. However, if this is taken to be the case, it turns out that, as realizations of conditions-1, conditions-2 are really subjective existents.

The problem which surfaces here is that if conditionality and subjective existence really are mutually irreducible, conditions-1 and conditions-2 would relate in such a way that conditions-2 would (or could) be viewed as both conditions-1 and subjective existents. And given the postulated irreducibility, that would not seem acceptable. Consider the following. If no object traveling at fifty miles per hour can cover a distance of 200 miles in twenty minutes, no taxi driver with a governor on his vehicle restricting him to fifty miles per hour can claim to have a valid alibi for a murder that took place twenty minutes ago by saying that he was then 200 miles from here. The actual circumstances do not meet the conditions which obtain. But if the taxi driver had claimed to be fifteen miles away at the time of the murder twenty minutes before, conditions are met in actual circumstances. Have conditions-1, as stated in the first case, now *become* actual circumstances and thus subjective existents in the second case? This problem must now be examined. Are conditions truly irreducible to subjective existence? In a correlation of irreducibles, can one relation turn into the other?

2.4.1   Conditions and principles

Let us now try to get at the difference between conditions-1 and conditions-2 by considering what we mean by principles and by the expression "in principle." Approaching the problem in this way will allow us to see that the difference between nomic conditions and subjective existence can remain a difference of irreducible correlatives even when we also distinguish between conditions-1 and conditions-2.

The attitude of legalism, conservatism, or traditionalism is in part a reluctance to distinguish between fundamental principles and their cultural expression. What I have in mind is this. People express respect for one another in greeting rituals of various different kinds. In certain cultures men may express respect by taking off their hat to each other. Let's say that after some time people no longer actually raised the hat all the way, but just lifted it slightly. Still later we see people justd touching the hat. In the end all that remains is raising a hand. We can distinguish here between a principle (i.e., expressing respect) and actual patterns of behavior (i.e., various actions with the arm relating to headgear). One could say that the behavior embodies the principle or gives expression to the principle.

In spite of all that varies, something "in principle" remains invariant through all this historical development. The behaviors vary, but "in principle" something maintains its identity in continuity. This continuity in principial invariance also gives continuity to the varying behavior; in fact, this continuity of principle allows us to recognize the varying behaviors as variations within a single pattern and thus as a continuing development. Something "in principle" makes the different behaviors identical. This "something" is the fact that respect is being expressed.

It would be wrong to tie this principle to a particular behavior in such a way as to conclude that only those who lift their hat all the way are showing the proper respect. That view could at best be the temporary and transitional opinion of the more conservation-minded participants in the culture in question. If such an opinion were to degenerate into traditionalism or legalism, we would have a case of a faulty identification of principle and actual behavior. The legalist who claims that those who just tip their hat are in principle not showing the proper respect is making the same mistake as the nominalist: he is failing to distinguish underlying principles in their invariance from the observable patterns of variant behavior.

This example once again raises the question: What is the difference between the reality of lifting one's hat and the reality of greeting or of showing respect? If we say that lifting one's hat, tipping one's hat, and raising one's arm all have something in common in that we designate them as greeting, are we postponing dealing with the question: What is greeting? One cannot properly, that is, with regard for the historical realities, say that we just happen to have various conventions which are all used arbitrarily to greet and to pay respect. These different behaviors are—and were—connected, both historically and in principle. And these two connections are themselves connected.

What, then, do we mean when we refer to something as such-and-such *in principle*? One thing we can say is that the principle allows us to distinguish one action from the other, even though the two actions might seem the same on the surface. Touching one's hat in a baseball game would be one thing if it were done to signal to a player, and another thing if it were done to greet a fan. The two actions, if viewed on film, might not be distinguishable. Seen as a mere pattern of physical motion, the reality would not have meaning in a social context. The same physical action—or one that is apparently the same—would mean one thing when embodying x-in-principle and another thing when embodying y-in-principle.

What lies behind the signaling behavior in baseball and the greeting behavior in other contexts, making the apparently similar behaviors different in principle, is a difference in decisions. We intend the behaviors to be different. In our culture it has been decided that a certain behavior will designate greeting. And in baseball it has been decided, perhaps precisely because of the deceiving similarity, to use the greeting behavior for telling someone not to run. Such decisions are not fundamentally different from a decision to designate all traffic on a certain street as one-way traffic. So long as we abide by them, both the latter and the former decisions will *condition* our behavior, determine our reactions. Such decisions set the limits within which certain behaviors have the meaning they have. We see here the same sort of reality as we have been discussing in the case of conditions. In our present terminology, we might say that earlier we were discussing that subjective existence behaves as though there are certain intentional conventions and explicit decisions about its behavior.

What the shift in terminology makes clear is that if we compare the conditions-1 of the former discussion with the "in principle" of the present discussion, the problem of conditions-1 becoming conditions-2 is not necessarily a problem at all. There is nothing problematic in asserting *both* that "in principle" what we call greeting or paying respect must not be reduced to certain concrete behaviors, *and* that no greeting or paying respect is possible except *in* certain concrete behaviors. Along similar lines, there is therefore no necessary contradiction in saying that conditions-1 are irreducibly different from subjective existence, while saying at the same time that the conditions-1 which obtain will not take effect in existence except in conditions-2. In this way a consideration of "in principle" reality can help clarify certain problems for us. The same is true for a consideration for "in principle" existence.

To make it clear that "in principle" does not mean unreal or non-existent, I should go on to observe that a decision which has been made "in principle" has really been made. The action on the decision may still have to be postponed. There may be a politically risky course of action on which a government must make a decision. Let's say that a decision must be made on whether or not to explore for gas and oil in an area sensitive to environmental problems. Those who oppose such exploration will oppose all possible versions of any decision to go ahead. The proponents of the exploration may differ among themselves on how to go about carrying out a decision to explore. If the government, in such a situation, decides to go ahead with the exploration but to continue debate on the various approaches to exploration, it can announce that it has decided in principle to go ahead. It cannot be said that the government has decided nothing, for it has in fact decided—on the most profound level. The reality of such a decision that has been made can be experienced in the heated debates in parliament, the objections raised in editorials, the demonstrations in front of government buildings, and many other observable events.

In principle the government has decided *that* it will go ahead. Once again the term *that* enters the discussion. We conclude *that*, we agree *that*, we stipulate *that*, we say it is a fact *that*, we refuse to acknowledge *that*, and so forth. Whenever we use the word *that* in such a sense, the problem of a certain "unreal" reality emerges. To decide *that* gas will in fact be exploited differs from exploiting gas. "That such-and-such will happen" refers to a real future event, but it is not an event. Even though the event has not yet happened, we know a good deal about it. This is because we have a concept of a structural pattern which we know will be realized in the future event. Only if the structural pattern is real can we truly know that the event will be such-and-such.

To decide "in principle" is to decide which structure will be realized. To say that behavior item x is a greeting is to say that it realizes the structure of greeting. Greeting "in principle" is the structural pattern of greeting. What history tells us is that relatively invariant principles, during the period in which they obtain, may be concretized in very different events and behaviors. Conditions of universal scope are met in events, and principles of equally universal scope are realized in actions. Conditions-1 for x can be regarded the same as x-in-principle. The condition-1 becomes embodied in a variety of individually differing subjective existents, which then become known as conditions-2.

Conditions-1 may be viewed as conditions-2 in principle. A genus can be said to be what a number of species are "in principle."[39] We could clarify this point by going back to the variety of greetings mentioned earlier. In order to overcome traditionalism in history, it is necessary to recognize lifting a hat, tipping a hat, or raising an arm as greetings. These are not merely physical arm movements. Neither are these movements, as such, greetings. What happens is that the behaviors originate in an intent.

In the intent the structure of a relationship is recognized: showing respect. The behavior which externalizes the intent takes on the reality of the structure. The real character of the behavior is its origin in that structure. The behavior has the reality of that structure as realized in subjective existence. Behavior which is subject to the conditions of greeting (showing respect) becomes conditioned in that way. One could also raise one's arm to stop a car, or one could tip one's hat to indicate "hat" to someone learning English. But when the behavior of touching one's hat originates in the intent to show respect, it takes on the structure of greeting. The behavior then becomes conditioned, contextualized, or determined (limited) thereby.[40]

Nominalism would result in either establishmentarian conventionalism or revolutionary anarchism.[41] Either only lifting one's hat all the way counts as greeting, or anything I choose is greeting. The recognition of "greeting in principle" makes it possible to avoid both conservatism and chaos (in the fear of which conservatism often originates). Helpful objections to legalism or traditionalism sometimes get formulated as follows: Instead of following the tradition literally, we must follow it in spirit, even if it takes on a form that differs from the one with which we are familiar at present. What is meant in such a formulation is this: It is necessary to preserve the "in principle" core of the tradition, its real principle, which appears to get lost at times in its realization. Any principle, when formulated and specified, takes on more limited ranges of meaning in a specific realization. The specific legal code of a given nation will always be narrower and more time-and-place oriented than the principle of justice permits in its universality. Traffic codes for right-hand driving codify the same principle as traffic codes for left-hand driving; there is no difference "in principle" between the two.

This consideration of matters of principle leads me to the conclusion that when we speak of conditions-2 as embodiments of conditions-1, we do not mean that irreducible conditions have thereby been reduced to subjective existents. The principle does not become the behavior. Raising one's hand does not take the place of showing respect; rather, it takes on the meaning of showing respect. Thus conditions-1 as conditions-2 still maintain their own reality as conditions-1 and can be distinguished from a particular specification in conditions-2 by being specified differently. Furthermore, this consideration of principles also shows that a nominalist attitude would not allow us to account for certain historical phenomena. These historical phenomena, however, can be explained adequately with the help of the reality of principles.

Finally, I use conditions-1 and conditions-2 to clear up a *terminological* confusion, which is itself due to not recognizing the irreducibility of nomic conditions and subjective existence. The fact that in our *language* we can refer to both by using *conditions* does not imply that the two are reducible or that there is a contradiction.

2.4.2 *Platonic realism rejected*

A look at conditions as principles seems to have helped us understand how conditions obtain in subjective existence: they determine and limit things and events by holding for them. They validate what they condition. But the concept of principle also made it clear once again that there is a difference between subjective existence and the reality of these principles. Principles are standards for subjective existence, but they are not subjective existents themselves. Doesn't this commit me to Platonic realism? Can I avoid positing two separate worlds—one of appearances which we experience and which change and vary from time to time, and one of stable principles of existence that can only be rationally discerned? And isn't this just what the nominalist objects to—the notion that there is one world that is observably real, and another world of nonobservable, reified word-references or concepts? If the need for principles makes nominalism unacceptable, how does one avoid the objections which nominalists voice against realism?

Plato's "knowable world" contained the identity principles of the things in our world. These identity principles are referred to as "things in themselves" or simply as "things themselves." Although that world might seem much like my posited order of conditions and principles, there is at least one important respect in which Plato's ideal world was not at all unlike our world: in addition to positing the irreducibility of that world to the world of our experience, Plato also viewed it as an ideal model for our world. Our world was an imperfect and multiple copy of the model.

The model, however, was not simply a model: it was much more like an ideal copy of the model. Both worlds, then, were basically of the same kind. This may well be what inspired Aristotle's "third man" objection: if all men were copies of an ideal man, whom did he copy, since he too was a man? If individual men were "conditioned in principle" not by an ideal man but by conditions for being a man, the "third man" argument could be invalidated.[42] But the ideal types were not conceived of as types or principles; they were viewed instead as perfect examples of themselves, to use an expression of Wolterstorff (UN, 267).

No doubt the Platonic positing of two worlds was intended to convey the radical and irreducible difference between existence and its conditions or standards. The standards, however, became perfect samples, like the perfect sample meter preserved in Paris. The meter in Paris is what I would refer to as a condition-2 meter. Plato's ideal world was a perfect and singular condition-2 kind of world apart from our world. For Plato there were two worlds—one containing many imperfect samples, and another containing one perfect standard sample of each kind of thing. It could even be said that Plato had no standards, but only perfect samples serving as standards.

There is a tremendous difference between standards and standardized samples. A standardized sample can be an example, even in the sense of a condition-2, for example, the meter in Paris. A standard is different. The difference here is comparable to the difference between the all-American halfback and the standards set for being a good halfback on an American team. "Meeting the all-American player" and "meeting the standards" are different concepts entirely. The conditions that some entity must meet to be a dog, the conditions that determine whether or not something is a dog, the principles of possibility for being a dog, the limits there are to being a dog, or whatever else one might call that with which I have been dealing in this chapter—none of these is a dog. They do not bark or bite. "Being a color" is neither green nor red nor any other color; it is just not colored.

The Platonic concept of distinguishing standards from entities that meet standards, then, is not acceptable. I say this not because it seems that the Platonist approach appears to be a less likely view than other approaches to the problem of standards, order, conditions, and principles, but simply because the evidence is against it. Although the evidence points to the reality of standards and the like, there is no evidence that standards are like ideal issues of the imperfect appearances in our world. They are not, in that sense, perfect archetypes.

Of course this does not mean that all forms of realism can therefore be rejected on the same basis. One could speak of eternal ideas in the mind of God, of the necessary existence of abstract entities, and so forth. There are many approaches. At least two forms of realism will be rejected at this point. One is the form of realism that interprets conditions along conceptual lines and refers to them as concepts, ideas, abstract entities, forms, or the like. Earlier in this chapter I argued that because such entities are the conceptual grasp of something, they require a referent. Thus the characterization of order along logical or analytical lines is really a postponement of the problem, in which conceptual entities are hypostatized and projected on conditionality of all kinds.

The other form of realism I will reject is that which postulates the eternal existence of conditions or order. Such a postulation is founded on arguments that are purely inferential, without the introduction of any other evidence.[43] In fact, it postulates the ultimacy of inferential procedures. Later I will explain in more detail why this, too, must be rejected.[44] But since the explanation depends directly on ultimate religious assumptions, it must be put off till the Appendix (see especially 8.1.1).

2.4.3   The experience of conditions

Although I have rejected realism, I still want to accept the reality of order.[45] Thus nominalism needs to be rejected too. This can best be achieved if we can argue for the experience of order or conditions, for isn't the nominalist right in rejecting anything of which we have no experience whatsoever?[46] In fact, the nominalist is justified not only in demanding some experience of anything introduced as real but also in demanding that the experience be intersubjective. Can an argument be made for the experience of conditions-1?

I believe the answer to this question is yes, but the validity of the argument will depend on what we understand experience to be and on what we believe can be experienced. Suppose someone were to say that we can experience only a space-time thing or a behavior. Combinations of these in relationships are also admissible. What this would come to is that only the behavior of space-time physical entities in their mutual relationships is really experienceable. Now, suppose someone were to raise the question of the existence of other minds, or even of minds in general. Since I am after intersubjective experience and not private experience, it is immaterial whether the problem is raised in terms of itself or just in terms of the question whether others besides me have minds. Even if I could be sure of my own mind, at least, I might still need an argument for the fact that others could experience my mind.

Suppose, then, that the problem of the *experience* of minds is raised. If we mean by a mind a nonmaterial space-time entity which is capable of behaving in certain ways, it will be difficult—if not impossible—to construe an argument to the effect that such an object has ever been experienced. But what if *mind* simply refers to the fact that people are capable of behaviors of which certain other creatures are not capable, which behaviors we then refer to as mind? One might wish to quibble over just how this is to be conceived, but at least it would then be possible to introduce behavioral categories.

Of course we need not limit our characterization of experience to a description of the entities that can and cannot be experienced. In fact, such an approach would be inadequate. It is also necessary to specify just what is going on when something is being experienced. Suppose someone were to say that experience is knowing something through the senses. We can experience what we can touch, smell, see, hear, or taste. If such an affirmation were to be strictly interpreted, one might say that no one has ever had the experience of love. On the other hand, we might interpret the affirmation in a much looser sense and take it to mean that whatever is experienced must not entirely bypass sense perception. One would indeed have a hard time explaining an experience of love in which nothing was ever seen, heard, touched, tasted, or smelled.

Let me now restrict what I mean by *experience* in at least two ways. First of all, no experience can be devoid of any and all relations to sense perception. Secondly, no experience can be devoid of any and all relations to what we call material things in time and space.[47] If I had nothing more to say than this, the experience of conditions might be hard to establish. Fortunately, there is more to be said. To begin with, it is necessary to point out the variety of experience correlated with the variety of realities to be experienced. Having a feeling of discomfort, seeing a fire, being indignant, disliking tomatoes, conceiving of other possibilities to raise funds, voting against the present government, buying a scarf, loving one's child, and praying to God are all different sorts of experience of different sorts of reality. To insist that loving your child can be a real experience only when it is like seeing a fire is to reduce experience to some of its dimensions without having any good grounds for doing so. Of course one could arbitrarily limit the meaning of the word *experience* to instances that are like a case of seeing something, but it would be unfair to expect everyone to then accordingly limit our experience of what experience is.[48]

Now, if I were to say that people do experience order, conditions, principles, and laws, what could anyone say against this? Would it be fair to say that this would commit me to the existence of immaterial things such as redness? I don't believe so. If I were to use the term *redness*, I would use it as a name for the conditions that must be met if some color is to be red. And those conditions would obtain universally for any possible occurrence of red. If there are said to be any conditions that actually do not obtain universally, they are simply not included in whatever is named by *redness*.[49]

Thus I do not accept the argument that experience of conditions or the like commits me to the existence of immaterial things.[50] It commits me to conditions, and it also commits me to the indirectness of experience. One cannot focus attention on conditions or principles except by way of words and concepts. One cannot directly weigh or measure a principle, for example. The way to get at it is to name what is grasped conceptually. But surely this cannot be judged unacceptable. Words have references, and so do concepts. That people make up words with pseudo-references (unicorn, Alice in Wonderland) or construct pseudo-concepts that are speculative (that than which nothing greater can be conceived to exist) does not mean that words refer to nothing real or that concepts are human machinations. Even when a word only refers to a concept, we can still ask what reality is grasped in the concept.

It seems that philosophers have always had difficulty admitting that conceptual activity could count as experience. I personally do not have such a problem, and I am at a loss as to what I should adduce as an argument for such experience. Perhaps the tendency to reject conceptual activity as experience is due to ascribing such activity to an immaterial thing called a mind, which resides in a material thing called a body. I reject this idea of mind. But conceptual activity remains. Philosophers and scientists engage in this sort of activity full-time. What better argument can be offered for the reality of conceptual experience? That conceptual experience is fraught with danger, that the road to a valid concept is full of traps, that the world of concepts is populated with pseudo-concepts and false concepts—all of this, surely, does not count against the possible reality of conceptual experience.[51]

If the right rules are followed, conceptualization is neither arbitrary nor devoid of experience. In fact, no human experience is humanly possible except with the presence of conceptual functions. The identity of any entity as an entity of a certain kind is crucial to all human experience. But the identification is impossible without conceptual functions. The conclusion of an argument, of course, is conceptually or analytically experienced, and what the conclusion refers us to is often indirectly experienced. But why shouldn't we say that it is even then a real experience of something real? It is perfectly true that if experience is limited to individual material entities, it would be hard to classify analysis as experience. In analysis we experience individuality as a limit. We can only name it; we do not conceive of it. On the other hand, even the experience of individual physical entities without conceptual awareness would not be human experience but at most animal awareness.

Perhaps the fact that conceptual-analytic experience points to realities we accept on the basis of certain evidence is a problem. Perhaps belief, that is, the acceptance of some entity as real, is not admissible as experience. But again I would ask: why not? Virtually the entire world accepts the reality of the Afghanistan conflict on the basis of the reports in the newspaper. Such belief constitutes a major portion of all our experience.[52] Of course we must be able to trust the source of the reports we are asked to believe. But if we do, we all are prepared to act on the basis of our beliefs.[53] In the case of conditions, laws, and principles, however, the evidence is scientific evidence and the people who report about laws and concepts are scientists. Our culture has always accepted evidence of that sort as the best attested.

I conclude that there is no reason to believe that conditions cannot be experienced, neither because of what conditions are nor because of what experience is. How do we experience conditions-1? By way of conditions-2. If we are in a theater where a magician is performing, he may say to us: "I hope you can all see that the card I am holding up is triangular and red." There is nothing unusual about such a statement. What he said was: you can *see that*. "Seeing that" is an expression for seeing an instance in which certain conditions have been met. *Seeing that* something *is red* is seeing that the conditions for being red were met in this instance. What we are seeing "qualifies" as red. Therefore what we see is red. "That it is red" is seen. Normally we do not regard this as an abstraction. If we want to abstract "that it is red" from seeing that it is red, we need conceptual or analytic focus. Then we view the propositon "that it is red" as our conceptual grasp of an instance of "being red," and from there we can analyze what "being red"entails. We then experience that something is red in a different way, but we still experience it. First we met "being red" (a condition-1) in this red card, and then we abstracted it. This, too, is an experience.

2.4.4   *The reality of conditionality*

I have said that experience must be related to material things and to sense perception. I have said also that conditions-1 can be experienced because as conditions-2 they meet the requirements of what experience should be. However, my ontology remains thin. All we know so far is that whatever I am talking about, it is a reality that relates universally to the things in our material and perceivable world, although its own reality is unlike anything concretely individual. Whatever it is, it holds for or obtains with respect to the world of individual entities. This I have taken to mean that order, conditions-1, principles, laws, and whatever it is that we grasp in concepts and name in words relates to the world of individual entities by ordering it, providing structure in it, limiting it, making it possible, and the like.

Is there any more that can be said? Can we legitimately contrast order with the ordered world and say that whatever is characteristic of the ordered world is not characteristic of the reality of order? As a general procedure this seems unacceptable. The fact that the world of individual objects is knowable is not a reason to conclude that conditions are not knowable. But what about characteristics of the world of individual things in correlation with the order of conditions, and from the point of view of that correlation? If the correlation presents us with irreducible correlates, can we find characteristics of irreducibility on both sides?

My postulate is that the relation between subjective existence and the order of nomic conditions is such that conditions make subjective existence possible, whereas subjective existence is dependent on conditions. Here we seem to have a relationship which is correlative and irreducible. On reflection, however, it is not clear just what characterizes the irreducibility. In what way are conditions unlike subjective existence, and in what way is subjective existence unlike conditions? The introduction of the distinction between conditions-1 and conditions-2 has still left us with an ambiguity on this point.

It is possible that the ambiguity is primarily semantic in character. It may be that what we call conditions-2 are just the evidence that conditions-1 are at work in subjective existence. It is possible that no event or occurrence as such is ever a condition. If x is only possible on the condition y, it may be better to say that an event y_e is the fulfillment of the condition. In y_e the condition has been met. Yet y_e is not the condition; rather, y is the condition. In the case of the conditions for the birth of a calf, one might say that one of the conditions is that an egg cell *must* be fertilized. The fertilized egg cell is not a condition as such but the fulfillment of a condition. The condition has been met.

But this brings us back once again to the reality of conditions. The hypothesis I have postulated proceeds from the assumption that the world is ordered, structured, has continuity, and displays lasting identities. All the functors functioning in relationship in our empirical space-time world have that order in common. It is they who display structure. It is they who are the concrete elements in a coherent totality called our world. And my postulate is that the ordered world with its continuity of common features depends on nomic conditions for its being so ordered and continuous. It is these nomic conditions, so my postulated hypothesis goes, that explain and account for all we want to or need to explain and account for in our world. As principles of the ontic given of an ordered world, they also serve as principles of explanation. They will explain the realities of our empirical world.

How will they explain the empirical world? In the same way that a set of bylaws, orders in council, and similar binding decisions, together with the submission of motorists, cyclists, and pedestrians to those conditions will explain and account for the traffic patterns in Toronto. The common features of our world, its regularities and continuities are what they are in subjection to conditions which obtain in our world. That the reality of an order of conditions will explain all we need to explain I hope to show presently. It may be objected, however, that the fact that x will explain y is no guarantee that y exists or that x is real. I grant this. On the other hand, a hypothesis that accounts for how and why the world is as it is, and that also accounts for how we can explain how and why the world is as it is, does just about all that one can ask of a hypothesis. My hypothesis does no more than this: it says that we all experience an ordered world, that in science we conceptualize and name the order of our world, that whatever it is that we so conceive and name is a reality, and that in appealing to that reality we can both successfully explain our world and account for that explanation.

Let us put it in another way. We can account for and explain why blood is red. To do that we have to understand the structure of light and of the perception of light, the physics of blood particles, and much more. That is, we employ previously found lawfulness, fit the unaccounted for item within its pattern, and thus account for what we need to explain.[54] However, though we can explain why blood is red, we cannot with equal success explain why red is red. All we can do is point to a set of complexly interrelated lawful patterns and say: that is red. When some entities function in subjection to that set of lawful patterns, they are red. But are we now entitled to ask how or why red is red? Is red red? Blood is red. Cardinals are red. Some sunsets are red. Much wine is red. By "is red" we mean that all of these meet the conditions for being red. Those conditions we can discover (through conceptual analysis) and name. What more do we need or want?

Well, we might say, with traffic laws we can go much further. We can explain their history. We can show you who made the decisions. How about the lawful order of conditions for being red? What is their history? What is their origin? Well, what of it? Why are these questions even legitimate? It took philosophy some time to realize that to ask of "red" why it is red was simply not appropriate. But how appropriate is it then to ask whether "red" has a history? Here, I believe, we meet an inveterate trait of human nature. We want a satisfactory explanation for everything, not just first order reality. If in order to explain the empirical world we appeal to an order that is to be found neither among the functors of our empirical world, nor among any of their actual and concrete functions, nor among any of their actual and concrete relations, then we want an explanation of that order. And especially in our culture, if we cannot explain it, we will not be inclined to accept it.[55]

It is permissible in our time to assume that theoretical hypotheses about problems as theoretically ultimate as our problems are framed in the light of our deep-seated commitments.[56] Whether we are naturalists, secularists, atheists, theists, Platonists, Christians, or whatever, will likely make a difference in the position we take in the present discussion. We *may* say: obviously the world is ordered and it is also obvious that the ordered things are not the same as the order. But the order is not further explainable. It is just there. It is as we find it. Or: the order evolved with the world and in interaction with it. Or: it has been here from eternity. Or we may say: there is a world order and what we experience as such is what the Creator of the world wanted the world to be like. In this case we see world order according to the analogy of human beings ordering their society. Christian theists may follow such a route. But we may also say: all that there is in the world is just what we can see. We see no more than functors functioning in relationships. And these are all concretely individual entities. They are all there is. What we say depends on these positions we can take as well as on what we think of the ultimacy of our powers of explanation or of the finality of the authority of the rules of inference.[57]

Philosophically we cannot enter into the matter of how these positions and our commitments function in devising a world hypothesis. All we can say is that the positing of the reality of a world order, of a coherent set of nomic conditions which must be distinguished from the world as ordered, is a reasonable theoretical move.[58] From the point of view of responsible theorizing it is as reasonable as the move made in metaphysical realism or in nominalism.[59]

2.5   *Approach to the Problem of Universals*

Now that I have distinguished between conditionality and subjectivity, I will make an approach to the problem of "universals" in terms of that distinction. What I intend to show is that the postulated distinction allows us to deal with the traditional problems associated with the universals controversy in a new way. It will allow us to reject the existence of things which are universals, and also the existence of things which are purely individual. Whatever it is that has the universality of a universal will not be found among the entities, objects, things, that we find in our empirical, subjective world of individual existents. And an individual will bear evidence of universality. Each individual sparrow has "being a sparrow" predicated of it. *It* is what *is a sparrow*.[60]

It is, then, more to the point to speak of the traits of universality and individuality. Universality I propose to see as the way in which conditions relate to subjective existence, while individuality I propose to see as the way in which subjective existence meets conditions. Thus I will deal with universality and individuality in terms of the conditionality-subjectivity relationship, that is, in terms of the two directions of that relationship. I will go back to some of the problems I raised in the first chapter to see whether the approach adopted in this second chapter can help address them.

2.5.1   *The holding of conditions and validity*

There are judgments which are said to be universally valid. One such judgment or proposition is "Being human is being mortal" or "If anything is human, it is mortal." Why is such a proposition universally valid? If it states what has been conceptually grasped or understood to be a condition for humanity, it articulates something that is universal in scope. If the scope of the condition in question is indeed universal and if it has been correctly grasped, the universality of the condition-existence relationship is transmitted to the propositional statement.[61] Universality then means that the sentence asserting the proposition truly states a universal condition and should be universally accepted.

What makes a propositional statement true is that it correctly states what has been conceived correctly. In a so-called universal proposition, then, a person has conceived correctly that a certain relationship holds universally. If something is human, it is mortal. Whatever is of a certain kind, in this case, human, is mortal. Whatever is human is necessarily mortal.[62] Whatever is of a certain kind is what it is in subjection to a nomic configuration of order. The relationship between what is and what determines that which is, is a universal relationship from the side of the determining principle of conditionality. Orders of conditionality hold universally for the subjectivities for which they do hold.

The condition is not "a universal" in the sense of an existing, subjective entity which has certain properties.[63] The universality is simply the relationship between conditions and that which is conditioned viewed from the point of view of the conditions. The same relationship going in the other direction is one of individuality. Subjects meet conditions uniquely, even when it is the same condition they meet. No two frogs are the same, even though all frogs are frogs. The responses of any two frogs to the conditional order or configuration which we might call "being a frog," which determines the reality of any possible frog, are individual responses. Since they are responses to one and the same condition, there is structural continuity and similarity as the context of individuality.

Just as a principle of conditionality is not "a universal," so the concretely existing object is not "an individual" but rather an individual frog. But the individual frog, in being a frog, is never *just* individual. Because the principle determining the existing frog is not itself a frog, it is confusing to refer to the conditional order for frogs as "The Frog," for the order of conditions is not a frog at all. And it is equally confusing to refer to frogs as "instances" or "examples," since that would make particulars into sorts of conditions.[64]

2.5.2 Universality as a relation

The traditional concept of universals is, as I see it, a view of the way in which conditions relate to that which they condition. In that view "universals" are reified relationships or reified conditions characterized by the way in which they relate. If this description is correct, then the *problem* of universals can be addressed as the problem of how we view conditions or principles of order. Let us say that the scope with which conditions hold is the area within which, without exception, particular existents can exist as valid, normal, and well formed. That scope and area are then our understanding of how conditions obtain universally. And the existents in that area respond individually. The reality of the conditions is then such that they hold without exception for everything that appears within their area of conditionality, that is, for all things subject to them.

It is important to understand that not all particular subjects that respond individually do in fact respond to the conditions holding for them in keeping with what those conditions require.[65] The conditions obtain universally regardless of whether they are being held to. Also, the conditions obtain universally regardless of the fact that all responses differ individually. The conditions for being a frog require that frogs have four legs. Not all frogs that come into the world do in fact have four legs. Moreover, some frogs have stronger legs than others. Yet these facts do not alter the requirement that wherever and whenever we look for a frog, we are required to look for a four-legged animal. Finding a frog born with three legs, however, leaves it a frog. It is deformed. We are justified in calling it deformed only if to be well formed it is necessary to have four legs. If not, then we have just found a new species.[66]

Of course, if subjects deviate from the conditions that hold for them, there are consequences. Frogs with weak legs get caught; frogs with no legs don't get around much to find food. Conditions are for existence, and therefore noncompliance with conditions interferes with existence. Individual compliance with conditions gives the holding power of conditions specific relevance. Subjectivity is not just human. Other existents are also subjective and not the same as that which determines what they must necessarily be. No individual subjective existent is a necessarily "standardized" sample—always to be trusted to indicate the standard correctly.

Since there is room for both deviation and variation, that is, subjectivity and individuality within the scope of the conditions, the investigation of conditions by way of the structures of actual existents often leads to conclusions that are at best general. Individuality and deviation show up in the statistical nature of many of our statements of law. The only way analysis can get at conditions is by way of what conforms to them. Rules of inference allow us to relate various conditions to one another, but there always remains the problem of determining which premises are correct. True premises are not always possible. The noncompliance of subjective existence as well as analytic noncompliance interferes with our efforts to state conditions validly. Often we are aware of this and therefore regard certain conclusions as probable, or as statements of trends, or as being generally—but not universally—applicable.

The difference between conditions and that which is conditioned, along with the relation between the two, implies that since universality is genuinely characteristic of only the conditional order, the quantification of universality would require a statement in terms of a number of subjective existents—whether all, some, one, or none. But this would involve stating the nature of conditions in terms of empirical existence, or universality in terms of particularity. The reality that is universal, the holding of the conditions, is irreducible to empirical existence. Therefore a proposition of the form "All ravens are black" is a singular empirical proposition. Moreover, it is a false proposition, for it does not recognize the existence of albino ravens. And it ignores the possibility that not all individuals conform to the norm. Finally, it can properly refer only to all ravens actually observed. The quantification of a universally valid proposition would have to take the form of a statement of a condition relevant to all objects to which it applies, such as "All normal ravens must be black."

The problem of dealing with one side of the universal-individual correlation in terms of the other side becomes even more involved if empirical reality is our only clue to a possible condition about which we are far from certain. Take the following as an example. It may be that in a particular state there are two categories of persons who, generally speaking, tend to vote for a particular political party, that is, farmers and business people. The statistical odds that either of these two categories of people will vote that way may even be high. Yet this does not make voting for the party in question a condition for voting in the case of the two categories of people. Neither does having to vote for the party become a condition for membership in either of the two categories.

Such relations would not even be likely if all the people in both categories voted for the party in question all the time. Even if the statistics all pointed in the same direction, it would be risky to formulate a statistical law. At any rate, the evidence does not allow us to explain or predict the voting behavior of any particular individual. The behavior of all members of a given class does not necessarily point to a universal condition, though it can. In the present example the regularity involved points to the likely conjunction of certain structures, though it may be difficult to detect what these structures are.

From the perspective here worked out it will be clear why universality and class membership are related, though not the same. Conditions are what determine what does and what does not belong to a class. Conditions determine what properly belongs. So universality and class membership are correlates. But this also implies that universals themselves are not classes or a class. For that would again be talking about conditions in language applicable only to the conditioned. Classes are always classes of subjective existents. Universals are never such existents. Consequently there are no classes of universals and there is no class of universals. Universality is not a predicate predicable of existents called conditions. A peculiarity of our language enables us to refer to conditions with words from the world of the conditioned. That ability confronts us with problems similar to those of God-talk (cf. 7.4). But these problems are not solved by actually conceiving of conditions as a sort of conditioned.

The irreducibility of the correlation between universality and individuality implies that we cannot simply move back and forth between universality and all individuals. Although individuality is conditioned, it is never universal. Individuality, as such, is never fully and only determined. But the individual entity is more than individual, and thus it is determined to some extent. What individuality guarantees is that the existing subjects do not merely respond automatically or mechanically to the universal conditions. Not all individuals respond identically; this is simply not a part of the necessity that comes with conditions.

In fact, individuality occurs within the scope of universality. The individual existent actualizes one of the possibilities provided by the conditions. The only necessity is that the limits of possibility are not transgressed. Whenever they are transgressed, as in deviation, existence is in danger. The conditions universally establish limits within which there are a variety of possibilities. This makes for the incommensurability of individuality and universality. There is a strict correlation between conditions and subjects, but the talk about either side occurs in a universe of discourse irreducibly different from the other.

2.5.3 Individuality

Individuality and universality are traits of a relationship such that concretely existing entities are neither universals nor again fully and only individuals. Existing entities display individuality, as well as a relation to universality; that is to say, they display being conditioned as well as being responses that are unique. Thus I have denied that there is such an object as "the universal," and I have also denied "the individual." What I mean by the latter denial is not just that individuality is not an object or thing or property, but also that no objects or entities are just individuals. When we use *individual* to refer to a particular, we do so to refer to the unique way in which each entity has its own relationship to the conditions that hold universally, thereby differing individually from every other entity of its kind.

The American philosopher John Dewey regarded individuality as a trait of organisms only; furthermore, he regarded it as a trait which organisms progressively develop. Genuine individuality is an authentic trait only in human beings who have developed individuality. The Dutch theoretical physicist M.D. Stafleu, on the contrary, is of the opinion that all particulars (including atoms) have individuality.[67]

What different concepts do these two scholars have in mind? What Dewey has in mind is that the difference between two hydrogen atoms on the one hand and President Nixon of the United States and Chairman Mao of China on the other hand is a very obvious difference. Although two atoms may in fact be different atoms and not the same, it would still be difficult to describe the difference in terms of the individuality of the one and the individuality of the other. And although Nixon and Mao were both human beings, it is hard to find ways in which they were significantly similar. Dewey's conception of individuality is such that he looks upon it as a growing trait of responsibility for what we make of ourselves in freedom. Stafleu, on the other hand, is satisfied to locate individuality in some evidence—no matter how small—of unique difference. That difference could show up in the different places which any physical particle must necessarily occupy, or it could show up in the physical indeterminacy relation.[68]

What both Dewey and Stafleu were concerned with is entitary individuality, that is, the individuality of some material thing capable of relatively independent action. The difference in their approach shows that individuality is appropriate to the kind of reality such an entity displays. The individuality of a person (Dewey's concern) differs from that of physical, microscopic entities (Stafleu's concern). But one can also speak of individuality in terms of parts of an entity, or in terms of relations into which entities enter and actions which they perform. The latter have individuality in terms of the sort of reality they display. Actions or parts, then, would likely have individuality *as* actions or parts *of* an individual entity. The entitary individuality, then, is what is central to individuality.

This is understandable, in the view I develop here, for individuality is a trait of entities in virtue of their unique response to the conditions holding for them. Such responses are always dependent on action centers. Arms do not respond—but people with arms. Walking does not walk—but horses do. Individually acting entitary wholes, then, are primarily individual. Individuality, then, is characteristic of action centers which differ *in being of the same kind*. The individuality is always commensurate with and correlated to universality.

Individuality is not limited to people, however, or even to conscious beings or to living entities. Of course the individuality of an intentionally acting person differs considerably from that of a mechanically moving molecule, but both are to be regarded as individual entities. The fact that the intensity of scope or degree of individuality is less in an atom than in a person is not a ground for denying the presence of individuality in the one case while accepting it in the other.

The major problem with individuality, as with universality, is that it is a primitive notion which cannot be understood in terms of other more basic notions. Conceptualization is possible only when we are dealing with universality, that is, with conditions, or with the consequences of the holding of conditions, namely, in structures. For a concept is our grasp of conditionality. Consequently, about all that we can understand about individuality is that we all know it. We intuitively grasp it, though we do not have a concept of it. That is why proper names behave as they do. They do not name anything conceivable in its individuality.

I have already referred to Armstrong's difficulty with keeping universality and individuality strictly irreducible. The problem of individuality further contributes to this difficulty. He tries to deal with individuality as itself a property. The particularity of a particular, according to Armstrong, must be distinguished from its properties, but at the same time, in his opinion, particularity is a property. Universals are parts, constituents, and actual dimensions of a particular in Armstrong's view, but they remain universal for him as well. What makes his particular a particular is its particularity, which is constituted with its particularizing property (USR1, 102, 111, 113; USR2, 64). Any attempt to explain individuality by subsuming it under an explanatory condition would mean precisely that whatever can be so explained is therefore not individual. *Individuality* is a word we use to describe something we experience and about which we can say something to one another with words. But it eludes our conceptualization. It is unique and incomparable. It is an experience that cannot be broken up into distinctions, is not divisible, is in-divisible, is in-dividual. We might also have called it atomic. But by now we all know what we mean when we say *individual*. It's just that we have no explanation or definition for it. It is always that which is defined. Perhaps this is what Loux has in mind when he takes Wolterstorff to be saying that we cannot get underneath individual entities (SA, 158; see also 165). Or what Quinton has in mind when he interprets Aristotle as saying matter is closed to understanding (29). (See also Kripke, NN, 52.)

2.5.4 *Existence and universality*

The major problem concerning that which we refer to by way of the term *universals* has been: Do they exist? If my approach to the problem of universality via conditions is to be considered as acceptable, the problem of existence will have to be addressed, at least. Is it possible to address this question successfully? If the problem of universals does indeed relate to the problem of conditions, there are a number of questions that can be settled. Conditions *are* not subjective existents but *hold for* subjective existence. Conditions are thus not material things, and neither are they minds or mental objects or creations of consciousness. Consequently, they are not local or temporal: genuinely universal conditions obtain anywhere and at any time, that is, wherever and whenever.[69]

This raises the following question: Do they exist independently of or apart from the subjective existents of the empirical world? The answer to this question cannot be simple and univocal. If "apart from" means somewhere else apart from our locations, we would still be ascribing location to them. And if "apart from" means completely independent, there would be many reasons for denying independence to conditions. Conditions are independent as conditions in the sense that *they*—rather than what is conditioned—do the conditioning. But since they are correlates of subjective existence, conditions cannot properly be viewed as independent in the sense of unrelated.[70] There is a real sense in which nothing is independent of real relationships in any strict sense.

The word *independent* itself has a very dependent sense, for it depends on the nature of the independent thing in question. In the case of conditions, *independence* means independence from being conditioned, but for a person *independence* means being free to be responsible. In no case, however, does *independent* mean standing in no relationships. In terms of relationships, in fact, conditions do have both temporal and spatial relationships, for they are related to things in time and things in space. In that sense they also have material relationships and are related to human consciousness.

What must be said, then, about the reality of conditions? Just this, that they are real *in* that they hold or obtain. If *existence* is the term we use to indicate the reality of subjective entities, that is, entities and their actions and relationships, all of which are *subject to* conditions, then we need a different term to indicate the reality of conditions. For again, nothing that is a standard can be an element of what must meet such a standard. That is the core argument against subjectivism. And subjectivism must be rejected.[71] Instead of speaking of "existence," we should say that conditions hold or obtain with respect to what exists. Existence is the reality of what is subject to conditions, while obtaining is the reality of what determines existence.

In that case, what about all the terms associated with the universals debate, such as *genus, species, category, kind,* and the like? What are they? Do they stand for anything? I believe they do. They refer to conditions and thus to realities which, rather than existing, simply hold or obtain. They are real in that they obtain. They are names for the fact that in the relationships between existing entities and their conditions, there are specifically conditioned and limited areas of relationship and concentrations of conditionality which are discoverable and theoretically isolatable. The set of conditions essentially required for instantiation in a horse is what I will refer to as a kind or species.[72]

2.6 Popper's Rejection of Institutions

I now want to look briefly at an ontology which is realistic with respect to some entities and nominalistic with respect to others. The view is Karl Popper's. (See 1.2.1 in the previous chapter.) He does not accept the reality of social institutions beyond the various relationships among individuals which are made up by these individuals or others in their culture by way of conventions or tradition. We could therefore call Popper a sociological nominalist. He does accept the need for a third world of abstract entities as the foundation for his theory of truth in the natural sciences,[73] but he rejects a conditional order for human society. Now, what sort of valid objection could one make to the acceptance of conditions that obtain universally for social institutions? This question seems particularly relevant for a scholar who is in principle willing to accept such conditions, a scholar who accepts them for the so-called natural world but rejects them for social reality. Why would the institutionalization of trothful love in marriage not be recognizable as a universal condition to be met by human beings, at least by those who wish to be married, whereas "being a frog" is recognizable as a condition which every frog must meet?[74]

There are some immediate factors which are often appealed to in order to deny the universality of an order such as we see realized in marriage. One of them is that some people simply do not marry at all. Another is that marriages are so different from culture to culture, from historical period to historical period within the same culture, and from marriage to marriage within the same period that it hardly seems feasible to speak of universally obtaining conditions. A third factor is that people are assumed to be free in how they arrange their lives. Universal conditionality would be a compelling factor in human affairs and would severely limit human freedom. Popper's association with liberal Anglo-Saxon political thought would certainly make it difficult for him to accept any sort of social compulsion or inevitability. Inviolable principles of order may make one generation of frogs the same as the next and the same as the previous generation, but with human beings it simply doesn't work that way.

The distinction between order and structures goes a long way toward satisfying these objections while maintaining a continuity of order in the universe at the same time. With such a distinction one can allow for real conditions underlying social institutions and also do justice to human freedom and responsibility. What this distinction allows us to do is to make room for the empirical factor of historical change and cultural relativity as well as for the reality of order.

Empirical social science is correct in pointing out the almost limitless variety of concrete forms which social institutions have taken on. This applies to political institutions, educational organizations, marriage bonds, and many other social relationships. At the same time, there is a continuity of structure throughout the ages and from culture to culture such that certain constant features in these relationships can be recognized at any time in any culture.[75] If one is not already prejudiced by notions of human freedom which prevent any sort of social continuity beyond human control, how can one do justice to both sorts of facts, that is, the empirically observable change and variety on the one hand and the equally empirically observable continuity in structure on the other?[76]

Without adopting a priori assumptions forbidding the acceptance of inviolable principles of social order, one can readily accept such principles and still maintain a healthy view of history and social change. The social order as an order of nomic conditions is, as little as the physical order, a description of the concrete reality of social relationships.[77] Social order can be viewed as a directive to which people give historically relative shape in cultural situations. By "historically relative" I mean both related and relevant to the particular situation of the moment and open to change in the direction of another situation. Principles or norms of justice, troth, frugality, care, dignity, and others can be inviolable conditions for human culture without any infringement on a person's freedom and responsibility to arrange things in keeping with those principles. Moreover, a person remains fully flexible in the actual arrangements set in place. Such a position would prevent both relativism and conservatism.

If there is indeed such a social order, some societies clearly do a poor job of incorporating this order in the actual relationships established, and others do not do so at all. Yet this fact should not be viewed as an argument against the reality of social conditions, for the reality or holding power of conditions can never depend on the responses to them. Just as a weak or a sickly lion does not undermine our belief in great strength as a characteristic of lions, so varying or failing circumstances in social reality need not undermine our belief in the permanence of a social order. At least such circumstances are not sufficient ground for denying the reality of a social order.

That certain people never marry, that others crusade for the abolition of marriage, that there are polygamous marriages as well as monogamous ones—in short, that the actual response of people to some condition of social order has been varied and has had its ups and downs is not empirical evidence to suggest that the universal conditions in question do not in fact hold universally. All it really indicates is that there is greater latitude in responding to social order than in responding to physical order.[78]

2.7 Conclusion

In my view, an investigation of the realities with which scholarship deals leads to the conclusion that there is an order of the world which conditions all of empirical existence, including the existence of rational processes. Therefore I posit the thesis that the existing empirical world has an irreducible correlate in the order of the world. When I approach the problem of universals from the point of view of this thesis, the difference between my view and the traditional views is immediately apparent. Natural kinds, social order, norms for behavior, and laws are all real (to mention only a few items), even though they are unlike anything in the empirical world. In fact, they are so unlike the empirical world that comparison is likely to fail.

These universally holding realities are required by science and are in fact assumed in all science. They do not need rational justification; rather, they justify rationality. If one rationally analyzes the issues raised in the traditional problem of "universals" but without assuming the ultimacy of rational justification, the reality of an order of conditionality irreducible to—but correlative with—empirical existence appears well justified.

In summary, I accept the reality of the nature of things, though I cannot for that reason accept the realist position. I also accept that essences or whatever one wishes to call the nature of things are not things, entities, or beings such as we encounter in the world of empirical existents, though I cannot for that reason accept the nominalist position. Finally, I see a special relation between concepts and the nature of things, though I cannot for that reason accept the rationalist or intellectualist position. I do not believe this lands me with the anti-intellectuals, the irrationalists, or even the subjectivists. The best I can do is describe my position. Both individuality and universality are real. They are also mutually irreducible and correlative. They are in fact traits of a relationship, namely, the relationship between the nomic conditions that hold universally for what exists and the empirical existents that individually and subjectively meet those conditions or are subject to them. And understanding what something is, is grasping in a concept what the conditions for its existence are.

Chapter III
Functors and Functions

DEVELOPING AN ONTOLOGY OF UNIVERSALITY is one of philosophy's most basic requirements. The fact that the problem of "universals" has persistently engaged the attention of the philosophical world for more than two thousand years is evidence of this. Further evidence is found in the fact that philosophers of science or theory develop essential dimensions of their views in terms of entities that are characterized by universality, such as laws, principles, rules, canons, structures, conditions, statements, dispositions, properties, kinds, predication, explanation, and prediction. None of these topics could be discussed successfully without making significant use of materials that arise from the study of universality.

The postulate I examined in the previous two chapters is that a basic distinction must be made between the ordered empirical world and the world order. The former is our familiarly experienced world of subjective existence, while the latter is the order of conditions to which the empirical world conforms.[1] This fundamental correlation of irreducibles I take to be the ground for the categorial distinction made in philosophy between that which is universal and that which is individual.[2] It can thus be said that the relationship between universality and individuality is the most important relationship in philosophy. For if all of concrete reality, that is, the world of individual existence, is approached by science, theory, and philosophy in terms of a conceptual framework, then that conceptual framework is the conceptual grasp of the structure of our world. And that structure is the existential evidence of world order, the order that holds universally for the world of individual existence.

However, even though the problems connected with the relationship of universality to individuality are fundamental to philosophy, understanding this relationship is not sufficient by itself to enable us to construct a complete ontology. To establish a full-fledged philosophical approach to the world, we need a number of additional categorial distinctions. If we approach the world in terms of empirical existence and its order, all we really have in terms of the observable world is one large concept without any diversity. All we would then know about our world is that it is ordered, that it exists individually, and that the individually existing entities must meet the order of conditions. More is needed if we are to gain a view of the general structure of our world, which, after all, is what philosophers are expected to construct.

The categorial distinction I will discuss in this chapter and the next is the distinction between functors and functions, that is, the distinction between the entities in the world and the actions they perform.[3] There is a good reason for dealing with this topic at this stage: now that the world has been introduced as conditioned, we can gain some insight into the sorts of things there are in the world. With the introduction of the functor-function relation, the world becomes populated. Furthermore, as we consider what entities are and what they do, a number of important issues will come to the fore. As we shall see, functionalism (or dealing with entities as reified functions), reductionism (or dealing with an irreducible manifold as though it fundamentally were a variety of one kind), and absolutization (or dealing with one aspect of a relational situation as unconditionally determining the other aspects), are approaches to the world that are related to the problem being explored in the context of the present chapter and the next. These approaches are never just of philosophical significance. When on assembly lines people (functors) are treated as functions of the line, destructive consequences follow. We will also see that a discussion of substance, property, and analogy is appropriate in this context. Finally, it is my expectation that the need for discussing other categorial distinctions in later chapters (such as unity-diversity, structure-direction, and the concept of relation) will also become apparent.

The key to the problems discussed in this chapter is the conceptual scheme we need to understand the relationship between a unit of functioning and its functions, a particular and its properties, a substance and its qualities, a thing and its attributes.[4] I will deal later with the relations among them (5.1).

Thoughts do not think, and feelings do not feel. *I* think and *I* feel. And I am neither a thought nor a feeling. Something that is not a thought thinks, and something that is not a feeling feels. Something, some one thing, both thinks and feels. Is the I who thinks a thinker? Does the thinker feel? Or is it possible that the I who feels is a feeler, and that the feeler thinks? Is there perhaps some other approach that is also possible and even fruitful? Does the thinker do anything besides thinking? Is the thinker the same as the feeler? Is the "I" just the whole collection of thoughts and feelings, of functions and actions? We will see that these questions direct us to the nature of totality, coherence, and diversity.

Thus before I can deal properly with the concept of a functor and its functions, I must first deal briefly with the nature of totality, coherence, and diversity; even though this topic will be treated again later (6.2). Here I deal with coherence and totality only as the context of a specific problem. Later I will deal with them more in general. Having set the context, I will then deal with the functor-function distinction.[5] Since the scientific tradition in our culture manifests a marked tendency to reduce things to their functions and to reduce functional multiplicity to one or two kinds of functioning, I will discuss the problem of reductionism after the nature of functionality has been explored (3.3 below). That discussion will be followed by a discussion of analogy as an interfunctional relation. Finally, I will briefly indicate the main irreducible levels of functionality which, in my view, the world displays.

3.1 Totality, Coherence, and Specificity of Functioning

There are certain action words in our vocabulary which do not seem to name any specifiable and recognizable actions even though they name items from the active life of human beings. Consider my making on a given morning a list of things to be done during the day. The list could quite meaningfully contain the following items: 8:00 a.m., take a shower; 8:30 a.m., have breakfast; 9:15 a.m., call my lawyer; 9:30 a.m., drive to work; and so forth. Suppose that in the middle of the list there appeared the following entry—3:20 p.m., love my neighbor. That would be a strange entry, no matter how we choose to read it. If the entry is interpreted as a planned act of adultery, it would be strange because one would not expect such a thing to be so soberly and methodically planned. If, as is more likely, the entry refers to my conviction that I must respond to the norm for all people to live in a loving relationship to all other people, then it is strange that I should be planning on doing so with respect to some specific person at a specific time. Why, for example, did this matter of loving one's neighbor not play a role with regard to the 9:15 a.m. entry?

The point I am driving at is this: although all entries refer to what human beings do or must do or can do, that is, to human action, there is a marked difference between the 3:20 entry and the others.

The 3:20 entry does not seem to point to any specifically recognizable action which can easily be distinguished from other actions. Instead it seems that although the 3:20 entry names an action in some sense, it refers to something that must characterize all human actions rather than just some actions as distinguished from others. What does this very obvious difference mean? What can we learn from analyzing it?

This will be the problem for this section. I will argue that action words point to different levels of integration of human functioning, and also that if we are to understand the functioning of entities, we must introduce concepts that will help us to recognize different structural patterns within which our actions and the actions of other entities are organized.[6]

3.1.1   *Action patterns*

Although the difference between "loving my neighbor" and "calling my lawyer" is obvious in terms of the specificity of the action indicated, the nature of the difference is by no means immediately clear. It appears that "calling my lawyer" refers us to some specific action, while "loving my neighbor" does not. But is this really so? Could it not be argued that "calling my lawyer" does not refer us to any specific action at all? There are still other, more specific actions that are involved in calling one's lawyer. These other actions seem more immediately clear in connection with "calling my lawyer" than the actions that might come to mind in connection with "loving my neighbor."

Surely calling one's lawyer is not a single act. I must walk to the phone, reach out to grab the receiver, put it to my ear, dial a number, listen for someone to answer at the other end, and then finally have my conversation with my lawyer. Isn't this a specified list of many actions? Therefore, couldn't it be argued that the relation between "picking up the receiver" and "calling my lawyer" is of the same sort as the relation between "calling my lawyer" and "loving my neighbor"? I was calling my lawyer not only when I walked to the phone, but also when I did the other things.

This line of questioning can be pursued even further. In his book *Prolegomena to an Anthropological Physiology*, Buytendijk has argued that many of the apparently autonomous processes going on in the human body can also be meaningfully interpreted as actions performed by responsible persons. Although breathing, dreaming, metabolizing, sweating, and sleeping (to mention just a few) may not be consciously and intentionally performed, they can nevertheless be understood as the actions of an individual self. Characteristically, they appear to fit the personality of the person engaging in the action. Naturally, such actions are in turn made up of muscle coordinations, sensations, nerve activity, and many other processes.

Are we now to speak simply of an increase in complexity from the mechanical actions of electrons in our bodies right up to loving our neighbor—or is it possible to recognize genuinely irreducible patterns, that is, structures of activity that are themselves integrators of the functioning of an entity? Do we have only the larger and larger clusters of atomic interaction, or do we have action patterns that can be understood as structural wholes in their own right?[7]

If we further examine the problems involved here, the suggestion arises that there may be distinguishable levels of subjective functional integration corresponding to conditioning configurations of integration. For example, it might be the case that "loving my neighbor" is an integrator of complex actions, that "calling my lawyer" is a complex action which integrates many functions, and that "stretching out my arm" is a function that integrates subintentional processes. In other words, it may be that there are levels of organization of actions, determined by configurations of conditions, such that whole actions integrate specific functions, and specific functions integrate less determinate processes.

That this seems a possibility is quickly suggested by even a superficial examination of the examples introduced. Such an examination reveals that the difference between "dialing a number," "calling my lawyer," and "loving my neighbor" is not simply a matter of increasing complexity, although at first sight such might indeed appear to be the case. I *can only* love my neighbor *in terms of* certain specific actions such as calling my lawyer, and I *cannot* call my lawyer *except* in terms of such actions as dialing a number.

This seems a simple progressive relationship. However, closer examination reveals some discrepancies. Although "loving my neighbor" needs to be enacted in terms of other actions, it seems not to have those other actions as its specific constituents, whereas "calling my lawyer" does seem to have the actions in terms of which it is performed as its specific constituents.

An example will clarify the point. "Loving my neighbor" is something I can do in terms of "calling my lawyer" or "removing snow from someone's driveway" or some other specific action. Yet those particular actions are not such that if I have not performed them, I can at all times be said not to have loved my neighbor. Not only people who have lawyers and people who live in snowy regions can love their neighbors. On the other hand, "calling my lawyer" (if by this we mean telephoning) can only be done through dialing a number, picking up the receiver, and so forth.

As we look further at these examples, we see still more differences. Dialing a number is not (normally speaking) a meaningful action in its own right; only when it constitutes an element of some more comprehensive action, such as "calling my lawyer" is it meaningful. If I were to perform the action of dialing a number at a telephone repeatedly without ever speaking to anyone over the telephone, other people in the room observing me would wonder about me if I responded to their question as to what I was doing by saying: "Oh, nothing in particular—just dialing some numbers." But if I were to respond to their inquiry by saying, "I'm trying to call my lawyer," there would be no problem.

3.1.2   *Possible philosophical categories*

It appears that the three sorts of action words (i.e., "loving my neighbor," "calling my lawyer," and "dialing a number") point to distinct phenomena that are structurally quite different. Is it worthwhile to inquire into these differences? There is no end to making distinctions. Is the kind of difference I have pointed to here a significant one? Should a set of different and precise terms be adopted? We all know that some actions are more complex than others, and that some are more complete than others. What is involved for people in what we might call "being a nation" is obviously extremely complex, for it involves many people, a great variety of actions and functions, many levels of activity, and vast networks of intricate relationships. A person trying to listen for the sound of a bird in a tree far away is doing something considerably simpler in comparison.

But is there any advantage or point to trying to unravel this sort of difference in complexity on a philosophical level? Is there a comprehensive problem here similar to the problem of universality? The latter problem turned out to be of significance for all of philosophy, and we discovered that it has very clear practical implications as well. It is related to such items as norms and standards for human behavior, the reality of social institutions, and other worthwhile issues. Can a similar case be made for the present problem?

I believe that such a case can indeed be made. Just as the issues related to the problem of standards of behavior (such as human freedom, responsibility and authority, and individuality) have important interfaces with the problem of universality, so the problem of the nature of action has similar interfaces with these same issues. What is an action that can be addressed as such? Who enacts an action? If we want to have control over events, whom or what do we address as action center? Can only a person or a thing be an agent? If so, can a government be responsible for anything? What sorts of action are recognizable as definite units of action? Can cultures "do" things? Do events, actions, and functions differ?

We may have intuitive answers to these questions, and many of those answers may be correct. But the degree of specialization in our present culture and the consequent isolation of minute phases of activity into institutions that decide things by themselves requires the development of a more overtly recognizable, explicit picture of how actions, actors, and related items do in fact relate and how they are structured. However, theoretically responsible reflection on these social problems requires in turn that an ontology of actions and actors be developed. It may well be that the categories of "actor" and "action" can be considered as exhaustive of all that exists. "Actors acting in relationship" is a fair summary of what occurs in our world.

If it is true that there is no end to the making of distinctions, is there a guideline we could use in making distinctions so that we will not get lost in the process? Could it be meaningful in some contexts to introduce a category called "means of transportation" made up of both human products (e.g., trucks, planes, ships) and things that are not made by humans (e.g., donkeys, horses, elephants, floating trees)? In a complex society it may indeed be helpful to introduce the study of means of transportation as a definite category of entities. Yet it is hardly a category of ontological significance. One might also introduce a distinction between the top of the figure "1" and the rest of the figure. Letter designers might find this a highly significant distinction, but it is not a distinction of such wide significance that the study of it should be introduced in a course which first-year university students of all kinds are required to take.

What is needed before we can speak of the necessity of introducing an ontological category? Such categories would have to apply to all of reality in some significant way—and not just to figures or to means of transportation. Hence ontological distinctions are very high altitude distinctions. Ontological categories can be "seen" as meaningful only if we have achieved enough distance from the details that only the main features remain visible. The distinction between world and world order as discussed in the two previous chapters is a very general, widely applicable, exhaustive distinction and is therefore a good candidate for being introduced as a philosophical category.

The branch of philosophy called ontology studies the most general structure of what there is.[8] It would appear that the category "entities active in relation to each other" is also a very general category. There does not appear to be anything in the realm of empirical existence that does not fall under this heading. On the basis of the information gathered in the first two chapters, I believe I can now say that categories of broad application must refer us to very high-level configurations of order, perhaps principles of order, so wide in scope that they structure immense areas of existence. In this sense, the above-mentioned very broad category of "entities active in relation to each other" points us to three very crucial principles of order, namely, the principles of "being an agent," "being active," and "relating." Such principles structure (i.e., integrate through their "holding" for existence) all of what exists. Two of these principles will be examined in this chapter and the next, that is, those of "agent" and "action."[9]

As philosophical categories, the principles of "agent," "action," and "interrelation" are so universally applicable that they seem uninformative. As broad organizers of experience, they take in much that is itself very diverse.[10] In the previous section I pointed out that the category of "action" refers to a complex field of reality which is itself in need of being understood in terms of subcategories. At this point I will therefore reintroduce the provisional levels that were pointed out in the previous section to see whether they can actually help us in organizing our experience in the face of complex and real problems. To facilitate the discussion, then, I will refer to such actions as "loving one's neighbor" as *first-level actions*; to actions that can more or less be understood as relatively independent, for example, "calling my lawyer," as *second-level actions*; and to activities that definitely appear partial and in need of a context, for example, "dialing a number," as *third-level actions*.[11] These rather rough terms will later be dropped. All I am looking for at the moment is a temporary handle on a very complex problem.

3.1.3 *An example*

Let me now introduce an actual problem which is being widely discussed today by philosophers of theory, that is, the problem of ultimate beliefs and commitments as ingredients of high-level theoretical paradigms. I shall attempt to show that my three-level distinction will in fact help to address this problem. I will use the difference between Marxist and capitalist economics as my example of the relation between ultimate commitments and paradigms for actual theories. I choose economics because it deals with matters that appear to allow for a highly quantitative approach (at the very least, economic matters are in fact approached that way), while at the same time its subject matter is very intimately related to matters of human decision, taste, evaluation, and so forth.

I will distinguish three levels of approach to economics: the level of actual theory concerning a specific economic problem (e.g., the relation of inflation to unemployment); the level of overall paradigms (e.g., the approach of Friedman); and the level of the commitment underlying the paradigm (e.g., a capitalist, right-wing, profit-oriented, individualistic, free-enterprise conviction pattern). Today it is recognized as meaningful to distinguish Marxist economics from capitalist economics. Both are quantitative and "exact," but few people would seek to distinguish between the two as scientific theory over against ideological theory. Both are ideology-oriented, and both are trying to be scientific.

Now let us look at what it means to be an economist. Can one be both a Marxist and an economist? Of course! But being both of these does not seem comparable to being both a garden enthusiast and an economist. "Being an economist" and "being a garden enthusiast" clearly refer to a variety of activities within the framework of a certain sphere of organization. Both are fairly recognizable as being *second-level activities*. They organize specific actions in a specific pattern. They need specific actions, and they also stand out as quite specific themselves and can be distinguished from others. Given our provisional categories, however, "being a Marxist" is to be categorized as *level one*. It is not very specific, and it permeates—or should permeate—all that a person who is a Marxist is likely to do.

"Being a Marxist" is likely to be characteristic of much more in a person's life than "being an economist." It has implications for lifestyle, educational strategies, political decisions, attitudes to organized religion, and a host of other strategic areas of action. "Being a Marxist" seems not to be confined to a single area of a person's life, but "being an economist" or "being a garden enthusiast" clearly is. A person can thus be an economist *in addition* to being a good many other things. On the other hand, a person is a Marxist *in everything* he says and does. In that latter sense he is not anything *else* (on the same level) in addition to being a Marxist.

When we analyze action only in terms of the different kinds there are, we are bound to come to the conclusion: there is a difference between gardening and forecasting economic conditions. We might go on to say that one must be careful to keep the two distinct, lest the one kind of activity begin to encroach on the other. In the same vein one might conceivably say also that one should keep being a Marxist quite distinct from developing theories about inflation. If my earlier attempt at categorizing action patterns is at all fruitful, such a statement could be misguided and could lead to confusion, for "being a Marxist" cannot be kept separate from the many activities in which the person who is a Marxist engages.

It is clear to me that all past debates about the relation between ultimate commitment (level one) and doing science (level two) have suffered from not making the sort of distinction I am making here. Can similar observations be made about the failure to distinguish level two from level three? I believe the answer is yes, and I will try to make some observations in this area. When the problem of the relation of commitment to theorizing is discussed, we sometimes come upon the following objection to a positive evaluation. We are told that when it comes to looking through microscopes, observing facts, calculating relationships, and other such operations in the academic sphere, things are essentially no different from one person to the next—and if they are, there must be something wrong. How accurate is such an objection?

Upon analysis the objection seems inappropriate. Suppose a capitalist and a Marxist have both entered a fishing competition. Would the difference between them result in the capitalist only fishing for largemouth bass with live minnows, while the Marxist only fishes for bluegills with Mepps No. 1? Even though different approaches to consideration for the environment, selfishness, sportsmanlike conduct, and similar issues might in fact produce such contrasts between certain people, I believe that the Marxist and the capitalist could indeed fish for the same species with the same bait. Thus it would appear that picking a species to fish for and choosing a kind of lure are not ideology-prone.

Let me now distinguish participating in a fishing contest as a *level two* activity from putting a certain bait on one's line as a *level three* activity. Something similar can be done with looking through microscopes. Such activities do not lend themselves to being discussed on their own terms without being related to the context within which they are performed. Level three activities are of such a nature that they are not meaningful apart from the context within which they are performed. Consequently, if there is any basis in fact for the distinctions I have provisionally introduced, we could conclude that a discussion of the relation of *level three* actions to *level one* actions without considering *level two* actions as context is bound to have inconclusive results.

It should be understood, of course, that what I am asking for at present is not a consideration of the merits of the problems used as examples but a consideration of the sorts of problems involved. To me it is clear that they are much related to important distinctions between kinds and levels of action. In other words, certain important issues in our culture demand that we make high-level distinctions with respect to the nature of action. A correct understanding of the nature of human responsibility may be precluded without inquiring into this matter.

The distinctions I have in mind are what we might call high-level categorial distinctions. We distinguish between items on the basis of different configurations of order. The three different levels of action which I have provisionally (and even hypothetically) introduced could be seen as different ways of understanding how actions are organized and integrated. They might indicate structural patterns within which certain concrete actions take place. The pattern of the activity called "taking a shower," for example, is such that one removes one's clothing before standing under the descending water. But removing one's clothing is not by itself a meaningful action sequence. It is something we do before going to bed, before taking a shower, before going swimming, and before entering the doctor's examination room. Anyone who made it his or her business to determine how the act of removing his or her clothing is meaningful in itself and therefore something one could perform for the better part of a day would be declared mentally off balance. It is helpful to understand that such actions usually require the context of other actions to make them meaningful. We could say that those other actions integrate or organize those otherwise not so meaningful actions into a meaningful pattern.

3.1.4 Closer examination of one level

Now that we have briefly considered a hypothetical approach to the problem of categorizing levels and kinds of actions, I will look more closely at one of the levels, that is, the one I have provisionally called level one. The question I wish to raise is this. Although it is doubtlessly true that "loving one's neighbor" has the appearance of an action concept and although it certainly appears that it can only be realized in some other actions, is it really helpful to conceive of "loving one's neighbor" as an action itself? In semantic terms it definitely comes across as something one does as an action. Yet this can be misleading.

If I were asked about my brother's line of work, I could say: "He is a salesman." I could also say: "He sells shoes." "Being a salesman" is something we say one is, while "selling shoes" is something we say one does. In this case, of course, the two expressions add up to the same thing. But this is not always the case. One cannot always state "being something" in terms of "doing something" in such a way that the two are really equivalent. An example is "being a person," which is hardly something one does—at least, in any specific sense. If I were to ask "What is Susan doing?" I would hardly expect to get an answer along the following lines: "She is being a person, but I will go and see whether she could possibly stop doing that and come to the door for a moment."

Of course, it is impossible to be a person and never do anything. One could not possibly be a person and do absolutely nothing. Even a person who was in a coma from birth on would still have to breathe, digest and metabolize food, and regulate various body organs. At the same time, "being a person" cannot simply be understood as the integration of all sorts of activities. Actions require actors, doings require doers, and functions require functors. Being a person cannot be understood solely in terms of actions. Being a salesman, on the other hand, can indeed be understood in terms of actions alone.

In the present context, "selling things for a living" is an adequate way of describing "being a salesman." Yet "metabolizing," "selling," "eating," "driving," and any number of other actions together would never do to adequately characterize "being a person." Still, one could not successfully be a person without doing any of these things at all. In a certain sense, then, the concept of being a person is much like the concept of "loving one's neighbor"—in the sense that although it does not seem to be an action itself, it does not exist except in terms of actions. Being a person is also like a *level one* phenomenon in the sense that no matter what might be the case, one is always a person. Salesmen are persons, and so are police officers, professors, wives, queens, and so forth.

Persons and *level one* phenomena cannot all be expressed as doings, but they can all be understood in terms of what someone or something is; that is to say, being a person or being a capitalist is not something someone *does*, although being one does indeed involve doing certain things. In terms of the actions involved, I suggested earlier that we look at some as *level two* actions and others as *level three* actions. Can something of this sort be done with persons? I believe it can. There are specific and distinguishable things that a person can be at the same time which are relatively independent centers of one's being a person. Examples are being a father, being a police officer, and being a prime minister. These examples are comparable to actions in the *level two* category. Being a father is not everything that a certain person ever is; yet it takes a person to be a father.

How about *level three* phenomena in line with being a person? Here I believe the present scheme breaks down. There do not seem to be clearly parallel structures of three levels of *acting* and three levels of *being*. Still, it remains quite clear that there is a difference between acting and being if we take this as an expression of the difference between what it is to act and what it is to be the performer of some act. We simply cannot give up the distinction between actions and the performers of actions. Of course, the two are correlated. Neither one is possible without the other—at least, normally speaking. All the same, the two are different.

Now, is there anything to the similarity between being a person and *level one* action? With respect to their relation to actions and the performers of actions, they have two similarities in common. *Persons* (as a category in the realm of actors) and *level one actions* (as a category in the realm of actions) have this in common: they both need to be expressed or realized in phenomena less comprehensive than what they cover as category and both need to be recognized as totally involved in all of their realizations.

What I am saying is this. Of all the various things one can be as a person, not one of them is the same as being a person. All of them are less than being a person, and no person can be a person without being some of them. In being any of them, a person always is what she is completely and totally as a person. The same can be said with respect to being a Marxist. Is there any reason why these two categories are so similar? Might it be that on the level of human reality, being a person and being a Marxist are the most complete categories for actors and actions? According to principles of integration and configuration, do both integrate the whole of their area of integration?

3.1.5   Total integrators of human existence

For the moment I will concentrate entirely on categories that point to the structures which totally integrate either a human action field or a human actor field. Thus I am considering conditions that would totally integrate all human actions or fully integrate all of what a person is. For now I will stay away from the question how these might relate, given that actor and action are correlates.[12]

In all of our actions, no matter what they are, how wide-ranging, or how specified, we are always called upon to act wisely and to do the right thing. We are expected to meet the norms for acting by being truthful and loving. We are intended to do all of this always. And this can also be said of persons. I must be a wise, good, truthful, loving person. It seems impossible to determine whether these categories apply to actors rather than actions. It seems to be the case that actor and action are integrated in the human world when we consider these categories. One might say that as irreducible correlates actor and actions are integrally one in those instances in which the actor acts to meet the requirements of being wise, good, loving, and truthful. We may say that an actor in her actions appears to be acting in this way with all that she is. In this way all the actions of the actor can be said to be one; they all are wise, good, and truthful. The actor is one with her actions; she acts with integrity.[13]

For our present purposes, a short elaboration of this peculiar feature of human action will suffice. On a number of occasions I have referred to the fact that human beings can know the conditions that hold for their actions, especially by way of their analytic powers. They can also will to act in accord with the conditions that hold by using their powers of decision. I will simply postulate now that the combination of the decisional and cognitive powers in their intent is that which I earlier spoke of as *level one* action. This intent is not any specific act, so to speak; rather, it is the person's attitude toward the entire complex of what she takes to be the conditions that hold; together with the effect of the holding of these conditions. Consistency in intent and action together, as well as the continued holding of a conditional configuration, will make for a person with integrity and will explain continuity in identity. A person who lives in harmony with the order of the world is a person who will be recognized as wise, good, and truthful.

3.1.6   Transition

So far the point of the discussion in the present chapter has been to explore the need for—and possibility of—finding high-level ontological categories of order which could help us to understand and explain the patterns along which human existence and experience is organized. This exploration suggests that knowing such categories may clarify certain significant areas of our experience. However, do any of the categories introduced provisionally have value beyond the facilitation of the initial discussion? Is there a promise here of categories for use in a broadly ontological context?

One distinction used in the previous section which has always been of value in philosophy is the distinction between actions and the agents of actions. Agents acting in relationships make up all that there is in empirical reality. However, our experience of this is a structured or ordered experience. And the first two chapters have led to the postulate that our world, in which this is all that there is, is an ordered world. Has our initial exploration of levels of action indicated a possible order of agents and actions? Can we find orders as integrators of our experience? It seems hardly likely that we can simply rest content with a world in which the whole diversity of agents of action is not further understood in terms of other categories. An ontology with only three categories (i.e., agent, action, and relation) would be a very reduced ontology in which many high-level categories of understanding would not be recognized. We would not be able to distinguish people from horses, a baseball game from a state banquet, or a marriage from a business contract, for these are the same as actors, actions, and relations.

Thus we need more differentiation—though not because our earlier ontological reduction is useless. The primary set of categories of actors acting in relation is fundamental, for it helps us to realize that in order to relate effectively to an action, we must address an agent. A marriage is not a person, an event, or an agent-like entity of any kind. It is important to know this. In a human situation one cannot "blame" a marriage for anything since "blame" is a category of human action which is truly applicable only to human actors, that is, to persons. The categories of agent, action, and relation do give us a first and basic orientation, but this is far from sufficient in itself.

Our interest remains ontology, of course, which means an interest in categories with a very wide scope. The categories of interest in the context of ontology straddle all the specialized inquiries of specific disciplines. Ontology is focused on ordering concepts which are more general than those of specialized inquiry. Physics is also interested in actors, actions, and relations—but only insofar as they are physical. Philosophy, on the other hand, deals with ordering concepts whose scope spans all special interests and whose meaning is assumed in all other inquiries. In the sequel of this chapter, therefore, I will explore how the basic ordering concepts of agent and action help us to detect ontic categories of lesser scope, even though they are still wide enough to span more specialized interests.

3.2   *The World of Functors*

I will discuss two concepts. One of these concepts is to be discussed in this section, the other in the next (3.3). The concepts to which I refer are "action" and "agent of action" as introduced in the previous section. I will use the terms *function* and *functioning* to refer to action concepts, and *functor* to refer to concepts of acting agents. In this section I will deal with functors, then.

Functors as action centers, as acting entities, are to be understood as relatively complete and independent units. What I and no functors are functions. No functions are possible except as functions of functors, and no functors are possible except as having functions or functioning. There are no entities, no matter how small or how simple, which do not at least appear to be centered, organized concentrations of energy. Thus, all functors function. At the same time, no actions can be observed which do not refer us to a point of origin in some action center which is not itself just an action. There are no functions except as functions of functors. There is no running if no one runs, no suffering if no one suffers, no change if nothing changes, and no action if nothing acts. At the same time, there are no runners if no one runs, and no sufferers if no one suffers. Nothing changes without change taking place, and nothing acts without action.[14]

Functors as action centers, as acting entities, are to be understood as relatively complete and independent units. What I mean by a functor is not such that my arm is a functor. Here we may be confused by the language people use. If I say that my arm hurts, I am not saying something which in the present context could be interpreted as "It is my arm that is doing the hurting," for this would leave us thinking of my arm as a functor in this situation. In such sentences as "My teeth clatter" and "My heart hurts," we are not to conclude that teeth and heart are functors. The fact that a certain word can operate as the semantic subject of an action word must not be taken as an indication that that to which the word refers must be understood in ontological terms as a functor. Teeth and hearts are not independent agents. Functors must be capable of independent action, at least relatively speaking. Persons are actors, and so are sheep. Fuchsias are functors, and so are stars. They all exist as acting, functioning, doing.[15]

Now, when we observe the category of reality called functor, two ordering principles with a wide scope concern us on a philosophical level. One is the category of irreducibly different kinds of functors, and the other is that of the irreducibly different roles to be played by the functors. The former I take to be a matter of different realms or communities of functors, while in the view I develop the latter refers us to a division of labor among functors.

3.2.1 Realms

We have seen that an answer to the question "Who or what functions?" is: a functor functions. Breathing is a function. But monkeys breathe, not their lungs or their breath. And persons think, not their brains or their thoughts. Of both functions and functors there is a great variety. That variety is irreducible in both cases. There is not, so to speak, an entity called a functor, of which all the functors we know are species. The functor, as an actually functioning entity, does not exist. There is no actual, concrete, empirical entity called a functor. There are monkeys, people, trees, computers, and stars in the universe. These are functors. But among them is not also a separate class of entities called functors, nor is there an arch-functor which is just a functor.

Functor is a name for a certain kind of reality, that is, the kind which is capable of acting, of functioning. As a very high-level category, it is too wide in scope to be of interest to any specific discipline.[16] The specific disciplines begin to come into the picture when we look at the different realms of functors there are. The highest level of diversity to which we come is that of the realms or kingdoms of entities, that is, mineral, vegetable, animal, and human functors. Once we arrive at this level of scope, there are at once some special disciplinary points of view which can claim such an area as their specific interest. Thus, the physical sciences study the *realm* of *physical* things and processes (astronomy, physics, mechanics, chemistry).

For every realm, then, we have special areas of study. And in spite of attempts at developing a more unifying view, the four realms remain irreducible in our understanding.[17] No animal is a complex kind of plant, and no plant is a sophisticated physical system. On the other hand, the various realms do presuppose one another. Organisms cannot exist unless there is a physical realm; animals need organisms; humanity is supported by all three realms. Furthermore, each realm incorporates the lower realms into its own existence. Within the organic realm there are physical processes; within the animal realm there are vegetative functions.

No functor can be understood as a functor of a certain kind apart from these four realms. Reduction of these realms has proved to be impossible. Principles of physical explanation do not suffice to account for the reality of an organism. Biology cannot account for psychic phenomena, and human behavior is not reducible to concepts applicable to the animal realm.[18] Of course, there are certain forms and processes of existence which do not at present clearly allow us to classify them into one of the traditional four realms. Yet this hardly invalidates the obvious success of classifying most of reality in this way. For the time being, there is really no generally acceptable alternative to the four-realm theory.[19]

From early times on, reflection within Western civilization has yielded four basic realms of existence. It may be that this division into four was speculatively connected with the adoption of four basic elements in Greek thought (i.e., fire, air, water, and earth). It may also be that these elements were themselves chosen to give some primitive account of what always seemed an obvious division of nature into four realms. The differences between a slab of marble, a geranium, a rabbit, and a person may always have been intuitively primitive. No modern attempts at further reduction have been thoroughly successful. Since this is the only widely accepted division we know, I will maintain it so long as no clearly superior alternative is proposed and widely accepted.

Actually we face a similar state of affairs here as we noted at the beginning of this section. We can never say about animals and plants, or about functors in general: here is a collection of animals; some elephants, some ants, some dogs, and some that are just animals. *Animal* is a name for a realm of functors. And within that realm of functors we note something similar with further divisions. *Mammal* is a name for some sort of animal. But no animal is just simply a mammal. Dogs are mammals and monkeys are mammals. Next to dogs and monkeys there are not also "just mammals."

According to what principles do we arrive at such classifications? This question becomes more complex, though also better understood, when we see that classifications may differ according to the purpose of the classifier. Philosophers make classifications of a very general kind. Their classifications are intended to be applicable to the widest scope thinkable. Zoologists have a lesser scope. Classifying animals according to their power and ability to pull a load would yield different criteria still.

Classifications can be made according to many principles. If I place together in a single collection a Frenchman, an Indian, a piece of chalk, a bottle of milk, a Bushman, and a rusty nail, and then ask someone to select the three objects that are of the same kind, that person may with perfect legitimacy select the Frenchman, the piece of chalk, and the bottle of milk. The criterion for such a selection would have to be something along the following lines: all three have the property of being white, and none of the other three items are white.

This would seem an odd choice to make. It might be construed to be a white racist choice. But would it be a philosophically improper one? Selecting the three human beings, of course, would have meant that more inclusive criteria were used. But why should one select a complexity of criteria instead of just one criterion?

3.2.2 Kinds

What does it mean to say that human beings are one *kind* of functor? Using the postulate of the previous chapter, kinds (natural kinds) would be configurations of conditions or structural frameworks. A kind of functor is a complex of conditions met in functors which all exist within the bounds of and exhibit characteristics of the same type of structure. "Kinds" of functors, then, are functors sharing a structural similarity. They normally share an identical set of properties.[20] And a condition for the existence of entities of this kind is that these properties occur jointly. Consequently, concepts of kinds imply concepts of properties, for the connection of properties in kinds is nomic. But kinds of functors are not the only kinds there are, for anything whatever in empirical existence must be of some kind or other.[21] There are also kinds of functions and kinds of relationships.

All male and female persons who are husbands and wives of one another share a relationship of one kind, that is, marriage. And "being of pale blue appearance" is a kind of function which is shared by many more things than just birds' eggs of certain kinds. The kinds we know are to be characterized as configurations, that is, the constant interwovenness of a complexity of conditions.[22] In all kinds this interwovenness is itself typical and relatively invariant, which is what makes for the type we recognize. The kind "scissors," for example, is interrelated with other complex patterns such as tools, steel, cutting device, and so forth, into one broad kind. And the broad kind can in turn be subdivided into various more specific kinds of scissors.

The typical interrelationship of characteristics is such that one cannot simply group properties together arbitrarily to form kinds. Being blue-eyed, having fair hair, being fond of milk, being fourteen years old, and being in my back yard right now is not a useful type. Both our son and our cat exhibit these features. Here we do not have enough difference within sameness to speak of a genuine kind. Genuine kinds exhibit a structural type which analysis reveals to be based on a natural order. One way to form a rough estimate of whether or not a type or kind is genuine is to see whether there exists a word in the language to stand for the kind, and also whether the word is used successfully by the culture using the language. The successful use of language depends on the reality of the kinds of things (nouns), actions (verbs), and relations (adjectives, adverbs, connectives) named in the language.[23]

Cat is successfully taken to refer to a real kind in English-speaking cultures. The same can be said of *tree, marriage, father, relative, blue, pain,* and thousands of other words. *Bonk* is not a successful name for a kind since what it names as a proper name is my son—and only I call him by that name. But even if many other people began to call him *Bonk*, this would not make my son into a kind. No word exists for the configuration of properties which I mentioned earlier, the properties that both our son and our cat possess. People have never noticed these particular properties to be conjoined in any particular nomic manner so as to recommend reference to them as a kind. Neither is there a single word to cover the piece of chalk, the bottle of milk, and the Frenchman. Perhaps we could make up a name: three objects having the property of being white. Still, this does not make the three into a naturally ordered kind.

What finally determines whether or not a kind is a kind is whether the connections between properties and relations characteristic of the kind can reliably be identified as nomic conditions. Or, to put it differently, kinds that are real fit within and display a nomic order. Thus, each kind will in the first place belong to one of the four realms of natural kinds. These realms determine the broadest types of functoral community. Within each realm the functors naturally divide according to lesser kinds. Within the realm of humans these lesser divisions are easily identifiable as divisions of labor within the one community, that is, the functor takes on peculiar roles—mother, manager, cabinet maker, teacher—in order to contribute specifically to the continuity of the entire community. In the other realms, however, these specific roles are becoming just as clear. Modern ecological science makes us aware of the irreplaceable contribution of each member of a realm to the maintenance of the whole.

So each functor is both *one* of a kind (i.e., this unique one) and one of a *kind* (i.e., the same as all others of that kind). In this way each actual, concrete functor shows both universal and individual traits. Within the functor we will find typical structural features of continuity pointing to a continuity of order that universally holds. At the same time the functor is a genuine individual displaying irreducible features of subjectivity, conforming to laws, and meeting conditions in unique ways. This "one of a kind" feature is also found in functions and relations. The individuality of the functor is not just a matter of one feature, a matter of one of its properties. Rather, though the functor may, with many others, be animal, mammal, cat, and Angora, it will not only be a unique cat, but also an individual mammal and animal. In its own peculiar unity, its own peculiar circumstances, its own peculiar genetic line, and many other factors, the individual is unique. And as a unique individual, its properties and relationships will also be unique.

3.2.3 Differentiation and development

So functors are members of communities of functors that are of one kind, and each functor is a unique member of a kind. Both approaches are needed if we are to attain a proper understanding of a functor as agent for some action. They bring into focus the irreducible uniqueness of each functor as well as each functor's dependence on an invariable order of nomic conditions. The world has both constant continuity and unique individuality as correlative features. But in actual temporal existence these correlative poles of order and uniqueness show up in a situation that is more fluid and ambiguous than what we have seen so far might indicate. In the world as we know it the order of universal necessity becomes a structure of general trends; constancy and invariance show up as regularity and continuity. Individual functors come into existence, exist, and pass out of existence. While they exist, they may be of a kind such that they go from birth and immaturity through maturity to decline. The history of individuals of some kind often shows that there is development in the kind itself, even if and when the kind is bound and limited by certain constant features. Functors and their world develop and differentiate.

When functors interact, they form new relationships, and they must respond to new challenges. In many ways they are continually challenged with what is new. The fact that every functor belongs to some kind or other and that every situation and every relationship is also of some kind or other guarantees that the newness and novelty of each challenge will occur in a framework of continuity that will allow us to recognize what is happening. But the newness is also genuine. Real change and development have features as unique as individuality. Appropriate response in such a world requires creativity. The principles of order may be constant and invariant, but fluid general structures and trends develop all the same. New functors, functions, and relations occur.

Development gives rise to a process of differentiation, that is, to a process in which new structural interrelations are formed. At the same time, the new interrelations acquire a stability that allows us to speak of new kinds. Structural relationships that were only real as structural possibilities before now become actual. New kinds that come about in this way often arise to meet a challenge which has grown historically and which continues to confront the existential situation.

We may expect such development and differentiation to remain bound to the principles of order which determine the ultimate boundary of the development that takes place. Therefore no development takes the newly arising forms of existence to a point where they escape from the hold of the bounds of order within which they arose. Differentiation of structures will not, as it were, give rise to new structural realms fully discontinuous with the ones in which they find their origin.[24]

This is illustrated in the developments within the educational relationship between parents and children. At simple cultural levels parents are equipped for the job of rearing their children. Such a task entails the preparation of immature members of society for responsible participation in that society. This will always involve more than just the gathering of food and the avoidance of danger, that is, more than just the skills for self-preservation. One must learn to participate in the social process. In simpler cultures, however, almost all members have all the required skills at their control. Hence parents can informally supervise and encourage their youngsters to learn by participating in immature ways in the process itself. Transmission of culture comes about as children grow up within the context of the community. Family, friends, and neighbors naturally educate youth, which then involves only a minimal amount of formal instruction. What instruction there is will itself be taken up in the daily routine and will not be something set apart. Learning is by supervised doing.[25]

As the culture gets more complex, tasks and skills may differentiate to the point that some skills can no longer be supervised by every adult member; otherwise learning by participation in the actual process would become risky. Then certain traditions can only be passed on by those who are trained in them. The parent may lack the training required and may also lack the time to supervise learning. Then education will no longer be a natural task engaged in by all. Instead it will be the special task of some. But at first education per se will not be a special task; rather, the focus will be on training in special skills—with different skills being handled by different people. It is only when a further step is taken that special members of society take upon themselves the special task of educating as such. Many different skills are then taught by the same person, who becomes the educator in the basic skills and traditions.

Such differentiation and specialization can go a long way. In fact, they can develop to a point where the link between education and preparation for responsible participation in the actual life of a concrete society is no longer experienced. At that point all awareness of the original limits is lost. But if we take those empirical conditional limits as obtaining nevertheless, then we will regard such a development as degenerative. Therefore differentiation and specialization can be successful only when there is respect for the original structure and the original relation in which that structure occurred. If differentiation is not to become fragmentation, it will have to be a simultaneous process of integration according to original principles of order.

Sometimes such integration can take place when all the specialized developments are pulled together in one organized context in which the original principle is observed. This happens, for example, when all the educative tasks and specializations are institutionalized in schools. The various skills are then placed in an educational context and therefore are not seen as a series of abstractions. But the school itself, of course, may also become too specialized. This can be prevented only by observing the original task of education in relation to the rest of society.

It is this sort of differentiation and integration that gives rise to institutions and professions. The original ordering principle of the educative relationship between parents and children has given rise to the structural kind of being a teacher. But "being a teacher," of course, does not take the place of "being a person." In fact, the person, whose own being is much dependent on being a member of a community (i.e., on being a participant in an integrative relationship), for that reason remains an essential foundation for the process of integration. Wherever specialization threatens to undo the integrity of being a person, the process of overdifferentiation will almost always receive counter-impulses.

It would not be possible, then, to say that "being a teacher" points to any new kind of functor in a radical sense, that is, in the sense that in addition to persons there are now teachers as well in society. A teacher is a functor in a subsense of being a functor. Overspecialization may give rise to the idea that people are persons in addition to being teachers, but such an idea is always the result of a lack of integration and therefore of depersonalization.

However, there is another side of the question to be considered: Don't the institutions to which these developments give rise present us with genuinely new functors in the radical sense? Aren't the school, the government, the church, the supermarket, the stock market, and the university functor-type entities which are truly action centers? Don't states do things? What does such a headline as "Canadian Government Sends Stiff Protest to Soviet Union" mean? Don't we have two individual functors relating to each other here? Or would it be a mistake to think so? States and other insititutions may have individuality, but are they for that reason functors?

This problem cannot be fully discussed here without taking the nature of functions and relations into account. However, it can be said at this time that institutions could be understood as social role specializations rather than functors. Just as the individual person can specialize as teacher, so the human community can specialize as school. There is the tradesperson and the market, the artisan and the industry, the preacher and the church. The human community differentiates as well as the person. These institutionalized community relations can all be individual as well, but they need not be viewed as functors. They need not be individually acting functors, if they can also be accounted for as specifically structured relations.

3.2.4 Irreducibility of functors and functions

Although the term *functor* is peculiar to my approach, the term refers to something with which most philosophers have struggled. Use of the term *functor* is simply a matter of terminological efficiency. It semantically helps to express a correlation, since a parallel term can be used for the other side of the correlation (in this case, *function*). I could just as well have used the words *actor* and *action*. But *entity*, *substance*, *object*, and *thing* are too problematic. *Entity* is used in the literature to mean anything capable of receiving attention, which would include functions and relations. *Object* is often taken to mean exclusively a material object. Further, *object* is contrasted with *subject* in a way that is not helpful for my purposes. (Cf. 5.4 below.)

So different terms name the matter and concept under discussion, but the matter itself is clearly recognized. Of course, philosophers do not all have the same point of view on it. However, when Aristotle speaks in the *Categoriae* about "that which is neither predicated of a subject nor exists in a subject," he is clearly talking about functors. I could express his point by saying that whatever is one of a kind and functions without itself being a function is a functor. The fact that talk about this occurs in different contexts and gives rise to different theories does not diminish our recognition of a common reality.[26]

But in spite of recognition by philosophers of a commonly accepted reality, serious conflicts of interpretation arise. When William Kneale, in a discussion of G. Frege, mentions that the term *object* is used in such a way that "objects include all things that are not functions," one is inclined to think of a functor-function correlation such as I propose. However, "not only sticks and stones and men, but also numbers and truth values" are viewed as objects (Kneale, 499). So "objects" here may at times appear to be like what I have called functors, but that would be a misunderstanding of my view. For in my view numbers and truth values cannot be functors. If functors are genuinely existing entities, a unique one of a kind, and not themselves functions, then they must always have a physical or material existential basis. What I mean is this. If a functor is an agent of action and if the action is to be real, then we need to do justice to the fact that genuine action is originally physical in nature. Action that is real is causal and effectual. And cause and effect are only real if they have a material dimension. (See Quinton, 46-53.)

Yet I do not wish to hold to a materialist doctrine. People are not thinking rocks. I have acknowledged four irreducible realms of functors, and only one of those realms has functors that are simply material objects (the realm of physical reality). On the other hand, I also pointed out that all functors have physical functions. Although it is true that not all functors are simply material objects, it is also true that there are no completely nonmaterial functors. No existing functor can be devoid of dimensions of physicality. For in that case we would have a functor incapable of acting effectually.

For that reason numbers cannot be functors—at least, not in my view of functors. Numbers do not have independent existence as entities capable of action. Numbers are functions of functors and of relationships. These relationships have an invariant order and we can name the invariants and analyze their relations to one another. As relations of order, however, they can never be functors. Functors are concretely existing entities, while numbers are kinds of quantitative relationships. And kinds are not functors. There are kinds of functors, but functors are not kinds.

The problem in giving definitions of irreducibles such as functor and function is that the definition may trip us up. After giving some examples and descriptions, Stebbing writes: "These are things because they *have* characteristics; they are not characteristics *of* something else. But common sense distinguishes between a *thing* and *its states"* (266). But in her view, states also have characteristics. Are states both things and not things? While it may be true that my breathing (a function) is heavy (a characteristic of my breathing), two things can be said about this. First, if a thing is a functor, it must not only *be capable* of functioning and having functions but must also *be incapable* of being a function. Although breathing may be heavy, it is never a functor. The other remark that can be made is that my breathing is not an independent functor with respect to its being heavy. I breathe, as functor. And my breathing, for purposes of analysis, is not heavy. Rather, when I breathe this way, *I* breathe heavily. Breath, however, cannot breathe heavily. Hence it is a semantic trick that makes us think that breathing can be heavy.[27]

The complexity on either side of the irreducible functor-function correlation is so vast that simple definitions will likely lead us astray. A passage in Wolterstorff's *On Universals* illustrates this. The passage (UN, 221) runs as follows:

> Thus far in our discussion we have been dealing with what I have called *predicables*. We have distinguished predicables from nonpredicables, or substances; and we have drawn this distinction by using the concept of (nonlinguistic) predication. A predicable is what can be predicated, a substance is what cannot be predicated.
>
> It turns out, on these definitions, that the class of substances is a very mixed bag of things. Not only exemplifications, but also cases of predicables are substances; for example, not only Napoleon, but also Napoleon's brashness. And among those substances which are exemplifications of predicables are to be found not only events and physical objects and persons, but also such entities as poems, symphonies, species, classes, groups, organizations, stuffs, and propositions. For though, to give but one example, one can of course predicate *being Bartok's Fifth Quartet* of something, one cannot predicate Bartok's Fifth Quartet itself.

This passage is an instructive example of why it is necessary to distinguish not just functors from functions but also conditions from existence, and why these are distinctions of correlated irreducibles, even though all of them are closely interrelated. What good reason might Wolterstorff have for concluding that the definition of substance as that which cannot be predicated entitles us to refer to cases of predicables as substances? Wolterstorff claims that he is aligning himself with a "long philosophical tradition" when he refers to substance as that "which cannot be nonlinguistically predicated" of anything (UN, 65). But just how far-ranging can such a definition be in its scope? One might ask, for example, whether "that which cannot be nonlinguistically predicated" served in that tradition as the name-definition of something which in other contexts was also known as substance, or whether it served to define substance in such a way that whatever could not be predicated in that way would therefore be substance.[28]

If I refer to Italians in Toronto as members of the ethnic community living around West St. Clair Avenue, I do not thereby claim that anyone and everyone found in that area is Italian. Wolterstorff takes it that "that which cannot be nonlinguistically predicated" refers to substance in such a way that whatever cannot be so predicated is thereby defined as substance. Yet this is certainly not a doctrine that can be generally ascribed to the tradition on substance. In so far as Aristotle started that tradition, he may have held/taught that properties are always general or universal. And the point that Wolterstorff makes here is that the actual property of an actual substance is itself individual. No one who is brash is brash like Napoleon is brash, even though all who are brash exhibit the same property.

By defining substance in such a way that other uniquely individual things also are included (for nothing uniquely individual can, of course, be predicated), for Wolterstorff things other than substances, namely, their actual properties, also become substances. Such a view is confusing and leads, if not revised, to illegitimate reduction. Predicates which refer to conditions cannot in the same way refer to existences subject to those conditions. Whatever meets the conditions for being brash "is brash" we say. But in that expression "is brash" cannot at once refer to both those conditions and to their existentially having been met. So if "is brash" refers to a property and "brashness" to property conditions, the fact that Napoleon is brash does not indicate that there is such a thing as Napoleon's brash*ness*. Such an individual universal or universal individual only brings confusion.

This problem of the irreducibility of predicates to existents is interrelated with the problem of the irreducibility of functors to functions. Napoleon's brashness is a function of Napoleon. Napoleon is a genuine functor, that is, a "substance" which has properties and which neither itself nor its own individual properties can be predicated. In this passage, then, Wolterstorff has confused functors with functions and also kinds with cases. Brashness is indeed a kind, but Napoleon's brashness is a case. And if it is a case, a genuine case, it can never be treated as a kind. Napoleon's brashness, in fact, is not brash*ness* at all. Napoleon is *brash*. Napoleon's *case* of being brash is not itself some *kind* of brashness but only a case of brashness. But this also helps us to see that brash in the case of Napoleon cannot be a substance. If we wish to use substance terminology, we must say that "Napoleon" names the substance.

3.3   The Nature of Functions

Functors and functions are irreducible correlatives. There are no functions without functors and no functors without functions, nor are some functors functions, or some functions functors. The discussion of functors must now be amplified with a discussion of functions. Functions are what functors do, are, or have: birds fly, persons walk, mothers give birth, ants are industrious, Mary has a beautiful voice. Flying is a function of birds (among others). Giving birth is done by human mothers (among others). Industrious is what we call the way in which the ant acts. A beautiful voice is what Mary has. Yet these are not really sufficient characterizations, for although certainly functors do things or have characteristics, it also seems that functions themselves can play these roles.

Is it not the case that an action can have characteristics? Doesn't the singing of a bird wake up a sleeping camper? The bird's singing wakes this snoring camper. If so, then is a function well defined when I refer to it as always being the function of a functor? A functor can never be a function, but if the singing of a bird is a function and if it functions to arouse a sleeper, has a function thereby become a functor? If so, is it really possible to conceive of the functor-function relation as one of irreducible correlates?

A simple solution might be that though we may choose to use the semantic expression "The singing of the bird woke the sleeping camper," we could just as well say: "The bird woke the camper." The difference is simply that the former expression is a bit more specific than the latter. The fact that the function of the ontic subject has been made into the grammatical subject of the sentence does not make the function of the ontic subject itself into a subjective functor.[29] Functional complexity is sometimes so vast that it takes very specific language to make clear what we are concerned about in speaking of some state of affairs.[30]

"That pink is lovely," said the lady, "but it upsets my husband." What she is talking about, of course, is a dress which is pink in color.

In explaining to the salesperson why she herself liked the dress although her husband would not, she turned to the color. The color of the dress is what she is talking about. If that color were the color of some other object, she herself would presumably like it again whereas her husband would be upset by it. Even though we often write and talk as though functions also function, it is always possible to translate the expression in question in such a way that it is a functor that winds up functioning.[31]

3.3.1 Reduction

It is my position, then, that functors and functions are irreducible. When I talked about functors, I also maintained that they are mutually irreducible. I did not simply mean by this that one functor is itself and never another. That this is indeed the case can be plainly seen by anyone. According to the principle of identity, any particular object can just be itself. What I was referring to in connection with irreducibility in the case of functors was irreducibility in kind. There are also kinds of functors that are irreducible—humans, animals, plants, material objects. Within them one can distinguish subkinds which can be reduced to more inclusive kinds.

What is meant by reduction here? In one way the principle of identity makes all reduction impossible. Everything is what it is and nothing is something else. But science tries to simplify our world. It tries to develop categories of understanding that allow us to view many different things as one in kind. Finding a common denominator science calls reduction. And irreducibles have no such common denominator. Pears cannot be conceived as apples, but both can be taken as fruits. However, no real category of functors allows us to treat humans and plants together. This means that some reduction is legitimate, while other reduction is illegitimate. In my view, taking humans as basically organisms is an illegitimate reduction. Taking apples and pears as fruits is legitimate. Irreducibles simply are barriers for reduction.[32]

Can we take a similar approach when it comes to functions? Are there ultimately irreducible categories of functioning? This question is clearly of considerable importance. One duty of science is to devise explanatory theories of a high level of explanation, that is, to develop theories that take in as much empirical reality as possible. Very general theories can be constructed only when the scope of the theory is very wide. Width of scope, of course, requires the inclusion of many entities, which in turn calls for very inclusive categories. The category "animal" is more inclusive than the category "horse." Functor, function, and relation are ultimate categories of empirical reality. A next level of categorization would indicate that these levels, though all, for example, levels of function, are irreducible to each other. In dealing with kinds of functions, what level of irreducibility can science achieve?

This crucial question of the scope of explanatory power has engaged the minds of academics for centuries. Until very recently there have been many scientists who tried to devise one general method for the explanation of all phenomena—hopefully, an exact method. The strategy of many scientists has been to use mathematical or physical explanations for all of empirical reality. But if such an approach is to be valid, it must be possible to reduce all phenomena to basically one kind, that is, the kind that allows for mathematical or physical explanation. Is this really possible?

This is not the same question as the question whether a functor can be reduced to its functions. Functionalism tries to do just that. It deals with functors in terms of systems of functioning and rejects the notion of functors as action centers.[33] My present question is a different one. Granted that functions cannot themselves be functors, what I want to know is whether all functions can be taken as being of one or at most a very few kinds. Is all functioning physical interaction? As I just indicated, I am now speaking of the actual functioning of actual functors—and not of the use of the term *function* in a merely semantic sense. Is all real functor activity physical? Is it possible that there is instead an irreducible diversity of functioning? Is sensing understandable and explainable in terms of physical interaction? Can the organic search for food be declared the basic form of analysis as the search for solutions?[34]

This last question relates the problem of reduction to the univocity of scientific terms. If we say that an animal searches for food while a scientist searches for a solution, have we then isolated a common category univocally named *search* under which we can subsume both food gathering and analysis? This would require that analysis and food gathering are structurally similar in such ways that we must regard them as members of the same kind. If we talk about "DNA" and "information" and "codes," do we then signify that my telling my wife (in a prearranged way so that the children will not know about the surprise we have in store) that I have just brought in a cake is a relationship of the same *kind* (i.e., having the same structure) as that between DNA, RNA, and organic processes? Does saying that RNA provides information *explain* anything beyond the type of explanation we give when we say that wine is soporific?

The scientific use of one term for a variety of phenomena where the term has the same import in all instances of its use requires that the phenomena named all be one in kind. The term must name the kind in question. That is, the term must name a configuration of nomic conditions. Methodological reduction presupposes underlying ontic identity. If we want to reduce the concept of life to that of physical interaction, the term *physical* must then be used univocally and must then indicate that life *is* indeed physical. Recognizing patterns in the vast variety with which experience confronts us requires generalization and the recognition of the need for reduction. No two phenomena are exactly alike in all respects. Neither are there any two entities that are unlike one another in all respects. What are the shared features, and what pattern do they display?

In the recent past the legitimate scientific concern to reduce individual variety to a common denominator has led to the almost unchallenged assumption that all the empirical diversity of phenomena should be reduced to one kind. Such was the unchallenged ideal for many scientists. All existence must be physical existence. All science must be quantitative. Contemporary theorists increasingly challenge that assumption, arguing that some of the reduction attempted is illegitimate. Today reduction*ism* is being challenged from many sides. This is an important debate from my point of view, for my own position involves the multiplicity of a large number of irreducible levels of functioning. I believe there are many kinds of functions that are irreducible and that do not have a more basic functional common denominator. Most anti-reductionists are open to three or four irreducible kinds of reality, but from the point of view I am developing here that would still entail a great deal of illegitimate reduction.

William Kneale raises a relevant problem of reduction when he discusses our attempts to express mathematical continuity in numerical terms, that is, in terms of discrete quantity. Can the numerically discrete or discontinuous be used to understand geometrical continuity? Geometry must make use of such numbers as *pi* or square roots which, as Kneale says, "give rise to perplexity" as early as the Greeks (390). The perplexity here, of course, relates to the fact that some of these numbers seem to miss the discreteness or exactness of a number. *Pi* is not discrete. That very fact may indicate that spatial continuity is not fully expressible in terms of numerical discreteness, or else such perplexing "numbers" as *pi* would not occur. As Kneale puts it, "our enlargement of the number concept is really an extension of the usage of the word 'number' to cover entities of various types . . ." (397). Thus, the *concept* number does not really fit all the entities that the *word* number covers.

Kneale concludes that the continuity of geometry can be treated in terms of numerical discreteness or discontinuity only if we allow ourselves to treat space *as if* it were numerical and then submit space to rules of numerical relations. But the price we pay, says Kneale, is that "we cannot use number expressions of higher types in the same way as we use ordinary numerals . . ." (397). And what this means is that what space essentially is cannot be reduced to what number essentially is. Numerical reality can at best approach the reality of spatial continuity in numbers such as *pi*. Such a number itself approaches that continuity in the infinity of our effort to calculate its exact value. But spatial continuity and numerical discreteness remain irreducible kinds of functioning.[35]

Nevertheless, as Susan Stebbing puts it, "science tries to reduce the diversity of things in the world to mere differences of appearance, and treats as many things as possible as variants of the same stuff" (21). Science must and does accept the legitimacy of reduction. But do we also understand reduction in a legitimate sense? Let us take an example from Stebbing herself. I will quote an entire paragraph (176), and for convenience in later reference I will number each sentence.

(1) A primitive concept and a primitive proposition are, then, *primitive* only in relation to a *given* system. (2) The selection of these primitive notions and primitive propositions determines a given deductive system. (3) What is a theorem, or demonstrated proposition, in one system may be a primitive proposition in another; what is defined in one system may be undefined in another. (4) Hence, it is meaningless to say that a given primitive proposition is *indispensable*, or logically presupposed by other propositions. (5) This may be made clearer by considering the logical relation of physics and mathematics. (6) There is a sense in which physics presupposes mathematics, since physics cannot be developed without reference to mathematics, whereas mathematics can be developed without reference to physics. (7) But it would be a mistake to argue from this that mathematics is *in an unqualified sense* logically prior to, or necessarily presupposed by, physics. (8) To say that *p is necessarily presupposed by q* would be to say that *q implies p*, i.e., that the falsity of *p* follows from the falsity of *q*. (9) But this is not the case. (10) Physics does not imply mathematics; it might be false though mathematics were not. (11) Physics might be true even though there were no general laws of mathematics. (12) Similarly, the special sciences presuppose the principles of logic; but these principles are not *implied* by the special sciences.

(13) Mathematical propositions are verified inductively in so far as physics, deduced by means of these propositions, is true.

The thoughts expressed in this passage are not exceptional. Many will likely agree. The paragraph deals with deductive systems, that is, with human creations. It does not deal with world order or system in any "natural" sense, such as we might meet in what is called the ecosystem. I can readily agree with the general sentiments expressed in the first three sentences. However, the "only" in sentence 1 as amplified in an unqualified sense by sentence 4 poses a problem.

It appears that sentence 4 wants to assert that a "given primitive proposition" is not "logically presupposed" by propositions that do *not* belong to the *given* system. The primitive propositions in a system such as Stebbing has in mind are not defined or proven within that system. But they are needed for the proof and definition of other propositions in that system. They therefore serve as basis for such proof and definition. She now means to say that we cannot speak of certain propositions as necessarily prior to any and all propositions whatever, occurring in any and all deductive systems whatever. This may be too strongly expressed.

What is said generally in the first three sentences is made into a universal principle that applies to all deductive systems whatever. It is a self-referential statement which may unnecessarily create a Russell paradox.[36] But even apart from that, the notion that no proposition is ever primitive in principle (as opposed to being primitive with regard to a given system) might be counterintuitive. If primitivity were completely relative to particular systems, the coherence of all systems would be a matter of circularity.

Be that as it may, Stebbing herself clarifies what she means with an example. She wants to consider the "logical relation of physics and mathematics." What might she mean by this? Is there a relationship between mathematics and physics—as systems—such that both are elements within one logical, deductive system? Is Stebbing referring implicitly to the possibility of the reduction of the whole of mathematics and physics to logic? Since the debate about the relation of mathematics to logic is still unsettled, the inclusion of physics in the debate is probably not what she has in mind. Of course, principles of logic must be obeyed by both mathematicians and physicists, but does this create a logical relation between the two disciplines?

Principles of logic must also be observed by biologists and legal scholars, but is there a logical relation between biology and jurisprudence? It may be that Stebbing is using *logical* in the sense of orderly, since she defines order as logical (201). Perhaps the question she is asking is this: What is the nature of the relationship between mathematics and physics? That relationship can never be purely logical, for the simple reason that logical order is an order of propositions alone. But mathematics and physics—as systems—depend for their truth not only on propositional correctness but also on truth of reference. Moreover, the realities referred to in physics differ from those referred to in mathematics. Therefore the use of *logical* for both "orderly" and "inferential" is confusing. It is not at all clear that the implication relation, as a formal logical relation, can serve to test the relation between mathematics and physics. The logical implication relation and a disciplinary foundational relation are by no means obviously the same.[37]

The material problems in which Stebbing gets entangled because she confuses *logical* and *orderly* can be seen when the material truth of her argument is tested. Physics and mathematics deal with realities that are irreducible. What Kneale pointed out with regard to the relation between quantity and continuity can also be applied to the relation between quantity and physical reality. Just as geometrical relations cannot be fully reduced to numerical ones, so physical relations cannot be fully reduced to ordinary mathematical ones.[38] And there is an order of priority in that relationship. Stebbing herself points out the order in sentence 6. Physics needs mathematics, but mathematics is independent of physics. In sentence 7, however, we find Stebbing saying that this is not necessarily so, that is, there is no logical necessity. For logical necessity would mean logical implication. But in sentence 9 she asserts that there is no logical implication. I agree, but does that mean there is no necessity?

Indeed, there is no logical necessity. Yet this is only relevant if we assume that the relation is a logical one. Her assertion comes to nought in material terms, then, as we can see from her assertion that without general laws of mathematics, physics could still be true. What might this mean? If there *can* be no physics without mathematics, no physics at all, it is hard to see how there could be true physics.[39] Even apart from that consideration, what are we to make of the claim that physics as a deductive system could be stated without being supported mathematically?

What the Stebbing paragraph demonstrates is that the problem of the relation of clearly distinct areas of reality that appear irreducibly dissimilar is a difficult one. Stebbing realizes that reduction is legitimate, and also that there is a significant difference between two fields such as physics and mathematics. Yet she gets entangled in the ambiguity of her use of the term *logical* in considering the relation between these fields. This problem has been noted by others, most acutely by Toulmin.

Toulmin has been especially aware of fallacies of reductionism whenever science depends too exclusively on a formal-logical point of view. In his view modal terms such as *necessary* and *possible* are field-dependent (AR, 36). Mathematical and moral necessity both have the real force of necessity. But criteria for arriving at the conclusion that something is necessary depend on the field. Toulmin then introduces the important question (AR, 39): ". . . are the differences between the standards we employ in different fields irreducible?" By this he does not mean that certain areas of reality are not accessible to logical argument, or even that some areas are more accessible than others (AR, 40).

I believe that the problem is indeed not whether logic is universally applicable. Rather, the problem is whether all order can be reduced to logical order. Thus the problem is whether or not there is an irreducible variety of kinds of order. One can maintain the irreducibility of kinds without sacrificing the universality and universal applicability of kinds. The question whether logic can be applied to all sorts of other realities is not equivalent to the question whether the other realities can be reduced to logical reality. The nature of what is logical and the nature of what is physical differ. But this difference does not preclude the application of logic to the material world.

The irreducibility in question can perhaps be stated as follows. Strictly speaking, only feelings can be felt, and only thoughts can be thought. Relations and functions of a certain kind are all of that kind and have the order of that kind. On the other hand, feelings themselves do not feel and thoughts do not think. It is a person that does the feeling and the thinking. And in feeling and thinking, the person thinks about other things than thoughts and feels more than feelings. All functions of the same functor are integrated, centered functions. Wholes relate to wholes in functionally diverse manners. Toulmin helps us to see that when these complex states of affairs are oversimplified in a reductionistic way, a logic that is itself reduced and reductionistic "cannot keep in serious contact with its practical application" (AR, 147; see also 169-70, 207).

In order to see this, one must of course see more in distinctions and classifications than convention. Karl Popper believes that "all this classification and distinction is a comparatively unimportant and superficial affair. *We are not students of some subject matter but students of problems*. And problems may cut right across the border of any subject matter or discipline" (CR, 67). But the fact that some problems may be interdisciplinary seems to be no reason to think that the disciplines or subject matter have no distinctness. Students of problems are found outside of science as well. Pastors and psychiatrists are also concerned with problems, but their problems would hardly be recognized as scientific, precisely because they are not at all interested in the recognition of *kinds* of problems *as* kinds. Also, they are not interested in studying the validity of certain methods in certain areas. Science, however, does concern itself with these problems.

In fact, Popper's attitude to classification is relativized by his belief in the *limited* applicability of certain approaches: "The belief that any one of the calculi of arithmetic is applicable to any reality . . . is therefore hardly tenable" (CR, 211). Underlying this statement is a positive attitude with respect to the problem of illegitimate reduction. In principle, at least, Popper does not think that all reality is accessible to certain approaches. But if he is indeed of this opinion, it is not clear how one could help oneself observe the right limits without becoming aware of irreducible differences in kinds of reality. Popper's above quote comes as he remarks on the significance of Gödel's theorems and he remarks in this context that formal language and number theory are irreducible. If this is so, there seems to be no ground for Popper not to allow for the significance of inquiring into the nature of such irreducibility. What are the boundaries between these two phenomena? To what kind of thing does the one point, and to what kind of reality does the other point? Sorting this out is clearly a matter of broadly ontological classification.

If ontological classification can indeed be seen as a designation of the ontic limits of reduction, such limits will themselves appear to be varied and considerable in number. If one is aware of this, like Polanyi, a strong anti-reductionist, one is likely to see that science has in general taken its task of reduction too seriously and has allowed formal logical considerations to level out too many irreducible levels. Polanyi rejects illegitimate reduction on a number of levels: of wholes to their parts, of wholes to their functions (PK, 330), and of levels of functionality to one another (PK, 342; see also De Jager-Seerveld). Polanyi also recognizes that such an anti-reductionist stance poses a special problem for the evolutionary approach to the origin of species.

Indeed, if kinds of functors—as well as functions—are irreducible, how could they ever have arisen out of one another? (See also 3.4 below.) "The evolutionary process forms a continuous transition from the inanimate stage to that of living and knowing persons; how can it then bring forth an additional . . . (irreducible) level—two in place of one, three in place of two?" (PK, 345). If orders of kinds are irreducible, can things of certain kinds still arise from things of other kinds?

Polanyi accepts a process which generates new levels of reality. "I have dealt before with . . . features that characterize the vegetative level; let me now sum up the new features that are added to these on the active-perceptive level. They are *sentience* of motive and knowledge; an effort to *do right* and *know truly*; a belief that there exists an *independent reality* which makes these endeavors meaningful, and a sense for the consequent *hazards*" (PK, 363). But he also views such levels as irreducibly different. "Lower levels do not lack a bearing on higher levels; *they define the conditions of their success and account for their failures, but they cannot account for their success, for they cannot even define it*" (PK, 382). Even "the rise of new forms of life . . . is likewise undefinable in terms of physics and chemistry" (PK, 383). "For no events occurring according to the known laws of physics and chemistry can be conscious" (PK, 389).

Polanyi, though convinced that modern scientific advances have blocked off the overly zealous reductionism of the immediate past, is not optimistic about quick acknowledgment of, for example, the irreducible difference between the physical and organic levels of functionality. "Scientists will not be prepared even to consider such a suggestion, unless they have completely accepted the fact that biotic achievements cannot . . . be ever represented in terms of physics and chemistry; and very few do realize this" (PK, 399). Polanyi here shows himself to be one of a new generation of thinkers who have come to the conclusion that there has been too much illegitimate reductionism and that science must consequently explore alternatives.

Ervin Laszlo is another of that new generation. He favors exploring the possibility that actual existence may be much more resistant to reduction than science would like. However, he also views reality in terms of the development of a whole hierarchy of irreducible levels from a single origin. "Adaptive self-organization inevitably leads toward the known biological and psychological systems" (SP, 42). A natural system gives rise to life and intelligence autonomously from within itself. "Given the self-organizingly adaptive property of natural systems, their mutual adaptations are more likely to result within any given time-span in a multi-level hierarchy than in a nonhierarchical structure" (SP, 48).

When Laszlo suggests the possibility of "a vertical law of organization by deduction from horizontal laws of interaction" (SP, 49), he appears to be thinking here that interaction on one level gives rise to new levels. How does he consider it possible to hold to the emergence of new levels while at the same time subscribing to their irreducibility? His basic approach is that properties combine to form new properties. "Fresh 'qualities' can emerge in the hierarchy in the form of new transformations of invariant properties. Such *nova* are accounted for by the consideration that systems at each level contain systems at all lower levels plus their combination within the whole formed at that level. Hence the possibilities for diversity of structure and function increase with the levels, and one need not reduce the typical characteristics of higher-level entities to those of lower levels but can apply criteria appropriate to their particular hierarchical position" (SP, 49).

In this kind of system, the wholes of lower levels function as parts on the higher levels immediately above them (SP, 51). We are to understand this in such a way that the result is an ordering of "natural phenomena into a 'vertical' order wherein any given system, with the exception of those on the lowest or *basic* level, is both a supra system in regard to its components, and a subsystem in regard to the totality which it forms together with other systems in its environment" (SP, 52). Whether Laszlo is indeed successful in combining emergence with irreducibility in a hierarchy of systems is not the point at present. What is important for our purposes is that he moves science in the direction of greater respect for irreducible kinds. (See SP, 52, 159, 169.)

At the same time Laszlo wants to leave room for the more traditional approaches—at least so as to keep from unnecessarily offending their adherents. This comes through clearly in the following statement. "The radical distinction between physical and biological nature can be overcome without entailing the labyrinths of the mechanism-vitalism controversy by the simple expedient of analyzing physical as well as biological phenomena in terms of a general theory of natural systems. Specific differences are not overlooked by such systems-analysis, but are accounted for in terms of structural *isomorphisms* (rather than identities). At the same time these isomorphisms guarantee the unity of the established phenomena in the significant organizational respects" (SP, 69).

In my view, Laszlo's attempt to combine genetic continuity with discontinuity of order or structural irreducibility remains problematic. (See, for example, SP, 187, 190.) The problem is that the emerging higher levels have in principle first been smuggled into the lower levels (SP, 151, 152). In this way the problem of irreducibility actually disappears. Another problem is that combinations of properties of a certain *kind* hardly account for a new property of another *kind* (SP, 152). And a third problem is that the appeal in a general system to the order underlying all existence can also be used to point to the irreducible kinds required by that order.

Günther S. Stent has, in fact, reflected on attempts to find laws other than physical laws to explain life. Successful attempts of this kind could possibly indicate that an irreducible order itself guarantees existential irreducibility. He concludes, however, that these attempts have failed, and he addresses the problem that remains: how to account for life anyway, since life's structures *are* irreducible.[40] Stent is convinced that physical laws cannot fully account for biological problems. Thus he, too, rejects the absolutization of certain methods, for he is aware that physics is insufficient. He rejects the view that "all biological phenomena, no matter what their complexity, can ultimately be accounted for in terms of conventional physical laws" (391).

Stent actually accepts the view that life phenomena cannot be reduced to physical laws, but at the same time he accepts the idea that there are no other laws whereby to explain anything besides physical laws. Thus his anti-reductionism results in a kind of agnosticism. "Perhaps *this* then is the paradox: there exist processes which, though they clearly obey the laws of physics, can *never* be explained" (395).

Although the above review shows that the discussion of irreducibility remains halting and uneven, it also shows that there are arguments for developing a greater respect for the irreducibility of dimensions of reality. Functors and functions, parts and wholes, levels of functionality (of matter, life, sentience, rationality, value, etc.), laws and processes subject to them, and others have been examined as candidates for irreducibility. I have already discussed my view of some of these irreducible correlates. But now I wish to concentrate especially on the irreducibility of functional kinds, on levels of functionality that must be understood on their own terms.

3.3.2 *Order and irreducibility*

If irreducibility is indeed a genuine feature of our world, we would expect to find it not merely in the structure of empirical reality but also in the order of conditions which makes this reality possible. In the first two chapters I concluded that the empirical world and the order of its conditions are correlates as well as irreducibles. We saw that this implies that no principles of order are subjective existents, while no subjective existent is a principle of order (condition-1). Further implications are that nothing in the empirical world is without structure and that no order is real except in relation to existence.[41]

I will now argue that principles of order that are irreducible to one another in their mutual relationships nevertheless "coincide," as it were, in structuring the same subjective existence. What I mean is this: although physical and biotic reality are irreducible in kind, we need not conclude that we will never find both kinds of reality present within the functional patterns of one and the same functor. Some functors would then function both physically and biotically. And organisms in fact do function in this way. Kinds of functional reality that are in principle irreducible to one another can nevertheless be part of the structure of the same entity.

I will argue in favor of this position by connecting the order-existence correlation with the functor-function correlation. One likely consequence of the correlativity of order and existence is that a fundamental distinction such as that between functor and function is itself both grounded in the conditioning order of things and a feature of empirical existence. If functors and functions are kinds of existence, we may expect that they are related to an order of functors and functions. Just as there are kinds of functors and kinds of functions, functor and function are themselves kinds of reality. By means of this construction we can account for both irreducibility and continuity, namely, by viewing functors as units functioning on a multiplicity of irreducible levels of functioning, all according to irreducible nomic conditions. The empirical world is structurally complex. This is because many irreducibly distinct orders simultaneously structure wholes of existence in their functional complexity.

We come upon an example of this complex interweaving of structures when we consider the question whether organisms can be understood at all in terms of physical and chemical principles. In the literature on this subject (e.g., the literature on the vitalism-mechanism controversy, or the literature on the origin of life), we find people taking a variety of positions which are all based on evidence. As we saw above, Stent believes that all known organic processes obey physical laws only. Polanyi's view is that physical principles, by their very nature, cannot account for organic reality. Hempel holds out hope for a purely physical explanation of all reality. Is there any way to approach these problems that will do justice to the empirical phenomena without at the same time getting hung up in fruitless and speculative controversies?

One possibility might be to distinguish between organisms as biotic or organic functors, on the one hand, and the biotic or organic functions of organisms in distinction from other functions, say physical functions, on the other hand. The concept of a living organism, in and of itself, does not require that all processes occurring within the life of the organism must themselves be living processes. If chemistry can fully account for and explain certain interactions occurring within the organism, there is no need to assume that these interactions are anything other than genuinely chemical processes. The problem is of a different nature. As Stent viewed it, whatever can be explained fully in terms of physical and chemical properties does not suffice to explain all that goes on and all that there is.

In such a case, it seems misguided to search for other *physical* laws. It would be better to search for laws of a different sort—perhaps organic laws or laws of sensitive life.[42] It would appear than an actual living organism functions on a multiplicity of levels. Some can be accounted for wholly in terms of mathematical principles, while others require the additional understanding of physical-chemical laws. Still others need a level of explanation called biological. Biological laws do not defy explanation, as Stent would have it; they only defy physical explanation. The order of conditions underlying the organic world may not be known in the same way in which the physical order is known, but the reason for this may be because it is a different order, an order irreducible to the order of physical reality.[43]

Many of the well-known laws in science come from the physical and mathematical disciplines: lawful states of affairs are articulated in exact formulae with a strictly universal bearing. In many cases, such statements can even be completely formalized and quantified. Many scientists regard such statements as the goal they are striving for. Yet it may be that such precision cannot be achieved in the case of typically organic and sentient processes. The complexity of those worlds may well prevent us from establishing quantified, universal formulae.[44] If Heisenberg uncertainty relations and Gödel incompleteness theorems relate to simple physical and formal mathematical systems, one would expect them to apply even more dramatically in the case of organic systems.

But why should this deter us from acknowledging that we are already acquainted with many law-like relationships that clearly point to underlying structures and conditions? We know that there is regularity in the organic world, and we also know that it is not fully of a physical kind. Even though there may not actually be such a thing as the "law of measles" in medicine, measles is a well documented and understood *kind* of phenomenon which displays abberration in a well-defined structural area. The conditions for its occurrence are known, the symptoms for its recognition are well-defined, and procedures for cures are accurately described.

We know that if youngsters do not crawl before a certain age they are likely to experience adverse affects when later they have to learn to read. We know that rigid hysterics ought not to be suddenly introduced to significant change. We know that in our society the solution to inflation worsens unemployment and that relieving unemployment is hard on inflation. We know that in matters of religious faith people pass through definite stages, as they do in developing intelligence. All these examples point to lawful behavior and thus to underlying conditional patterns. So far their complexity has prevented us from formulating exactly what is the case. But their reality is too evident and the scientific community's hold on them too tight for us to deny the reality of order in every corner of existence.

It is true, of course, that many realities are too complex and the individual variety of their occurrence too multiple for us to reasonably expect that we should be able to state their underlying conditions in the same way that we state the law that for every five units of empirical existence we will always have only three left if we remove two. We can state this law as: $5 - 2 = 3$. This mathematical relationship is not one that applies to numbers; rather, it applies to things. If I have five pigs and sell two, I will only have three left. Yet this does not mean that mathematical laws will fully explain all that can be known about pigs, even when such laws fully explain this situation.

Surely we should not expect to be able to state in the same manner what the structure of emotional maturity is. However, if recent developments in the explosion of psychology are any indication, "personality types" understood as "laws," as allowing us to explain and perhaps even "predict" some behavior, are now much closer to scientific status than before. If feelings were numbers and if sensations were atomic forces, we might expect mathematical and physical laws to suffice. On the other hand, if feelings are functional realities of another *kind*, the inability to explain them mathematically and physically would be the expected and rational thing.

What the discussion has brought to the surface here is that there appears to be a difference between (a) viewing wholes in terms of other wholes, and (b) viewing wholes in terms of some of their functions rather than of others. Let me illustrate. It is one thing to view an organism (a whole functor) as a machine (another whole functor). It is another thing to view an organism (functor) from the point of view of its physical (functional) level of existence.[45] If functors are functionally complex, one need not reduce functors (wholes) of one kind (plants) to functors (wholes) of another kind (machines) if one is a materialist. On different grounds it would still be possible to defend the difference between these functoral wholes while at the same time taking the plant primarily as a physical system.

In the latter case one does not take a machine view of the plant but a physicalistic view; that is to say, the kinds of functional multiplicity in the plant have been reduced to one functional kind. In fact, the distinction between functors and functions introduces yet another reductionist possibility, namely, the one in which being a functor is explained entirely in terms of functional complexity, which involves a rejection of the need for an irreducible distinction between functor and function. A functor is viewed as just the complexity of its functions. In more traditional language: substances are viewed as bundles of properties. This latter type of reduction would pose a problem even in the case of the analysis of a machine. As Polanyi has shown, even a machine, as a functoral whole, cannot be explained in terms of any or all its parts and functions if an attempt is made to analyze it entirely on the basis of physical-mathematical models.[46]

The renewed interest in anti-reductionist approaches is too recent for us to be able to make an accurate and generally valid assessment of the situation. At least it is fair to say that fully reductionist approaches are no longer left unchallenged today. There is a definite interest in differentiating sharply between physical processes, life phenomena, and psychic events, while maintaining that all remain lawful. There seems little reason not to acknowledge a great variety of irreducible empirical reality as well as a correlative order for this empirical world. Still, this does not necessarily mean a revival of simple dualisms like the theory of the Cartesian ghost in the machine. Functionalism has made it clear that more sophisticated theories are needed to account for conscience, sentient functioning, and the like.[47]

Renewed attention to wholistic analysis is intended to counteract purely functionalist and reductionist approaches which are no more satisfactory than the theory of the ghost in the machine. At the same time, there is a great deal more to wholistic analyses than a speculative positing of the existence of immaterial spiritual substances. Included are trends toward acknowledging a functional multiplicity, structural irreducibility, and the unity of wholes within their functional multiplicity. An important question in this context concerns the variety of functional multiplicity being acknowledged. So far in this section I have been preoccupied with irreducibility and order on every level of existence. Now I want to come to the question of how varied the irreducible levels of functionality might be.

If functional complexity is distinguished from functoral unity, will it not follow—at least as a matter of possibility—that functional variety need not run parallel to functoral variety? What I have in mind is this. Earlier in this chapter I argued that functors are basically of four irreducible kinds, called realms or kingdoms. Does this mean that we must also accept four basic levels of functioning? It is not hard to see that this might commit us to *at least* four levels, so that we could distinguish physical, organic, sentient, and human functioning. The latter could be called rational, cultural, spiritual, normative, or moral, for example. But must we limit it to four? The many possible designations for "human" point in another direction.

The possibility of different levels of functionality in one realm can be illustrated by introducing one of Zeno's well-known paradoxes, that is, the one concerning a moving object which, since it will always (as Zeno saw matters) first have to cover half the distance before it can cover the whole distance, will never be able to move very far since distances are infinitely divisible. Because the series 1/2, 1/4, 1/16, and so forth, is infinite, the 1/n distance will never be reached except in infinity. However, we know that objects do in fact move in space.

This problem, of course, is usually taken to be entirely solved on a physical level with quantitative principles. However, even this relatively simple phenomenon appears to reveal to analysis a number of irreducible levels of functioning and also the necessity of distinguishing between functors and functions. The moving object is an entity in action. An event is taking place. One of the first things overlooked in the paradox is that the complex event "object in motion" cannot be resolved simply in terms of the quantified spatial relations. Motion across a space by itself is not a reality. There is in fact an object that moves, a functor that functions. Without such an object there is simply no "moving some distance" at all.

However, this is not the only reduction we encounter, as a result of which we cannot account for the phenomena. The paradox also ignores the irreducible difference between the functions of spatial extension and motion. Although it is undoubtedly true that any moving object has a path of motion, the motion cannot be fully accounted for by mathematically approaching it in terms of its path of motion. Extension and motion are irreducibly different kinds of functions.

The facts of the one function (spatial), its relationships, the methods we use to account for them—all of this will not suffice to account for the other function (kinematic). In this sense one might say that there is even a difference on a purely spatial level between extended surfaces and an extended path. The latter is a relation of spatial functions to phenomena of motion, while the former need not be. What Zeno's paradox shows us is that if we ignore the irreducibility of levels of functionality, we will not be able to account satisfactorily for the givens of empirical reality. For dealing with one level of functionality in terms of another is itself paradoxical.

The relatively simple phenomenon of a moving object reveals many dimensions of irreducibility. First there is the irreducibility of order and existence. The concretely traveling object cannot be reduced to laws of motion or to any other laws; it is an actually existing entity in action—not a law in action.[48] Yet it obeys laws. We can understand and explain dimensions of the process according to these laws. But the laws and the process of an acting object are irreducible.

Furthermore, the actually moving object is not the same as the sum of mathematical, mechanical, and energy functions. The object is an individual entity which has these functions. We can use the functional dimensions and their laws to explain the event. Since the many functions are all functions of one functor, they all help to clarify what goes on. But the functions do not *add up* (in a mathematical sense) to the event. Finally, the functions themselves are irreducible to one another. As functions of one object, they interrelate. Since motion is indeed along some path, spatial relations help us understand motion. But when we start treating motion as though it had the properties of space (as Zeno did), nothing will move. At the same time, the irresolvability of the quantifying operation has pointed to the fact that such irresolvability exists in connection with motion: the number $1/n$ itself moves on and on without stopping.[49]

Even in this simple example, there is much to be said for the adoption of an approach that counts on finding many irreducible levels of functionality in reality. The attempt to reduce the given multiplicity to illegitimate covering categories will only frustrate us if it turns out that the multiplicity cannot in fact be so reduced. At the same time, science simply could not be where it is today if there were not some validity to reduction. The principles of *order* cannot very well be just as diverse as existence is *individually* varied. Furthermore, there is the principle of the economy of analysis to be considered. It is only proper to try to find as simple a picture of things as possible. A complex picture may not be inaccurate, but science will always want to know whether the picture could not be simplified with the same explanatory power.

Yet, our intuitive sense of diversity is offended if there are too few principles of explanation. Philosophers may be materialists, but ordinary experience tells people that the world is more than just physical. The approach to this problem must be in terms of the structures of reality. What one begins to look for is *levels* of *generality*—not individual variety. Science must account for the irreducible levels of reality in terms of structures, conditions, and principles of order. The limits of reduction are in the first place limits of the order of possibilities.

When science discovers certain relationships of order that appear to be invariant, we then have some scientific categories to work with. In recent decades, there has been an enormous amount of scientific development, which has resulted in an immense amount of specialization and the introduction of innumerable scientific categories. One of the reasons why science is placing more emphasis on the reduction problem of late is that the specialization of categories has created a great need for scientific integration, for organizing categories that will allow us to conceive of the body of the sciences in a more encyclopedic manner.

Given the move away from unwarranted reductionism, the need for new categories of integration is much in evidence from this point of view as well. Now, if what I have argued in the first two chapters is true, namely, that regularly observed patterns of reality and experience point to structures and orders and that these structures and orders give rise to our ordering categories, then I believe that the considerations brought forward in this section can lead to a number of categories that are basic to our understanding of reality. These categories may in turn point us to fundamentally irreducible principles of order.

The model I am working with posits the most primitive categories of existence to be those of functor and function in relation. Empirical existence is most basically "made up" of functors and functions in relationship. In the view I am developing this happens in subjection to the order of reality, that is, the order that obtains for reality calls for the existence of functors and functions. That same order also gives rise to categories of functors and functions that are mutually irreducible and would thus guide science in the search for appropriate methods and concepts in each irreducible field. I searched earlier for kinds of functors; now I will explore the likelihood of irreducible principles of functionality.

3.3.3   Irreducible functions

Functions of existence can be understood as irreducible in two senses. On the one hand they are irreducible to functors, and on the other hand they are irreducible to one another. Functions and functors cannot be reduced to each other; functions of one kind cannot be reduced to functions of another kind. The reason why the category of functor cannot be reduced to that of function is that functioning itself is impossible (empirically speaking) unless there is integrated and centered existence which operates functionally, that is, which performs the functions. The integrated centeredness of a functioning entity or a functional whole is not itself one of the functions. It is precisely the functional multiplicity that needs to be centered and integrated. This requires a centered unit of functioning.[50] What I am after in this section, however, is not this irreducibility but the irreducibility of one kind of function to another.

Earlier I suggested that the number of irreducible kinds of functioning may be greater than is now commonly assumed. Not only is physicalism unacceptable, a division into four realms of functions also seems too limited. Whenever a method appropriate for the understanding of one kind of functioning turns out with unsatisfactory explanations, we may suspect that the method is being (illegitimately) applied to a different kind of functionality. In the case of the moving physical object, it may be necessary to distinguish levels of number, space, motion, and energy as functional dimensions. Empirical research strongly suggests that sentience and life should also be treated as irreducible functions of reality. Can abstractive intelligence be explained in terms of these, or is it irreducible as well? What about religious experience—and our evaluative approach to things?

If all functions are always of some specific kind, and if kinds of functions can be grouped into more ultimate kinds, then do we finally arrive at kinds which are mutually irreducible? This matter is the object of much controversy and much experimentation. Is it possible to develop criteria whereby one determines the basic kinds of functionality? Are there principles of analysis which can help us to detect these functional categories?

There does not exist a discipline which has developed methods for discovering irreducible levels of functionality. Moreover, the concern for analyzing the nature of natural conditions of irreducibility is recent. All the same, there may yet be approaches readily available which can be explored. I will look at four possible varieties of approach in this section. (a) The first is the approach via the history of the development and specialization of science into a number of distinctly different disciplines. (b) The second approach is via our understanding of paradoxes in the analysis of empirical reality (e.g., Zeno's paradox). (c) The third is via the analysis of the relationship of an irreversible natural order in reality (e.g., where mathematics is fundamental to physics but can exist without physics). (d) The fourth avenue toward an order of irreducible principles of functionality is via the experience of functional inappropriateness (as when, e.g., functional concepts used to organize the running of a hospital or a business cost lives).

a.   In the history of science we find an increasing diversification of special disciplines. The world of learning is divided into many branches of scholarship. There is not any single known method that will allow us to unify science through a single approach; in other words, a single, unified scientific method does not exist. Methods of analysis differ with differences in subject matter. The existence of actual divisions and specializations in science should help us to recognize functional kinds. The divisions that do exist among the disciplines are there for a reason. Psychoanalysis is not likely to lead to a discovery of the properties of helium; diets are not likely to reduce the national debt; computer analysis is not likely to explain to me why I dislike a certain vegetable. Certain kinds of subject matter can only be approached with the use of certain methods.

As we survey the history of science, we see that the need for methodological diversification has taught us much about the diversity within the total subject matter. It is undoubtedly true that historical factors and the exigencies of administration have also put their stamp on the present organization of the disciplines. Yet, this does not invalidate the concept of disciplinary variety pointing to a variety in subject matter such that we can see a preference for certain methods above others while other approaches are excluded altogether. In fact, one might even speak of the irreducibility of disciplines and of the methods of the sciences. Undoubtedly there is a basis in the subject matter investigated by the disciplines for this observable difference.

b.   In the detection of antinomies we have a more easily recognized structural approach to irreducibility. However, an antinomy is not the same thing as a contradiction. If I say that I am a bachelor and that I must meet my wife within an hour, I am contradicting myself. A contradiction is illogical or anti-logical, but an antinomy cannot be resolved by logic. In fact, we can only arrive at an antinomous conclusion by following the principles of logic rigorously. An antinomy occurs when the order of reality is wrongly represented in the premises of an argument, when the mentioned state of affairs is not in accordance with the actual order of things.

An antinomy is created when one's view of the order of reality commits one to conflict within that order. Principles of logic may then take us along a formally correct route but will make us come up with conclusions that are not acceptable. Zeno's categories were in conflict with the order of things; consequently, he could not account for the empirical givens. On his theory, nothing could move. But things do move. If, theoretically speaking, something which in fact occurs is declared logically impossible, we have an antinomy. The declaration of something as impossible when it is in fact both possible and actual is an antinomous declaration.

The root of the declared impossibility is the use of a category of explanation that is not in harmony with the structure or order of the explanandum. But since the declared impossibility is in fact a possibility and a reality and since possibility is determined by an order of possibility, there must be other categories that will allow us to explain the phenomenon. Concepts of motion will allow us to explain motion where concepts of space will fail.

A modern example of a problem in which the detection of an antinomy could lead to recognizing an irreducible functional order is an argument of Günther Stent. Stent claims, as we saw, that physical laws do not explain biotic phenomena, and that therefore we may never be able to account for organic life. But an equally valid and possibly more promising argument could have been that since science is in principle competent to account for empirical reality, we should not look for physical laws. The problem is probably not that biotic processes are inexplicable, but that they are simply inexplicable by references only to physical laws. If physical and biotic functioning are irreducibly different, Stent's problem will not arise unless physical principles are the only known principles of explanation. If used in this way, the principle of antinomy can help us in the search for irreducible kinds of functioning.

    c.   A founding relation is a relation in which a is founded on b, while b is not founded on a and can exist independently of a. Such a relation is another obvious tool in helping to detect irreducible differences in functionality. Certain kinds of functioning assume other kinds of functioning. Hearing presupposes organs; that is to say, sensing is founded on organic reality. Such an irreversible order of functionality is basic to all of empirical reality. Life requires a physical basis, sentient life occurs on an organic basis, the process of intelligent generalization requires a perceptive grounding, and so forth. The one kind of functioning is impossible without the other, although the other can quite well occur independently.[51]

d.   The proper nature of a phenomenon can also give us clues to irreducibly different kinds of functions. This occurs in a certain area of investigation when we detect realities that seem inappropriate, irrelevant, or otherwise improper as a result of our own attitudes. We are all familiar with the adage, "Business is business." When people in business are involved in situations with unpleasant moral or emotional overtones, we sometimes hear it said that business is business. Business transactions obviously have their own proper structure which, if ignored, can lead to unhealthy economic decisions. Since business is concerned with economics, it is pointed out, one must not be overly concerned with morals or feelings when doing business. Business can be hard.

In many cases in which the adage is used, there may be an illegitimate reduction going on. Many people look upon all transactions involving money as primarily business matters, for which the laws of economics must first be met. Some people regard being a doctor as a way of making money. For them practicing medicine is a business. And since business is business (i.e., governed by economic principles), it obviously makes much more sense to treat six patients per hour than three. It may be that treating six per hour is less therapeutic—but business is business! In this case, moral concerns are reduced to economic concerns, or at least, subsumed under them. The moral concerns can no longer be addressed on their own terms. Therapy can no longer be therapeutic. When the structure of therapy is subsumed under business principles, therapy will inevitably diminish. When the use of a certain functional concept clashes in this way with reality, we may suspect that an illegitimate reduction has taken place.

The approaches to the discovery of irreducible areas of functionality are not, as it were, methodical principles which can be employed in a vacuum. They cannot be used, for example, in the way one would use a mine detector—sweeping a field without knowing in advance whether the objects one is looking for are present in it. These approaches are likely to be useful when one is already open to the concept of the irreducibility of ultimate functional kinds and when one is in fact employing a number of categories of irreducibility. In other words, when we are on the lookout for difficulties in analysis and for possible category mistakes of a reductionist nature, then these approaches can be helpful. In such a situation one can ask: Is there a special discipline investigating the matter with which I am concerned? Is reduction a possible ground for the paradoxical results I keep getting? Is the constant failure in coming to terms with some reality due to an inappropriate treatment of it—perhaps a reductionistic treatment? Naturally, these approaches are also useful for the detection of other mistakes besides reductionism.

3.4 A Special Problem of Reduction: Evolution

One way to test the legitimacy of a reduction is to establish whether or not there are genetic or developmental ties between the two phenomena in question. Genetic "deduction" or developmental differentiation may imply reduction as a legitimate approach, and evolving realities may point to resolvable structures. The touchstone for a theory of irreducible realities is whether it can account for both continuity and change, and especially for simpler origins of a complex universe. Irreducibility suggests lack of connection. Genetic and developmental continuity suggest evolution as an uninterrupted process. To account for continuous development, for the relation of genuine change and real continuity, more is needed than the fact that functions are integrally related in functors or the fact that functors are interrelated.

This is not the place for a discussion of the problems of continuity and development.[52] At the same time, irreducibility is an essential feature of my ontology. How, then, are history and genesis possible? I will take one major problem area relative to irreducibility and continuity (i.e., the problem of evolution) and discuss it from the point of view developed here. Since evolutionary thinking has become a major paradigm for modern science, a discussion of its outlook will do more than a discussion of philosophy of history or a discussion of the theory of genetics to lay bare the hurdles that need to be overcome by a theory intent on emphasizing irreducibility.

The doctrine of evolution, which may have started as a scientific model for explaining how the organic world hangs together, has become a philosophical approach for many disciplines. If *evolution* is simply taken as a word for change or development of any kind, there are no immediate problems; but from the very beginning the doctrine of evolution introduced reductionist ideas that went far beyond the sort of reduction that had been thought possible up to that time. The doctrine suggested a common origin for all forms of life, and it was expanded to suggest the development of life out of matter.

It is important to distinguish between the doctrine of evolution as a philosophical theory and the theory of evolution as a scientific conception of how the various organic species might be related to one another. As a special scientific theory, evolution struggles with the problem of the genetic continuity of empirical existence and posits the hypothesis that genetic continuity is more basic than structural discontinuity.[53] But evolutionism as a philosophy or a world-and-life view posits the autonomy of the natural process, an autonomy that is not affected by any relation to an order that is irreducible to the process.[54] Evolutionism views this autonomous process as propelled by such forces as the struggle for survival, the clash of life and death, and the tendency for the fittest organism to live on.

An evolutionistic universal philosophy puts evolutionism on a par with any other total approach. As a philosophical view, evolutionism claims for itself the authority of science, which it places over against faith in the authority of revelation. Evolutionism is a rational and scientific view of reality, and it makes total claims. A person who was a Christian could have great difficulty in adopting evolutionism in the garb of philosophy, whereas adopting evolutionary theory as a scientific hypothesis concerning the origin of species might be an option.

Since no important theory is philosophically sterile, the theory of evolution cannot be wholly separated from evolutionistic philosophy. Therefore I will first present some considerations about evolutionism as a philosophical approach. On this level there can be no question of viewing the discussion between Christianity and evolutionism, for example, as a discussion pitting faith in revelation against a rational acceptance of the results of science.[55] When reason or science is taken as the ultimate authority, even if only within science, the Christian faith is then confronted with commitment to science or faith in reason. On a philosophical level there is a clash between kinds of faith, kinds of authority, even kinds of revelation.[56]

A Christian committed to biblical revelation may have insuperable barriers to overcome with respect to evolutionism and its commitments. Evolutionism has no room for a creator, and it leaves no room for an order of reality to which the natural process is subject. Nature itself creates and orders itself autonomously.[57] Moreover, this autonomous development is viewed completely from the standpoint of one kind of development, that is, organic growth and organic genetic relations. Continuity in growth becomes a basic category for interpreting all change and all development. This requires an absolutization of the concept growth, for which there can be no other ground than a commitment to growth. The wide variety of individual existence is interpreted as basically an organic variety. All forms of existence are regarded as life forms. Evolutionism leaves no room for an irreducible variety of functions and functors beyond the boundaries of organic existence.[58]

Evolutionism involves a commitment to belief in life as a mystical absolute, a substance, force, or thing which has meaning absolutely, that is, in itself. From other points of view, however, this is nothing but a projection or extrapolation of the meaning of the organic dimension of reality. When this dimension of existence is absolutized, a Christian interpretation of the distinction between life and death or of the origin of reality becomes impossible.[59] When these basic concepts are also used as ideological background ingredients for the special theory of evolution, the concepts obviously founded on these ideological bases will seem suspect to those who are not committed to this ideology. However, one can certainly view the special theory of evolution on its own merits.

As a result of the above, crucial concepts implied in the special theory of evolution will look different from the point of view of a theory committed to an order of irreducibility. The special theory of evolution is not simply a scientific proposal about certain genetic mechanisms but a theory which provides an integrative and encyclopedic model for all the biological sciences, at least. Evolutionary theory is a hypothesis which attempts to provide a model for integrating all biological knowledge. As a model for the unification and integration of scientific theories of a more special nature, it is a theory of a high level of generality and therefore may legitimately be called a comprehensive philosophical biology. It is on this level that I will present certain problems.

My own fundamental assumption is that the failure of evolutionary theory to account satisfactorily for the empirical givens is the reason for the contemporary return to a serious consideration of the possibility that existence is a larger complex of irreducible factors than had been hoped.[60] There appears to be one crucial conceptual approach implied in evolutionary thinking, which I will discuss in terms of four problems generated by this approach. The crucial conceptual foundation can be described as follows: all of reality is basically to be understood as either material-physical or biotic-organic in kind. The immense variety of forms of existence with which we are acquainted is a result of the interaction between living organisms in and with their environment, including their physical environment. The life functions themselves originate in matter functions.

Whatever functional variety we are acquainted with beyond material functions (divisibility, extension, mechanical interplay of forces, motion of objects, energy) is to be understood as an evolved diversification and specialization of life functions. Therefore the world consists of physical systems and organisms. All functors and functions are either physical or organic. All that is organic has its ultimate origin in material processes. All present forms of organic life have their origin in the behavior of the interacting organism. Within the organic world there is a strict continuity from a single living matter to all the complexity of life as we know it today.

The first of the specific problems to which this underlying conceptual view leads—and because of which evolutionism has not succeeded—is the neglect of theory as an approach to the structure of things, distinct from the description of the history of individuals. The nature of this problem appears very clearly in the literature on the relation of history as a science to general laws of explanation.[61] This discussion has not yet been resolved satisfactorily. With regard to the patterns of empirical connections, we are left with a gap between real events as unique and not repeatable, on the one hand, and universal laws without which nothing could be explained, on the other hand. The same discontinuity applies to evolutionary theory, which jumps over this gap without justification.

Theory deals with common structural patterns shared by many individuals. For this reason theory moves away from individuality and uniqueness. It is by this route that it arrives at concepts of structural continuity, which is a continuity of individually shared and common structures in virtue of individuals being subject to an identical order. Such structural continuity is very different from genetic continuity among individuals. The individual relationships do indeed occur within the framework of a common pattern, but they cannot as such be reduced to that framework.[62]

The fact that a number of individuals of a certain kind share structural features with individuals of another kind is not a sufficient ground for asserting their common ancestry. The nature of genetic relations militates against the view that all organisms share one common ancestry. Evolutionary theory is led by its commitment to organic continuity to draw conclusions which are less than supported by the evidence.[63]

A second objection which flows naturally from the first is that if evolutionary theory is to guarantee both continuity and the sanctity of evidence, it must posit concrete events which are impossible according to its own view. What I mean by impossible events is events which have not only not been observed but which—on the basis of what we know today—could not have occurred. One such event is the spontaneous generation of life from matter. Our present understanding of physical laws and organic patterns of interaction prohibits the occurrence of the generation of life by a physical system. But any theory which declares on the one hand that some *kind* of event is *now* impossible and on the other hand that such an event did once occur unobserved in the past is relying on unwarranted and unjustified postulates.[64]

Comparable to this is the positing of the concept of all complexity of behavior as life forms without being able to use the basic concepts of biology to account for observed events. Fear of communism is an observed event, but it can hardly be explained in terms of complex cell theory. Neither can theories which do account for such fear be explained as derived from cell theory. This implies that the postulate of the continuity of life forms is not connected to continuity in empirical reality. The discontinuities are not explained. If biological explanations do not suffice to explain known phenomena that are postulated to be life forms and if theories that do explain these phenomena are not structurally connected to biology, there appears to be a discontinuity which no postulate can bridge.

That same postulate of the continuity of life harbors another theoretical problem which is never addressed by evolutionism, even though it is a real problem that evolutionism cannot solve. The problem is that the term or concept "life" is used without any real specific meaning. On the one hand the word *life* is used in a way which suggests that it is an entity. It has a definite reified or substantialized use. On the other hand real entities such as living organisms are regarded as forms of life even when it is clear that organisms in their totality are much more than mere life forms. They have many dimensions to their existence, including dimensions that certainly cannot be viewed as manifestations of life in any biological sense. Here the evolutionistic continuity postulate again serves to obliterate irreducible differences, without ever touching on the problem in question. Life, of course, is not an entity; it is a property of certain real entities. They are living—but they have other properties as well. What essentially happens here is that on the one hand the distinction between functors and functions disappears from view, while on the other hand the variety of functionality is basically viewed as all of one kind. Functors, that is, real organisms, are viewed as substantialized or reified functions—and as functions of one basic kind, at that.[65]

In addition to these three related problems, there is a fourth problem of reduction. Here the irreducibility of certain dimensions of empirical existence is apparently avoided, by focusing on a form of existence in which it is less obvious that a clear difference is being ignored. On the level of macro-experience, it would appear that the irreducible differences between a block of marble, a geranium, and an elephant are well established. But the clarity of these differences cannot so easily be captured on a micro-level or in borderline cases. This, however, is hardly a ground for declaring that such differences are only apparent. In this way the problem of irreducible differences is itself reduced to the problem of our theoretical inability to explain borderline cases.

On the basis of these problem areas, I have come to the conclusion that the widely held view of evolutionary theory—despite all the good it has been able to do—has not made it possible to conclude that certain differences which were once thought to be irreducible really are reducible after all. But this does not mean that a theory upholding the irreducibility of kinds of functioning as well as the irreducibility of functors and functions has established itself as acceptable. The effort to account for a continuous history remains a problem for which no adequate solution is available at present. And if no solution to the problem is theoretically possible, one would at least expect an explanation as to why we must consider such a solution impossible. Yet this is not clear at this time either.[66]

Does this mean that irreducible functions and functors are barriers to understanding an integrated and coherent world? I don't think so. Thus far I have indicated at least three ways in which interconnection is established. One is via the continuity and universality of order which prevails in the diversity of empirical existence. A second way is via the integration of a multiplicity of functions in the existence of one functor. The third way is in the fact that functors function relationally. The coming together of these factors in acts and events does in fact give us an experience of orderly and integrated reality. I will conclude the present chapter with this.

3.5   Acts and Events

A discussion of functors and functions—abstractly considered—would naturally lead us to think in terms of a disconnected world unless further structures of interrelationship were also discussed and the place of functors and functions were determined in that context. Functors must be seen in action, as it were. And functions or actions do not normally come to our attention except in bigger contexts, mostly known as events. What I have in mind in speaking of a function will not generally be a recognized unit of macro-experience, for example, but much rather a phase of such experience. Let me illustrate. As I do so, I shall limit myself to human behavior.

If a child is reminded that he should first go and brush his teeth before setting off for school, we may witness something that can be called a concrete, recognizable, meaningful unit of action. We can go to the bathroom and watch the child go through a number of motions which, in their integrated wholeness, we recognize as the brushing of teeth. By means of this illustration I can clarify the distinction between functions and acts. By a "function" I mean all the behaviors that go into the making of an act, behaviors which themselves do not normally occur in isolation, even though they can also show up in the context of other acts. All the action which cannot normally stand alone will be called "function," while the integration of such functions into a unit will be called an "act."[67] The functions will not only be conscious behaviors but also the activity of the brain, subconscious breathing—in short, whatever goes on as it becomes focused in the act. But the functioning, even though it is integrated and patterned and organized in terms of the act, can nevertheless not be understood as the functioning of the act. The functions involved in brushing the teeth are functions of the child, as is the act. *The child* organizes the functions into the pattern which defines the act in question.

It is important to recognize that there is a difference between functions and acts, even if the difference is not easy to pin down.[68] The unit of action called an act, of course, is not an isolatable unit in any strict sense of the word; it is relatively recognizable as an act of some identifiable sort because it can stand relatively isolated. Putting toothpaste on a toothbrush is not meaningful unless one intends to brush one's teeth. Letting the faucet run is not meaningful unless one plans to wet the brush and rinse the mouth. Making the brushing motions is not meaningful unless one is doing it with a wet and pasted brush and provided one did not also go through the same routine three minutes before.

Brushing one's teeth, as the act is called, is only meaningful in a larger context. The point I wish to make here is that certain dimensions of an act are to be viewed as functional within a pattern. This simple fact is basic to our experience. It is assumed in giving testimony before a court, for example. When certain partial actions are described, a pattern emerges and it is accepted that the act has been witnessed. If we did not ourselves instantly group such a report in the context of a known act, the testimony would be without meaning.[69]

In the case of human beings it can certainly be said that the number of functions and even the number of complex patterns that make up the simplest act is beyond the imagination. It is likely that even the variety of functions of one kind (e.g., all of the physiological functions of some simple act) are too varied and too complex to be described completely. There is a large host of subconscious functions which are habitual involuntary and which fall into complex patterns mechanically. Even then they remain functions of the actor, and even then they are meaningful in terms of the act situation.

It is the functor that is doing the subconscious and involuntary functioning. It may be true that I am largely unaware of this as I breathe, that I must do so even if I do not want to, and even that I will continue to do so when I do not want to. But it is *I* that breathe, not my lungs.[70] The functor integrates the functions into the act pattern. Yet the borderline between acts and functions is not easy to draw. One could not lay down a carefully formulated rule such that any and all activity of a person could be faultlessly recognized as either an act or a function. Generally speaking, however, we can distinguish between them as integrated units of activity and the activities that go into the making of such a unit.

A human act is something that is done intentionally or purposefully. Where a unit of integrated functional diversity is present without purpose, decision or design, one cannot speak of what I here mean by act; it could be better described as a functional process, perhaps going on habitually or subconsciously. Although breathing, as a functional process, does integrate and coordinate many other functions, it cannot itself be understood as an act. An act manifests an integration of functional processes from a purposeful point of view.[71]

Of course acts do not occur in isolation either; they occur in larger patterns. But although these larger patterns manifest interrelationships between acts, they are not as invariantly structured as the acts themselves are. Taking a bath, getting dressed, eating breakfast, and brushing one's teeth are different acts which together make up the familiar event "getting ready in the morning." Events consist of acts that can be left out, postponed, sometimes done by others, substituted by other acts, and so forth. The event "preparing a meal" includes the acts of peeling the potatoes, washing the vegetables, setting the table, and many more. Some of these could be performed by any one of a number of people, and some could be left out if a member of the family suddenly discovered that she had to eat very soon. One might even substitute doing rice for doing the potatoes. But once an act is decided on, it requires certain functions, and those functions require a centered functor.

The recognition of act patterns is well known. Let me describe what happens when someone who is not aware of a certain event receives an update from someone else. Suppose the latter speaks of a number of people gathered near a body of water, with some of them going in and out from time to time, and so forth. For us to identify what is likely to be an event of some kind, more information is needed. The present information by itself could indicate swimmers, divers, religious people holding a baptism, or some other event. Is the body of water a pool, or is it a natural body such as a lake or a river? If the former, is it a pool for swimming or a fish pond? If it is a swimming pool, did there seem to be a pattern to what was going on, with people in charge, or was the activity apparently quite random? In other words, was it a pool party or a swimming competition?

Usually we gather such information quite quickly, with one or two well-chosen questions which themselves integrate a lot of information. Of course we would normally know the word for what we suspected was going on, and so we could ask: Was it a party? But perhaps our spokesman is Hungarian, and although we know a certain amount of Hungarian, we do not know many words in this context. Hence we ask questions using words that we do know and then make our identification. Such an identification is not made on the basis of a complete description of all the details, complete with a description of how everything relates to everything else. What normally happens is that a few crucial points add up to a certain pattern which fits our knowledge of *kinds* of patterns that belong to *kinds* of acts and events. We do not know and will never know the *particular* event in question, but we can recognize a *pattern* all the same.

When the information gives us a picture, we know what went on in this particular event from a description of a pattern. If at regular intervals a number of persons jump into the water simultaneously at the blowing of a whistle or the shot of a gun, and they all swim in the same direction for the same distance as fast as they can, and other persons sitting around clap and shout when the first of the swimmers arrives at a certain point and stops swimming, and soon thereafter they all stop swimming—then we can conclude with very high certainty that we have been informed of a swimming competition.

What is meant by the pattern we have recognized? If we recognize it as a kind of pattern, this implies that we have knowledge of a structure indicating the presence of an ordering mechanism, a pattern of order. A multiplicity of acts and functions of different kinds hang together in a definite or defined way. A merely physical or just biological description of the events will never serve to identify them.[72]

The many levels of functioning in an event such as I just described include emotional functions, informational functions, logical functions, social functions, and so forth. Actually, what we recognize in such a case are not functions as such but acts of some kind. The blowing of the whistle and the shooting of the gun are both acts; they are symbolic in kind. But this does not mean that the blowing of the whistle is *purely* symbolic. The act in question included many functions, but all of them are centered around and integrated through the dominant role of the symbolic function. The symbolic function determines the *kind* of act that it is. A description in terms of physical, physiological, psychical, and other functions would never succeed in getting at the central significance of the symbolic function of the act of shooting the gun or blowing the whistle at a competition. In fact, the function in question is so significant that the person who repeatedly performs this act at a competition becomes identified in terms of the act: she is called the starter.

The dominant feature of some functions in acts and of some acts in events is an invariant characteristic of the order of all functions and acts. The dominant functions and acts are a central point of reference around which all action and functioning is grouped, organized, and integrated. Such integration will always manifest an underlying pattern of invariant definiteness. The blowing of the whistle to start the race is an example of a function-integrating act. It is a very short act, but it is unmistakably an act. It is performed purposely and integrates raising the hand that holds the whistle, blowing into the whistle, observing what goes on, choosing the right moment, deciding to blow, and so forth.

The brief deed is consciously and purposefully executed. Its essential nature, that is, the kind of deed it is, can be defined as the giving of a signal. Its symbolic function is central to its successful execution. When to blow, how loud to blow, in what characteristic way to blow, how to interpret the blowing—all of these questions are determined by an understanding of the symbolic function. There are many other *kinds* of functions involved, with many different properties. Some are physical, some mechanical (the production of sound by blowing air into an instrument), some sentient (making the sound audible to those concerned), some formative, and there are many others. Yet the main function is symbolic. The symbolic function will determine the movement of arms, lungs, and lips. It will determine the posture of the starter and the direction in which she looks. The act receives its structure from this particular kind of function, which integrates and qualifies all the others. It becomes the characteristic or defining property.

In addition to the defining function or qualifying property, there is also a level of functioning which serves as the *conditio sine qua non* that is typical for this sort of act. One might say that the latter is the foundation upon which the act is built. Without it, the qualifying symbolic function cannot even occur. In the case of our example, it is the mechanical production of sound, the forcing of the air through the instrument in a certain way. Without this the whole act would not even be what it is. Yet the production of the sound is not the characteristic act. The characteristic act has its identity through a symbolic convention about producing this sound in a certain context in a certain structured way. If the sound is not produced subject to the conditions of that symbolic convention, nothing will occur—or perhaps only a false start.

If I were to analyze more acts and events, it would always appear that these integrated units of functioning called acts are patterned around two pivotal kinds of functions, namely, one which typically serves to give the act its peculiar definition, and one which serves as a *conditio sine qua non*—both in a characteristic way for this *kind* of act. I will refer to these two functional levels as *the qualifying function* and *the founding or foundational function*. They are characteristic features of all acts and events.

A sports event, for example, has a qualifying social function and a founding formative function. The competition, that is, the competitive performance of skills and competitive demonstration of that which is much more than exercise, is the basis on which the whole event rests. However, the actual sporting acts, such as swimming the one hundred yards, running the mile, broad jumping, and so forth, are not what qualify the event. The event is not staged in order to engage in the exercising of certain skills. The skills are demonstrated, shown off, displayed. In the demonstration the sport is promoted, and in this way a social ritual is established. The whole event is qualified by the social meaning of the excitement, pride, and glory belonging to the competition. The event is staged and planned in a certain way in order to achieve this social ritual.[73]

The example of a large sporting event is a good indication of just how the social and formative functional levels shape one another. In their mutual interrelation, they mold one another and become the focus for everything else. When we see an athlete performing a certain skill all by herself, we do not get the same picture as when we see the act of performing that skill integrated into an event for which it serves as a basis but which is really a social ritual. In the latter case the athlete wears clean and colorful sports clothing. She is nervous and excited, she does not exercise but performs, she wants to please, and so forth. When she is exercising, she is a different person. Her exercise only serves to improve her skill. The formative function then qualifies what she does.

When the performance act takes place as part of a sporting event, however, it is still a formative act, but it is placed in a social context. At the same time, the social ritual called a sports event is quite different from a visit with a neighbor over a beer. Because the former is a social event based on the performance of skills in competition, it is colored in a way that makes it completely different from a social visit with a neighbor.

I will speak of this peculiar structure of interrelation as the x/y (read: x over y) structure of an act or event. The x refers to some qualifying function, the y to some founding function. One of the typical characteristics of this x/y structure is that it makes the x function y-oriented, and the y function x-oriented.[74]

Up to this point I have spoken almost exclusively about acts and events as function organizers and integrators. Only occasionally have I made reference to the crucial role which functors play in this complex interrelationship. I will now have to make up for this obvious shortcoming. Functions, acts, and events can be what they are only if there are functors to actually function and integrate and organize. Functors must function in the pattern prescribed if there is to be an act or event of some kind. In this context I must briefly raise a matter that will later be discussed in more detail, that is, the difference between human and nonhuman functors as being function-specific in their role as functors. Physical functors, animal functors, and organisms are function-specific. What this means is that the total pattern of their existence as functors is integrated by the peculiar pattern of functional structures on one irreducible level.

Human beings are different in this respect.[75] The entire existence of an organism is determined and integrated from the point of view of its biotic functions. The animal is sensitively integrated. The human being, however, is not integrated from any specifically functional point of view. Other functors are functionally limited in what they can do and in what purpose they serve. A worker ant is just that—and all its functions are geared to being a worker ant. A human being, on the other hand, has multiple roles to play and is not exhausted in any of them.[76]

The starter of a race is more than just a starter. Persons do fully take on certain special functional roles. Function-specific roles then result in special patterns of action and relation to which we give a functor name, such as starter, coach, or swimmer. Functors integrate their actions in specified ways and get specialized in those ways. By constitution they may be especially suited for a specific role. Such functor specialization also has this peculiar x/y structure. The *conditio sine qua non* of being a father is biological, but the ultimate integrator of that role is moral. For this reason the act designed to result in one's becoming a parent must also take place in a moral context. Moreover, that specific moral context gets its special character from being based on organic ties.

Through these functor specifications, persons are connected in specific ways and specific kinds of functions, acts, and events. Fathers are found in families, nurses in hospitals, teachers in schools, and cabinet ministers in governments. Where functors functioning in relationships give rise to enduring active relationships of specific structural kinds, we witness the rise of organizations, institutions, and other forms of human organization. These are organized as specialized functor communities. They also display an x/y structure.

Chapter IV
An Order of Functions

A KEY ELEMENT IN SCHOLARSHIP is developing concepts that allow us to conceptually "reduce" subjective, empirical existence to *kinds* of things, *kinds* of functions, and *kinds* of relations.[1] What the zoologist aims to understand is not every individual elephant but rather the species or *kind* of elephant.[2] If we extend the analogy of the zoologist and the elephant, we might say that scholarship is kind-reduction. At the same time, the scholar must be wary of the danger of reduction*ism*. The first three chapters have assumed throughout that scholarship is impossible without universality or kinds. Scholarship without the proper awareness of the limits of reduction transgresses its boundaries.[3]

A zoologist interested in studying the characteristics of the kind elephant may spend a great deal of time with a particular herd. But however many cattle egrets might appear to be permanent fixtures in the herd, none of them must ever be counted as belonging to the kind elephant. Egrets must not be reducted to elephants. No egret is an elephant. Here there is no room for reduction. All the elephants in the herd can be reduced to the kind elephant, but reduction*ism* is wrong. The egrets do not belong.

On the whole, scholarship is more interested in and occupied with functional relations than with functors. There are relatively few scholars working on functors as functors.[4] The problem of reductionism is less pronounced when it comes to scholarship dealing with functor kinds. A probable reason is that the irreducibility of functors as functors is intuitively obvious. Another reason is that those who work on functors *as* functors have probably already decided that functors cannot be reduced to functions. When it comes to the study of functionality, however, reductionism has been the main trend. In our century, especially, scholarship has been characterized by the attempt to reduce all functioning to a quantitative understanding.

There have indeed been scholars who opted for a more varied interpretation of functional reality, but most of them stopped at recognizing two—or at most three—levels of existence. If reality was not judged to be all physical, then it was no more than biophysical, or psychophysical; or at most material, living, and spiritual. Among those who allowed for two or three realms, there has never been significant agreement about the real meaning of such terms as *living*, *psychic*, and *spiritual*. Hence we have materialism, panpsychism, or psychomonism as attempts to reduce all levels of functionality to one, or mind-matter approaches as the so-called anti-reductionist views. Contemporary philosophical literature is giving renewed attention to the possibility that there are many more irreducible levels of functioning than was popularly believed.[5] It is now being more and more widely accepted that approaches to functionality have been overly reductionistic. I will devote this chapter to a description of a great variety of irreducible kinds of functionality.

First I will simply and briefly introduce my view of the kinds of functionality I think there are and introduce them in their cosmic order. I will then devote a section to discussing what is meant by irreducible kinds of functions—how they are recognized, how they relate, why their order is as it is, how the variety of functionality found within a kind or functional field is structured, and so forth. In the section that then follows I will select three of the irreducible kinds of functionality and discuss them in more detail. In the next section I will give a brief characterization of all the levels I have distinguished. Finally, I will briefly discuss the relation of the fundamental category of functionality to our concept of properties, explaining my view that properties are identical with functions. In the entire chapter I will be following very closely the view of functionality and its kinds developed by Herman Dooyeweerd and analyzed extensively in the second volume of his *magnum opus* entitled *A New Critique of Theoretical Thought*.

4.1   *The Irreducible Functional Kinds and Their Order*

I will use the technical Dooyeweerdian terms *mode* or *modality* to designate the entire area or field characterized by one ultimately irreducible kind of functionality. Thus mode or modality will have to be understood as very complex. A specific mode will include both the principle of order that determines a given kind as the kind that it is, as well as the richly varied occurrence of structured functions in empirical reality that conform to the order of that kind.[6] As I will explain in more detail later, each mode displays an inner order in which its own inner diversity is arranged. The specific way in which these modes are arranged will be called *modal order*. Thus the term *mode* covers the entire correlation of order and empirical existence developed in chapter 2 and applies specifically to the concept of function developed in chapter 3.

The modes or modalities are understood to be arranged in a special serial sequence. The significance of the serial sequence, in turn, is understood to depend on the end from which one proceeds in interpreting the sequence. I will refer to this sequence as modal order. The order of the modes proceeding from one end is not the same as the order of the modes when proceeding from the other end. All of these concepts will be developed more fully later on (in the remainder of this chapter and in 6.3). For the present we will have to make do with a very brief characterization of the different order directions. The series of functional modes is viewed as constant in terms of the relative place of each mode. Thus, with the exception of the two end modes, each mode will always be found between the same two other modes, just as in the number series. Four is always between three and five, although whether it comes before or after three depends on the direction in which one is counting.

The importance of this difference can quickly be illustrated by means of a relationship carefully analyzed by Polanyi, that is, that of the functioning of DNA as a source of information relative to a living cell, and then viewed in relation to the fact that DNA, as a chemical compound, cannot by virtue of its chemical properties alone be sufficiently explained when it comes to its informational role.[7] Now, the relation of DNA as a chemical compound (one modal level) to its function in a living cell (another level) is such that the existence of the cell is impossible without DNA as a chemical, whereas the existence of DNA in its specific role is impossible except on the basis of the presence of the living cell. What we have here, therefore, is a foundational relation in two directions. The two levels mutually support each other. The claim being made for the order of modes is that the series in its entirety displays this feature of "basing" in two directions.

These two directions can be characterized as follows. Going through the series in the direction lower to higher (from physical, to living, to sentient levels) will be called the *founding direction* of the order. This terminology is connected with that used to refer to the x/y structure discussed in 3.5. The lower level functions in a foundational way as support for the existence of higher levels, as in the foundations of a building. If we went through a house from bottom to top, that would be the foundational order in going through it; it would be impossible to start going through it from top to bottom. The basement supports the first floor, the first floor the second, and so forth.

It's the same way with functional modes: except for the first or lowest of them, they all need the support of the previous ones. Life functions are supported by material functions; immaterial life is impossible. But another direction of modal order is the order in which lower functioning is enriched as a result of its being made serviceable to a higher order. Chemical compounds within living structures are immensely more varied, more complex, and more diversified in their functions than those found in the physical environment only. Life has a chemical foundation, but life also opens up the potential of the chemical mode of functioning. This will be called the *developmental direction*.

For purposes of this section I will do no more than present the modes in their order. The names I use to refer to them will be sufficiently clear to gain an initial orientation, even though the complexity of meaning involved in them will later require some refinement and explanation. There remains considerable discussion among those who use this model of approach as to what the modes are, what their order is, how they are to be characterized, and so forth. Hence I will present my own version of the theory here. Since the levels are taken to be irreducible, the names given to them cannot easily be explained or recast in terms of other, simpler, clearer terms. Most of them are names borrowed from an area characteristically recognized as being a level of a certain kind, though the names are not specifically designed to name anything like *the* essential property of the kind. The terms will name some one essential property that is known, even though they are intended to stand for the essential core nature of the whole mode. The term may have a typical action meaning, or more of a state denotation, or even functor associations. The important thing to recall is that the terms are *used* to designate an irreducible mode of functioning, although in other contexts they may well conjure up meanings that could be confusing.

The modes, in the order I take them to have, are as follows: numeric, spatial, mechanical or kinetic, energetic or physical, biotic or organic, psychic or sensitive, technical or formative, symbolic, analytic, social, economic, juridical, ethical or moral, and pistic or certitudinal. What I mean to assert in presenting such a series is that any function, state, action, property, characteristic, or relationship of functors can be conceived as minimally belonging to one of the modes or kinds of functionality named in this series. Furthermore, I am claiming that each kind of functioning mentioned in this series is only possible on the basis of the preceding level. Finally, I am claiming that each level of functioning opens up the functional potential of the preceding level.[8] Since the number of modes and their order is a matter of much discussion, I do not mean to present this specific model as the last word. All I am doing is presenting certain claims and working out the implications, for I will in fact be working with this model in this volume.

4.2   Characteristics of Functional Modes

Modes as ultimate functional kinds show us the ordering principles in the functional dimension of reality. In the previous chapter, I used the term *function* to mean all that a functor can be, have, or do.[9] This includes states, actions, qualities, attitudes, properties, and the like. As such, "function" is a very high-level concept, covering the reduction of an immensely varied diversity. The concept must be well understood if it is to be theoretically serviceable. Two couples enjoying dinner by candlelight can be said to function, while a line as the distance between two points is also said to be a function. The series of functional modes summarily introduced above does not by itself help us much in gaining a clearer notion of the functional order. In this section, therefore, I will first discuss some general characteristics of functional modes in their interrelation, before going on to characterize these modes themselves.

4.2.1   Analogy as functional interrelation

In the various functional modes we find actual functional realities about which we may wonder whether they belong in one mode rather than in another. These functional realities are expressed in terms that we know as analogical in meaning. They are at first sight what might be called functional metaphors. The concept of the force of an argument is an example, as is the concept of the growth of the economy. Force is normally thought of as physical. Growth is normally thought of as organic. Do economies really grow? Do arguments literally have force? If we examine the possibility of finding terms and concepts in which we rid ourselves of these metaphorical or analogical usages, it appears that this rejection is impossible. No science can function without analogical concepts. It is not possible to express realities in any functional mode without use of terms that seem borrowed from or that seem to refer to other functional modes. No science can develop without the use of especially numerical, spatial, kinematic, and physical analogies. What would we do if, for example, we could no longer refer to "higher" and "lower," simply because they are, strictly speaking, spatial references? In this section I will attempt to clarify this interesting phenomenon with reference to the figure of intermodal reference. These analogies, I claim, demonstrate that, though the various ultimate modal categories are irreducible, they do not occur in isolation.

People do not, on a routine basis, overtly and systematically *classify* things in their experience. All the same, they *relate* appropriately to things according to their kind. Furthermore, people are able to see at a glance whether things are of a certain kind or not. Intelligence tests routinely make use of the "class" consciousness of people, even though classifying is not an operation that people have been specifically taught. In intelligence tests we are asked to identify—at considerable speed—the stranger in a certain series. In the series "Beethoven, Bach, Brahms, Mozart, Brecht," the one that does not belong could be either Mozart (whose name does not start with a B) or Brecht (who was not a composer). One could also name Mozart because his name is the only one lacking an h. There are many common structures and properties shared by things. Depending on the common property one has in mind, one may note that one element in a series is missing that property. It is certainly remarkable that people are able to pick out classes and agree upon them at a glance and without having been trained to do so.

It is equally remarkable that the classes recognized by an untrained person are often significant. It appears that the actual structure of things is genuinely known to the normal person. Imagine the complexity involved in the following situations and the ease with which we identify them. The elements are four people seated around a table with some props in some environment. People walk by and identify the scene as bridge, lunch, coffee, Monopoly, or a discussion. A mere word identifies what has been spotted at a glance. A small change requires a new word: fifty-two cards, a brown paper bag, a cup of coffee, a piece of board, and no props. Each time there is a change the whole situation changes. We take in the whole scene and identify it, naming the whole reality with a simple expression— sometimes a mere word. We have many expressions for people taking in food, and we normally know exactly which one is appropriate—going out for dinner, having lunch, taking a tea break, going on a picnic, grabbing a sandwich on the run.

Is there structural order underlying such identification patterns? I believe there is, and I will now introduce one type of order, be it for more technical purposes than would be useful in everyday practice. I am referring to the x/y structure as a device allowing us to classify all sorts of gross and complex events into very broad categories. As we saw earlier, this x/y structure was intended to grasp the notion that there are two sorts of functionality standing out in all concrete acts and events. The first of them so colors the whole act or event that we can refer to it by the name of the mode to which that function belongs (of which irreducible kind it is), for example, a social event, a religious gathering, an educational organization, an economic contract, and so forth. The second sort of functionality plays so basic a role in making acts or events possible, that without this sort there would not be that act or event at all, for example, organic functioning in the family (the blood relations between parents and siblings and among siblings, the sexual relation between the parents), the physical reality of a territory for a state, and the sensitive awareness basic to any genuinely cognitive human act.

This x/y structure is related to the two directions I mentioned in characterizing the two directions in the series of modes or functional kinds. The y kind is basic and supportive, while the x kind so colors the entire structure that it qualifies all of the structure's dimensions. As a conceptual scheme, the x/y structure posits that for every structure of a concrete thing or act or event there will be two modal dimensions such that functions of one mode typically support the existence of the thing in question as a *conditio sine qua non* specific to that entity, while functions of a different modal kind typically characterize, integrate, and organize the entire structure in question. What I mean here by "typically" is that this structure will obtain in all individuals of this kind.

If I use the x/y structure as a classification device, I can first classify the most basic kinds of existence there are according to the sort of x function they have.[10] I can then subdivide the whole class according to the different y functions that are related to the same x function.[11] For example, friendship and marriage would both be understood as moral relations (i.e., relations requiring faithfulness and troth), but marriage is the subkind founded in organic relations while friendship would be a subkind founded in psychic relations. At the end of the previous chapter I referred to x functions as *qualifying* functions and y functions as *founding* functions.

In classifying all functions or entities that occur in an x/y structure, we may note that the actual interrelation between x functions and y functions is evident in both. We may note within the x functions that they have a foundation in y and we may note in the y functions that they are qualified by x. Just to give an example: if we take an organism and roughly take its x/y structure to be that of life functions/physical functions, then we can note that life functions are functions of physical constellations, while the physical constellations are peculiar to the organism. Thus we may consider the y functions to be x-oriented and the x functions to be y-based. Here, I believe, we may have the key to ontological metaphors or unavoidable analogical structures. I will come back to this.

This analogical nuance can be expressed in the formula as follows: x_y/y^x. This more complex formula expresses the role of y as supporting x and shows that relation within its own structure. We write x for organic functioning in its broad modal sense and y for the energy level of functioning. The chemical energy exchange, though modally bound to the laws for energy exchange, functions in close relation to the organic modal functions and manifests this in its own complexity and relations. The enriched chemical functioning is then represented as y^x. At the same time, the life functions that are typically supported by chemical processes can be indicated as x_y.

The new formula, as an attempt at demonstrating the nuances of complexity, hardly begins to indicate the actual complexity of a concrete reality. For example, take the real occurrence of what we recognize as a soccer game. The complete reality of such a game is even more complex than that which is structurally typical of it. That which is structurally typical of it in a modal sense (its x/y structure) differs from the full reality of the game. Typically, one might argue that a sporting event staged for the public is to be understood as a socially qualified event stimulating the development of bodily skills. Even if one might argue for a different qualifying function or founding function, just supposing those two to be accurate, one would then conclude that a soccer game for the public would be a socioformative event.

But this is far from sufficient for an understanding of the reality of the event. If anything is to be actually real in the world of empirical existence, it must ultimately be founded in physical reality. If we were to fully analyze human or cultural realities, we would come to the conclusion that in some fashion or other, all levels of functioning are either directly or indirectly (actually or at least potentially) involved in whatever we choose to analyze. Now, if the symbol for merely indicating the global boundary conditions of a certain structure, when analyzed on a very general modal level, turns out to be as complex as x_y/y^x, we can appreciate what sort of a complex formula would be needed to express the actual functional complexity.

Without attempting anything of this kind, one can surmise quite easily that even the reality to which the simple x_y or y^x point is ex-

ceedingly complex. The point I am trying to make is this: if all levels
(to say nothing of actual functions on such levels) of functioning can
actually be present in any real act or event or functor, then the complexity of the interrelationships of functions, that is, the structural
complexities of these interweavings of functions, would manifest an
intrafunctional diversification of immense proportions.

The same point can be made in another way. It has been
repeatedly asserted that functions do not function and that actions do
not act. Actors act, and functors function. But functors, typically, are
immensely complex. In a functor that functions well, all functions are
correlated, coordinated, and interrelated in a coherent and orderly
way. The functor will function integrally, in a unified way. All the
functions of that functor are the functions of one and the same—or
identical—functor. If this is really apparent to us (as it is in our everyday experience), it is because right within each act, within each function, we have the evidence of integrity and unity. All functions are
"fine tuned" for each other. If this is the case, might there in fact be a
principle of modal functioning, which structures functional interrelationships in a way that would account for this?

In the history of philosophy a number of different strategies have
been developed to account for the interrelationships of levels of existence and of functional dimensions of human experience. Among
the approaches are parallelism, interactionism, and occasionalism. In
parallelism the levels never really interrelate. The identity of the
functor on all levels of functioning is conceived of in parallelism as the
hidden harmony. On this view, the feeling of sadness and the physical
process of shedding tears go together, but there is no real connection
between them. In interactionism there is mutual influence, as the
term suggests. In occasionalism the lower levels provide an occasion
for the higher ones to be enacted.

The view I am developing here represents an attempt to learn
from the various traditions without opting for any one of them exclusively. In my approach to the problem of interrelation, I will pay
special attention to the core or essential characteristic of a mode in
order to maintain a clear view of its irreducibility, while also trying to
account for the variety of characteristics of richly nuanced functioning within each mode in order to understand the coherence among
the modes. I will use *nuclear moment* as my technical term for the
concept of the irreducible core characteristic of a mode, and I will use
analogy or *analogical moment* for the variety of functionality within
a mode, characterized by that nuclear moment, but bearing evidence
of relations to other modes.

We find an example of the analogical characteristics of a mode in the discussion of the antinomy of Zeno. Zeno tried to reduce motion to the numerical division of a path of motion. The calculation process is a genuine numerical process. There is nothing unusual about the series 1/2, 1/4, 1/8, 1/16, 1/32, 1/64, and so on. But there is nothing in the series itself to suggest that it should never stop. Yet it does never stop if we wish to calculate at which point the moving object really takes off across the center of one of the segments of its path of motion.

The series can be seen as an attempt to calculate a path of *motion*. The irreducibility of the nuclear moment of the mode of functioning called kinetic (the mode of mechanical functions of motion) does not allow a reduction of motion to a number phenomenon. However, when the kinetic function is approached in terms of a numerical function, this shows up in the infinite "movement" of the number series. The same is true for the number *pi* as a number related to the circular path of a heavenly body. I will often have occasion to refer to this phenomenon of analogy. It always shows up as the *appearance* of the property of one mode of functioning within the modal area of another function in an *analogical* way.

Another example: what kind of phenomenon is growth? It is clearly a function of something, for example, of a child, or of grass. Growth is not something that appears by itself. It is certanly not a functor. Growing is what some functor does. What about growing economies? We speak of them often. The newspapers are sure that economies grow, whether slowly, quickly, or hardly at all. Is such talk meant literally? Growing grass makes sense. Is growing in an economic sense anything more than a metaphor? Do we feed or fertilize an economy? Do we give it water, or protect it from too much sun? Do we just have a peculiar use of language here, or does the language point to something more basic?

Let me give an example in which it is very clear that we have nothing more than a figure of speech, a semantic peculiarity, or idiomatic usage, as opposed to a word usage that appears to be more than merely figurative, or idiomatic. If a person is wrong about something, we say that he is "all wet." We do not need to say that. Yet this is a manner of speaking which tells us what is going on, provided we understand this particular English idiom. There is no connection whatsoever between persons being wrong and persons being soaked with moisture. If a person were literally wet, this would have no necessary connection with being wrong. And a person's being wrong need never be stated in terms of being wet. The use of such an expression is limited to English idiom.

On the other hand, it can be stated in any language that the number series in the Zeno example keeps *going*. And in no language will it be possible to refer to the phenomenon observable in the number series without referring to phenomena of space (it stretches without end) or motion (it never stops). Yet the number series is not truly extended or moving. Still, the reality observed is incomprehensible if we do not understand extension and motion. Thus there does appear to be a difference between metaphor and idiom. Metaphor can express a genuine connection, a functional analogy—not merely a semantic peculiarity.

The scientific disciplines are literally filled with terms of an analogical character. Economic science needs to refer to "expanding" markets and to a "growing" economy. If we are impressed that economies do not grow by feeding, watering, sunlight, and the like, we may suggest speaking only of expansion. But how does an economy expand? Sideways? In miles, or feet? At what speed? Can the rate of expansion be calculated in somewhat the manner in which one can calculate the rate of increase in motion? There is something going on in the economy that can only be expressed analogically. If we treat these terms nonanalogically, our understanding of economic reality suffers.

It is not always possible to show just what the connections in reality are. In the case of economic expansion it is fairly obvious. Expanding economies need expanding markets, which in turn need expanding territories. The connection of "larger territory," though real, is still an economic one and cannot be comprehended simply in terms of geometric relationships. To say that one has a market of 2600 square miles is not economically meaningful unless this is translated into economic terms. The geometry needs to be economically enriched, while at the same time the economy has to be geometrically based, as it were. There is an x/y structure at work here.

Thus the economy really does behave *as though* it is growing and expanding, whereas a person who is wrong does not behave *as though* he is soaked, any more than a person who was overcharged for some item he purchased behaves as though he got soaked. What is the underlying reality that cannot be ignored here? What might be the more-than-semantic reality of the likeness between economic growth and plant growth; between length of time and length of lines; between a lively calf and a lively poem; between the scope of a piece of land, the scope of a vision, the scope of an argument, and the scope of power; between following a deer and following an argument?

In none of these cases *can* we do without metaphor. This is true for ordinary language, but it is also true for science—circular argument, DNA codes, span of life, decline of health, and so forth. Even formal languages will make use of definitions from which metaphor cannot be absent. The very meaning of the term *formal* is metaphorical. The expression *stands for* is likewise metaphorical. Element, inclusion, and relation are all metaphorical terms. Is the semantic metaphor a pointer to ontic analogy? Does functioning in each irreducible mode also point to the other modes?

If we are determined to bring out a contrast with metaphorical semantic meaning, we need words that have a direct, original, nonanalogical sense. For each irreducible mode, can we find a word that refers unambiguously to the nuclear moment or core nature of that mode? Such a term would then point us univocally to the core reality of a mode, in terms of which it could then be determined whether certain phenomena belong properly to this mode or that one. For the series of modes I mentioned earlier (i.e., numerical, spatial, kinetic, energetic, biotic, psychic, technical, symbolic, analytic, social, economic, juridical, ethical, and pistic), an attempt can be made to find such words. One might try the following: quantity, extension, motion, force, growth, sense, and so forth. So far no attempts to complete the series in a fully satisfactory manner have found unanimous acceptance among adherents of the theory.

A certain amount of arbitrariness at this point is unavoidable. Language cannot be expected to accommodate a theory fully. Thus, if we look for nonanalogical terms for the mode of human functioning which is characteristic of human thought, that is, conceptual abstraction or generalization, every suggested term will be seen to refer beyond the area of thought in its original or etymological sense. Such words as *analytic, logical,* and *abstracting* may all sound very original, but they do have their origin in references to breaking apart, or words, or reasons (which in turn refer to rations).

The use of words derived from Greek or Latin only hides this fact. This state of affairs appears to suggest very strongly that reality is interfunctional in such an integral way that even though irreducibility is a clear fact, evidence of fully continuous interrelationship is just as clear. The difficulty of drawing unambiguous terms for modal cores from existing language should not be interpreted to mean that irreducibility is hereby shown to be unfounded. Language also shows us that analogical terms do in fact have analogical meaning, which would make no sense if there were no original sense to which our experience appeals. Analogy depends on originality. If one uses a single term to cover the reality of more areas of functionality than is possible, equivocation will result.

An example would be John Dewey's attempt to reduce analysis in its most rudimentary form to organic behavior. He realized that his continuity hypothesis called for such an attempt.[12] Therefore he characterized analysis as search. Once he had done this, he was satisfied that he had demonstrated the organic origin of analysis, to the point of seeing rudimentary analysis in all organisms. However, his definition necessarily became so equivocal that it was no longer possible to avoid using the term *search* for the behavior of a river "searching" its way down a mountain. Yet it is impossible to convince anyone that rivers engage in a very rudimentary form of analysis. In fact, Dewey insisted on the irreducibility of life and matter—at least in the sense in which typical organic behavior did not have typical properties in common with physical behavior.

To come back to the argument: there are irreducible areas of functioning. Yet it is not possible to translate this into as many unequivocal and original semantic terms of the existing language as there are irreducible areas. In every irreducible modal area we are bound to use terms which, in their meaning, are not original for that specific area of functioning. In the case of some terms, the reason for this is that within the modal area in question there is indeed a relation to some other modal area. In such an instance we are justified in using an analogical term. In other cases the analogical term is used in an original sense; that is to say, its analogical semantic meaning is misleading since it does in fact point to an original sense.

In a way, of course, each analogical term has this dual status. *Growth*, as an economic term, has economic meaning; and *scope*, in arguments, has analytic meaning. Yet these meanings can only be understood with reference to other modes of functionality. We cannot understand arguments and their nature except on the basis of our understanding of spatial relations, even though no dimension of an argument in its analytical sense has any spatial function in its original sense. So we can use *growth* in an original sense in biology and in an analogical sense in economics.

From this point on I propose to use the term *original* as the qualifier of a term used to indicate univocally the irreducible, nonanalogical core nature of a functional mode. What this usage implies for other usage is that no term indicating an actual modal function will ever be anything but an analogical term. Any functional term—except the one indicating the irreducible core nature of a mode—will depend for its meaning on the reference it has to some other mode. But this calls for an explanation beyond the general claim that all modes are interrelated.

What I am saying at this point is that all actual functioning is analogical. But in saying this I do not simply mean to indicate that the interrelationship of irreducible modal levels is established by the fact that all actual functioning requires a functor integrating functions, with the functor guaranteeing functional interrelationship. Though this in fact appears to be the case, the reason why all functioning is analogical must be sought on a deeper level.

Suppose it is indeed the case that whenever we analyze the actual function of some functor we discover that it displays evidence of an x/y structure. The function may have the nature of x_y or of y^x. This indicates that in addition to a function being of a certain irreducible mode itself, such a function contains an implicit reference to another mode. But in that case one would expect such a universal fact to refer to a correlated nomic condition, to a principle of order.

The conceptual model I will use to acquire an understanding of the intramodal order of functioning is as follows. Each mode will be assumed to have an irreducible core nature which determines the irreducible nature of all functions of that mode.[13] This core moment of a functional mode does not correspond to any real function within empirical reality; rather, it determines the nature of many different sorts of functions of the same ultimately irreducible kind.[14] This modal nucleus is a principle of order determining the relative serial sequence of the levels of functions, and determining the nature of each irreducible modal kind.

Within each mode I assume an order of analogies whereby each mode internally relates to the other modes. If the relative position of a mode is such that it is founded on six other modal levels, it will within its own internal order contain analogical references to these six foundational modes. Analogies within a mode which refer back to earlier modal levels will be called *retrocipations*. Analogies which refer to the nature of another modal level which is higher in the modal order will be called *anticipations*. Thus the minimal order of any mode of functioning is that it has a modal nucleus and that it has as many retrocipations as there are modal levels founding or preceding it (which is nil for the lowest level) and that it has as many anticipations as there are modal levels following it (which is nil for the highest level).

Thus, in this model, a modal nucleus is surrounded by analogical moments of both an anticipatory and a retrocipatory character. The retrocipatory analogies are evidence of the foundations of a modal level in other levels, while the anticipatory analogies are evidence of the potential opening up of a mode through its founding of higher levels. What is postulated here is that the possibility of the x_y/y^x structure is guaranteed in a principle of modal order. This principle determines that the modal order is analogously reflected within each one of the modes.

A simple example can illustrate how helpful it can be to work with an ontological model which accounts for both modal irreducibility and modal interrelation. Suppose a son and his father have both enlisted in the army. The son becomes an officer, while the father remains a private. Does the son now have the right to give orders to his father? Suppose further that the older man, the enlisted man, is a wise person and that the younger man is both a minor (under twenty-one years of age) and an upstart. Wouldn't the father expect the son to listen to him rather than the other way around?

This sort of problem is a characteristic sample of what certain scholars would call the dialectical structure of reality. In treatises on ethics these situations are supposed to illustrate the nature of moral and legal conflicts. One might even encounter the opinion that such a situation demonstrates how irrational, individual, and subjectivistic our moral choices are in conflict situations. But is this really the case?

Let us take active functional relationships of these two persons to each other into account. These relationships differ irreducibly in kind from the one situation to the other. The father-son relationship does not occur within the army; it is a functor specialization which, although it undoubtedly also has juridical dimensions, is not qualified as a relationship of an original juridical kind. The qualifying function of the father-son relationship is originally moral in kind. If the two men were to spend a weekend back home, the father-son relationship would have to prevail there.

In the army, of course, there are no fathers and sons as such; the army knows enlisted men and officers. This is originally a juridical relation which, though it has its own moral dimensions, does not have these in an original sense. Within the proper setting, the lines of relationships are quite straightforward and are not at all irrational and dialectical. And with the help of an analysis which has room for modal irreducibility as well as modal interrelation, this situation can be acceptably classified.

4.2.2   The unity of functional diversity

Up to this point I have attempted to account for both functional continuity and irreducible functional diversity by means of a theory which posits irreducible modes of functioning. In these modes the modal core or nucleus guarantees modal irreducibility and the functional analogies guarantee intermodal coherence or continuity. I now want to come back to the problem of the continuity of empirical reality. If our experience and the world of our experience confront us with the fundamental wholeness, unity, and integrality of things, then a theory which insists on the irreducibility of functional modes has a special problem in accounting for continuity. So far I have addressed this difficulty in two ways. In the first place I have pointed out that functions become integrated in their diversity when we see them as the actual functions of one functor. The functor is a unit which functions and so guarantees the integration and continuity of functioning. In the second place I have pointed to the functional analogies as bringing about coherence in functioning. But are these two approaches sufficient? Each of them brings continuity to functional diversity "from the outside," so to speak. The functional modes remain as such irreducible and thus discontinuous.

What I shall attempt in this section is to establish that functional continuity is also an internal functional given, considering the fact that the concept of "function" refers to a reality which all functions have in common. "Function" points to a fundamental principle of order which serves as the basic common denominator of all functional diversity. Each mode of functioning is irreducible to any other mode. But in being a mode of functioning, each mode points to a deeper unity, namely, the reality of being a function.

If the unity of all modes of functioning is to be a genuine unity and not just a name for a formal concept without real content, all modes of functioning must ultimately be one. Such a unity must at the same time not undermine the irreducibility of the functional modes. Thus, the unity of the modes is not a unity characterized by *one* of the modes of functioning. Obviously the unity of all the irreducible levels of functioning can never take on the nature of one of those levels; otherwise we would have to conceive of all the other levels as reducible to that one level. If being physical or being organic is just *one mode* of functioning, the unity of all functioning cannot be that all levels are ultimately physical or ultimately organic. But what, then, is the unity of the modal levels of functioning?

As we have seen, it is the nature of the functor to function. Functioning is essentially functor-oriented. I do not here refer to the fact that actual functors in empirical reality function on a multiplicity of levels and in this way integrate a diversity of functioning. Rather, what I have in mind is that the *order* of reality *requires* that a functor function. The unity of functor and functions is determined by the order of reality. So too is the integral unity of the functor. But I have argued that the functioning which the functor is determined to do occurs within a modally diverse order of functioning, and that this diversity is irreducible. One modal level of functioning cannot be reduced to another.

However, as modal levels that limit some *ultimate kinds* of functioning, they have a deeper identity in being levels of the *functioning* that the functor does. The essential nature of *any and all* functions of *any and all* kinds is that they belong to functional subjectivity. Modes are ways of subjection. Moreover, this subjectivity owes its nature to the order of reality. One might say that all functioning of each mode refers back to the order of the modes. This order determines that functions are ways of being subject to the order of reality. Functors and functions are subjects and ways of being subject to the order of things. A functor is a unit of subjectivity; a function is a specific way of being subject. We will need to find the ultimate subjective unity of both functor and functional diversity in the nature of subjectivity.

This point can be clarified by means of a familiar illustration. Each child, at a very young age, comes to a certain stage in its development, a stage that is signaled by many repetitions of the question "Why?" No answer ever appears to be sufficient. Each answer is experienced as insufficient *in itself* and therefore in need of further justification. This, I believe, is the child's implicit growth of awareness of the fundamental nature of all reality. The child senses that reality is insufficient in itself, that its ground lies outside of itself, and that the order that determines subjective reality refers us back to the origin of that order. The relation of each empirical phenomenon to that order is that it subjects itself to the order of reality which originates in that origin.

Now, the insufficiency of any one functional mode is apparent in that even though the mode as such is irreducible, it refers us to a functor as well as to all other levels of functioning. Each mode of functioning is only relatively original. Its original irreducible nature is original with reference to the other kinds. But it is also founded on the reality of the other levels of functioning and points toward the other levels. One might say that reality here displays a restlessness, a relational insufficiency. This restless insufficiency surfaces in the problem of relativity. The relativity of all empirical reality is simply the nature of its insufficiency. And the ultimate unity of functors and functions, found in the origin of what makes all empirical reality subjective, is at the same time a point of orientation in the relativity of our world.

The modal reference to the origin of all that is relative is evident in the analogical order of the modal levels. In that order each original mode reveals that its originality is not absolute. Each original modal limit of functioning can be understood only in coherence with all the other modal levels as modes of subjectivity, ordered to be subjected to the principles of order, and their origin.

An example of this restless relativity is our contemporary experience of justice. Within the modal limits of what is legal we still find anticipatory moments of a higher order. These higher functional principles are themselves founded on what is just. At the same time they are anticipated within the order of justice. The jural modal principles of equity and legal security are anticipatory analogies of the principles of troth (ethical) and certainty (pistical) within the limits of juridical reality. The original meaning of these principles is jural, but they refer to the original principles of higher modal levels. The equity and certainty they refer to, as principles of legal morality and legal faith, have their original meaning outside of the juridical order.

The reality of modal boundaries and simultaneously the irresistible reference beyond them is evidence of the subjective tendency of reality to refer to an original unity. We see this at work in the actual relation of morality and justice. In a modal sense, there are acts which are legal from a juridical point of view but that may nevertheless be immoral from a moral point of view. Acts that are legally forbidden may likewise be moral. Immorality is not a juridical phenomenon, and illegality is not a moral phenomenon. But the unity in origin of these two irreducible principles of functioning is manifest in that negativity in the one cannot long be related to positive experience in the other. Modern legislation concerning homosexuality is clear evidence of the irreducible difference between what people may believe to be immoral and what they determine to be illegal. Even in anticipating the moral within the legal, we must maintain the bonds of justice as the foundation of legality. But the jural is also the foundation for the moral. Today there is widespread experience of legal situations that are clearly unjust. The existing legislation is no longer determined by the fundamental principles of justice. This in turn gives rise to situations which are immoral, since the foundations of morality are out of kilter. Morality cannot be legislated, but neither can it be founded on injustice. Justice founding morality must itself anticipate the moral in legal equity.

Another example is a similar relationship between the economic order and the legal order. Here the legal is not the foundation for what is economic, as in the case of morality. Morality is impossible in an unjust society, but in the case of the economic order the reverse is the case. A just society is impossible without an economic order that anticipates justice. A society that sets its economic priorities in a way fundamentally at variance with the order of reality will not be able to provide a foundation for justice. A distribution of goods which is unfair fundamentally promotes injustice. The economic life of a society, in its own irreducible *modal* sense, can never be unjust but at most uneconomic. But to argue such a thesis in the face of the testimony of millions today that the distribution of goods is unjust would be to treat reality as if it were only modal and irreducible.

Intermodal order determines that economic imbalance necessarily results in injustice. If, according to the presently understood nature of the prevailing economic patterns in a given society, it is fundamentally uneconomic to do basic justice in such a society, the prevailing economic pattern is at variance with the nature of the economic order. The true nature of any economic order is to reach out to the order of justice in an anticipatory fashion, as evidence of anticipating the fundamental unity of all functioning in the origin of the order of reality.[15]

Another example of both the unity and modal irreducibility of a function is pain. Pain, in its concreteness, is something that first of all confronts us with a total situation. Someone is in pain. A person has touched a hot stove. A contorted face, muffled expressions, a hand waved to and fro—all of these indicate what the situation is. Pain in the concrete fullness of the situation points to functors in functional relationship and comes to expression on all sorts of levels. For a brief or extended period, someone's pain may dramatically dominate an entire situation.

But pain can also be looked at in modal terms. Pain is a phenomenon of a specific kind and is distinguishable from phenomena of other kinds. Pain is at heart a sensitive phenomenon. The crashing of the stock market may hurt many people, but (apart from its own concreteness) it is an economic phenomenon from a modal point of view. Pain is a sensitive phenomenon. Being in pain is never characteristic of nonsentient creatures. Plants whose flowers are cut off do not experience pain. Therefore we do not feed aspirins to a pruned bush to reduce the pain, nor do we comfort a tire that has been cut. From a modal point of view, pain, as such, is irreducible. But further reflection will also reveal that even though it is irreducible, it cannot be set off from the rest of reality but is one with it.[16]

What I have in mind here is not fitting pain into a fully real situation as described above but rather the unity of pain with the rest of reality right within its irreducible modal limits. As a sensation, as a feeling, pain has its foundations right in the organic and suborganic functions. Pain primarily is sensitive awareness of damage, tension, or strain in those lower functional areas. It is possible as a phenomenon ordered by a retrocipatory sensitive principle. A person in pain is a person aware of something wrong within the organism. It is not just an awareness of an organic state of affairs but an awareness of it as wrong, dangerous, destructive. Pain calls for restorative action or for avoidance. Modally, it is a sensation which can only be felt. It is not itself organic; it is a sensation.

As a sensation, however, pain falls back on organic functioning in two ways. In the first place, what is felt (by the functor) is that the organic functions (of the functor) are malfunctioning somewhat. It is a feeling especially in touch with the organic dimensions. But there is even more: those organic functions themselves are opened up, through the nervous system, to be able to register a sense of wrong. The functor that senses something wrong on the organic level (is in pain) does so psychically. But the organic functions themselves are prepared for that interrelationship; they are the foundation for that sensitivity. Certain cells do become the seats for sensitivity. It is not that they do the actual sensing; it is the functor that senses, and the sensing that goes on is not organic. But the organic functions are opened up to the sensing and make it possible. An x/y structure is present here. The organic functions are developed as sensors (y^x) and the sense functions have an organic base and reach out to the organic level (x_y).

4.2.3 *The identification of a modal kind*

Given that functions are characterized by both unity and irreducibility, reality may appear to be overly fluid and indeterminate. Can anything actually be identified as being of one mode rather than another? Doesn't modal analogy give functions a mysterious indefiniteness? The importance of this difficulty can readily be understood. A phenomenon that is modal in kind can properly belong to only one level of functioning. Emotional language, for example, is either sensitive in nature or symbolic—but not both. Whereas interrelationship of functions can make identification difficult, irreducibility demands that the right kind be indicated.

In our everyday experience we do in fact seem to recognize irreducible levels. Suppose we encountered a person serving in the army as an enlisted man who refused to take an order from an officer on the grounds that he was the officer's father. We would say that the enlisted man was confused as to the *kind* of relationship in which he stood to this officer. Politicians who try to enforce their morality on the nation through legislation can be said to be confused about their proper authority and competence. Scientists who define emotional problems in terms of chemical imbalances may be mistaking a foundational relation for the suprastructure functioning on that basis.

On the other hand, although it is true that economic problems cannot be psychologized away or resolved through psychotherapy and that real emotional problems are not genuinely resolved by increases in salary, there are indeed relationships here. Because all functional areas are interrelated, people who have emotional problems may find that their economic abilities suffer as well. So an increase in salary may in fact relieve certain tensions. How, then, do we find out what's what?

This is not an easy problem to solve. It could be pointed out that no method properly belonging to one modal field can serve to deal with phenomena on another modal level; methods that yield an understanding of things on one level will only confuse us on another level. Logicians have long known that the nature of arguments is properly studied by logicians—not psychologists. But this approach presupposes that one already knows what level to relate to. Further, phenomena on one level cannot in the final analysis be properly understood if we do not understand the role played by foundational functions on lower levels. Modern biology is impossible without mathematics. It is true that biological concepts are not reducible to mathematics, but it is also true that biological concepts cannot be developed without mathematics. There can be organic functions only as functions of functors that have preorganic functions as well; in fact, the organic functions are founded in the preorganic ones.

As long as we speak formally, the distinctions seem clear enough. Difficulties arise in connection with the search for patterns of identity in a multifunctional reality. Functions of phenomena that are empirically observable occur as dimensions of entities that have many interrelating functions. Moreover, even within one functional mode, the very principle of its irreducibility as the core of its nature is in fact the core nature of a variety of actual functions. And these actual functions refer to other levels. No patterns of functional identity are empirically observable in their purity and in isolation.

Further complicating the problem is the fact that none of the analogical functional realities can be understood merely in terms of the levels to which they refer. They must first of all be understood in terms of the original concept of the irreducible nature of a mode—yet in relation to the understanding we have of other modes. Genuine theoretical penetration into the nature of any functional structure requires approaches proper to the nuclear nature of that function. The most basic concepts of a field of functioning must be original to that field.

There is no easy way out of this difficult problem. The minimal requirement is the development of special methods and special concepts. Thus, if a phenomenon is being approached as genuinely physical, does it make sense to inquire about the weight and dimensions of the phenomenon? Once we are aware of a number of fundamental concepts proper to a field of functioning, that is, concepts whose appropriateness to the original nature of the field are well established, it will be possible to determine whether such concepts are applicable to some problems we are studying. This task should ultimately not be too difficult for a scientist who is always busy with the viewpoint of a special field. Within the field there will exist a number of basic concepts proper to the field, concepts whose applicability can be more or less successfully tested out.

However, there are two qualifiers that must be taken into account here. One is that by no means all scientists are busy with a field which is limited, functionally speaking, to one irreducible modal kind. Where a scientific field is functor-oriented and not function-oriented, that is, where the point of view of the field is oriented to kinds of functors with a multiplicity of functions rather than to functions of one kind, the basic concepts are not limited to one mode. There is still unity of point of view, however, since the functor will also be of some kind. And the kind of functor it is will be determined by a qualifying function which itself has a specific foundation. In this way, the point of view will still be functional.

The second qualification is that the study of functional fields is to be distinguished from the study of functor wholes. Since a functor is qualified by its highest actual functional level as being a functor of some kind, a student of one of the other functional levels of this phenomenon may believe that the entire phenomenon—including the mode which characterizes the qualifying functions—can be reduced to *his* field of study. Simply because organisms do in fact have functions other than organic functions and because it is entirely proper to study organisms from various functional points of view, there is a temptation to reduce both the organic functions and the entire organism to the functional field in question. But this temptation must be resisted. The physical study of organisms is entirely proper. But the point of view of the organism must set the context for this physical study, not vice versa. This remains true even if the organic phenomena investigated are genuinely physical in nature.

By correctly assigning a function to its proper mode and by understanding its reference to other modes, we form genuine analogical concepts. Such concepts may help us to detect relationships that could otherwise remain hidden. There are, for example, many emotional phenomena here that are patently incapable of being reduced to levels of functioning other than the psychic mode. But at the same time, these phenomena show the interrelationship of psychic functioning with other kinds of functioning, which helps us to see how we can best understand such phenomena. We can easily appreciate this in the case of strained relations, tension, feeling closed in, and being depressed. These are clearly psychic moods, attitudes, states, or feelings. But they also refer to other modes. What does this tell us?

If the difference between a mere figure of speech and a genuine analogy is appreciated, one can understand that "feeling closed in" is related to the uncomfortable proximity of walls or people. The sensed proximity of those walls or people is experienced as uncomfortable or, as in the case of claustrophobia, as very threatening. In all likelihood the walls or people are not truly closing in, but such feelings nevertheless have a basis in reality. The same is true for tension. Muscles do in fact tighten up when people are tense. The tension is a feeling, but a feeling which does more than just refer to physical reality, for it actually has a basis in that reality. There is actual tension of physical forces. Muscle relaxants can help people get over tensions that originate in the psychic realm and have no origin elsewhere.

Another example is distance as a social phenomenon. The social distance between an executive and her chauffeur should not be understood first of all in original spatial terms. One would not say, for example, that we distinguish the social distance between the executive and her chauffeur from the social distance between the gardener and the chauffeur by noting that the former is two miles and the latter three feet. Nevertheless, if the distance were very pronounced, one could put it in this way—as a manner of speaking. This is possible because social distance requires—or is expressed in terms of—physical distance. The social distance between two people is not originally spatial, though it refers to and is founded in spatial relations.

People who are socially at a distance to keep their distance in an original physical sense, depending on how strong the social need is. In terms of living area, the chauffeur will be farther away from the executive than another executive will be. In many instances, the chauffeur would quite literally keep his distance. A society where these differences disappear and where one easily changes from chauffeur to executive is spoken of as a socially mobile society, to indicate that there is social movement which can cover the distance.

A last example is that of a market area. This is an economic concept which refers us analogically to spatial functions. As such, it cannot be treated geometrically, that is, with the tools of original geometry. Of course, if a market area is to be real it cannot be a merely economic function. Where real markets are found, a geographical area has been economically opened. Within that area we can find the occurrence of slow-moving products. This, too, is an analogical concept, but it does refer us to the actual time it takes to move a product from one area to another, for example, from the trade location to the customer's home. The actual economic relations that confront people from day to day do in fact have kinematic and spatial bases, which reveal their roles in economic analogical terms.

4.2.4 *Primary functional order*

So far in the discussion of the various characteristics of the order of functional modes I have given little attention to the difference between analogical concepts of a retrocipatory nature and those of an anticipatory nature, although this difference has been mentioned several times. Retrocipatory analogies are those that refer to earlier modal levels, while anticipatory analogies refer forward. This difference needs to be fleshed out somewhat.

The order of retrocipation is the order of the foundation of possibility. The conjoint functional order of a mode in which we conceive all of its retrocipatory analogies forms the primary order of that mode. Those retrocipatory dimensions, held together by their nucleus, are the minimal foundation for any modal level. They are the constitutive elements of a mode, its primary or unopened order, without which there would be no functioning of that kind. The constitutive order ties down the nucleus of that level of functioning to prior foundations which support that kind of functioning and in terms of which it comes to expression.

The primary order of all psychic functioning is that it is tied down to its organic substratum. Without sense organs—or at least sense-adaptable cells—there could not be any sentience. This still does not imply that, even on the most primitive level of psychic functioning, one could reduce the primary structure of these functions to their organic substratum. The primitive functor that functions as sensor is the primary given. The sense function of that sensor opens the organic substratum. But even though no mere organism is capable of sensing, sensing is fully dependent on there being an organic foundation for it.

Quite distinguished from this primary order is the opened or anticipatory order. In more highly developed animals, the organic foundation for sensitive functioning is opened up in the formation of specially organized sense organs. Furthermore, it is easy to distinguish between unopened or closed-down sense perception as it occurs in even the highest animals, on the one hand, and the sort of perceptiveness that has been opened up toward human analytic functioning, on the other. The perception of conceptual relationships—or better, the perceptive support for grasping conceptual relations analytically—requires that sensitive functioning no longer be rigidly tied down to organic sensory substrata but be opened up to higher levels of functioning that could not be sensed unless these levels became operative in the sensor.

4.3 Some Specific Functional Modes

Thus far the discussion of various characteristics of modes of functionality has been formal and abstract. Therefore some actual functional modes should now be discussed. A major difficulty in discussing functional modes is that concrete examples can never be given. Modal levels of reality do not occur in isolation or abstraction. One can give examples of biotic functioning in order to illustrate something about the biotic mode of reality, but biotic functioning is the actual functioning of a functor which functions on many levels. In this section, therefore, it will be important to remember that the discussion takes the point of view of modal *aspects* of reality, even when the illustrations tend to call a fully concrete reality to mind.

This must be remembered especially when the illustrations concern even less than a functor. Thus, to ask whether or not a certain decision was morally responsible when discussing the moral modal *aspect* of reality might create the impression that the decision as such is a modal phenomenon. In such a case the moral *dimension* of the decision, which is itself a complex reality, must come to the fore in the example. And it is the dimension that we must focus on, even though we could never get at the dimension except by calling to mind something more concrete which has such a dimension.

We can appreciate this point if we bear in mind that even parts, which as such are multidimensional and considerably more concrete than modal aspects of reality, cannot be isolated. But since they are physically separable, it does appear as though their reality can be more easily examined. We can take out a heart, snip off a piece of lung, or extract a tooth. Such parts can then be examined. However, we do not then get any picture of their actual and real role, for the isolation has distorted our view. Parts of a living body die almost as soon as they are severed. This is even more dramatically the case when it comes to modal aspects. They can only be severed conceptually, and in being severed they lose their reality.

On the other hand, this point must not be overstressed. If we bear in mind the nature of abstraction and also the point of view of the reality from which we are abstracting, then abstraction, though difficult, is quite legitimate. Without a conceptual grasp of orders and structures, our human ways of knowing would be impossible. Numbers can be isolated conceptually, and they can also be symbolized and studied. The same can be done with curves and motions. In economics we can isolate price and competition. At the same time, the more complex the reality from which we isolate, the more difficult it becomes to apply what we have learned in isolation to the complexity from which we have isolated. It is easier to accurately apply what we learn about the relation of speed, distance, and time to a moving target than it is to apply what we learn about price and competition to a modern market economy.

Many of the phenomena studied in science are multimodal, even when a given phenomenon is studied from the point of view of one mode. However, science sometimes isolates the phenomena of a specific mode. This is easier in the case of the lower or more fundamental modes of reality. Numerical relations can quite easily be isolated. Spatial relations are not so hard either, even though we must instantly depend on number relations implied in these spatial phenomena. When we come to the kinematic aspect, the laws of motion as studied in mechanics take on an unreal character: in order to isolate motion modally, we must speak of the rolling of balls down an incline *as though* there were no friction. Real motion never occurs that way, yet it is necessary to view motion as a modal abstraction in such terms. And as we go on to the more complex levels of the modal order, the abstraction becomes ever more difficult to perform. Nevertheless, it is possible conceptually to isolate modal functional principles from the point of view of the irreducible nuclear nature of that mode of reality.

The example of Zeno's problem of the arrow that can never cover the distance it must go may help us see the problem. The actual event of the shooting of an arrow is extremely complex. If it occurs in the setting of an actual ancient war, we have many modal aspects to consider, such as legal dimensions, moral aspects, technical sides, and so forth, if we hope to do justice to the entire event in its actuality. But suppose we confine our discussion to the arrow flying to its target through the air. This is in itself an abstraction, an isolation; it is not a real event that can actually occur unless we take into account someone shooting the arrow with a bow. But the arrow flying through the air is still real enough.

It is not a hard isolation. If we consider that we are aware of its having been shot with a bow by a person for some reason at some target, the only abstraction involved thus far is that we have taken a segment of a real event which possibly retains its full concrete reality. That segment can be looked at in the context of the whole event. We can take account of the x/y structure of the whole event and recognize our segment as qualified by whatever x function is the qualifier. The event could be an execution, a practice shot, an ancient Olympic game, or part of a strategic battle. But we can also look at the more abstract physical event of a moving object, disregarding the context in which it happens.

The flying of the arrow, in its physical reality, is one of the less complicated kinds of physical reality that we can be confronted with. Yet we all know that, as such, it is still very complex. Even modally speaking, it still manifests functioning on the four levels of the numerical, spatial, kinematic, and energetic modes. This is not to say that the event as physical has four functions; it probably has an unoverseeable number of functions. What modal analysis says it that the event, as physical, has functions of four modal *kinds*. The actual number of functions in these four levels is innumerable.

Once we begin looking at more specific phenomena, however, they tend to fall into categories of functional kinds. The flight path is a spatial phenomenon. That the flight path is not a straight line but a curve shows that we are dealing here with the space of moving objects, which is analogically expressed within the spatial dimension of functionality by the curve. If we study the motion side of the flying arrow, we have to do with problems of the sort that are studied in mechanics. The ballistics expert will use numerical and spatial measuring techniques for his calculations, but these will manifest the anticipatory enrichment of being functions of a moving phenomenon. The curvature of this particular motion is that of a trajectory, not the surface of an object.

From a modal point of view, then, the concept of a "flight path" is still very complex. It is a spatial concept belonging in the spatial functional mode of reality. This is the *kind* of function it is. It needs to be understood from a spatial point of view. But within the complexity of phenomena that do have such spatial functions, this one shows us a kinematic analogy. It anticipates the characteristics of motion without itself being motion. This sort of abstract functional point of view in relation to very real phenomena that are very complex will continually challenge a philosophical modal analysis. In what follows the point of view will always be abstractly modal, although the examples and illustrations will be as concrete as—or even more concrete than—that of the flight path of a projectile.

4.3.1 *Technical or formative functioning*

The first modal dimension of reality which I will discuss in somewhat greater detail is formative functioning. I have in mind the *kind* of functioning we recognize in our methodically controlled relations with our environment, that is, the instrumental and purposive relationships between conscious creatures, the design of action, the moment of choice and decision, and the means-end relationship. Why do I think that this sort of phenomenon should be understood as modally irreducible, that is, as being a kind functioning apart from all other kinds? We can approach this question by seeing first of all whether the characteristics I have just mentioned can be differentiated from other realities while all remaining of one kind. The second step would be to try to understand whether or not these kinds of things are reducible to other, more fundamental kinds of functioning.

The phenomena I mentioned are easily distinguishable from other phenomena. Making something with instruments for some purpose is known as a specific type of activity in any society. Not all our actions are of this kind. Plants or physical systems don't act like this. Making, designing, crafting, creating, forming, building, producing things is so specific that we recognize a special class of people as crafts people. The skilled use of tools as a means to reach some end we recognize as the occupation of crafts people. They have a special trade. We distinguish their activity as a kind from all other sorts of activity.

As a very fundamental mode of functioning we can expect making to be present in almost all human activity. But it is still distinguishable from mere action and reaction or action and consequences. Making is not just causing, a product not just an effect. Plants, in *this* sense, do not *make* sugar. We just *say* they do.[17] But animals do make nests. When skills get well developed and when methods and techniques become fundamental to a society, society recognizes this in the special study of this kind of functioning. I have in mind such disciplines as engineering. Other fields of study also have this point of view: medicine, agriculture, and education, among others. Engineering itself has a clearly universal application: we speak of medical engineering, chemical engineering, and all sorts of other technologies.

So there is reason to take all what is studied in engineering, technology, education, and other such fields as being of one kind. The same can be said of all that is specific about skills, crafts, instruments, the means-end relationship, tools, and methods. All of it can fundamentally be characterized as the conscious, controlled form given by aware functors to the objects, functions and relationships with which they come into contact. This control is not an end in itself but a means to another end, an end of which the functor is aware. This kind of activity is characterized as the reaching of a goal through means that can be controlled by the functor wanting to reach the goal.

This kind of functioning does not occur on the physical level of action or on the merely organic level of functioning. No merely physical object or merely living organism is capable of the use of means to reach some end. Action viewed as the most primitive organization of all functioning on the level of physical entities is a purely mechanical sequence of determined action and reaction in which all the patterns are irreversible. The process whereby an organism takes in its environment as food on the vegetative level is also not to be characterized as pursuing a goal by certain means. Though organic action is indeed not merely irreversible but is characterized by restoration, it is not purposive on the part of the individual organism.

Thus "forming" is at least a kind of activity that is only found among sentient creatures. Formative functioning cannot be understood in terms of any of the functional levels that are prepsychic. At the same time, no other postpsychic levels contain this sort of functioning in its original sense as an element of their original constitutive order or can themselves be reduced to this type of functioning.

Though it is true that all postformative functioning is founded on our ability to plan, design, and skillfully use tools, instruments, methods, and techniques, such functioning is also much more. For one thing, all postformative functioning can be regarded as an end and not as a means. But the end of a means is just that: to be a means and not an end. Skills and methods are by nature never ends, but only means for ends.

Where the means become ends, the ends to which the means were means either will not be reached or will become deformed. Making music is never pure skill or technique. Understanding something is more than the use of logical method. In contrast, what is preformative is neither end nor means. Thus it is inappropriate to treat moods and feelings as planned and designed. Rather, we just have them. This does not mean we are not responsible for them and especially for what we do with them. But they are not planned or formed. We feel what we feel.

The irreducibility of formative functioning to other levels of functioning becomes even more apparent when we consider the relative place of this modal level in relation to other modes and when we explore its primary order.[18] One level of functioning that is quite clearly presupposed in all purposive activity is consciousness. Design requires awareness—if only awareness of differences between the goal and the method used to reach the goal. Consciousness itself is to be understood as opened-up sensitivity. Where sensitive functioning occurs in its own closed-down primary order, the sentient organism responds directly and mechanically to a sensed stimulus with a motor response. The relation is a direct one-to-one correspondence. There is no such thing as an indirect awareness of what is sensed. The stimulus and response belong together.

The sensing of the conscious creature is sense opened by purposive activity. Drive and instinct are not forms of sensing that are conscious or aware. One would hardly speak of a unicellular, sensitive organism as conscious. But in the so-called higher animals we do find behavior that is much more than merely a mechanical reaction to a sensed stimulus. In the higher primates, evidence of conscious control and design is arguable. I will attempt to demonstrate this point soon, but first I must point out more dimensions of the primary order of formative functioning.

What I have indicated just now is that design, differentiated behavior as to goal and road toward goal, and controlled pursuit of the goal are constitutive dimensions of formative functioning, and also that they refer back to sensitive functioning itself opened up to become conscious. This is further based on organic relations of differentiated functional specificity. All formative action must show design based on organization. This organization is achieved by the skillful use of organs developed for the purpose of organic integration in carrying out our design. And if the functor who is to function formatively is to be able to organically integrate and consciously coordinate its activity, there must occur an adaptation of the organism itself into specific functions and organs.

The skillful use of organs as instruments in turn requires that the action patterns become timed; that is to say, they must be regulated and controlled. In purposive action one cannot merely act physically, that is, in the patterns of physically and chemically determined equilibrium of forces. On this level, action itself must be controlled—held back till the right moment. All of this shows that formative functioning does have an analogical order that is quite specific and that is founded in opened-up analogies of more fundamental levels of functioning.[19]

Formative functioning is a mode of functioning found in the animal as well as the human realm. When some animals have certain avenues of behavior blocked off, they become resourceful in their response. There is "indirection" in their behavior. This indirection, which has the character of being there as a means to an end, cannot be explained in terms of a pure stimulus-response pattern, which is organic in character, or even in terms of merely sensitive reaction patterns. Animals search, hunt, court. In some cases they teach and instruct young animals. They solve problems. In some species we find organized labor with a division of tasks—in other words, efficient cooperation. Much behavior is controlled.

It is true that many animal behavior patterns are genetically endowed and seem mechanical, that is, performed within a rigid pattern of instinctive action. Nevertheless, we cannot fully explain them on the basis of the immediacy of sensitive awareness of things, especially because this kind of awareness is so unwavering, so direct, so immediate, and so without hesitation that it cannot account for the mediacy and indirectness of instrumental behavior as means to an end. Nests, ant hills, and beaver dams require skill and control in the molding and shaping of materials. At the same time, we must not be misled into thinking that the formation of delicately shaped "artifacts" suffices for classing behavior as formative. The "forming" of antlers, snails' shells, and the like does not even have to be explained on an organic level; a chemical explanation within an organic context will suffice. The "accomplishment" of that which seems difficult and delicate to us and appeals to the eye should not be interpreted—anthropomorphically—as purposive formation on the part of a sentient creature.

Many dramatic stories are available from the animal world which highlight resourceful behavior. I have myself received a reliable, firsthand eyewitness account of how a beaver came to the rescue of a small trout. The trout was wounded in the gills by an angler. Upon having been thrown back into the water the trout appeared in difficulty and could not get enough oxygen. A beaver then appeared and did what anglers know is helpful: it pushed the trout around in the water till the trout had regained enough strength to go it alone again. And a story reported in the *Weekend Post* in South Africa relates how an old goose acts as a blind guide for an old goat. The goose not only leads the goat around the farm by calling, but also wards off other animals by hissing. It goes without saying that such behavior is known to be neither intuitive nor learned. It is, rather, what must be understood as creative behavior.

To see formative control on a more developed level, it is necessary to go to human experience. As it occurs in animals, where it is directly founded on sensitive and organic functions which are themselves not opened up any further, formative control is closed down and primary or primitive. But even as a human mode of functioning, formative control is to be understood as presymbolic and preanalytic. If symbolic or analytic functioning could themselves be reduced to formative modes of action or the reverse, one would have to adjust one's analysis of formation as a specific mode. But "symboling" is a much more complex and fundamentally different kind of functioning than the means-end skilled manipulation of actions in the environment.

A symbol—and symbolic activity is meaningless without a symbol—is itself to be understood as the symbolic retrocipatory figure that points to the means-end relation. The means-end relation is basic to symbolic activity, but "symboling" is more than formative control. For one thing, symbolic functioning is indirect in a much different sense than the indirect course of purposive control. Formative control, in all its forms, requires a direct relation to the environment, a direct relation to what is being formed and controlled. In the symbol it becomes possible to relate to that which is being "symboled" in a completely indirect manner. A symbol can never be understood as a mere tool. In the case of a tool and in the methodical means employed to reach a goal, there is no hint of the sort of distance reached via a symbol. Via the symbol, action can be stopped, postponed, changed, or resumed in arbitrary ways.

The animal, through opened-up awareness, is capable of being conscious of the relation between one thing as means or instrument and another as end or goal. It is controversial whether any animal is also capable of a perceptive awareness of the means-end relationship as such. The animal can see a concrete thing as means, and another thing as goal. On that basis it can act in organized fashion. But the perception of the relationship as such would require an opening up of consciousness to a stage of symbolic awareness, and it is not clear that an animal is capable of such an awareness.

That animals "communicate" is clear, but it would appear that their use of signaling methods may be no more than a means to reach an end.[20] If this level of functioning is indeed the cutoff point between typically human and animal functioning, then formative activity is not exclusive to human beings. The sensitivity of lower animals found in drive and instinct is opened up in higher animals to conscious and purposively directed behaviors which differ in principle from the mechanical and automatic structures of behavior.

Many animals do not just have organs which, with faultless chemical patterns, do the job of keeping the organic functions balanced to promote the growth of the organism, nor do they develop organs such as limbs merely for locomotion or sense organs for awareness; they develop organs as instruments, as well as activity that is instrumental. Some animals can extend this beyond their own bodies. Food is stored in the place remembered. A thorn is used to get at food otherwise impossible to reach. A bush is used for cover. We say that the animal capable of all this behaves intelligently, that is, as perceptive of purpose and aware of distant goals. Being conscious of goals, the animal now uses organs and entities in the environment as ways of manipulating, controlling, and molding its own actions or the environment.

In people, this type of behavior and this type of functioning is opened up and developed. Whereas for animals it is (possibly) the highest form of functioning, in human beings it is a foundation for other kinds of action. In human history this level of functioning becomes institutionalized; it becomes the foundation for culture. We have developed a world of techniques, of engineering, our means for culture. We go beyond the craftiness and cunning of a lion's hunting strategy. We have developed a storehouse of means, methods, tools, instruments, and raw materials. We are not just sensitive to goals and aware of consequences; we foresee them and plan ahead, and even

avoid certain actions by having foreseen the consequences. Organization, planning, deliberation, and weighing alternatives are formative
or technical functions of human society that anticipate higher forms
of functioning such as analytic, social, and economic functioning. But
they, too, are founded in the perceptive integration of our sensitive
presence in the world.

4.3.2   *Pistical or certitudinal functioning*[21]

In the series which constitutes the modal order which I have
adopted, there are (as there would be in any other version of the
series) two terminal levels. Either of these terminal levels can be basic
or first; it depends simply on the direction one adopts in approaching
this series. One of the terminal levels is the pistic or certitudinal mode
of functioning. The name *pistic* is derived from the Greek word *pistis*,
which means faith. People are the only ones who can function as
pistic functors, although other entities can enter into pistic relationships as pistic objects. They then function objectively in the pistic
mode of reality; that is to say, they are objects of human faith or objects of certainty.[22]

In modern and contemporary philosophical literature one would
not expect to find much discussion of this "theological" subject matter. Existentialists may have devoted some attention to faith, but on
the whole the devotion to rationality in the West has made faith
a suspect phenomenon.[23] However, the contemporary philosopher
Michael Polanyi has made this dimension of human existence a cornerstone in his analysis of our experience.[24] He refers to it as commitment and makes it clear that no theory of human experience can be
complete or even sufficiently explanatory in itself.

The pistical mode has peculiarities that relate to its place as a terminal mode. One can see this, for example, in the function of belief,
which is a dimension of certitudinal functioning. Belief is crucial in contemporary analytic philosophy. It functions there as a way out of the
impasse created by the demise of foundationalism. Many recognize
belief as something that cannot be explained completely in terms of
rationality, even when belief relates to propositions.[25] Nevertheless,
belief is seldom recognized as a phenomenon of faith, even when its use
is acknowledged to be fundamental, that is, providing a foundation.

What kind of functioning is certitudinal functioning? What is
the irreducible nucleus of its functional nature? Its essential nature
characterizes our acceptance of or surrender to a trusting relation to
something, to its truth, its reliability, its certainty. Since ultimate
reality confronts us most clearly in connection with this dimension of

our experience, faith is most often correlated with surrender to what we take to be the ultimate. Thus *faith* could be taken to be a word for the concrete attitude that is characterized by this mode of functioning. Yet faith should not be regarded as required only in the face of the ultimate or in the face of that which overwhelms us and to which we surrender irresistibly and give ourselves. Characteristically, however, it is in relation to the ultimate that the faith dimension is highlighted. For the ultimate is regarded as the final basis for anything.

The ultimate itself has no basis on which it can be accepted. It must be accepted on its own terms. It compels us to accept it and often overwhelms us. If we do accept it, it reveals its own meaning to our committed acceptance.[26] It becomes the ultimate basis for all our actions as it determines our priorities and shapes our fundamental loyalties.[27] We experience the world in its light and from its point of view. It is in this sense that the pistic function is assigned the basic role as seen from the terminal point at its end of the series. Pistic functioning relates reality to its ultimate foundation.

However, pistic functioning is not only found in confrontation with the ultimate. Reliance and acceptance—and surrender—occur as relational ultimates in our relations to all things. Since nothing subjective, in the final analysis, is sufficient in itself as basis to gain our trust and reliance, we must give it our acceptance. In most of our experience this happens routinely; it is habitual, unnoticed. We appear to accept things on all sorts of bases—trust, evidence, argument, threat. We surrender to many things in many ways—to fate, to love, to other people, to the inevitable, to joy and sadness. When we have accepted them on their own terms, we have surrendered to them. We commit ourselves to being on time for an appointment, or we commit ourselves to a job or to helping a person through a difficult period. But not one of these is in itself a sufficient basis on which to accept it always. Ultimately, we need an ultimate ground for the acceptance of anything.

Perhaps we could put it as follows: ultimately all acceptance is ultimate and is acceptance of the ultimate. This ultimate acceptance of what is ultimate is the core character of certitudinal functioning in a modal sense. It is the Luther experience: "Here I stand; I cannot do otherwise." Cutting ties with one's ultimate foundation is what makes people suffer and brings them into states of great fear, anxiety, and guilt. Not having surrendered to the ultimate and having no ultimate basis for commitment makes people untrustworthy, incapable of joy, insecure, and fundamentally unstable.

The place of this functional level of human experience is cosmic in scope. Our ultimate reliance plays a role in our relation to the universe and also influences the development of the world. As evidence I need only point to space travel, environmental interference, the existence of vast numbers of species of plants and animals that are affected by human culture, and other such indications of human entry into the other dimensions of the world. Because of these relations, pistic functioning is not limited to human experience; it is also a terminal function of the rest of the world. All normal human beings, in all of their experiences, are guided and directed by their ultimate beliefs concerning themselves, their world, their fellow human beings, and that which constitutes the origin of it all.

From the point of view of faith, the lives of individual persons, organizations, institutions, cultures, and civilizations are founded on this ultimate experience. Belief in progress, belief in science, belief in economic growth, belief in the autonomy of human reason, belief in the rights of the individual, belief in free enterprise, belief in profit—all these beliefs and a number of others as well have, either alone or in relation to one or more or all of them, shaped and directed the course of modern world history and thus have affected the world both within and outside of human culture.

These beliefs are either based on other beliefs or accepted ultimately on their own terms. When such beliefs are accepted as ultimate, they become the source of our fundamental commitments. Such acceptance is ultimately not based on rational or factual evidence or on observable realities. In the foundational order, pistic experience is indeed founded in analytic levels of functioning along with others, but in the reverse order the acceptance of the ultimate makes analytic functioning itself possible.

The point I am making is that pistic functioning is irreducible. It cannot be equated with other conscious functions. It is not just sensitivity or awareness. Yet it is aware. It is also not understanding. But this does not mean that it is irrational. In its core faith is different than sensitive or rational functioning. Even if we have ultimate belief in reason or science, such belief is not the same as rationally justified acceptance of science or reason. Belief in reason is based on the assumption that science or reason is itself ultimate. Belief in reason is its own ground. And what we accept in faith is a basis for whatever else we accept. This is the fundamental or founding character of this level of human experience.

At the same time, the terminal level of faith is itself based on all the other functional levels in the founding order. This makes it possible to be critical and open believers. Yet we never ultimately doubt our ultimate ground; this is an impossibility, for such a thing could only be done on the basis of an acceptance (if only for the moment) of another ultimate ground. Nevertheless, we are always conscious—or should be conscious—of our ultimate surrender, of what it means and implies, of what it demands, of the loyalties and priorities it requires of us. If we do not do this, we will be manipulated by the hidden faith of others. But if we are indeed aware of our ultimate commitment, we can be open to feeling secure on that ground and can be open to experiencing the world rationally as an orderly universe. If the ground we accept leaves us insecure or makes our world appear irrational, we can justly demand that such a ground legitimize itself. For then it will not support the world we live in, whose ultimate ground it must be experienced to be.

It is not always possible to exchange one ultimate acceptance for another. The exchange is called conversion, the radical turn from one ultimate commitment to another. We cannot live without such commitment. Anyone who thinks she can is in the grip of a hidden commitment to which she is not open. A person who is open to her commitment will also be willing to accept that in the grip of this commitment she believes and accepts what is seen from its point of view. Such acceptance is the correlate of a process of revelation. Seeing, believing, accepting, and deciding in the light of what we take as ultimate is the medium of revelation. Ultimate grounds are known through our commitment and determine what our decisions, choices, priorities, convictions, and believings must ultimately be. A genuinely open, conscious life is a life open to the commitment supporting it. In touch with our commitment, we will be aware of how it shapes and directs all of existence.

The pistic mode as a terminal level is a basic level of existence. Is there any point in trying to determine whether it is more or less basic than the other terminal mode of functioning? If the question is formulated in this way, it will seem too abstract. Since no mode of functioning and no actual function is thinkable apart from the real existence of a functor, the question can be reformulated as follows: Is human surrender (viewed as a real act of persons) more or less basic to the universe than physical reality (taken as the realm or kingdom of physical or material entities)? But even in this form the question cannot be answered. The answer that is in fact given depends on the ultimate vision of reality held by whoever answers the question.

If the world is believed to have an ultimate origin beyond itself, that is, an origin which transcends the world, then that origin will be held to be the world's ultimate foundation. The question of the foundational levels of functioning is then a question of the functional foundations of empirical existence. In that case a question about which terminal function is foundational needs another question: fundamental in which sense? From the point of view of bare existence the physical basis is indispensable for all of empirical reality. However, from the point of view of what the ultimate criteria are for the fundamental intent, meaning, purpose, and direction of the universe, the act of commitment is fundamental.

As a terminal level of functioning, this level will only have analogies of one kind, that is, retrocipatory analogies; but it will in turn be anticipated on all the other modal levels. All of the rest of human experience serves as the primary structure of pistic functioning. Whereas sensitive functioning, for example, is possible just on the basis of biotic and prebiotic functioning and is itself a foundation for all postpsychic functioning, in the case of surrender we can say that it occurs on the basis of all other human functioning.

Consequently, the healthy and normal functioning of our call to surrender and to accept the world in which we live is undermined by any malfunction on any other level of human existence. At the same time, none of the other kinds of functioning will be sufficiently integrated into the wholeness of a person without open surrender to our ultimate identity, openness to our ultimate beliefs on all levels. If we are emotionally disturbed, if we understand the world poorly, if our economic affairs are out of kilter, if we live unjustly or immorally, these malfunctions will undermine our ability to accept and surrender. On the other hand, the chances of correcting such malfunctioning improve with a strong personal commitment to what we take as ultimate in our life.

This simultaneous double foundation in all our functioning is understandable if we recall that functions do not function. It is functors who feel, think, act morally, and believe. The functor acts on all levels of functionality simultaneously, and so provides integration on all functional levels. The surrender of our feeling life to our ultimate choices will at the same time provide an emotional basis for accepting these choices. A healthy emotional life will recommend its acceptance and will at the same time be founded in a feeling of ultimate security. Thus the primary functional order provides the foundation for acceptance, while surrender and commitment direct all of one's functioning to and anchor it in the ultimate.[28]

The foundational order gives experience a bottom, while surrender keeps experience open. Experience is kept open when we do not allow any kind of functioning to become closed off in itself or to be looked upon as the foundation for all things or as the ultimate point of reference for all things. This includes pistic functioning, which, in functionally effectuating personal surrender, does not accept itself as ultimate. For this reason certitudinal experience can also remain open—open, for example, to the testimony of other dimensions of life as to whether or not they flourish in the face of the ultimate commitment that has been made.[29]

The core or essence of pistical functioning will express itself in terms of functional analogies directly related to the preceding modes. Words taken from the natural vocabulary of this dimension of human experience make that clear. Such words abound: commitment, surrender, faith, acceptance, ultimate, sacrifice, confession, ritual, belief, creed, vision, certainty, reliance, justification, and many others. *Commitment* refers to the primary constitutive moment of pistical functioning. It indicates the level of retrocipation in which faith is both founded on troth and simultaneously transcends the functional level of troth, that is, the ethical mode of functioning. This ethical troth, opened up to pistic functioning, displays an anticipatory moment in trust. This trust becomes the direct foundation for commitment. Commitment is the primary constitutive moment of faith and is founded directly in trust. They are related in an x/y manner. Such analogy shows the relation of faith to morality or keeping troth as well as its irreducibility to that dimension.

Within the modal order of pistical functioning, commitment is founded in conviction, which is the justification of one's commitment. It is the nature of commitment, of course, that the ultimate ground to which one commits oneself, justifies one's commitment. But this requires that commitment is based on being convicted by the ultimate. Such conviction makes one's surrender right. It is intermodally founded, in the foundational order of functioning, by an analogy of opened jural functioning, that is, justification. Opened-up jural functioning enriches jural meaning from being just to being justified, that is, being grounded ultimately in being right. One is right and just in the face of the ultimate. The judge who convicts the accused thereby accepts responsibility for—and surrenders to—the verdict that the accused is guilty before the law.

Moving now to a much lower level, pistical functioning needs a deep grounding in belief, which is the pistical reference to analytic factuality. Belief is an analytic analogy, an analytic retrocipation within the pistic mode of functioning. Belief is grounded in the acceptance of one's conceptual grasp of the structural order of things. Contemporary research in both logic and epistemology makes it clear that propositions are indeed believed, though belief itself is not simply a matter of argument or conceptualization, that is, an analytic function. Developments in the philosophy of science have led to the contemporary conviction that no conclusion of an empirical argument can be conclusively verified in a rationally acceptable manner.

The process of inference arrives at conclusions. These are the proper analytic entities. To become facts, these conclusions need to be accepted, believed. A belief is an accepted proposition, while a fact is a believed state of affairs. In our belief system we surround ourselves with our conceptual grasp of the structure of our world, its basic patterns, its fundamental continuities. These are, indeed, the facts we believe, the things we take to be the case. Belief is one of the "that" structures of our experience, which, as we saw in chapter 2, always relates our experience to its structure and order. Irreducible conceptual functions and irreducible pistic functions show themselves as analogies of one another in facts and beliefs.

The variety of analogical moments within pistical functioning and the variety of analogies to which these appeal and refer is virtually endless. I will merely mention some. Sacrifice is a certitudinal reference to the economic mode, fellowship to the social, regeneration to the organic, integration to the energetic, and discernment to the analytic. Other examples of reference to the pistic mode in the other modes are investment in the economic, verification in the analytic, control in the formative, security in the psychic, and reverence in the social mode. All of these show both the irreducibility and the integrality of the modes of reality.

4.3.3 *Psychic functioning*[30]

The last level of functioning that I will briefly discuss is the psychic or sensitive mode. In terms of human experience, it is a very foundational mode of functioning. The contemporary preoccupation with emotional health makes us more aware than ever of the crucial role which our sensitive relations to the world around us play in our lives. This particular area of irreducible functionality is the one studied by psychology. At first glance it might appear—on the basis of a survey of psychology textbooks—that the scope of psychology comprehends all of human behavior. Of course such a view is not satisfactory if it is indeed true that the psychic mode represents just one irreducible level of functioning.

The fact of the matter is that human behavior is studied by many other disciplines as well: economics, sociology, theology, epistemology, and logic also study human behavior. And what those disciplines focus on certainly is not covered in psychology. How, then, is psychology's field to be delimited? What is the principle of order that limits the viewpoint of psychology as a field? Some have said that psychology focuses on the individual behavior of the organism, rather than on group behavior. This answer, too, is unsatisfactory. In the first place, there are many organisms that psychology does not study—think of plants, for example. And even within the domain of human behavior, there is individual behavior which does not, in any straightforward sense, belong to the field of psychology. Further, psychology of groups exists as well. What is needed here is a specific, functional point of view which will then leave open the possibility of exploring virtually all of human and animal behavior from that point of view. Psychology would then be the study of human behavior from a specifically irreducible modal point of view.

The point of view dominating all of the psychological literature is that of sensitive functioning. This is what indicates the nature or core moment of the psychic mode of functioning. The easiest way to understand what is meant by sensitive functioning is to view it with reference to its most rarified form, that is, the experience of "psychics" or people who can feel or sense things in unusual ways. Among these ways are clairvoyance and telepathy. Telepathy is sensing or feeling from a distance. The functional dimension which allows a functor to sense or to be sensitive to the environment cannot be reduced to any organic or biotic functions. Organs or cells cannot sense unless they are the sense organs of sentient creatures, that is, organs of functors that have a sense function.

The primary structure of this sensitive level of functioning manifests its first and foremost intramodal level in the retrocipatory structure of sensory functions as these are founded in organic specializations of the cell, whether primitive sensitive cells or specially adapted sense organs. That sensory process, in its primary structure, is always directly linked up with the integration of the sensed stimulus into a reaction pattern that asks for a motor response. These phenomena (feelings, perceptions, emotions) are in turn closely interwoven with the substructure of organic and psychical functions. The very internal structure of sense experience betrays these foundations in the retrocipations within the psychic mode. Emotionality, feeling intensity, vital feelings, sight, sound, and smell all put us in immediate contact with the subpsychic founding functions, even though these psychic functions themselves retain their truly sensitive character. The fundamental order of sensitive functioning is the sensitive awareness of ourselves in our environment.

There is a criterion by which the sensing functor directs the sensing integration of experience and behavior: we look for situations that are joyful, pleasurable, happy, satisfying. When what is sensed comes across as fearful, painful, and the like, contact is broken off and the sensitive reaction is to withdraw, run away, flee, stop tasting, hide. This primary structure of sensing becomes tremendously enriched in human sensing. In the healthy person, who can trust her senses and the appropriateness of her feelings, sensitive awareness of the world is fundamental to all else that is done or experienced. The entire postpsychic order of functionality is intimately interwoven with the anticipatory order of the sensitive mode. We develop a sense of justice; we can feel the injury to our dignity in indignation; we can feel insecure if we are unable to surrender; we can perceive the identity of things in their structural continuity. In many ways we give evidence of this interrelationship.

4.4 *Characterization of the Areas of Functionality*

Since the development of modal analysis is in an early stage of infancy, it is hardly possible to present a thorough, clear, and systematically organized description of the order of each mode. Such a balanced overview would require a clearly irreducible characterization of the nuclear nature of a mode as well as convincing examples of each of the analogical moments, in terms both of their conditional order and of examples of actual functions of such an analogical kind. The present stage of analysis is not sufficiently advanced to allow this. However, for the sake of clarity in the development of themes in future chapters, a brief characterization of each modal area can be given.

Pistic or certitudinal. This is the modal area readily associated with faith, creed, and cultic ritual. In the act ultimately qualified by this dimension we surrender ourselves to the origin of the universe as the ultimately secure foundation of reality in which we can rest secure.[31] Its core principle of order is the call to surrender. It is institutionalized in cultic organizations such as the church. Among the activities typically qualified by functions of this modal dimension are worship services, rites, prayers, and confessions. Creeds are certitudinal entities. All certitudinal action, whether personal and private or institutionalized in public communities, is essentially to be characterized as the fostering of certitude in life. These activities ground us in the ultimate to which we are committed.

It is important not to confuse the certitudinal mode with the nature of religion.[32] Although the certitudinal functions should rightly guide all of human experience, these functions can be distinguished from that which is not certitudinal in human experience. A prayer is not the same as a petition addressed to the prime minister, and communion is not the same as supper at home. But religion is to be understood as the integral totality, the radical relation of all of human experience to the chosen origin of reality. *Religion* is a word for consciously undertaken human subjectivity to the order of reality as directed by the origin of that order. The certitudinal functions of life provide us with a functional avenue through which this radical integration becomes functional in our lives. Yet religion is of such a nature that all functional dimensions are at bottom radically one in being ways of subjectivity, while subjection is the character of religion. It is also to be understood that all people function certitudinally and that all people are religious; that is to say, all people are subject to the one order of reality, and all people are in functional contact with the ultimate meaning of that order through faith.

Ethical or moral.[33] This functional mode must not be confused with the general demand on human functors that they consciously submit to the order of reality, that is, that they respond obediently and in truth to the normative order. If that were taken to be the meaning of the term *moral*, one could indeed characterize all human behavior as being either ethical or unethical, moral or immoral, since all human activity occurs within the dynamics of the order-subjectivity relation in an aware manner. In the terminology I am employing, however, the use of the terms *good* and *bad* to characterize our manner of response to norms in general is not a moral usage but a religious usage. Good and bad are the results of obedient or disobedient response, true or false response. These are religious terms, then.

What I mean here by *ethical* and *moral* in a restricted functional sense is a kind or mode of functioning to be characterized by troth, loyalty, faithfulness. The older English word *troth* is found back in terms related to friendship and marriage—*pledging troth, betrothal.* These are relationships typically characterized as ethical bonds, bonds of fidelity. Keeping troth is standing in permanent relations of trust, keeping one's promise. Keeping troth is the subjective ethical response to the call for truth.

Juridical. This area, in principle, is characterized by the call for justice. In terms of retrocipations it is founded in retribution or restitution, which is an economic retrocipation within jural functioning. Retribution is the constitutive moment of the primary order of all action characterized as just. Without restitution of rights or retribution for injury, no justice is possible. At the same time, opened-up jural functioning will anticipate ethical troth in meeting the principles of equity and will anticipate certitude in acting in good faith. The institutionalization of justice is found primarily in a legal code, which is the regulator of social justice. The legal code is either public or private, though it is all organized by the state (government, police, judiciary) as the institutional protector and promoter of a just social dispensation.

Economic. Economic functioning is characterized by its specific address to two characteristics of our world that demand human choice and decision, namely, the multiplicity of possibilities with which the order of the world confronts us and the limited nature of all realization of possibilities. In the face of the necessity of choosing, persons are required to achieve a maximum realization of potential which demands a determination of priorities. The use of our time, talents, and resources requires constant choice and constant determination of priorities. To make these decisions responsibly, that is, to achieve the maximum that is possible in a responsible way, is what economic functioning is all about.

The optimal use of resources, talents, and the fruit of our labor (raw materials, services, and goods) requires a network of relationships providing for the exchange and distribution and optimal use of these fruits, talents, and resources such that excess and waste and exhaustion are avoided. We both use and care for our world. The vast network of relationships created for this purpose in a modern society is what is called the economy. It is a network designed to meet all the needs that arise in our call to service in the world.[34] This network is known by us in the institutions of trade, commerce, money, and markets. In our modern age there is a global economy in which we attempt to manage the affairs of a civilization with respect to the distribution of resources and products.

Since the economic order is so fundamentally misunderstood in our time, I will make a few further remarks to try to prevent any possible misunderstandings that might arise from the remarks made above. All human beings have an economic task insofar as all of them must responsibly manage their own affairs. On the other hand, there are some who have a special task of managing certain affairs on behalf of all of us in a social sense. The latter are the coordinators of manufacturing and producing goods and services in society—the trade and commerce people. They have a specific economic task. What is economic is not to be confused with a "job," and a "job" is not to be confused with earning money. Neither is the government to be perceived as being "in charge" of the economy. Its task is justice—not management.

Now, in our society the "economy" has become an institution on which we depend. It is very important that the economy remain afloat. In order to be able to do so, it needs to retain resources, goods, and services for itself. This is what we refer to when we speak of the profit involved in the economic enterprise. Making the economy profitable, however, only means enabling it to continue to serve in managing the production and distribution of the goods and services needed by all of us to fulfill our legitimate tasks. Money is an instrument for the formalization and universalization of the economic order; that is to say, it facilitates the economic task. A person active in the economy must never be understood as "being in business to make money." Neither is it any other person's right to view an "occupation" as being in "business" or as making money, if that occupation is not genuinely *qualified* as economic.

Social. Intercourse is the word that best characterizes this mode of functioning, even though this word has been strongly reduced in meaning by many people. *Intercourse* is still defined in the *Oxford Dictionary* as first of all meaning social communication or dealings between individuals. What is intended here is not simply a broad reference to relationships or even to human relationships. A social relationship is a specific kind or mode of functional interrelation. It is intended to convey the consciously practiced development of relationships between people in which the fostering of relationships is an "end in itself," as it were.

The social functional dimension is an actual, distinctly different, irreducible level of functioning in which interhuman relations are practiced, are deliberately formed and nurtured, and have norms of their own. The social visit or social call is an act typical of this kind of functioning. Hospitality and etiquette are social phenomena. The fabric of overtly recognized practices in which we form these relationships and recognize their variety is what constitutes the web of etiquette. The core nature of this level of functioning is given with our call to dignity and respect. A funeral (when we pay our last respects) is the final social relationship we have to a deceased person.

Differences in functioning all have their social dimension in terms of the manner in which we show our respect for the person in that function. The practice of social cohesion in the ways designed for promoting such cohesion is essential for the maintenance of a healthy society. Our economic system, our jural order, our ethical relations, and our seeking of communion are all founded in the existence and maintenance of a fabric of social relations and dependent on the practice of social relations.

That social interaction is more than mere relationship is evident in the fact that, though we speak of being related to the sun, of standing in relationships to the sun, we never associate with the sun. Association or intercourse are irreducibly different. Social stratification, the neighborhood social center, the club, the reception to meet people, the church picnic, the fellowship hour, and many more phenomena point to the irreducible specificity of this mode of functioning.

Analytic. Often we mean by "analytic" the characteristic of a proposition that simply makes explicit what is already implied in the nature of a concept. "Bachelors are unmarried men" is analytic. But that is not what I mean by "analytic" here. I have in mind the irreducible modal nature of those functions which are typically found in analyzing, thinking, conceptualizing, arguing, reasoning, inferring. That functional level I refer to as the analytic, conceptual, or logical mode. Functioning of that kind, that is, acts and events qualified by functions of that kind, is found in the world of science and scholarship. The university is the organized community of people professionally busy with analysis in a predominantly occupational way. The order of analysis which determines the validity of this sort of functioning is found in the rules of inference, and the study of this order is what we mean by logic. By following the maxims and canons discovered in logic, we gain a conceptual grasp of structures, laws, order, conditions, patterns.

In the analytic process of verification we anticipate—though never achieve—pistical certainty. In argument we justify our conclusions. By means of the principle of parsimony, we simplify and systematize our conclusions. The scientific practice of reduction is a matter of rational economy. These are all anticipations of higher levels of functioning in our thought-life. The first opening up of our analytic functioning is in dialogic analysis. The first constitutive level of analytic functioning is the collection of terms and propositions in which we symbolically lay down our grasped order. It is the defining of what we have distinctly identified. The terms and propositions make it possible for us to give sensible (word-pictures and word-sounds) shape to our analysis; without this no human thought would be possible. The typical analytic operations are contrast and comparison, that is, the making and classifying of distinctions. These are formative retrocipations of analysis and are founded in the perceptive grounds for understanding the identity of things conceptually in their differences.[35]

Symbolic.[36] My use of the term *symbolic* should not be understood in exclusively semantic terms. The semantic form of the symbolic is a socioanalytic development of symbolic functioning grounded in the formative organization of elementary relationships of structure. As a system in which we convey information to one another, language is patterned after the structure of human experience. Almost all words are conceptual vehicles or names for concepts. They are grammatically related in the way in which we find the structure of reality relating to the concepts themselves. The syncategorematic words that do not fall under this heading are symbolic connexives or symbolic indicators of realities which help individualize the universal scope of concepts. Thus language is symbolic, and all that is semantic is symbolic. Language is the symbolic as carrier of conceptual meaning.

But semantic reality does not exhaust the realm of symbolic reality. Symbolic functioning is the typical instrumental allusion to individual meaning in reality.[37] Symbolic functioning, in its primary structure, always retains the fullness, richness, and uniqueness of individuality, beyond which its perceptive foundation cannot reach. The symbol always remains irreducible to the precision, distinctness, clarity, and universality of concepts, although it can anticipate all of this in words. The fact that symbolic functioning always requires a symbol points to its formative substructure, which is in turn founded in imagination as the symbolic production of a sensed meaning. Whether or not animals are capable of functioning on this level is a crucial question which I will not seek to answer for the present.[38]

Technical or formative. This is the functional area of tools, instruments, skills, methods, and techniques. Its principle of order is control, and it introduces the means-end relation into reality. The latter relationship, in its own formative way, refers back to the physical action-reaction pattern. Aptitude or a formative "feel" for things is a psychic retrocipatory moment, while organization and development are organic anticipatory moments.

Psychic. This is the modal area of sensitivity, feelings, emotions, drives, stimulus-response, and perception. The psychic mode is that kind of functioning which is most likely to be regarded as the functional integrator of the centered individuality of animal functioning—at least, of lower levels of animal functioning.[39]

Biotic. The biotic mode of reality is a crucial mode for science. It plays an important role in addressing the problems of continuity and discontinuity and of monism and dualism. Its typical phenomena are quite familiar: growth, reproduction, metabolism, restoration, birth, genesis, and maturation are some of the concepts we associate with biotic functioning. It is customary to associate all of these phenomena with life and to view life as originating on this functional level.

The meaning of the word *life* is greatly reduced, however, if it is understood as referring primarily to the typical biotic functions of organic existence. Such usage implies conceptually that physical existence is dead. But surely only entities that were once alive can be spoken of as dead. When we bear this in mind, an expression such as "dead matter" makes little sense. I therefore prefer to reserve the term *life* for characterizing a total functor as subjectively meeting its ordered expectations.[40] In this sense of the term, life for a human being would be infinitely more than mere vegetative continuity. One might say that for human beings, organic functioning is a boundary condition for life. But what is meant by the phrase "human life"— indeed, what everyone means by the phrase—is the whole of our human existence.

What, then, is the core meaning of the term *biotic*? What I mean by this term is the functional specification and interdependent integration of all functions of the entity such that they become parts of a coherent and singular whole which functions to generate growth, that is, which continually generates and regenerates all of its parts for its own continued development and existence. Molecules are concentrations of energy that hang together by equilibration and/or traction. Unlike the physical entity, the organism is not merely held together by a balance of forces governed by mechanical laws. It cannot be adequately understood the way we understand merely physical entities, as different concentrations or quantities of energy in different positions, arrangements, and force relations.

The physical entity is not a cooperative interfunctional integration but a mechanically explainable interrelationship of mass points whose charges hold them together and whose interaction of forces, whether severally or together, follows the laws of motion and energy. Of course there is also orderly relation in the physical world, but one cannot speak there of functional differentiation and integration or of any inner center which governs the totality to continue its own existence. No purely physical system seeks to continue its own existence. A physical system has no "defense" against an outside force.[41]

Operative in the organism is a principle (the core nature of the biotic order) which directs all the material functions into an organic integration and interdependence. This irreducible principle, in a central way, encloses all physical functions and subjugates them to its order. In a literal way, physical elements are incorporated into the organic corpus. Such entities as the atom and the sun, however, are not bodies in exactly that sense, with differentiated functions. The sun is a large concentration of energy, but its structure can be fully explained on the basis of principles of energy and motion. Such an explanation can even fully cover its parts independently from the whole and can cover the shape of the sun.[42]

Energetic. It is important to distinguish *this level* of functioning from the multifunctional operations of an *actual physical* functor. The functor is qualified throughout by its energy functions, but as a whole it has functions of at least four kinds, with energy functions constituting only one of the modal levels, be it the qualifying one. The energy functions are known to us in the phenomena of mass, force, matter, and the like. Cause and effect, as a physical relationship, is a characteristic of a functoral interrelationship between energetically qualified entities. Therefore cause and effect may be called a physical relationship rather than an energetic relationship. In order for any entity to be a functor, it must at least be physical; that is to say, it must function on the four foundational levels that are qualified or integrated by functions of the highest or energy level.

Kinematic. There are no functors which have this functional level as their only mode of functioning, nor are there any with this one as their highest function. The functional realities of this field are abstracted in a science such as mechanics. The nuclear nature of this mode is motion.

Spatial. The core character here is continuous extension. Geometry studies these functional relations; that is to say, it takes the spatial viewpoint in its analysis. The inescapable and universal use of spatial terms and images in our language shows the position of this mode in the modal series.

Numeric. The area of discrete quantity studied in mathematics. It was Frege's view that number was the most primitive and universal sort of existence, which is perhaps his way of articulating that the numeric mode of existence is a terminal mode and the most foundational of all.[43]

Among the functional modes currently recognized in the Dooyeweerdian tradition, these are the ones I find most acceptable. Moreover, I have presented them in the order I find most plausible. Other areas have also been recognized, for example, the aesthetic and the lingual. I deal with both of these in terms of symbolic reality. There are also some other proposals regarding the order of the modes. The most common one is: psychic, analytic, formative, symbolic, social, along with an additional mode (the aesthetic) placed between the juridical and the ethical. Other questions arise as well. It has been suggested that the numeric and the spatial are not really modes but rather the physical evidences of the universal characteristics of unity-diversity and continuity-discontinuity. There have been discussions among natural scientists about the justification for distinguishing modally between kinematic functioning and energetic functioning. For the time being, my position is as outlined in this chapter.

4.5   Functions and Properties

At the end of my discussion of the order-world and functor-function correlations some brief remarks are in order about the relation of this discussion to elements of traditional discussions of properties. For in my treatment it will not be clear whether I view what are called properties as functions or as order.

To get into this issue I must first go back again to my distinction of world and order as an irreducible correlation. When I call whatever structures and orders our world order, condition, law, or nomic, I am using words borrowed from a certain area of human experience. Most of the terminology here derives from public administration. Laws, rules, orders, conditions, and the like are phenomena of governing human relations. Some authors use terminology deriving from physical-spatial areas. They speak of constraints or boundaries. Words like cause or determination are also physical. Others have dealt with the matter in terms of ideas, words, concepts, reasons. They view the problem from a rational or logical perspective. My point is that all these are ways of getting at necessity and possibility from a special point of view. What we are after is whatever makes for necessity and possibility in our world.

The terminology and model we construct can never be literally the case. They are at best terms and models which, because of the meaning they have in our experience, allow us to get at what we need to focus on. Existence exhibits features that suggest constancy, continuity, necessity, pattern. Existence also suggests to us that it is self-insufficient, that it is not self-caused, and not its own origin. We combine these two givens in theoretical or conceptual models which account for our world. The only thing we can mean by saying our model is true is that, as far as we can see, it achieves what we expect from it: it explains and accounts for things satisfactorily. For this reason we reject nominalism. But nominalism persists, because nominalists are sensitive to the fact that our model, conceptual construction, or theory cannot be literally true. It is a model. And it does explain things. But if we should be tempted to treat it as really so, many problems come up that cannot readily be answered. And that gives rise to nominalism.

In the model I have constructed here I hold that order and existence are correlates and irreducible. Nothing *exists* that is not *subject* to order. At the same time, nothing that exists *is* order. Order is not an existent. And no order holds for what cannot possibly exist. There are no negative universals. I also hold that in existence there is a correlation of functors and functions which is irreducible. Consequently, no functors exist without functions, and no functions exist unless as functions of functors. Together with the first correlation, this one implies an order for functors as well as for functions. In this order functors are ordered to have functions, and functions are ordered to be functions of functors.

One reason why this model appeals to me is that it allows us to settle certain questions about properties that otherwise remain puzzling. These questions can be settled if we deal with them in terms of this model. The questions I have in mind are questions like: are there negative properties? are properties universals? do properties have properties? if properties are universals, are they sometimes individuals? and others like them. What we must do is decide whether in talking of properties we are talking about order or about existence. Are we talking about the red of my shirt? Or are we talking about that which all red things have? I have decided that the red of my shirt is a particular, individual characteristic of my shirt. The red that my shirt is cannot be the red of anything else, for it concretely exists right there and it now colors my shirt.[44]

But then what do all things red share? Only this, that they meet the property conditions for being red. The red of my shirt is a property. What all things red share is not their actual red, but their meeting the same property conditions. So I shall distinguish between properties and property conditions. And all properties are individual and particular. They are the actual, concrete characteristics of actual subjective things.

Can properties then have properties? Or can property conditions themselves be subject to conditions? On the basis of the positions I have taken, the answer to both questions must be negative. Properties can be complex. Perhaps all properties are complex. Or at least properties as we experience them are complex.[45] But then what of saying that the red of my shirt is fading? Does that not indicate a property of red? No, it does not. It only shows that my shirt is both red and fading and that the red of my fading shirt is therefore the actual, concrete, particular red that it is. It is not properties that have properties, but things. And things have complex properties. Such complexity is integrally interrelated, which clearly shows itself.

The same goes for property conditions. They are not themselves subject to conditions. Only properties are. But property conditions can be complex and can show necessary relations. When I say that red is a color, I do not say that being a color is a property of red. Rather, I say that this indicates that things which have the property red must be colored. Property conditions are interrelated and these interrelations are laws.[46]

So we have properties and property conditions. These are irreducible and complex. The relations among the former are determined by the latter. And by properties I mean functions. *Functions* is a word for properties, states, actions, qualities.[47] But how about functors? Surely they are not themselves properties of functions. They have properties or functions. I have rejected the view that functors would just be bundles of functions. Functors and functions are correlative irreducibles. Nevertheless, is "being an elephant" not a property of elephants? If no elephants had that property, how could any elephant be an elephant? My answer here is nevertheless that "being an elephant" is not a property. It, too, is a name for conditions, for nomic order. For that reason alone it cannot, given my model, also be an actual, particular property. Rather, it is a nomic configuration determining the nature of functors. That nomic configuration determines what properties any functors (thing, substance, object, functioning unit, etc.) must have that we know as elephants. If anything is to count as an elephant, it must and will have such and such properties. That is what "being an elephant" is all about.

So, properties do not have properties, but things do. Functors function, not functions function. But order determines that functors by nature do have such and such properties. And "by nature" means: it should have these properties if it is well formed. But it may not be well formed. There are, exceptionally, white elephants.

But what of negative properties? Are there any? My answer is: yes and no. Yes, if by that we mean: there are nomic conditions which make for the impossibility of something. Rather: all nomic conditions, in making some things possible, also make other things impossible. And it is necessary that some of these things are impossible. These *things*. It is impossible that there be any such thing, such functor, as a human being who can leap across the Atlantic in three steps. Whether or not that impossibility is itself possible or necessary is a bogus question. It is things and their qualities that either are or are not necessary. Conditions make them so. But conditions are neither necessary nor possible. If they were, they would be things. But they are not things. And that's why as conditions they are neither possibilities nor necessities. They only determine the possibility or necessity of things and their qualities.

But indeed, some things and their qualities are impossible. And these impossibilities are not properties of things. If negative properties were real, all things could have all properties; provided that some were positive and some were negative. That just makes no ontological sense, no matter how attractive to formal logical considerations.[48]

Chapter V
Special Relations

TO THIS POINT, I have developed a number of fundamental ontological categories. These elements of a conceptual framework are general enough to include all of reality in their scope. I have developed this framework in such a way that the most radically irreducible distinction in reality falls between the order for the world and the existence of the world. The general outline of this view is as follows. Both the world order and the ordered world are real. In the world, the two irreducible dimensions of existence are those of function and functor. For both of these dimensions there is also a corresponding order. This is to be expected, because the irreducible realities are at the same time correlative realities. Order and existence are correlative; function and functor are correlative. Thus, functor and functor order, as well as function and function order, are correlative. But so far I have not dealt much with any of the irreducibles in relation, aside from showing how they are correlative. In this chapter I shall discuss three special ways in which things interrelate in our world: the part-whole relation, the subject-object relation, and the enkaptic relation. Before entering into these discussions, I will first devote some attention to a more fundamental question: What is a relation?

5.1   What Are Relations?

Relations are puzzling.[1] Is a relation an entity in its own right, just as relata could be? If it is, then can one also ask about the relation that exists between a relation and its relata?[2] This is one sort of problem. There are others. Suppose we have admitted the reality of relations as ontic realities. Where could we "place" them ontologically in terms of our previous categories?[3] Is relation a function, a functor, or is it neither?[4] Moreover, do we say that relations are all of these, that is, functor as well as function, condition as well as conditioned? Any possible answer to these questions seems to generate more problems. If relation as a category is exclusively a subjective existent, then apparently there cannot be any relation between conditions, orders, and structures. We know this because my previous analysis found all subjective, empirical existence to be radically irreducible to the order which obtains for it. However, if relations were simply conditions, then there would likewise not be any existential relationships. If one would say that relations are both an order for relationships and actually existing relationships, then we would be at a loss to explain the resulting relation. It would connect order and existence, and would itself be neither.

These problems all occur when we try to account for, or explain, relations. However disturbing these problems may be for analysis, they do not exist from the point of view of our experience. Even if we could never explain or account for relations, they are so firmly established in our experience that we would still subscribe to their reality.[5] They are there and they are known. I am related to my children, for example, and the tides are related to the phases of the moon. Being a cow is related to being a mammal, and the drastic changes in climate of the last decade may or may not be related to our interference in the environment.

Perhaps it is difficult to give an account of these relationships or to place them logically within a system. But who can deny relations? And who can say that relations are simply unknown? Knowledge, although not unrelated to concepts, is not necessarily just conceptual in kind. Knowing is clearly more than having a concept or grasping a proposition.[6] It is possible to know something without being able to explain or account for it. We may be thoroughly familiar with something, and relate to it quite adequately, but we still might be unable to account for it. I love my wife, for example. I know it and do it knowingly. But I cannot fully account for it, give adequate reasons for it (although some reasons can be given), or even explain it. In fact, the opposite sometimes seems to be the case. A love relationship may appear to be so unprecedented that it seems unreasonable for the relation to exist at all.

But knowing that I love my wife is not mystical. I can say things about my love relationship that contribute to knowing it. Many of the things I can say are clear, reasonable, and open to explanation. I can relate how we have similar interests, complementary personalities, and the same deep convictions about life. Yet I cannot successfully explain why I love my wife. It is not a mystical experience, but it is a mystery. Knowing a mystery, like knowing a miracle, is a form of knowing that surpasses understanding. Such knowledge may not fit the epistemological prejudices of certain traditions, yet it can certainly be empirically experienced.

The nature or essential characteristics of a mystery remain inscrutible to logical argument. At least, logical argument according to the rules of inference does not allow us to come up with a clear, clean, well-balanced, and logical picture. Relations appear in many ways to be known in that fashion. They may be the sort of reality knowable only as a mystery. The essence of relation may not take a well-defined place in a well-defined system. It may defy definition. However, it may also still be possible to say clarifying things about relations. Although a full explanation may be impossible, logically coherent characteristics can still be noted. This appears to be the case especially when one investigates specific relationships, rather than simply the formal topic of relationship. The relation between employer and employee can be investigated, or the relation of smoking to cancer. With this thought in mind, I will now take a specific relation and analyze it for the sake of understanding it *as* a relationship.[7]

The example I shall use here is that of marriage, a relation between husband and wife. Two persons, upon entering the relationship called marriage, take on the function of being husband and wife. The terms *husband* and *wife* stand for functions of persons who stand in the relation of being married. Do we have three elements here, or two, or more? There are in any case at least two relata, namely, husband and wife. Is the relation between them a third element? Is it merely a matter of semantic convenience to speak of the relationship in distinction from the relata as they relate, or is there more to it? The relata are thus named because they relate. They are relata only as relating persons. Is there an entity, a phenomenon, or a reality which is separate, distinct from, and in addition to the relata, and which is called relation?

This is a thorny issue, because I am asking if there is a difference between a relationship and the functioning of one functor with respect to another. Is distance a relationship? If so, how does it differ from a spatial function? If it does not differ from a spatial function, then at least in this instance one might have a case of the identity of a function and a relation. What happens if I tie my bicycle to a lamppost with a chain? Is the chain the relation between lamppost and bike? Perhaps it is not; relationship and connection may differ. In this case the chain connects the bike to the post. But one might say that the relation between the bike and the post is something else. In distinction from the shorter post of a parking meter, a lamppost is suitable for securing a bike. That is the relation and it is established by means of a chain.

And what would the relation then be? Would it be more than just the fact that the lamppost is tall, preventing one from simply lifting the chain off? The lamppost is also solid, it is in the right place, and connecting a bike to such a post with a chain would prevent it from being stolen. Do I here dissolve the relationship into the functions of a bike and a post? The question whether relations are functions could also be reversed. Is a function possible which does not establish a relation? Is there a difference between functioning and relating? If not, then one might conclude that in the functor-function distinction the reality of relationship is also covered. Different relationships would then be different functions, that is, functions of a different kind.

But here another difficulty arises, for there may be relationships that are not functional relationships. Let us return to our marriage example. In analyzing a marriage, the relationship can perhaps be partially reduced to the functionings of a male and a female human functor. But what about these two functors and their relation to the conditions they must meet in order to function appropriately in their marriage? Husband and wife must meet certain conditions; being husband and wife they are also subject to certain norms. If these are not met, the two people have in fact dissolved or begun to dissolve the marriage. Now, even though these conditions must no doubt be met *in* functioning, nevertheless a functor-function relation appears to differ significantly from a functor-condition relation. Whereas one might conceive of functions as functor-functor relations, it is unclear whether the same thing is true of functor-condition relations.

Let me pursue this for a moment; perhaps the problem can still be resolved. If a husband loves his wife in subjection to the norm for love, it is indeed clear that he sustains two relations: he is loving his wife and being in conformity with a norm. But are not both relations understandable in terms of the functioning of the husband? It is certainly true that the relata differ. But from the point of view of the functor, is the relation to his wife a function, and the relation to the norm not a function? The function which he has in relation to the norm is one of subjection; the function which he has in relation to another functor is, in the case of marriage, one of loving. But are not both cases still examples of functioning? Perhaps so, but that would seem to result in another problem: the relation between condition and empirical existence becomes a function of empirical existence. And it seems unacceptable that a relation can be a species of one of the relata. How can this be resolved?

What I have observed so far suggests that perhaps when a func-

tor is in relation to something, that relation is a function of that functor. Both the functor's relation to other functors and to conditions
could be functions of the functor. But a difficulty emerges, for this
seems to imply reducing the relation between nomic conditions and
subjective existence to a species of one of these. However, is this implication necessary? And even if it were necessary, would that be objectionable? If one says that in marriage the relation between the husband and the wife is simply that they function as husband and wife,
has the relation then been reduced?

The answer depends on one's notion of relation. If relation is seen
to be a third and distinct entity, apart from the relating relata, then
the perspective changes. But I see no need for this. By taking relation
in terms of relating relata, relation is reduced to relating. And why is
that objectionable? I see no reason for it. It is difficult, if not impossible, to come up with an example of a relationship between functors
which is not simply a matter of the functors functioning in certain
ways. To return to our marriage example, the husband loves the wife,
or the husband stands in the relation of loving to his wife. The two
ways of stating the case amount to the same thing. So by taking relations such as this to be functions, relations are not eliminated; their
orderly place in the scheme of things is simply identified.

But have I now succeeded in identifying relations and functions?
No, I have merely said that in the case of functional relations there is
no relation distinct and apart from the functor functioning. Could
that strategy also be followed in other relational contexts? Is there no
relation between nomic conditions and subjective existence except for
the existing-in-subjection of the ordered world and the determining of
the world order? In the case of functioning in subjection to conditions, that appears to be unobjectionable. When we talk of the relation between particulars and the nomic conditions for particulars,
why should there be an entity called a relation in addition to the individual subjecting of all empirical reality to these conditions? When
two functors relate, that relating appears not to differ from each of
them having a function of some kind with respect to the other. Cannot conditions and empirical existence relate in the same manner?
Cannot the conditions simply determine empirical existence, and empirical existence in turn be subject to conditions?

Following this strategy does not eliminate relations; rather, it
deals with them in terms of the actuality of their variety. Stated simply, there are relations because nothing in reality is real in and of and
by itself. What is real is functors functioning in subjection to conditions that order their functioning. To say that functors relate, is sim-

ply to say that they function. And similarly, conditions will relate because they condition. Functors also function in relation to conditions, because they are subject to conditions. Everything in the world is in relation. The relating is sometimes conditioning, and at other times it is being subject. This was already noted in the first two chapters, which discussed the most general, mutually irreducible correlation. These were correlations. This meant that neither of the relata made sense without the other.

What are the implications of this approach for the reality of irreducibility and for the reality of a phenomenon such as marriage? Is a marriage merely a husband and a wife? Is a relation just relata? Although there are no relationships as phenomena apart from, distinct from, or separate from relata, this does not mean we cannot put our finger on what is real about what we call relationships. One might ask whether my analysis leaves us only with relata, but I would answer that relata are nothing but relating functors or relating conditions. And apart from or in addition to the relating relata there are no relations. The specificity of a marriage does not thereby disappear. Simply, a marriage is a relating of some specific kind between functors of a specific kind, subject to specific conditions. Marriages are not separate entities apart from, in addition to, or distinguishable from husbands and wives.

But this does not mean that marriages cannot be distinguished from carnivals, or from business contracts, or from client relationships. And husbands and wives are, of course, distinguishable from persons, in the sense that husbands and wives are persons in specific roles. The persons playing those roles also have many other roles to play. Marriages and carnivals are distinct ways in which functors function in connection with other functors. These different or distinct ways also have a different or distinct order. They display certain patterns which appear to be relatively constant and continuous. Because functors function in subjection to order, we can give names to them when they are functioning in certain ways. The order guarantees that the name can be used repeatedly to name the same thing. This makes it meaningful to speak of a specific way of functioning as a relationship of some kind.

So I have apparently not denied the reality of specific kinds of relations such as marriage. But what about irreducibility? Is all of reality now reduced to either relations or to relata, or to relating relata? Does this mean that order and existence are not as radically irreducible as they have seemed up to this point? I do not believe this to be the case. For one reason, our semantic reference (by means of the terms *relation* and *relating*) to the fact that we know nothing in reality is alone or by itself does not necessarily imply that the fundamental reality is that of relations, of which all that is real is a species. My view is not meant to suggest that the most fundamental category of all of reality is that of relation or relata. I do not wish to make the claim that, essentially, reality is relata. *Relation* as a term is just a name for what we know; none of what we know to be there actually exists by itself. There is no such thing as the entity or stuff called relatum, of which all of reality is made. In fact, what I have tried to do is minimize all chances of reifying relations and relata, without denying that relations are real.

Suppose that someone holds a view of reality, as I do, which states it can be known in terms of three radical irreducibles: the existing world, its order, and the origin of world and order. Using the language appropriate for ultimate references, such a view of reality could be articulated with reference to God as Creator, the world as creation, and the order as creation order.[8] In my view there is no problem of maintaining the ultimate and radical irreducibility of these three references. If God is not some sort of creature and no creature is God, and if God is in no way creaturely and nothing creaturely is divine, so that God and creature are mutually irreducible, it would still be possible to say that both are there and both are real. Such a commitment to the reality of both does not commit me to the reality of "reality" as a separate entity, which is instantiated both in the case of God and in the case of creatures. God and creatures can be real, can be mutually irreducible, and can be radically irreducible. The same thing can be said about God and order, and about order and creation.

This position can also be maintained while knowing that God and creatures are in relation. Their being in relation does not make them into one basic sort of thing, namely, relata. God can be God to creatures; conditions can also condition creatures. Order can be ordered by God. Creatures can be subject to order. Such a view does not entail the separate reality of relations or relata. All it entails is a view about how these three are real *together*. The presence of these three together does not add anything. Such a view does not require the reality of relations apart from relata or the reality of relations as either God, conditions, or conditioned. These three can be in relation, relation can be real, these three can be radically irreducible, and yet there need not be separate entities called relations apart from these three.

The preceding discussion should not be taken to be an explanation or an account of relations. Rather, it is intended as an explication of my understanding and use of the term *relation*. It sets forth in a reasonable manner what I know relations to be and what role I believe they play in my view of things.[9] I have said that the term *relation* refers us to something real. Yet I have not wished to say there are separately identifiable realities called relations. Meaningful, sensible things can be said about relationship. But in the end we return to the mystery. If we simply had the world, its order, and its origin, irreducible and by themselves, we would not have the world and world origin I know and to which I am committed.

My view of relations stems from my commitment. Thus I am committed to working on a view which allows for the Creator, the order of creation, and creation to be there for each other, without thereby having to add another basic reality or without reducing these three to the one reality of relating relata. These three are related and so is all diversity within them. Relationship is everywhere but has no separate being. Everywhere, relationships have the character of the relating realities. Without those elements between or among which relations exist, there would be no relations. To say that all things relate is simply to say in a very general way that all that is there, is there actively, doing something together in concert. Reality is something (re-ality is thing-like) and reality is work-like (is *wirk-lich*). Reality as relating is realities referring to, going back and forth among, each other. Whatever is there is active in its own way, God acting divinely, order being orderly, and creatures behaving creaturely, all relating to one another in their own way.[10]

I have been able to say rational things about relations, but I have also concluded that relation is a mystery. But people generally will not use the term *mystery* to refer to their inability to explain relations. They will use more philosophical terms, such as *indefinable*, or *basic given*. They may call *relation* a primitive term. Or they might say they can clarify, by means of examples, what is meant. Armstrong notes that philosophers "have often been puzzled by relations" (USR2, 76). Stebbing says that it "does not seem possible to define *relation* without presupposing notions no less in need of definition. All that we can do is to make some observations that will help us to grasp what exactly a relation is" (166). In my view, however, this inability to define relations is the same as what I mean by relation being a mystery.

5.2 Part-Whole Relations

Without defining relations, I believe I have sufficiently clarified what they are. I can now proceed to discuss three philosophically important relations, that is, relations significant to all that exists. One of these is the part-whole relation, whose main importance lies in an ongoing controversy. Can a whole be explained by the properties of its parts, or is a whole more than the sum of its parts? The second, the enkapsis relation, is an innovation of Dooyeweerd. He developed it in order to do justice to some apparent part-whole relations which mislead us when we treat them as such. Upon further analysis these relations turn out to be quite different from the part-whole relations.[11] And the third, the subject-object relation, is traditionally important in epistemology as the relation for the knower-known scheme. I will first look at part-whole relations, then the new enkaptic relations, and finally the subject-object relations.[12]

Examples of the part-whole relation abound: window frame and window, arm and body, rod and piston, and engine and car. The last examples show a progressive series of parts, all of which belong to a whole. Parts can indeed have further parts. But can parts ever be genuine wholes? Are pistons and engines true wholes in one context and true parts in another? I believe there is some significance in raising this sort of question. A proper understanding of the part-whole relation is important not only for analysis, but also for everyday experience.

Here are two examples of everyday significance, based on the fact that people have accepted certain theoretic views. These examples also testify indirectly to the fact that theoretic understanding of the part-whole relation is important. Suppose a nation upholds the view that the state is a whole, of which all citizens are parts in all their relations. The state, in such a view, might be an organism; and families, businesses, churches, schools, individuals, and so forth, are the parts. As a whole, the state embraces all of these other relations. In this view—which in my opinion is mistaken—the government has a basis for meddling in any affairs whatsoever. The government of the state assumes government of the whole, whose parts comprise all the other social relations.

Now suppose we take the opposite view. One might think that in human society there are only individuals; no real social structures exist in society. Reality consists solely of individuals who sustain various relations. I believe this view is also misguided. There would be very little basis to counter the arguments that whatever the individuals wanted would be proper. Both views—that the state has overall power to finally decide all issues, or that there is no reality to any social structures except the individual wills of the people—can serve to destroy genuine social interaction. In our time they provide the backdrop for the endless seesaw between civil libertarians who hold the will of each individual to be sacred, and governments who see no limits to their power. A nuanced view of the reality of wholes might break through such an impasse.

In the world of science we can also find a prominent example of the signifance of the part-whole relation. *Gestalt* thinking, holistic thinking, and systems thinking are recently in vogue. This partly is a result of earlier analysis of wholes that did not take the point of view of the whole in analyzing the parts, and which to certain scholars has proven to be misleading. Consequently, some have taken up the vitalism-mechanism controversy again and there is considerable discussion surrounding the revival of that debate. Polanyi has contributed much to this discussion.[13] In understanding organisms, he says, we cannot reject the view that, as wholes, they differ from the mere mechanical relations among material systems which are not genuine wholes. He argues that even machines, as mechanical systems, are wholes which cannot be explained merely by taking into account the various properties of their parts. Polanyi demonstrates how a difference in view about the nature of a whole can have significant consequences. It may, for example, alter our chances of reaching a satisfactory conclusion to an important problem.

So, a correct view of the part-whole relationship has its importance. But it is also hard to achieve. In the Gestalt school of psychology, one doctrine has been the cornerstone of all significant insights: a whole is more than the sum of its parts. Many important contributions have been based solely on the consequences and implications of this doctrine. So, if that doctrine is correct, is it not impossible for anything to be both a part and a whole? Are they not irreducible correlates, like functors and functions? Or are the properties of parts and wholes interchangeable, so that what in some contexts is a part, would in other contexts be a whole?

From this perspective, a piston might be a part of an engine as a whole, even though the engine might be a part of a car. Or, the problem could be even more complicated. Is there a difference between the doctrine of the parts and the whole and the doctrine of the functions of a functor? The one thing known as a whole is, in fact, a whole or a unity in a great diversity. Cars have engines, doors, wheels, and windows. If this were not the case, then there would not be a part-whole problem. But is there a difference between the car's functions and the car's parts?[14] And is there really a difference between what we call a whole and what we call a functor? Is *whole* not just a word for the functional integrality of a functor?

Langer treats parts as constituents differing from other elements in a totality. "Since the related 'parts' of a structure may not be parts at all, but may be physically inseparable qualities, aspects, locations, or what not, just as well as actual ingredients, I shall not refer to them as related *parts*, but as *elements* of the structure" (47). Langer apparently believes that parts are not just any diversities within a unity; they are specific sorts of diversities. She does not view members of a class, for example, as parts (113). Of course, Langer is not just playing a word game. One might conceivably argue that the elements of a molecule are also its parts, and chemists speak of atomic entities as elements. Hence, Langer would be wrong.

But that is not the point. Obviously Langer is indicating how she finds the term *parts* to be inadequate; in her opinion it does not name all the diversity that exists within the context of some entity. In the case of classes, her point is clear. A class does comprise the entire collection of its members. But together they do not constitute a whole, although one might say they are the whole class. This use of the term *whole* simply indicates completeness or entirety. But apart from those members, there is nothing of which they are parts, not a whole constituted by parts. The class of all people is nothing more than the sum of all of its members.

Let us consider Langer's statement again. She implicitly distinguished the part-whole relation from a good number of other relations and pointed out how these other relations should not be taken as a part-whole relations. What we understand parts to be, apparently does not apply to certain aspects of a thing. The location of an entity is not taken in any straightforward way to be a part of the entity. Langer seems to think that parts must be physically separable. In itself this is hardly applicable to all parts, unless she means they must be separable whether or not it causes the death or destruction of the entity. But the physical separation of the brain is quite a different matter from taking a tire off a car. Otherwise, her point seems generally well taken.

But what happens if we reverse her perspective? What are now called parts would not allow us to refer to aspects or qualities as parts. But what if I were to suggest that parts are aspects? And in terms of my own approach, what would happen if I suggested that parts are functions? If one makes a study of the increasing complexity of reality as one moves from the physical realm, through the organic, to animal, and to human existence, many of the parts we recognize are no more than a special physical integration of various functions. These parts provide a foundation for increasing functional specialization. From a mere photosensitive cell we move all the way to an eye. Being photosensitive is a function of a cell. Why could the eye also not be a function of an animal or a person? Is there a good reason to suppose that the relation of the whole to its parts is at best a mere specification of the relation of a functor to its functions?

Perhaps the best way to approach this problem is simply to confront it as a question of the relation of a unit to its constituents. We can do this without first settling the question whether whole and functor are parallels, and whether part and function are parallels. Then later we can return to that more specific issue. The problem still perplexes contemporary scholars. Popper offers this remark about the theory of social wholes: "I do not assert that it is mistaken. I only assert the complete triviality of its content" (Adorno, PD, 297). Consequently he sees no problem in reducing social units to their constituent elements. When Adorno writes that the whole is nothing *apart* from its members, Popper takes that to mean no more than: there are social relationships (Adorno, PD, 297).

This Popperian sentiment is reflected in the thought of many scholars who maintain a positivist orientation. Hempel echoes similar thoughts: "If a characteristic of a whole is counted as emergent simply if its occurrence cannot be inferred from a knowledge of all the properties of its parts, then, as Grelling has pointed out, no whole can have any emergent characteristics" (ASE, 260). By emergent characteristics Hempel means characteristics of a whole which cannot be explained by laws used to explain the parts of that whole. Emergent phenomena exist on a new level that cannot be explained on a lower one. Hempel apparently does not agree with the point that is made by emergentists. He says their claim is not rational; they do not allow the laws and terms used on the new level to be entered into the resources used to make the explanation.

But this is exactly the point. New directions *not present on the old level* cannot be explained unless we introduce new terms, new concepts, and new explanatory devices. As is evident from his support for Grelling, Hempel thinks that the whole can always be explained from the laws pertaining to its aspects, parts, and functions, so long as we introduce enough of those laws on enough levels. But the doctrine of the whole and its parts does not make the absurd claim that the whole is not explainable. This doctrine only asserts that it requires more principles of explanation than those which only apply to its parts.

Let me give a simple mechanical example, one which adopts the same level of analysis as Hempel. The game called Lego, which is intended for children of all ages, consists of many kinds of building blocks. Some are simply plastic squares and rectangles, others are spheres. Althogether there is a great variety of shapes. These shapes may become parts of anything an imaginative child may build.[15] But from the properties of the building blocks one cannot possibly deduce what the child will build.

But now the child brings an imagined plan, a structure, to those blocks and integrates them according to the structural demands of the plan. Once the blocks are put together and understood in the context of the final structure, it will be fairly easy to explain the whole from the blocks that are now its parts. But that is precisely because the whole has been brought into the picture. Its point of view now enters the explanation. Without the introduction of the whole, however, the parts were not even parts of that whole. And then the whole is analyzed, the parts receive a certain definition from being contained within the structure of that whole. The whole qualifies the parts and is, furthermore, assumed in accounting for the whole as a whole. The whole is not simply more than the sum of its parts; it is something entirely and irreducibly different from what the parts might, in total, produce.

Once again, this is more than just a semantic issue. When Stebbing discusses difficulties associated with the making of an "assertion about the whole of the class or about part of the class" (46), she is not, in fact, discussing my problem, although semantically this might well seem to be the case. Her discussion makes good sense in English, but she is assuming the terms *part* and *whole* to have different meanings than I do here. One can use *part* in the sense of a slice, a portion, or a piece. In an investigation of an airline crash we might hear this expression: "Parts of the plane were found at great distances from the place of impact." The term *parts* may refer then to the items one gets in the parts department of the repair shop, but most likely it refers to fragments. From the expression, "The whole crowd moved forward at once," we know that all the people moved forward. But the crowd is not a whole in the sense in which I am now using that concept. The conceptual and nonsemantic issue being discussed here concernscon-*stituent* elements of an integrally *unified* entity; we are looking at an *organized totality*.[16]

The existence of these wholes, of course, is disputed by philosophers like Hempel. Popper also rejects this concept, although his disagreement may be limited to social wholes. But there are also contemporary scholars who strongly subscribe to the concept. Polanyi states that "the understanding of a whole appreciates the coherence of its subject matter and thus acknowledges the existence of a value that is absent from the constituent particulars" (PK, 327). Laszlo agrees with this point: "The concept of *wholeness* defines the character of the system as such, in contrast to the character of its parts in isolation. A whole possesses characteristics which are not possessed by its parts singly. Insofar as this is the case, therefore, the whole is other than the simple sum of its parts" (SP, 36). However, he dismisses any "mystical interpretation" of the doctrine (SP, 38). And finally, Maslow expressed his opinion on the matter as follows: ". . . a quality of wholeness is something which pervades the whole and is lost by dissecting" (62).

Armstrong discusses this problem in terms of the reality of conjunctive properties. These are not new properties in addition to the properties which make up the conjunctive property (USR2, 30). They are not properties "over and above their conjuncts" (USR2, 31). He does, however, allow for two features of conjunctive properties that go a long way toward explaining the doctrine of the whole and its parts, namely, first that they may be conjoined nomically and thus be structural properties (USR2, 36-38), and secondly that the causal power of conjunctive properties differs from the separate powers of the properties combining to form the conjunct (USR2, 35). Since Armstrong's most powerful argument for the reality of properties is their causal power, he seems to overlook his own doctrine that different causal powers point to different properties (USR2, 44). Even though he denies the doctrine that the whole differs from the sum of its parts, he expresses it when he allows conjunct properties to have different causal powers and he reinforces it when he allows conjunct properties to have the force of laws.

I conclude two things about a part-whole relation in its technical sense. First, the whole is not just a collection or aggregate. It is an integrally organized unity in which the complexity of the diverse and constituent elements all have different roles to play. These roles all enhance the unity of the one entity and its particular purposes and requirements. The many constituents all form a coherent and diverse entity.[17]

Second, the unity of the resultant whole is other than what the constituent elements could constitute by themselves as an aggregate.

The whole is more than, other than, over and above, or in addition to, the sum of the parts. A whole is an integrated, or integral, coherent totality that, as an individual unit, characterizes all of its parts. It has a unique identity as a whole simply because all of its parts function within a pattern of coherence and unity, although each does so in its own way. The structure of the whole is such that the order of the whole appoints the parts as *its* parts; the parts themselves have no meaningful existence separate from that whole.[18]

At the same time there is no whole apart from its parts. A part is in itself something which is not separate or independent from the whole, but does make its own peculiar and necessary contribution to the whole. It has a character all its own. A part of something is in this sense not a mere particle or piece. It is a functioning and functional contributor to the totality. It is a function which has been crystallized into a concrete and permanent member of a body. It cannot function alone; its existence is not meaningful outside of the whole. At the same time the whole is lost, damaged, or incomplete without the part.[19]

Let me now return to the two problems mentioned earlier. First, are parts and wholes interchangeable in different contexts? Second, is there a similarity between the part-whole relation and the functor-function relation? Building on the discussion to this point, I can begin to deal with these issues. Can parts sometimes be wholes? Can wholes sometimes be parts? This question can only be partially covered in this section. The problem of whether there are apparently "independent" entities—entities capable of independent existence in their own right, functioning while being included in the existence of another entity—will be discussed in the next section on enkapsis. In this section, however, progress can be made concerning whether a part can sometimes be a whole.

Wholes that function as parts, or apparently function as parts, will be said to be functioning in enkapsis. Parts functioning as wholes—the concern to be settled now—do not really exist. The point worth remembering is that in order to be a genuine whole, the part to be functioning as a whole would have to exist apart from a whole and function independently, as a functor in its own right. And there are simply no examples of such parts. A piston is part of an engine. But an engine, although it has parts, is not a whole. For an engine does not exist meaningfully apart from a car or some other machine which needs an engine. An engine is a part of a machine that needs to do work. An engine is a complex part, but that does not make it a whole.

What about the possibility of interpreting wholes as functors? Stated in this way, a problem does not actually exist. Certainly no whole can exist, yet not be a functor. Nor can there be any question whether there are any functors that have no parts. All wholes are functors and all functors have parts. One question remains: Do some functors display a diversity within their unity of more than parts? Or rather, is the diversity within the functor a diversity of parts in *addition* to a diversity of functions? Is there a difference between functions and parts?

To answer this question I think we can best look upon the whole-part relation as one in which any complexity of either properties or things displays a structure, such that a nomic configuration conditions the arrangement of interrelating elements. In that structure the function of all elements is directed by the role they play in the configured boundaries. And that configuration can never be explained or accounted for simply by the summative qualities of all the elements separately. If we look upon the part-whole relation in this way, we need not necessarily limit it to the physical parts of a physical thing.[20] The meaning of *parts* need not be limited to the sort of gross physical entities made available in the stock rooms of manufacturers. A whole will be anything capable of separate meaningful existence whose elements are bound in a nomic configuration. And a part will be anything whose meaningful reality is limited to the role it plays within the boundaries of a whole. The heart can be a part to a human being. But so can the aorta be a part to a heart. A genuine part can never be a whole, since as whole it could exist meaningfully on its own and thus not be a part. But parts can have parts.

What we may finally say, thus, is that to be a genuine whole, something must be capable of independent existence as an independently functioning unit, that is, a functor. But the part-whole relation extends to the elements of parts. Any element both constitutive of and dependent on a nomically configured complexity will be a part.

5.3   *Enkaptic Relations*

One specific problem which needs more attention than it was given in the previous section is: Can wholes sometimes be parts? Genuine, actual parts can never be wholes. My definition of the term *part* implies that a part cannot exist by itself, separate from the whole. But what can we say about wholes that sometimes appear to function in a part-whole relation? These wholes may play a special role in the context of a larger whole. And the larger whole may relate to the lesser whole just as it does to genuine parts. How, for example, do we conceptually relate to the place of a person in a family? We usually say that persons are members (parts) of a family. But are families wholes? Persons do function as functors, and not as functions; a person is not a function of a family.

Is the function of membership in a family, however, the same as being a part of the family? Are persons like arms and legs? This is not really possible, because arms and legs cannot exist apart from persons, but persons can exist quite well without being mothers or fathers. Do all structured wholes present the part-whole structure? Is a person a part of a family? Or is a family not a genuine whole? Do all totalities that have numerous elements necessarily have *parts* as their diversity?

At the end of the previous section, we saw that in a complexity not all elements are like parts. Then do not all of the elements within a whole need to be parts of the whole? Can other wholes belong to a whole? Here is the problem: What do we do with that class of relationships in which independent wholes are clearly indispensible elements in another whole and are, in their functioning within that other whole, apparently bound by it? These relationships, in particular, are the ones we meet so often in society. Persons, as independent, individual entities, relate to wholes, which in turn structure their roles as persons. People as functoral wholes enter into relations which have structures that clearly bind and limit people's functions within the relation. These structured relations behave to their elements as wholes do to parts. I am thinking of marriage and family, or state and citizenship, for example. This sort of relation also figures in ecological problems. Is a tree part of a forest as well as a part of the environment? Is the environment a genuine whole? If you alter the environment, can individuals survive?

The question comes down to this: Are there wholes that have among their constituent elements some phenomena which strike us as parts, but are clearly wholes with their own functoral unity? If a family is a whole, or an environment, or a state, then there seem to be such wholes, for they apparently have persons and other individual functoral entities as their constituents. And if they are wholes, we can ask whether these particular, constituent elements are parts.

What is a whole? In the previous section I concluded that a whole is an integrated, coherent totality which, as an individual unit of functioning, characterizes all of its constituent elements. It *is* a whole simply because all of these elements function in this coherent and integrated way. All of the parts are subsumed under the dominant structure of the whole. The structure that integrates all of the constituent elements provides for the completely "other" character of the whole. That structure will constantly and invariably direct all of the constituent elements to serve the coherent whole.

If this is indeed the character of wholes, then families, states, and chess clubs are, in fact, wholes. But then what are the constituent elements of wholes—only parts and other functions, or also other wholes? Do families, states, and environmental wholes also have functors as their constituent elements? Do persons belong to families as constituent elements?

In the earlier discussion of functors and functions, the larger wholes that integrate functions and interrelate functors were never called functors. A person is a functor and so is a frog. But a family is not, and neither is a state. Families and states appear to be structural wholes, but not functors. One characteristic of a genuine functor is that it be an independent unit of action with actual physical functions. A genuine functor must have weight, for example, and it must take up space. But families do not have weight or size: a six hundred-pound family or a seven-yard family is nonsense. And it also seems no more than a figure of speech to say that a family is an actual functor, itself an action center, capable of independent, centered functioning.

I want to distinguish wholes that are functors and have parts from wholes that integrate functors. In the second instance, the whole that is the functor does not get submerged into the whole that integrates functors. We might say that it is not really persons who are members of a family but mothers. And persons are not members of the state; citizens are members. Of course, citizens and mothers are persons functioning in a certain capacity. If they did not play these roles, then there would be no families or states. But as mothers and citizens, people are, in these functions, integrated into wholes such as families and states. The whole person is a mother and the whole person is a citizen, even though each of these roles is only one of the many functions they perform.

Now, when we have what seems to be a structure into which functors are integrated because they play an indispensable role, I will call it an *enkaptic* relation.[21] The word is derived from the Greek term for enfolding. In the relationship between a functor and this type of complex structural relation, the functor can be viewed as "folded into" the relation. In that role it temporarily suspends other roles which it could play in different contexts. I am not suggesting that persons can be persons without having a number of these enkaptic roles. Nor am I saying that persons cease being persons when they take on these roles. My point is simply that a functor, a whole, functions in the context of such a complex structure without becoming a part of that structure. A person suspends his or her full range of possibilities by serving the complex structural relationship in which the role is played. A person can be removed from a family without ceasing to be a person. The same cannot be said about a genuine part, such as an arm or an eye. The part-whole relation is a special instance of a wider relation, here called an enkaptic relation.

I should make it clear that I have indicated only one kind of enkaptic relation. There are also enkaptic relations between full functors, rather than between nonfunctoral wholes (family) and functors. Thus, the relations between material elements (atoms and molecules) and cells is such a relation. Molecules functioning in a cell do not lose any of their character as physical functors. They are only temporarily bound by (enfolded into) the organism. The relation, again, is an enkaptic one. A genuine whole temporarily functions in the context of another genuine whole; it suspends its independent possibilities by serving the whole into which it is enkaptically bound. So molecules are not genuine *parts* of a cell.

So I conclude as follows. The relation between elements of a complexity which displays a structure subject to a nomic configuration is broad. Its main character is that the elements of the complexity function integrally in such a way that the total functioning of the complexity cannot be accounted for by the characteristics of the elements or their arrangement. One example of this relation I will call enkaptic. And the part-whole relation is another example of this relation in which the complex structure is a functor, that is, one of the primary action units which as such are members of either the physical, vegetative, animal, or human realms. Of the many relations of this broad kind, only some are part-whole relations.[22] Others are enkaptic relations.

5.4   Subject-Object Relations

The last special relation to be discussed is that of the subject to the object, a well-known focal point for discussion in epistemological literature. The terms *object* and *objective* as well as *subject* and *subjective* have many meanings. A study of their history and the ways in which they relate, though helpful, cannot be attempted in this context. I will only mention the more obvious meanings.

Object as a noun refers to the object of a verb in a sentence; a thing; anything known by a knower, except that which is in, or of, the knower who does the knowing. *Object* as a verb means being opposed to something. *Objective* can mean a goal to be achieved, or the state of being detached and unprejudiced in one's opinions; it can also refer to conditions that prevail apart from all subjectivity or individual arbitrariness. Many of these meanings have been pivotal in the history of philosophy, although these terms have often been misused.

Subject, as a noun, can refer to the subject of a sentence, a project for study, spoken or written material, something to talk about, a person, a knower, inner states, or mental states. As a verb, *subject* means to put under one's rule. *Subjective* refers to something personal, private, or not dependable. As not dependable it is characteristic of something that is under the rule of conditions outside of itself, yet which does not sufficiently bring those conditions into account.

5.4.1   *The epistemological subject-object relation*

The relation that has been particularly important philosophically is the one in which the subject-object relation has been conceived in the context of the knower-known relation. Traditionally the knowing subject (mind, reason, soul, understanding, spirit, perceptive behavior) in this relationship has been viewed both as merely subjective, private, individual, and personal, *and* as objective and constitutive. Its knowledge of the object could be subjective, but it could also be objective. In the latter sense, objective knowledge could be understood to be valid and impersonal, but also to be constituting the object. On the basis of ambiguities in the history of this theme as well as in the conceptions themselves, many mutually contradictory views have been held. In general, many philosophers have wanted to establish the absolute objectivity of knowledge. Today there are more and more people who wish to demonstrate that all knowledge is by definition subjective, that is, it is the knowledge of a knower.

Let us assume that the most prevalent and dominant tradition of understanding the subject-object relation in Western thought gives us an interpretation of that relation as a knower-known relation. What sorts of acceptable insights can be found in this interpretation? I can agree at least that there are knowers and things known, that is, knowers, knowing, and knowns. Among the knowns are mostly things that themselves are neither knowers nor knowings; we know mostly phenomena that lie outside the realm of knowing.

But one might say that, at least within traditional epistemological approaches, some of the phenomena known are concepts and similar abstractions. We might use the term *known knowings*. Within Western epistemological traditions one could say there are thinkers, thoughts, and things thought about. And most of the things thought about are neither thoughts nor thinkers. This seems to be an agreeable proposition. Accepting it does not imply a commitment to minds and material objects as the only things in existence.

I would like to look at one possible implication of the idea that there are thinkers, thoughts, and things thought about, and that things thought about can be thinkers, thoughts, and whatever else there is in the world. We can place this discussion in the framework of my previously developed categories. Some functors will function in a way that is predominantly analytical; the analysis is mostly directed at nonanalytical reality, although it can also be directed at analytical reality. In many situations one can be satisfied with an analysis which demands an analytical subject and an analytical object (both in the grammatical and logical sense). But something that can be thought about (grammatically: the object of thought) can itself be the subject (in the grammatical sense).

When in the latter case the various senses of subjective and objective become confused, we are presented with a difficult puzzle: subjective knowledge (i.e., knowledge of—subjective genetive—a subject) can be objective. Knowing *as* done by a subject is, in that sense, subjective. Knowing, in the case of a specific object, can be (if the object is respected) objective. If the object is a subject (the knower is a known), will the knowing be objective, subjective, or both? For if the object is a subject, it can also be respected.

Puzzles like this arise when shifts in meaning occur. When we call knowledge objective, we often intend to say more than "the knower is respectful of the object." Such objective knowledge is often regarded as no longer subjective. The knowledge, apart from being merely valid, might even become the origin of validity. The origin of this trend in Western thought stems from the epistemological revolution in Hellenistic thought, which proclaimed the knowing subject to be the origin of order.[23] In this sense the term *objective* means something very different from merely "being of an object" (objective genetive). Objective now means "not subjective," but in the sense of being a universal standard of validity.

Two fundamental meanings of the term *objective* are traded off here. If knowledge of an object is called objective and what is meant is "of an object" as in objective genetive, then the knowledge remains subjective as well, that is, it is also the knowledge of a subject (subjective genetive). And this has to be honored epistemologically as subjectivity in all theories of knowing. When knowledge is taken to be objective (i.e., not subjective in any sense), it takes on the character of knowledge without a subject. It becomes knowledge not in need of a knower. Knowings arise without knowers; knowings arise that are not known. Objective knowledge becomes possibly unknown knowledge binding on all knowers as a standard of validity.

When we look at the uses of *object(ive)* and *subject(ive)* in literature which assumes that these terms have commonly accepted unproblematic meanings, it turns out upon examination that the problems are surprisingly many. This is not so much the case in documents that set out to deal with the problem and in which the terms are both carefully defined and consistently used. It appears more frequently in more damaging situations which assume an innocent use but which unwittingly create confusion.

W. Köhler introduces the technical term: *objective experience*. What is experienced objectively is experienced as outside myself, Köhler suggests. This experience is also defined to be independent of myself. "When . . . I use the term 'objective experience' it will always have this meaning. For instance a chair as an objective experience will be something there outside, hard, stable, and heavy. Under no circumstances will it be something merely perceived, or in any sense subjective phenomenon" (GP, 16).

This explanation appears to be straightforward and commonly accepted. But it seems to beg a question: Why is a chair an objective *experience*, and why is it not just an objective *entity*? If we say it is experience of a chair that we are after, and not just the chair, then another question needs to be asked. Can experience *as* experience be objective at all? Can there truly be an experience (if that description *is* intended) that is not "in any sense" subjective? Is the experience of the chair "objective" in the same sense in which the existence of the chair, independent of my experience of it, is also objective?

This somewhat misleading use of the term *objective* is still very common. Laszlo uses it to introduce two fundamental perspectives on systems of the world. He distinguishes a physical realm of "scientifically observable objective events" and a mental realm of "mind events" correlated to "cognitive systems." The mind events are ones which "can only be observed by introspection and which make up the immediate, felt experience of each of us" (SP, 119). The tension between these two realms should be obvious. The cognitive systems of which Laszlo speaks must, of necessity, include science. But the objectivity of the world, he says, is scientifically observable. Science, however, as a cognitive system, will have to be part of the world of introspection. Once we radically divide the objective realm, which is physical, from the subjective, which is mental, the place of objective knowledge becomes uncertain.

One often gets the impression that, in this area of concern, terms are used in a random fashion. They are employed without a sense of the problems involved, and thus uncritically. As a result, we see usages which, upon reflection, almost appear to be nonsensical. For example, Imre Lakatos, in his debate with Popper and Kuhn, makes this statement: ". . . *the—rationally constructed—growth of science takes place essentially in the world of ideas, in Plato's and Popper's 'third world'*, in the world of articulated knowledge which is independent of knowing subjects" (180). What are we to make of *articulated knowledge* apart from *knowing subjects?* Essentially, Lakatos is introducing unknown knowledge. But unknown knowledge is an impossibility. Using an Aristotelian figure, one could perhaps speak of unknown knowers as an analogue of unmoved movers. But unknown knowledge is an impossibility; it would be equivalent to an unmarried spouse. Knowledge is what is known. Nothing *can* be known without being known by knowers.

Is it any wonder that in the same context in which Lakatos's comment arose, Kuhn is becoming confused about the meaning of objectively known entities? In bewilderment he writes: "But is sensory experience fixed and neutral? Are theories simply man-made interpretations of given data? The epistemological viewpoint that has most often guided Western philosophy for three centuries dictates an immediate and unequivocal, Yes! In the absence of a developed alternative, I find it impossible to relinquish entirely that viewpoint. Yet it no longer functions effectively, and the attempts to make it do so through the introduction of a neutral language of observations now seem to me hopeless" (SSR, 126). Kuhn's bewilderment is not so strange if we consider that, in the brief discussion so far, we have already met views of knowledge as "unknown" and of "objectivity" as a species of subjectivity.

Thus, we see two odd notions, one of unknown knowledge (Lakatos) and the other of objective science as a subjective system (Laszlo). Both notions reappear and are explicitly defended in Hempel's view of objectivity, stated in terms of intersubjectivity, and in Popper's view of objective truth. Popper consistently speaks of objectivity when he discusses standards of truth to which all our subjective knowledge must appeal. Such standards are then referred to as objective truth. Popper discusses this theme in the context of his explicitly stated awareness that it is difficult to hold that knowledge is human *and* that it can be objective, that is, having to do with standards.[24] Popper makes this bold assertion: ". . . the objective theory of truth . . . allows us to make assertions such as the following: a theory may be true even though nobody believes it, and even though we have no reason for accepting it, or for believing that it is true . . ." (CR, 225). As we noted in the work of Lakatos, this notion suggests there are theories that no one, in fact, entertains.

Hempel's attempts to save objectivity by means of intersubjectivity are also fraught with the dangers of irresolvable conflict: "A rational reconstruction of the standards of scientific validation . . . has to be based on objective criteria" (ASE, 10). Obviously no "subjective matter" can provide such a basis. Thus he is looking for transsubjective standards or nonsubjective reality. However, in his dealing explicitly with different understandings of objectivity, a problem emerges. He first states an underlying agreement between two camps (one of them his own). He then says both have emphasized experiential meaning "as a necessary condition of objectively significant discourse" (ASE, 123). Experience, a subjective matter, becomes a ground for genuine objectivity. *Subjectivity* becomes a *condition* for *objectivity*.

In order to save objectivity, Hempel appears to move in the opposite direction from Popper. Popper cuts objectivity loose from its relation to subjectivity; in contrast, Hempel develops objectivity in terms of subjectivity. Objective, scientific knowledge becomes objective "in the sense of being intersubjectively certifiable" (ASE, 141). Subjectivity is simply a constituent of objectivity, or perhaps objectivity is even a kind of subjectivity. "What matters is, I think, to be aware of the extent to which subjective factors enter into the application of a given set of concepts," says Hempel, "and to aim at a gradual reduction of their influence" (ASE, 146). There is no evidence that the reduction, in his view, is heading towards elimination.

Thus, we find Hempel and Popper trying to save the notion of objectivity in its more traditional sense by, in essence, aggravating its inherent tensions. Other contemporary philosophers have been more candid in acknowledging a more fundamental impasse in traditional notions of objectivity. They have engaged in radical attempts to reform the concept of objectivity. The work of Abraham H. Maslow and Michael Polanyi is part of that trend toward the development of an entirely new frame of reference for the treatment of objectivity.

Maslow tries to describe a kind of objectivity other than the scientific variety, which he views more or less in traditional terms. "Briefly stated, my thesis is: if you love something or someone enough at the level of Being, then you can enjoy its actualization of itself, which means that you will not want to interfere with it, since you love it as it is in itself. You will then be able to perceive it in a noninterfering way, which means leaving it alone. This in turn means that you will be able to see it as is, uncontaminated by your selfish wishes, hopes, demands, anxieties, or preconceptions. Since you love it as it is in itself, neither will you be prone to judge it, use it, improve it, or in any other way to project your own values into it" (116). Maslow here develops a notion of objectivity in which the subject is not eliminated; it relates to the object by letting it be itself, and by not maintaining it in a subjective manner.

Polanyi develops a rather elaborate, alternate theory of objectivity, one which also touches on science, in *Personal Knowledge*. His first three chapters deal with objectivity, probability, and order. If we are after objective knowledge, Polanyi argues, then based on a certain view and according to certain criteria, we must rely on theory. "It seems to me that we have sound reasons for thus considering theoretical knowledge as more objective than immediate experience" (4). But as Polanyi moves on, he finds that an honest consideration of the facts leads him to a problem. Theory itself is inescapably subjective. "Speaking more generally, we may say that there are always some conceivable scruples which scientists customarily set aside in the process of verifying an exact theory. Such acts of personal judgment form an essential part of science" (20).

Polanyi concludes that objectivity functions within our experience in a way that cannot be cut loose from our subjectivity. "On these grounds I suggest, quite generally, that the appraisal of order is an act of personal knowledge, exactly as is the assessment of probability to which it is allied" (36). As he comes to the conclusion of this opening section, Polanyi envisions a solution. "We see emerging here a substantial alternative to the usual disjunction of objective and subjective statements . . . [and] we may yet avoid the sterility and confusion imposed by these traditional categories" (48). In the last paragraph he makes this statement: "It is the act of commitment in its full structure that saves personal knowledge from being merely subjective. Intellectual commitment is a responsible decision, in submission to the compelling claims of what in good conscience I conceive to be true" (65). In the second section, which deals with the tacit dimension of knowledge, Polanyi then asserts: "But both *verification* and *validation* are everywhere an acknowledgement of a commitment: they claim the presence of something real and external to the speaker" (202).

In the third section of his book, Polanyi sets out to justify this personal knowledge. He assesses what he has achieved to this point: "By now I have surveyed a series of facts which seriously suggest a reappraisal of our capacity to acquire knowledge. This reappraisal demands that we credit ourselves with much wider cognitive powers than an objectivist conception of knowledge would allow, but at the same time it reduces the independence of human judgment far below that claimed for the traditionally free exercise of reason" (249). Polanyi then explains how a demand for precision in the new theory is misplaced, whether it be for precision in universal clarity of terms or in logical rigor. "When the act of meaning is thus brought home to a person exercising his understanding of things by the use of words which describe them, the possibility of performing the act according to strict criteria appears logically meaningless" (252). By saying this, however, Polanyi does not intend to issue license for sloppy thinking. He only asserts that "laying down precise rules for making or testing assertions of fact, is condemned to futility from the start" (254).

In the development of Polanyi's arguments, the chapter on "The Logic of Affirmation," which opens the third section, is particularly important. Here we find the crucial section on the *fiduciary program*, in which the function of belief is identified as the source of all knowledge (266). "This then is our liberation from objectivism: to realize that we can voice our ultimate convictions only from within our convictions—from within the whole system of acceptances that are logically prior to any assertion of our own, prior to the holding of any particular piece of knowledge" (267). Polanyi comes to this conclusion: "Innocently, we had trusted that we could be relieved of all personal responsibility for our beliefs by objective criteria of validity—and our own critical powers have shattered this hope" (268).

The last phrase, dealing with "our own critical powers," may still tie Polanyi in with the rationalist tradition of Western thought. For, on his own terms, it is not primarily his critical powers but his different faith that shattered the hope. But perhaps the polemical context can be a factor here; otherwise, it is clear what he intends. Here is Polanyi's own summary statement on the matter: "On such grounds as these, I think we may distinguish between the personal in us, which actively enters into our commitments, and our subjective states, in which we merely endure our feelings. This distinction establishes the conception of the *personal*, which is neither subjective nor objective. In so far as the personal submits to requirements acknowledged by itself as independent of itself, it is not subjective; but in so far as it is an action guided by individual passions, it is not objective either. It transcends the disjunction between subjective and objective" (300).

The very last paragraphs of Polanyi's book once again tempt us to interpret his overall thought as still within the context of the rationalist tradition in Western thought. If "every manifestation of life" is in fact a "knowledge of nature" (404-5) for Polanyi, then his specification of the uniqueness of humanity in terms of "the only centres of thought and responsibility" (405) leans heavily on a view of knowing as epitomized in thinking. However, his inner critique of rationalist conceptions of thinking would still give Polanyi a unique borderline position within the Western tradition on rationality. And at least his view of objectivity is fully extracted from traditional rationlist roots.

5.4.2 *Development of an alternative view*

Serious ambiguities are inherent in the traditional positions on subjectivity and objectivity. In addition, radical approaches to a solution are now being proposed. Let me first summarize what appear to be the three major problem areas. First, there are the problems related to standards of validity. Special problems arise in the area of standards of validity for knowledge. Second, problems are found in the association of "subjective" with "mental," and "objective" with "physical." Finally, there is the problem of relating grammatical subject-object relations to logical and ontological ones. Additional problems can probably be discussed in conjunction with these three, so I think this is a fairly accurate summary.

Let me begin to discuss the problem of objectivity and subjectivity in relation to the first problem—the nature of standards, criteria, laws, and conditions of validity for human behavior. We have no apparent reason to limit this problem of objectivity to the area of objective knowledge. We know, *prima facie*, that standards are to be met in many areas of human behavior, not just in epistemological matters. The evaluation of phenomena according to standards, and the possible controversy over the "objectivity" of these standards, is a problem in economics, the law, the arts, and a good many other areas. In any case, we commonly refer to supra-arbitrary, constant, transsubjective standards of judgment as "objective" standards. And the knowledge of such standards has come to be called objective knowledge. But knowledge validated by these standards has also come to be known as objective knowledge. Thus, we find there are views of knowledge which, in turn, suggest that all knowledge worthy of the name is objective in kind.

This now gives us three meanings for the term *objective*: having to do with standards that are supra-arbitrary; having to do with knowledge of such standards; and having to do with knowledge meeting such standards. If we further develop this argument from the viewpoint (not held by me) that standards are always rational standards by definition, then standards will be made conceptual or cognitive by definition.[25] As a consequence, the entire problem of objectivity and standards becomes a matter of epistemology. And since one cannot possibly conceive of knowledge without taking subjective dimensions into account, the arguments for rational objectivity appear contradictory. At the very least, the problem of standards, seen in the light of rational objectivity, becomes fraught with internal ambiguities.

Sometimes the relation of objectivity and standards can become further confused. This happens when we add the difficulties connected with the second set of problems, namely, those associated with the physical and mental realms: the realms of objectivity and subjectivity.[26] It is easy to see what complications will arise if objectivity is associated with both reason and physicality. However, the objectivity associated with the nonmental realm, and the subjectivity associated with the mental realm, usually has less to do with the validity of things than with their reality. Physical things are objectively real; mental things are only subjectively real. For that reason, physical reality may also give rise to more objective knowledge and so be raised once again as a standard (e.g., physics as a standard for all science). Knowledge of physical reality (i.e., of objects) is objective (i.e., of objects), while knowledge of mental reality is subjective (i.e., of subjective things).

The character of the known is transferred to the knower in this approach. Whereas in this view all knowledge should be subjective by virtue of being mental, only that of subjects is subjective, while knowledge of objects is objective. Once this view is superimposed on the first set of problems, described in the preceding paragraph, we have an irredeemably complex and confusing view of objectivity. Now subjective knowledge is drawn into the realm of "merely" subjective reality; then, by definition, no objective knowledge (meeting standards) can be had of subjective states. At the same time, standards, which are certainly not physical, will nevertheless parade as objective. And when standards become rational in the sense of a creation of the mind, mind becomes objective, although not physically real.

We could hardly expect this situation to become more confused, but it does. There is yet a third set of problems which can get drawn into the arena. In grammar, the distinction between the terms *subject* and *object* is that between an active actor and that towards which the action is directed and which passively suffers the action to be directed at it. The grammatical subject is thus different from the logical subject. And the ontological meaning of "subject" may be incompatible with both the logical and grammatical meanings. Yet the close relationship between semantic realities (words as names) and logical realities (words as concepts) in the grammar and logic of statements, sentences, and assertions can undermine the distinction between logical and semantic meanings.

It may seem foolhardy to attempt to disentangle this web of confusion. One can try to define clearly one's own use of certain terms, but the meanings that others habitually attach to these terms still cause difficulty. This problem is most evident when the intended meaning and the received meaning are irreconcilable. Nevertheless, I believe that any philosophical model which is intended to relate to its environment needs to have precise terms to distinguish between subjectivity and objectivity—even if these terms are somewhat confusing. And I might even add to that confusion when I introduce my own use of *subject* and *subjective*.

As will become clear, my usage will not always be easily accessible and certainly not very familiar in the present philosophical climate. I have so far used *subject* and *subjective* in the sense of whatever is subject to standards, subject to laws, limited by laws, or conforms to conditions. All things in the empirical world are subject to conditions that hold for them. As a result, I have referred to empirical existence as subjective existence. So whatever in our world is not a standard will herein be called a *subject* or a *subjective* existent. According to this definition, subjectivism would be the mistake of letting that which is subject to a standard serve as the standard itself.

But according to my view there is as such nothing wrong, or unreal, or undependable about subjectivity. Furthermore, in this view, the standards to which such subjective existence is to be subjected are not called objective standards. My use of the term *subjective* in relation to standards has nothing to do with what in my alternative approach I will call *objective*. What I will call *objects*, and whatever is *objective*, is not related to any view of standards. Moreover, subjectivity, in the sense of being subject to conditions, has nothing as such to do with subjectivity as it functions in the subject-object relation. In fact, in the view I will develop, both the subjects and the objects of the subject-object relation are subject to standards and thus, in that sense, can be called subjects.

So I use the terms *subject* and *subjective* with two quite unrelated meanings. In one case, subject is a correlative of law or condition, while in the other case subject is a correlative of object. In the former case, subject comes from the law-subject relation; in the other case from the subject-object relation. These two important relations both have a relatum referred to by the term *subject*. That seems confusing. However, we need to use these two senses of *subjective* and *subject* because they conform to common usage. To express what I have in mind, I cannot avoid these two meanings. When the basic relation between creatures and order is discussed, the notion of having to meet standards or nomic conditions is best expressed by the term *subjectivity*. And when the subject-object relation is discussed, the term *subject* should not, in that relation, be replaced by another term. This relation is well established, although conflicting notions of its meaning may still cloud the issues. I will distinguish the two uses by referring to subjects, as the correlates of conditions, as subjects$_1$; correlates of objects will be called subjects$_2$.

I can now begin to discuss the subject$_2$-object relation. What scope does this relation have? In our discussion so far, we have kept to what I perceive to be the case in the Western philosophical tradition: discussions of this relation are mostly limited to epistemology. In that context the subject$_2$ is always the knower, mind, reason, spirit, soul, consciousness, or cognizer. The object is seen to be that which differs from subjects$_2$ viewed in this way. The character of the epistemic object is: (a) that it is in a relation of being known or being knowable to the subject$_2$ who knows, cognizes, contemplates, or thinks; (b) that it itself is unable to do what the subject$_2$ does to it (viz., knowing); and (c) that in being known the object places limitations on the subject$_2$ who does the knowing.

The scope of this relation, whether or not the epistemological context defines it for us now, can be demonstrated to be much wider. If the s-o relations (as I will henceforth refer to it) is indeed characterized in the same fashion as the knower-known relation—namely, as an active agent relates to some passive phenomenon, an action of which the passive phenomenon is incapable, but in which the agent is limited by the passive phenomenon—then that relation has a very wide scope indeed. We buy and sell objects, we worship things, we see and hear entities, we kick a ball, we squeeze a lemon. In fact this relation might not even be limited to human experience. Animals also see and hear. Birds build nests, beavers build dams. Plants metabolize minerals. All of these relations do appear to have the same structure just described in the knower-known relation. Some $subject_2$ acts upon some object, the object is incapable of performing that sort of action, and the $subject_2$ is limited by the object. All of the objects have a special relation to their $subject_2$, and none of the objects is capable of performing the functions which the $subject_2$ performs in relation to it.

What sort of relation is this s-o relation? First of all, the specificity of the s-o relation is largely due to the object. It is not always the case that a $subject_2$ performs an action with respect to objects incapable of performing it themselves. Knowers need not only know entities which are incapable of knowing. One can know other knowers and one can even know oneself. In that case I would not say a $subject_2$ knew an object; this would only add more confusion. Rather, in a relationship in which one entity performs an action with respect to another, which the second could reciprocate, I will speak of a $subject_2$-$subject_2$ relation, henceforth an s-s relation.

A soccer player may kick a ball and be confident never to be kicked back by that ball. This is a s-o relation. But if he kicks a player—especially if he does it more than once to the same player—he may certainly expect to be kicked back! That is a s-s relation. So in the s-o relation one is concerned with entities that have a limited capacity with respect to an action performed. A functor functions as an acting $subject_2$ and acts toward or upon some entity (hence: object); in that relation the object does play a role characterized by the relationship. The knower knows an object and the object becomes a known. In the knower-known relation, the object plays an "as known" role.

Thus we can safely indicate as one of the characteristics of the relationship that the object is unable to perform the action that characterizes the relationship. But the object does take its own peculiar place in the relationship. A knife cannot kill or commit injustice. But it can become a murder weapon. Potassium cannot digest or metabolize, or generally feed or grow, yet it is an important ingredient for organic existence. DNA is an even better example. It is a chemical, a fully physical entity, and a macro-molecule. But it is never found except within the boundaries of a living organism; it is an organic object. It is an "organicized" physical entity. The object is placed in certain relations and contexts. In those relations it functions and plays roles that are peculiar for this relation to its $subject_2$. At times the object even takes on the characteristics of that relation. Organic chemicals are chemicals. They are fully physical. They obey physical laws. But they have taken on characteristics determined by their organic object functions, by their functioning as objects to the organism. Outside the organism such chemicals are never found.

We can add to this now that the object limits the relation; it restricts the actions of the subject$_2$. Iron ore can be sold for many purposes, but not for the use of snacks with cocktails. A small penknife could be introduced as a murder weapon, but not likely as the instrument with which someone felled a Douglas fir, especially if the storyteller claimed the feat was accomplished in one day! DNA requires an organism to be an organic compound, but it also limits what the organism can be.

Using concepts developed in previous chapters, we can give this description of the s-o relation. First, it is a relation between two functors; thus it is a functional relation. As a functional relation the s-o relation will have the functionally dominant characteristic of one irreducible mode of functioning. So it will be a psychic s-o relation, or an economic s-o relation, or an analytic s-o relation, and so forth. That s-o relation has as one characteristic that only the functor performing the actions which functionally dominate the relationship is subjectively$_2$ or actually capable of functioning on that dominant level.

For example, iron ore has no subjective$_2$ economic functions. It cannot perform the actions characteristic of economic subjects$_2$, that is, economic functor subjects$_2$. Ore does not buy or sell or make choices. Only a person can be an economic subject$_2$ functor. Only a person, an economic subject$_2$, can act economically with respect to ore. Ore is then taken up in that relationship and performs its own economic role in that relationship. But it is not capable of being an economic functor in any subjective$_2$ sense. It is an objective economic functor. It cannot sell or buy, but it is sellable. It has economic potential, and that potential is being realized by an economic functor.

At the same time, the economic functioning of the subject$_2$ is limited by the ore. The ore's economic potential is limited, which in turn limits the subject$_2$. The performing functor, acting subjectively$_2$ and economically, is the subject$_2$, while the undergoing functor is the object. The object passively undergoes the relationship, but is itself active as subject$_2$, although not as an economic subject$_2$. It is a physical subject$_2$, and as such it limits its own role as an economic object. In turn, it also limits the economic subject$_2$.

So, in a functional s-o relation of a specific modal kind, we always find that a subject$_2$ is what it is for a specific object, and that the object is what it is for that subject$_2$. What is meant by the term *objective* here? Formally speaking, *objective* is whatever is characteristic of the object. But in this relation what is characteristic of the object? It is that the object places limits on the subject$_2$, and those limits are the limits placed by that object on any subject$_2$ to which it is the object that it is. Iron ore has economic potential, but that potential has objective economic limits. The object places objective limits on the subject$_2$, that is, upon the normal, healthy, well-formed subject$_2$. To a sick person, for example, sugar may not taste sweet. To a deaf person, falling objects make no sound. To a greedy person, ore mining has no limits. Nevertheless, the functioning of the object in the relationship is not changed by the ill-functioning subject$_2$.

So in the s-o relation the objective functioning of the object is a limit for the subject$_2$. The object is not actively involved in the relation on the level of functioning characteristic of that relation. But the object keeps its own characteristics even as its potential on the other level is opened up. Ore has economic potential, but its limits must be observed. It has characteristics as a functor as well as those it presents as limitations to the subject$_2$. The subject$_2$ is incapable of altering those limits; they are objective. Within those limits the potential of the object can be opened up, but *only* within those limits.

There are objective limits to our knowledge of the location of a subatomic particle at some given moment. And a rose by any other name would smell as sweet. Any normal-smelling subject$_2$ can either like or dislike the scent of sweet-smelling roses. But there is not a thing that can be done about the objective state of affairs which determines the scent to be that of roses. If someone denies that roses smell as roses do, then that is no longer an objective statement.

We can, of course, make all sorts of errors and try to impose certain things upon the object. But objectively this is unwarranted. Such is the reference of the term *objective* in the s-o relation. Roses do not go around smelling other roses. To one another they have no smell. Smelling a smell can only be done by a sensitive subject$_2$. The smell itself is an objective function of the object. Roses do not smell subjectively$_2$. But the subject$_2$ smelling a rose is objectively bound by the limitations of the object to smell only a rose.

The meaning of the term *objective* which I have just discussed accords well with what *objectivity* conveys in epistemological literature. For that reason, we must clearly distinguish our meaning of objective from the notion of "according to standards." At the same time it will help to relate objectivity to standards. Although objectively a rose smells as it should, an actual rose is not likely to be a standard for any person who smells it. A concrete rose can be a standard neither for smelling, nor for sweetness, nor for roses. Concrete functors and functions must *meet* standards. A rose and a person are both subjects$_1$.[27] Subjects$_1$ exist in subjection to conditions, laws, norms, and standards. They are consequently not themselves norms or conditions, since nomic realities and subjective$_1$ realities are irreducible correlates.

As subjects$_1$ in the smelling relation both the person and the rose play a subjective$_1$ role—the one as subject$_2$ and the other as object. The smelling is a subjective$_{1,2}$ activity. Only the person is, as subject$_2$, a subject$_1$ to the conditions for smelling. The rose is subject$_1$ to the conditions for being smelled, that is, for the conditions relevant to the opened-up potential for being smelled. If this is so, then clearly the use of the term *objective* to mean both "according to standards" and "subjectively$_1$ limiting the actions of a subject$_2$," is very confusing.

But at the same time it is clear that the s-o relation is itself subject$_1$ to standards. It is a relation with an order of its own, having its own peculiar characteristics. And because the s-o relation is subject$_1$ to conditions, one might easily be tempted to superimpose the two meanings on one another—"according to standards" on "objective." It is quite apparent that there is a difference between "objective" and "according to standards," as well as between "objective" and "being a standard." Objective has a meaning that imposes limits but leaves room for individual and subjective$_1$ differences. Not every rose is equally sweet. The smell of one rose is not the standard for how another *should* smell. The smell of any rose in particular is neither *the* exemplary example or outstanding instantiation, nor is it the universal condition.

The special nature of objectivity in the s-o relation can be concluded from an analysis of the existence of s-s relations and the absence of any object-object relations. Let us take a look at conceptual or analytic relations between entities. It is clear that many functors are not capable of subjective$_2$ analytic functioning. Mountains, shrubs, and goats do not analyze or form concepts. They are incapable of performing operations people need to perform in order to generalize or abstract. They can at best be analytic objects, that is, people can have concepts of them.

If only analytic subjects$_2$ existed, there would not be analytic objects. But now there are analytic objects, that is, entities nonconceiving though conceivable. But there is no analytic object-object relation. As I have defined it here, an object must be an object for a subject$_2$. Something may be a potential object, but even then it is a potential object for some possible subject$_2$. For that reason, o-o relations cannot exist by themselves. There can, of course, be a relation between objects via subjects$_2$. The concept of a rose, which is an analytic object function of a rose, can be related to the sweet smell of roses, which is a sensitive object function of roses. But the relationship still requires a subject$_2$. And the management of that relationship has objective foundations. But smells and concepts do not, in and of themselves, relate.

Objectivity, then, is not separate from subjectivity$_2$. Objects are not objects for other objects. Between subjects$_2$, however, there can be s-s relations. For example, in the analytic s-o relation between functors (say, a molecule and an analyst), the object is passive analytically (*not physically*). But in an analytic s-s relation between persons we can have one subject$_2$ analytically active to the other, while the other actively participates. Both can be analytically active. There can in fact not ever be an analysis of the analytic functioning of a subject$_2$ unless the latter can submit a "piece of analytic functioning." In essence, analytic interaction is needed. In the s-o relation there is no analytic interaction. In the s-s relation there must always be interaction.

This difference contributes to the fact that in the analytic s-o relation, the chances of error are less than in the s-s relation. Error, which in this case would be analytic, is behavior contrary to, for example, the rules of inference, or to certain analytic conditions or standards. A rose can never make such an error.[28] That factor makes an objective concept less error-prone. But as a concept it is still subjective$_2$ and therefore capable of being wrong. Because there is no object apart from a subject$_2$, a *purely* objective concept is a contradiction in terms. Every concept is, necessarily, analytically subjective$_{1, 2}$, both in the sense that it is subject$_1$ to the conditions for good analysis, and subjective$_2$ in that a concept is the result of analytic activity itself. Therefore it cannot be analyzed objectively.

The importance of this distinction can be seen in an illustration: every concept, *as a concept*, is subjective$_2$. All the same, it can conform to the relevant standards for concept formation. And in being the concept of, for example, a cell, it can be a properly formed concept of an analytic object and thus be objective. A well-formed concept would in this way be a true concept. But in spite of its "trueness," it would never be just objectively true. As concept, it remains subjective$_1$ *and* subjective$_2$, even though it is also true to standard and objectively true. However, this does not make such a concept less true for not being merely objectively true. Many concepts are, of course, formed in a s-o relation. They can be objectively true, insofar as they correctly observe the objective limits of concept formation in this context. But they are never *just* objective.

From time to time in the analysis of the s-o relation, I have spoken of both objects and object functions, of both subjects$_2$ and subject$_2$ functions. This terminology is related to the functor-function distinction and to the fact that all s-o relations are functional relations. So far I have paid no attention to the difference between functors and functions in this respect. Can anything be said about the difference between objects and object functions, and between subjects$_2$ and subject$_2$ functions? There is indeed a difference here; neglecting it would lead to reductionism. By calling a functor an object *of some kind* or a subject$_2$ *of some kind*, I refer to the fact that they sustain a relationship which is specific, which is *of some specified kind*. In the analysis of a rose, the rose functions objectively. I have called the rose an *analytic* object in *this* relation and I have then also spoken of the analytic object function of a rose.

If we call a rose an analytic object, do we reduce the rose to its analytic object functions? Do we not imply in this case that some subject$_2$ (a rose) is what it is only as a function of its passive relation to another subject$_2$? Or when a person is called an analytic subject$_2$, is that a reduction of the entire functor to its analytic subjectivity$_2$?[29] Reduction is certainly not what I intended in these various references. Rather, since in s-o relations we deal with functors from a functional point of view, a term referring to a functor from the point of view of that relation can only be partial in its reference. A known object or a seen object is, in fact, what it is taken to be only *as* known and *as* seen. This does not imply there is an object "in itself" which is not known or seen and which cannot be known or seen. The whole entity is known or seen. But there is more to the entity than what is known or seen.[30]

In order to understand this better, it is helpful to remember that the terms *subject$_2$* and *object* are functional indicators of functors. So far I have used these indicators in a global way. In a functional relation of a specific modal kind between two functors, we have said that one of these functors participates actively on the given functional level and the other does not. The active contributor on that level has been designated as *subject$_2$* and the passive one as *object*. So I have spoken of *subject$_2$* when in fact I was dealing with *subject$_2$ functions*, and I have spoken of *object* when I was discussing *object functions*. This terminology is not sufficiently clear. Especially not when, as we will presently see, there is a difference in the impact that certain s-o relations have on a functor in distinction from other s-o relations.

It is possible to distinguish between functors just *in* s-o relations, and functors so characterized *by* this relation that they can be called objects. So, in the context of the s-o relation, it is better to clearly refer to subject$_2$ functions and object functions as well as to subjects$_2$ and objects. In the latter case a functor in a s-o relation becomes specifically qualified in a functionally dominant way by its object functions. I will refer to that functor as an object. Modern vegetables, for instance, are specifically grown to have shapes, colors, crispness, and other attributes (i.e., subject$_2$ functions of vegetables) to enhance their marketability (often at the cost of their worth as foods). So they can be characterized as objects. They are not merely functors with an objective economic function. As organic subjects$_2$, their relation to human economic functioning has invaded their very inner structure. The inner development of their physical and organic functions to economic needs so dominates their organic qualifying function that they have become definite economic organisms. Their very physico-chemical structure has been economically objectivized.

Objective functions can thus have a drastic effect on the subjective$_2$ structure of a functor. Does this undermine the sense of objectivity I have tried to characterize? In this instance does the subject$_2$ in the s-o relation really transgress the limits of the object? In the example of the vegetables it appears that, instead of the economic subject$_2$ being limited by the object functions, that subject$_2$ molds the object functions at will. But here a subtle difference emerges between the realization of the full potential of some entity and the (ultimately) destructive straining of its limits.

In human culture the s-o relation is an important relation. Its structure characterizes our relationship to our "natural" environment and to all of the technical artifacts, utensils, instruments, and so forth, which are such important parts of modern culture. All tools, for example, are technical objects. They are shaped and designed according to a human plan out of natural materials, which never appear in their own environment in that form. Their existence as natural materials is bound up in the technical design of the instrument as a subjective$_2$, technical, human function.

We all know there are certain limits to the potential of some material. The objective technical functions of ice, for example, dictate that its use for building foundations would not be recommended in areas where there is a long and warm summer. We are also aware of the almost limitless uses to which materials can be put by modern technology. The laser beam or the computer bit are splendid examples of the technical development of the physical potential of natural phenomena. But there are objective limits nevertheless. Tomatoes will tend to lose their nutrient value if they are especially treated just to serve the market needs of the producer. And ultimately this loss of food value will invade the market area too, and will result in a loss of sales. If objective limits are not observed, then subjective$_2$ functions will ultimately be affected as well.

Perhaps the nature of objective functioning can be further clarified by using the concept of analogical functioning. If we view the objectivity of functioning as analogical functioning in a certain type of relation, this may clarify the limiting role of the objective function. It may also clarify the integration of objective functioning with the subjective$_2$ functioning of another functor. Functional analogies, as I treated them earlier, are functional evidence of functional interrelationship. When two functions, both of an irreducibly different kind, are in relation to each other because they are both functions of the *same* functor, then the functional relationship between them shows up in intrafunctional analogies. But there appears to be a close relationship between the s-o relation as I have discussed it here and the relations of functional analogies. The possibility of functional analogy has been based, to this point, on the relation of all functions to a functor. That functor was always seen as multifunctional. Its unified and integral existence as a functor demanded functional integration. Lower kinds of functions anticipate higher ones, while higher ones refer back, or retrocipate to lower ones. And the s-o relation now introduces the possibility of functional integration between different functors when they function on irreducibly different levels.

The natural world abounds with examples of functional integration between different functors through the s-o relation. DNA is a molecule with its anticipatory area of functioning opened up. Many Fibonacci numbers are numerical anticipations of organic relationships. These anticipatory analogies did not arise in the physical molecules or in the numerical relations except through the presence of a s-o relation. The analogical functioning does not originate in the functor whose function shows the analogy in question. Rather, the analogical functioning stems from another functor whose subjective$_2$ functioning opened up the anticipatory function in an objective way.[31]

However, this does not explain the nature of the more simple and by far the most common s-o relations. The gross, natural entities of our macro world are all visible, audible, and touchable. These functions, as object functions, do not show developed analogical functioning. There is no necessary evidence of internal development of the structure of things as a result of being observed, heard, or touched. It is here that the s-o relation depends on functional analogies in the functor whose subjective$_2$ functioning is involved. The very chemistry of the brain must contribute, for example, to the formation of a visual retinal image, lest we never actually see what is visible.

To be sensitively aware through sight, hearing, or touch of physical objects requires the physical functions of the sensitive functor to be opened up in anticipation. The physcial contact on a subjective$_2$ physical level through physical interaction (touch, soundwaves, lightwaves) must, within the body of the sensitive functor, correspond to sensitively opened up physical and organic functions in order to really enable the functor to hear, see, or touch. And the correspondingly sensed object functions must objectively be capable of making possible an adequate relation between the two functors. The objective sensory image of a seen object, to which one cannot reduce the reality of the seen entity, must nevertheless form an adequate objective foundation for the interfunctoral relation in the s-o relationship.[32]

Various patterns of order in the s-o relationship can then be observed with the help of the concept of functional analogy. First, no s-o relation can exist unless the functor which delivers the subjective$_2$ dimension to the relationship has an opened-up substructure allowing subjective$_2$ contact between the functors. All s-o relations must ultimately be founded on physical interaction, that is, the s-o relationships have s-s relationships as their foundation. No relationship between functors is possible at all unless there is a s-s basis of interaction to the relationship. Second, in many cases this interrelationship only presupposes the subjective$_2$ opening of anticipatory functions in the functor functioning subjectively$_2$ in the s-o relation. Third, the s-o relation, however, may also further develop the anticipatory functions of the objective functional relations. These will be objective anticipations. Examples of the difference between developed and undeveloped functions abound. There is the old discussion about whether objects that fall in places where there are no hearers do or do not make sounds; this is simply a matter of an undeveloped s-o relation. Noise or sound is an actualized, simple, object function. *Sound* is a name for the sensory awareness of contact between airwaves and eardrums. Apart from that relation, there is no sound.[33]

This same relation can also exist in a developed way. It is possible to control soundwaves in such a way that the sounds produced will constitute music. Similarly, soil is not just fine particles of rock, but earth related to vegetation feeding on it. Soil is organically developed matter. It is an organic object. It has objective anticipations in relation to vegetation. If the vegetation deteriorates, the soil will erode and become desert. Beaver dams, ant hills, snails' houses, foxes' dens, and other animal artifacts are also examples of developed s-o relations. Similarly, the nest of a bird is not an aggregate of twigs, pieces of paper, straws, and saliva. It can only be properly understood as a psychic object. It is so constructed that the proper functioning of a bird, that is, a functor functioning subjectively$_2$ in the psychic mode, can take place in the physically developed object functions of the nest. In that nest the bird will feel at home when laying eggs, hatching them, and feeding the young.

It will by now be clear that I can amplify my statements in the opening parts of this section to the effect that we know the s-o relation traditionally only from epistemology. The whole literature on primary and secondary qualities is also concerned with the s-o relation. But here again, tradition has limited its discussion mostly to psychic object functions of taste, touch, sight, hearing, and smell. The debate has been about whether these are or are not qualities of the entities in question. In my discussion of the s-o relation two things have become clear. One is that indeed there is something unusual about those properties I have called object functions. They are properties of things, but only in relation to other things. Secondly, the secondary qualities, so called, are vastly more complex and occur much more often than in the case of sensed qualities. Concepts of nonhuman things are also object functions. So are prices. So is signification. Whenever something is in relation to another entity which has subjective$_2$ functions lacking in the former, "secondary qualities" are qualities of the former, designated in kind by the functioning of the latter.[34]

Chapter VI
Integration

TO DO JUSTICE TO THE UNIVERSE we live in, more needs to be said about relation than was said in the preceding chapter. Rice in a jar, for example, contains countless little items in relation. But our understanding of the world is much more complicated than the relation of grains of rice in a jar. Many things not only relate, but they do so in patterns, orderly manners, and meaningful ways. And there are unordered relations; not all things fit each other. But in general, we inhabit a coherent universe. Most things fit in the environment to which they belong. Relations are integrated. Thus, the world is ordered in such a way that people can be at home in it. If we do not spoil the environment, then we can breathe the air, eat the plants, and drink the water. The world does not consist of people and objects that merely pass each other like ships in the night. It consists of meaningful patterns of relationships. People are parents and children, husbands and wives, employers and employees. Birds eat insects. Tears wash our eyes. The sun helps make things visible. And rain makes plants grow. Everywhere we look, there is coherence in the universe.

But there is not only coherence in the universe; there is also unity, a similar but significantly different phenomenon. When we use the term *coherence* we suggest that things relate in integrated interrelated patterns. Well-regulated traffic in a large metropolis, for instance, may move in coherent ways. But the coherent traffic movements do not constitute a unity. The many different elements in the coherent pattern are not related as they would be in a diversity within a unity. Cars, traffic lights, and police officers do not have an intrinsic relation to each other in the way that parts of a body do. Coherent diversity and diversity within a unity are quite different. So, if we are to understand our world in a more integrated way, rather than just as a world with relations, we need to look at both unity and coherence.

But even then we will still not have a complete understanding of our world in its thorough integrality. The world picture will not be complete without an understanding of its temporality. The coherent interrelation of units of existence functioning in relationships, all subject$_1$ to universal order, is first of all a temporal world. Things relate dynamically; they change, and they come and go. The entities in our world not only relate coherently, but they do so in temporal relations, in development and growth, in rise and decline, in appearance and disappearance. Time separates things and brings them together. So in this chapter we will take a look at temporality and discuss it along with unity and coherence. For time, it will appear, is a relational category.

6.1 Unity and Diversity

The concept of unity as a broad ontological category has been discussed by philosophers in different contexts. Unity has been viewed as the problem of the one and the many, as in the traditional discussion of universals. That is not what I have in mind here. It has also been discussed as the question of the one and the whole universe in relation to the manifold it contains. That comes closer to what I have in mind, but not close enough. Even more to the point and certainly related to what I shall discuss in this chapter is the problem of the whole and its parts. But, as I hope will become clear, I believe that the problem of unity in ontology is more inclusive than that of wholeness. In fact, I will even be discussing totality in a next section as distinct from what I have in mind here.

Let me first illustrate the problem of unity and diversity as I understand it. Many things in our experience can be understood either from the point of view of unity or from the point of view of diversity. Things appear to be both "one" and "many" at the same time. We can speak of parliament, and also of the members of parliament. We can refer to a book, or we can be conscious of pages, front and back covers, letters, chapters, and page numbers. Sometimes we refer to a meal simply as dinner, and sometimes we refer to it in terms of soup, potatoes, meat, vegetables, and pudding. A cup of tea can be viewed in terms of a cup, a saucer, hot water, and tea leaves.

In taking these different points of view—either of unity or of diversity—is there any priority? Are things essentially one, or are they basically many? Or is this approach even correct? Is it better to say the one is impossible without the other? Perhaps it only makes sense to speak of unity in relation to diversity. And how should we view diversity in the examples mentioned above? Are they not all just examples of things belonging together, that is, things together within a unity? A cup, a saucer, hot water, and tea leaves in any haphazard relation will not constitute a cup of tea. Diversity and unity, as I intended to show in the examples, are themselves in relation.

The problem of unity and diversity is not easy to analyze. Upon reflection, some basic meanings which at first seem clear and evident begin to elude us and shift focus. Does unity have anything to do with a unit? How should we view army units, or units of vitamin C? Can the unity that may result from ties among people be meaningfully referred to as a unit? In the army, a group of people acting in unison and tied together in other ways may be called a unit. Are people who act in unison at the voting booths a unit? Unity may occur, apparently, as a characteristic of relations as well as of entities. But unity is not characteristic of anything that is merely one unit without any diversity. A unit of mass, as in an atomic particle, may not be a unity; there is no diversity within it. The number "one" does not primarily stand for unity but for unit, even though we may be said to become "one" when we unite.

Perhaps we must conclude that there are, in fact, many kinds of unity. We might need to look for an advanced yet general concept to include them all. Would the categories already introduced in this study be of any help in settling this issue? Is unity a function? Might it be a condition? Is the phenomenon of unity to be found on both sides of any of our previous correlations: order and subjectivity$_1$, functors and functions? If we mean a whole as only one sort of unity, then how do other sorts of unity differ from the character of a whole?

I will enter into this maze of questions by introducing a problem. One would think that the unity displayed in some diversity is not one element of that diversity. The unity of all the diverse elements of "x" is not itself likely to be an element of "x," for then the unity of "x" would be included within itself, which would seem to be contradictory. But we also cannot take the unity of some diversity to be the same as the totality of that diversity. By unity we do not mean the same as all elements taken together. Then unity would have diversity as one of its own constituents. Unity would then just be the whole diversity. We need both unity and diversity, with respect to one another, or as correlate dimensions of something. The totality of a thing includes both its unity and its diversity, so the thing's totality cannot be the same as its unity. Unity is neither all there is to something nor a moment of all there is to something.

This is a thorny problem. It seems that unity and diversity differ; yet together they also constitute a diversity; and at the same time in unity all diversity comes to one. Obviously there are problems here. One of these may be that we take the term *unity* too formally and univocally. Different senses of unity may be merging with each other, although we are not noticing them. A way out of this dilemma is to give the terms a defined context. So let us begin by noting that unity and diversity appear to be correlates. In the context of the problem we are discussing here, unity is impossible without diversity, and the two are also irreducible.

If diversity and unity are correlated irreducibles, then the term *diversity* does not refer to just any indiscriminate multiplicity. The discussion up to now may give the impression that by diversity I just mean any multiplicity. But since I am speaking here of unity and diversity as correlates, we assume that the diversity of which I speak is that sort of diversity in some phenomenon (entity, system, event, etc.) which is correlated to the unity of that same phenomenon and which therefore is a coherent diversity. In this context diversity is the multiplicity we find correlated to a unity. All the things collected on a garbage dump would then not be a diversity of items but a mere multiplicity of things. From here on, I will use the term *diversity* in that sense. And I will use the term *unity* to stand for more than just unit. I will use it to indicate specifically that some diversity has unity. Unity will not merely stand for any multiplicity joined in some fashion or other. A garbage dump is not a unity.

The picture of the unity-diversity relation may now be hard to distinguish from the part-whole relation analyzed in the previous chapter. The sort of arguments used to arrive at the concept of a whole might not be different from those used to arrive at the concept of unity. In part that is because a whole is a good example of what is meant by a unity. But parts are not all that constitute a whole's diversity. Further, a whole is always a functoral whole. Unity may also occur in other contexts. What we call thinking may be a unity having a great diversity of moments. But thinking is not an individual whole with parts. Enkapsis also results in unity, and enkapsis was brought into the previous chapter to introduce a relation that is wider than part-whole relations. And the unity of a movement cannot be expressed by either the concept of a whole with parts or by enkapsis.

It is still hard to explain what is meant by unity, in spite of the gains that result from considering unity and diversity as irreducible correlates. As is the case with relations, unity is a firm given of our everyday experience. But even in that context, a definition of unity is elusive.[1] For example, someone may remove my bike, which I had securely locked to a post. Now, even if that person left behind my lock and the front wheel, I will still say my bike was stolen. If, on the other hand, all I notice is that someone took the front wheel, I will not conclude that my bike was stolen. What if only the frame has been taken, but the seat, wheels, and rear reflector are left behind? Did someone then steal my bike or just the frame?

There is not likely to be, of course, an exact conceptual point at which speech passes from one mode to another in this case. I believe the reason for this can be found in the correlative relation between unity and diversity, which is an irreducible correlation. The one can only be understood in relation to the other as a result of the correlative relation, although not as a result of the irreducibility. Diversity indicates a multiplicity within a unified field. When the field has been sufficiently disturbed, the remaining elements will no longer be grounds for making a judgment about the former unit. Unity is characteristic of some diversity only when it is held together in an integral way, although not by any moment (part, function, relation, etc.) of that diversity.

So it would be a mistake to view the unity of some entity as a separate, distinguishable dimension or aspect. We may express the irreducibility of unity to diversity by saying that unity transcends diversity. There is no harm in making that claim so long as we only mean that the unity cannot be reduced to merely the linked, or joined, or added diversity. However, we should not suggest that unity somehow lies beyond the entity, or that it must be found outside of the entity that we actually experience as a unity. In that case the phenomenon of unity has been made into a substantialized and severed formal concept. Then the problem of unity has been "solved" by projecting the unity beyond where it needs to be to solve anything, namely, within the context of that which *is* is a unity.

A bike is a unity and *its* unity must be explained. This example of unity may give us a clue to what we should look for. Perhaps if we take a closer look at something that is supposed to be a unity but is not, or something that is an imperfect unity, then we might find out what is missing. If unity is absent, then what is missing? What is not "in order" when unity is lacking or imperfectly present?

To begin the search for the missing unity it may be helpful to recall that a unity (perhaps a functor, for example) is not something static. When we speak of a functor that is a unity, we are referring to an entity functioning *in* unity. Its unity is not a separate dimension, but characteristic of all the moments of the diversity as together they *function in unity*. It *acts* unifiedly, is being a unity, and functions all in one piece. The expression "unity is lacking" makes sense in a certain context. A scratched-up bike needs to have a paint job; it does not need to have its unity restored. A federal cabinet in which a prime minister and a colleague of influence continually make incompatible decisions does not need its appearance improved; it needs its unity restored. What, then, is the unity of a thing? And when it is present, is a new element added to the diversity? Can it be both present *and* not present in some entity? What is the difference between a broken marriage and a harmonious one? How do we distinguish between a hung jury and a unanimous decision?

One helpful approach is using the radically irreducible correlate of nomic conditionality and empirical subjectivity$_1$. Unity could be explained when something, with all of its diversity, is ordered or structured to function in unity. The radical correlate of conditionality and subjectivity requires that structural characteristics of empirical reality be related to nomic order. Something whose structural conditions or order call for unity will act or function as a unity when it behaves in conformity with that order. This does not mean that whenever something does not completely or fully conform to its conditions, then that unity is, in this instance, or in all instances, absent. But if something is conditioned or structured to be "one" but does not meet its conditions significantly, then it will exhibit a lack of unity to the degree that it does not conform.

This concept of unity is, of course, a very formal one. Nothing is said about various kinds of unity. The unity of a paragraph in a book and the unity of a person throughout the lifetime of such a person obviously are present in response to different requirements. The concept of an action center or of centered action may be appropriate to a functor and may not be required at all of a family as a unit. At what critical moment of malfunctioning a unity will have ceased to be depends on the structural requirements for the unity in question. Unity may, as the case may be, diminish, break down, or disappear. When some dimensions of a unity act against their intended role required by the thing's structure, unity may just be undermined. But in all cases unity results from a thing's functioning in unity as required by its structure.

So, on this view, an entity is a unity when it meets the conditions for functioning as a unity. This view may seem to conflict with the requirement that an entity's unity must not lie outside of it. My view of conditionality and subjective$_1$ existence as an irreducible correlate may be seen to require conditions for unity to lie outside of the actual unity of an actual entity in empirical existence. What something is meant to be, and what it is in fact, are not the same. What a thing is meant to be lies in its condition. This, however, is only an apparent problem. The relation between the conditional grounds for the existence of things and those things themselves is not one of reality and less reality, or reality and nonreality. If unity exists when conditions for unity have been met, the actual unity is not the same as the conditions for unity. If an entity exists when its order is met, the order is not the thing.

The unity of an empirical entity is subjective$_1$ unity, not unreal unity or apparent unity. But as subjective$_1$ it needs to be grounded in an order. Thus, an entity is one when it acts as an entity in correlation to an orderly requirement for unity. Unity is a structural requirement. *Why* it is a structural requirement, of course, we do not know. Things *are* that way, and we *find* them that way. We can explain this situation if we accept that it is structured in this particular way. And this may be all we can say from a theoretical point of view.

6.2 *Coherence and Totality*

I have introduced the concept of unity as a correlate of diversity and have indicated that the evidence of the correlation lies in the fact that the diversity in question coheres. It is a well-ordered diversity. This suggests the question of whether all coherent diversity is necessarily a unity. Could there be coherence and not unity in a phenomenon? Could there be a cohering totality of diverse elements which as a totality is not a unity? In philosophy, especially today, renewed attention to these questions is likely to be helpful.[2]

Suppose a person lacks concepts of coherence and totality. How can this person then distinguish between the links that peas in a jar have to one another, and the connections between parts of a cell? How does one distinguish between mere conglomerates and immense actual totalities such as the earth, a nation, or a solar system?[3] Perhaps one does not have such concepts. At the very least, this would create difficulties in understanding some phenomena of everyday experience. At worst, it could imply that one does not experience these phenomena integrally, though perhaps they should be. Integration in one's world picture can be achieved only with the help of concepts of integration, such as unity and coherence.

Coherence and totality concepts provide integration in specific ways. Not all relationships are coherent and not all related multiplicity is a totality. Coherent relationships are ones that display reciprocity, mutuality, dependence, organization, necessity, and similar characteristics. If I am a collector of stamps, for instance, and I keep them in one large cardboard box, then there is no actual coherence. Even if I fasten them neatly in rows on the pages of notebooks, but in random fashion, then that shows no coherence. If I decide to group them by country, in the order of dates of issue, and in issued series from the lowest value to the highest, then a pattern of relationships will develop. This determines where stamps *belong* in relation to each other. They not only relate, they co-relate. And when the correlations are complex and continue, we speak of coherence. However, the particular coherence of a stamp collection is not the result of its unity. Unity, as defined in the previous section, is characteristic of unitary functioning. A collection of stamps, coherently displayed, is not a unity in that sense. It may be complete and a unit, but the many stamps do not function together as one. On the other hand, the collection is a totality. It may not be a unified whole, an action unit, but it is a totality.

How do we distinguish totality from unified whole? The latter is, of course, also a totality. How, then, do the two differ? And what would not constitute a totality? A totality I define as a diversity to which all the moments of that diversity belong. Any other elements of what is in the world do not belong, even if those elements are in some fashion of the same kind. Thus, a collection of all the stamps of the Dutch East Indies, which as a colony of the Netherlands no longer exists, can be a complete collection. It can be said that of all the stamps in the world there are those that definitely belong to this collection and others that do not. The collection has definite boundaries of completion, inclusion, and exclusion according to known structural patterns. Such a diversity of elements is a totality. But this totality is not a unity; nor is it a unified structural whole. It is a diversity of elements with a structure and boundaries, but it has no functioning unity of existence.

So of all totalities, one that is a coherent unity is the more integrated, and a centered unity the most integrated of all. But a totality need not be a unity, and yet it can still have coherence, as we can see in the stamp collection. From this we might conclude that unity and coherence also do not need to coincide. Something can exhibit coherence without being a unity. And what about totality and coherence? Are they related? In the case of unity and coherence, one could say that unity presupposes coherence, that is, nothing can be unified and yet not be coherent.

Now, how should we view totality and coherence? Is totality possible without coherence? And is coherence possible without totality? Coherence is indeed possible without totality, if by totality we mean a diversity characterized by definite patterns of boundary, inclusion, and exclusion. Speech, for example, is necessarily coherent if it is to be well formed. But instances of speech, however systematic and coherent, need not be complete; definite boundaries do not exist for any given occasion. Similarly, a coherent set of relationships can very well be open ended.

What about the possibility of totality without coherence? That, it appears, is as impossible as unity without coherence. Totality brings together a diversity of elements according to *some* criteria of structure inherent to the totality. There must at least be a criterion for exclusion and inclusion and a boundary. So totality will always show *some* degree of internal interrelation. But totality misses functor focused unity of functional interrelationships. It does not correspond to an order of coordinated functioning which determines the unified being of an entity in which all diversity is similarly concentrated.[4]

In conclusion, philosophy has a need to recognize the existence of wholes, unity, totality, and coherence. The elements of the universe cannot be adequately comprehended without understanding the context of integration to which these elements belong. And we cannot understand these elements unless we understand the degree of integration that is proper to the pattern concerned.[5]

6.3 *Time*

Readers may be wondering what a discussion about the concept of time is doing in a chapter on revelational integration. However, the view of time that I will develop here is crucial to my entire perspective. Whether or not things actually cohere, concretely relate integrally, will depend on whether they do so *in* time. In fact, what I mean by *temporal* will relate to more than our empirical world.[6] *Time* will be viewed as the most inclusive term for cosmic interrelation. The view of time employed here is unusual.[7] As a preliminary orientation to time and temporality, I would offer the following overview. In this chapter, as well as in the previous one, I depended a lot in my exposition of relation and integration on the radically irreducible correlation of nomic conditionality and empirical existence. We have seen how these interrelate: conditions hold universally, and subjective$_1$ reality responds individually. Now I wish to introduce time as the integrator of that relationship.

The word *time* refers to the integral interrelation of conditionality and subjectivity$_1$. All things are ultimately related in time. Yet time
does not relate conditionality and subjectivity$_1$ as if time were a third
item. Rather, what we experience as time—and it is precisely to this
experience of time that I wish to appeal—can be analyzed as the interrelation of order and empirical existence. This is the line of thinking I will now pursue: the interlocking of ordering and subjecting$_1$ as
time.

This view of time is unusual. So I will need to develop it not only
in relation to an account of our everyday experience of time, but also
to what other traditions have had to contribute on the topic. Let me
repeat what I think our account of time should be. Time, I will argue,
is the actual relation between order and existence. As we once again
discuss that relation, it will become clear how that relation is what
time is all about. This perspective is important in the context of the
discussion of this chapter. In explanations of why a certain relation
prevails, why something is integrated in a particular way, or why
things cohere or are a unity, I have constantly resorted to the notion
that such is the order of things or such is the nature of relations. But
how do we finally account for that relation of order and existence?
How is *it* integrated?

My answer is that in our understanding of time we grasp the
manner of integration of the universe. So I will relate time, that is, our
experience of time, to order and subjectivity$_1$ in their relation. And I
will in turn relate this perspective to other accounts of time.

In everyday experience, the concrete, actual existence of things is
a completely temporal existence. Time is experienced by us as change,
development, growth, genesis, decay, progress, finitude, mutability,
contingency, limitation, and individuality. The words we use to indicate the opposite, or correlate, or parallel of these words are often
associated with another realm, namely, the nontemporal or eternal.
Constancy, necessity, permanence, universality, infinity, immuta-
bility, and the like are not to be found (so it is thought) in this world,
that is, in the realm of the temporal and the realm of actual existence. Now, the relation of the view I am proposing to this popular
understanding of time and temporality is quite evident. I believe that
whatever is of value in this understanding of time is related to the correlation of conditionality and subjectivity$_1$. And I believe that such a
conceptual link is also easy to recognize in the more philosophical
views of time.

In philosophy there has been a long-standing question related to
the problem of time: How does change relate to permanence? How is

it that things pass in and out of existence and yet we still see continuity and constancy? How do things change and yet maintain their identity? The perennial questions of philosophy demand something to be constant underneath (substance) or beyond (realm of essence) the fleeting appearances.[8] What abides and what goes? Is anything beyond decay? Is there anything exempt from demise or decline? These problems, too, can easily be approached from the point of view of the basic correlation of subjectivity$_1$ and nomic conditionality as they relate individually and universally. For conditions in principle hold abidingly and universally, while things respond subjectively$_1$ and individually. Subjective$_1$ individuality comes and goes; universal conditionality remains. It is in this very relation that I want to look for our explanation of temporality.[9]

6.3.1 Basic ontology of time

Everything we know in our world is temporal. In this respect, the scope of concepts of temporality seems to coincide with the concept of subjectivity$_1$. Let me give a dramatic example of one aspect of time, namely, its relentless limitation of our powers. Suppose we are aware of miners trapped underground where water is creeping in. Or we know of negotiations between freedom fighters and a government to avert war. Let us also suppose that with respect to one of these situations a newspaper would carry an extra large front-page headline: *TIME IS RUNNING OUT*. What would that headline mean? In terms of the present discussion, we would say that with respect to the life of miners, or with respect to the peace of a nation, the forbidding invariance, universality, and necessity of order has entered into the very uniqueness of a situation. Order and existence have been dramatically integrated in our awareness, they are indistinguishable. We all know *that* people will die, *if* something does not happen very soon. The conditionality is there (*that* and *if*), the typical dynamic of time is there (*happen* and *soon*), and the utter dependence of subjectivity$_1$ on conditions is there. This, I maintain, is the integrality of a temporal world. It is what we experience as time.

We all know what time is when we experience it. But who can explain it? Even in the fourth and fifth centuries, great thinkers such as St. Augustine were aware that we both know, and do not know, time. We must learn to understand time, but we do this not to learn that it exists, or to point out to people where they can experience it. We know it is all around and we are able to recognize it. What we need to find is the nature of time. That we do not seem to know. And herein lies the difficulty, for there does not seem to be anything in our experience that is both as universal *and* as unique as time. Explanations, especially theoretical-conceptual ones, require comparisons and a common denominator. But of what fundamental kind of reality is time a species? To what shall we compare it? In what context of known things, and in relation to what, shall we explain time? It is not like numbers, although it does have characteristics of succession. It is not like space, although it exhibits simultaneity and being stretched out. And it is also unlike physical reality, even though it seems to move.

Let me introduce some examples. I might say, for instance, "I have no time to read this book now." In this situation, what am I saying? Am I suggesting that perhaps the person to whom I am speaking might have some time, and thus give me a portion? In certain circumstances, that is not an impossible construction. If I have no time for something, then I have already chosen to commit myself to do something else. If I am already engaged in one thing, then I cannot do the other. But if someone would take over what I am currently doing, time is made for me; someone has given me some time.

But what is made for me, of course, is not a stuff or some entity. It is, perhaps, an opportunity that has been made for me to do something. But opportunity is not necessarily the same as time. A gift of $200 is also an opportunity. "Time" is "money" in the sense that it can create temporal space because we do not have to use it to gather food or to do other necessary things. But the opportunity created by $200 is not the same as that created by someone who takes over my task. If I am very committed to what I am doing, I might buy someone for $200 to take over my work, but still not be able to change my commitment. Nevertheless, spending is what we do with both money and time. To spend the one I need to spend the other. Is time like money? Could one compensate suffering with money, that is, time spent or lost in suffering? Judges, for example, seem to think so.

We could have many discussions of time such as this. They would all have the same characteristic: what is talked about is known and clear, yet for lack of definition it is also mysterious. In that way time reminds us of relationship. How can an ontology of time be developed? I think this is possible to a certain extent by "placing" the phenomenon of time within the context of categories of reality developed thus far. The notion of time which then emerges can be used to account for its characteristics. So where do we place time?

Clearly, time is connected both with conditions and with subjectivity$_1$. Concrete things are in time; they come and go. But time is also conditioned. Simultaneity and succession are time orders. What occurs in succession cannot also occur simultaneously. Some things can occur only in succession or simultaneity. Death comes only after birth. One can only be young first and old later, not at the same time, and not in reverse order. You can only be married to your spouse simultaneously with your spouse being married to you. Time is definitely found in a relationship between a relatively (i.e., relating) constant or invariable order of conditions and a coherent world of subjectively$_1$ responding entities in active functional relationship. The conditions relate, the subjects$_1$ relate, and the conditions and subjects$_1$ relate coherently and integrally. They are inexorably connected; one thing follows *after and from* another.

Things stay together, relate and exist in time, as they continue to develop within limits. Things come into existence, exist, develop while they exist, and pass out of existence. While anything which exists must exist physically in some sense, nothing physical is lasting, and many things exchange all of their physical elements completely many times over while they exist. A multitude of characteristics join together to constitute the phenomenon of time: the continuity of an order of coherence; the continuity of the relative identity of things in the midst of changing relationships; the disappearance and discontinuity of things; and the relative constancy of conditions. Continuity of coherence is really a continuity of relations. Actual relationships show order and structure, as well as functionally shifting constants and variables.

In addition to the term *temporality*, we also use *relativity* to name what I just described. And so, as the current usage goes, all is relative, all relates. Relativity is as wide in scope as temporality and subjectivity$_1$. Relativity and time are closely related. Both are to be understood in terms of changing points of orientation, shifts from constancy to variability. Time is not merely duration; it is also cessation. In fact, time has only been used in connection with duration to characterize it when it has a finite character. Often, duration without end has been associated with eternity, and eternity has been contrasted with time. Relativity and finitude are hardly distinguishable.

Is it accurate to approach time in terms of relativity? Are they the same? Is time the stuff that relates things? Is that why we say we are "in time"? Is it the glue holding things, functions, parts, and especially subjects$_1$ and conditions all together? Is it the great receptacle? If we suggest time is connected with relativity or relationality, we do not need to substantialize or reify time. This is the nature of relations; they are nothing in addition to what is related, as we discovered in the previous chapter. That would account both for the mysteriousness of time and, concurrently, our inability to understand it fully. The dynamics of relativity as temporality takes on new meaning in the light of what we discovered earlier: there is a lack of absoluteness in the subjective$_1$ world. We also noted that even order has its own origin and does not need to subsist by itself.

In the previous chapter I argued that the world is restless, referential, relational, and relative. It has no absolutes within its limits and its limits are relative to their own origin. Thus, a view of time as relationship, especially the relationship between limits and subjectivity$_1$, could be illuminating. The constancy we experience in a temporal world is always a relative, that is, timed constancy, always temporal and sometimes temporary constancy. In this regard we might look at Heisenberg's uncertainty relation and Gödel's theorems of incompleteness. Both of these positions indicate the complete lack of closed, finished, stable, constant, timeless duration even in a highly formalized and simple system. The relative constancy is found in the continuity of response to stable structures, so that certain patterns of response as well as units of response show relative durability. Functors (actors, relators) endure so long as they continue to abide within the limits of their order. Patterns or structures endure so long as they make principles of order concrete in meaningful, expressive ways. These are relative points of orientation within the coherence of functions and relationships, which make up the moving stream of time.

Our world, in other words, is a thoroughly historical world. Not just human culture has a history. The simplest form of existence we know, physical interaction and energy exchange, calls for change. Stars and planets have their history, their process in time. In organisms the core demand of existence is growth. When existence becomes still more complex and functors become sensitive, processes of maturation in emotional development are unthinkable without development. Going further in the modal series of functional complexity, we cannot conceive of skill without learning. All of these show us that not only subjective$_1$ existence is temporal, but that the order of the world is a temporal order in its calling for change, growth, development, learning, creativity, and so forth.[10]

That temporality must not be seen exclusively in terms of change and all the other characteristics of time I mentioned, but rather as change within limits, ordered growth, structured development, and so forth, is evident from the presence of evil in our world. Evil in its core is destructive, annihilative. Speaking in religious terms: the wages of sin is death. We do not know of a world where there is no evil. Still, the universe continues to exist. In one way that makes no sense. But in another way it does. If temporality is not just subjectivity$_1$ but ordered subjectivity$_1$, then the evil of existence is limited by an order which in principle is constant and invariant. It can be resisted, but not violated to the point of annihilation. And that order keeps calling existence to growth, development, and creativity. And that calling could account for how the universe, in spite of the overwhelming amount of evil, continues to exist.[11]

What we need to flesh out is the difference, in this context, between the use of the terms *temporal* and *temporary*. What could temporal mean if it did not need to include the temporary at some point? It could mean precisely what the idea of time as relativity highlights. If all things exist in relationship, relativity is essential to all things. Constants and traditional "absolutes" can then be relative without creating a contradiction. Relativity as relationality then has a primary meaning: things are what they are and mean what they mean, not primarily and exclusively in, of, and through, themselves. If, within this context, the difference between subjectivity$_1$ and conditionality is one of different sorts of relativity (as we discussed in the previous chapter), we can speak of the relativity of order as relative although not temporary. It is tempor*al* but not for a limited time. Conditions are limits. Their temporality is not limit*ed* but limit*ing*. The temporality of subjectivity$_1$, on the other hand, is a limit*ed* temporality. Such temporality is tempor*ary*. Conditionality and subjectivity$_1$ are related—both meet in time—so they would have the same relation as temporally limiting does to temporally limited. Limiting and limited would themselves be temporally related and relative.

Suppose time was to be contrasted with eternity, and God was viewed as eternal. Would this jeopardize the notion that everything is in relation? If God is eternal, and thus not temporal, would that mean God is not in relation? This is indeed a traditional (Aristotelian) view of the eternal absolute: something which is what it is, in and of itself, in relation to nothing for all time. But in the same context mentioned above, an alternate view seems possible. If we say God is eternal, we can mean that time originates in God. Being eternal can refer to another special temporal notion, namely, that of originating time. Rather than being limited or limiting, God could be the origin of both; God places everything in relation, within the limits of relation. Being the origin of time is not the same as being unrestricted temporally, or being out of time. Eternity can constitute a unique relation: being origin to both conditions and conditioned.

Now, if things stay together and constants are constant only "for a time," how long do they endure? What determines their duration? This depends on conditions, or it does so at least within temporal relations. The subjective$_1$ temporal processes are correlated to conditional limits which in principle remain stable. Nevertheless, these conditional limits are also relative because they determine reality in constant relation to each other. The different functional relationships and their relative constants, however, are patterns and units of response. These point to principles of order which are truly nomic conditions, limiting time and rising above subjective$_1$ temporality.

Temporality is in *this* sense the essential characteristic of what we experience as the subjective$_1$. Thus, time has its limits; things are temporally limited. For all things there is a time, and time does not swallow up what exists. Whatever exists in the empirical world exists subject$_1$ to conditions. But these conditions do not eradicate existence. The subject$_1$ is limited, but not in a deterministic way. There is time for what exists to be itself, but within certain limits. On the other side of these limits we find the origin of existence. That origin is not a reality outside of time; it rather is above and beyond conditions. When temporality is the ongoing coherence of subjective$_1$ existence within its limiting conditions, then the origin of these conditions is eternal.

6.3.2 Traditional temporal categories

Suppose that the preceding discussion of a time ontology is satisfactory. I should then be able to deal satisfactorily with all the specific notions of temporality through which philosophers have understood the concept of time. Some of these categories of time are duration, simultaneity and succession, past-present-future, periodicity, developmental stages, rhythms and genesis, to name only a few.

One basic time term is *duration*. Using the concept to which it refers, I will deal with some of the others. The continuity of duration is limited. This is what we recognize as change. Things do not stay the same forever. They endure, but only for a time. In physical interaction, such as dynamic motion, force is not merely movement in circles, which was the ancient picture of eternity. The force of dynamic motion presents us with change which is indeterminate, even for physical reality in its individual atomic or electronic existence.[12] This feature of duration is also the basis for other characteristics. The dynamic duration of anything is always related to the specific duration of a thing or function. Duration is unique for the kind of thing it is, however much leeway there may be for individual variety within those limits.

As things endure, they do so before, or after, or together with other things. The successions of *before* and *after* are distinguished by the terms *past* and *future*, while simultaneity is *present*. *Past, present,* and *future* are our names for the relations of succession and simultaneity. Some things that are all in the past can still have a *before* and *after* relation. But this does not imply that *before* and *after* are different than *past* and *future*. All it tells us is that in different contexts we may not use the same expression or word. Any event that occurs before another is in its past, any later event is in its future, and any simultaneous event is in its present.

Events are not the only phenomena that can be temporal and display these characteristics. Anything that occurs is temporal, and all subjectivity$_1$ is occurrence. In our ordinary speech, we distinguish between the constants and the variables in a fairly standard fashion, due to our need for orientation and stability. Nevertheless, it would be incorrect not to say that a tree occurs. Wolterstorff argues that trees do *not* occur.[13] But in my view trees are not, as he argues, sub- or trans-temporal substances *to* which, in any sense, events may "occur." Trees are themselves occurrences. If we say the sprouting or demise of a tree occurs, but the tree does not, then we are looking at a tree apart from its sprouting, maturing, and dying. That is the traditional substance notion, which illustrates a misunderstanding of "being a tree" as a natural kind.[14]

Apart from sprouting, maturing, and dying, trees do not exist; we are left with only the conditions for this process, this occurrence. Because these are the limits of the tree's occurrence, these conditions do not themselves occur. But if we say that trees do not occur, we misunderstand the thoroughly temporal character of all subjective$_1$ existence. There are realities that can have occurrences which are not occurrences themselves.[15] But the realities that have occurrences (traditionally: instantiations) are not empirical existents like trees. They are kinds. Their "exemplifications" are their occurrences.[16]

How should we view such typical time phenomena as periodicity, cycles, and rhythms? The present framework can account for them quite adequately. They all have to do with the specific limitation, the particular shape, of temporal duration subject$_1$ to each nomic configuration or kind. Temporal categories such as youth, incubation, period of mourning, speed of light, and others all tell us about human experience with respect to the duration of things. They show roughly how long a typical phenomenon will be subject$_1$ to its specific conditions. This is dealt with in particular by the "historical" sciences: geology, genetics, developmental psychology, paleontology, history, and so forth. They all must deal with difficult phenomena which are both unique and orderly, and occur just once and in a structured world. So these sciences deal specifically with the dynamics of temporality as the integration point of order and subjectivity$_1$.

The history of human culture, in which individual variety and the individuality of decision and freedom are greater than in any other realm of existence, offers special problems here. But historians of human culture also relate the uniqueness and individuality of their subject matter to patterns and constants of structure.[17] In certain ways time will always retain its mysterious character, because it is our experience of the most integral relation that exists, and relationality always has this mysterious side. But at the same time we can form some relevant concepts to explain and account for time. The integration of fixed and universal order with a universe functionally grounded in physical interaction, with motion and change as characteristic moments, shows how time can be seen as a dynamic development, one that is structured, not chaotic.

6.3.3 *Expansion of time categories*

Traditional time categories with which we are familiar can be accounted for within our present view of time. But we must not conclude that this particular view can account for these categories as they are traditionally understood. What is particularly unusual about our view of time here is its explication in terms of the many levels of functional irreducibility. Time as the integrator of order and subjectivity$_1$ becomes known in the functional dimensions of this subjectivity$_1$. Functionality, one of the two most fundamental dimensions of empirical reality, can only be understood in its interrelationship if it is viewed as a temporal dimension. Functionality is held together and set in a context of dynamic development in time. It is in time that functions coherently relate, that is, in the dynamics of the relation between order and subjectivity$_1$. For that reason, we may expect the irreducible functional modes to manifest their own irreducible ways of being temporal.

"Clock time," as measured duration of motion, is a physical dimension of time. Time in that context has always been viewed philosophically as the great coordinate of space. Our existence "in time and space" has always been a fundamental characteristic of empirical reality in Western philosophy. Considering the position of space and motion in the modal order, it is easy to appreciate their fundamental nature. And if time is especially understood by us in its physical sense, then we can see the foundational role played by physical reality in the constitution of our universe. However, to see time only as related to space, motion, and physical reality would be a reductionist position. That would account only for the numerical meaning of time (succession), the spatial (simultaneity), the kinematic (motion), the energetic (change), and at most the organic (growth or development). So I now make a case for a modal or functional expansion of categories of time.

Let me take, for example, the time one has to wait for the outcome of an important event: the result of an examination, the verdict of a jury, a report from the doctor's laboratory. We know that waiting for only a few minutes of "clock time" can sometimes take a long, long time. Conversely, if the hours spent on a certain project are absorbing, exciting, interesting, and immensely pleasing, it seems to take very little time, even if many long hours were indeed passed. Are we now to say that our feeling of time is less real than its measure? Or is it just as realistic to say that physically we can measure time, while psychically we can feel time?

In more technical terms: are the conditions for existence relative to moving objects only integrated in *measurable* durations, or can we say that the *sense* of integration of conditions and empirical circumstances is just as real. Felt time is still duration and it retains its succession and character of simultaneity. And in physical time, the measurement is not the time itself, only the measure of it. Can what we measure and feel not be the same thing, namely, the integration of nomic conditionality and empirical existence? If that is so, then what would be the best way to know time? If we say temporality is primarily what clocks tell (as relative as that notion is, following Einstein's discoveries), then we may be reflecting an age-old prejudice in scholarship: we want to tie genuine knowledge in with what we can count and measure.[18]

Perhaps these considerations open up some new questions for us. Do psychic and physical time really differ? Or are they just different dimensions of time? Is it the physical time that is felt? Or is the felt time what we measure? What are we to make of being able to tell time without being able to consult clocks? Is such time not that of organic rhythms? And is it not true that these rhythms are known as felt messages of the organism? What to say of the sensed significance of light and dark? How do birds tell when it is time to migrate? How should we regard patience? Is it not primarily an experience of time that is inexpressible in terms of physcial motion? For example, how long does a particular lecture last? Is it a long time, or forty minutes?

Do all lectures of forty minutes last equally long? If we feel a sense of boredom is that because we also sense something temporally out of kilter, that is, in the integration of conditions and existential reality? The reality of time is also clear in these statements, which are literally inaccurate, but nevertheless descriptive: "You never wipe your feet," and "You always yell." Strictly speaking, such statements are seldom true in any factual sense. But do they not portray something real?

Measured continuity of motion does not seem to be an adequate model to explain the temporal meaning of processes such as maturation, gestation, and growth. Theories of developmental stages in human growth show definite patterns of structure. But they cannot relate to time as physical time only. Seasons cannot be reduced, one would think, to the number of revolutions made by the sun. They are all processes of continued duration. Because they are empirically real, they also have physical foundations. But why should that dimension be singled out as the best indicator of what time is? In social relations, certain things disappear. They have had their time. When their social meaning is lost, they no longer appear. Could that phenomenon of social change adequately be expressed in terms of physical change and physical time? We no longer make a deep bow before a person of higher rank, for example, but is that comprehensible in terms of physical time? It is a matter of time, but is it a matter of the number of some year?[19]

Human experience of time has always included the reality of suitable time, social time, historical time. An expression like "the time of Caesar" does not normally make us think that we are employing a metaphorical sense of the term *time*. Here, too, time does have a physical basis, but it amounts to more than that. Historians tell us that the division into measured periods of what they experience as historic time is simply not accurate. Historical periods cannot be properly described when they are forced into a mathematical or physical model. But are we then suggesting that historical time is not real time? Is historical periodicity less real because it is unlike chemical periodicity?

I would propose that all of these temporal expressions do refer to real time. But none of them can be reduced to the others. When time is the integrator of order and empirical reality in terms of dynamic process, then the variety of subjectivity$_1$ will have a corresponding variety of temporality. If physical subjectivity$_1$ is foundational, then physical time will be as well. But if there is more than physical functioning, then there is more than physical time. I recognize, therefore, how there is functor time as well as function time. The time of a plant, an animal, and a mountain all differ. Physical, psychic, formative, and economic time differ. For every irreducible mode of functioning there is an irreducible kind of temporality. All of these have their appropriate ways of integrating order and subjectivity$_1$ and therefore their appropriate time. Each has a characteristic duration, and characteristic possibilities for succession as well as simultaneity.

In terms of the model of reality I am exploring in this text, it is also possible to consider another approach. Some philosophers might suggest that time is primarily a physical phenomenon; all different senses of time would be analogical moments of temporal reality. The argument might proceed as follows. Just as growth is a genuinely economic concept pointing to actual economic realities, it nevertheless does not have original meaning in economic reality. Originally, growth is an organic phenomenon. Economic growth is not organic, but it is real growth nevertheless. The meaning of growth in an economic sense can be seen as an analogy of original organic growth. Why could we not use this model for time?

Could we say that time is a category for every level of functionality, although only in a physical sense is time actually original? In all other levels of functioning, is time analogical? I do not think this can be a solution. With the exception of certain scientific or philosophical literature, time is seldom referred to as originally physical. When we say we have no time for something, we are not speaking analogically, although we would also not always be able to explain our lack of time in terms of measured motion. If we can all agree that an hour after one's wife has died is not a good time to go to a party, we can also agree that, in spite of the physical foundation to this temporal experience, the actual reality of "not a good time" is not reducible to physical time.

6.3.4 *Temporal direction*

Each genuine temporal expression is in many cases not reducible to physical time and yet it has physical time for its foundation. Here we have a reminder of the foundational direction of the modal order. Existence is ordered so as to build on physical foundations. In the world order, physicality comes before the organic.[20] This aspect of temporal expressions also has implications for our understanding of conditionality. In the temporality of the order-subjectivity$_1$ correlation, nomic order manifests its reality in existential structures in a certain sequence. In the duration of time, the time order requires certain events to precede others; physical conditions must be met before organic processes can occur. The modal order is, in this very sense, a thoroughly temporal order. There is a direction to temporality. Change, movement, growth, development, and progress take place in a certain direction. The past must come before the future, before precedes after, and the future comes after the present. The temporal series displays an irreversible direction of past, present, future. Time moves out of the past and into the future.

This direction of time relates to a particular pattern: as time integrates order and subjective$_1$ existence, it must follow order. In the sequence of time, as order and subjectivity$_1$ are integrated in concrete events, the terms *before* and *after* are used to express order, that is, necessity.[21] Events are directed; and they are directed by anticipation. The directing is done by something toward which the process moves; for that very reason, however, this "something" is not really present. The anticipation of the future directs the present. At the same time, the anticipated future is entered securely on the basis of, and supported by, the present. In scientific research, for example, data support a hypothesis. The data are real and present. The hypothesis, a future fact, directs the research. Here we see the anticipatory and retrocipatory features of the modal order manifested as temporal order (the founding order and the opening or qualifying order). Time has an anticipatory qualifying direction as well as a retrocipatory founding direction. The latter direction is the existential foundation of all possibility, while the former directs the temporal process. They may be referred to as the founding and directing orders of time. They temporally found and direct the dynamic of reality.[22]

Certain things must happen before or after others: seeding before harvesting, for example, and the hostages were freed after the Shah died. This is a matter of temporal priority determined by the order of reality, and experienced in the actuality of events. It is in the actuality of events that order and subjectivity$_1$ are integrated in time. Events move within structural limits and in a certain direction, so they are directed and supported at the same time. As a result, a diversity of moments are pulled in time into a unity of direction. In time, that unity and diversity also become fully integrated, for then the order of unity is met in an actual integral unity of functioning. In this way unity and diversity are also temporal moments. The movement of all things, the genetic process of growth, the ontic structure of anticipated meaning—all of this activity is a phase of the temporal process being directed toward fullness, totality, and fulfillment. Everything that is real must start somewhere and have its foundation in something. But everything also goes somewhere and has a destiny.

If we look at reality from the point of view of the future, then that future directs the present. Through anticipation, the future becomes a basis for the present direction of things.

6.3.5 *Integration and differentiation*

The anticipatory, or opening, or directing temporal order together with the retrocipatory or founding temporal order are known to us by the terms *before* or *after*. These terms describe the temporal succession of duration. What happens to the temporal category of simultaneity? Change, growth, and development do not only occur in successive stages; they also appear in simultaneity with other developments. In fact, all change is really a complexity of simultaneously occurring moments of change, being joined together in patterns of order. Temporal simultaneity is the joining together of many forms of existence into existential coherence and unity. The categories of integration discussed earlier in this chapter are, in the final analysis, themselves also temporal categories. The dynamic temporal process gives rise to both an increasing diversity of things and to an increasing integration of things.

There are always two simultaneous processes taking place: entities and functions increase (interaction, genesis, newness), and they are being placed in functional interrelations. This is really a historical process in which integration and differentiation are simultaneous temporal realities. Temporal simultaneity implies that in the integration of order and subjectivity$_1$, existential coherence takes place, not just an *order* of coherence. Real things cohere according to their order, and they do so in time. Unity and diversity are integrated in this way. The entitary unity of things in a functional multiplicity shows us how the diversity is integrated in a unity. The unity is also expressed in a diversity.

A moving, changing, growing, developing, progressing world gives rise to new functions, parts, functors, and relations that enrich and support the opening up of reality and increase the fullness of meaning. The differentiation is integrated; the specialization is totalized. Within contexts and unities the variety of things coheres in time. When sensitivity is unfolded in the organism, we get a development of special organs which fit the sensitive functioning into the coherence of the total organism. This temporal genetic process is not limited to organic functions of organisms, but is a feature of all reality. The temporal world specializes and integrates an ever-increasing variety of functors and functions.[23]

Education is a necessity of life. And as culture develops and becomes more specialized and interdependent, each newborn member of the human race must learn more and more to deal with his or her society. As we well know, education becomes ever more specialized, although if such specialization is not at the same time oriented to integrative patterns, things fall apart. We can only responsibly exercise our calling if we are fully at home in the environment in which we find ourselves. Education allows us all to catch up with the race. In contrast, a young animal can assume its own care very quickly, since in all the generations of its parents, the needs for such care remain unchanged.

Things are different for young children. Even years of being close to their mothers does not make them capable of self-care, as in the case of animals. At the age of six, children can look after themselves in terms of feeding, hygiene, clothing, and so forth. But they are only able to care for themselves in terms of vital functions. They can maintain their organism, so to speak. But they still are not emotionally mature. And to be fully human they must be ready for a position of social responsibility, being a member of the body of humanity. That body will need specialized members to do its work.

At earlier stages of civilization, young people could become educated by staying close to the adult members of the society for a number of years. Children could watch their elders perform the tasks belonging to their stage of culture. Some verbal instruction was perhaps necessary, but mostly it was a case of practice. The main tasks would be hunting and food gathering, building homes, and so forth. By about twelve years of age, children in these cultures were considered as adults, so they could be initiated.

As things have grown more complex, learning has also become more difficult. A special time now is devoted to education. Special persons have taken that educational task upon themselves. Gradually the function of education, which formerly had gone almost unnoticed, now has become an institutionalized activity. It requires regular meetings, a schedule of activities, a unique building, and a professional educator. But that process of specialization, differentiation, and integration never stops. The next development is special teachers, special subjects, and special schools. As with all specialization, we will see a process whereby new developments will be integrated into the continuity of the main stream of development. And this integration, according to the temporal order, should be simultaneous with the specialization.

Chapter VII
The Special Place of Humanity

DURING THE COURSE OF THE PRECEDING CHAPTERS I have at times made remarks that seemed to exclude humanity from the treatment given to the rest of empirical existence. In the chapter on kinds and functions, for example, I analyzed the pistical function as a way in which human experience is kept open beyond empirical existence. There have also been references to the Appendix, a section in which I deal more specifically with the nature of the commitment underlying this study. The present chapter looks at some unique and special features of human existence. I will examine some problems here that have arisen in the history of philosophy as a result of humanity's unique place in existence.

Human existence is obviously continuous with the rest of the empirical world. People must be physical to be real, they must metabolize their food, and they must open their eyes in order to see. But at the same time, people occupy a special position in the world, by virtue of their dominant position. Although empirical existents must all respond to the conditions that hold for existence, a person is called to respond *responsibly*. So an analysis of the human world confronts us with special problems. It also presents a crucial test for any philosophy that tries to provide a conceptual framework for all empirical reality. Can the framework developed so far do justice to the peculiar position of our humanity?

I will begin by discussing the special problems of humanity in terms of realms of existence. The human race belongs to a special realm, one which displays continuity and distinctness. Because the human realm *is* a realm, it is continuous with other realms in the order of time. The human realm is distinct, however, because it has unique characteristics, *as* a realm, not shared by other realms (except objectively in their relation to human culture).

After I have further elaborated on the concept of realms of existence, I will explore the human realm. Its functional uniqueness and the spiritual dimension of reality will both be investigated. It will not be possible to postpone all of our discussion of elements that lie beyond the reach of philosophy, which properly belongs in the Appendix. If human commitment is constituent of being human, then in a discussion of the phenomenon of humanity, the nature of commitment cannot be omitted. So the Appendix will be anticipated much more closely in this chapter, particularly when I discuss human spirituality. The discussion of these matters will be followed by a section on dualisms. These have arisen at various times in the course of Western thought as philosophers have tried to deal with special problems of human existence. The closing section will briefly touch on a critical issue: can the human relation to the origin of the universe be part of a theoretical, philosophical discussion? A negative answer to this question finally clarifies the need for the Appendix.

7.1 Functor Realms or Kingdoms

When I talk of realms of existence I talk of the major categories or kinds of functors. *Realm* is thus a technical term which denotes only an ordering of reality into the four basic functoral kinds of mineral, vegetable, animal, and human. The categories world order and ordered world are not, therefore, realm categories. Realms are categories of existence according to principles of order. And whatever belongs to one realm must completely and exhaustively belong to that realm. At the same time whatever belongs to one realm must be continuous with whatever belongs to other realms. All functors must belong to no more than one realm, no functors must not belong to any realm, and no realm must be without functors.

There is no agreement, not even agreement in principle, on this matter of realms. It is not even widely accepted that the realm division is a functoral division. It is not uncommon for philosophers to refer to a principle of order as an "entity," in continuity with naming, say, a fish an entity. Among the realms of things, they might say, there is also a realm of order. But even if we should agree that the realms of things are realms of subjective$_1$, empirical, physical, temporal existents, then we still do not find agreement as to what realms there are. Some would admit just one realm of material entities.[1] Others admit material and living things.[2] The latter might further subdivide the realm of the living into organisms and animals, and the realm of animals into beasts and humans. But a two-realm theory might also divide things into material and mental, rather than material and living.[3] Probably the most realms introduced into Western thought are five: material, living, sentient, rational or mental, and spiritual.

The division into realms is historically related to both the diversity of functors and the diversity of functions. The two are, of course, related, since functor realms are primarily determined by the different qualifying functions. It will be recalled that I count myself among the four-realm theorists. But I do not characterize the human realm primarily functionally. Let me explain. The characterization of the first three realms as physical, organic, and sentient is based on the qualifying functional level of existence of these entities. The human realm is frequently characterized by just one of the human functional levels, one which only people possess subjectively$_2$, namely, the level of the analytic, often called the rational. I do believe that only human beings are rational, but I find evidence of reductionism if we characterize as rational all of human functioning that is specifically human. In addition, I also believe that the specifically human cannot, in the final analysis, be fully understood in functional terms. These are the phenomena that I wish to focus on in this chapter.[4]

Nevertheless, I do opt for the traditional conceptual scheme of dividing reality into mineral, vegetable, animal, and human realms. I believe that modern research in the so-called life sciences, as well as in the behavioral sciences, supports the opinion that reductionist attempts of the last century have not proven to be satisfactory.[5] The four-realm model may, of course, have its own problems, and in many cases this theory may appear to be both uncritical and speculative. Nevertheless, there does not seem to be any available evidence to show that the four-realm model must be wrong. Evidence does not steer us clearly in the direction of an alternative view. The four-realm model is at least consistent with the adequacy of everyday experience. It seems unnecessary to question the rightness of the four-realm interpretation of things common to our everyday world.[6]

The division of reality into four realms has at least two implications. First, if an entity is truly to exist in our space-time world, then it must either be a physical thing, an organism, an animal, or a person. Whatever is not one of these four will have to be accounted for in terms of functions of these four, or relations of or among them.[7] There is also another implication. The human realm may be one of the four realms of subjective$_1$ existence and thus continuous with all subjectivity$_1$, but it is still a realm of its own and will provide us with room to look at the uniqueness of humanity. If we classify humanity as one kind among the animals, however, understanding this uniqueness is much more difficult. Later in this chapter I will deal extensively with the uniqueness of humanity. For the moment it is necessary simply to recall that in my view the realm of human existence is not reducible to that of animal or organic existence nor, for a stronger reason, to that of physical existence.

This does not imply discontinuity. Human beings function on the physical levels and also on the biotic and sensitive levels. But they do so, of course, in specifically human ways. And those human ways show both the discontinuity and the continuity to be present even on the levels shared with other existents. Moreover, the human being as a whole also functions on many other levels in subjective$_2$ ways. On those levels other entities only function objectively, because they do not have certain subjective$_2$ functions of their own.[8] Thus, the natural sciences and psychology may perhaps be adequate to deal with physical, organic, and animal entities, but they are unable to account for economic reality, ethical levels of functioning, or the experiences of justice, faith, language, and so forth. There are, as we have seen earlier, realms of functioning which do not subjectively$_2$ occur in the animal, plant, and physical worlds. Consequently, if there are functional levels not found subjectively$_2$ in the first three realms, one looks for entities capable of functioning on these levels in another realm.

There is a further difficulty: in my view a person cannot be reduced to functional existence. Human functioning is centered in a way that qualifying functions cannot fully account for. The integral identity of the human person transcends human functionality. Human responsibility and accountability point to another dimension of human existence besides the functional dimension, namely, the spiritual. The spiritual in humanity cannot be *fully* understood as functionality, although it can be understood *only* if we understand it *in terms* of functionality. For this reason, too, we need to acknowledge a specifically human realm of existence.

Admittedly, the four-realm theory I am proposing here has its special difficulties. For example, this division does not leave room for creatures that do not belong to the four categories mentioned. In the case of evolutionism's possibility of transitional entities, the problem is not so severe. Perhaps some other realm must one day be introduced, as the theory of evolution keeps developing. Evolution theory makes the four-realm theory problematic. Present ways of characterizing concepts, which would help us to classify existents as either organisms or animals, have not proven to be universally applicable. This may imply that our present categorization is too rich, and perhaps we really need only one category for animal and organic existence.

But our present categories may also be too poor. It might be worthwhile to see whether there are entities in both the plant and animal kingdoms whose nature cannot properly be categorized as either plant or animal; their reality might call for redivision into new realms of functors. The animal realm, as it is currently understood, might really consist of more realms. Using the functional order proposed in an earlier chapter, one might begin to speculate. In the animal world there may simply be sentient creatures whose existence is a combination of drives and need-satisfaction, others who are capable of environment manipulation in a conscious way, and still others capable of symbolic behavior.

There is still at least one other problem for a four-realm theory, namely, the uniqueness of human existence in terms of the spiritual dimension of persons. The existence of this dimension of humanity cannot be explained in terms of the functional configuration of realms, as a result of which the four realms cannot be fully commensurate. In the area of functional structures, there is no common denominator for the acceptance of human spirituality in these four realms. However, the human person is in fact spiritual, and humanity's existence is continuous with the rest of empirical existence. To solve this problem without falling into dualistic discontinuities, "ghost of machine" theories, or *deus ex machina* introductions, will be my special challenge in this chapter.

If there are indeed four realms of empirical existence, how can we begin to classify all the entities that exist? The exceptional place of humanity will be treated at length later on in the chapter, so I will largely confine myself to the subhuman realms. All functors in these realms have one particular characteristic: their unity is the result of being subjected$_1$ to a typical configurational order. This order structures the temporal unity of the entity by determining its qualifying functions as the highest level on which the entity can function subjectively$_2$. In the case of physical objects, for example, the highest level on which they function as subjects$_2$ is that of their energy functions. These functions typically qualify, integrate, and open up all functioning of the physical entity. Any functional whole that has no higher kinds of subjective$_2$ functions than energy functions will be an entity belonging to the physical realm. These qualifying functions determine how a material thing is defined.

We must realize that this is true primarily of physical entities in their so-called "natural" state, and not as they have become affected by human culture. In the latter case we see things as they have become characterized by certain kinds of objective functioning. In their functor identity, characterized by their involvement in the human realm, they can belong to that human realm objectively. Cultural artifacts such as machines would be appropriate examples. In that way the so-called "natural" world also is taken up (objectively) into the guidance of the development of the world through human commitment. But "natural" physical entities are energy functors, centers of interactions of forces. And all functional levels in that sort of entity are oriented to this physical functioning.

Organisms include all entities that are biotically integrated functors. Their subjective$_2$ functioning extends beyond that of physical entities because they have biotic subjective$_2$ functions. But this does not mean they are simply physical things functioning on another level. Rather, they are, in their entirety, vital or organic functors; they are growth units, centers of organic action. All their functions, parts, and relations are subordinate to the vital integration of these dimensions into integral biotic functioning, that is, growth and survival. The other levels of functioning do not, by being so integrated and subordinated, lose their specific identity as functions of a different kind. They simply do not play a leading or qualifying role in the functoral unity of the entity in time.

In the case of what we now call the animal kingdom, the situation is more complex. Animals function at least in a sensitive way. Some of them appear to have formative or technico-manipulative functions, while others may be capable of genuine symbolic behavior. Whether all animals are capable of formative and symbolic behavior, however, is controversial. And there is also a question about animals' social behavior. Do they merely display group behavior, or is there evidence of real social relationships with a social order? Many researchers seem to conclude that animals are in any case not capable of generalization, that is, of forming abstract concepts. They do not have any analytic functions.[9] The other transpsychic functional levels have been ascribed to some animals by researchers, but not without arousing controversy.

There are still many hurdles to be overcome. For example, what constitutes behavior of one functional kind? How do we know whether certain organisms are sentient? When do we conclude that a particular behavior is symbolic, and what are the criteria? On the animal level, what constitutes evidence that such behavior is present? There is also a concern about the validity of any experiments conducted to settle such questions. We may conduct experiments, for instance, in which animals are taught certain functions by humans. But can we safely conclude from these experiments precisely what these animals are "naturally" capable of?

Whatever the case may be with animals, there seems to be no reason to abandon our model for looking at a functor. We can still view a functor from the perspective of the integrating and qualifying role of the highest subjective$_2$ functions. That model goes a long way in accounting for many perplexing states of affairs. It helps us to understand how organisms can have physical functions which do indeed obey physical laws, even though the methods and laws of physics cannot account for the life and the growth of the organism. And it explains that although animals do have genuine organic functions, these functions are not sufficient to account for the whole reality of what we know to be an animal.

In animals, the organic functions will not have the dominant leading role that integrates all animal functioning. Animals are sensitively, or otherwise, oriented. Their lower functions are developed and structured by higher functional levels.[10] So in animals the organic functions as a sublevel of functioning, unlike in the case of organisms. But these animal organic functions do keep their own organic nature, even though they become the organic functioning characteristic of animals and not of plants. At the same time, the organic level of functioning serves as the foundation for those higher levels. And this organic level of functioning is itself developed in anticipation of these higher functions.[11]

We have evidence of organic functions in animals that are qualified, developed, and integrated by higher functions. The vital organs of an animal, such as the heart and lungs, are not merely organs needed to maintain an organism's vitality, in any limited sense of that term. These are not just organs of viability. The animal body has organs that support self-motion, feeling, and so forth. These functions are not found in mere plant organisms. If we explain feelings by means of the organic substratum that supports them and makes them possible, then we are merely acknowledging how feelings are integrally interwoven with the organic functions. And we also acknowledge that these organic functions, in serving the sentient functions, have been developed by them. Eyes, nervous systems, legs, grasping hands or feet, blood (not just juices or liquids) are all indications of what I have in mind here. But the eyes do not see, nor do the nerves feel. They are the organs of a functor that does see and feel, one that has sentient functions. And plant organisms do not have such functions.

Thus, a creature that belongs to a certain realm is integrally unified, in a manner typical of the nature of that realm. A physical entity is simply that. And an organism and an animal cannot be other than what they are. But this does not mean, for example, that the only organic functions found in an animal are anticipations of the higher functions. If the organs that are organic anticipations of psychic needs are to function genuinely, then they need a support system that is genuinely organic. On every level of functioning there are anticipatorily developed functions. But there are also the supportive, retrocipatory functional levels that seem to be, and are, fully organic, although they do not give evidence of being locked into the psychic anticipation. They are not, as such, part of the animal body; they are enkaptically interwoven organic entities. They are taken up in the animal structure as food and used as support. But when they are not taken into the animal structure, they would be capable of independent organic existence.

Functors do not, of course, exist in isolation. Especially in the last few decades, research in the natural sciences has demonstrated how the earth presents us with a number of very delicately balanced systems of interrelationship. These are ecological units, environments of very specific structures, biospheres that are in perfect, yet delicate, balance. In these environmental systems or habitats, we find specialized physical conditions (climates of recurring patterns of constancy), certain types of vegetation, and specific animal populations. The interrelationships are delicate and easily disturbed, although if left alone they are continued by their own internal organization. They are coherent totalities, but not functoral unities or action centers.

Deserts, tundras, and boreal forests all are examples of these vast interlocking systems. Marshes, moors, or woods are smaller units. A beaver dam is an even smaller unit. A galaxy or a milky way is a completely physical, organizational system. Others have more realms interlocked. From these examples it appears that functors do not exist in splendid isolation and, furthermore, even realms do not exist by themselves. Every concrete situation shows realm-interdependence. Not only does vegetation serve as food for animals, but animals contribute to specific patterns of vegetation. They fertilize flowers, spread seeds, and provide manure. Thus we not only have functional interrelations in functional analogies, but also functoral interrelations in the subject$_2$-object relation.

Such interlocking and fairly well-defined systems have an integrality and unity of their own. They are totalities, although they are not functors. A desert is neither a functor nor an individual unit of action. Deserts are functor and function integrators. They are not merely the sand. Rather, they are complex systems of subject$_2$-object interrelationships that do have the character of individual totalities, but not of functoral unity. Can these unique totalities be categorized? Are they examples of a kind? Do they exemplify structurally constant relationships? Are their typical structures known? Does each desert have a totally unique organization? Is it possible to indicate a structural type which all deserts exhibit?

Although the systems are delicately balanced, this is not sufficient for them to be unified wholes. We can pile up a number of articles in such a way that if the pile is disturbed at any point, the whole structure will collapse. What is true here of physical balance can also be said of interrealm balance. Nature seeks to favor relations that exhibit stability, regardless of the cost. After any disaster, some balance will again be established. But it may be that former participants in the system are gone and new ones have been introduced. In that respect there seems to be no preestablished order that ordains which entities belong to a particular system. On the other hand, there appear to be natural cycles and rhythms which, barring disaster, run their own course. Marshes, lakes, and deserts all have known origins and destinies.

7.2 The Human Realm

Within certain broad limits, people are not bound to any particular environment. Most animals are habitat bound. Loss of habitat often leads to extinction of a species. This is not so for humans. Bushmen live in deserts, Eskimos on ice fields, certain Indians in rain forests, New Yorkers in vast structures of steel and concrete. At the same time, all humans do live in some environment. But we are all adaptable to many existing environments, even when we have especially accommodated ourselves (only temporarily, it seems) to our particular environment. This adaptation can be seen in habits of dress, food, recreation, shelter, feelings of comfort, language, customs, and so forth. In many ways we do not merely adapt to the environment; we use its elements to adapt that environment for our habitation.

There are definite limits to the specifically human interrelation with the other realms. Human control has its own boundaries, as modern environmental awareness is showing us. What exactly is that human realm like in its continuity and discontinuity with the other realms? Clearly, the human realm is fundamentally continuous with the other realms, as we have already noted. We need air to breathe, water to drink, seeds or meat to eat, the earth to walk on, and the rivers in which to swim. Without trees to burn or to make shelters, animals to ride or to pull our burdens, and the natural resources to make our utensils and instruments, human existence would not only be impoverished, but we would be unable to exist. We not only have functions on levels shared with others, but we also depend on other realms for our existence. By our existing in communal continuity, the environment is objectively developed in farmland, raw materials, domestic animals, dams, canals, planted forests, and now even in attempts to harness the energy of the sun. All of these objective cultural realities have a great impact on the "natural" environments. Insofar as humanity is one with the rest of nature, however, these impacts are human, though not unnatural.

In nature, separate from humankind, and also on preanalytic human levels of functioning, higher human functions develop lower levels. All of this is well documented. The erect posture, the position of the thumb, the volume of the cranium, certain unique brain centers (speech, for example), the difference between copulation and lovemaking, and many more human functions testify to this development of lower levels of functioning. In all of this humans do not differ from the other realms. But humans are in certain ways also discontinuous with other kinds of creatures. For this reason I will now take a look at the special place occupied by humanity. Then I will examine some of the specially human realms of functioning.

7.2.1 The exceptional place of humanity

In terms of the patterns discussed so far, the exceptional place of humanity in the world points to some very important differences between persons and other entities. We can begin to understand some of these differences if we look at one very important fact. In the life of a person, there is not a single qualifying function that structurally unites and integrates all of human experience. Later we will see how, in all aspects of human behavior, there are specific kinds of qualifying functions for specific kinds of behavior. However, none of these functions qualifies all of human experience. Other functors are functionally *defined* by a qualifying function. But no functions fully determine functionally who the total human being is.

There is one functional level of experience which does guide all of experience and helps keep it open, namely, that of the pistic functions. But it structurally qualifies, that is, functionally determines and defines the nature of only a certain number of specific human acts and relationships. These are acts of faith, and phenomena such as prayer and worship. Moreover, the specifically qualified faith relations are found in institutional relationships such as the church. In all other human functioning, the faith functions only guide human life and keep experience open. Since there is no higher function to which this opening up can be directed, it is directed to the origin and unity of all of reality. This source, we will recall, is also the origin of unity for human existence.[12]

The fact that pistic functions have no other functional level to anticipate and the fact that all other functional levels do in fact anticipate that level of functioning in the qualifying direction of the cosmic modal order gives pistic functioning a peculiar place. Pistic functioning, however, is not closed off for lack of another level of functioning it can anticipate. Rather, it provides for the openness of human experience to what lies beyond the limits of subjective$_1$ existence, namely, the origin, order, and destiny of existence. All human experience is in that way directed to the ultimate destiny of the world. And given the place of humanity in the world, all existence becomes consciously directed to that destiny. And that destiny in turn is given shape through what people believe it to be.

In this way we may say that in the qualifying direction of the modal order all things are not only temporally defined and qualified in their nature by their qualifying functions, but all things are also ultimately *guided* functionally through human faith in the world's destiny. Human pistis thus functions as guide to the destiny of the world. And the x/y structure of things (i.e., their having qualifying and founding functions) is taken up into a $\frac{e}{x \cdot y}$ structure. The qualifying nature of a thing is not its ultimate destiny; rather, its being taken up and being guided through human faith to the ultimate destiny of the world determines its final place in the order of things. The origin and destination of the universe is the ultimate orientation of all things through human functioning in faith.

Thus we can see how a human being is functionally open to what lies beyond the limits of subjectivity$_1$. A person's life is not functionally closed off. It is open to being committed, through faith, to the acceptance of the ultimate. This acceptance of the ultimate is not without ground, however. A person will only accept what is experienced as acceptable. But the ultimate acceptance of our ultimate ground is a matter of experiencing it *as* ground, which is then *itself* the ground *on* which we accept it. At the same time, this experience of acceptability is seen to be far more than mere subjectivity$_1$. Committed acceptance of the ultimate is always an act of submission to revelation.[13] This will hold true whether the ultimate is the creator of all things or the autonomous freedom of humanity as the origin of all that is meaningful. Epistemologically we see this submission in the notion that some of our ultimate beliefs are basic. They are seen to be based not on other beliefs, but on the evidence of the ultimate itself.

The belief content of such commitment is basic in three senses: what is accepted as ultimate is basic; the belief in the ultimate is basic; and the function of such basic belief in the ultimate will control all other beliefs. This supremacy of our basic belief in the ultimate will constitute what is experienced as revelation.

Thus pistic functioning, as terminal functioning for human experience, is quite special. The x/y structure of things requires some function—namely, x, the qualifying function—to be the one that temporally closes off the subjectivity$_2$ of the entity, the one that defines its nature. As an organic entity, a plant cannot function in a subjective$_2$ manner beyond its organic nature. But it can still be developed functionally in an objective manner. Beyond its own qualifying function, an organism can objectively be developed by animals and people. And this also makes a plant open to being guided in a certain direction through human faith. But in the case of people, there is no such thing as a highest subjective$_2$ function which qualifies human behavior and closes it off or defines and fully determines the nature of humanity on that functional level.

Furthermore, there are many x/y structural relations in human society in which the x function is not the pistic function. If that were not the case, all human institutions would by nature be religious worship communities like churches. And that is, indeed, not the case. The market, for example, has an economic x function. As a human relationship, it is economically qualified. As a subjective$_2$ human phenomenon it is also economically closed off, even though it is guided toward an ultimate destiny by human faith, and even though the temporal, economic destiny of the market can be anticipatorily and objectively opened up to higher levels of functioning such as justice and morality. However, in being guided by faith, such a phenomenon remains fundamentally open to what lies beyond the limits of subjectivity$_1$ and subjectivity$_2$.

No human experience is closed off by a qualifying x function. All concrete, typical, human experiences do have an x/y structure. But that specific x/y relation only characterizes these specific human kinds of behavior. It does not characterize all of human behavior, nor does it essentially define what it is to be human. Every specific kind of human experience or relationship, although relatively determined in its functional characterization by an x function or qualifying function, remains open to the guiding function of faith. And in faith it remains open to what lies beyond the limits of humanity. Human faith, as a subjective$_2$ terminal function of human experience, keeps human life open to what lies beyond the subjective$_1$ realm. In this way all of subjective₁ reality in humankind is open to the order and origin of reality, that is, open to what people in faith take to be the order and origin of reality, and to which people in faith also commit themselves. Humankind is functionally open to this perspective. As a result, we are able to participate in directing existence to its origin, which is also its destiny. Through humankind, existence functionally receives direction.

What emerges from this discussion is that we must define humanity as that functoral community which as a realm of functors in relation to the other realms is called to be an agent for the direction of the world. And by viewing humanity as subjective₁ director of destiny, we view it as spiritual. When I speak of human spirituality, I mean human openness to what lies beyond subjective₁ empirical reality. We are spiritual in that we are not closed off functionally. We are in touch with the intended direction of things, with the destiny of temporal development, and we are able to be conscious of the order of things. In the spirituality of humanity, all of empirical reality is open to direction and is temporally aware.[14]

We may refer to the human being either as a body or as a spirit. In both cases we will be speaking about the entire person. A person is a body as much as a person is a spirit. As body the person is spiritual body. As spirit the person is bodily spirit. Seen as a body, a person fits functionally into the world as we know it, displaying many different functional dimensions which all interlock comfortably with the world on all levels. Seen as a spirit, a person is united, is one through being oriented to the origin and destiny of the world, is an integrally functioning agent of developmental direction in the universe. The unity of a person is itself a matter of the directional integration of all human functional diversity. This diversity is being concentrated on the ultimate destiny and origin of all reality.

Spirituality, as I see it, is not in addition to the human body. A person is not a body *and* a spirit. The human body, as noted above, is a spiritual body and the human spirit is a bodily spirit. The entire person is a body; the entire person is a spirit. Spirit is not a separate entity dwelling within a body. The human body is not simply a physical corpus or an organism. A person is referred to as a spirit simply as an indication of the specific and peculiar centeredness of all human action. It is not centered by any of the human functions. Rather, in humanity the concentated integrality of all functional diversity is found in the openness of the person to the origin and destiny of the universe. And a person is able to be an integral and centered being in conscious concentration on this origin and destiny.

The concentrated orientation of the universe through human-kind on the origin, order, and destiny of existence is what constitutes humanity as spiritual. This is also what both unites all members of the human race and constitutes the unity of the individual person. Truly human integrity or simplicity is found in spiritual integrity. This spiritual unity is expressed in a diversity of functional structures which together in their coherence are known as the human body. In the foundational, temporal order, the person is a body, while in the developing order of reality the person is a spirit. The person as a spirit or the person as a body are simply the same person seen from a different perspective.[15]

From this viewpoint, it is clear that dualisms in anthropology are not acceptable. Cartesian or Platonic approaches to the spirituality of humankind must be rejected. However, this does not mean that a materialistic monism is accepted, or that what used to be called the rational soul of the person can simply be explained in terms of certain levels of human functionality. All human functions are spiritual because they are the functional diversity of a spiritually centered unity. The physical and organic functional dimensions in persons are spiritual dimensions. At the same time, the analytic, moral, or faith functions of a person are dimensions of human corporeality; they are bodily dimensions. The spiritual in human existence is not some functional dimension. It is the specifically human centeredness of all functional levels.[16]

7.2.2 *A typically human event*

In its unique spiritual place among other realms, the human realm confronts us with a number of special problems. One of these is how we should deal with "worlds" within realms: the worlds of education, language, trade and commerce, government, religion, and so forth. In our complex civilization they seem more and more to be worlds apart. Spiritually, however, all of life is potentially one. If all people shared the same commitment, there would not be any division in humanity, only functional diversity. The basic divisions in human society are ideological, ultimately religious, divisions. Functional diversity does not really imply division.

That functional diversity is immense and ever-growing. There are numerous social totalities and communal wholes with qualifying functions on different levels. They give us the impression that they all belong to a unique realm, one which differs from other human realms. To these human relationships among functions and functors, that is, among acts, institutions, and communal relations we need to pay some special attention. To make a beginning I will discuss a complex but presentative event, namely, the signing of a peace treaty.

What constitutes the signing of a peace treaty? How do we know what belongs to that particular event? Should we include negotiations that precede it? What about the preparations of a great hall, or the protests outside of the building? Or is the event marked only by the ceremony itself?[17] If that is the totality, then what belongs to it? Is the arrival of the invited dignitaries also part of the signing? Or does it all start with the opening speech, gong, bell, or trumpet blast? A reporter might announce, "The ceremony is about to begin." Then, suddenly, after a short, specific period of time, he adds, in more hushed tones, "The ceremony has begun."

As we can see, this is not an easy matter to decide. For the moment I will simply concentrate on the boundaries and typicality of the actual ceremony. All the other events can be regarded as foundational in the order of time. They constitute the manner in which an event is interwoven into the coherence of the rest of human experience. The actual ceremony begins at precisely 2:30 p.m. Consequently, it is immediately interwoven with the rest of human experience, because sometime before 2:30, people must cease other activities and make their way to the hall. Later the reverse situation takes place. When the ceremony is over and the champagne has been drunk (the hour for leaving having been determined at 4:30), the guests depart to take up other activities, some of them, no doubt, related to the preceding event.

Is this event a unity of some kind? Is it comparable to a desert, which has interrelated ecological dimensions? Or is it analogous to a centered entity? Although its duration is certainly much shorter than that of a desert, this need not deter us. Some organisms or chemical elements also have a very short life span. But they can still be reckoned as units of functionality. In the case of a treaty, there is apparently a factor pleading for its interpretation as a functional unit: it is reasonably possible to determine what does and does not belong to the event. On the other hand, can we treat the event not just as some totality, but as a centered unit or independent functor? This would require it to be found only in certain relational contexts. In addition, it would need to be relatively independent to act.

In the case of the signing of a peace treaty we might argue that it makes sense only in a larger relational context. It is then to be understood as merely a moment in, or a function of, a relationship between two nations. In that case, we might say there are many different activities which are coordinated, integrated, and made coherent because there is only one predominantly functional level of reality which characterizes all the activity. The dominating kinds of acts may be founded in acts and functions of other kinds, of course. But one level of functioning might be said to functionally integrate and organize all other functions and relationships into one coherent totality. Thus, we might say all actions and functions and relations that are formative in kind characterize what goes on. The formative point of view sets the tone. More specifically, the pistic anticipation of this level of functioning (ceremonial acts and relationships), founded in the analogy of force (historical power), provides the integrating point of view.[18]

What I have tried to indicate with the above description is that in order for us to place functions, acts, and events in our experience, we need to see them in terms of the structures that define them. In the context of the structures of their relationships we see humans acting in ways that we recognize as events of some kind, organizations of some sort, institutions of some type. Within their contextual boundaries the activities take on meaning. And theoretically we can begin to deal with such structural boundaries when we can identify their x/y relations.

7.2.3   *Structural types in human society*

The introduction of structured functions, acts, and events as contextual organizers of human behavior will start to give us an orderly sense of the complexity of human society. In that manner we may be able to understand the existence of relationships between actors which not only seem to have a greater degree of permanence than momentary acts and events, but in some cases seem to have the character of actors or functors themselves. Examples of this phenomenon are referred to in ordinary speech by words we take to be actor identifiers. The *school board* has decided. The *government* has refused. The *church* is inactive. The *school* is celebrating the birthday of the nation. Do these sentences indicate acts or events, performed by actors or functors, which are named by the nouns, that is, by the grammatical subjects in the sentences?

Discussion of this problem is important. In the case of human society, will my views allow us to account for, or explain, certain concrete problems? Human society today is seriously undermined by nominalistic and individualistic views of how the world "hangs together." Interrelationships are seen as personal choices rather than configurations of ontic order. Could the categories developed in the preceding chapters suggest another approach? Is there reality to the unity and orderliness of a phenomenon such as the school?

With the help of the categories discussed earlier, I think it can be said that schools, school boards, governments, banks, shopping centers, tax review agencies, and so on, are all *kinds* of human association in relationship to the world in which they occur. As relationships, they are more than mere happenstance contacts. They presuppose, in a structural way, a type of functioning called socializing. We are *related* to the sun, although we do not *associate* with the sun. The institutional relationships I have in mind are all associational relations; they are related to purposeful, conscious, planned acts of association. Furthermore, the institutions I have in mind are related to an important way to buildings, territories, and other physical phenomena. The totality we refer to as school, church, government is as complex a phenomenon as an ecosystem. The social system of a modern university or a modern government bureaucracy is very much like an ecosystem. But is the university a system of integrated and coherent relations? Or is it itself a functor? What is the nature of its totality or coherence?

We will recall that prehuman reality exists in the realms of minerals (physical entities), vegetables (organisms), and animals. As realms, they each differ according to their qualifying functions. The same approach can be used here to make sense of human social realities. The whole realm of human behavior can be seen to exist in subrealms of functional types according to the different modal levels of functions which qualify and integrate types of relationships. For each human subject$_2$ function we can find a wide realm of human relations. Human association, guided by such a function, provides patterns of integration that help us to recognize definite types of such association. Further, different combinations with contrasting founding functions are possible. This gives us an ontological classification model which has easily recognizable patterns and also wide application.

As an example, we can look at human types of behavior which are qualified as typically ethical, as having their nature in being directed by bonds of troth. Three obvious forms of this association would be marriage, friendship, and family. All are ultimately qualified by the responsibility to keep troth. For this reason James Olthuis called his book dealing with these three relations *I Pledge You My Troth* (Harper & Row, 1975). These types of relationships typically involve fidelity or loyalty, which is further deepened and guided by commitment on the certitudinal level of functioning. But not all of these relationships have the same foundational functions.

The marriage bond is so all-encompassing as to be founded in the physical or bodily unity of a couple. This is the relation to which sexual intercourse typically belongs. Here intercourse finds its proper destiny, and outside of this relation it degenerates. Sexual intercourse has a specific character. It not only fits exclusively within a committed fidelity situation, it fits particularly in the one that is physically founded, which we recognize and refer to as marriage. In the family bond of troth and commitment, the typical bond is founded in the genetic (i.e., organic) origin of the typical compatibility relations. And the friendship bond is founded in emotional or psychic affinity.

This sort of example can be multiplied almost infinitely over the range of associational relations in human society. In addition to troth associations there are cultic associations (churches, support groups), economic associations (businesses, banks), jural associations (state, government), and many more. A police force would be a form of human association based on power (a physical retrocipation of formative functioning) and qualified by enforceable justice. The juridical qualifying function would have its own retrocipatory meaning in being retributive power. The actual power displayed by a police force would, in turn, be anticipatorily opened up by justice. This power would have to be legally justified.

What are we to make of these forms of association with their typical arrangement of qualifying and founding functions. Can a family or police force truly be regarded as actors, functors, or unified wholes? Is there integration that will make the social unit itself become a whole, capable of human action independently? The human persons involved in them seem to be enkaptically interrelated. Do they give up their identity as action centers in favor of the centered action of an entity such as a family or school? This is obviously not the case. The school, although it is a human enterprise, cannot be a person. But it is an organization, that is, an organized, interactional, interrelation of persons in a specified environment, such that the interaction has organizational centricity. There is a principal, a school board, and a chairperson. The organization takes the form of an action center because it has centered action.

Now, human relationships may be integrated, organized, and associated into institutions and societies, but this does not make independent entities in the sense of functors out of them. An entity, that is, a functoral whole, has to function subjectively$_2$ on the first four functional levels. Its numeric, spatial, kinetic, and energy functions must typically be those of a subjective$_2$ physical foundation. But marriages or governments do not have these typical subjective$_2$ functions, even though a marriage is physically founded. What might account for the subjective$_2$ physical functions of a government or a marriage? They do not have weight, mass, or dimensions. The physical dimension of these interrelationships is the objectively opened-up function of the soil as integrated enkaptically in the state as its territory. And the human physical body is enkaptically interwoven within the marriage.

But the state or the marriage do not have any typical physical functions that are subjective$_2$ functions of these relations. All of these relationships are, quite simply, just relationships. In spite of their centered organization, they do not become independent action units. This holds true even though the spiritual community of the persons involved becomes a dimension of the typical, associational forms of interrelationships. People who share a common spirit will in any form of association be united by that spirit. United, they will pursue a common destiny.

It is important, however, to view these relations in human society in terms of a variety of recognizable structures. The recognition and identification of these relationships is not, of course, in dispute. We all know what is meant by a family and a government. We all recognize the mother-son relation. We are able to identify a church. What is important is that we accept the patterns of order underlying these recognized realities in order to be able to acknowledge the proper sort of tasks, authorities, competences, and other functional relationships that structurally belong to any given social arrangement. Earlier I alluded to the impropriety of sexual intercourse outside of moral commitment relations. Today, the question of the extension of government powers is very much in vogue. My position here is that these questions are not simply a matter of what we decide. The real question is what we *ought* to decide in the face of relatively invariant structures, recognized patterns of order which define the proper boundaries of the bodies in question.

Thus I want to avoid two problems. One is the view according to which social totalities are nothing but the relationships that individuals happen to want to institute according to their subjective$_1$ desires. I accept the reality of social order, that is, of nomic conditions which transcend human arbitrariness. And I also want to avoid a substantialization of these social totalities as though they were themselves persons who can be treated as such. The ultimate centers of action and responsibility remain people, though these people have roles to play that are integral dimensions of ordered social relations. But persons cannot hide behind institutions. Neither can they deny institutional realities.[19]

7.2.4   *Ultimate divisions in society*

I will now continue the discussion of the spiritual dimension of
human existence. A picture of human society that allows us to understand the diversity of structured social relations is not complete unless
it also deals with divisions in society. When I talk of divisions I do not
refer to mere differences, but to obstacles which threaten the unity of
human society in a fundamental way. Such divisions cannot simply be
reduced to differences of opinion based on contrasting analyses, or to
other functional reasons. The latter differences have always existed
within larger contexts of unity: the people, the nation, the folk, the
culture, the civilization. In our history, such expressions as "the
American people" or "Western civilization" formerly stood for largely
binding and unifying realities. Now these realities are not as commonly shared. In some instances they are not shared at all. As a body of
people, even most Western nations are deeply divided. How can we
explain this lack of unity?

Human relations are communal relations. What this means is
that the spiritual unity of a person is integrated in the spirituality of
human relations. Where communal relations are genuine, they have a
common spirit and the community is spiritually united. There are
many individual tasks and responsibilities faced by human communities. These call for functional differentiation into many specific
task communities such as governments, schools, and other forms of
associated behavior for a specific functional purpose. But the same
communal bond of unity can be expressed here in the context of functional specificity. These various organized functional relations between organizations and institutions, the special interrelationship of the
various people and task communities into one community can be a
meaningful reality so long as there is an underlying spiritual integration.

The total human community cannot be integrated by one of its
segments. Human society is not a state, a church, or a school. None of
these can be the total integrator of all human functionality into a
functionally organized pattern. Nevertheless, typical structured interrelations among social wholes may lead to a community binding
together many task communities. They become characterized by a
common territory, climate, culture, commerce, language, history,
and so forth. All of these common functional elements may be shared
by a society. But underlying the integration was always assumed to be
the expression of a common spirit.

Unless the ultimate bond is spiritual, it cannot create typically *human* integration. Where all of the structural bonds do have genuinely spiritual integration, a corresponding, genuinely unified people may exist. But in an age of secularization, nominalism, and individualism, commonly held spiritual unity has been eroded. Consequently, there is hardly any large segment of people in Western culture that can be referred to as *the* "so-and-so" people—a spiritually united community with all the normal dimensions of such a community. *The* American people, for example, no longer exist as a community in that way.

This problem is not as imaginary as it may intially appear. In our time, many individuals, movements, and political parties claim to be speaking for "the people." Who are *the* people? Does someone who speaks for "the people" speak for all of them, most of them, or simply a minority? In order to deal with this problem we must first ask ourselves whether there are such things as human society or humanity. Is humankind a recognizable, typically structured entity? As a totality, what is its nature? Of course, there is a sense in which everyone knows that human society and humanity both exist. But what is their identity? Is it of some type? We can send a letter to the government, the school, or the church, for example. These are deliberately organized and instituted forms of association which we can identify and locate. They have specialized the function of correspondence into a position filled by a secretary. This cannot be done with "the people" in most normal situations.

The moment we begin to define what is meant by "the people," and as soon as we state what their characteristics and needs and aspirations may be, then many people want to opt out. They say that others are not speaking on their behalf. This problem is inherent in the question which is before us now. We may get agreement about the four basic kinds of existents: minerals, organisms, animals, and people. In that sense the people are *of* one kind, and all people are *one* of that kind. But the nature of this kind is not functionally closed in terms of functional orders of interrelation. "Human," as a kind, is spiritually open. And spiritual differences, when they exist in as profound a manner as we see them today, make us question whether humanity does exist as a unit. When "the people" of one persuasion come to power in countries ruled by military force and violence, those who belong to "the other people" are shot or incarcerated. If you do not join the spiritual definition of the kind, you do not belong to it.

When we speak in general terms about "the people" and not simply about the people of my neighborhood, those of my church, or of the eleventh congressional district, then what am I talking about?

Surely no one can be exempt, in spite of what happens, for example, between the social right and the far left in Oriental or South American situations. All people must be members of the kind "humanity." Any person is human, at least insofar as that person meets the conditions for being human. But what happens if someone meets those conditions in a spirit alien to such conditions? A person may go spiritually counter to what the conditions call for. People become inhuman. Are such people still human?

We do not want to exclude a certain race, nation, or profession, as such, from the qualifications for being human. Any black, suburbanite, prime minister, or white is human. However, many spiritual movements (religions, political convictions seen as ultimate, nationalisms, etc.) have a tendency to exclude those who do not join with the movement in spirit. Excommunication and execution are radical forms of this exclusion. Ostracizing a person may also be such a form of exclusion. On this level the human race is apparently divided into irreconcilable commitment communities. People become alienated from one another. And everyone, at some time or another in life, will have to choose to join such an ultimate commitment community. In order to really belong and be accepted, people seek out these spiritually unifying movements.[20]

Individual persons are responsible for what they make of themselves, for what they do with their "being human." Each individual is called to be a member of the community of humanity and is therefore a candidate for responsible membership in the body of humanity. Each person is meant to be an individual locus of responsibility within the entire human community. The responsibility of humanity as a whole is carried via the responsibility of each person. And the various tasks of humanity as a whole are structurally and spiritually related. People together can be spiritually one and functionally differentiated in the same way that, as individuals, they have these two characteristics. The relation of the person as spirit to the person as body is the same relation as that of humanity to its members.

Humanity is in this sense a body, a communal relationship without specific functional organization. That body is possible as the spiritual integration of all specific task communities and all particular members of humanity. Humankind is a spiritual kind. Humanity cannot just be bodily integrated, but must be spiritually united. Human unity is impossible unless there is spiritual unity, that is, unless there is a shared orientation, destiny, perspective, commitment, and ultimacy. People must act as one, face-to-face with the message they accept about their origin, task, and destiny. People must move in one direction, whether individually or communally, in order to be one, in order to experience integrity. A person or community finds unity and integrity in taking a stand in response to the task to which all are called, namely, to be human in all specific acts of being human. If this unity is present, differences such as race, nation, talent, and type of work would not become divisions (a lack of unity), but merely distinctions of task, specialization of labor (differentiations). Differences that are only differentiations can maintain a unified perspective.

This peculiar feature of humanity could be called the religious nature of humankind. If human society were to be one, it would have to be religiously one. This is not, however, the case. The human race is deeply divided. In Western civilization none of the former unity contexts still prevail. Humankind is fundamentally divided in its response to the task of being human. There is no unity of ultimate conviction about the nature and destiny of humanity. In the present situation no faction, political party, conviction group, or movement can truly maintain the pretense of representing *the* people. These groups are simply assuming that if *the* people know what is good for them they will follow the lead of a particular movement or organization. In that movement, the people are supposed to see the true task and destiny of humanity.

So today even the expression "the people" has a variety of meanings. In the past, a political speaker could possibly have addressed rallies in some country as the representative of "the people," knowing that the citizens of that country were basically united for more than just a specific purpose. The speaker might know that the present leadership had violated the people's sense of destiny. But this type of unity has been absent from Western society for a long time. Now the expression "the people" has a clear, concise meaning only in certain, specific contexts. "The people of Denmark" is a category that only makes limited sense. It suggests people share a common culture in some location. It does not mean people are spiritually united.

At the same time, in some country, province, town, or other geographic region the inhabitants *could* be very united in an ultimate sense by a dominant view of life or a civil religion which gives spiritual conviction to most of life. In the United States, there may at one time have been an American way of life, defined in somewhat "Waspish" terms: a vague and uneasy truce between incompatible convictions of protestant, white, Anglo-Saxon traditions such as democracy, church attendance, patriotism, free enterprise, bourgeois norms, and so forth. Such a civil religion may once have made it possible to say the leading American forces that dominated most of life were united. As a consequence, the people may have been recognizable as *the* people (the rest being un-American). When such a dominating force is in power as an integrating element in society, reinforced through mandatory and centrally organized public education systems, churches, and the media, one can in a limited yet meaningful way speak of "the American people." But after the Vietnam War and the counter-culture movements of the late 1960s, this sort of unity may be gone forever.

Today Western civilization only knows a plurality of spiritual communities.[21] Yet in a time when our culture is falling apart, people deeply need a sense of identity that satisfies the spiritual communality of human nature. Ritual cults tend to flourish during these times, even among the most sober, empirically minded people. Others look for the uncompromising absoluteness of racial or ethnic ties. Through centuries of geographical proximity, genetically common origins, and identity of language and traditions, national ties can provide temporary bonds of a pseudo-spiritual nature. Proximate goals (national security, a prosperous economy, the protection of my own life) can in our times easily function as ultimate destinies, requiring absolute loyalty (patriotism), and even ultimate sacrifice. Yet none of these bonds can transcend history, and none will be maintained through time. Spiritual unity must ultimately be spiritual in origin.

Ultimate spiritual incompatibility makes for rejection, excommunication, judgment, condemnation, and whatever else excludes people from the body of humanity. People are excluded in this way from families, schools, churches, work forces, nations, and whole cultures. That gives our times urgency and seriousness in the face of the predicament that we are both growing into a world civilization and we are divided as never before. Perhaps for the first time Western civilization is facing seemingly irreconcilable spiritual division. Every government must contend with major segments of the nation who are spiritually alienated from the spiritual affinities of the ruling body. The task which now faces humanity is to find ways of living together across divides that seem unbridgeable. This probably involves the art of living with the unacceptable.

What it also involves is understanding that no specific task, no specific function can serve to unite people. Whatever truly unites people is ultimate sharing of ultimate destiny. Sharing on that level around safety, national security, ethnic identity, wealth, economic growth, job security, or whatever else is concrete and specific entails treating these as ultimates. And all of them are only relatives. They will betray the trust of all who treat them as ultimates. The unity of humanity and the true unity of every human community requires sharing in what we hold out as our ultimate destiny on the basis of what we recommend as the ultimate source of trust.[22]

The responsible person, in community, is responsible for the destiny of the universe. This is both the point of entry for evil into all affairs of the world and the point of entry for the derailment of good intentions. The distinction between good and evil is the distinction between that which happens in the world in keeping with the ordered destiny and that which develops in resistance to that destiny. As a result, evil is no arbitrary designation of things. Things are not evil just because they are called that. They are evil because they resist what is good, they destroy, break down, cause sorrow. The less we are spiritually in touch with the order and destiny of our existence, the more arbitrary the order of things will seem to us and the more we will tend to go for what evil design has come to call good. But in the end only the order of the world originally intended as directive toward an existence of justice, peace, and joy can lead to that end. Only that is good which in the end leads to what is good and directs existence there.

The spiritual calling of human beings requires them, however, to spell out what they have come to know as the principles of good existence. These principles are themselves only directives, spiritual pointers. They need to be concretized into actual goals. Joy, peace, community, justice, truth, beauty, happiness, and all other ingredients of what is good remain in principle identical throughout all ages. But in every age their concrete shape needs to be fashioned anew. This translation process of spiritual directives into concrete goals has dangers both of conservatism and idolatry. Conservatism identifies the principles of world order with the concrete shape they take on in a certain age. In that way the genuine power of world order to be a directive toward the good life becomes historically petrified and fossilized and loses its power for goodness. The opposite attitude rejects the principled continuity of order in favor of whatever happens to feel good to the present generation.

More dangerous, however, is to tie a whole culture down to the ultimacy of an originally legitimate but still limited goal. Economic growth can be a legitimate goal for some generation, at least in some areas of life. National security, too, can become an important objective for a time. But where such goals become the supreme touchstone for all our decisions and for judging all our actions, they become idols and their destiny is evil and death. Then we try to achieve security via weapons systems that threaten the very security they are meant to protect.

7.3 Dualistic Views of Human Nature and the World

Understanding human unity as spiritual is almost as controversial as the idea of such unity itself. In the history of Western thought many traditions have viewed with suspicion any notion of a fundamental, original unity to human existence. Dialectical themes, which prey on genuine dualities in the world, have influenced people in the direction of dualistic interpretations. The view I develop here is incompatible with dualisms. I do, of course, accept many dualities, such as fundamental correlations: conditions and subjectivity$_1$, unity and diversity, part and whole, subject$_2$ and object, and functor and function. And I admit that there are both the spiritual and bodily perspective of human nature. But it would not be right to offer dualistic interpretations of what I intend. Dualisms threaten to undo the integrality of experience. They promote the same fragmentation of experience cultivated by nominalism and individualism. So it is important to follow up my discussion of human nature with a clear rejection of all forms of dualism.

In my opinion, there are many correlations that confront us with duality, with pairs. These are not necessarily dualistically viewed relations. We do not need to acknowledge duality and correlation in a dualistic fashion. There *are* legitimate pairs: universal-individual, law-subject$_1$, body-spirit, and structure-direction. In the history of thought these have become interwoven with each other and mixed with other pairs that are less legitimate. By this I mean such pairs as nature-culture, knowledge-experience, knowledge-faith, faith-reason, fact-value, or nature-freedom. When the character of legitimate, illegitimate, and incompatible pairs are mixed, problems inevitably arise.

It is easy to see how a contrast such as good-evil can only be superimposed on the spirit-body pair (good spirit—evil body) with far-reaching consequences. That pairing can, in turn, lead to a faulty rational-physical dualism. Or imagine a view in which humanity as a rational divinity is placed over against chaotic nature. Here dialectic approaches also arise. Contrasts may be superimposed on correlations, or harmless correlates could be viewed as basic polar opposites in great tension. This is especially noticeable when things that are dialectically opposed are interpreted from the point of view of a logical identity.

Logically, according to the law of identity, only one "x" can be "x"; whatever else is in the world is not "x." For correlates this is not necessarily a harmful point of view. If we understand "one is not many" to mean "one is not-many" (unity is identical with non-diversity), rather than "one is-not many" (unity and diversity are not the same), then unity is conveyed in terms of diversity. This can sometimes be helpful if unity and diversity are correlates. But in a strict sense all that is not "x" comes to be viewed in terms of the correlate of "x." Master is not slave. Is "master" the same as "not-slave"? But butter is also "not-slave." The potential for confusion and dialectical speculation is seemingly endless.

In the remainder of this section I would like to examine a number of these dialectical themes. We can see how, in a dualistic fashion, they interpret correlations as opposites or contraries. They break patterns of integration into patterns of opposition.[23] The themes to be treated are all closely related. I will analyze nature-culture, freedom-determinism, fact-value, soul-body, and norm-law. They are so closely interwoven that, upon closer inspection, they may turn out to be variations on one theme. They demonstrate the interweaving of the good-evil contrast with the divine-human distinction and the law-subject$_1$ distinction. These themes then are in turn interwoven with the distinction between the peculiarly human functions and other empirical levels of functionality. The dialectical tensions are usually worked out logically, although the basic opposition often becomes spiritual, ultimate, or religious in nature. Whether the two themes are seen as originally one (ontological monism), or as fundamentally dual (ontological dualism), is of less importance here. In this discussion I will view dualisms as dialectically spiritual interpretations of reality.

7.3.1 Nature-culture

I will begin with the nature-culture dialectic. The term *nature* has several different meanings which must first be established. *Nature* can refer to the basic principles of order, or to the essential conditions for something (as in "the nature of humanity," or "this is the lion's natural inclination"). But *nature* or *natural* can also refer to the world as it is unaffected by human interference (as in "we spent a day in nature"). And there are ambiguous meanings as well. A *natural* product is made of ingredients produced by forces other than human, although these ingredients were then used in human production (as in "natural butter"). In this instance, *natural* is opposed to artificial. And in the term *supernatural* there is probably a mixture of the first sense (principles of order) and the second (unaffected by human interference). There may be other shades of meaning, but I will omit them for the moment. What is important for my purpose is to consider what is understood by the term *culture* in relation to the meaning of *nature*.

Culture is often used to name the specific results of human activity. I has been used in a narrower sense to indicate what is associated with the so-called fine arts. Or in a somewhat broader sense it may indicate the outcome of developed, skilled human activity (craft), insofar as it is positively appreciated. I will neglect these latter uses. Instead I will concentrate on the reference to specifically human products, whether they are made with raw products of nature or with materials already produced by human labor. My question is whether there is a special problem of nature versus culture.

I could ask if culture is natural. Is human nature also cultural? Are people both natural and cultural? If an artifact is made of both natural and cultural materials, is it both natural and cultural? Are materials that are used to produce synthetic or artificial materials also not natural? Is a newborn child a nature product or a culture product? Is that child a natural being or already a cultural one? As we can see at a glance, all the material for an involved dialectic is present here. This is especially the case if the variety of meanings for the terms used are taken into account, the more so if in the dialectic they are confused and neglected.

Let us try to avoid problems from the outset by asserting that a person, too, is a natural empirical being. When a woman goes into nature, for example, she goes into her own environment. If she is estranged from nature, she is thereby estranged from herself. In the context of this discussion, *nature* will mean all that subjectively$_1$ exists according to its proper conditions. To use a play on words that includes both of the definitions of this term, *nature* is all that is *natural*. The term *artificial* describes what human beings produce according to natural patterns, but using different materials, that is, not the same ones that would have been used without human interference.

In nature I will regard specifically human work as cultural. But it is natural for people to be cultural. Culture products are in this sense no more or less natural than the products made by spiders or beavers, or the effects of the miraculous "coding" role of DNA. What DNA effectuates is no more natural than homes or gardens. Human products are, of course, human. They are not animal or vegetable products (nests, beans, or nuts). But they are natural just the same. When we use the expression "human products transcend nature," we divide nature into two realms, which can then only be reunited through an unnatural dialectic.

An unnatural dialectic is probably the main reason for the tension in the nature-culture problem. What Max Scheler called the "Sonderstellung" (exceptional position) of human beings among their fellow creatures has not been approached with enough care. In this chapter, I have taken the view that humankind does occupy a special position. But this theme has a curious history, particularly when humanity (seen as the autonomous creator of order, for example) has been placed over against nature.

If the nature-culture theme is intended to distinguish *how* people *are* people, that *only* people are people, and that in all of nature people have a special responsibility for nature and a special place among all other creatures—then this distinction may yield some fruitful insights. Of course, the mere insight that only humans are human is not enough to yield anything special. Only frogs are frogs, but we do not have a frog-nature distinction. We do not lift frogs out of nature for their uniqueness. Nevertheless, each kind that exists is the only one of that kind. It possesses unique traits, giving it an exceptional position.

However, even on this level there is already something quite special about the human kind. People do function on all functional levels shared with other entities, which allows people to be at home among all the other creatures. We do have functional continuity with all creatures, that is, we have physical, organic, and sentient functions just like rocks, oaks, and horses. Yet humankind also has functions not shared by other creatures, at least not subjectively$_2$ shared. No other creatures can think, trade, or believe, to mention just a few possibilities. And, as we will see, these specifically human levels of functioning are a good foundation for human spirituality. That spirituality is the characteristic which makes people unique among the entities of the universe.

People are not unique merely from a functional point of view; in a functional way plants also transcend rocks, and animals transcend plants. Humans are exceptional in having more than just an increased variety of subjective$_2$ functionality. The spiritual dimension of people goes beyond mere functionality, even though it does permeate the functional dimensions at every level. Spirituality even goes beyond the assumption that humanity is free while the rest of the world is determined. (I will in the next section discuss this dialectical theme. In essence, I wish to argue that people are as determined as they are free, while the rest of reality is as free as it is determined. But that will come in the immediately following section.)

We are able to see the exceptional, creaturely position of humanity because of a difference that is fully transfunctional, although it is not afunctional. We might even say it is prefunctional and human functionality is the expression of our uniqueness. I am referring to human spirituality. Because that spirituality is the human orientation for all our functioning, the difference between humanity and the rest of empirical reality cannot truly be expressed simply in terms of functional differences.

If the reality characterized by the peculiarly human group of functions is together viewed as culture, and assumed to be identical with what I have called human spirituality, then a problem arises. This argument will lead to a divided perspective on empirical reality and will undermine the continuity of human nature with the rest of nature. Instead, we need to preserve the bodily continuity of humanity with the rest of nature. At the same time we cannot dualistically distinguish this continuity from the person as spirit. The person as spirit is related to the total and integral orientation of humanity to the origin, order, and destiny of reality. This is the basis of the unity in every person and in the community of humanity. All human functions are, in principle, expressions of this concentric relation. They are dimensions of human centeredness in the relation of humanity to the order and origin of the universe and, consequently, related to our openness to the destiny of the world.

The peculiarity of the human creature as a spiritual being is expressed on all levels of functionality.[24] And those levels of functioning are continuous with one another, both opening up lower levels as well as founding and anticipating higher ones. However, through human continuity with the rest of the universe, human spirituality implies that, through the person, the rest of creation is also open to the directing dynamics of order and origin. The functional levels that the person shares with the animals are in humans functional vehicles of spirituality. But as functional levels they cohere fully with earlier levels of functionality and do not come to stand over against them. Humans sense in the same functional way that animals sense. But human spirituality enables that sensing to become a spiritually open sensitivity to the world. Human formative functioning, shared in one way with the animals, is, in another way, open to order and origin. Consequently, it takes on the meaning of dominion. Signs have their meaning deepened to become symbols. These functions, which are not only human, clearly show the peculiarity of humanity in its functioning. Human culture is unthinkable without formative and symbolic functioning. Yet these functional levels may be shared and continuous with animal functioning. And, at the same time, these functions display in persons with peculiarity of the human spirit.

The functional levels that lie beyond the symbolic realm show in an even more dramatic way how spirituality and functionality are integrated in persons. Analytic functioning gives us a grasp of order. Economic functioning provides the spiritual knowledge of priorities and, consequently, the ability to make decisions in a complex world. As a juridical subject$_2$, a person is able to administrate the order of the world among the subjects$_1$ of that order. As an ethical creature, a person is able to form bonds with other persons and other creatures which transcend the centeredness of an entity in itself. And as a creature of faith, a person reaches beyond the limits of subjectivity$_1$ to the ground and origin of being.

All of these human functions are fully natural and in continuity with all that is natural. Humanity, together with all other subjects$_1$ is fully subject$_1$ as well. And all human functions are dimensions of subjectivity$_1$. To refer to all that is functionally human as *culture* can do no harm, so long as *culture* does not take on the meaning of determining nature (i.e., making nature subject$_1$ to the cultural creator of order). Functionally and bodily speaking, a person is all nature, all service, all subject$_1$. But the human being, a functional body, is truly a spirit, that is, an aware and conscious administrator of order in submission to that order, in touch with the origin of order. A person is not merely centered functionality, but a spiritual functor. In that way persons transcend functional relativity. They become directors of functional existence.

7.3.2 Freedom-determinism

If we conceive of nature and culture in a dualistic and dialectical fashion, then we misinterpret their relation. There is no division in the world between them, and they do not relate as dialectical opposites. All we can possibly do is refer to the peculiarly human way of being in the world as a cultural way. But then we will have to clarify that this is, indeed, human nature; and human nature, being cultural, is in continuity with the rest of nature. In all of the functions that are peculiarly human, the person is natural. In all of the functions shared with other creatures, the person is cultural and human. Thus, people are one with the world, although they are still unique. They know the order of things. Being spiritual, they are called to give leadership to the temporal development of the world as a historical world. And they are aware of the direction in which reality moves toward its destiny.

The culture-nature dialectic is not the only way in which this state of affairs is misinterpreted. The peculiarly human position in the world has also been interpreted via a freedom-determinism model. This theory deals with the peculiarity of humanity not so much through the difference between peculiarly human functions and those we share with the rest of nature, as through the correlation of order and subjectivity$_1$. How does the determination of processes relate to human freedom? I will confront this problem by using the categories already introduced. And I will defend the view that being free is not opposed to being determined, but that only what is determined can be free and only what is free can be determined.

Determinism is closely related to views of causality. When we use the word *determined*, we often mean "causally determined." Many contemporary views of causal determination have arisen from physicists' recent discoveries in the physical sciences. These findings have been markedly different from what was expected, based on classical views. Hanson observes that: "Newton gave new meaning to causal explanation. Mechanics became the paradigm of a causal theory. Thus its central concepts—force, mass, momentum—were sometimes regarded as ultimate causal powers" (911). However, he also notes that moderns disassociate themselves from this approach. "Causes are related to effects as are the links of a chain, or the generations of a genealogical tree. It is all one plot with two themes . . . like a novel by one of the Brontës. But this simplicity is unreal . . ." (51).

It is surprising how this notion of the failure of the mechanical model had already penetrated into texts of logic by the 1930s. Stebbing confidently asserts "that the notion of cause as exerting compulsion . . . no longer merits serious consideration. Nevertheless the activity view dies hard" (261). She contributes to the debate by introducing the "distinction, so vaguely conceived by common sense, between *cause* and *condition*" (270). In reviewing this distinction, she helps us understand the bearing of laws, kinds, and order on the actual subjective$_1$ process in empirical reality. Nevertheless, she still confuses nomic conditions with conditioned circumstances, and this does not add to the clarity of her discussion (274).

In the analysis of causality and determination, the correlation of order and subjectivity$_1$ plays an important role. This is basic to my argument on freedom and determination, and I believe this approach is also implied in the work of Hempel. He distinguishes the causal relations among entities from the relation between entities and laws, as we see in this reference: "laws of motion and of gravitation cannot properly be said to *cause* the free fall of bodies . . ." (ASE, 301). There is a difference between what a law determines must be the case if some event takes place, and what in an event causes other events.

Thus, Hempel distinguishes between the problem of causality in relation to kinds and in relation to individual events (ASE, 348).[25]

Toulmin hints that, although causal references are mostly absent in physics, we do find reference to causality in applied physical sciences such as engineering (PS, 119). We could account for these references if science deals with order (as I believe it does), while applied science deals with empirical process. Consequently, recent discussions about the problem of determinism have begun to emphasize the distinction between laws and subjective$_1$ processes.

Recent literature also supports the view that freedom can be approached in terms of the order-subjectivity$_1$ correlation. Fewer and fewer scholars now believe people are simply free and able to escape all determination. This opinion holds not only for the so-called natural dimensions of people, but also for what has been viewed as the free cultural dimensions of humanity. As Eibl-Eibesfeldt writes, "Human beings are generally convinced that they act of their own free will . . . . In many respects we behave like programmed computers" (8). The same sentiment can be detected in the work of Lorenz and Leyhausen. "Certainly being equipped with hereditary features which virtually cannot be influenced represents a considerable limitation on our objective freedom" (46).

Based on his research into animal movement, Leyhausen also criticizes the notion of the arbitrary freedom of motion of animals. "No free-ranging animal . . . has freedom of movement, i.e., moves as it pleases and at random" (99). Views which relate freedom to lawful determination are not going unchallenged, nor is the old notion of completely subjective$_1$ freedom quite dead. On the contrary, a very modern thinker such as Laszlo still speaks of freedom in terms of not being "determined by any factor other than the subject . . ." (SP, 234). A correlation of freedom and determination in all human subjectivity$_1$ is not easily accepted by contemporary thinkers.

Very novel and creative views on freedom and necessity are found in the work of Michael Polanyi. He succinctly describes the problems in terms of the forces of science on the side of order, and the forces of subjectivity$_1$ seen in human responsibility. "We have seen how perilously poised is the balance between the intrinsic claims of a subject matter, and the passion for exactitude and coherence, e.g., in the scientific study of sentient beings; how the tendency towards a universal mechanistic conception of things may threaten completely to denature our image of man" (PK, 160). Polanyi is especially persuasive in showing how a freedom-determinism dualism becomes a dialectical trap in which opposite intentions are, in fact, achieved.

"The great movement for independent thought [freedom] instilled in the modern mind a desparate refusal of all knowledge that is not absolutely impersonal, and this implied in its turn a mechanical conception of man which was bound to deny man's capacity for independent thought [determinism]" (PK, 214). Polanyi then comes to a surprising conclusion. In terms of traditional notions it sounds paradoxical, but if those notions were themselves dialectical, the conclusion may well make perfect sense. *"The freedom of the subjective person to do as he pleases is overruled by the freedom of the responsible person to act as he must"* (PK, 309). I come to similar conclusions. By applying the order-subjectivity₁ correlation to the problem of freedom and necessity, we can relate to the peculiar position of the person in the context of the empirical world.

I believe freedom can best be understood if we analyze it from both a functional and a spiritual perspective. From a functional perspective freedom involves freedom to function, having the "room" to function according to one's nature. If we have functional freedom, we are *able* to function, in that we have the capacity to give a valid or invalid individual response to a law which holds universally. The order of conditions determines the response, that is, provides a limit or conditional context for the expected response. In that sense there is room for an individual variety of response and for complying better or worse with what the order or nature of things might prescribe. Responses in that sense are typically right, good, to be expected, below expectation, not well formed, imperfect, and so forth. This holds true for any creature.[26]

Now, the individual response, which is more or less in compliance with order, may be determined, but it is not the same as *what* is determined. What is determined is *that* an entity is expected to respond in certain ways, and *that* the order for it is such-and-such. But the actual response, although it is in correlation and, we hope, accord with the order, is not the same as the order determination. Response is possible only for individual units of response, that is, action centers, actors, functors. Individuality of response requires maneuverability. Determination is a characteristic of order, laws, and conditions. Empirical subjectivity₁ does not determine; it is determined. However, being determined does not imply the necessity of the determining order. It is necessary *that* certain processes comply with certain conditions. But no two processes necessarily comply in identical ways, nor does any given process necessarily comply, whether completely, in part, or at all.

Determination is universal and necessary. But the process in which the response—the subjection$_1$ to order—occurs is one that is determined only in principle, in the conditions that obtain. The subjective$_1$ process is not thereby eliminated. But it is an individually subjective$_1$ process. The difference becomes apparent in truly universal statements of law, and in statements which describe, statistically, what happens as a matter of general tendency on the subjective$_1$ level. Such statistical laws are not matters of precise determination and prediction. They forecast expectations based on the subjective$_1$ performance of large numbers. And the variety of performance indicates that subjective$_1$ performance cannot be reduced to orderly universality and necessity.[27]

Causality must be understood in precisely this context. It is a subjective$_1$ phenomenon. Causal relations exist among concrete individual things and events. All events have their conditional framework, which determines an order of response. Events are related to one another and in this relation they are correlated to conditions. This temporal interrelation is the locus of causality. Conditioned events in time have causal relations. In physical events the relations between actions and reactions are irreversible. The pattern of irreversible action and reaction in a physical sense, as determined in a conditional order, is what we mean by the mechanical cause and effect relation.

But the organic stimulus and reaction relation, although no doubt founded in physical relations, is not reducible to them. Organic causality, having a different order and occurring among irreducibly different kinds of events, is not the same as mechanical causality. The same holds for the psychic reflex relation and the technical means-end relation.[28] All are causal and temporal relations among subjective$_1$. They have an order which determines the relationship. But they also have a subjective$_1$ individuality; they have room in the relationship. Furthermore, not all are of a physical or mechanical kind—they are not all irreversible. The combination of physical irreversibility and determination (the *order* for physical causality), when confused with actual subjective$_1$ events of which most are not merely physical, creates what we know as determinism.[29]

Once the categories of response and individuality are accepted as characteristic for all realms of subjectivity$_1$, we must recognize that all concrete functors must have some degree of freedom in the sense we have just introduced. They must have room to move. Indeed, even the most elementary particles in physics can only be understood causally in the context of indeterminacy relations, as Heisenberg has demonstrated. Causality is not the same as determination. Individually concentrated subjectivity$_1$ requires freedom; without freedom there can be no individuality.[30]

Individuality is, in a basic and important sense, irreducible to principles of order. Two seeds, for example, may be sown under the same circumstances and, for the rest of their existence, subject$_1$ to the same conditions and exposed to the same circumstances. But two different plants may grow up, one always sickly and the other always bristling with health. This is a matter of subjectivity$_1$. We should not try to reduce this difference to an initial determination hidden in the seed, or a minute difference in the total state. Here are two different individuals and therefore two different responses to the same universal conditions. Similarly, the actual position of any molecule in a gas is in principle indeterminable; this reflects the same principle of individuality. Responses to conditions are necessarily made by individual subjects$_1$.[31]

At this point I would like to introduce the principle of modal order to explain ranges of freedom in reality. Perhaps an analogy will be of some help. It is well known that in human society, the more insecure and immature a person is, the less responsibility such a person can assume. This person needs the support of simple and concise rules, of authority, and of decisions which, for a more mature and secure person, would be unnecessary. In this analogy we can see that the less capacity for individuality there is in empirical reality, the less ability for subjective$_1$ response there is. Consequently, there will be more need for determining order and structure. Less individuality leads to less possibility for freedom, and the need for a more specified and detailed conditional framework.

We can make the point again in the human context: a mature and responsible person, who is capable of doing the work expected, normally only needs a hint to understand what is required and to start doing the required task. A person who is minimally talented, not very mature, and not very responsible needs to have almost every detail of the work spelled out. Every move must be prescribed. An analogous relationship between ability to respond and detail of conditions can be observed in the modal order of functionality.[32]

In the case of the modal order of functions, we see how these functional levels increase in complexity as they increase in their founding direction. As things function on higher levels, they gain more lower levels of functionality for support. This explains why we find a decrease of determination as complexity increases, that is, a decrease of determinative specificity. For functors in the physical realm, the network of determining conditions is so vast, compact, and detailed that individuality is minimal and freedom is barely existent. So all the rest of reality, as it were, can depend on the proper functioning of the physical world. We need not reckon here with much possible deviation. The physical world is so full of restrictive and determinative laws and principles that we could almost be satisfied with a deterministic and mechanistic view of empirical reality.

Organisms, however, have much more room, are more flexible, display more individuality, have restorative power in destructive situations, and easily show up defectively. With increased freedom comes increased vulnerability. In the higher levels of functionality, we can detect that patterns of universality and necessity decrease. At the same time, the kind of order given merely in principle is on the increase. With an increase in individuality and responsibility, there is an increase in functional freedom and a decrease in constancy of order. In each new functional level, the distance between order and subjectivity$_1$ increases, the dependence is lessened, the order becomes more elastic, and the subject$_1$ is better equipped to shape its own limits in structured responses to principles of order.[33]

When we speak of freedom in this manner, we are not making any distinction between human freedom and the freedom of the other creatures. It is, and remains, a freedom that is characteristic of all subjectivity$_1$. This freedom is a foundation of subjectivity$_1$ and a condition for individuality. It is defined in relation to principles of determination, necessary orders, and universality. It is freedom as subjectivity$_1$, freedom to be subject$_1$. It occurs only within a framework of orders of determination. Yet there is no entity that can be reduced to mere principles of determination. Thus, even mechanical processes cannot be viewed deterministically. Humans are determined in their freest acts; atoms have room to move in the most determined situations. If all atoms lost that freedom, everything would cease to exist. That would be what the physicist calls *absolute zero*.

But a question naturally arises at this point. Is not our discussion of freedom and necessity incomplete? So far, I have at best discussed ontic foundations of human freedom. But a more uniquely human view of freedom still awaits discussion. To complete the picture I must talk about freedom not only from a functional point of view, but also from a spiritual perspective. This second perspective is necessary if spirituality in some sense transcends subjectivity$_1$ and involves freedom to participate consciously and responsibly in reaching our destiny. In essence, we have just discussed freedom of the body, but we also need to discuss freedom of the spirit. In that way we will acquire a notion of freedom which is uniquely human.

Indeed, if we always intended freedom to mean spiritual freedom, then truly only people are free. Nevertheless, we would still have to accept the idea that other creatures are not fully determined. Since a subject$_1$ cannot be a law, no subject$_1$ can have the same universal and necessary reality as a law. At the same time, we must understand that a person is a subject$_1$ and there can be no subjects$_1$ without conditions. So human freedom not only has limits, it also is a freedom in which subjects$_1$ are not free to be their own law. They cannot be a law unto themselves. Human freedom is not autonomous with respect to the world order.

These considerations bring us close to the core of our problem. Although human beings cannot be a law unto themselves, people are creatures with functions on less restrictive modal levels. Higher-level human functions are not only less restricted, they also call for the subject$_1$ to concretize principles of order into structural patterns. These patterns have the force of order, even though they are brought into the picture by the subject$_1$. People mold principles of order into concrete patterns. They do so according to their own subjective$_1$ appreciation of the situation, their insight into the principles of order, and their view of the order-subjectivity$_1$ correlation. In the process, we help develop the world order into the direction in which we want to see the world develop toward its destiny.[34] The human creature shapes history in a unique fashion. This freedom to decide on the actual shape that order will take is human spiritual freedom. Humanity is called to function responsibly and to codirect the response of all subjective$_1$ existence. The freedom to contribute to the destiny of the world is human freedom; it is our spiritual freedom.

Spiritual freedom, then, is a freedom to have dominion. We are free to respond individually to the one calling of all humanity to be open to the directives of the order and origin of reality. This freedom belongs only to human beings. It is not a separate kind of freedom, apart from, but in addition to, functional freedom. Nor should the term *functional* (mentioned in our other perspective on freedom) lead us to think that spiritual freedom is not functional. Rather, two sides of freedom, two orientations or perspectives, are united and integrated in humankind: the foundational order and the directive development of empirical reality. In humankind the opening of existence to its destiny receives its functional origin. A human being, to be truly free, will use the available functional room to serve the rest of reality, that is, by helping to lead reality in moving toward its destiny.

It is this freedom which also creates the possibility for transgression of norms, the possibility for us to be evil. Evil is an attempt to misuse our freedom and to lead existence into the path of a fatal destiny. Humankind is not free to be evil, nor do we have the freedom to do wrong. There is freedom only in true subjection$_1$. If a person were "truly" free to do wrong, this would reflect autonomy rather than subjectivity$_1$. In that case, we would not need to account for what we have done with our responsibilities. Atoms are free to act and move. Organisms are free to grow. Animals are free to feel happy and to play. People have the room to have dominion over nature. But our human freedom is not to be understood as the rejection of all authority, nor as the origin of human autonomy.

7.3.3 *Facts and values or laws and norms*

I have discussed both the relation between human culture and the rest of natural empirical existence, and the nature of freedom and determination or necessity in the context of the irreducible correlation of order and subjectivity$_1$. This gives us a natural backdrop for a discussion of the traditional fact-value problem. That problem arises in the same context. It concerns our responsibility for establishing what is real, necessary, or the case; and our role in acknowledging or in changing the state of affairs or course of events in which we find ourselves. For this problem concerns the principles that hold for the specifically human levels of functionality. The question arises whether these are not themselves of a spiritual nature, such that their holding power differs from laws of nature. This problem is also of dualistic and dialectical origin. I will discuss it too with the help of the concepts already developed.

We often assume we must distinguish between the laws of nature and the conventional norms of a cultural tradition. The laws of nature, we assume, will necessarily be obeyed, but norms are our own values which we can either follow or choose to ignore. Natural laws are said to be factually objective and constant, but norms are subjective values which are at best historically variable. I think this model is confusing and I will try to illustrate this confusion in some of Hempel's pronouncements.

Hempel has written a study of the problem of fact and value as he conceives it. In this study he brings to the surface a crucial connection. "Categorical judgments of value, then, are not amenable to scientific test and confirmation or disconfirmation; for they do not express assertions but rather standards or norms for conduct" (ASE, 86). However, he also concludes that rules for scientific testing are rules for conduct and not amenable to testing. ". . . The justification of the rules of acceptance and rejection requires reference to value judgments" (ASE, 92). The upshot of this is that standards of conduct and standards for scientific testing are both related to human evaluation.

What Hempel says here about rules for conduct is accepted today as characteristic of all rules, laws, and universal statements, namely, that they are not verifiable, in any strict sense. In this respect, scientific assertions do not differ from moral assertions. Scientific statements, which for Hempel too are statements about rules, laws, and nomic connections, are not about individual empirical facts. Hempel escapes this problem by asserting the subjectivity$_1$ of all standards. "All that is needed in either context are *relative* ultimates, as it were: a set of judgments—moral or descriptive—which are accepted at the time as not in need of further scrutiny" (ASE, 96).

What is not specifically discussed in Hempel's essay on this problem is the important distinction between a judgment of empirical status and a judgment concerning standards or rules, whether in the natural sciences or in the area of morals.[35] Scientific assertions of individual facts cannot be fairly compared to ethical categorical judgments. "Stealing is bad" should not be compared with "this mountain is 12,000 feet high," but rather with "light travels in a straight line." The comparable statement to the one about mountains is "Jim stole this bike." On a factual level, the status of both the mountain and the bike can be checked in equally accessible ways. Strictly speaking, the statements about the ethics of stealing and the direction of light are both unverifiable.[36]

The whole matter of factual assertions is much more complex than might appear from the simple disjunction between statements of fact and statements of rules or standards.[37] However, that distinction is crucial. As Hempel discovered, not all that presents itself in the realm of science is purely factual, that is, descriptive of an actual entity or event. There are a number of potential sources of confusion. I will mention five. (1) The difference between order and subjectivity$_1$, for example, must not be overlooked. This is often expressed as the difference between rules and facts. (2) And the difference between human realities (whether order or subjectivity$_1$) and nonhuman realities should also be observed. (3) Moreover, we must not confuse the first difference with the second in either a full or partial manner. (4) There is then the added difficulty that in a person everything is human, including the functional levels shared with other creatures. And we should mention one final complication. (5) In *statements* of order, subjectivity$_1$ as well as order is involved; the statements, although they refer to order, are themselves subjective₁ realities.

We can now ask this question: Are standards, rules, or laws more dependable, certain, true, or constant in the case of nonhuman reality than they are in human reality? When Popper says that error or doubt implies the idea of standards of rightness which are objective, he appears to cut through the distinction assumed in our question.[38] Apparently he believes there are standards for subjective₁ reality that transcend the subjectivity₁ of entities. These standards, Popper suggests, are not subject₁ to arbitrary behavior by entities. In all cases of judgment these standards are there as necessary correlates of entities and events. Polanyi, who would not want to deny the reality of such standards, whether in the case of morals or in the case of prehuman reality, observes, however, that we ourselves are always involved in standards, even in these transsubjective ones, whenever we use them. "Indeed, we cannot look at our standards in the process of using them, for we cannot attend focally to elements that are used subsidiarily for the purpose of shaping the present focus of our attention" (PK, 183). Is there a solution to this puzzle?

At least three crucial notions have played a role in the traditional fact-value dichotomy. Understanding them may help us find an approach. *One* is the deterministic theory that prehuman subjects₁ do not play a role through their responses in the development of conditional structures. A *second* notion derives from the mistaken comparison of prehuman subjective₁ *processes* with *standards* for subjective₁ human behavior. And the *third* notion comes from a failure to appreciate the spiritual nature of the human contribution to a concretization of standards.

With respect to the *first* problem we must realize that the nature of all subjectivity₁ presupposes subjective₁ processes in individual responses. The nomic conditions to which empirical processes conform are realized temporally in terms of structural patterns within subjectivity. All subjectivity is an active response to conditions. These nomic conditions are concretized in time. All subjective₁ reality is historical in that sense. Stars and mountains, for example, have existed a long time. But they are not eternal. When we look at the physical universe from a genetic or developmental point of view and say that there is development in the physical realm, such physical genetics is not popularly thought to be real. But physical change in the universal process of becoming does not exclude the possibility that the structure of macro interrelationships in space need not necessarily be the way we find it now.

Physical facts are not static constants. Recent data concerning

Saturn relayed to scientists by Voyageur I have made this point dramatically clear. The subjective$_1$ side of standards in culture will shift and develop faster than physical structural relations. But this, in principle, is only a relative difference, regardless of the immensity of the difference. Consequently, the factual description of actual, empirical physical functors, functionings, or events (apart from being incapable of capturing the individual subjectivity$_1$) can never be taken as stating just nomic and thus necessary relations.[39]

The *second* problem also occurs when reality is dualistically split into human and prehuman dimensions. As I just pointed out, this gives rise to ignoring the subjective$_1$ character of physical reality. But there is a further problem here. One realm is exclusively discussed in terms of subjective$_1$ process and the other only in terms of laws and universal necessity. In this situation we are confronted with the impossibility of comparing two incomparables. This confusion leads some philosophers to discuss human conditionality in terms of what it conditions (dealing with subjects$_1$ as laws), while in physical reality, conditioned processes are themselves treated as conditions (dealing with laws as subjects$_1$). In addition to a denial of genuine subjectivity$_1$ on the prehuman side, this confusion often results in a view of human reality as merely and thoroughly subjective$_1$ and devoid of truly dependable standards.

In this confusion we find the basis for the traditional fact-value problem. Objective natural facts are contrasted to subjective$_1$ human values. Facts are thought to be universally acceptable, while values are accepted only as a matter of individual choice. We are *free* to accept values; facts, we *must* accept. Both the culture-nature and the freedom-necessity dualisms are clearly evident here. However, very few facts are actually accepted universally. And all value judgments do appeal to transsubjective$_1$ standards. Furthermore, facts are often the result of evaluation, and many assertions are made in the realm of value in such a way that values are asserted as fact. There is a key to the resolution of these problems, however. The human subjective$_1$ factor is involved in constituting the nomic conditions for human behavior in a more unusual way than is the case for nonhuman functioning.

When assertions are made concerning subjective$_1$ human behavior or standards for such behavior, we are always dealing with statements that in any case have the nature of factual statements, whether or not they are taken to be good samples. A fact is always what someone takes to be the case and then asserts to be so. A statement of fact is a successful assertion that something *is* in fact the case, and is believed to be the case. When it is believed to be the case, it is always believed that *in fact* it is the case. This is what we mean when we believe something to be the case. Whether it is in fact the case, even if no person believes it to be so, is merely an academic question. In any event, this question never plays a significant role. If something *is* the case but is not *believed* to be the case, then it is not *known* to be the case.

So a factual assertion is simply an assertion of some person (or of immense numbers of persons) who takes something to be the case. This holds true whether we assert that snow is white or that stealing is wrong. There is a difference in how one actually arrives at the statement. But both make a claim of fact. There is another difference, however, one which is crucial. There are many realities which are not in principle affected by the factual assertions we make about them. There are also realities that may be seriously affected that way. Snow will be white regardless of whether I assert it to be white. Whether or not some act will be perceived as stealing and is therefore wrong *will* be affected by my assertion that it is. How can we explain this situation?

The crucial function of assertions in human behavior is due to the place of the analytic level of functioning in the modal order. Whatever is postanalytic in nature has analytic functioning as a constitutive part of its own nature. In postanalytic functioning, the analytic functions are foundational. The fundamental nature of subjective$_1$ analytic behavior with respect to social, economic, jural, moral, and pistic functioning is simply determined by the order of reality itself. Preanalytic reality functions analytically only in an objective manner.[40] But postanalytic reality is always analytically subjective$_2$. In these realities, our concepts are constitutive. Our marriages are, for example, in part what we conceive marriages should be. In most human functioning the analytic functions are constitutive in a different way than in the physical, organic, or animal realms. If we make an assertion of fact about some prehuman reality, our assertion is not part of that reality. The assertion will never be a subjective$_2$ function of the prehuman reality. But we can never say this about many areas of human life. Consequently, it is impossible to speak about them with analytic objectivity.

This lack of analytic objectivity, however, has nothing to do with the dependability of postanalytic order in reality. Nor does it mean there is no such thing as transsubjective$_1$ order in postanalytic functioning. Our experience of moral functioning is not possible unless we make assertions. And our knowledge of moral standards is dependent on making subjective$_{1,2}$ assertions. This implies our subjective$_1$ analytic involvement in the functioning of certain levels of order. That is certainly peculiar. But it does not give us grounds to deny such order. All it means is that the order which is present, itself requires human analytic involvement in some of its actual relations in time. Analytically objective assertions about postanalytic reality are therefore impossible by definition. But if postanalytic reality has its own order, there is nothing in the nature of reality to prevent judgments about postanalytic reality from being subjected$_1$ to universal and necessary relations. So there is at least this much ground for the fact-value dialectic: there are assertions about postanalytic reality which cannot be analytically objective.[41]

There is still a more important ground for the otherwise mistaken fact-value dualism. This is connected with the *third* problem, namely, a failure to properly understand the spiritual perspective. Viewed from a spiritual perspective, human functioning is transfunctionally integrated. In the transfunctional spirituality of human functioning, the subjective$_1$ character of that functioning is opened to transsubjective$_1$ dimensions of reality, that is, to the order, origin, and destiny of reality. In light of this, human beings, although fully subjective$_1$ and fully functional, take on a peculiar role. People take coresponsibility for the direction in which the world develops in time. In the face of a choice about the origin and destiny of the world, a person is not only aware of the order of reality, but also makes a decision as to where that order must lead. This is a free decision in commitment to origins and destinies.

So in human subjectivity$_1$ we have to account for the involvement of the subject$_1$ in shaping subjectivity$_1$, and for the subjective$_1$ shaping even of conditional structures. But we also have to be aware of the free responsibility which the human subject$_1$ has in this respect. The human subject$_1$ must *will* to be subject$_1$ and can decide not to be subject$_1$. A person is the only creature capable of deciding not to accept the order of things. It may be stupid or even evil to do so. But it is done, and we must acknowledge that this is possible.[42]

In deciding to disregard order, to be autonomous, and not to respond as a subject$_1$ (irresponsibility), a person becomes unfree. If a person does not *co*operate in the *co*rrelation of order and subjectivity$_1$—that is, does not freely, consciously, willingly decide to act as subject$_1$—then the order of reality becomes destructive and the person becomes unfree. This all implies that human subjectivity$_1$ is normed subjectivity$_1$. Whether order prevails or history develops in orientation to world origin and world destiny are, in part, matters of human choice and decision. In recognizing the origin of order and the destiny of temporal development, it is possible for the spiritual subject$_1$, a person, to give true guidance in history.

In open commitment to the origin and destiny of the world, the universe unfolds as it should. Such commitment is possible only through humans. This implies that, in the case of the human subject$_1$, the order of things *depends* on willing subjection$_1$.[43] The opening up of reality in true anticipation of its destiny is dependent on human cooperation. All of reality is a foundation for human existence. No human can exist in isolation from the world. Human existence is dependent on all that exists. People are completely dependent and for that reason utterly vulnerable in the world. At the same time, the destiny of everything depends on people. This is the nature of their subjectivity$_1$ and responsibility, and the expectation of their response.

We refer to this peculiar spiritual relation of humanity to the order of reality as normativity of order. In relation to humans, order not only holds, it also depends on our evaluation. The fact-value split is dualistic and dialectical, but not because we lack a reality to which it appeals. The fact-value split appeals to the difference between subjectivity$_1$ in relation to the supraarbitrariness of order (the constancy and invariance of conditions), and subjectivity$_1$ in relation to the spirituality of the human subject$_1$. This second relation ties the holding power of order to a decision of subjects$_1$. It is called *value*, while the former state is called *fact*. But it is incorrect to interpret these two in opposition. In the realm of value the order of things then loses its constancy, invariance, and supraarbitrariness; and in the realm of fact, no subject$_1$ plays any real role. The correlation of order and subjectivity$_1$ are split. The two sides are then imposed on the ill-conceived realms of nature and culture, or of necessity and freedom. Ultimately the human subject$_1$ is made to appear autonomous.

Thus, in the genuine meaning of normativity, we experience the relation of human subjectivity$_1$ to the spiritual dynamic of the order of reality. Two things need to be pointed out in connection with this definition. First, the problem of history as the concrete temporality of the universe becomes intertwined at every point with the place of humanity in that dynamic and orderly process of genesis and development. History is eminently human. In our time, we are beginning to appreciate this quality, even with respect to the astronomic universe in outer space. All principles of conditionality are at the same time principles of development, involved in genesis at every level.

The universe is historical. For this reason, the historian is always uniquely confronted with the joint presence of invariance of order and uniqueness of subjectivity$_1$. History as a discipline is the venture in which, to use the terminology of the dualistic dialectic, fact and value are one. In all disciplines that are in this sense historical, the analysis of subject matter is not only or primarily an explanation and an account for something; it also is an interpretation. Thus, historical disciplines, one might say, are not just scientific but hermeneutical disciplines.[44]

I should also point out that human normativity is not limited to any realm or to certain dimensions of human existence. For persons, all order is normative. In our time, we are also beginning to appreciate how persons need to take responsibility for their functioning on every level of existence. We are not only responsible for our uniquely human actions, thoughts, and feelings, but also for how we function on organic and physical levels. Our physical and organic functioning are also our own actions. We only need to consult the vast literature in the phenomenological movement to appreciate this quality of humanity.[45] A person is not a machine-like physical body in which a responsible spirit dwells. A person is integrally one and, as a person, is entirely responsible for all of his or her activity.

7.3.4 *Body-soul*

In our discussion of dualisms and dialectic we have at various points referred to the unity of the person and rejected any body-soul dualisms. But if we are going to complete this discussion of dualisms, we will also need to deal explicitly with this body-soul dualism. In Western thought, indeed in Western culture, this dualistic view of the human person has been very prevalent. It suggests that human functionality is to be understood as a dichotomy. Usually, the higher functions together are seen as the soul, or as the soul and the spirit, while the lower functions are viewed as the body. This view is thoroughly interwoven with the other dialectical themes presented in this section. I reject this dualism because it appears to contradict contemporary human experience. Fortunately, much contemporary scholarship also rejects it.[46] This view cannot do justice to the unity and continuity of human experience.

The deepest origin of dualism can be found in a fundamental misinterpretation of the spiritual or religious antithesis in the world.[47] By this I mean the fundamental opposition between good and evil. That distinction is, as noted earlier, a spiritual distinction which bears on the direction in which the universe moves toward its destiny. The world through humanity is either responding to the true world origin in subjection$_1$ to the intended direction of the world's order (out of its origin, toward its destiny), or the world is moving in other directions in violation of the order of reality. The good in this world results from harmonious relations in the order-subjectivity$_1$ correlation. Evil results from brokenness in that correlation, primarily through human rebellion against the nature of the world and even against human nature itself. This primeval opposition in the world is the source of dualistic interpretations.

How does this religious antithesis between good and evil give rise to dualisms and dialectics? Good and evil, as spiritual directions in the world, are reified when we project them upon a dimension of reality. We might say order is good and subjectivity$_1$ is evil; humanity is good and "nature" is evil; God is good and creation is evil. Evil is identified with an actual dimension of the good world, rather than with the pervertedness of human decisions. It is basically an attempt to rid us of the responsibility for evil. Evil cannot be comprehended; we can at best accept responsibility for it as a personal choice. Evil does not, as such, *belong* in the world; there is no explanation for evil. We can explain whatever has a legitimate place in the scheme of things, but evil has no such place. People bring it into the world when they decide autonomously that their freedom as a spiritual being gives them the right to arbitrarily determine the nature of things.

But people do not want responsibility for the consequences of those bad choices. Consequently, they project what originated in themselves onto what lies beyond their responsibility. The body is evil, sex is evil, blacks are evil, nature is chaos, Jews conspire to overthrow our culture, owners of wealth are the source of misery. Of course, as a spiritual distinction, the good-evil conflict appears concretely only in the empirical realities we know. But good and evil are not the same as the realities in which they become manifest. Whenever the good-evil opposition is thus superimposed on some legitimate distinction, that distinction comes to be interpreted as a dualistic opposition: body-soul, nature-culture, capital-labor. Because the good-evil distinction is in fact one of irreconcilable opposites and the other dualities are not, the dualities give rise to dialectical themes. In human society they promote absolutisms. When Marxists come into power, for example, they must deny others the right to be right-wingers; and vice versa.

In my view, the human community and the human person individually are intended to be radically and integrally one. That is human nature. The root of that unity is human spirituality. In relation to the true origin of reality and in true submission to the actual order of the world founded in the origin of the world, the human person will be integral and one. Without this spiritual integrity, however, the person disintegrates and societies will eventually disintegrate. Spiritual integrity will determine human unity. In the case of spiritual schizophrenia, a person could conceivably become a body and a soul. But that would go against human nature and would be the result of evil. It would be the struggle in a person to be free in spirit from subjection₁ to the order of the world, while being functionally bound to that order. Speculation about human nature using this kind of split basis has produced many sorts of dualisms: the free cultural spirit incarcerated in a natural body; the rational soul imprisoned in an animal body; and the mind trying to make something of a physical body.

Many modern writers reject these dualistic views. Nevertheless, they inherit the problematics that come along with the dualisms. Usually they reject the crude ghost-in-machine dualism forwarded by Descartes. But many philosophers, whose rejection of Cartesian dualism does not for them imply crude materialistic monism, retain a view in which human functionality, and indeed all of the functional complexity of the world, is viewed as a dichotomy. For example, Gerard Radnitzky writes: "Notice that rejection of this [Cartesian] dualism by no means implies rejection of a dualistic ontological groundplan, i.e., one which distinguished between perceptual (physical) and phenomenal entities—a distinction which must be made, much as the distinction between individuals and characters" (259).

Thus we are confronted with the rejection of mind-body dualisms but a simultaneous promotion of many other dualisms: sense and knowledge, faith and knowledge, matter and life, inner and outer, and so forth. Most of these dualisms have lost the spirituality of their origin. They are now habitual patterns in which Western scholars view reality. For Western thinkers, these dualisms are paradigms with very deep roots; they are second nature. The implication of reducing a multidimensional reality to such a dualistically viewed universe is seldom understood. This is probably because the world does exhibit a number of irreducible correlates which serve to hide these misinterpretations.

An instructive example of contemporary struggles is found in the systems philosophy of Ervin Laszlo. He is sensitive to the vices of dualisms, unable to overcome them, yet always struggling to do so. Even his phrasing of the problem contains the dilemma of dualism, so this makes solutions unlikely. Thus, at one point Laszlo is looking for a "consistent viewpoint from which to view the organic as well as the inorganic natural organizations" (SP, 73). He is convinced that his theory removes the dualistic perspective, "leaving only specific differences among basically isomorphic systems" (SP, 73). Having invested all diversity in this basic distinction, however, Laszlo cannot avoid a dualism. As a result of his dichotomist reductionism, real unity is absent in his theory, while most of reality's irreducible diversity is hidden. This becomes clear when what he sees as the physical and the mental realms are related in his view called *biperspectivism*. But this view assumes the validity of dividing things into "the realm of physical events, as well as that of mental events . . ." (SP, 119). Now at least three basic divisions exist for Laszlo: physical, organic, and mental.

The influence of a dualistic problem orientation is clear in the following reference: "the 'bifurcated' theory of nature is indeed unsatisfactory, whether it is in a Cartesian or Lockean formulation. Yet the difficulty which these theories try to overcome is real: it is to exhibit, within one system of consistent relations, mental events such as the redness and warmth of fire, and physical events, such as the kinetic motions of molecules of carbon and oxygen and the radiant thermal energy acting on the sensory receptors of the body. It is only in the last decade or so that experimental findings have encouraged an approach which sometimes takes the form of an affirmation of body-mind *identity*, or in a somewhat weaker sense, of body-mind *correlation*" (SP, 147). Laszlo is not able to solve these problems even to his own satisfaction. "Our approach, however, recognizes irreducible differences between sets of mental and physical phenomena, and attempts to integrate them through the discovery of invariances. It thus flirts with dualism" (SP, 159).

Dualisms cannot be overcome unless we assume the fundamental unity of the world in its origin and in its subjection₁ to an order of the same origin. Radical and integral unity derives from the relation of all reality to its one origin. For human beings this implies the spiritual unity of the individual in relation to the spiritual unity of the human community. Such unity calls for many responsibilities, all united in one common commitment. But there are also many dualities in the world and there are radical differences among a variety of irreducible levels of functionality. Diversity is as fundamental as unity. This is as true for the rest of the world as it is for human beings in this world. In a philosophy of human nature we cannot look at unity without examining commitment, responsibility, and community. It is dualism itself which has banned these from empirical analysis. Growing numbers of contemporary thinkers, however, do pay attention to these dimensions of human existence. Maslow, Kuhn, and Polanyi come from very different backgrounds, yet they all show an openness to the spiritual, religious, worldview dimensions of philosophy. And their approach remains scientific. Polanyi speaks in this regard of "the explicit acknowledgement and endorsement of the philosopher's personal judgment as an integral part of his philosophy . . ." (PK, 253).

Polanyi's view of the unifying function of commitment as a factor in the unity of humankind, both individually and communally, shows us how depth dimensions of philosophical discussion are necessarily involved in overcoming dualisms. "Any attempt to define the body of science more closely comes up against the fact that the knowledge comprised by science is not known to any single person. Indeed, nobody knows more than a tiny fragment of science well enough to judge its value and validity at first hand. For the rest he has to rely on views accepted at second hand on the authority of a community of people accredited as scientists" (PK, 163). The same holds true for the relation of science to the rest of human culture (PK, 203). Every word I speak to others presupposes unity with community (PK, 209).

This communal nature of the human endeavor Polanyi sees as founded on commitment. He deals with it in terms of four coefficients of social organization: "the first is the *sharing of convictions*, the second the *sharing of a fellowship*. The third coefficient is *co-operation*; the fourth the exercise of *authority or coercion*" (PK, 212). Commitment, for Polanyi, is the ultimate human source of unity in individual persons, the human community, and the world. Commitment, unity, and community are perfectly interwoven. "Since both individual and interpersonal commitments are related socially and established institutionally, the perspective of commitment widens here to the whole of humanity pursuing its course towards an unknown destination" (PK, 328). In this commitment Polanyi also sees the unity of the order-subjectivity$_1$ correlation. "We observe here a mutual correlation between the personal and the universal within the commitment situation" (PK, 302).

I interpret some of the concepts used by Polanyi to have different meanings. I would suggest the "unknown destiny," for example, is a chosen and knowingly pursued destiny. Nevertheless, the formal structure of Polanyi's argument seems to agree with views I have developed to this point. Indeed, I can subscribe to his judgment that ontology is, in a basic sense, an ontology of commitment. The inner factors leading the universe to its destiny are determined by human commitment. This viewpoint, I agree, implies "the acceptance of our calling—for which we are not responsible—as a condition for the exercise of a responsible judgment with universal intent. Our calling was seen to be determined by our innate faculties and our early upbringing within our own culture, and these conditions were made to subserve an act of commitment by relying on them for fulfillment of standards believed to be universal. Calling; personal judgment involving responsibility; self-compulsion and independence of conscience; universal standards; all these were shown to exist only in a relation to each other within a commitment. They dissolve if looked upon non-committally. We may call this the ontology of commitment" (PK, 379).

Polanyi is saying that dualisms can only be overcome when we believe in a view of reality in which commitment provides the perspective for unity and this unity is pursued spiritually. Perhaps human unity is basically the same as human spirituality. Thus, if a person is opposed in spirit to dimensions of himself, herself, or the rest of the world, that person will view the world dualistically and will inevitably be self-divided. From a physicalist or materialist perspective, the world may be grounded in those dimensions, but it will still fall apart. Basing one's view of things on the perspective of diversity will presuppose, yet hide, unity. The unity of humanity in and with the world appears only from the perspective of the human relation to order and origin in spirit.

In commitment to the unity of all things we can and do experience the world as one. This calls us to be religiously or spiritually at home in the world, trusting its origin and order, and accepting the ground of being in commitment. Not to do this will result in evil in the universe. The relation between good and evil is such that the two do not mix; they do not tolerate each other and are antithetically opposed. They are, of course, a twosome; but they are a special instance in which one element is destined to try and overcome another. Dual*isms* arise when this type of relationship is seen in all duality in the universe. Good and evil as opposites cannot be equated with law and subject$_1$ as correlates, with spirit and body as perspectives, nor with "x" and "not-x" as complete distinctions from a logical point of view. If we confuse these dualities with one another we will encourage dualisms and dialectic. Further dualities such as subject$_2$ and object, part and whole, or functor and function can also be brought into the confusing viewpoints, which only adds to the complexity of this mistaken approach.

So I reject any body-soul dualism. If I were at all to refer to the person in terms of body and soul, I would mean by body all the manifest and experienced functions of being human. All these functions are functions of the body. In their irreducible diversity, however, they are functions of one person. And that one person is one. A person is a unity in the concentration of all functionality on the fulfillment of the human task in commitment to the origin of the universe, through which we are directed to our destiny. If for the fact that a person may thus be one and may in that integrity of identity exist forever we use the term *soul* or *spirit*, then soul is no more than the human body viewed from the point of view of its destiny and its own role in getting there. But there is no more to the soul than there is to the body. Soul is just another name for that body which is the body of a person. It is a name for me when I have in mind my total origin and destiny. At death this integrally united person disintegrates. What we bury is not the body, but the physical remains of the body.

Body in this view is not identifiable with physical functions. No full explanation of who we are as humans can be made from the point of view of physics.[48] And that, I believe, conclusively settles all claims against materialism. At the same time, the human person as soul or spirit is not a mind. Mind is at best a name for certain levels of functioning, notably functions of awareness, skillful goal achievement, communication, and rationality.[49] And there is no good reason for lumping these together into a quasi-substance called mind. In my view persons do not have minds. Nor, for that matter, do they *have* souls or spirits, no matter how conceived. But, as is clear from my view of irreducible multifunctional bodiliness, I also reject monism of all kinds.

7.4   End and Transition: Philosophy and God

The discussions concerning the nature of humanity, as well as those examining dualistic views of the human person and the human world, have led us to the limits of what is often taken to be a proper study of philosophy. Matters of faith, commitment, and religion do not normally enter into philosophy in the manner they would have to beyond this point. At least, this has been the persistent view for more than a thousand years in Western thought. Certainly it has been prominent during the last five hundred years. Thinkers such as Polanyi have tried to show, however, that this view has been detrimental to philosophy. Without commitment, our realm of study is bound to be a philosophy without truth. I agree with the new trend toward an opening up of philosophical study. But at the same time I disagree that a theory of God is possible.

Theorizing without commitment is impossible, but so is a theory of the ultimate ground of one's commitment. For this reason I have saved some of my final declarations about important problems for the

Appendix. There I will discuss what I confess to be my ultimate commitment about many problems of philosophy. But before I yield the discussion to that Appendix, I would like to look at one more problem in a philosophical context, even if that context has certain limits. Although we need to be committed in philosophy, we cannot philosophically analyze the ultimate ground of our commitment. How can we resolve this problem?

Because I am a theist and believe in God, I would like to examine why in philosophy we cannot "deal" with God. Speaking or even thinking about God is not irrational.[50] Nevertheless, God transcends rationality.[51] As a limited philosophical exercise, I want to clarify why I do not discuss my faith in God here, but rather in the Appendix.

It may seem strange, considering the view discussed in this study, that I devote no chapter to the theory of God. The most radical distinction in my ontological model is world, world order, and world origin. As will be apparent in the Appendix, I do believe that the origin of the world is the God in whom Christians have faith. God is the Creator of the world and has given the world its order. So I have referred to empirical entities from time to time as creatures. And in this final chapter I have begun to speak of religion and of the spiritual destiny of the world. Readers of this text may have come to the conclusion that a theory of God, who God is, what God's relation to the world is, God's existence, and other topics would probably need to be discussed. So it may seem strange not to find this discussion forthcoming. Why should I deal only with the world and world order and not with God as Creator of both? Many themes in this study are based on the assumption that God is the Creator. Why can the assumption not be developed in a theoretical way?

I can offer two explanations, both of which may be challenged. First, the ultimate assumptions of a theory do not belong to the theory in the sense that they can be theoretically explained and accounted for. They are the foundation for one's analysis and they cannot themselves be analytically justified. We believe them in the pistic or confessional sense of the term *belief*.[52] Second, the structure of analysis is bound by the order of the world. It is only possible to analyze whatever is within those bounds. God is the origin of order. Theoretical analysis of God would require God to be within those bounds. But God is never subject$_1$ to an order, nor limited by any structure.[53]

If what I have just said is true, then it will not be possible to justify our commitment through analysis. I can only explain my beliefs through clarification, exposition, examples, and illustrations. So, in essence, the difficulty with developing an adequate theory of God is that God must then be subject$_1$ at least to logical laws.[54] To make valid theoretical assertions concerning God, rules of inference must normally apply. But God would then have to be subject$_1$ to these rules. My rejection of this is related to the Christian belief that the Creator is the origin and ground of everything other than God. I take this belief to imply that rules of inference and all other order must also have their ground and origin in God. If my understanding of this Christian belief is applicable, then we cannot in any straightforward way assume the Creator of the laws of logic to be simultaneously subject$_1$ to them.

However, there is apparently a valid objection to what I am asserting here. If God is not subject$_1$ to rules of inference, then how can I argue this and find it implied in a belief? If we cannot use rules of inference to conclude certain things said about God to be true of God, then how can we use a logical operation (this argument) to find a logical relation (implication)? How can anything be validly said or thought about God if no ordinary rules for speech and thinking straightforwardly apply? If Christians think the Bible speaks dependably about God, how could they also think the laws of speech and logic do not normally apply to God?

Here is an initial response to this objection. Although God is not subject$_1$ to logical laws, people who think about God are certainly subject$_1$ to those laws. However, for such speech or thought to be true, it may be said that the laws must also apply to God. This seems fair enough. Although logical operations are limited operations because they are one kind of functional reality, they nevertheless must be applicable to whatever we do think or speak about. Consequently, it must be possible to have concepts of God, and concepts we use with respect to God may apply to God. Only concepts and propositions can be analyzed. We smell an odor, we lift a weight, we price a car, and we analyze concepts or propositions. We do not smell a proposition or conclude an odor. And if we think about an odor, we think about the concept odor with reference to an odor.

The rules of inference are for arguing, concluding, and the like. They are not for smelling or lifting. So, to have a valid theory of God one would have to have a concept of God, and propositions would have to apply to that concept. But to have a concept of God we need to be able to grasp and logically conceive the nature of God, the *kind* God, the order to which God, in being God, is subject$_1$. We need to determine the properties of the *kind* God. And if God exemplifies some of these properties, then truly God *must* have them. All this, I believe, is in flagrant contradiction with biblical teaching.[55] But then what can we do about this argument?

These problems would not be so bad if Christians did not think or speak about God or, if in doing so, they would do it only "as a manner of speaking." But Christians do think about and speak about God, and they believe what they do is right, true, and valid. So how can we understand this in conjunction with the denial that God has a nature? Can we even deny God has a nature? Now, we could point out that Christians do not believe God has an elbow or has weight, although the Bible does say God has a right arm and sits on a throne. And Christians also refer to God as the rock of their salvation. Why can Christians not understand all speech about God in this way? Who could object if we said all speech and thought about God is metaphorical, figurative, nonliteral, and creatiomorphic? If God reveals creaturely to creatures, God's self-revelation could be viewed in terms of God taking on creaturely dimensions and functions. Such creatiomorphic revelation would then also be subject$_1$ to the order of creation.

So if we speak and think about what is revealed of God in speech, we must follow rules of speech and inference. The use of concepts is then subject$_1$ to logical laws. But then we are not saying that God as God is subject$_1$ to this order. So if a visible manifestation of God comes in the form of a wind, a cloud, a person, or an angel—as these are described in the Old Testament—the order that applies to winds and clouds and persons and angels will apply here as well. They might do so in an unusual way, but the application is still possible. The same would hold true for speech. And by the unusual nature of the cloud, the wind, the speech, or the burning bush we could see how God in self-revelation is not really the same as these; God is not subject$_1$ to their order as they are. So the bush will burn but not be consumed. The wind will sound as if speaking. And the speech will be characterized by use of a term such as *omnipotent*.[56]

If this approach were taken we would not expect formal theoretical argument and formulation to be valid in abstraction, although contextualized thought and speech would be. So this is what I have in mind. The meaning of a section of the Bible will be what it intends to proclaim in that context, not what might or could be formally inferred from it in abstraction. And what people concretely say about God makes sense within the full context of human experience, from the point of view of faith, but not in conceptual abstraction. Thus, in one context we might say God is sovereign. Or in another context we might say God is omnipotent. These could be pastoral contexts in which some person was worried about God's ability to heal or control things. But if we were to work out an abstract theory of sovereignty and omnipotence, we would see that such a theory would yield untenable conclusions.

If something in any clear way exhibited certain structures, we could draw logical conclusions from what we know about such structures. But if God exhibits no structures at all except as a mode of self-revelation, then God may reveal God first in one way, then in another.[57] The Creator would not be both a wind and a person at the same time and in the same sense, although God might at different times appear as either of these. As normal entities these two would have certain incompatible properties. But this is not the case when they are used as media of revelation. Indeed, God has no name in the Bible and it is not possible to make an image of God. We can refer to God in any creaturely way, as the Bible does. But God is none of these creatures in the sense of having a nature of the kinds they are or with the properties they have. God is love, but if we generalized, abstracted, and took this statement out of context, it would be absolutized. Love in the Bible is a matter of obedience. Whom would God obey? To see God as a person, in the sense in which people are persons, would be equally wrong.[58]

So we can experience God concretely and contextually, but when we speak or think generally and out of context we lose the *right* to speak and think. So this makes a theory of God, as a description of the structures which define God, impossible and any statements here become theoretically invalid. My remarks are not simply theory, however, but a means of drawing out the meaning of some beliefs I confess to hold within the context of this chapter. A theory of God is impossible, but this does not deny God a role in theory. God is present in theorizing if a theorist believes God's revelation and allows his beliefs to influence his theorizing, without thinking they can be rationally justified. We can relate to God on the basis of Scripture just as we can relate to people on the basis of what Lewis Carroll, C.S. Lewis, or J.R.R. Tolkien write about people in *Alice in Wonderland*, the *Chronicles of Narnia*, or *The Lord of the Rings*. In the case of the Bible, people who believe in it also hold it to be trustworthy beyond any book.

But this also suggests we cannot abstractly base arguments on Scripture if they are general arguments taken out of their biblical context. The Scriptures say that God is love and God is a spirit. May we conclude that love is a spirit? Again, God is love and does love all who love God. I love God. But is it biblically sound to say, as a matter of general theory and abstractly true proposition, that God *must* love me? There is nothing God *must* do; God has no such obligations (although the Bible does speak of covenant faithfulness). So we can clearly see the problem. All of our concepts are very system-dependent. But those beliefs that involve concepts related to ultimates (beliefs that are the content of faith commitment) are apparently more system-dependent than any other belief. Everything we believe depends on them and they gain their meaning in functioning as a basis for other beliefs. Any beliefs of this sort, when taken out of context, are ultimately lost.

There is something arbitrary about the Western tradition of philosophy. It claims that no laws hold for God, but that the exception to this rule is logical laws. Most Christian writers hold that God is not subject$_1$ to the law of gravity, for example. But why would God be subject$_1$ to *any* law, order, or rule if God is the sovereign ruler of all that exists? God reveals in terms of the creation and does not shun anything in that creation when it comes to divine self-revelation. Creation has many properties, including logical ones. But it is unclear why logical properties should be singled out from others and said to apply normally to God.[59] This is especially true when we look at the implications: according to rules of inference it will be determined what other properties God may or may not have. All of this appears itself to be illogical and arbitrary. It seems indeed paradoxical that what we already believe about physical reality—namely, that God has no physical properties—is also true of all other reality in terms of which God reveals, including speech. But it is just for this reason that, if we speak of God, then we cannot speak univocally.

All of these problems, of course, are not new. In the history of philosophy they have given rise to negative theology: we can only say what God is not. They have also given rise to agnosticism, which claims we cannot know God. I do not accept either position. God is known. Nevertheless, this does not mean we have accepted certain propositions about God as true in the univocal and logical sense of "as true." The knowledge of God is not simply acceptance of true propositions. It is a contextual knowledge, and the truth of propositions in that context *requires* the context. Why do we accept that God is not physical? Do we say it is because God is a spirit? In this study I conclude that people are spirits, too, and we certainly have physical properties. If we allow for subjection$_1$ of God to logical rules, then theology and philosophy will autonomously decide on the nature of God, guided by arbitrary, philosophical, and logical prejudices.

So when God's self-revelation comes to us in terms of a rock, we cannot take that univocally. But then if God's self-revelation comes in terms of a book, a sentence, or some other semantic reality, why must we take that univocally? But can we then trust the Bible? If we believe in it, then we can trust it. If it says something about God in a context, we can trust what it says in that context, without spinning off abstract inferences. The Bible says we see God through a glass, darkly. God is known when we surrender ourselves trustfully to the terms of God's revelation. We walk with God as we obey. We relate to God as we relate to our neighbor. And we love God in loving our neighbor. In all of our creaturely relations we relate to God, knowing that God is not a creature.[60]

So speaking, thinking, or concluding things about God is not forbidden, meaningless, nor invalid. But these acts must be fully contextual and in integral relation to everything else we are and do. And we must take seriously what God is not, as well as what God is, in terms of God's own revelation to us. God is not a subject, and is not a creature. That conclusion, in fact, is the whole point of this transitional section. God is not a creature and can therefore be approached via creation only indirectly, whether physically, semantically, or logically.

In certain life contexts it will appear necessary for us that God is believed to be this or that absolutely (as a manner of speaking). But in another context, such an affirmation may be harmful. No concept applied to God can stand by itself, yet all concepts may apply in certain contexts. We may not claim such a conceptual description is logically satisfactory. But this does not mean God is not dependable. What we know of God is not to be taken as scientific information, publicly observable, and inferentially accessible to everyone.[61] God invites us to trust and surrender ourselves in a logical sense as well. To say this is, of course, also a matter of language, with the inherent consequences. So we must not think we know logically what this relationship amounts to, exactly and clearly. We know only through faith and commitment. We act by what we know as trust. And we trust that we can trust God.[62]

Appendix
A Concluding Prescientific Postscript

IN THE PRECEDING SEVEN CHAPTERS I have presented an approach to ontology. I have proposed a simple model for the reality of our experience in terms of three irreducibles: the origin of the world, the order for the world, and the existential, empirical, ordered world. Our world order and the ordered world are irreducible correlates. In the ordered world there are functioning functors, active and structured in relation to their order. All of these elements are in relation, and the relations provide an integral world in which humanity plays a special role. This point of view has appeared to be consistent and coherent with what was *seen* from that point of view. It has seemed possible to construct this view of the world in an orderly manner and to include all that is real.

Two things, however, have been conspicuously absent from this discussion, although they were present by implication all along. One of these has been a forthright exposition of the relation of world and world order to world origin. The other has been an outline of the content of my commitment. Ever since the modern period began, it has seemed more and more appropriate for philosophers to place these sorts of "speculative" and "metaphysical" questions outside the domain of rational philosophy. However, I have stated in the preceding chapters that what I believe about the origin of the world and about commitment is important for the views I have set forth. At the same time I agree that a discussion of these items is not properly philosophical. For that reason I have chosen to introduce these questions outside the body of the discussion, but close enough for any interested reader who wishes to consult my beliefs about these matters.[1]

Needless to say, the discussions and explorations of this Appendix can hardly be explanatory, nor will it be possible to give rational justification for the ultimacies I introduce. But I do believe them to be true. And that belief brings them into the discussion. They are the basic assumptions through which I account for my positions in the preceding pages. These assumptions ultimately explain what has gone before them. What follows can at best be an exposition and clarification of what I believe. Toward the end I will try to provide an explicit tie between these beliefs and the theoretical approaches of the preceding chapters.

It is difficult for us to face an awareness of our ultimate assumptions. The difficulty is increased when the articles of faith are in direct relationship to a global, theoretical, philosophical discussion such as an ontology. Even when we try to explain these assumptions, it is hard to know where to begin.[2] We might say that the basic support for my discussion, to this point at least, has been taken for granted. We often do that sort of thing, and we are not disturbed by taking things for granted. A person who is an overnight guest in a friend's house takes for granted that upon coming downstairs in the morning there will be an opportunity of some kind to eat a breakfast. A person who walks to the sink to get a glass of water assumes that upon turning the tap, water will be coming out. In presenting the arguments in this text I have similarly taken for granted that certain basic beliefs were supporting my presentation.

In taking things for granted, of course, we are not guaranteed that the future will turn out as we expect. Something may go wrong. We are aware of such possibilities, even when we make certain assumptions. The person coming down for breakfast will be displeased if the rest of the family has already gone to school or work without leaving some food or at least a note of explanation. But that unpleasant turn of events is certainly a possibility. The person going to the sink for water may find that city maintenance crews have just turned off the main valve. That, too, is a possibility.

Some of the things we take for granted also include certain impossibilities. Breakfast at a friend's house will not likely be served by three pigeons. In fact, this is taken to be an impossibility in our assumptions. And I would not believe my senses if I opened the faucet, tested the liquid, and thought it tasted like gin. I would not believe, that is, that the liquid was actually gin. There is a difference between taking for granted things which usually occur with great regularity, and taking for granted things that are without exception. When someone is pregnant, for example, we do not merely "take for granted" that the "someone" is a woman and that she is expecting a child rather than a rabbit. When I refer to expectations of this sort, I will henceforth speak of assumptions. An assumption will be an expectation, an attitude, an awareness that is resistant to doubt, whether mildly or very strongly.

When something is assumed, I am not suggesting there is always a lack of foundation for the assumption, even when we assume things that *appear* to have no foundation. When we critically examine notions and concepts, we use certain assumptions for support. Most of those assumptions provide a basis allowing us to explain to people why we hold them. Of all the women I know to be pregnant, for example, I now assume none will give birth to rabbits. But this does not mean I cannot account for my assumption. Nor can we expect all people to have the same assumptions.

Many assumptions must be taught and explained to children. They must learn to assume we should never cut through a live electric cable with a saw. Other assumptions do not enter our knowledge until some definite point in the history of our culture. We have learned that it is safe to assume an eclipse of the sun relates to the position of the moon relative to the position of the sun. Some assumptions also disappear. Many people no longer assume the world was created. And there are assumptions not shared by everyone. Not all people share the assumption that businesspeople have a right to make as large a profit as the market will bear.

There is a category of assumption so fundamental that it appears to function as a ground for other assumptions, although it does not appear to have easily discernible grounds itself. When we check into this category of assumptions, they initially appear to have some ground. But soon we discover how these grounds and these assumptions are more or less circularly involved with one another. Take, for example, a belief in the reality of God. I may make this assumption on the basis of believing the Bible, which I may believe on the ground that the Bible is trustworthy. This, in turn, I believe because God tells us in the Bible that the Scriptures are trustworthy. But if God says in the Bible that it is trustworthy and I believe this, then I already assume God is there.

Such assumptions are not completely held without ground, nor do they appear in a vacuum. There may be many different cultural and biographical reasons why I have come to believe any basic assumption. But upon critical examination, we end up with a few beliefs apparently going around in circles. We may hold them not *on* some ground but because, *as* grounds for whatever else we hold, they appear to do their supporting job very well. In that sense, very fundamental assumptions are in a way "upheld" by what they support, that is, they support well what we hope for them to support.

In many cases we find ourselves holding these fundamental assumptions without any coherent explanation of why we should do so.[3] We find ourselves in this position without realizing precisely *how* we came to hold them. Yet our experience of having held them seems to have been good for us much of the time. Probably these ultimate assumptions are beliefs constituent of our ultimate commitment.[4] They are not shared universally, but only by the people so committed. They are not unintelligible or irrational, nor do they lack definite meaning. They might be called primitive or prototypical beliefs. They seem to be accepted because, with their help, things that are not otherwise clear may now become clear.

The "big bang" theory or the "great soup" hypothesis about the origin of the universe are such assumptions. They are not the kind of beliefs that are the only possible, intelligible, or rational grounds for holding or explaining other things.[5] They are ultimate assumptions by people who feel their beliefs ought to have the semblance of a scientific hypothesis. They are committed to scientific respectability. Why should anyone want to be so committed? Perhaps people make this kind of choice because their world somehow is made to appear more meaningful. These beliefs are, in turn, grounds for other beliefs, which really do not have comparable grounds. One does not explain these beliefs, although these beliefs might themselves explain a good deal, if they are true. All the rest of our knowledge seems compatible with these assumptions.

For a long time the analytic climate in philosophy has made it difficult to take a serious and critical look at the matter of assumptions. The spirit of positivism had convinced serious philosophers that truly rational and scientific thinkers assumed nothing except one or two self-evident propositions. And they admitted that perhaps it was valid to proceed according to the known rules of inference.[6] All that one believed had to be eminently justified, and nothing could be believed that could not be justified in this way. That belief in the need for and in the validity of such justification, of course, could itself not be justified in this manner.

This self-evident truth, however, was not apparent to those inspired by positivism. Holding, without criticism, the belief that all beliefs should be held critically is not inconsistent with the nature of beliefs which belong to our commitment. We make commitments and, having made them, we find our lives meaningful in light of them. We believe what we see in the world in the light of these commitments. Not all people, not even all philosophers, are committed to the belief that we ought to assume nothing unless it is rationally tested and justified. So the matter of commitment and the meaning of various assumptions is open for examination.[7]

8.0   *Introduction to Ultimate Assumptions*

Some assumptions have a particular nature because they are elements of our ultimate commitment to what we hold to be ultimate. These I will call *ultimate assumptions.* I take it that our ultimate commitment to the ultimate contains beliefs which may be called *ultimate assumptions.* Ultimate commitment is not only a matter of holding beliefs. But our ultimate acceptance of the ultimate also does involve beliefs.[8] Some of the beliefs that are part of our commitment may be said to be constitutive of our commitment. If I am committed to the God of the Scriptures, for example, I must believe that there is the God of the Scriptures. Belief in God is constitutive of commitment to God. And this belief also is in reference to God. Not all beliefs constituent of one's commitment need to be direct beliefs about the ultimate; but some, in fact, are. If we believe God is real, this belief is both constitutive of commitment to God and concerns God. Other beliefs among those constituent of commitment may also appear to be basic. Barring some circular sense of ground, some beliefs do not appear to have any grounds in other beliefs. And finally, some other beliefs constituent of commitment are held in such a way that none of whatever else we believe should be in conflict with them.

To sum up, I have briefly introduced ultimate beliefs that are part of one's commitment. They have the following characteristics: they are ultimate, they concern the ultimate, they are ultimately constitutive of commitment, they are basic to other beliefs we may hold, and they constitute a ground for rejecting beliefs not in harmony with them. Such beliefs are, apparently, very basic. But how could something be *very* basic? Let me explain. I may at any time have a belief which functions as a basis for other beliefs. I may believe the streetcar is now on its way; as a consequence I may believe I should wait and board it rather than walk to where I am going. The belief that the streetcar is now coming may be the result of some noise I heard, rather than being a belief based on some other belief. But I believe I should board the streetcar partly because I believe it is coming.

Now, the belief that the streetcar is coming may be said to be basic to the belief that I should board it. But the class of belief I am discussing in ultimate assumptions is quite different. The beliefs introduced at the beginning of this section are constitutively basic to any possible belief that I may hold. They are assumed—although sometimes very indirectly and very distantly—in all I believe and they will also be the outcome of all I believe. Wherever I turn in my examination of beliefs, these will form my point of departure; they will be ultimately basic and they will be the end of the chain if I should examine my assumptions. The image of the end of the chain is not meant to suggest a simple linkage of single beliefs connected to other single beliefs with one final single belief at the end. Ultimate assumptions come in clusters which mutually support one another: God, the Bible, and faith, for example, in the case of Christian commitment.

If that basic ultimacy or ultimate basicness of these beliefs is a fact, a discussion of ultimate assumptions will necessarily involve these very assumptions. In all comprehensive discussions, some things must be taken for granted and others assumed. Now, if ultimate assumptions are taken to be the beliefs which ground all others, then these ultimate assumptions must be involved in an investigation of all beliefs, including those known as ultimate assumptions. In a discussion of ultimate assumptions, their role will be assumed to be that of true beliefs. We will not find any ground for undermining our acceptance of them. We may examine such beliefs and ask questions about them in order to understand them better. But they will be assumed and, in that sense, remain unquestioned. If any discussion with respect to beliefs can possibly be neutral, objective, or unprejudiced with respect to ultimate assumptions—which I think is not the case—in any case a discussion about ultimate assumptions cannot be thus unprejudiced.

I am not saying that human beings can never doubt any ultimate assumption on any ground whatsoever. Some Christian believers have come to doubt the reality of God. Some atheists have come to believe God is real. We may be converted and there is no a priori way of knowing how, why, or on what ground this may happen. Perhaps our world or our worldview caves in. Perhaps a persuasive person capitalized on some doubt or unhappiness. If whatever was supported by ultimate assumptions gives way, we may be forced to look for other assumptions, or we may accept our fate. We may change allegiances and find something better on which to rely.

Normally we experience a compatible relationship between ultimate assumptions and interaction with the world. Nevertheless, we often observe what may seem to be a pronounced conflict between ultimate assumptions and the rest of our experience. In philosophy, the presence of evil has been taken by many people to be incompatible with belief in the God of the Bible. Why are some ultimate assumptions not very compatible with what our experience, our world, or our world picture appear to tell us?

An answer can be found in the special relation between people and what they assume in an ultimate way. What is ultimately assumed as a belief does not have other beliefs as its ground. Such an ultimate belief is much more an accepted belief than an understood fact.[9] We understand and explain many things by reference to other things we know and understand. With ultimate beliefs this is not possible. They are accepted because of our commitment. They are a part of our commitment. And the commitment is made in trust. The meaning of the world is given to those who accept what they see in the light of these assumptions. Examination, exploration, explanation, and argument are founded on these assumptions, and what comes to light is accepted in trust as fitting the assumptions. Our commitment makes it possible to have this trust, even when other factors might seem to call into question the validity of our commitment to these assumptions.

We believe what we see to be true about the world in the light of our commitment, which contains ultimately assumed beliefs. This is known as believing through revelation. What is meant by revelation, at least in this context, is not a secretive process of sending messages, nor a private, coded, series of whispers in our inner ear. It is simply what is made known to us through commitment to an ultimate. Something is revealed if it is made known to us. A newspaper might carry this headline, for example: "Government reveals plan for energy conservation." That meaning of the term *reveal* is no more or less than what I have in mind here. But I will use the term *revealed* only when I speak of something made known to us through commitment to an ultimate.

It will be clear that what I believe concerning ultimate assumptions is constitutive for what I am now writing about ultimate assumptions. I am describing what I ultimately believe concerning my own ultimate assumptions. They are my fundamental beliefs about commitment and its belief content. And I am committed to these beliefs and their ultimacy. I am even bold enough to believe that what is characteristic about my own ultimate beliefs may be characteristic about all ultimate belief. I find myself believing this and at this time I cannot do anything else.

In the light of my own commitment, I see others also being committed. Some people will accept as real, true, or reliable only what science can explain or account for. Such people may, for example, ban to the realm of fables all talk of unidentified flying objects, angels, or gods. These people claim to base their trust in science and observation. They do not trust any observation that science cannot explain. Science is the ultimate authority for them. They accept all of its revelations. That some observations need to be explained away by science does not bother true believers in science.

The ultimate source of what people accept as reliable knowledge can be referred to as their god. Whatever people give their ultimate allegiance to is, essentially, what they worship. In that way they may be committed to science, themselves, fate, progress, profit, the God of the Bible, or the deity of some other religion. The worship of a god need not necessarily be expressed in terms of standard rituals and other cultic practices. It can also be exhibited in terms of a willingness to die for some ultimate faith, or to wage war and shed blood for its protection.[10] Worship need not be recognized as ritual worship. It can simply be an attitude whereby all argument is forbidden in the face of the ultimate. No matter what this ultimate is, those who are truly committed do not question it so long as its ultimacy is unchallenged.

The ultimate, or what becomes known in the light of our commitment to it (i.e., is revealed and accepted), may not be perfectly understood and might even be held to be relative. Perhaps some believers' experience of the ultimate and its revelation is such that relevant statements may need constant correction and revision. The dynamics of history, the change, development, and progress occurring through time all call for a continual revision of our ultimate beliefs in order to keep them contemporary and significant. Revelation, because it is temporal, is always progressive. Consequently, the history of commitment is progressive, whether it is the history of positivism or of Christianity. But in all of this, people relate to their god. They practice their religion in ultimate trust and confidence.[11]

I am not referring now to cases in which doubt sets in and the commitment itself is weakened or perhaps even destroyed. I am talking about those situations in which, underneath all development, the ultimate commitment is retained. Then the ultimate beliefs are confessed and understood to be the beginning and the end of all questions and answers. We might say that questions asked *at* the source *about* the source are also asked *of* the source *from* the source. If science tells us it is founded on observation and it also tells us UFO observations are fictitious, then anyone committed to science will believe this. And if one is committed to a belief in rationality which avoids all commitment, then one will truly believe that commitment to rationality is not a commitment at all. Lakatos notes that Popper declares commitment to be criminal.[12] I believe Popper says this because he is committed to intellectual honesty.[13]

In my opinion, truth and certainty flow authoritatively from the source of our commitment. The ultimate assumptions are the confessed beliefs of those who do not doubt what they hear, see, or discover in the light of these assumptions. This view of ultimate assumptions implies that all talk of them is unavoidably circular. We always start from ultimate commitments in the justification of any belief and we assume them throughout. And eventually we have to come back to them as the ultimate ground. From within my own beliefs and commitment I not only know I am doing this, I also see others doing it as well.[14] If other possibilities were observable, I admit that from my perspective I would not be likely to see them.

Having made these introductory remarks about ultimate assumptions, I must now introduce a refinement. To this point I have written of ultimate assumptions only as confessed beliefs in the core of our commitment. But now I want to pursue ultimate philosophical categories. What is the relationship, if any, between ultimate assumptions and these categories? I believe ultimate beliefs function philosophically as ultimate assumptions in terms of the fundamentally irreducible categories of philosophy. A simple statement of our ultimate beliefs (the beliefs constituting the core of our commitment), and a simple statement of how we philosophically believe the world to be actually composed, are as close together as the two sides of a coin.

A philosophical view of the world is, by definition, a total view. But if philosophy is theoretical, a philosophical view of the world will state in a few propositions what are the basic components of the world.[15] The world is ultimately what we take it to be in the light of our ultimate assumptions. If we state in terms of the most general propositions possible what the world is like, we will have to state what becomes visible from our ultimately accepted point of view. I will not go into the differences between conceiving and believing, nor set forth the nature of theory and philosophy. But I will present an exposition of a number of fundamental beliefs from the point of view of their ultimacy. This will be followed by an exposition of these beliefs by way of the propositions they imply. These can serve as philosophically ultimate categories.[16]

The difference between these two kinds of expositions needs some further elaboration. When we believe, this is not always the same as believing propositions. Believing a person does not always mean simply accepting someone's assertions. It is true, however, that believing often does involve propositions. But believing is more than this. Perhaps an example will help to clarify the problem. Christians subscribe to the Apostles' Creed. Thus a Christian will be able to confess: "I believe in God the Father, Almighty, Maker of heaven and earth." This confession of belief *in* God is not just asserting a belief in a proposition. It consists of much more than accepting as true the propositions asserted about God. Belief in God as Creator and Father brings along a whole life, a fundamental way of being in the world.

This belief is confessed. As a confession it is not to be contrasted with a known fact, the way one might contrast a fact and a belief. Belief in God, for a Christian, is more reliable than any fact. One important Christian document says faith is sure knowledge.[17] The first article of faith in the Apostles' Creed should not even be read as a proposition. To *confess* "I believe in God" is not the same as to *assert* "*that* I believe in God." The second statement is a component of the first, which, in turn, is much more than an assertion or acceptance of that proposition. Of course, propositions are the subject matter of philosophy. In philosophy we would be occupied with propositions about God's reality and the conceptual knowledge that God is real. These would be general truths and concepts. But these philosophically interesting points would be too logical, abstract, general, atomistic, and denuded to serve as expressions of faith.[18]

Here a difficulty arises. Although I do not pretend to be espousing philosophy in this Appendix, what I do is nevertheless *for* philosophy. I am attempting to relate ultimate assumptions to the study of philosophy. What follows cannot be a meditation or a sermon. But neither is it philosophy. I will explore my ultimate assumptions with a view to the service my stating them here may perform. I hope these statements will provide a basis for some philosophical categories. Thus, if I were to make a statement of my ultimate commitment in some other context, it would not look like the one that follows. We can state our most fundamental convictions for use in philosophy, in framing a political platform, and for many other purposes. Naturally, in all contexts such statements would have a common root if they were articulated clearly by a person with integrity and conviction. But in what follows I will state and clarify certain core beliefs of my commitment in such a way that they can be seen in relation to philosophy. At the end I shall restate these confessed core beliefs as conceived ultimate assumptions for philosophy.[19]

8.1   Core Beliefs of Commitment

I will introduce five areas of belief here. They are not single propositions, but complex realities.[20] All five are related to the most general distinctions I have made in the preceding chapters. The first area is that of belief in God as Creator, that is, the actuality of what I believe concerning the origin of the world. The next area of belief concerns God's Word and Spirit, whose reality is philosophically apparent in our experience of order and direction in the universe. Third is my commitment to how Creator and creatures are related—the nature of relationships. Then I will discuss some beliefs about creation. Finally, I will look at some beliefs pertinent to the role played by the Bible in the formation and justification of Christian belief.[21]

8.1.1   The sovereign God

In relation to the creation, God is known as supreme ruler, Lord. God's authority is singular, above all, underived, and complete. This is implied in the term *sovereign* when we use it to describe God. The sovereign God is not the same as the "Absolute," however. I do not believe in any absolutes, insofar as that concept implies the notion of being something in and of itself, completely out of relation to anything else. I do not hold such a belief. When the term *absolute* is intended to mean dependable, constant, and invariant, its use could be harmless. But usually the idea of isolated arbitrariness is implied; then it is not a useful Christian notion. Absolutes are strictly nonrelative; God's self-revelation is not that way.

When we say God is sovereign, we include the notion that only God can be trusted to make God truly known to us, to truly reveal God as God, and as we can and must take God. If, for some reason of our own, we should feel compelled to believe God is or must be something else, which may even be in conflict with what God has said, then we must be in error. God is only what God says, not anything else. We do not know God "in God's essence," for example, because God has not made any self-revelation known in that way. We do not even know whether God is anything "in essence." God makes self-disclosures known in the way God chooses and in no other way. We are totally dependent on God for knowing God. No source of knowledge of God is known to us other than what God has designated.[22]

Similar things can be said about creation. It is what God says it is, not something else. We have no "ways of our own" to find out what creation is, only the ways of God. We do not know better than God or Scripture what that creation is, nor do we know if it could or could not have been different. Our urge to infer may lead us to think about the order of things and to conclude that we know what is necessarily the way it is, and what is not necessarily the way it is. But we have not been told that it is so, nor are we aware it could have been otherwise. Once we know how trees have been created, for example, we may infer and know what we can expect individual trees to look like. We know what trees must of necessity be if we know the order God ordered for them. But we do not know that trees could or could not have been different. We find them to be as they are created and beyond this we are merely speculating without warrant. Neither God nor creation (ourselves included) are what we might declare them to be apart from what God tells us.

What things are, must be, could have been, could not have been, or what we would like them to be is all beyond us. This includes laws of logic. Our thinking must obey these laws. But what we must think is not the same as what God must do. Since it is not up to us to say, we are not able to assert it in any dependable or trustworthy way. God only knows. God is who God is. God is faithful and trustworthy. God is not arbitrary but abides by self, Word, and work. Although humanity has brought evil into the world, things basically are still called to be what they were created to be. We may interfere with what happens to creatures, but our will has little influence on what God intends as Creator. In any case, on that we do not have a bad influence. Essentially all things are what they are called to be, because God keeps calling them by the names given them, even when existentially their response is not what God calls for.

All our beliefs are dependent on God. So, in whatever we believe, we not only believe God but we also believe what we believe *in* God. When we say we believe in God, we are saying we believe God as the author, judge, and ground of all we truly believe. What God makes known, whether of will or work, is fundamentally made known to us in God's Word. We can truly believe God because, although God is not subject, to that Word, God is not beyond it either. God is its origin, speaker, and author. God reveals the Word and abides by it. And the same is true of God's work. God both transcends that work and abides by it. In this way God is sovereign. God is faithful, also to God's own will. And God speaks that will in the Word. That Word is reliable and steadfast, although not static, absolute, or beyond temporality.[23]

When we talk about the sovereignty of the Creator, we are not suggesting independent research is invalid or that for Christians only theology is a worthy enterprise. I am not saying "faith" is dependable and "knowledge" is not.[24] I have not said the Bible is to be our only source for knowing things. Rather, I have described how God is the sole, although not arbitrary, arbiter of what is valid for us to know. And by implication, all we are to know must be rooted in, directed by, and critically adjudicated by what we believe in the context of our commitment to God.

Our belief in the sovereign God includes the belief that God transcends creation, including the human creature. Again, we are not suggesting God is absolute. God is not transcendent to us in the sense that God is unrelated to us or beyond us in a complete and total sense. God is within our reach, but also beyond our grasp. God is within our sphere of influence, yet wholly beyond our control. When we think we can control or grasp God, we will find God also beyond our reach. This is because the order to which we are subject$_1$ in whatever we do is, in fact, God's to set and maintain. God is sovereign and transcendent, and is thus not what we are; God is not a creature. Nor is God subject$_1$ to the order set for creatures. At the same time, those conditions and no others are the limits of whatever is creaturely possible or necessary.

Because God is steadfast and faithful to self and work, we can speak of unquestionable aspects of our lives. We can be committed, we can trust, believe, surrender, and be sure. We can rely on the constancy and invariability of the order of God's work, even though we may misunderstand this order. If we rebel against the order God instituted, we cannot rely on anything, however. The sovereign God is a dependable resting point for restless creatures who will rest in God. How do I know this? I believe God says these things. I believe that whenever we are willing to take something completely for what it is at its own testimony and accept such testimony as authoritative, then we are face to face with our god. It is, of course, very important for us to have the right god, in case there is only one. I trust what I believe through what I accept as the sovereign Word of the sovereign Creator. This has to be my final word, because God's Word is final. It is final, the first and only, the last, and the beginning and end of all things.[25]

These beliefs have implications for our understanding of God. We are saying God sovereignly proclaims the conditions to which creation is subjected$_1$ without exception, although God is not subjected$_1$ to these conditions but faithful to conditions and works. It is always up to God to say what God wills. God calls forth order, God determines what the Word is. Not only *can* we depend on this, we *are* in fact dependent on it. It would not be proper for us to arrive at independent conclusions in a so-called objective, abstract, unbiased analysis, as to what the universally obtaining conditions of the universe are.[26] Even less would it be proper to say on the basis of knowing these conditions what God must necessarily be like. This would at least assume that God, too, is subject₁ to these conditions. But this is not what we understand God to say.[27]

Thus, a belief in the sovereign God is a belief in the Creator and origin of all that exists. God sets the limits and bounds to everything.[28] God is the source of all knowledge and truth. Because God is the author of existence, God is also the only true and original authority; God needs no justification for anything. We can fully depend on God. God's authorship is the central, immovable, unshifting, dependable point of orientation for any and all relations, including those between God and others. Only God is God. God's authority is that of the only and one true God. Whatever else is real owes its reality to this God. Nothing besides God exists in eternity with God. Not even the laws of logic hold in that way. God made creation with its logicality. Logical creatures may not conclude God had to do it this way, however. To suggest there are laws holding coeternally with God, and God must obey them without knowing their origin or having ordained them—this is mere speculation outside of biblical revelation. A belief in such coeternal laws is in conflict with belief in God's sovereignty.[29]

8.1.2   *God's Word and Spirit*

The sovereign Creator made the whole world through Word and Spirit.[30] A contextual and relational study of many Bible passages has led me to believe the Word and Spirit of God are fundamental to our understanding of creation.[31] As the Word and Spirit of God they are sovereign, but because they originate in God they are also dependent on the Creator. The Word of God, according to the Bible, is the express declaration of the will of God for all creatures and for what they are as creatures.[32] The Word of God is the beginning of all creation, is itself created, and is also God. God creates through the Word in the presence of the Spirit. The Spirit directs what the Word creates. Through the Spirit the Word takes concrete, real, historical, temporal effect.[33]

Word and Spirit have ontic significance, that is, they are confessed to be the ways in which God's will comes to the creation. Together they are one, although not the same.[34] Things are what they are through the Creator's Word and Spirit. They can be known by humans only in knowing subjection₁ to Word and Spirit.[35] The Spirit is the divine origin for the direction the Creator intends the world to have. In the Word we see the divine origin of the order of the world. In the unity of Word and Spirit, world order and world destiny are also one.

For philosophical purposes, we may assume the Bible's references to the Word relate to God's order for creation.[36] God's Word orders creation to be as God wills or ordains it to be. Through the Word, creation is called to order. "Word" in the Bible can be taken to mean the unity and totality of all God's ways with creation. In that same context the Spirit of God directs and guides creation through time to be subject₁ to the Word. Creation will move in the direction God wishes to lead, when directed according to the Word. Word and Spirit are the origin and destiny of the world. And they are one. The Spirit is the Spirit of the Word only, and the Word is likewise the Word of the Spirit. The Spirit is the direction of the Word and the director and guide of the Word. The Spirit directs and guides according to the Word of God. For the Spirit, the Word is the path and the way for God's work.[37] Only in the Spirit can the truth be known. To worship God in Spirit and in truth, we must be truly worshiping God in spirit.

By implication humanity is called to direct itself according to the Spirit in this world.[38] Our spirit must be in accord with the Spirit of the Word as we walk in God's way. In philosophical terms, meeting the conditions for being is necessarily a spiritual affair. The spirituality of all creation is its dependence on the Spirit of God directing the spirit of humanity to reach its destiny in truth. The *way* of God through the Spirit (confessionally, the Word; philosophically, the nomic order) points to God's order. Submission brings peace, obedience yields blessing, and subjectivity₁ leads to universal order, cosmic harmony, coherence, and shalom.[39]

In their unity, Word and Spirit are one with God, are of God, are God's Word and Spirit. They are so fully God's witnesses that, as *one* with God, they *are* God. Where they are, God is. In full dependence on God they make God known to creatures. They bring God's will to God's work. They direct God's work to respond to God as God wills. Between Creator and creation they are the link, the way, the tie, and the connection. God comes to creation in Word and Spirit; creation comes to God through submission to Word and Spirit.[40] Word and Spirit are there for creation, and they are God present for us. They direct all things to God and away from themselves. They do this out of God as they mediate between God and creation. Christ, as redemptive mediator between a fallen world and its God, is redemptively fulfilling the role which the Word and Spirit had from the beginning of creation.

The meaning of the term *Word* should not be taken simply to be that of *symbol* or something lingual or semantic. Nor should *Word* be fully identified with logicality and rationality. The Word is not merely a word, nor is the Logos merely a reason. On the other hand, the choice of precisely these terms to convey particular meanings is not arbitrary. It is, in fact, probably quite significant. The Word is, after all, a *declaration*. It is an assertion, a proclamation, a revelation of God's will, and as such it is the origin of order in the universe. Both in the sense of declaration and in the sense of order, the term *Word* is meaningful.

Order is not to be taken primarily in the sense of logical order or rationality (to which we often reduce order), but in the dual sense of command and of the regularity coming from submission to the command. The Word makes God's will effective for creation and makes it reachable by humans. What God wills of all creatures is that they be subject₁ to the Creator as their sovereign. They must be part of God's rule, God's reign, and God's kingdom. That rule is one of shalom and order. The order is one of harmony, life, fruitfulness, growth, love, and communion. This order is not statically fixed, but designed to bring change, development, and movement toward ultimate destiny.

If this is indeed what the Bible reveals to us as the Word, we should be cautious not to look at the Word as a synonym for the Scriptures. Scripture can be identified *as* the Word, identified *with* the Word. We can legitimately refer to it as the Word of God. But the Word cannot be exhausted in the Bible.[41] The Word is the order of the universe *in principle*, that is, the fixed or established *origin* or *arche* of all order. Nothing that lacks an origin in the Word can be orderly or peaceful. The Word is the only origin, the only principle of peace. It orders creation constantly, it is invariably dependable, unwavering when creatures rely on it. That order is full and total. It would be a mistake to reduce the fullness of the Word merely to logical order, or to historic, genetic, legal, or economic order.

It would also be a mistake to understand the Word in a deterministic or absolutistic way. As an order for response and responsibility in time, the Word frees and allows room for creaturely individuality and history throughout creation. The Word sets the whole creation free. Creation can exist as it was intended to be. All creatures can be themselves, according to their own nature. And the Word places this freedom in a specific context: evil has been overcome in the redemptive sacrifice of the Word Incarnate, Immanuel, the Prince of Peace. The creation, which responds individually, is the correlate of the Word's order making all things possible. The Word makes possible whatever *is* possible, according to and in keeping with that Word. And freedom is freedom to be and to become what the Word ordains.

The order that is in principle the Word of God is intended for all creatures in all of their dimensions. This order calls them to be themselves, that is, to be what God wants them to be. The opening chapters of *Genesis* can be read from this vantage point. *Genesis* is then seen not so much as a report of how things were made, but rather as a proclamation of their beginning, their origin. *Genesis* proclaims what things are in principle, that is, originally, and how they depend on God as God speaks the Word in the Spirit. In the Bible the phrase *Word of God* often seems to stand for the totality of all that God asks of us, and for the unity and totality of God's will. Christ, the Redeemer of the fallen world, is called the Word because Jesus incarnated the will of God completely and totally, through perfect obedience to the will of God. Christ became the will of God alive in the flesh. The Word is the concentrated unity of what God makes known for us of what God wills. Having rebelled against the will of God, the world has been brought back on course by Christ. Jesus fully submitted to that will even to the point of accepting voluntarily the price for rebellion—death.

In the Spirit, the Word comes to the creation. *Spirit* is a motion word in the Bible, conveying motivation. *Spirit* stands for guidance, leadership, and direction. The Spirit of God is God's moving, motivating, and directing presence in creation. Through the Spirit God leads and directs creation as, and where, God wills. People can follow God's commandments in spirit and in truth when they follow the Spirit. The Spirit opens up the true meaning of the Word and makes people wise. With the help of the Spirit, the Bible becomes more than a mere letter; it becomes a life-giving force. In both creation and redemption (understood as re-creation), the Spirit is present together with the Word.[42]

8.1.3 *The covenant as bond*

The mediating position of Word and Spirit in what Scripture calls the covenant is of cardinal importance among the commitment beliefs noted in this study. We recall how the chapter dealing with relations was pervaded by a sense of mystery about them. This theme can now be taken up again in terms of the biblical notion of covenant. The mystery of relationship can be approached spiritually, receptive to the Spirit who makes the Word concrete as a relation between Creator and creature. Word and Spirit are the mediators of creation and redemption or recreation. As the very Word and Spirit of God, they are divine. Because they are insufficient in themselves and born of God, they are also said to be creaturely.[43] Since they are both divine and creaturely, we might say they are by nature in relation to both Creator and creation.

I do not mean to say God and creation are opposites between which we need to have ontic mediation or some such thing. There is no original ontic need for reconciliation between creation and its Creator. The need for reconciliation is not given with the nature of creation. Only when evil was introduced into the creation by the creature was the bond between Creator and creature broken. But from the beginning Creator and creature were in principle bound in relationship through Word and Spirit. And in the redemptive recreation it is through Word and Spirit that God accomplishes reconciliation. The Word and Spirit are always God's way to the world and the world's only way to God.

So the key to our view of relationship is actually the way of Word and Spirit. Now, this crucial tie between Creator and creature in Word and Spirit is referred to in the Bible as the covenant.[44] In the covenant God regulates and constitutes the relation between Creator and creation in the Word. It is the pledge of the sovereign Creator to which God and creation are held; God in faithfulness, the creature in obedience. God's covenant promises goodness and life to the creation.[45] The covenant, the relation between the Creator and the creation, is ordered and regulated by the Word, and directed and guided by the Spirit. If the creation responds to the Word in the way directed by the Spirit, existence is meaningful and harmonious, blessed and peaceful. If creation goes its own way it will disintegrate. The creation is the realm of the Sovereign's reign. Here God rules according to the Word and calls for obedience to the Word, always with the promise that God will care for the world. Christ, the incarnate mediator after the relationship had been broken, says this prayer: "May your Kingdom come."[46]

The creation finds its limits in the Word. Only within these limits is it possible to be a creature. The Word thus provides the conditions by which creatures exist meaningfully in a subjective$_1$ manner. The Word is the only condition, so it is the only way for a creature to be. Each creature must necessarily be what God calls it to be.[47] God's Word is the condition for, and limit of, all that is possible. The Word is given to creation by way of commandments, ordinances, laws, words, statutes, ways, principles, rules, and directives. In these laws we see as great a variety as we do in the realm of creation. The diversity of creation has its correlate in a diversity of creative orders. In origin and principle, all of these have the same meaning: creation is called to be subject$_1$ to the Word, to follow the Spirit, and to obey.

World history is the scene of the struggle between God and a creation fallen into destruction. By not wanting to be what they must necessarily be, creatures become self-destructive. But God wills their life, wills for them to be what they are necessarily called to be. This is not just a New Testament theme. Even in the Old Testament we see clearly the sovereign rejection of evil, for example, in *Genesis* 8:20-22, *Isaiah* 57:16-19, and *Hosea* 11:9.

In terms of the focal point of the covenant in the God-humanity relationship, obedience is an act of love. We see this love if and when humanity walks with all creatures before God according to God's Word. Love is also seen in God's faithfulness to the Word of life and shalom. The Spirit of the Word is the Spirit of love; God and creatures are in active temporal relation through the Word and the Spirit. Love is the summary of the covenant and the Word. The nature of the relation between God and creatures is one of love. In obedient people, God is present on earth. They are God's image. If people love each other and love all their fellow creatures—rocks, rivers, forests, marshes, birds, animals—by doing God's work in the Spirit of the Word, then God will be present on earth and God's love is presented to all creatures.[48]

Although there is only one Word for creation, we might say the Word comes to all the creatures in their own way through many different principles, orders, laws, and commandments. The Word itself addresses all creatures with authority in principle only. It is the origin and beginning of all creatures; yet those creatures, guided by the Spirit, are left to structure their own existence in time, in historical development. The Word, the origin of all that exists, leaves each thing room to be itself. The order of the Word as the order of mediation is an order of, and in, principle. It orders the creation's authenticity and validity in principle; it commands in terms of directives for a guiding Spirit. In that sense the Word, whether in its unity or its diversity, is not as fully concretized, diversified, and specified as creation is concretely varied and individual. It calls creatures to freedom in freedom; it sets us free.

The Word is the firstborn of all creatures; it is creation in principle and the beginning or first fruit of God's work. The Word makes the rest of creation possible, while being creation in essence itself. It is the principle of being a creature, and the origin of all that is possible. The Word is not a creature which derives its possibility from the principle of creation. The Word is creation in principle and not creation as subject$_1$. In order to redeem all fallen creation, however, the Word took on the form of a subject$_1$. The Word reconciled the world to God through death, the necessary atonement for a creation rebelling against the very Word that now saved creation.[49]

That same Word is known to us primarily in three ways. It is supremely known in Jesus Christ, the Word become Subject$_1$.[50] We also see it revealed in verbal, literary form in the Bible. Here, explicit statements draw attention to a Word that fallen people could no longer understand in its natural form, that is, through obedient fellowship with those creatures originating in the Word. Thus, creation, Scripture, and Christ are the three ways in which we come to know the Word. These three ways require one another; one way is not sufficient to know the Word, yet the three make the one Word known in terms of each other.

Since the Word is the Word of the Spirit, a spiritual Word, and one with the Spirit, it can only be known *in* spirit and *by* a spirit.[51] Knowledge itself is, in fact, spiritual. Human knowledge cannot be understood merely as the presence of an analytical and functional dimension in human experience. Rather, it is an aware relationship to God, Word, Spirit, and creation of which only a spirit is capable. A person, being spiritual, is a person who can know. We are equipped to be knowing persons with a subjective$_2$ functional diversity exceeding that of any other creature.[52]

In order for the mediating Word of life to be the true source of life, the Spirit must guide creatures toward submission. They must obey the Word spiritually and in principle. Then creatures will be moving in the direction given by the order of the Word—creation moving toward its destiny. In the diversity of commandments, statutes, and laws, the unity of the Word is maintained in spiritual integrity. Since the order of the Word also has an annihilating, destroying, death direction (when it is disobeyed), creation requires the help of the Spirit in order to move in this direction of life. Here, humanity becomes the focal point by providing the openness to the Spirit for creation. This implies that the universe needs a spiritual integrity in the human community in order to develop as it should. The path of the Word can only be a path of life if people live in spiritual integrity. Together, Word and Spirit in the mediating covenant position make the difference between life and death, existence and nonexistence. They hold God and creation together.

The covenant, one might say, is the scene of history as the unfolding of creation, where humanity is given the task of being God's earthly representative. In that way of viewing things all reality is a dynamic temporal movement from origin to destiny. God, as origin of the historical and temporal universe, is then God of history in history.

God, too, is historical; all things are from, through, and unto God. God's place in history is designated by the temporal term *eternal*. God being eternal is not God being out of or beyond time. Rather, God is God of time or is the origin of time. In the covenant, the full interrelation of God and creature in time, the human creature has the gift of living forever, if indeed the human creature lives in obedience. But living forever is not the same as being eternal.

8.1.4 Creation as meaning[53]

Let us examine two different approaches to creation. We might say it is God's work, or we might say it is a response to God's order. Both approaches are legitimate, although either by itself would be one-sided. Both views are incomplete and need each other. In the first instance, the authorship of God is stressed. In the second formulation, the full calling of creation is emphasized. But each reference alone is insufficient.

Here we can see how Creator and creature are fully distinct and have nothing in common. There are no analogies. God is God and only God. Only Yahweh is God. God is not a creature in any way and is not *like* a creature in any way. God has no creaturely properties in creaturely ways, even though we might hear God speak in this manner. And no creature is god or divine in any way. Creatures are fully creaturely and beyond them there are no creatures.

God and creatures, however, are in relationship. They are there for each other. God fully determines all things.[54] All creatures are out of God, for God, through God, and unto God.[55] They relate to each other in Word and in Spirit, both of whom are divine and creaturely. Word and Spirit do not deterministically govern creation; they do so in principle and in spirit. Creatures, although never autonomous, are fully themselves in obeying Word and Spirit. To know God and to know creation they must be known according to the Word and in the Spirit. Whatever we understand of either God or creation that is not founded in the Word and not uncovered by the Spirit is ultimately untrue. In the relation via Word and Spirit, God remains God and creatures remain creatures, both maintaining themselves as they are.

So creation has its own reality. Only *it* is what it *is*. But its reality is nevertheless dependent. Because it properly has a character all its own, it is to be totally distinguished from God. Yet we must also stress that nothing creaturely real is, or exists, or stands, in itself, of itself, or by itself. No creature is out of itself, nor unto itself. Creation is not absolute. No creature is absolute or an absolute. Neither is creation or any creature autonomous or free to be a law unto itself. Autonomy and absoluteness exist nowhere in creation, at least not legitimately or with valid claims. (Both are terms for erroneous views or ill-conceived notions of reality.)

No creature is a sovereign either. Only God can be sovereign. We must even deny that any creature is a substance, if substance is taken in a traditional and technical sense. When we claim a creaturely being stands in itself (*ens in se stans*) or stands under (*sub stans*) all appearances as permanence in change, we have absolutized the Word taken as a subject$_1$. The notion of the proper identity of creatures in continuity is acceptable and so is the notion of their real individuality and of their room for response. But no creature is *sui generis* or of its own origin, nor is any creature *self-evidently* what it is. No creature is *causa sui*.

Within Christian commitment, all of these are matters of ultimate belief. There is, of course, a process whereby we arrive at these beliefs. We do not come to believe in the dependence of creation in the same way we come to believe our feet are cold. We are taught by other believers, or we believingly read the particular book accepted as the canon of faith, which in the Christian tradition is the Bible. And then we either accept or reject what we are taught by fellow believers according to the Bible, and what it teaches us through our faith. So we cannot argue, as it were, from universally accepted premises that the world is as I believe it is. But if we do believe it is so, then our view of the world can be quite intelligible.

So, in the light of this view, the referential nature of reality makes much sense. Creation is seen as relational or relative. Within creation all things relate to other things, and all things are what they are in relation to other things. This interrelatedness and relativity of subjective$_1$ existence is in turn related to the order of things, which in turn is related to God as the origin of all that exists. However, in contrast to a relativistic view of relationality in which there would be neither end nor beginning (and certainly no stable orientation in all relativity), a creational view of reality can have room for both relativity and for stability. The relativity comes from the interdependence of all creatures in their dependence on the order of creation. The stability is seen in that all creatures and their order are from, through, and unto God. In God they live, move, and have their being. In God, they are what they are.

Apparently no creature is anything in and of itself. Moreover, a creature is what it is only in relation to the other creatures in subjection$_1$ to the Word. These features constitute what we call the meaning character of creation. When I mention creation *as* meaning I am not referring to some dimension of creation. I am speaking about the very essence of its reality as subjectivity$_1$. Essentially, meaning and subjectivity$_1$ are the same; meaning and being in a creature are the same. I am not suggesting that there are creatures and they *have* meaning, however. Meaning is not intended as something for creatures to have.

Within this framework it is not possible to refer to anything apart from its meaning and then ask what its meaning is or what meaning it has. Something *is* what it means; it *is* its meaning. So, instead of saying creation is subjectivity$_1$, we might also say it is meaning. The use of the term *meaning* in this context highlights the dependence and relativity of all creaturely existence. It emphasizes how all creaturely reality relates and points to the reality beyond itself. And this process, instead of having an infinite regress, comes to an end in God. From God each creature receives its meaning, its being, its call to respond to God's order.[56]

So, existence can be seen as essentially meaning; existential reality is always restless, referring beyond itself to find its rest in God. It is not contingent, however, in the sense of being accidental, absurd, arbitrary, unnecessary, irrational, or a chance happening.[57] Creation, which is ordered and ordained by God, is in its original sense quite apart from the introduction of evil. In that sense there are no traces of incompleteness, imperfection, or negativity in creation. The necessity of a thing to be what it is ordained to be is not incompatible with the freedom of creatures. Nor is the lack of human ability to understand, conceive, or explain all things an indication of irrationality. This only shows how human limits and the origin of all limits are to be found in God, not in reason. Creation is good, wanted, and willed by God. The Creator was pleased with it.[58] Evil has caused the degeneration of what was created good. But evil in the form of spiritual rebellion—a movement against the limits of creation while in subjection$_1$ to them—still is incapable of destroying God's intentions. It is even incapable of making God abandon those intentions.[59] Although evil is manifest in the very structures of our world, it leaves the Word as it is.[60]

There are two possible ways in which we may refer to creation as contingency. As a concept, "contingency" may legitimately refer to the dependent character of the conditioned existence of creation in its thorough interrelatedness. This does not imply anything about creation being accidental or nonessential. Contingency in this sense is what children discover when they begin to ask all their "why" questions. Each answer is contingent on another one. Each reply indicates that the reality pointed to in one answer is in touch with reality of another kind. This shows contingency in the form of interrelation and interdependence.

But contingency may also legitimately refer to particular circumstances; each thing that happens will do so in just the way it does. The conditioned dependence of things is tied to a unique configuration and array of concrete events and circumstances. And this uniqueness goes beyond conceptualization and explanation. The correlata of creation and order are irreducibly different. Consequently, order can account for why things exist as they do; but order is not the same as what is subject$_1$ to order. The uniqueness and individuality of the concrete subjective$_1$ situation will point out how things do not happen and exist as order, but as ordered events.

No event in its uniqueness is predetermined to happen as it does. The same conditions leave room for events that may differ from this one. And yet this particular event in its uniqueness is what it is and could not have been different. An actual event, once actualized, is what it is. It is there as given, and must be accepted as is. It has a unique individuality which analysis cannot fully explain. The sentence I am now writing has now been written this way, on this typewriter, with this word order, and with a black ribbon. This sentence now has achieved an identity which no other sentence could have had. Whether this actual sentence could have been different is beyond discussion. It is now an actuality, not a possibility.[61]

All that is the case in creation, everything that actually happens has two sides, as noted at the beginning of this section. Each creaturely reality reveals both its own reality, which is proper to itself, and its dependent reality on God. In one sense each event is a concurrence of events which make for a uniquely individual occurrence. God's order leaves room for the idiosyncratic character of created reality. Created reality is not divine, part of the divine, in part divine, or divine emanation. It is itself, is what it is, in its own uniqueness; which uniqueness it has itself. But creation, as an event that happens, is a response to a conditioning order. The order guarantees that nothing "just so happens" inexplicably and accidentally, as a purely chance occurrence.

At the same time, however, everything in its own uniqueness happens just so and not otherwise, and inexplicably so. The totality of an actual event is more than order will allow us to explain. Order is the order of possibility. Creaturely events are unique actualities. And this is true not only for creation in its many individual events, but also for creation in its entirety. There are many creatures and many events, but just one world and one creation. And that one creation in all of its orderly coherence also has a uniqueness and individuality which raise it to a level of contingency going beyond full analytic penetration. The creation is, so to speak, God's first miracle and all creatures are miraculously made.[62]

8.1.5   The Bible

I have explained what I believe regarding God the Creator, God's Word and the Holy Spirit, the creation, and the relation between them. These beliefs are derived from what the Bible has to say about such realities. I believe my account is consistent with biblical revelation and is relevant to a philosophical exploration of what the Scriptures teach us. I hold that my beliefs as set forth are in accordance with the Bible. This is important because, for a Christian who philosophizes, the Bible is an authoritative canon. A cardinal belief of the Christian faith holds that the Bible plays that role in the life of Christians. Whatever we believe, hold in faith, or accept and proclaim as certainly true must be in accordance with the Scriptures.[63]

The Bible is authoritative as *the* creaturely statement about ultimate truth. Within creation, Christians have no other touchstone for the veracity of their beliefs. The Scriptures themselves announce that they are a reliable witness to God's Word and a reliable indicator of what our response as creatures should be to God's Word. Even Christ, the Word incarnate, customarily grounded his witness to the truth by referring to its basis in the Scriptures. As a creature, the Word itself accepted the creaturely touchstone for veracity. Christians accept this literary revelation of the Word in faith. Nevertheless, this does not guarantee, of course, that Christians are always right when they proclaim some assertion to be biblical.

To many scholars, including some Christians, the attitude toward the Bible which we have just described seems to imply an abdication of our critical faculties. Many recent texts have shown how neutrality and objectivity have for centuries been perceived incorrectly in our culture. Yet there is still a great reluctance to admit that faith based on the Bible can be an acceptable factor in scholarship.[64] Scholars will admit that we must accept belief as unavoidable, although some beliefs are in many cases neither self-evident nor evidently rational. So an element of faith is connected with all belief in modern literature. But few scholars, if any, will allow religious beliefs and faith into the arena of scientific beliefs and rational faith.[65] Centuries of dogmatic scientism and rationalism have conditioned us in this way, so their reaction is understandable.

For my part, however, I cannot commend this view. I fail to see why things cannot be accepted as reliable just because they have not been rationally justified, empirically verified, or otherwise approved by the test of critical investigation. But such reliability is the only option from the point of view that our critical faculties are ultimate. From another point of view this position is contradicted by contemporary investigations. Modern research has shown how critical investigation itself is at least partially dependent on uncritically accepted attitudes and beliefs. Furthermore, the history of science in our culture does not inspire as much faith in its ultimate authority as it did only a few decades ago.

Many people in our culture still opt for critical rationality, or something similar, as their ultimate, reliable guide to certain knowledge. Such an option, then, is itself a type of faith. The choice of our critical faculties as an ultimate guide is still a form of commitment. As such, this choice has nothing better to commend itself than does our faith in the Bible. Both faiths recommend themselves equally to believers and are unacceptable to nonbelievers. And this is the normal state of affairs for all faiths and all believers. They all hold their faith commitment to be ultimately more reliable than any other. This is natural because believers have made a committed surrender. Once we have surrendered in commitment, the ultimate ground we have accepted will reveal things to believers and we will accept them unconditionally as the truth.[66]

How does the Bible figure in this approach? Christians believe it is a trustworthy declaration of the Word of God. It is intended for people who, by their own nature, are unable to hear the Word as it is knowable through whatever else exists by its power.[67] All creatures exist in response to the Word and as they are called into being by the Word. In this way all creatures reveal the Word. But the evil existing in our world, our specifically human rebellion against the Word, obscures knowledge of the Word through creation. Humanity in sin confronts the Spirit of the Word and interprets creation according to spirits foreign to the Word. Yet people can still believe that God has, in Christ and through our faith, reopened the way of the Word through creation again. We can understand the Scriptures as a revelation of the Word, and in light of the Scriptures, we also comprehend creation. Through the Scriptures, believers can once again view creation as God's revelation.

The preceding chapters detailing a worldview in which world origin, world order, and ordered world were the most fundamental elements, were in fact chapters about God the Creator, about God's

Word and Spirit ordering and directing creation, and about the creation as originating in God and existing in submission to the directives and directing of Word and Spirit. I have, of course, written about them philosophically. But there is no possibility of finally declaring oneself on the ultimate meaning of the philosophical concepts used here except in faith. And as Christian faith, that faith must be bound to the Bible. I do not accept natural reason investigating nature unaided and coming up with the views I hold. I believe that the role played by biblical revelation is essential to what I have done. For that reason I need to declare myself on what I take that Bible to be, without which at least this piece of philosophical reflection is unthinkable. If to anyone it looks like the preceding chapters were written without appeal to the Bible, then it is time now to remove that impression, because it is erroneous. The links may have been hidden. But they were there all the time.

For Christian believers the Bible is the objective record (for faith) of God's acts toward creation.[68] In these biblically recorded acts, God declares the Word. When we accept them as such, the Scriptures declare the Word. But the Scriptures do not declare the Word in all of its diversity, except from the perspective of faith and ultimacy.[69] The Word as the ultimate perspective on reality is what the Scriptures ultimately reveal. They were written and chosen by people directed by the Spirit. Believers saw their recorded text as the Word of God. The same Spirit opens the Scriptures to reveal the Word to believers.

Although the Scriptures are not themselves the Word, they still reveal it. They are God's word about the Word. They made the Word known in a trustworthy and authoritative manner. They also make known to us how the Word became incarnate in Christ. The Scriptures show how faith in the incarnate Christ can reopen our lives to the Word as a means of redemption. Thus a Christian believer accepts the Bible and surrenders to it in commitment. When we believe the Scriptures, they enable us to believe in God *according* to them.[70] Whatever other beliefs we may have, they ought to be compatible and in accordance with the Scriptures, as we understand and believe them.

To say the Scriptures are a standard or norm as we understand or believe them does not imply a subjectivistic or individualistic point of view. It is not possible for the Scriptures (or any other norms for that matter) to be obeyed unless they are believed. And we cannot believe them unless we accept them in faith. Of course, this situation results in a variety of interpretations, some of which are even in conflict. But the Christian tradition guards against the dangers of subjectivism and individualism here by stressing two points. First, humanity is a community, and people are communal in their existence. In this way the Christian Church has stressed the interpretation of the Bible not as a private matter, but as a means of knowing where the Spirit leads the Church. Because community is essentially a spiritual unity among people, and individuality is a matter of membership in a spiritual community, the individual subject, has a safeguard against arbitrariness in communal acceptance of the biblical canon.

And there is a second safeguard; we stress the ordinary, literary quality of the Bible.[71] The Bible is usually confessed to be a literary whole; the continuous identity binding all parts together is the revelation of the Word of God through the Spirit to the Church. So, arbitrary interpretations are also checked if we insist that any interpretation of a part must fit the interpretation of the whole. In any literary document, a text will only derive its meaning from its context. And the context will always be interpreted in relation to the overall intent of the author. Further, the text itself will have to be able demonstrably to bear the burden of any interpretation; demonstrable, that is, to faith.

We have a special need for our beliefs to be in accordance with the Scriptures, even if it is hard to determine at times what they mean. This need is caused by our inability to hear the Word directly from our understanding of creation as the Spirit testifies to the Word in the works of God. There are two main reasons for this dilemma. One is our human inability to trust ourselves, because of sin, to understand the Spirit and the Word; we are inclined to reject their testimony. The other reason is that no creature can be fully trusted to respond truly to the Word in the Spirit. Thus, no creature can be trusted to be a safe mirror of the Word.

Human sin has entered into all aspects of the world. Our contemporary awareness of the environment will drive that point home clearly. All creatures are affected by our failure to manage the earth as God's stewards. So no creature is, as such, a trustworthy indication of what God requires. But in the Bible, God meets humanity in this predicament. The Bible not only proclaims what God's Word is, it also comments on what responses are true and which ones are evil. The Scriptures, as a creaturely statement, are designed to overcome our handicap in a creaturely way.

So the Bible is fully a creature as well. The Scriptures are not divine; they are a book. Our reference to them as the Word of God can be misleading, especially since they do not refer to themselves as a whole in this way.[72] Through the Word and Spirit they reveal, the Scriptures are a unified collection of human documents: poems, historical records, prophecy, and letters. In these literary forms, God addresses humanity. Through the Spirit, God speaks in the Bible to faith, through faith, and for faith. The Church believes that, guided by the Spirit, God's people selected these writings as a specially inspired and trustworthy canon for faith. The focus of these writings is on the way in which they address themselves to faith, and through faith to the rest of creation, that is, to all of human life and all the other creatures.[73]

The Bible becomes the canon for the opening up of creation, for humanity's task of guiding creation to its destiny. As creaturely writings, the Scriptures are relational and relative, receiving their constancy as a canon from the Word they reveal. But even the Word itself is not the origin of all things. It points beyond itself to the will of the Creator.[74] Furthermore, the Bible is also relative and relational in a cultural-historical way. The texts were concretized in a specific temporal medium, although they were intended to reveal the Word for all times. As such it becomes the duty of each believer to hear, through the contextual specificity of the text, the underlying universal proclamation, re-contextualized in the present.

The specific temporal character of the Bible requires a three-sided interpretation. On the one hand (1) the Bible must be read fully within its historical context, lest the original text and its way of communicating be lost. The text-transcending Word cannot be heard unless it is understood in the context chosen for revelation. The authority of the Word will disappear from the Bible, and its canonicity and power will be lost, when we attempt to isolate Word from Scripture. At the same time, when Scripture is heard in its context (2) the Bible-Word transcends that realm and (3) is transported into the context of the hearer. If the Word in the Bible is not seen to transcend its context, then the same loss of canonicity and authority will occur. Only when we see the text in this many-sided role—within a context, transcending the same, and entering another—can we trust the Bible as the Word of God addressed to us. Then the written traditions in which Word and Spirit presented themselves for all times allow us to understand them and experience them reliably and with life.

The only proviso here is that we also must submit to and live by what we hear. In that correlation the Bible is the authoritative declaration of the Word of God. Stated in another way, the authority of the Bible extends only to its authorized use. What the text proclaims in its own context and what is thus heard by the readers in their context, only this is truly the Word of God. Implied teachings, extracted doctrines, logical implications, and other derivations from the text do not have the authority of the Bible-Word or the biblical inspiration of the Spirit. Thus, many of the things that follow from an analysis of the biblical text do not belong to the authoritative revelation of the Word.[75] Similarly, many propositions that the text could with logical justification be said to imply often do not belong to the authoritative canon. The texts do not even authoritatively proclaim what they assume.

Although the Bible is designed to meet humanity in the predicament of human sin, it is incapable of redeeming people from sin. The written Word does proclaim, however, that the Incarnate Word is offered to our faith as redeemer. Only when that Word is accepted in faith does the Spirit renew the human spirit and allow it to be open again to the Word in truth. Apart from Christ, the reliability of Scripture vanishes. The Bible acquires its trust when persons also entrust themselves to Christ. In that way the Bible, which otherwise would be a mere book, becomes worthy of belief. If we believe that the Bible itself, *in* itself, is the Word, it will become an idol and the unspiritual tool of conservatism and legalism. The power of the Spirit will be absent and the texts will cease to proclaim the Word. Instead the texts will proclaim the theology of the reader.[76]

As we noted above, the Bible can only be believed to say what we believe it to say. So, it is especially important for believers to always be open to the sovereign authority of the Word and open to the necessary limitations of our own viewpoint in coming to Scripture. Thus, the Bible will tend to confirm a Reformed perspective as biblical when the Bible is read from this vantage point. These dangers can be mitigated only when the Word is approached always new and renewing, refreshing, and different. Otherwise the Bible becomes the easy victim of strife, heresy, and violent misinterpretation; it will be unable to bind believers together. The Word is then subjected₁ to the authority of dogma, confession, theology, or another faith tradition. Such pseudo-authority cannot transcend church and history. The Bible will then leave the Word stranded in some distant phase of history.[77]

The relativity of the Bible as creature is vital to our proper understanding of its meaning. The term *relativity*, when used in the context of a revelation of God's constant and abiding Word, may sound inappropriate. But the meaning of relativity in this context is (as it should be) a reference to how the Bible should be properly accepted as the Word of God only in relation to other realities and not in and of itself.[78] Otherwise the Bible will lose its creatureliness and no longer be accessible to the human creature. In the Bible, the Word is embedded in creation in a certain way. And an understanding of creation according to the Bible is necessary for an understanding of the Bible creationally, and vice versa.[79]

Thus the Bible's trustworthiness is relative to, dependent upon, and related to our understanding of other things. It does not exist in a vacuum. As a book, the Bible must be understood spiritually. And all of these interrelations are tied together in Christ, who is Word, Spirit, and creature.[80] Word and creature are to be taken correlatively. They must be understood in terms of each other, even when one is the canon for the other. Word and creature are for one another; one is norm, the other is event. As the law and as that which is subject$_1$ to the law, their roles differ. But we can only understand them in their mutuality; the believing subject$_2$ acts in subjection$_1$ to the canon, while taking the canon to be what it is in relation to the subject$_{1,2}$.[81]

Biblical relativity, as correlativity, shows the progressive character of biblical revelation. The Word is present for a historical, temporal creation. It entered history in its incarnation, and also in its inscripturation. When we take the Word in its original cultural context in the Bible, and then hear it in our own context, the horizon of its meaning is widened. We can also see a history and unfolding of the Word through the Church. In their temporal correlativity, Word and creature progressively unfold their meaning to us.

As a canon, the Bible is closed. We do not add more authoritative books to the present collection of Holy Writ. We might say it is a finished standard of interpretation, or a final rule for understanding. The Word is willing to be taken *according* to *these* Scriptures. But our interpretation of what the Bible says in any given circumstance depends largely on what the Spirit (according to the Scriptures) says to the Church about the Word at that time.[82] The Bible is a closed canon with an open dynamic. The Word shows its relationship to the Bible by coming to us in accordance with these sacred writings. But the Word is neither exhausted in, nor imprisoned by the Bible. It is the Word of freedom; in all its fullness it is not bound by the Scriptures. Instead, the Scriptures are bound by the Word, which allows itself to be taken according to the Scriptures.

8.1.6 *Knowledge and truth*

The legitimacy of introducing the Bible into the spectrum of human knowledge as a canon (i.e., as a standard for what is true) has certainly become an issue in Western thought.[83] There has been a tradition in the study of knowledge to exclude any possibility of the Bible as an authoritative source of knowledge. For this reason alone we should say a few things about what the Bible says about knowledge. In addition, various issues raised throughout this study have been an occasion for me to repeat my personal position: I am operating with a view of knowledge that deviates from the major Western tradition. I hold beliefs about knowledge that are, I believe, biblical in origin. Incidentally, some contemporary publications appear to call for a view of knowledge which, for other reasons, displays many of the same characteristics.[84] To clear up this problem, then, I will herein state my pivotal beliefs about knowledge.

The biblical viewpoint on knowledge is, I believe, a definite notion of knowledge. The use of the term *knowledge* in the Bible is not just coincidental. This term, which has a certain reference and sense in today's common English usage, is not used in a totally different manner in the Bible. Nor is the biblical usage figurative or metaphorical. Both biblical and Western scholarship refer to the same reality when they use the term *knowledge*. But their interpretations are fundamentally different and perhaps even opposed. Modern biblical scholarship is quite agreed on this point.[85] The meaning of the term *knowledge* in the Bible should not be interpreted through Greek views we have inherited.

At the same time, modern Western scholarship is also pointing to many deficiencies in our traditional rationalistic views of knowledge which are now surfacing. Many such contributions mutually reinforce each other.[86] Positivism, objectivism, neutralism, scientism, logicism, and other perspectives which overemphasize certain dimensions in our Western views of knowledge are increasingly being exposed for their inaccuracy. It is pointed out that many scholars have mistakenly stressed the predominantly rational nature of knowledge and have tended to contrast such knowledge with belief or perception. Through a particular view of knowledge they have naturally concluded that science had to be the perfection of knowledge. Moreover, rational knowledge was seen as especially connected with certainty, truth, and justification.

In contrast to this intellectualistic Greek inheritance, we have the biblical tradition. Here, knowing is usually related to communion, living, loving, and obedience. These religiously cognate phenomena have their roots in our willing subjection to the divine call and in intimate fellowship. We are called to be one in spirit with God and our fellow creatures. Knowledge in the Bible is equated with obedient (human) communion with God and (human) communion in service to our fellow creatures. Such communion is referred to as love, life, or knowledge. *Truth* is the term that conveys the characteristic of authenticity, of having made the mark with respect to such active communion. Truth from God refers to God's dependability: "I AM." I will faithfully abide by my Word. In human terms, truth means responsibility and submission to the Word in spirit and according to the Spirit. And both are focused in the dynamic relation of Word and Spirit to God and creature. "Eternal life" is "to know God," and obeying God (Old Testament: fear, New Testament: love) is the principle (beginning) of knowledge. To know someone in the biblical sense involves relating in a bond of communion, aware of the nature of oneself and the other, and aware of what is expected of the relationship. When we authentically follow the Word we are "truly" being Christ's disciples. The truth is not just for "being known" in a logically abstract sense. We can also do the truth or stand in it.[87]

Biblical notions of truth and knowledge are compatible with, and form the context for, certain Western notions. Standards of intersubjectivity, reliability, and rationality of knowledge are dimensions of what the Bible calls knowledge.[88] Sometimes the Bible draws attention to these very dimensions in its own usage. But these specified usages must always be integrated into the full biblical context. The biblical notions of truth and knowledge encompass all of human experience. Knowing includes all of human existence before the face of God. The limitation of knowledge to a justified belief in true propositions is a notion entirely foreign to the Bible. The Scriptures would not regard such a believed proposition as knowledge if it were not integrally part of what the Bible sees as knowledge.

8.1.7   *Humanity's special calling*

The various areas of belief introduced to this point have been primarily concerned with human beings and their faith. Indeed, belief and commitment are phenomena only associated with human experience. But the ontic significance of human faith and commitment apparently go far beyond the limits of human experience. They are said to be related to the very destiny of the world. This very special connection of human beings with the ultimate destiny of the world is, of course, itself a matter of faith and commitment.

In humankind, creation has an open recipient for the relation between Creator and creature. Humans are open to what lies beyond creation, and are not closed off in body while being in relation to God in spirit. So, through humanity, creation is in touch with the intended direction of things. In people, creation is open to order as God's

Word. People are called to be spiritually one, a united community of spiritual integrity.[89] The person as spirit is open to God; the person as body is one with creation.[90] Human life originates in the presence of God's Spirit in humankind.[91] So the human body may be of the earth, and earthy, yet it becomes a living, that is, spiritual body. Humanity is called to represent the Creator on earth as a servant bearing authority, that is, as a creature representing the Creator.[92]

The Bible refers to this representation as the image of God. Humanity is called to be in the image of God.[93] As representatives of the Author of creation and of the Creator's will for creation, the human person has been empowered by God. This is the meaning of human authority and it gives humanity a unique position among the creatures. Because humanity is not the author, people have this authority in a creaturely way as servants. They can exercise it only in obedience to God's will, which they represent. Having to perceive God's will in Word and Spirit calls for humankind to be a spirit. As a spirit, a person can relate knowingly to the ways and directions in which the Word calls us to walk.

In this fashion, humanity is called to involvement in the development, the opening up of creation, following the direction intended in the order of creation. In the human spirit, creation is open to its Maker. Thus the human community is specially called to administer the opening up of creation. The human office is designed to guide creation in its differentiated integrative development. We are to direct it in the path of the Spirit through history, limited only by the order set by the Creator. Human beings are authorized to act decisively with respect to time. We must implement the future and speak with finality.[94] Humankind is placed in charge of history; the human creature represents its Maker before the other creatures. To be human is to be like God, although a person is not God and is not even divine. In the human community God has a representative on earth. In obedient people who administer God's will, we are supposed to see what God is like, what God wants. In humankind, God is among the creatures. The Word has, from the beginning, been the mediator: the way between God and creation. The human calling has, from the beginning, been to be Immanuel: God with us. In people, God has wanted to be with creation.

So this is the intended relationship between God and humanity: the whole creation in humankind submits in service to God through Spirit and Word. The characteristic integrity of human existence, which results from this submission, is revealed in the Bible as love, obedience, knowledge, service, truth, and life. In these terms the whole relation of creation to the Creator is concentrated. Every human action and function is in principle intended to be an expression of this central relation. But that relation must be understood as the concentration point of all human functionality. Having dominion, serving with authority, and representing the will of the supreme Author is fully functional. Our special relation has brought humanity very special functions which no other creature has: reflection, decision, choice, troth, and commitment. But these are firmly founded in the rest of creation: the physical, organic, and sensitive sharing with the other creatures.

Now, even these qualities become spiritual instruments of humanity's calling to freely administrate the Word to creation in submission to that Word. Directed by the Spirit we are called to be directing spirits and to follow the directives of the Word. The fullness of all callings, norms, rules, laws, standards, and expectations for creation are concentrated in human obedience, responsibility, and commitment. For the human being, such concentrated submission is called life. In not meeting the callings that come to humankind, people lose life.[95] Commitment and life are one; they are the full involvement with all of one's self in being "one-self." In being oneself, one meets the conditions for being a self. In living submission, one is oneself in truth. Commitment in truth—true commitment—is life. And love is true commitment and living communion. In the concentrated existence of humankind, all of the most rewarding qualities of creation come together in a center.

In this context, human freedom must be understood as the freedom to be a spiritual creature and join the Spirit of God in opening up creation according to the Word. Within the room provided by the Word of God and by going in the same direction as the Spirit of God, humanity is free to be the ruler of the earth, to have dominion, and to administer the Word. Atoms are free to move and act, plants are free to grow, and animals are free to play. Similarly, people are free to rule the earth in God's name.

This freedom cannot be used autonomously, however. Neither can it be used to reject authority, nor to let humanity itself determine the order of reality. A person is not free to do evil. We are not supposed to be punished if we use freedom properly. If the human community sins, the consequences are death and destruction. Therefore, there is no freedom to sin. Freedom is positive freedom to obey the Word and follow the Spirit in our own individual way. We are to make our choices as full and worthy partners in the covenant relation with the Creator.

8.2 *Ultimate Assumptions as Philosophical Categories*

The sort of belief statements presented above are not customarily found in philosophical texts. But in our time we see a renewed search for new paradigms. Systems of conceptual schemes that are general enough to cover a universal ontology are, even now, quite scarce.[96] Commonly accepted concepts that can integrate large areas of learning are not widely available. So, I see no other alternative for philosophy but to bring our own foundations to the surface. Having done so, I must now also describe the road leading from the beliefs of ultimate commitment to the realm of philosophy. This road leads, I believe, via the ultimate categories used by philosophers, to the construction of an ontological model.[97]

If in philosophical ontology we must present the most universal order of reality, then the ultimate categories used to construct such a system will likely reflect the ultimate beliefs we have about the world. These categories are themselves philosophical concepts, so they are also theoretical constructions. Most people are not committed to a philosophical system the way we are to ultimate beliefs. But propelled by those ultimate beliefs we know these ultimate categorial concepts are not reducible to other concepts. They are, as it were, the limits of our theoretical constructions; they are as far as we are able to go. And such categories are then likely to be directly related to our ultimate commitment beliefs.

In the philosophical approach outlined in the preceding chapters, I have used a number of basic categories. These can now be visibly related to the beliefs of commitment outlined in this Appendix. However, the basic categorial distinctions I used do not cover all of reality. The category of the order-subjectivity$_1$ correlation, which has been called a radically irreducible correlation, is a partial view of a wider relation, namely, that of origin, order, and world.

The origin, although philosophically projected at various times, turned out to be the Creator, about whom in my view it is impossible to theorize. But something must precede the basic category of order and world. Hence my belief in the covenant relation between Creator and creation through Word and Spirit. In itself, that relation is resistant to abstract inquiry. But this belief does directly ground the basic concept of the order-subjectivity$_1$ correlation. So it may be said to form the link between my ultimate commitment and my philosophical conceptual framework. I will refer to this belief as the *radical distinction*.[98]

8.2.1   *The radical distinction*

The biblical beliefs concerning the covenantal relation between Creator and creation through Word and Spirit lead to a general conclusion: Neither the world nor its order are self-made; they are not *sui generis*. The origin of the world lies outside of both the world and its order. If we were to approach this question from a different perspective or commitment, we could likely come to a different conclusion. From the point of view of philosophical argument, we might well begin with the assertion that the world itself is its own beginning. If none of our beliefs conflicts with this statement, then nothing prevents us from asserting it.

There is no way we can prove or even justify the assertion that the world is its own origin. It is another belief to which we come without rational justification, conclusive evidence, or compelling grounds. It is, however, an assertion we might arrive at through a firm commitment to the ultimacy of empirical reality. There will likely be more support for this type of commitment in the contemporary climate than for a commitment to God as Creator. Nevertheless, I am committed to God the Creator and I reject all propositions about a self-originating world. So I will have to deal with the philosophical consequences of my beliefs on their own merit. At important points I know they will collide with opposing positions.

A similar and basic concept concerning order is also present as a result of the commitment I have outlined. Whether the world is ordered, and whether there is an order to be distinguished from the empirical world, are questions on which philosophers certainly disagree.[99] These issues also cannot be fully settled in a purely philosophical way. From the point of view I have taken, the world appears to be structured. But I believe our experience of structure in the world cannot be understood only as part of the subjective$_1$ world. The world is subject$_1$ to order, receives its order, and becomes structured all because it conforms to God's Word. And therefore order does not coincide with what is ordered but is distinct from it. But we only see this if we believe in the creation of the world through the Word of God—the expression of the Will of God to which the world is called to submit.

So all that is known or can be known must be either the world, the order of the world, or the origin of the world. Nothing else is real or can be known. And this belief is founded on a prior belief rooted in commitment to God the Creator, God's Word and Spirit, and God's creation. Merely to talk about the world and its order is insufficient.

Similarly, to talk only about the world and its Creator is also inadequate. Because we cannot construct a theory about the origin of the world, we can only deal philosophically with the correlation of world and world order. We know this to be the case even though the correlation is in fact part of the more encompassing relation between origin, order, and world.

These three are fully related, although they must also be understood to be irreducible. This irreducibility is not an occasion for discontinuity in relationship, however, because Word and Spirit relate world and origin. World and world origin have no properties in common. But Word and Spirit are both creaturely and divine. This creates a genuine relationship between origin and world. Only the world is subjective$_1$, and only the world order is nomic condition, law. But the world is subjective$_1$ because it is subjected to order. And the order is law because it holds for the world. The order does not hold for the origin, which is the origin not only of the world but also of its order. These three—origin, world order, and ordered, existential world—can be known only in relation to each other. Nevertheless, they cannot be reduced to each other.

Existentially ordered world, world order, and world origin are all spiritual. Such is the perspective of beliefs outlined in this Appendix. God is a spirit. God's Word, and consequently the principle of the order of the world, is truly spiritual. The order of creation is a spiritual order, one of purpose, movement, and history. The path of order is directional; it leads somewhere, and has a destiny and an end. And the destiny and end are the same as the origin: all things are from and unto God.

Yet the path to the end from the origin is not equivalent to a circle.[100] Its direction is ordered ever forward, into the future. And in this way creation is also a spiritual reality. In its responsive character, unified in the spirituality of humankind, the world follows the lead of the order in its direction. In this way the world is dynamic, a world of action, movement, growth, history, and development. None of the stability and constancy we find can be static. Although origin, order, and world are all spiritual, this is not a reason to reduce them to a common denominator of spirituality. There is no common denominator. The three are related but irreducibly different.

When I speak of the reality of origin, order, and the world, I also do not mean to indicate a phenomenon—such as reality—of which these three are subdivisions. There is no reality of which origin is one kind, order is another, and the world is a third and final kind. As a term, *reality* only indicates that neither origin, order, nor world is a mere postulation, hypostatization, nor imaginative creation. And when we speak of the reality of all three, we are simply indicating that all three are being referred to at once. They are not three levels of one substance, however, nor are they together the essence of "being." They are present in one universe of discourse, where they share a common term.

8.2.2 Basic categorial distinctions: order-world and universal-individual

My whole conceptual scheme depends on one ordering concept: the basic categorial distinction is given in the irreducible correlation of universal order and empirical subjectivity$_1$ as it responds individually. In philosophy, this correlation is the accessible side of the relation of origin to order and to the world. Via this correlation the ontological categories are directly related to beliefs of commitment. Thus I have a crucial distinction immediately tied into my views of the world as creation and of creation as God-ordered reality.

The relation of universality and individuality is directly connected with the relation of order and world as a result of my views of the biblical notions of creation and the Word. What we philosophically experience as universality is what I take to be our conceptual awareness of the unconditionally necessary relation of the Word to any possible creature.[101] What we philosophically experience as order, pattern, structure, coherence, and regularity in the world is our conceptual awareness that any creature or creaturely event or relation is concrete evidence of its dependence on the Word, as well as evidence of the Word's expression of God's will for an ordered and coherent world.[102] And what we philosophically experience as individuality is in fact the rich diversity of the creatures which exist as a varied host of servants of God. Each has its own peculiar calling, is known by God, and is known by us as something irreducibly real in its own right. And it is not exhausted because we know or comprehend it. Each creature is uniquely made and uniquely itself in responding to God's call.

Conceptually we cannot work out the beliefs of commitment solely on the basis of principles of inference. Our believing experience of the meaning of these beliefs limits inferential approaches. We will have to accept the conceptual meaning of these beliefs, without prior rational justification, for their own worth. Only then can inferential approaches to them be trusted. And this is normal. There is no "logical" necessity for the condition-1 that a cow should have four legs, for example. Why should there be? A cow is not a proposition nor a concept, so it does not need to be "logically" necessary in any part of its construction. We also accept that cows must have four legs. So if any cow is to be a properly formed animal, it must necessarily have four legs. The problem with beliefs of ultimate commitment is that they relate to matters which strain the limits of human knowledge. If we insist on the same conceptual clarity with respect to these beliefs as we do with our appreciation of the need for cows to have four legs, then difficulties will arise. These can only be resolved if we place the demand for logical clarity in subjection to the call for integrity of commitment.

We might say our belief in order as the limit of subjective$_1$ existence also implies our belief in philosophy (as a form of subjective$_1$ existence) to be limited by this order. Philosophy is itself conditioned, having an order and proper limits of its own. If we believe philosophy is subjective$_1$, and *subjectivity$_1$* means being subject$_1$ to order, then order cannot originate in philosophy. Nor can it be determined or even given its definition in philosophy. Philosophy must accept order as it is found if we are to proceed from the commitment beliefs presented here. If philosophy accepts this proviso, it will be able to benefit from knowing the order of reality as it is believed. In a purely philosophical and isolated context, we may at best expect order to be postulated as a possible way of conceiving the universe. But if philosophy accepts the givens of commitment, it can treat order as a known given.

Philosophy can then allow order, which originates in the will of God, to be able to transcend subjective$_1$ existence. Order will be seen as constant and inviolable, in the sense that subjective$_1$ existence can depend on the guaranteed uniformity, stability, and continuity of order. And order can be accepted a priori as universality because it holds for subjective$_1$ existence. As a philosophical category, order then becomes the transcending, inviolable, and a priori ground of regularity in the world. It is not a category which is entirely postulated. It does serve to explain the experience of orderly structures in the universe, which is too cosmic a notion to be limited merely to those who share the beliefs outlined in this Appendix. The will of God, as revealed in the Word of God, is not only inscribed in the Bible and incarnate in Jesus Christ, it is also evident in the patterns of creaturely continuity.

So the creation itself, the empirical world of subjective$_1$ existence, manifests its subjectivity$_1$ in its (ordered) response character. Patterns of order become interwoven in patterns of response; principles of order give rise to structures of subjective$_1$ concrete reality. The regularity of our experience shows a subjectivity$_1$ that is neither its own condition nor its own reality. We can experience the compelling, general, and continuous dimensions of each event *and* the unique spontaneity of every moment in time. In our experience of order, we know the structures are stable, but they are also relative and historical.

Science, as the committed art of the conceptual discovery of orderly structure in the world, shows this subjective$_1$ manifestation of order in its history. The discovery of order, proclaimed as fact, is itself a developmental process. Science aims to present information which is reliable and related to the invariance of universal order. But the laws which science discovers, isolates, and formulates are not static. They are continually corrected and often rejected or relativized. Scientific views can become outdated. Scientific discovery is genuine discovery, not just the gradual and rational uncovering of order. So the collection of scientific beliefs at any one time is experienced by the scientific community as a stated body of facts and laws which are *models* of structure and conditionality.[103]

The formulation of structure in science cannot be identical to the conditions-1 of reality or the principles of order themselves. Rather, science engages in a conscious attempt to isolate structures of subjective$_1$ reality. Then it can try to approximate the conditions-1 for subjectivity$_1$ and the universal order of possibility. This can be done through an analysis of the subjective$_1$ world. And the analysis itself is subjective$_1$. Thus, scientific propositions, theories, and models reflect the most up-to-date and stable understanding of the most general sort of stability to be discovered. It suffices as an explanatory device for the world as we know it. But both the development of empirical reality and the history of science prevent us from viewing the body of scientific laws at any one time as a fully reliable picture of the actual principles of order.

Via the subjectivity$_1$ of scholarship the beliefs of our commitment structure our philosophy. At the same time scholarship yields terms and categories which provide a satisfactory explanatory device from the point of view of *what* is being explained. And in this way the correlativity of world and order can, as we have seen, be detected even on the world's side of the correlation alone. However, although order is detectable in what is ordered, it cannot be identified with merely the evidence of order in subjectivity$_1$.

If we treat order as subjectivity$_1$, this analysis inevitably produces contradictions. If order is conceived as condition-1 *for* subjectivity$_1$, it cannot also be *subject*$_1$ to any conditions. World order and ordered world are irreducible components in a correlation. Order mediates the relation between origin and world. Order is there for the world and bears the evidence of this, just as the world bears evidence of being ordered. Moreover, order itself is evidently not self-sufficient, self-evident, self-explanatory, nor self-holding. But this does not mean order, as we see it in the world, is subjective$_1$. Order is in a mediating position with respect to world and origin. This is evident not only in its correlative irreducibility with regard to the world, but also in its dependence on the origin.

If we look at order, we see it is not "dependent" because it is ordered or conditioned, but because it originates outside itself. Order has been given to the world so as to hold for it. So order reveals its origin by having been called forth from the origin. It manifests its relation to the world because it creates orderliness in the world. Order shows its mediating position both by its ultimate character of being an inviolable and constant order in principle, and by its subjective$_1$ manifestation in relatively stable structures.

Order has characteristics which come to the forefront in mathematics and logic, for example. These characteristics reveal to us how order is above arbitrariness. But the characteristics of order also come to the forefront in the legal codes of nations, which move with history precisely in order to maintain the inviolable principle of justice. Thus, the philosophical category of order is a suitable conceptualization of the belief in the relation between Creator and creature through Word and Spirit. At the same time, order provides an acceptable model for a theoretical explanation of certain universal features of our experience.

Conditions have no other origin than as fundamental ordering principles for creation, which constitute the limits of possibility for subjective$_1$ existence. As such they were called forth to hold for all creation by the Creator. They are the Creator's conditions for the maintenance of creation. Order in principle is the point of origin for all that is subjectively$_1$ necessary and possible. It is an order of a priori universality with inviolable constancy. With respect to subjectivity$_1$, it is a transcendent conditionality. But as the correlative of subjectivity$_1$, we see how subjectivity$_1$ itself is ordered and structured. Order *for* subjectivity$_1$ becomes evident in the structure *of* subjectivity$_1$, that is, in patterns of regularity which are themselves subjective$_1$.

So the category of order in relation to the category of subjectivity₁ can provide an adequate explanation of reality from a theoretical point of view. But the meaning of these categories will still be derived primarily from beliefs of ultimate commitment. If we were to try to formulate the relation of order to subjectivity₁ from a formal logical point of view alone, we would not be able to arrive at the irreducibility and correlation of these two realms.[104]

We can now see how the correlation of order and world, and the universality and individuality of the two directions of this correlation, give rise to another interpretation of a basic category. The correlation has the dual character of both flowing from commitment and being able to account for generally recognized states of affairs. This allows us a certain interpretation of individuality. I refer to a distinction between the orderly and the directional features of reality. These features are related to the distinction between Word and Spirit. The spiritual dynamic of the Word of power is the way in which the Creator's will for the creation is addressed to a creation responding individually to God's will. The unique unity of each creaturely unit of response, which I called a functor, is the creature's own way of being itself.

In this way, the creation is not unordered chaos to which the Word is addressed and through which it becomes ordered. The creation is itself an ordered response; it is ordered in responding, and is patterned in being itself. But that "being itself" shows us not only variation and uniqueness, but also a capacity to respond according to the Spirit of the Word or the intended direction of the order. On earth only people, of course, are spirits. But all earthly creatures, in being free to have functional room, are able to be participants in the spiritual movement of creation toward its destiny. This is basically what individuality is all about: freedom to be oneself or itself, either in being a spirit or in being open to spiritual dynamics.

So within the context of universal order, each creature is individually active in contributing to the movement toward the destiny of creation. In participating in and contributing to that movement, each creature or functor is spiritual, whether it is a spirit or simply open to relationships *with* a spirit. The entire creation responds or corresponds to order together with and led by humanity. And the human community is not merely open to the guidance of the Spirit of God, but is itself spiritual and thus able to communicate as such with the Spirit of God. Thus the individual unity of each creature is forged in a spiritual process. All children, of course, are born human. But they grow up in a world in which their "being human" is thrust into the realm of ultimate destinies. They are called and held responsible for helping to guide the universe toward its destiny.

In being human, our actions can either be good or evil. And both the good and the evil, although they are spiritual realities, do penetrate the existence of all dimensions of creation. Every universal principle of order calls for a structural identity of response, even when each individual response is different and unique. But that principle of order also calls for an integral response made in the spiritual direction of the principle of order. Each creature is called to respond in a way that is good for itself and all other creatures. Translated into a belief of commitment, the direction to which every principle of order points is love. If a person is continually one and integral in response to the entire scale of order confronting humanity (i.e., is bodily and spiritually in touch with Word and Spirit), then that person will be one in all actions. All actions will be integrated in directional unity.

Thus the philosophical concepts of individuality, unity, and temporal direction are given their content through what we believe in the Spirit by means of our commitment. Given the meaning of commitment, these concepts help us to account in an orderly way for experienced patterns of regularity, as well as for events and certain kinds of phenomena. The simple commitment beliefs in Word and Spirit—who reveal and carry out God's will in relation to a creation called to respond to that will in its historical, temporal movement— these beliefs give us a point of orientation for philosophical categories such as the order-world relation, the universal-individual relation, and the concepts of individuality, unity, and universal structure in relation to historical direction. The structured functional diversity of things is unified in individual subjects$_1$. In a unique manner they participate in the movement of time, are structured by principles of order, and are directed by the spiritual leadership of humanity. Certain beliefs ultimately orient these basic categories. We believe creation exists before God's face in responding to the Creator's Word and Spirit.

This radical summary of beliefs of commitment helps us to pinpoint the interrelation of many basic categories. The creation as we now understand it could not exist in pure subjectivity$_1$. As evidence of this we can point out how creation has an ordering and directive side as well as a subjective$_1$ side. There is a concrete, responsive variety of units of subjectivity$_1$ as well as universal order. And there is individual subjectivity$_1$ as well as an ultimate unity of direction. The creation, as seen in our subjective$_1$ world, does display integral-universal order as well as individual and concrete responses of subjectivity$_1$. Both are sides of the subjective$_1$ world and are temporal, historical, and creaturely. They are irreducible sides of the same world. The world cannot exist without either one; neither side can exist without the other; yet the two sides are irreducibly different.

Apparently all concretely existing things have both sides. No creature is pure subjectivity$_1$. And all order is an order for subjects$_1$. Both sides of creation show how they are rooted in the unity of Word and Spirit. They demonstrate a fundamental diversity of patterned coherence as well as a directional unity. The directional unity of the integration of all order can be found in the spiritual call of love in creation. This call comes in a variety of principles of order, each of which presents the universality of all order. On the subjective$_1$ side, the directional unity of subjectivity$_1$ is an individual and unique unity of spirituality. It is manifested in a structural correlation of directive order and subjectivity$_1$. On each side of the correlation we find direction and order, guiding and founding, integrating and differentiating, unifying and diversifying all moments.

My commitment beliefs concerning God as Creator and the world as creation have influenced me in developing certain philosophical categories. In addition, my beliefs about knowledge and truth have had a direct effect on what I conceive to be the proper context of a philosophical inquiry. This, I believe, is as it should be in philosophy, even though that effect may seem at odds with what is traditionally or currently accepted as proper philosophical procedure.[105] But my beliefs *about* knowledge have not only shaped my *concept* of knowledge. Together, my beliefs and concepts have also determined the practice followed in this inquiry.

Thus, I have not proceeded on the assumption that philosophy or reason is autonomous. I have made a different assumption: philosophy occurs within a context of a great deal of knowledge that cannot be explained or accounted for in philosophy. I also assume that the truth of what I say philosophically cannot be determined by philosophical methods and standards alone. I do not subscribe to the perfection of knowledge in science, nor do I accept the correspondence doctrine of the identity of truth and true statement, proposition, or assertion. Rational analysis as a human activity, and rational analytic truth as the true results of such activity, can only be authentic if validated by a context and by standards which themselves transcend the limits of analysis and its results.[106] An appeal to faith or commitment as the ultimate horizon of our experience is deeply human. Strong traditions in Western thought have made philosophers suspicious of religious or fiduciary phenomena. It is therefore not wise to consult with philosophers about the reality or the nature of these things, for they have disqualified themselves from having respectable opinions in this field. There is, however, an ever-widening tradition of investigating the ultimate dimensions of human experience as a difficult but nevertheless fully empirical field of investigation, manifestly present in the lives of all normal persons. That tradition is making it apparent, fortunately also to an increasing number of students of philosophy, that without the horizon of faith no human endeavor either exists or is possible.[107]

Notes

Notes to the Introduction

1. CF, 59. The categorial framework in question could be referred to as ontology, metaphysic, world hypothesis, philosophical paradigm, or model of the general structure of the world, all of which I could use as synonyms.

2. Besides Holmes's book on worldview there is the similar book by Richard Middleton and Brian Walsh. Both of these books attempt to be as broadly Christian in the Evangelical Protestant tradition as they can. More specifically Reformed is a recent book on worldview by Albert Wolters. I find all three to be broadly compatible with my aims.

3. See Holmes, WV, 3-5.

4. For similarly simple models, see Wolterstorff (UN, 299-300) and Armstrong (USR1, 126ff.).

5. Every metaphysic, having stated what there is, also notes that there are some things that should not be there, or that there are some things that are not as they should be, or even that some things that are claimed to be there by others are not really there at all. We think that death and evil should not be there, that a child born with deformed limbs is not as she should be, and that ghosts are not really there. Many of these choices depend on our ultimate position. "To accept Naturalism is to reject such entities as Cartesian minds, private visual and tactual spaces, angelic beings and God" (Armstrong, USR1, 127). "The concepts and predicates which we actually employ are determined by our powers of discernment and our interests" (ibid., 39). The crucial factor is on what basis or on whose authority we decide what things should be there, should be different, or are not there at all. Without taking into account and accounting for this question and the answer one gives, no philosophy is possible.

6. See 235-36. Such objections are especially weighty if they are made by dominant traditions which in their own view need not critically reflect on their objections. See Rorty, PM, 172 and Radnitzky, 382.

7. See 236. Also see Rorty, PM, 330, who is happy with the sharp distinction between science and religion, but confesses that it is no longer clear that rational standards can be credited with being the basis for the distinction.

8. My intentions to bring to the surface what I consider to be my roots in the Christian tradition should not be misinterpreted as a claim to have succeeded in actually formulating a fully and consistently biblical philosophy.

9. For a brief discussion of the contemporary relation between philosophical interest in knowledge and philosophical interest in system, see Anthony Quinton, 112. For a discussion of the role of knowledge in Western thought, see Rorty, PM, especially 3, 38, 43, 190, 366, and 368.

10. See Rorty, PM, 51 and 53. Greek thinkers up to and including Aristotle were undoubtedly convinced that ontology was the basis for epistemology. But the subsequent struggle with skepticism shifted the accent from being to knowing in the struggle to determine who or what is the measure of things. Out of that shift came the general stance that world order is mental or rational order. See the opening chapter of Wagner.

11. "The manner in which a person classifies the objects of his experience into highest classes or categories, the standards of intelligibility which he applies, and the metaphysical beliefs which he holds are intimately related" (Körner, CF, ix).

12. I have in mind especially the recently founded Society of Christian Philosophers which publishes the journal *Faith and Philosophy*. The society includes in its membership philosophers from a large number of Christian traditions in Canada and the United States.

13. I am speaking here of North American attempts. I am well aware that Herman Dooyeweerd's extensive philosophical system is available in English. Unfortunately its philosophical style, the quality of its translation, and its background in the continental European milieu make his *magnum opus*, *A New Critique of Theoretical Thought* (4 vols.), hard to penetrate.

14. It is fascinating that a philosophical tradition which has been so firmly rooted in human autonomy has at the same time been so fearful of human subjectivity. For the dominance of the rational perspective see, e.g., Rorty, PM, 38 and 166.

15. Interestingly, these same worldviews and their implied ontologies have deeply influenced the history of Christian doctrine.

16. The most recent and shocking example for the dominant philosophical school is Richard Rorty. His work is often characterized as blatantly subjectivist and relativist. I believe, however, that such characterization makes sense primarily from the viewpoint of analytic philosophy. Not only does Rorty remain devoted to reason, but he also subscribes to standards and to truth. He just denies that all of us share these standards and that they are rational in nature.

17. E.g., "Popper *confesses* himself to rationalism and he supports it by reasons but he does not 'justify' it" (Radnitzky, 370). In keeping with this: "Belief may be a regrettably unavoidable weakness to be kept under con-

trol of criticism: but *commitment* is for Popper an outright crime"
(Lakatos, 92). Contemporary devotees to reason without rational
justification are not persuaded that other faiths should be allowed to com-
pete in the academy.

18. The rational point of view has seldom been viewed as another point of
view, next to, e.g., emotional, political, moral, or religious points of
view. It has always been seen as privileged over the others. But even if
that position is perhaps coming to an end, it remains necessary to reflect
on what in fact is the rational point of view and how it differs from
others. I give the rational point of view no priority with regard to truth.
But I do view it as the only explicit grasp of general structures of necessity.
I also do not view the rational point of view as certain (see Rorty, PM,
113). But I do accept the dependability of general structures. See Rorty's
long note (PM, 300) on truth.

19. Truth, I believe, appears in the empirical world wherever what exists
meets the standards for existence. Truth is not a characteristic only of propositions and assertions, nor even of human language more broadly conceived. Rather, truth is a characteristic of anything when it is as it was intended to be. According to this view, the truth of a philosophical
paradigm will not just depend on the universal acceptance of rationally
justifying arguments in its favor or on the absence of successful counter examples. This view of truth requires that philosophy not only embody a
relativized view of rationality, but also a relationship to whomever or
whatever it is that determines what the standards for existence are. If this
in turn requires a relationship to something beyond both humanity and
the rest of nature, humanism and naturalism obscure the quest for truth.
Further, if the proper nature of what exists in the world is determined by
the Creator of the world, whatever is not of that nature puts us in touch
with evil and, consequently, with human responsibility. For the true and
the good are identical, as are the lie and evil. And the origin of the lie and
evil is found in the abdication of human responsibility in favor of the
assumption of human autonomy.

20. See Gödel on the impossibility of self-consistency in formal systems. See
Polanyi on the unavoidability of commitment for holding to a conceptual
scheme. If, e.g., one makes the belief that God is omnipotent a pillar of
one's conceptual scheme, then a purely logical analysis might lead to the
conclusion that such a belief is contradictory (the familiar example of God
doing something he cannot do). But such conclusions have seldom led to
the abandonment of the belief in question.

21. The impossibility of rationally justifying rationalism undermines reason's
claims to be qualified to sit in judgment over us when we say that we
know something. See Rorty, PM, 212. I am not sure that Rorty distinguishes
sufficiently between the "permanent neutral framework" of philosophy
(211), which I also reject, and the continuity of order in the world, in
which I do believe and on which belief I think all of science is founded.

22. See Rorty, PM, 281, 286, 299, 315ff.

23. One might say that in our time we need "affirmative action" on this point. Until philosophers in general are no longer reluctant to make known the commitment they have and the role it plays, explicit and extensive attention to this dimension of thought should be fostered by those who are now prepared to do so.

24. In philosophy that tradition is mainly represented in the neo-Calvinist philosophy developed at the Free University of Amsterdam and in North America by the tradition oriented to Scottish common sense philosophy. See Hart, van der Hoeven, and Wolterstorff, *Rationality in the Calvinian Tradition*.

25. In theology this trend can be found clearly in the works of Calvin, Karl Barth, Herman Bavinck, and Gerrit Berkouwer.

26. An extensive bibliography and an introduction to Dooyeweerd can be found in Kalsbeek. There has been an Association for Calvinist Philosophy since 1935, which publishes the journal *Philosophia Reformata*. The movement has had considerable influence in the work of the Institute for Christian Studies in Toronto.

27. I consider John Dewey the most important American philosopher of this century. See my CC, 8-12. Also see Rorty, PM, 5ff.

28. This is the pair which Dooyeweerd refers to as the law-subject relation and which John Dewey calls the conjugate relation. Pairs such as these can lead us to view the history of Western thought in the light of the persistence of a dialectical theme. Philosophers have been fascinated looking at reality in terms of basic dualities and their relations. Examples of such pairs are almost endless: mind-body, form-matter, form-content, universal-individual, freedom-causality, value-fact, subject-object, thought-subject matter, concepts-data, spirit-matter, soul-body, substance-accident, church-state, individual-community, good-evil, infinite-finite, reality-appearance, constancy-change, eternity-time, rational-empirical, analytic-synthetic, language-fact, postulate-given, nonexistential-existential, ideational-material, reason-sense, necessity-contingency, philosophy-science, belief-feeling, knowing-believing, faith-reason, revelation-observation, concept-percept, essence-existence, idea-reality, etc., etc. These pairs have been seen as logically contradictory opposites, as correlates, as dialectical poles, as representing good and evil, as standing for the determined and what determines, and so on. That is, these pairs have very much been interpreted in terms of each other. In this book I will also deal with perennial problems of philosophy in terms of pairs.

29. Throughout his two volumes, Armstrong sees close connections here as well.

Notes to Chapter I

1. Aristotle did this in antiquity, but it is still fashionable today. Anthony Quinton speaks of individuals which have qualities and relations (3, 41, 249) and continues to refer to this threesome throughout his book. D.M. Armstrong introduces his discussion by referring to particulars, properties, and relations (USR1, xiii, 126; USR2, 19). He also continues to work with these three. See also Wolterstorff, UN, 80, 85 and Körner, CF, 4.

2. When I use *kind* I do not mean the same thing as *natural kind*. I use the the term as broadly as possible, so broadly that everything in our empirical universe can be said to be of some kind or other. Things are not just minerals, vegetables, animals, or humans. A kind of (whatever) is just a sort of (whatever).

3. All who admit that there are universals may be called realists. Realists may come in many varieties and may sharply disagree with one another. But all subscribe to universals that cannot be reduced to particulars. The disagreements are over such issues as how real they are, where they are, when they are, how they relate to particulars, what they are, and other problems. One may be a Platonic Realist and admit the existence of a realm of immutable and eternal universals separate from our empirical world. One may not want to go that far and still be in favor of independent universals and call oneself a Metaphysical Realist. One may also say that universals are merely actual dimensions of things right here in our world and not independent from particulars, though not reducible to them either. Such a person might be called a Scientific Realist. Alvin Plantinga and Michael J. Loux are examples of Platonic Realists. (See GN and SA.) Nicholas Wolterstorff would be an example of a Metaphysical Realist. (See UN.) D.M. Armstrong calls himself a Scientific Realist. (See USR1 and USR2.)

4. All who wish to admit no more than the reality of the particulars in our world may be called nominalists. Nominalists also come in a great variety. (See Armstrong, USR1, 12-17.) The differences are due to how far one wishes to remove oneself from acknowledging some sort of reality to account for the sameness in things. Things may in fact have nothing in common, or only a name, or just a concept.

5. Armstrong holds this (USR2, 4, 168) and so does Quinton (4).

6. An example is Wolterstorff (UN, 221).

7. Though he works in the tradition of this way of putting the problem, Armstrong certainly attempts to get away from the idea of a realm of entities in addition to or over and above and separate from particulars (USR2, 4-5).

8. See, e.g., Armstrong, USR1, 78, 87, 100, 112.

9. This is the view of Loux, SA, 96ff.

10. Armstrong, who calls his view Scientific Realism, sees a close connection between science and universals. What universals there are is a question for science to settle (USR1, xiii).

11. If it is true that universals can be construed as standards or criteria for what exists in our world, then without universals there might be no such standards. At best there might be conventions, and conventions are entirely dependent on subjective decision. So nominalism should lead us to reject the view that "objective standards" exist. Wolterstorff, for example, argues that kinds allow us to refer to "what is true of *normal*" entities of the kind (UN, 245). Combined with his approval of C.S. Peirce's view that such a kind "determines things" this may lead to the conclusion that kinds are needed both to find out what is normal and to make things normal (UN, 254).

12. Armstrong, Loux, Quinton, and Wolterstorff all seem to share this dissatisfaction with the traditional approach to some extent. But they remain realists. And the contemporary attack on realism by authors such as Hillary Putnam, Richard Rorty, or Bas Van Fraassen (e.g., at the recent World Congress of Philosophy, Montreal, 1983) would make them uncomfortable. My own views allow me to sympathize with the attack, while maintaining the concerns about relativism voiced by the realists. In his Presidential Address to the Western Division of the American Philosophical Association in April 1982, Alvin Plantinga stated in his opening paragraphs that the realism versus anti-realism dispute is still "center stage" today and that he, too, hoped to "mediate" in the lasting impasse.

13. From the reality of predication Wolterstorff moves to the additional reality of predicable entities existing over and above the semantic phenomena. (See UN, 105-27.) Armstrong rejects the idea that predication necessarily entails the existence of predicables or universals. (See USR1, 11-24.)

14. Actually, this is only relatively true. No particular person or group of persons need relate to particular trees or groups of them. However, deforestation, especially in the Amazon areas, profoundly affects world climates and oxygen supplies. In a more radical sense, humanity is essentially related to trees.

15. In the tradition and even today it is not at all uncommon to see universals treated as parts or dimensions or aspects of particulars. Armstrong does

this, and in so doing he sees himself as a Scotist. Scotus in turn can be viewed as holding a variant of one of Aristotle's positions on the problem (USR2, 3). One also encounters the treatment of universals as the many qualities of the one particular. (See, e.g., Quinton.)

16. A general law is, strictly speaking, a contradiction. A genuine law holds universally and not in general. What we call a general law is not really a law but a generalization in the literal sense, i.e., we expect exceptions. Though *general* as a characteristic of a *genus* or of *genera* does point to strict universality, in our vocabulary it has come to mean "in most cases" rather than in all. And the existence of statistical sciences which probe the characteristics of classes of entities more than their nature makes it useful to distinguish between general and universal.

17. Throughout the text I use terms such as *instantiate, instance, example,* and *exemplification* and others to indicate the relation of an individual entity to the kind to which it belongs. Strictly speaking, my view as it will be developed is not one of instantiation or exemplification. A person is not an instance or example of "being a person" in my view, at least not strictly speaking. A genuine instance of "being a person" would strictly speaking also be "being a person" and so would an example. My own view will be that an individual person is of the kind "being a person" by virtue of the fact that an individual person exists subject to conditions of a certain kind. So by *kind* in this technical sense I mean a specific set of conditions. Strictly speaking, whatever is of that kind does not so much exemplify or instantiate those conditions, but occurs in subjection to them. But for the sake of terminological continuity I will refer to "subjection to conditions" in this specific context by speaking of *instantiation* or *exemplification*. But, as Roy Clouser has pointed out to me, I do not really mean by this what is usually meant by it. In summary: I mean by *exemplifies* or *instantiates* just that something is subject to conditions of some kind.

18. Armstrong seems to think that universals may relate to one another in the same way as universals relate to particulars. He then suggests that the "higher order" sort of universal relates to a "lower order" universal in such a way that the latter may have to be viewed as a particular of a different order as the "first order" particulars (USR2, 133).

19. This, too, is a line of thought closely pursued by Armstrong, who refers to his view as Scotism and likes to look at universality and individuality as dimensions of particular entities. See, e.g., USR1, 108-13.

20. What Popper distinguishes here is related to what in certain professional discussions on universals is treated as a difference between pure and impure predicates, where impure predicates essentially depend on their relation to specified individuals. See Armstrong, USR2, 14-17. In the case of generality connected with statistical trends, we have to do with the behavior of some members of a class and not others. This specific exclusion of some other members makes the universal impure. The disposition in question can be stated in general, as a trend, rather than as a law.

21. The familiar problem of induction seen in this light is or is not significant depending on whether one looks upon universals in terms of all individuals or in terms of themselves. If universality is irreducible to individuality, observation of a universal state of affairs in particulars might be enough if it is observed in a few. But if universality were indeed just a matter of the class of all individuals, then the observation of the behavior of a few would not warrant a conclusion about all. See Toulmin, PS, 110.

22. An instructive example of what Laszlo is talking about is found in the following observation of Eibl-Eibesfeldt: "For all their multiplicity, all forms of greeting behavior really amount to one fundamentally quite uniform type of behavior in which the same behavioral elements recur again and again across the spectrum of culture" (196).

23. See also SP, 292-95 for remarks of a more speculative nature on universals and systems.

24. I will clarify the two meanings at length in 2.1 of the next chapter.

25. Armstrong views laws as nomic correlations of universals (USR2, 129-30 and 149-53).

26. Wolterstorff, in fact, comes to the conclusion that what are traditionally called universals are actually one sort of kinds (UN, 260). Is there a connection here with the nomic correlations of Armstrong? (See note 24 above.)

27. A merely conceptual view of laws would conflict, for example, with the following statement by Hempel: "A law, we noted, can support subjunctive and counterfactual conditional statements about potential instances, i.e., about particular cases that might occur, or that might have occurred but did not" (PNS, 57; cf. also ASE, 377).

28. See ASE, 264-70 and 377-79.

29. In this respect, Toulmin appears to agree with both Polanyi and Laszlo. With Polanyi he agrees that one can correlate "the presence of significant order with the operation of an ordering principle . . ." (PK, 35). Polanyi distinguishes empirical circumstances from an ordering principle (PK, 383-84). And with Laszlo he agrees that the occasion for speaking of laws of nature is natural regularity. As Laszlo puts it: "Nature supplies the limits of the interpretable perceptual patterns, and science supplies their interpretation" (SP, 210).

30. See also SP, 8, 11-12, 18, 20, 30, 32, 47, 55, 139, 176, 210, and 294.

31. In the professional literature on universals the concern with particularity is mostly directed at the problem of how universals become individualized. The second part of Michael Loux's *Substance and Attribute* is an investigation in this line. The problem of particulars is the problem of how universals are individuated into "fully individuated . . . substances" (x). Quinton's discussion of substance opens with a similar concern (12-32).

32. The relation between discussions of classes and traditional discussions of universals is outlined briefly by Kneale (624-28), who shows that the

problem at issue in the universality debate also crops up in discussions of classes, even though it had been assumed that approaching universals by way of classes would make it possible to avoid old problems.

33. See Armstrong USR2, 19ff. and 53ff. for discussions of predicates that do not correspond to or imply real universals. Cf. also USR1, 34.

34. Langer opens her treatment of formal logic with a chapter on form, her way of dealing with universality. She connects such universality with a long list of items, including none of the traditional ones and mentioning such phenomena as social form, personality type, norms, fashions, plans, and standards (24). She also points out that it is these forms that determine classes (116ff.).

Notes to Chapter II

1. See the opening of the first chapter and the first note of that chapter.

2. See SP, 8. Laszlo ultimately finds the question of whether or not the world is ordered unanswerable (SP, 18). But he proceeds on the assumption that it is minimally meaningful to relate to the world as though it is in fact ordered. Cf. SP, 8, 11-12, 18, 20, 30, 32, 47, 55, 129, 176, 210, 294.

3. See Loux, SA, 163ff., Wolterstorff, UN, 221ff., Armstrong, USR1, 116ff., and USR2, 61ff.

4. Loux and Wolterstorff approach universals through the medium of attribution and predication respectively. See SA, 3ff. and UN, 65. Armstrong and Quinton deal with universals primarily in terms of properties or qualities and of relations. See Quinton, 3 and Armstrong, USR1, xiii.

5. Armstrong has referred to his theory of universals as scientific realism. He thereby wants to indicate that science, rather than a priori reasoning, a consideration of the meaning of words, or the reality of predicates will ultimately have to tell us what universals there are. See USR1, xiii.

6. There are fundamental considerations of ultimate positions involved in this move. It can be argued that in our culture two fundamental positions on the nature of humanity have been significantly influential in ultimately shaping the universals debate to make it a controversy between realism and nominalism. One of these positions is grounded in the belief that ultimate human autonomy does not allow for any natural necessity, world order, or pattern of invariant norms determining human culture beyond human control and apart from a person's own decisions. According to this position, no traditions, myths or authorities outside ourselves must be allowed to shape our destiny. A strong commitment to this position shifts the burden of meta-questions in the universals debate toward nominalism. This position also occurs in a variant in which human autonomy is viewed in terms of a commitment to rationality. Whatever is necessary from a logical point of view will be considered necessary for God and creature alike. This variant belief in human autonomy is a belief in rational autonomy, and those who accept it tend toward realism. Herman Dooyeweerd has elaborately analyzed these

trends in terms of what he calls the "personality ideal" (no strictures on human autonomy) and the "science ideal" (human autonomy in terms of scientific control). He understands both of these ideals as variant views of how human freedom, as understood in Western culture, is in dialectical tension with natural necessity. Although this analysis is found in many of his writings, the most elaborate account is in NC, vol. 1, part 2, 167-495. A briefer account is found in TWT, 35-51. For my views on knowing God see the last chapter (7.4) and also DC. Because I am not committed to either of these traditions, I do not accept their force in the inquiry undertaken in this chapter. An extensive account of the commitment underlying my own position in this book can be found in the Appendix.

7. I have in mind here the same problem often referred to by Armstrong in his many objections to what he calls a priori realism, in which the reality of universals is established purely formally. See USR1, xv.

8. Obviously, this rule is coarse and primarily useful on the surface of the earth.

9. It is important here to differentiate between various kinds of necessity. Logical necessity must be distinguished from natural or metaphysical necessity (Kripke, NN) or broadly logical necessity (Plantinga, NN). Physical necessity must be distinguished from moral necessity. It is sometimes suggested that logical necessity is a deeper or more basic kind of necessity. (Kripke, NN, 122ff.) In my view, logical necessity pertains to the necessity with which certain analytic entities (propositions, terms, conclusions) are connected according to rules of inference. In all other instances, the question of whether there is logical necessity is, in fact, irrelevant. It is true that logical and physical necessity differ. But that makes physical necessity only non (not: less) logical, not nonnecessary.

10. For the moment, I am saying this without regard to whether these conditions can change, be controlled, originate in human decisions, etc. Later, I will take such questions into account.

11. Sometimes the fact that such-and-such is the case, especially where such facts seem complex, is referred to as a state of affairs. Dooyeweerd often refers to what he calls structural states of affairs which, once laid bare, no scholar can any longer ignore. (See, e.g., NC, vol. 1, 56.) He seems to mean by states of affairs complex interrelations of properties and relations in their universality. Armstrong speaks of states of affairs as particulars having properties and standing in relations (USR1, 113ff.). But so far in my analysis it is difficult to determine whether states of affairs are conditions-1 or conditions-2. Considering the confusion this could lead to I will not use *states of affairs* as a technical term, if at all.

12. See Armstrong, USR2, 61-63.

13. I am simplistically referring here to the complex of conditions to be met in fertilization and conception, gestation, etc. Laws of genetics, species determination, and other complexities all have to do with the continuity and preservation of kinds.

14. What I have in mind here is that the nomic conditions that determine the things of our world are not found among the constituents either of those things or of our world. Nomic conditions are neither functors nor any of their actual functions or concrete relations. Yet they are here postulated as real. Their reality is found, e.g., in the undeniable fact that they determine what things are like. Their reality has some consequence.

15. I find it necessary to distinguish between conditioning, ordering, or determining on the one hand, and causing on the other. In my view the condition-1 that if I am human I am mortal does not *cause* me to die, even though we may *say* that people die be*cause* they are mortal. The condition-1 *determines* that I *must* die. A coronary failure *causes* me to die. My death must come after my birth, but it is not caused by my birth. A purely conditional analysis of causation (as, e.g., that of J.L. Mackie) tends not to make this distinction. Armstrong also connects causality with conditional necessity, i.e., with the universality of properties, without making this distinction. See USR1, xv.

16. Cows can become mothers in the most wonderfully complex ways these days. The intent of the example is not to provide accurate information on the state of the art.

17. One factor in Hume's account of causality was his failure to demonstrate logical necessity in a relationship not itself logical. His attempt to treat physical necessity on the model of logical necessity resulted in denying physical necessity. But physical necessity is never logically necessary. Why should it be? Necessity is just that: necessity. Some of it is logical, some of it is not. Nonlogical necessity is still necessity. See note 9 above.

18. Logical necessity is often established by following the method of determining whether lack of necessity would lead to contradiction. But what is contradiction? To assert that so-and-so is a bachelor and married is to assert an uncontroversial example of a contradiction. How about that such-and-such a calf was born but never conceived? If the concept of having been born in the case of a calf would imply having been conceived, then it would be contradictory to assert that a calf, though never conceived, was born. But this is not likely to be an uncontroversial example of contradiction. Yet on the basis of such distinctions one may hear it asserted that bachelors are necessarily unmarried, in the sense that the necessity is logical; whereas if calves are born, the necessity of their having been conceived is not said to be logical, though it may be admitted to be necessary in a weaker sense.

19. I reject out of hand the idea that particulars resemble universals in any respect at all. If there is red and there is also redness, even then I do not see how red could resemble redness, since no one any longer considers the possibility that redness is at all red.

20. If it is correct to reject any arguments for the relation between particulars and universals that go the route of resemblance (see note 19 above), then

not only do particulars not resemble universals, but also the universals are not required to be like the particulars in any respect.

21. Subjective existence, it will be recalled, is the empirical world, seen from the vantage point of its being subject to conditions.

22. Language should not trip us up here. Sometimes we allow definitions and conventions to send us in directions that only these definitions and conventions require. E.g., if one defines substance as what cannot be predicated, then the actual case of a property (Napoleon's brashness) will turn out to be a substance. (See Wolterstorff, UN, 221.) If one defines property as what something can have or possess, pianos will turn out to be properties, for I can have a piano. Perplexities such as these direct people to look upon certain classes of universals as particulars, or to assign properties to properties. (See Armstrong, USR1, 116ff. and USR2, 133ff.) What I am after here is the clean break of irreducible realities. Once it is determined that existence is a category of things that are conditioned, conditions will not fall under the category. They do the condition*ing* and they are then not condition*ed*. One would, in that case, have two completely irreducible universes of discourse. What I cannot develop here is my view that actual discourse, i.e., semantic behavior, belongs to the world of conditioned existence. That presents special difficulties for the semantics of conditions-1. We *talk* about them. But in some fashion they do not yield to the ordinary conventions of speech. That may be one reason why predication and attribution are not good entrances to universals.

23. Carl G. Hempel almost always refers to laws as statements or sentences. See PNS, 19ff. He does say, however, that such statements may express a law.

24. The connection between nomic reality and language is powerful. To a creature not capable of speech we can communicate a relation to conditions only by elaborate training and conditioning. To a human being we can just *say* what is the case. Words, in fact, do nothing else but refer to the elusive nomic reality we have been dealing with. It is, therefore, not surprising to see words and nomic reality identified in the nominalist tradition. See also all the meanings of *logos*.

25. My uses of *logical* or *analytical* can be confusing. First of all, I use them as synonyms, or nearly so. In so far as they are synonyms they mean the same as my use of *rational* or *conceptual*. The way I use all four of these is to refer to (1) our activity of arguing, concluding, distinction making, abstracting, reasoning, forming concepts, making theories, conducting an inquiry as to what is the case, etc.; and to (2) the rules and procedures proper to that activity and thus the rules of inference, the rules of logic; and to (3) the capacity of things in this world to yield valid arguments, conclusions, and concepts. Let me give an example. A sentence is a semantic entity. A proposition is a logical entity. The reality of a sentence is semantic. The reality of a proposition is logical or analytic.

26. Or the stated theory, the named conceptual relation, or perhaps the conceived state of affairs.

27. Concepts and names can appear simple by the use of a single noun. But this need not mean that what is named or conceptually grasped is simple. *Red* may appear to name a monadic universal. But it may also name a very complex interrelation of universals. Perhaps there are no simple properties. (See Armstrong, USR2, 137ff.) However, in any case a proposition always grasps a complexity, always one thing in relation to another. In a concept we at least try to grasp a complexity in terms of a unity. The concept gold is an example. But in a proposition we always deal with two items in relation.

28. We may, of course, have a concept of what a concept is. That would be an example of conceptually grasping what is itself conceptual. But usually our concepts grasp what it is to be a frog, gold, or human. And being a frog, gold, or human is not itself conceptual.

29. For what I mean by analytic entity I refer to note 25 above.

30. It is important to note that the actual and concrete empirical entities are inconceivable. I cannot conceive actual entities. I do not have a concept of this or that thing, but of what it is to be that thing. Concepts do not refer to empirical entities, but to *what* it is *that these are*. We do not conceive of horses, but of being a horse. To say that being a horse is just that, a concept, is to fail to explain what we conceive. Especially a nominalist should balk at conceiving of material objects in their individuality. Having a horse "in mind" would just not do. Having in mind what a horse is, makes a lot of sense. But what do I have "in mind" when I have a concept?

31. See note 22 above. Once a terminology, definitions, and irreducibility have been decided, consistency demands that no subjective existent can ever be a nomic condition-1. Then it will also have been decided that no conditions themselves have conditions, because to be conditioned *is* to be a subjective existent. Nothing can be both a particular and a universal. On this I disagree with Armstrong (USR1, 79 and USR2, 133).

32. Whatever we call the nomic reality we are after, the terms will most likely always derive from what we empirically know of actual and concrete space-time existence. So when we refer to our nomic conditions as laws or rules we are probably using an analogy. The point is that whatever we essentially have in mind when we speak of laws and determination, that reality gives us a concept which allows us to deal with the problems of universals.

33. If it is kept in mind that conditions-1 are here viewed as rules, i.e., *regula*, then it will follow that conditions-2 manifest *regula*rity. Regularity or structure is the result of something happening "as a rule" (we say!); according to a rule, plan, or design. Rule or plan do not essentially differ; both have a nomic character. Rules usually refer us to the nomic conditions for behavior, while design may rule the shape of an entity.

34. The holding or obtaining of conditions determines things, but not deterministically. Thus, in the case of deviance there is not some other condition which holds. The deviant is deviant precisely because the original condition both holds and is (in existence) not met.

35. What needs to be shown, of course, is that nomic conditions also account for what we call properties, predication, kinds, and many other items that play a role in the universals debate. I will come to this later.

36. I remind the reader of the fact that I am aware that what I am postulating here may only be referred to analogously. Thus, if I refer to what I am postulating as law, I must be aware of the fact that laws usually originate in legislative chambers and that the use of *law* may direct me to questions that are not germane, though on the other hand they may be. See note 32 above.

37. Realism, certainly hardcore Platonic realism, has halted at this point and has not gone beyond universals to ask where they originate. They are eternal and immutable. (See, e.g., Loux, SA, 89-99.) For that view, conditions-1 are *sui generis*. Even where the fusion between realism and theism has produced the belief that many universals are ideas in the divine mind or are created by the Creator, there still remains the belief that the Creator is limited by certain rules, mainly those of a logical character. The laws of logic, at least, are regarded as constituting an order without origin. In the present context I will not attempt to penetrate these questions further. I have discussed the matter extensively with Wolterstorff. (See Hart, DC and Wolterstorff, CC.) An extensive treatment can also be found in Plantinga (GN). In this volume the problem will not surface again till the end of the last chapter (see 7.4) and in the Appendix (especially 8.1.1–8.1.4). Once again, I state my postulate in analogical language and the problem itself will have to determine whether the spin-off from such usage is relevant or not. But so long as the postulate serves the purpose it is intended to serve, it can serve as a genuine hypothesis.

38. I stress again that we are dealing here with a postulate and a hypothesis. The hypothesis is that the postulated reality will allow us to form a concept which will serve as sufficient explanation for the problems we are addressing.

39. The actual etymological meaning of "in principle" can be understood along the lines of "originally" or "in origin." So understood, principles are archetypes, i.e., originating kinds, kinds of *archai*.

40. See note 38 above.

41. If in denying the reality of "universals," nominalism is denying what I have been calling nomic conditions-1, then there are also no "objective" criteria for culture, no transsubjective norms. And that leads to either the slavish following of the empirical realities of the established situation, or (if the status quo is oppressive) to arbitrary reaction.

42. It is not clear to me whether or not all possible world philosophy implies some form of hardcore Platonism. In any case, Platonic problems remain when one adopts a possible world ontology to deal with conditions-1. For the danger now looms large that the "possible world" will be dealt with as some sort of "existing" world. Of course, a possible picnic is no picnic. A condition-1 which makes something possible, say x, does not thereby become an existing possible x. And the dangers become especially great when it is noted that possible world ontologies are built up in completely a priori ways. Cf. Armstrong, USR1, 36 and USR2, 5.

43. See Loux, SA, 89-99. Armstrong uses as a strong principle that no universal is a universal if its reality can be determined only in a priori fashion. See Armstrong, USR2, 11.

44. The ultimacy of inference is assumed in all forms of rationalism. This assumption commits philosophers to accept whatever formal logic appears to necessitate. It is one of the assumptions that play an important role in taking a position in the universals debate. See also note 6 above. I will deal with this problem more extensively at the end of the last chapter and in the Appendix.

45. Whether or not I have "rejected realism" is partly a matter of terminology. What I reject is the existence of any and all entities called universals which exist outside of and apart from a world of particulars. But since I accept the reality of what concepts grasp, and since I postulate a reality as a result of which this world is conditioned and determined, I may still be called a realist. If accepting the reality of laws of nature and other determining conditions-1, while at the same time suggesting that such reality is not found among the entities constituting our empirical world, makes me a realist, then I have not rejected realism.

46. I will never mean just sense experience when I use *experience*, although I will always include the role of the senses whenever I use *experience*.

47. I see no reason why the meaning of *experience* should be arbitrarily curtailed to sense perception. In "Wanted: experienced hostess" there are a variety of factors involved beyond sense perception. And I take it that *experience* is used genuinely here. At least, I use it to include this meaning. Those who find this usage vague when all ordinary people know what it means have placed upon themselves the burden of explaining why it is vague.

48. It may especially be objected by some that, if "having a concept" is to count as experience, then my principle that for anything to be accepted as real it must be possible to experience it, will have come to nought. I think this objection is arbitrary. In fact, it may well turn out that the "experience" such objectors have in mind turns out to be a logical construction unknown to normal human experience.

49. To distinguish various universals, such as red, being red, and redness is, in my view, absolutizing language and predication. See Armstrong, USR2, 9.

50. Conditions are, of course, immaterial. But "immaterial" is a negative predicate and it is immaterial in the sense of irrelevant. To say of something that it is immaterial and to say it with force is to assume that it falls into a categorial neighborhood which makes the disclaimer meaningful. But "material" is a property of entities in our space-time world. In that same world one could meaningfully say that the senti mental value I attach to some gift is not material. But if conditions-1 have a reality that differs from anything in our space-time world, then to say that conditions-1 are immaterial is as appropriate as to say that pains have no weight, but in an even more dramatic sense.

51. If one grants ultimacy to inferential procedures one's "experience" of certain arguments and conclusions as necessary seems unavoidable, even though to others such conclusions may seem entirely speculative. It is undoubtedly the felt quality of such an "undeniable experience" which helps a priorists to hold on to what others reject out of hand. There is, however, a way out of this. Science insists on validating a "purely" conceptual experience. It does not accept anything a priori. Positivism's verification principle may have gone the way of all flesh and pragmatism's insistence that the real must make a practical difference may not have been universally accepted, nevertheless these historical fortunes of certain emphases do not invalidate the conviction underneath both verificationism and pragmatism that a priori rationalism and consequently the acceptance of all entities which only logic compels us to accept are both rejectionable. Whether or not a theoretical construct has reality can certainly be discovered in our experience of the temporal universe, provided experience is not arbitrarily limited. (See J.J. Gibson.)

52. The analytic tradition's universal insistence on the general justification of belief as such is just an unwarranted extrapolation of the necessity that some beliefs be justified. Belief, just like that, needs justification as much or as little as the legs on which I walk. For "the" justification of belief it is not likely that a procedure will ever be found, while for the justification of some given belief the justification will depend entirely on the circumstances leading to our doubting the belief.

53. Pragmatism made that *the* characteristic feature of genuine belief, viz., our preparedness to act on it. In so doing it went back to Alexander Bain's definition of belief as that which we accept as basis for action.

54. I am referring here to the classic Hempelian way of explaining explanation.

55. In our culture a pervasive tradition holds that for anything to be accepted it must be justified, and to be justified it must be rationally justified. Our culture is religiously devoted to the rational. Surely it is this devotion to which Richard Rorty refers when he writes: "Culture is the assemblage of claims to knowledge, and philosophy adjudicates such claims" (PM, 3).

56. Michael Polanyi is not the only one who constructs the edifice of human knowledge on a basis of commitment. More and more the role of commit-

ment is widely admitted as crucial in all knowing, even rational knowing constructed along fairly a prioristic and formal lines. Cf. Plantinga, BIG, 26-27 and Wolterstorff, RwR, 66.

57. That order is there as we find it might be the position of Armstrong. Laszlo seems to hold that order evolves with the world. Loux posits an eternal order. For the bearing of our positions on this issue, see Armstrong, USR1, 127 and 129.

58. I am not saying that the move is acceptable here, only that it is reasonable. Thus, if as "rational" a philosopher as Michael Loux can assert that kinds are not to be viewed as being among the constituent elements of the particulars that are of that kind, I take it that a generalization of this sort of move is at least reasonable (SA, 164).

59. But the move is, of course, much more than just reasonable. There is also an underlying position from which the move is made. The relation of my move to this position lies outside of the limits of acceptable philosophical argument. For this position see the Appendix.

60. See Armstrong, USR1, 80 for the strict correlativity of the universal particular relation.

61. It will be recalled that "holding universally" is the very reality of all nomic conditionality.

62. See Kripke, NN, 138.

63. My general sympathy for the position of D.M. Armstrong breaks down at this point. In his desire to develop an empirical and scientific theory of universals, he declares certain existential realities to be universals and thus denies the individuality of a particular's properties (USR1, 86). There are, for him, no particular "cases" of a property. (See Wolterstorff, UN, 133.) By including universals among the entities of the empirical world he is also led to speak of the same entity as sometimes universal, sometimes particular (USR1, 79 and USR2, 133ff.). "A universal which falls under a universal is *ipso facto* a particular as well as a universal." The whole tradition of realism is, I believe, founded on the correct and inveterate intuition that standards and what they are standards for are irreducible to one another. Standards are not among the elements, constituents, or parts of whatever must meet standards. This intuition is lost in Armstrong.

64. Both nominalism and realism, as I have repeatedly stated, have a valid point to make. Nominalists are right in stressing that in our world there are only particulars, subjective existents. Realists are also right in claiming that our world is not *sui generis*, that it cannot account for itself. But the way of perceiving the problem of their disagreement has made solutions elusive. I think this is because the universals, both by those who affirm them and those who reject them, are on some continuum with the particulars. Particulars are individuated universals, so to speak; and universals are immaterial perfections of particulars. Both exist. No radical irreducibility along with strict correlativity is envisioned in the traditional

debate. In modern discusssions, of which Wolterstorff, Armstrong, and Quinton are good examples, authors are attempting to get out of the traditional problems. They feel sympathetic to both sides on some points. But as yet there is no solution.

65. It might be said that in this case one could not hold that conditions are what make things necessary. For if it is possible that some existent of which it is required that it have such-and-such characteristics in fact shows up without these characteristics, then surely it is not necessary that it have those characteristics and that they be required. But this need not be so. In Kripke's discussion of tigers as four-legged, he offers the possibility of meeting three-legged tigers, in which case tigers are not necessarily four-legged (NN, 119-22). But I think Kripke has in mind the possibility of three-legged tigers who would appear to be normal as three-legged tigers. And then, indeed, tigers need not be four-legged. But a single three-legged tiger existing due to a congenital deformity is a different story. Such a tiger would not cancel the necessity that tigers be four-legged in order to be normal tigers.

66. It is necessary that each individual member of the species Kalahari lion have four legs. It is also and equally necessary that each have a head. Yet we may find a deformed three-legged Kalahari lion roaming around, though hardly a headless one. What about that? In my view, all it means is that consequences of not meeting standards work themselves out in time at different rates. The survival rate of headless lions is nil. The survival rate of three-legged lions is low. But to show how *necessary* it is for a lion to have four legs is to ponder the saying: "There is no need for lions to have four legs, it's just convenient." The right response to the question "Why did this three-legged lion only live a few months?" is: It is necessary for lions to have four legs. See also the section on freedom and determinism in chapter 7 (7.3.2).

67. For a description of Dewey's use of "individual," see Hart (CC, 47). For Stafleu's views on individuality in physical reality, see IP.

68. When later on I develop my views further, I will argue that such traits as freedom, necessity, and individuality do seem to have a sliding scale sort of reality. The individuality of Johnny Carson seems more individual than that of a molecule. The freedom of Picasso seems greater than the freedom of a spider. The necessity whereby lions must have heads seems greater than that whereby they must have legs. (See chapter 7, sections 7.3.2 and 7.3.3.) It seems to me that when Armstrong or Quinton discuss individuality solely in terms of things like position, they reduce the complexity of individuality to the individuality of purely physical particulars like atoms. Clearly Armstrong and Quinton differ in more than their present address. (See USR1, 111 and 113; USR2, 11, 64; and Quinton, 20, 26, and 28ff.) Individuality as mere numerical diversity (Loux, SA, 165) is also not rich enough, even though all individuals will be numerically diverse.

69. Though traffic laws have served as a paradigm for conditions, I must now

enter a disclaimer. Such rules definitely do seem to be both local and temporal. Where we do meet with conditionality which seems local and temporal I will hold that we are dealing with structures and states of affairs rather than nomic conditions. For my views on time in relation to conditions, see 6.3.

70. See Armstrong: "There is no separation of particulars and universals" (USR1, 113).

71. This has bearing on Armstrong's claim that, scientifically speaking, nature may be a causally self-enclosed system; an admittedly controversial claim (USR1, 129 and 132). Science is not our only authority for what there is. And nature as a self-enclosed system goes against the principle that nothing should be *causa sui*, subscribed to by Armstrong (USR2, 93). According to that principle, our world needs an explanation. It cannot be its own cause. In our world there are no more than particulars. But why should our world be all there is? See Appendix, 8.2.1.

72. See Kripke, NN, 138: "In general, science attempts, by investigating basic structural traits, to find the nature . . . of the kind."

73. The realism here is obvious to Lakatos, who simply refers to "Plato's and Popper's" adoption of a third world (180).

74. It will be obvious that I do not subscribe to the is-ought distinction, at least not in a way that makes the condition here be an unnecessary one. See 7.3.3.

75. Laszlo discusses this problem in various places. See, e.g., SP, 199-200.

76. See note 6 above. Regularity, it will be recalled, is evidence of order.

77. A point made repeatedly by Hempel in his debate about laws of history. See, e.g., ASE, 233; also Carroll Goon.

78. See note 66 above.

Notes to Chapter III

1. It will be recalled that by *subjective* I mean whatever is subjected to conditions. Entities that so exist are subjects and they exist subjectively.

2. I have just used the terms *basic, fundamental,* and *ground.* They are now suspect in many quarters, because of the demise of foundationalism. I rejoice in that demise. But I do not take it to imply that terms which foundationalism had used in an unacceptable sense have now become unusable in every sense. It will still be fine for children to learn the basics of Latin. It will also be acceptable for politicians to defend our fundamental rights. And it will remain helpful for scholars to have grounds for conclusions. So I will continue using these terms and I promise never to use them (knowingly) in a foundationalist sense.

3. For a general treatment of what the construction of categorial frameworks involves, see Stephan Körner's *Categorial Frameworks.*

4. It will have become clear from the preceding chapters that my view of what "the problem of universals" (for me the relation between the universality of order and the individuality of particulars) is all about differs from other views. Some view that problem as the problem of substances and their attributes (e.g., Quinton). The attributes are the universals, the substances are the particulars. I reject this view. Each particular's attributes, in my view, are particular attributes. The problem of an entity and its attributes is for me a problem of phenomena in our empirical world *as* they (both substances and attributes) are subject to conditions that hold for them. Both Loux and Quinton refer to confusion on this score. (See SA, 143 and Quinton, 3-6.) I believe that if one sees the world of particulars, as well as their attributes, and their relations *as* particulars (though determined by a universal order), one can avoid confusions. Then we do not need to speak, as some do, about entities that are sometimes particulars and at other times universals (e.g., Armstrong, USR2, 133), nor do we need fear that the world is just a bundle of universals with whose particularization we have great difficulty (a problem throughout for Loux, Armstrong, and Quinton, but not for Wolterstorff). I also will not need universals such as substance universals or particularizing universals to individuate particulars, as do both Loux and Armstrong. So when I

talk about things and their properties I do not refer to particulars and universals. Things are individual things and properties are individual properties. And both are subjected to an order of conditions that holds universally for them.

5. I have already pointed out that in my view this distinction is not the same as that between universal and individual. Some readers may think that in this chapter I confuse the functor-function problem with the problem of the whole and its parts. But I also consider that a different problem from what I discuss in this chapter. Whole-part will be discussed later. (See 5.2.)

6. In other words, I will develop my view that what things are and do, their properties, qualities, states, and actions, can be viewed as a thing's functions. And the actual, existential, subjective, individual functions of a thing, i.e., its concrete functioning, occurs in subjection to an order of conditions, conditions for functions.

7. Here we face a major problem of reductionism. If things are reduced to their functions and functions to their elements then more and more we will be asked to adopt the view that the ultimate explanation of things will not occur until we can account for them in terms of atomic interaction. If, on the other hand, orders of conditions are real and if they require functions within boundaries that come in irreducible configurations, then an understanding of these boundary conditions will be essential for an understanding of existence. If "calling my lawyer" refers to a genuine structure (which it may not), then not even the elements of actions going into it (mentioned above) will explain fully what that structure is. This gives significance to an investigation of the authenticity of certain action categories. If Peirce, as cited by Armstrong (USR2, 151), is right in suggesting that lawful patterns of behavior have their foundation in orders of "universals," then it will obviously be important to investigate what such orders might be. For then it will be clear that a cluster of nomically connected conditions that explains the *physical* relations among atoms will not explain other relations that exist because other clusters obtain as well. These other clusters will then have to be found.

8. This is how Wolterstorff puts it (UN, xii). I agree, but I need to add that in studying that structure (which I view as the empirical evidence of the reality of an order that obtains) we are trying to approximate an (postulated) order. However, structure is subjective evidence of order and is therefore liable to both corruption and change. Therefore, our theories are bound to be incomplete at best. If we further mix in the consideration of our own subjective input into our theories, the hope of a lastingly accurate ontology must elude us all.

9. Readers who prefer a clinically clear use of terms to what may seem like my sloppy use are aware that I have referred to the same reality by using functor, actor, agent, thing, entity, etc. This is intentional and, rather than being sloppy, the intention is to be as clear as possible. Before I fix

the use of a term as technical jargon, I prefer to use different words of our language to get before the reader's mind as broad a feel for the technical application as possible. If what all these looser usages convey is indeed included in the technical use of one term, that term can only become clear by our getting used to that broad reference.

10. There are even difficulties in finding the right category for what we encounter. A simple example: Is a rock an agent? It surely is not an action or a relation. If all that exists is either agent, action, or relation, then agent is all that remains. My solution is to refer to the molecules or atoms that make up stuffs as agents and to refer to quantities of them as structured clusters. These agents will differ from clusters which are so structured that they themselves are agents, such as planets, for example.

11. The initial difficulty with this introductory way of dealing with levels of action is that the nonspecificity of "loving my neighbor" and its reality only in other actions stimulate us to believe that "loving my neighbor" is no action at all, but rather a disposition or state. But what I am holding on to at least provisionally, is the fact that "loving my neighbor" can meaningfully be said to be something I must *do*.

12. I am dealing here with what others might refer to as complex substance universals and conjoint properties.

13. Can similar remarks be made about nonhuman actors? In one respect, most people would say not. Humans respond to nomic conditions as knowing and willing creatures. They act intentionally, and they can be held accountable. Persons can decide—even against better knowledge—to disregard what ought to be done in the situation. This is not a possibility in the subhuman world. Apart from that, however, the subhuman world also displays the correlation between actions and actors, and there too the ultimate integrator of all action patterns shapes the identity and continuity of the actor. It is precisely this issue which has exercised philosophers when they have examined the relation between substances and their properties. What makes the particular entity the entity it is? Technical quests have been: What particularizes or what individuates? What bears the attributes? For this see especially the second part of Loux (SA) and the first and third chapter in Quinton. Zigterman (DTS) compares Aristotle and Dooyeweerd on this issue. Further, all agents function so that lesser action units take on their meaning in the context of larger action patterns. But the difference between *level one* and *level two* actions does not occur outside the human world. Only in the human world do we find the structure of intentional acting, which is bound up with a person's ultimate commitment. I come back to this very briefly at the end of this chapter and deal with it in more detail in the last chapter (7.2.1).

14. Roughly speaking, what I have said here can be treated as a truism. Is it also philosophically significant? Truisms of this kind exist because in terms of them we have successfully oriented ourselves in the world for centuries. But does this way of speaking also refer to a genuine ontological category?

This is a controversial issue. Property bundle theorists and bare particular theorists, i.e., those who only acknowledge the reality of functions and function clusters and those who allow minimal bearers of properties, are at odds on just this issue. And there are other positions besides. I shall simply assume here that only actors act and that the agents are not their actions. It is an intuitive insight which, if not shared, will not be accepted on other levels either.

15. From the point of view of certain traditions someone may ask what room exists in my scheme for the reality of sets, "mental" images, concepts, and the like. If my ontology only has room for material functors of the gross kinds such as people, animals, plants, and minerals, am I then not limiting the world too severely? Do I deny sets or concepts any reality? I do not. It is true, they are not *functors*. But why can a concept not be a *function* of human beings? And why can a set not be a numerical *relation* among things?

16. There is a general science of living things, biology; of animals, zoology; of material things, physics. But there is no general science of things. "Thing" is too broad and indefinite to have its nature inspected. At the same time, "thing" is definite enough to distinguish it from its functions. See Quinton, 41-46. In that sense, when I speak of a thing, I do not refer to any real thing whatsoever. What I mean here is an agent capable of acting and of having its actions ascribed to it. Consequently, even though special disciplines have no way of dealing with anything as general as the thing, philosophers have dealt with it throughout their history. Thing or functor is, in this sense, the highest sort of kind category there is, together with quality or function, and relation. See Loux, SA, 173-75.

17. If one is a materialist and believes that it is possible to reduce all that exists to a physical point of view, then one realizes that such a point of view is not just the received view of common sense. Rather, it is an approach in need of argument and defense. Our intuitions about reality go very deep. For example, no matter how well feelings can be explained with the help of physical models, it occurs to no one, not even materialists, that a plant might express pain or reveal hurt upon the abrupt removal of a part. We resist a view of sentient creatures as just physical or organic. For most people "being physical" or "material thing," "being alive" or "living thing," "being aware" or "sentient thing," and "being human" or "spiritual thing" represent categories, concepts, and realities too diverse to be grasped under one common denominator. Furthermore, once we say farewell to materialism we are still very divided as to whether we are then left with two realms (and which two), or three, or four. (See Quinton, 249.)

18. The human kind is included in the ordering of functors into realms, even though humanity occupies an exceptional place among these functors. (See chapter 7.) On the one hand, the human kind functions as an irreducibly different functor next to the other kinds of functors. Plants are

not complex physical systems. Animals are not mobile and sentient plants. Human beings are not thinking animals. Each is its own kind and must be understood as its own kind—though in relation to the other kinds. However, the difference between humanity and the other functors is so great that philosophers of all ages have questioned whether it is justifiable to place that difference on a continuum with the other differences.

19. The four-realm classification approach is a classification of functors, not of levels of functioning. There are also irreducible fields of functioning, such as physical functioning, the life functions, and the sensitive functions. But these levels of functioning, discussed in the next section (3.3) and the next chapter (4), though they relate to the division of functors into four realms, number more than four.

20. See Armstrong, USR1, 76 and USR2, 129; Loux, SA, 161 and 174; Quinton, 263 and 269; Kripke, NN, 127 and 134.

21. See Wolterstorff, UN, 7 and 249.

22. What Armstrong calls "a nomically united cluster of diagnostic properties . . ." (USR2, 64). The properties nomically united in a kind, say human, differ from the properties of an individual of that kind, say Ronald Reagan.

23. Wolterstorff uses true predication as a reliable index to what kinds there are (even though he also knows nonpredicable kinds). See UN, 3 and 13. Armstrong, to the contrary, denies any one-to-one correspondence between the (semantic) action of predication and the reality of universals. For Armstrong's views on language and universals, see USR2, chapters 13 and 17.

24. In section 3.4 of this chapter I briefly discuss the bearing of this on our understanding of the process of evolution. In the present section I do not discuss the bearing of evil on the reality of history. A complete account would have to do this, if only to become aware of the influence of evil on our ability to detect genuine order from the study of what is ordered.

25. The rich literature produced on this subject by John Dewey remains instructive, especially as he incorporates it into the wider contexts of anthropology, epistemology, and even logic. *How We Think*, *Democracy and Education*, and *Logic: The Theory of Inquiry* are classic examples.

26. See Kneale, 25ff. for a discussion of Aristotle on this point. His interpretation of what Aristotle is dealing with does not leave in doubt either the very different theoretical approaches, or the very persistent recognition of realities recognized by philosophers of all kinds.

27. The semantic problem is easily explained. Whenever we have complex property relations, we tend to use action words and spatial terms to refer to them. We speak of essences as lying behind or within things. We refer to them as doing things in places. But surely we should not take that language literally. Thus, when we describe a complex property we speak as though the properties of a substance make up the complexity. But

literally, a complex property remains a property and does not become a substance just because our language uses nouns and grammatical subjects. I thus share Loux's conclusion "that substance-kinds are irreducible to properties . . ." (SA, 162). See also Kripke, NN, 52.

28. Thus, e.g., Richard Rorty, PM, suggests that the view of substance to which Wolterstorff here refers had as its paradigm "an individual man or frog" (63).

29. See note 1 above.

30. See also note 27 above.

31. We do, of course, encounter the claim that properties have properties or that besides universals there are second order universals. At times it is also common then to refer to certain properties as substances and to certain universals as particulars. Wolterstorff provides an example of viewing properties as substances while Armstrong provides good examples for the other views mentioned. Now, in one sense properties having properties is no problem, *if* by this we mean that features of some kind are, e.g., necessarily related to features of another kind. And we may semantically express this as properties having properties. But if that semantic usage leads to the confusion of irreducibles, i.e., to first distinguishing substances and properties, e.g., and then having properties with properties that also become substances, though remaining properties, then one's ontological categories are not well defined. I believe that it is both possible to maintain the difference between properties and substances and to explain how we refer to certain realities as properties having properties. (See especially the last two chapters of Armstrong, USR2.) If a complex of nomic property relations is seen as itself a property, to which I can see no objection, then it will be unobjectionable to refer to that latter property with one term (P) and to refer to the properties making up P as the properties of P. That is not, however, sufficient ground for concluding that properties have properties, though it does explain the reality involved. If Armstrong claims that particular and universal are irreducible (USR1, 80), he cannot also claim legitimately that some universals are particulars (USR1, 79).

32. Often, whatever is irreducible on one level can be reduced to a higher level. Legitimate reduction is in fact no more than subsumption of different items under a higher category.

33. Functionalism is the view that substances are bundles of properties, or, in my terminology, that functors are just collections of functions.

34. John Dewey held this view. See my CC, 111-17. In my terminology, he thus reduced rationality to a form of organic interaction.

35. For a detailed treatment of levels of functionality in the realm of physical things, see M.D. Stafleu, TA, chapters 2 and 3.

36. "No primitive proposition is prior to all deductive systems" is a primitive proposition prior to all deductive systems. See the beginning of the Appendix to this volume and also the last two sections of my RC.

37. Stebbing only seems to discuss the mutual priority of deductive systems and not the priority of the areas of reality treated by these disciplines. But it is obvious that in the latter sense physical reality presupposes mathematical reality. The realities of the physical world simply are impossible without the numerical and spatial relations involved in them.

38. See Stafleu, TA, chapters 2 and 3.

39. When Stebbing was writing, of course, the notion of real necessity as logical necessity was predominant. Modern notions of natural necessity, as found in, e.g., Saul A. Kripke, Alvin Plantinga, or Hillary Putnam's recent work, were not generally popular. Natural necessity, on the other hand, is not a recently discovered phenomenon. Think, e.g., of the Greek notion of *ananke*.

40. He does not—not even for the future—share Hempel's view that in the vocabulary of "a comprehensive unifying theory . . . the notion of eventually reducing biology to physics" would become superfluous (PNS, 106). Hempel remains a modern reductionist not only in terms of levels of reality but also in terms of wholes as irreducible to their parts (see ASE, 258ff).

41. In Armstrong's words: ". . . although universality cannot be reduced to particularity, nor particularity to universality, particulars and universals do not stand in splendid isolation from each other. Particulars are particulars falling under universals and universals demand particulars" (USR1, 80).

42. If by laws one remains strictly universal conditionals expressed in terms of numerical or material relationships, it may be tempting to claim that laws occur only in physics or perhaps mathematics and logic. However, Hempel's extensive writings on scientific explanation all make the point that for science to explain anything satisfactorily implies that it subsumes whatever it wishes to explain under a "law," even when what we call law is no more than the formulation of a general trend. The fact that all science, including biology and psychology, is successful to some degree in explaining phenomena falling under its jurisdiction, implies that though such a science may not be successful in formulating an "exact" law, it still appeals to a regularity founded in lawful relations.

43. Polanyi (LT and LIS) has written clearly and briefly about these matters. See also Tim De Jager-Seerveld.

44. See Laszlo, SP, chapter 9, especially ii and iii; also, 159-63.

45. Polanyi treats this difference extensively in LIS.

46. See Polanyi, LT; also 5.2 below; and Dooyeweerd, NC, vol. 3, part 3. See also Tim De Jager-Seerveld.

47. Laszlo, SP, is a fine example of someone who resists both monism and dualism, pleading for a recognition of both continuity and irreducibility in nature. See especially chapter 9.

48. Galileo's laws characteristically pertain to balls rolling down inclines

without friction, i.e., an idealized situation to approximate the fact that the law for a function must ignore the total behavior of the functor.

49. This is a similar phenomenon as the one we met in the reference to the numerical oddity of *pi* earlier in this section. *Pi* as a number of circularity points to the character of circular motion.

50. See Polanyi, PK, 344 and LT; Herman Dooyeweerd, NC, vol. 3, part 1; De Graaff (AM and MM) argues at length for the concept of person as functional center.

51. Hierarchies of levels of functioning are discussed both by Laszlo (SP, chapter 3) and Polanyi (LT and LIS).

52. See 6.3 below.

53. See, e.g., John Dewey, L, 23-41; Polanyi, PK, 327ff.; Laszlo, SP, 35-53 and 165-80.

54. See, e.g., Armstrong, USR1, 126ff. Evolutionism requires naturalism.

55. Trials in the United States recently and historically in which creation and evolution have been pitted against each other have been based on a confusion of categories. Belief in creation does not purport to be a scientific or theoretical account of the origin of the world. It is a faith. Its rival is not the theory of evolution, but the postulate of naturalism, which also is a faith. Concerning origins one can have nothing but a faith, a postulate, a dogma. Any theories will need the underpinning of such a faith. The reliance of the theory of evolution on the naturalistic postulate must be made clear in such situations. When that is done, naturalism has as little scientific authority as belief in creation.

56. An analysis of the concept of revelation as the process whereby we get to know something by accepting what becomes known about it through a basic commitment yields the conclusion that all people who claim to know anything somewhere in their knowledge harbor beliefs in revelation. See my RC.

57. The dogma that no creator can exist rests upon another dogma, viz., that nature is ultimate.

58. See, e.g., John Dewey, L, 42ff.

59. If the concepts of life and death are spiritual-religious concepts with a normative meaning, any understanding of them in terms of organic growth and the presence or absence of biological vitality becomes unacceptable from a Christian point of view. Life in the Bible appears to be related to whatever exists in harmony with the divine will. All things can be alive, including stones and the sun. It is not that plants are alive, while rocks are dead. Rather, plants are or can be living organisms, rocks living matter. Life is not the well-functioning organism. And *death* is not a term for physical reality.

60. Laszlo not only proposes a hierarchy of irreducible levels, but also posits that hierarchy is due to laws that do not emerge along with the process

but that were present all along (SP, 32 and 35-53). Similar thoughts occur in Polanyi, LIS.

61. See, e.g., Carl Hempel, ASE, 231-44; Patrick Gardiner, PH, 51-105; William Dray, 4-20; and the paper by Carroll Goon.

62. Actual genetic continuity requires not only a shared set of determinative nomic conditions, but also causal empirical connection. And if we accept the discontinuity or irreducibility between empirical existence and an order of nomic conditions, it is very hard to see how the irreducible order of conditions could be caused (an empirical connection) by genetic connections.

63. The postulation that in the primal state genetic relations were possible that no longer occur now simply postulates what present scientific theory cannot cover. And that amounts to the positing of faith belief. No presently known facts can explain the sudden appearance of an immense variety of highly developed organisms, both in the plant world and in the animal kingdom.

64. The gap between living organisms and physical systems is unbridgeable, with the exception of postulates that may themselves support evidence but that are themselves not supported by any evidence. Matter does not strive to maintain itself, and it certainly does not restore or regenerate itself. In the process of living, a cell exchanges its material components many times over without losing its identity. Molecules, on the other hand, are held together by equilibration of forces. The list of irreducible properties is long. It is simply unintelligible to think that high concentrations of processes of one kind should as such, in and of themselves, be able to suddenly give rise to another *kind* of process. We may take a seed or a piece of plant and place it in water, moist soil, or even moist air, and we can expect a plant to be produced by the seed or by the plant part in its moist environment. A chemical analysis of the elements of seed, plant piece, and moist environment cannot by itself explain this reproduction. Further, there are elements involved which have a structure which only seeds or plants can produce. Such elements will not be found unbound in purely physical nature. Furthermore, today we are still not able to place together all the naturally free material elements in such a way that a process ensues which will produce the plant. Finally, even if in the future we would be able to do this, we would be dealing with a process guided by our knowledge of the nomic conditions involved, which is analogous to the creator-creature relation which evolution theory wishes to avoid.

65. I beg the question, of course, if sentience is called a life form. Clearly, only living creatures can be sentient. But if sentience is irreducibly different from the peculiar configuration of properties found in plant organisms, then treating sentience as a property of such a configuration begs the question.

66. If we are convinced that nothing is beyond the possibility of scientific explanation, the fact that some problems seem in principle incapable of be-

ing explained is an embarrassment. If, however, our worldview assigns a modest place to science, then we need not insist that all problems be rationally accounted for. See Rorty, PM, 365ff.

67. I begin again at this point the discussion of levels of action in the first section of this chapter (3.1). There I used the rough terminology of *level-1*, *level-2*, and *level-3* actions. Now a more discriminating conceptual framework must be devised.

68. The difference between functions and acts that I discuss here is what I earlier characterized as the difference between *level-3* and *level-2* actions.

69. The nomic connections among properties give acts their known structures. The complex property we name when we name the act has a known structure such that if certain minimal properties have been observed, we assume that all the other properties were also there.

70. F.J.J. Buytendijk's analysis of such functions as body posture, regulation of body temperature, breathing, and blood circulation shows how these functions are truly functor oriented and individually centered. See, e.g., 205ff.

71. Being depressed is thus not considered an act, even though in some sense I am not only capable of being depressed, but I can also be addressed as being responsible when I am depressed. Being depressed, however, like being tired, or having a pain, is a functional state, not an act.

72. In LT, Polanyi offers an elaborate analysis of how even a minute and exact description of all the physical properties of an event would never allow us to recognize the event as it is.

73. Analysis of qualifying and founding structures is complex and difficult. The results of one's analysis are easily open to criticism. I am here not so much interested in whether or not the actual functional areas indicated are rightly identified as in giving an example of what I have in mind.

74. This is further discussed in 4.2.1 below.

75. For a detailed discussion see 7.3 and 7.4.

76. I am referring here to what was called *level-1* action earlier on.

Notes to Chapter IV

1. By *subjective*, it will be recalled, I do not mean mental states, personal involvement, private experience, or the like. This term refers to the fact that all concrete empirical existence, the world of particulars in space and time, is a world which exists by virtue of its *subjection* to nomic conditions. Though the term may be confusing in relation to other well established philosophical meanings, there is no better term to express whatever correlates with nomic reality. And this meaning of *subject* outside of philosophy is well established. In fact, the meaning of *subjectivism* is tied up with my meaning here, since by subjectivism we mean an attitude which ascribes determining factors to what is determined or which sees criteria for judgment as set by that which is subject to those criteria.

2. In his debate with philosophers of history Carl Hempel stressed repeatedly that all scholarship fails to understand concrete individuality. See ASE, 233.

3. On universals as limits or boundaries see Armstrong, USR2, 64.

4. Concepts of so-called substance kinds or particularizing universals are usually assumed when research is directed at some dimension of the existence of particulars of such a kind. This does not mean, of course, that there is no scholarship attempting to describe and define functor kinds.

5. Nicolai Hartmann, Michael Polanyi, and Ervin Laszlo are modern authors whose worldview understands reality as many-layered. For them these layers are mutually irreducible.

6. The name for the property that appears for most to characterize the specific functioning of organisms is *life*. Technically, that term designates the core reality about organisms. In the view developed here such a term will be used to designate a mode of functioning. More particularly, it will designate the *core* principle of a *kind* of functioning. But it will not itself be seen as a function. Rather, all sorts of concrete functions, in being of this kind, are therefore organic functions. But life is not itself a single, actual, and concrete function.

7. See LT, 61 especially.

8. The use of language here should not confuse what I am saying. When I speak of functions "opening up" other functions, I do not wish to suggest that functions do things apart from functors. Thus, a more subtle formulation here would be: the integration of actual functions in the existence of a functor will have the effect that lower level functions are enriched by higher functions as they serve to base these higher functions.

9. Whether it is really meaningful to distinguish between what something is and what something does is controversial. "Having a picnic" is what we do, while "being a person" is what we are, or so we *say*. In that sense one could argue that what a thing *is* relates to so-called substance universals, i.e., to the order for its being the functor kind it is; while what a thing *does* relates to its properties and relations. On the other hand, one might also argue that one is what one *is* in relation to what one *does* in subjection to the proper order. Consequently, I do not intend to make technical distinctions between what something *is*, or *has*, or *does*.

10. It is likely that at least the subhuman realms of empirical reality are integrated in this sort of way. All their entities and relations are organized by functions of the highest modal kind for that realm. Physical things are energy systems; organisms are biotic wholes; animals could be one realm of entities capable of sensitive awareness. Possibly the animal realm is more complex than we indicate when we refer to the animal world as more than plant or organism and less than human. If it is more complex, the device of using x functions to arrive at a different classification would be intriguing. Are some distinctions in the animal world based on the ability of some and not others to function symbolically, of some and not others to develop and learn skills? These avenues of investigation suggested by the model used in this volume would open up untested possibilities for a renewed understanding of the nature of things.

11. Whether in the subhuman realms the analysis of different y functions within the same realm will lead to the discovery of natural kinds that reveal a genuine structure of subrealms is an intriguing question to which no answer is presently known.

12. See Hart, CC, 116.

13. See Herman Dooyeweerd, NC, vol. 2, 49-79 for a more extensive analysis of a conceptual model for modal order.

14. An ultimately irreducible kind of functions I refer to as a mode, and the way in which the various functions of a given mode display a peculiar arrangement I refer to as modal order.

15. What this discussion has attempted to do is to show that in their own way irreducible levels of functioning point to a deeper unity and integrality. But the formal noticing of this unity is incomplete so long as it is not given any content. Such content can only derive from assigning a value to our notion of subjectivity, to that way of being which has its nature determined by an order which itself points to a unity in origin. But the discus-

sion of the reality of this origin lies beyond the limits of philosophy. Answers to the problem of the unity of reality have to do with the purpose of existence, the meaning of reality. These answers do not come to us from philosophy unless we view philosophy itself as ultimate. When that is not the case, we face fundamental attitudes with which we come to philosophy and which originate outside of philosophy. These attitudes set the tone for what earlier I called *level one* activity. A proper discussion of this must wait till the Appendix. See also 4.4 in this chapter, especially what is said about *religion* in the opening paragraph on the *pistic*. And see 7.2.1 in the last chapter, as well as 8.1.3 and 8.1.4 in the Appendix.

16. I have no need to examine pain as private, inner, mental experience over against public, outer, physical reality. Pain is functional and real, but irreducible to functions of another kind. It is private as *my* pain, public *as pain*. It is inner if the pain is subcutaneous, outer if it is a burn or cut. It is as invisible as "expensive" or "stupid" is invisible; it is not a color or a surface. It is visible as writhing is visible, audible as yelling is audible. It is "mental" in that it is not an atom or a cell. It is not "mental" in that it is the actual and real function of functors who are real and who have cells and atoms as organic and physical functions.

17. The great variety of human language to name things, i.e., the varied means we have at our disposal to predicate properties of things, is not in itself a basis for concluding that things have the properties whose names we use in describing the things. A teacher who in a lower grade biology lesson helps the children understand that plants *make* sugar is not thereby teaching them that plants make plans, have purposes, and know how to execute them. The biotic order of reality determines that in organic interaction a chemical process mechanically yields chemicals known as sugars. If no more than that is meant when we speak of plants making sugar, then *making* is no longer a good word to use for what I have in mind in this section. The verb *to make* has then acquired an equivocal meaning of such wide usage that it no longer equals, e.g., creating. The "making" I have in mind here has elements of design, control, and skill. And these are always concentrated in tools and instruments, means and methods specifically oriented to the end which the functor has in view. For repeated analysis of the abuse of names or predicates as designators of real properties, see Armstrong, USR2, especially 7ff.

18. The primary order of a mode, it will be recalled, is the constitutive or essential arrangement of functions in that mode without which no functioning of that kind could exist.

19. Michael Polanyi has helpfully analyzed the difference between purely physical and mechanical interaction patterns that the laws of physics can account for completely, and physical action as it occurs in machines that are made as tools and instruments for human purpose and design. The planets act and interact purely mechanically. Machines do not. The intricate motions of flywheels in a clock are those of a machine. The mo-

tions of planets in a solar system are not those of a machine. See LT and LIS.

20. Symbolic functioning is never merely means. It also occurs as end in the consummation of the symbol in its enjoyment. Human play is both symbolic and consummative. Animals probably do not play at all. They frolic and dally. But symbolic and imaginative activity purposely engaged in for enjoyment only seems foreign to such frolicking.

21. James H. Olthuis has written extensively on this topic and I owe much to his work in this section. See especially CH. Fernhout offers another treatment of this level of functioning in its relation to the meaning of religion, where again he perceives religion not as a human function but as the central direction of the whole of human life. See FM, especially 182-95.

22. In the next chapter I treat *object* and *objective* as technical terms. See 5.4. They are used here in that sense.

23. Perhaps the singlemost important book by an existentialist on this topic is Karl Jaspers's *Der Philosophische Glaube Angesichts der Offenbahrung* (Munich: Piper, 1963). In this book Jaspers confronts science and theology of revelation as two avenues to truth, rejects both, and presents philosophy as his alternative. A long and varied tradition of literature exists on the relation of the Christian faith to science. See W. Brouwer, Coulson, Dooyeweerd in TWT, Hart in RC, Hart and Olthuis, Jeeves, McIntire, Mackay, Runner, Wolters, and Wolterstorff in RwR.

24. The concept of "commitment" plays a central role in his analysis not only of knowledge, but also of logic. See PK, especially chapter 10; see also Anastasiou, Joldersma, and De Jager-Seerveld.

25. See Plantinga, BIG and BGB; also Wolterstorff, RwR. The role of belief in modern epistemology differs from the roles of faith or commitment but is at times also clearly related to these.

26. Revelation is the process whereby we know what lies beyond our universe and beyond our experience of our universe. If we believe that the universe is not original, not *sui generis*, not *causa sui*, then we come to know its origin in faith. And by having that faith, the origin becomes known to us. That is revelation.

27. Faith provides us with beliefs as grounds upon which we are prepared to act. Beliefs are much more than justified conclusions of argument. They are action grounds.

28. "The ultimate" could, of course, be many things. It could be the God of the Christian religion. It could also be the ultimacy of humanity in humanism. It could be matter, fate, the universe, or the future of humanity. Whatever it is, it will ultimately direct and anchor our life.

29. Wrong ultimate choices inevitably reveal themselves, given time, as conflicting with the real nature of reality. Thus, if a relative good such as national security becomes an ultimate value, the protection of national security will become an obsession turning defense into a threat for those

defended. When relative ends become ultimate finalities, the world will protest being directed from and anchored in such a point of view.

30. See De Graaff, SO.

31. See Augustine's famous adage: "Our hearts are restless within us until they find rest in God" (*Confessions*, Book I, chapter 1). The ultimate is not accepted *on* some ground, but *as the* ground of all things ultimately.

32. On this see especially Fernhout, FM, 182-95.

33. See Olthuis, FV.

34. The reduction of our needs to a need of resources and goods, to material needs, also limits our ability to meet many legitimate needs. But normatively speaking an economy should establish a network of chosen priorities in which we are enabled to care for one another and our world in the most optimal way.

35. It may occur to some that what I am characterizing here is what usually is called reason. And it is indeed true that whenever I use *reason* or *rational* I use it in this context. But the problem with this more current terminology is that it is tainted with the history of rationalism. In my opinion it is really impossible to say what *reason* or *rational* mean in general. These terms have many meanings, some of them incompatible with others. I shall always curb all uses of *reason*, *rational*, and *rationality* to a close and narrow association with the functional dimension of logical reasoning, inference, and conceptualization. So it always refers to just one functional and irreducible dimension of our active life or to acts, events, and institutions qualified by functions of that dimension but having other dimensions of functions as well. The act of reasoning is rationally, logically, conceptually, or analytically qualified. But it has, of course, other functions as well: brain chemistry, perception, use of symbols, etc. Yet all of these occur within the boundary functions of the analytic dimension. Consequently, reason as I use it is much narrower than knowledge. All knowing has rational dimensions. But only some knowing is rationally qualified, i.e., is typically rational knowing.

36. The sequence I follow in the modal series here was first proposed by Calvin Seerveld. See FW, 143. In the sequence originally proposed by Herman Dooyeweerd in the opening pages of the *New Critique* he has psychic, analytic, formative, semantic, social, economic, aesthetic, jural, etc. For this section of the series, Seerveld has proposed the sequence psychic, formative, aesthetic, semantic, analytic, social, economic, etc. I follow this, but I do not believe that a separate semantic mode is needed. I collapse his aesthetic and semantic into one, viz., symbolic.

37. *Meaning* as I use it has reference to what may be called the referential character of both subjective existence and the nomic order of the world. Nothing in either world or world order is absolute or self-sufficient, *sui generis* or *causa sui*. The essence of all that is always turns out to refer beyond itself to something else. Our world is re-lative (relating and rela-

tional) and contextual. What things *are* always requires interpretation. So I believe that reality *is* what it *means*: both its existence and its order are what they are in relation to their origin. See Appendix, 8.1.4. Consequently, not just words have meaning or are meaningful, but all of reality. All of it is expressive, revealing, telling. We speak of the loss of meaning in life. We then do not intend to say that words have shifted in sense. It is that sense of meaning I here intend. And I extend this sense to refer to all of both world and world order.

38. When the symbolic functions typically qualify our actions and such actions are founded in the perceptive awareness of meaning, we land in that realm of human culture known as the aesthetic. The symbolic objects then are typically founded in color, rhythm, form, sound, or texture as the felt carriers of perceived meaning.

39. Whether or not animals can function formatively, symbolically, or socially remains a matter of much speculation. The position I have taken myself is that formative functioning occurs at least in higher vertebrates and that symbolic functioning must be seriously considered. Social functioning, if it indeed has analytic functioning as part of its substratum, does not come in for serious consideration. It should be pointed out that when we try to determine the nature of a mode, the question whether or not it is found in nonhuman reality has great significance. In the first place, such a question helps determine the nature of the mode in question. Secondly, it concerns the possibility of more irreducible realms included in the now recognized unity of the animal world. Thirdly, it has great consequences for our view of culture as specifically human. With regard to psychic functioning, we know that animals have it. As for analytic functioning, we know that only human beings are capable of it. These two "certainties" help us to determine the nature and relative order of the formative, symbolic, and social modes.

40. In my view terms such as *life, love, truth, good, knowledge,* and others are totality words or coherence terms. They do not so much indicate specifics, but rather the state of a whole when held up to its standards. They are words suited to refer to what elsewhere I have called *level one* activity. To know, to love, and to live are the positive names for our whole active being when our being and doing is good and true. So *life* has no specific modal reference as I use it. See 4.2.2 and note 15 above.

41. The relation of portions of matter, particles, or quanta, to the whole unit of physical action (atoms and molecules as physical systems with the structure of a whole) differs immensely from the relation of matter to wholes known as organisms, biotic systems functioning as wholes. Remove a quantum of energy from an atom and the whole entity is changed. It is its matter. The atom loses its identity with a change in its matter. But remove physical matter or even cells from an organism and the entity not only retains its identity, but it restores the injury. Physical systems cannot even be injured. They change completely. But organisms continually ex-

change their matter and even renew their cells. And the function of matter within the organism, such as the function of the chemical DNA, is physically unexplainable. Matter just does not have organismic properties. And these organismic properties are therefore irreducible to physical properties.

42. See Polanyi, LIS; also Stafleu, TA. The latter work explains in detail the nature of physical reality in terms of the first four modes of existence.

43. See Kneale, 488. The universality of numeric and spatial relations can quite easily be explained by reference to the fact that they are the two basic terminal modes of reality in the founding direction of the modal order. Their modal character also explains, via the concept of modal irreducibility, why we cannot ever hope to develop a universal language of science which is mathematical. These explanations seem sufficient to abandon as speculative all attempts to view the numeric and spatial modes as the characteristics of universal continuity and individual discontinuity, and to view mathematics as the discipline which studies the physical evidence of this continuity and discontinuity.

44. On the status of a color as a property, see Armstrong, USR2, 117ff. On the difference between "being red" and a case of this, i.e., the difference between property conditions and properties, see Wolterstorff, UN, 89.

45. On whether or not all properties are complex, see Armstrong, USR2, 19ff., 30ff., and 61ff.

46. For the view that relations between universals may be laws, see Armstrong, USR2, 148ff.

47. Only minerals, plants, animals, and humans can be functors. Consequently numbers, concepts, words, etc., are functions. The concept *"horse"* is our name for what some person or persons at some time understand horses to be. *Six* is our name for an aspect of all those entities that can be enumerated on all the fingers of one hand plus one finger of the other. And these are functions or conditions for functions. In Dooyeweerd's work these are sometimes called modal subjects. All that can mean is: an identifiable functioning of some kind.

48. See Armstrong about the rejection of negative universals, USR2, 23. What actual, concrete, particular properties there are is determined by our experience of them. And whether there are nomic connections among conditions such that they constitute a property is largely determined by science. And in determining these things it makes a great deal of difference whether or not the alleged properties or nomic connections do in fact make a positive difference in reality, i.e., whether they have actual effects. Armstrong discusses these factors throughout his two volumes.

Notes to Chapter V

1. See Armstrong, USR2, 75, who points out the long-standing recognition of this.

2. Wolterstorff thinks this is the case. See UN, 87-104.

3. The problems surrounding this issue have contributed to my speaking sometimes of a world consisting of functors, functions, and relations; sometimes of a world consisting of functors and functions in relation; and sometimes of a world consisting just of functors and functions. As shall become clear soon, the latter way of speaking was prompted by the consideration that at least in the empirical world, relations might just be functions. In that case speaking of just functors and functions would include relations. But in this chapter this lack of clarity on an important point needs to be resolved.

4. For the possibility of reducing properties to relations or vice versa, see Armstrong, USR2, 80-88. Quinton in one place suggests that relations might be thought of as properties (14).

5. An important assumption of this study is that everyday experience is a valid premise for analysis; at least generally speaking. Analysis may clarify and explain phenomena in our experience, but it does not constitute the validity of our experience. Analysis need not necessarily either "underwrite or debunk" (Rorty, PM, 3) our experience.

6. The concept of knowing developed by Michael Polanyi (e.g., in *Personal Knowledge*) makes this point convincingly.

7. My use of terms here is not intended to be precise. What I discuss here can be called a relation, a relationship, a link, a connection, or whatever else may serve the purpose.

8. For this see the Appendix.

9. When I say I know relations, then by "know" I do not mean the same as "have a concept or definition" of relations. I also do not mean to suggest that what I thus know is devoid of conceptual elements. All I mean to say is that I not only know relations, but I also know that what I thus know cannot be fully comprehended, understood, or grasped in a concept;

while at the same time my knowing is (partly) dependent on conceptual comprehension. If knowing is conceived as identical with understanding or comprehending, what I am saying here will make no sense. But in my view of knowing, knowledge always exceeds understanding. That makes, in my view, for an element of mystery in all knowledge. Mystery means no more, in my view, than: knowledge which goes beyond our conceptual grasp though it includes such a grasp. Nevertheless, of some things we can have an adequate concept. We have a concept of implication. We also have a concept of gravity. But as all great scientists will testify, that is not the same as taking all the mystery out of things. When I refer to the mystery of relations I have in mind a knowledge which combines several concepts that seem mutually irreducible and thus almost antinomous or contradictory. For I have said that creating, determining, and being creature or subject are completely and radically irreducible. But if all these are relations I may finally have said that they are reducible to being instances of relations. However, my view of reality is not such that reality is basically relations. All of what is real is related. And we can know what it is to be related. But we cannot have a single concept of what that is.

10. One might say that the mystery of relationship is the mystery of communion or fellowship. Relationship is there only when each does its share. And yet relationship adds up to more than just that, although there is nothing else. The "adding up to more" constitutes the temptation to take the proper reality of relationship as something in its own right. We can say much about a marriage. And much of what we say is rationally intelligible. But the marriage seems to add up to more than just a male and female person each doing his or her part in a relationship. The two functors are also in subjection to an order, and that order determines what more there may be besides the two persons. One could even add, if one's commitment allowed it, that God, who ordained the order, used it to call for the "something more" in the relation just so long as it is subject to the order. But from the point of view of analysis, this does not add anything. From the standpoint of analysis, relation maintains its mysterious character. And the mystery remains even when approached from the point of view of faith and ultimate commitment, in the language of confession. Communion, love, and knowledge are words of the highest order to express what we experience in a world full of relationships. But even though we know what they mean, these words do not give us a definition or a concept of the realities expressed. Ultimately the reality of relation must be accepted.

11. Dooyeweerd has elaborately discussed his theory of enkaptic relations. See NC, vol. 3, part 3, 625-780.

12. The meaning of *subject* here is not the same as that defined earlier, i.e., as in "being subject" to laws. I will define this new usage carefully in what follows.

13. In both LIS and LT, Michael Polanyi addresses problems in the context of

this revived debate. Throughout his discussion of enkapsis Dooyeweerd also refers to this controversy; see note 11 above.

14. Quinton (12) hints that a part (e.g., the roof of a house) may not be the same as a property (e.g., the shape of the house). He bases this on the idea that parts are particulars and properties are universals.

15. To suggest that the blocks *are* the parts, however, is risky. In some sense they are not genuine parts, but merely ingredients. The genuine parts are those constructions which are elements of the structure being built. If the structure is a house, then doors and windows will be parts.

16. The same confusion is found in Armstrong, who discusses segments of a line as the parts of the line (USR2, 121). That is not the concept of part which philosophers have in mind who subscribe to the doctrine that a whole is more than the sum of its parts. The parts of such a reality have no meaningful existence apart from the whole. Consequently, mere addition of parts is never what they have in mind when they speak of the totality of the parts. One can find a hint of awareness of this in Quinton's addition of a significant characteristic to the phrase "sum of its parts," namely, "suitably arranged" (98).

17. The denial of wholes (as constituted by parts which together as a sum or addition do not make that whole) implies the denial of certain universals. But it is not helpful to refer to sociological individualism as nominalism, unless one would further define it as sociological nominalism.

18. In many wholes, the parts would be different as soon as they were to be found apart from the whole. Organs die outside of wholes. Some parts cannot be investigated simply because they need to be taken out of the whole to be investigated and being outside the whole they no longer function as the parts they are. This indeed suggests that the properties of a whole are determined to be a nomic conjunction which forms the nature of the whole. And the whole's nature determines that the properties together function differently than if they were in a mere additive relation.

19. A whole as a whole is indivisible. Quite to the contrary, a chunk or whole portion of material is not a whole in this sense. It can be divided and the resultant portions are indeed less than the bigger chunk. But they are not its parts. But portions of human being are not themselves just lesser quantities of human being.

20. It seems entirely appropriate, therefore, that Armstrong discusses the problem in terms of properties. If properties are elements in a complexity they can be parts. But not every element of every complexity is a part. A part as discussed in the controversial part-whole relation is an element in a configured complexity. See Armstrong, USR2, 36ff.

21. I have adopted the term from Dooyeweerd.

22. Changes for the better in my view of the part-whole and enkaptic relations are due to discussions with Jon Chaplin and Bill Rowe.

23. What I have in mind here is the Hellenistic origin of the idea that the order of the world is not only rational in nature but is an order *of* a mind, i.e., is mental in nature. That thought pattern persists today. It results in seeing human conceptual understanding as the supreme measure of things. The contemporary revolt against this view is strong, though so far not successful. Cartesian rationalism or foundationalist empiricism are far from dead. It survives, e.g., where realists regard order as essentially known, save themselves from the subjectivity of knowledge by making order (as known) unknown by humans, and save themselves from unknown knowledge by having order known by God. The battles against these trends by, e.g., Hans G. Gadamer, Jürgen Habermas, Thomas Kuhn, Michael Polanyi, Gerard Radnitzky, Richard Rorty, or Stephen Toulmin appear as yet to have made little progress in those camps where the dominant traditions of the immediate and distant past still reign supreme.

24. See CR, 16. Kierkegaard also was aware of this problem. He believed that a notion of truth had to be *held* by someone in order for it to be true. He had objected to extreme objectivism which ultimately places truth beyond subjectivity entirely; it no longer seems to involve the subject at all. "Subjective" is not merely distinguished from "objective"—the two are, in fact, cut loose from each other. See, e.g., *Concluding Unscientific Postscript*, vols. 1 and 3.

25. I have often been told by colleagues that my insistence on a strong connection of *rational* or *rationality* with the human mind or with human inferential powers is misplaced. However, the origin of the usage which makes *rational* applicable to anything having to do with order, coherence, or being based on legitimate grounds, lies in the view that the nature of things is in the mind, or lies in seeing the rational mind as the measure of things. And so I have never come across significant theories of what is rational—whatever it is—that were not intimately connected with views of rational minds.

26. The gross reductions involved in basically viewing all of empirical reality in terms of a mind-body dualism will not be discussed here. But see 7.3.4.

27. Note that here I shift to the other meaning of *subject* (i.e., to subject$_1$ from subject$_2$).

28. Much reality contains concepts as constitutive elements of its nature. Almost all typically human products, nearly all of what we refer to as culture, cannot exist except through conceptualization. Without our having concepts of these realities we cannot produce them. But much of the concept in turn depends on our understanding of what we have produced. In this way most of culture is analytically subjective$_{1,2}$. It contains analysis as a constitutive subjective$_{1,2}$ moment. Consequently, no analysis of such reality can ever be objective. Nevertheless, it can meet standards and be true.

29. To refer to a person as a rational animal, to understand that the definition of a person is the rationality of the being, might well involve such a reduction.

30. The visual image of a tree is its psychic object function. In having my image of that tree, that tree functions in the image. But the actual tree is not the same as what I see, though what I see is a function of the real tree. What I have an image of is the tree as seen; rather, my image *is* the tree *as seen*. The image is not the tree. But it is a true function of the tree. And as a perceptual image it is also a function of myself. I have the image, it is my image. It is the tree as *it appears* to me *and* as *I look* at it.

31. The organic functioning of the DNA molecule is due to its functioning within the context of a living organism. The physical-molecular properties of the material components of DNA will never suffice to explain why this organic compound has the structure it has. Which is not to say, of course, that the analogical functions of the DNA are any less physical. One may compare this to the relation between a pelt and a fur coat. No analysis of a pelt will yield natural implications leading to the establishment of the human artifact fur coat. Nevertheless, the object function of having warmth is a natural object function and is founded in subjective$_2$ physical properties of the pelt.

32. The interesting thing about these particular s-o relations is that on the basis of just such a *partial* relation we succeed in adequately interacting with our surroundings. The seen tree and the felt tree are one tree. On the basis of just a sound, a smell, a touch, we can and do relate integrally to the whole entity. We do not, so to speak, just hear sounds and then compose a view of the entity. Rather, we hear a thrush. We hear a train. Only when in doubt might we say: I hear what sounds like a train. Or we might then say: the sounds I hear sound like they are the sounds of a train. Only in extreme doubt or ignorance do we "just" hear sounds. Then we are confused, because, as we know, something must make the sound and we don't know what does.

33. For a helpful discussion of a s-o relation in its complexity see the discussion of heat molecularly and heat as felt by Kripke, NN, 129-32 and especially 153. When he talks about the problem of "making molecular motion felt as heat" he appears to say that merely physical properties of molecular motion do not explain heat. He thus would not agree with Armstrong's contention that what we have always known as "secondary qualities" could be fully accounted for "solely within the vocabulary of physics" (USR2, 55).

34. See also Quinton, 47-50.

Notes to Chapter VI

1. I am reminded here of what Michael Loux says about substance and the impossibility to reduce the notion of substance to other notions. Such a fundamental or primitive notion, he says, "is given us at the beginning of the ontological enterprise and is not one that the ontologist must construct" (SA, 165). Richard Rorty appears to have similar convictions about the primitivity of unity. See PM, 154 and 155.

2. In my view, philosophy is an integrative discipline. In contrast to the specification, differentiation, and specialization of the various branches of science, philosophy draws things together. So philosophy is especially dependent on its own philosophical concepts of integration. Some philosophers have thought that unity and coherence are not inherent in the natural order of things. In their opinion the world is chaotic, except for the human institution of order into experience. This Kantian view still prevails in contemporary thought. Laszlo finds it impossible to refute this notion conclusively and leaves it as a moot point (see SP, 8-12, 18).

3. Is it true, e.g., that "the totality of things—the universe—is a particular," as Armstrong notes? (See USR1, 115, note.) As "a" particular, does it have the identity of a whole? The unity of a whole?

4. Armstrong speaks of "nomic connections" which tie together the functions of things "into a unity" (see USR2, 62).

5. Contemporary discussions about the institution of marriage and about sexuality in relation to marriage depend to a large extent on how participants conceive of possible relationships. They often do not ask which orderly patterns of unity, totality, and coherence are involved. Someone might not accept marriage as a totality concept, nor accept sexuality and commitment as some of the inclusion properties of marriage. Such a person will have a much different expectation of these discussions than someone who does accept these properties. I am not saying that one view is right or better. I merely want to point out how categories of integration and the recognition of concepts as integration concepts, make a crucial difference to our understanding of the world in our daily experience.

6. I owe this view of time entirely to Herman Dooyeweerd (NC, vol. 1, 22-34). His analysis is largely spread over a number of early articles available only in Dutch. See my PT. Though I owe my views to Dooyeweerd's original proposals, my own version should not be construed as an adequate rendering of his effort.

7. The view I develop here goes beyond one which takes our universe as spatiotemporal. In my view the relation of nomic conditions to our empirical universe is also a temporal relation.

8. It seems clear to me that science requires nomic conditions as well as complete constancy or invariance of some of these. If our world and its history are one, i.e., if world history has unbroken continuity, then without some abiding basic common denominator no comparison, classification, dating are possible. But without these the most rudimentary steps of the scientific process would be impossible. So if we believe that science is real and that its contributions are credible, some view about the order of things is unavoidable.

9. There is a terminological problem here. I have continually dealt with reality in terms of a correlation of order and existence. And I have often referred to existence as subjective$_1$ and individual. At the same time I have made it clear that any actual existent is not just, merely, or only subjective$_1$ and individual. Right in and through existence there are all sorts of evidence of order. The correlation is world order and ordered world. And an ordered world is not just completely subjective$_1$ and individual. Nevertheless, my language will often suggest that I may be saying just that. So I wish to make clear at this point that when I speak of subjective$_1$ and individual existence, I am aware that such existence displays its relation to nomic order right within itself.

10. The science of history, as we know it today, is usually limited to the study of the relation between temporality and human responsibility, i.e., to a study of the human factor in world development. But we cannot conclude from this that only culture is historical.

11. Customarily works in ontology dealing with the structure and order of things do not deal much or at all with evil. In that way they tend to stress the continuity and invariability of order. But since the evidence of order in structure is certainly open to the ravages of evil, a more complete account of temporality would also have to deal with time and evil, i.e., with change as destruction.

12. For an account of time as physical, see Stafleu, TA.

13. See GE, 4.

14. As a kind, i.e., viewed from the point of view of the nomic configuration to which existing trees are subject$_1$ (exemplifying a kind equals being subject$_1$ to an order in my view), *the* tree does indeed not occur. Rather, it determines whatever trees occur. But I do not see this distinction at work in Wolterstorff. For a detailed analysis and comparison of Dooyeweerd's

notion of nomic configurations for functors (called structures of individuality by him) and Aristotle's notion of substance, see Zigterman, DTS.

15. Here I agree with Wolterstorff. See GE, 5.

16. When Wolterstorff explains how events have to do with predicates (viz., the actualization, instantiation, or exemplification of what he calls properties, relations, and actions in UN), he suggests this notion in the context of his own views.

17. These two sides of the problem are the root of the debate about covering laws in history. This disagreement is focused on an exchange between Dray and Hempel as principals. See Dray; also Hempel, ASE, 321ff. For analysis of this debate from the point of view of this volume, see Carroll Goon.

18. The basic position of physical existence in the world does, of course, make physical time fundamentally important. It is hard to imagine any experience of actual time that would not be related to the patterns in which sun and moon revolve and in which the seasons change. Clock time is fundamental in that sense.

19. Physically speaking, clothing of a bygone age may persist. Clothes stay around in musea and in attics. Wearing them later, we step into a different time. In the present time they exist inappropriately.

20. This view would dictate that matter should never be denigrated, or called *dead*. Matter is the existential basis of all things, a foundation for all that lives. Matter is significant, meaningful, to be respected.

21. Consider the following statements by Hempel and Toulmin. Hempel writes: "In sum, the maxim that data should be gathered without guidance by antecedent hypotheses about the connections among the facts under study is self-defeating, and it is certainly not followed in scientific inquiry. On the contrary, tentative hypotheses are needed to give direction to a scientific investigation. Such hypotheses determine, among other things, what data should be collected at a given point in a scientific investigation" (PNS, 13). In this instance, the elements of temporal direction ("directs"), order ("determine"), and subjective$_1$ temporal process ("data collection") are clearly present as indispensible aspects of a reality. That is also apparent in this statement by Toulmin: "Before the scientist enters his laboratory . . . he must have guidance about . . . certain evaluations. This guidance can come only from a careful statement of his theoretical problem, and if one looks at the conditions of the experiment he performs one will find that they are tailor-made to suit his theoretical problem" (PS, 66).

22. The all-encompassing nature of this process can be seen in the fact that the qualifying functions of entities or relationships only provisionally close off the reality of such entities or relations. An organic entity is provisionally defined, limited, or closed off by the qualifying and directing functions of

a biotic or organic type. All functions of the organism are determined to be directed in this way and that is what essentially the organism is all about. But in its relation to the rest of reality, we see the interrelation of this organic reality with other realities and in that context the anticipatory and objective development of organic reality (in agricultural techniques, aesthetic enjoyment, scientific understanding, economic management, etc.) to higher functional levels. See opening paragraphs of 7.2.1.

23. In chapter 3 (3.2.3) I referred to this process of development and illustrated it with the progress of education. I will here use this example again. It will now illustrate temporality as an integrating factor in the specialization process of a developing world.

Notes to Chapter VII

1. Anthony Quinton is an example.

2. John Dewey is an example.

3. Ervin Laszlo is an example.

4. The German phenomenologist Max Scheler deals with the peculiar position of humanity in the world in his *Die Stellung des Menschen im Kosmos (Man's Place in Nature)*.

5. Ervin Laszlo, though aiming to be as reductionist as possible with his model of isomorphic systems, nevertheless documents the impossibility of reducing all of the empirical world to merely physical systems. See, e.g., SP, chapters 8-10.

6. Everyday experience refuses to see a plant as merely living matter, an animal merely as a moving or sentient plant, and a human being merely as a reasoning beast.

7. Whether or not there is, in addition to these four kinds of functors, a realm of spirits, angels, or other living beings in outer space continuous with these four realms in our empirical universe is a question for which, in any case, no sufficient empirical evidence is available to enter into a theoretical analysis.

8. For the meanings of objective, subjective$_2$, and subjective$_1$, see chapter 5, 5.4.

9. The fact that animals can learn, i.e., be taught to develop skills, includes the possibility of learning certain skills from human beings in the setting of being domesticated. Animals may become sensitive to humanly made distinctions and may respond adequately to what they sense. For that reason domestic animals are not adequate for the study of what native capacities there are to be observed in animal behavior.

10. Both Polanyi (see especially LT and LIS) and Laszlo (SP) have extensive discussions of what they call boundary conditions, a feature of reality whereby higher levels serve to reorganize functioning on lower levels.

11. For a discussion of the great differences in human and animal physiology, see F.J.J. Buytendijk.

12. In faith the human functions are committed to the origin and destiny of subjective$_1$ existence. Through humanity's place in all of existence, the world is guided to its destiny, all of prehuman existence is developed and opened up objectively, and thus in human commitment all that exists is guided to its fullness of meaning. See also 4.2.2, 8.1.3, and 8.1.4.

13. I use this term here as I earlier discussed it in the opening paragraphs of 4.3.2 and especially note 26 in chapter 4. See also my RC.

14. Our pistic functioning is the *functional* foundation for our spirituality, taking foundational in its developmental meaning, i.e., as basis for the opening order of functionality. A problem arises at this point, however. In a philosophical study, is it adequate merely to assert that human spirituality is equal with this openness and receptivity to order, direction, destiny, and origin? Is spirituality in people closed to argument, analysis, and explanation? I do not believe it is. But I do believe that our views about what constitutes spirituality in human experience are always intimately interwoven with our ultimate positions. And our ultimate positions serve as a foundation for much of the argument and explanation that would ensue. Consequently, when I will now discuss the person not merely as a bodily being in continuity with all other entities in empirical reality, but also as a spiritual being in distinction from all other empirical entities, I will have to anticipate many of my ultimate convictions. These are dealt with at length in the Appendix, wherein I discuss matters that reach beyond the proper limits of philosophical discussion.

15. All other functors that exist on earth are body only. Their functional integration into a unified whole is itself a matter of a nature determined by qualifying functions. That determining nature is temporal even in the sense of being fully temporary. But human beings as spirits, functionally open to what lies beyond subjectively$_1$ functioning existence and thus capable of orientation to and by what lies beyond, are potentially enduring without end. Human spirituality is temporal. But spiritual submission to the intended order of reality in the intended direction of that order (from its origin and to its destiny) makes for the possibility of life without end. This possibility for life everlasting implies at the same time that the person is mortal, destined to be cut off from life if spiritually developing in a direction that is destructive of self and other existence. In the Appendix I will deal with this further.

16. This ultimate point of view with respect to human nature will have a certain conceptual one-sidedness, because it simply analyzes an ultimate approach in describing a person. This is the case with ultimate positions on almost any fundamental issue. Certain salient features may be highlighted better in monisms and others in dualisms. However, my overall position denies all dualisms and all monistic reduction. Instead, I see human nature as essentially one, although with both a bodily and a spiritual orientation.

17. Whether or not something belongs within a particular context is in

general a vexing problem for theory. In everday life we decide both practically and contextually on our boundaries. (See Laszlo, SP, 24.)

18. I make no claim here for the correctness of this characterization. It would appear that the more ultimate role of pistic functions such as hope, acceptance, risk, and surrender are evident here. Nevertheless, all I intend to show here is how such a characterization might proceed in making use of the model proposed in this volume.

19. Extensive analyses of social institutions with the use of structural models discussed here can be found in Dooyeweerd, NC, vol. 3, parts 2 and 3. For a brief and lucid discussion of Dooyeweerd's analysis of the state, see Jonathan Chaplin.

20. Although most people will fit into some ideological community with some consistency, our confused times also make for allegiances by the same people to different and mutually exclusive ideological patterns. One person sometimes is a pacifist and a supporter of abortion on demand.

21. For extended analyses of this, see Dooyeweerd, WC and Hart, DD, CA, and ND.

22. It goes without saying that the task of the Christian church in this situation is first and foremost to live in unity out of a common allegiance to one God, thus to make visible its faith that unity is possible in the way of seeking ultimate spiritual community.

23. By *dialectic* I mean the treatment of legitimate dualities as logical contradictions, ontological divides, or moral-religious opposites. By *dualism* I mean the treatment of dualities as exhaustive and irreducible ontological divides, inviting us to see anything in reality as either being of the one kind or of the other, though the two sides of the divide are original in their opposition and cannot be viewed in terms of a deeper unity. Often the good-evil contrast is superimposed on the ontological dualism. But the superimposition of the good-evil contrast on an ontic duality also occurs in monism, when the original unity of things is viewed as giving rise to a basic split.

24. See Buytendijk.

25. Unfortunately this distinction, coupled with the rejection of determinism by physics, leads Hempel to reject the concept of universal laws (ASE, 89). He does not appreciate that, even if physics shows how processes cannot be causally determined, they may still be determined by laws. Confusion on this point leads Hempel to try and retain the possibility of some form of causal determinism. He appeals to the vague notion of the "state of the total system . . ." (ASE, 351). See also Armstrong, USR2, 153ff.

26. Subjectivity$_1$ and individuality, precisely because they are the one pole in the correlation of nomic condition and individual subjectivity$_1$, escape our conceptual grasp. It is structures and conditions we grasp conceptually. Individual subjectivity$_1$ we can at best give a name. But the name defies definition. However, if we were to describe what we experience in-

dividuality to be, we could say in the present context that individuality in subjective$_1$ existence is what we ascribe to every agent who, given the room there is to act and the variety of responses that are possible in any given situation, is the subjective$_1$ locus for making the actual response which was in fact given. Nomic conditions determine the response, provide the room. But the agent makes the response. And that makes the agent the source of individuality.

27. So necessity is a matter of nomic connections among nomic conditions. As they hold for subjects$_1$, these conditions require that responses be such and such if the response is to be in keeping with what is required. But the nomic conditions do not deterministically determine that the response will actually be according to what is required. The nomic conditions do determine and necessarily determine the nature of the response. But they do not bring about the response. Otherwise necessity would cancel out freedom, responsibility, subjectivity$_1$, and individuality. As it is, necessity is the context for freedom.

28. For a broader discussion of the differences between physical, organic, and cultural causal relations, see Polanyi, LIS and Stafleu, TA.

29. Armstrong is probably not a determinist, even though he links up causality with nomic necessity and therefore, in his view, with universal properties. In his view properties are causal agents. And properties are determinate universals. But though he, in my view, thus confuses nomic necessity and determination with causality, his view that there is more to reality than properties probably saves him from a purely mechanically determined universe. In fact, he even has theoretical room for divine exceptions to causal connections. (See USR1, 24 and USR2, 149 and 156.)

30. See Stafleu, TA.

31. Thus, in my model of reality, determination and causality are different realities. Determining is what nomic conditions do, while causing is what subjective$_1$ existents do, though both in correlation, of course.

32. See P.A. Schouls, MC, 65, note 68. The difficulty inherent in the problem I raise here is discussed by Schouls in terms of a number of pertinent and far-ranging questions.

33. On the level of realms of functors, the scale or range of freedom and determination is also clearly visible. Physical systems act and react irreversibly as a consequence of mechanical forces. Very little is indeterminate. Organisms are self-restorative and capable of genetic adaptation and variation. Animals are self-moving, can change location for self-maintenance, can flee and defend. Humans have a whole range of increases in freedom available. They can think about consequences of actions before enacting them. They can make choices and set priorities. They can decide to structure the laws that will determine their actions in keeping with the situation they are in. Humans have an ever more elastic relationship of subjectivity$_1$ towards nomic conditions.

34. Typically, the determinants of most of human life are given only in prin- ciple. Let's use an example. We are called to be just. It is ontically necessary for humans to be just if they want to be successfully human. Happy humanity is determined to be humanity that is just in its interrela- tions. But what it is to be just we seem to know only by intuition, via tradition, and through experience. The more concrete demands of justice are left up to us to conceive, encode, and enforce. The same holds for our social, economic, moral, and cultic-religious life.

35. He does discuss this in the context of his debate with Dray about laws in history. (See, e.g., ASE, 231ff.)

36. See Toulmin, PS, 79.

37. As Wolterstorff notes, universal connections have "normative . . . force" (UN, 245). All science is in that sense normative, since science studies nomic connections, relations among universals. The crucial question here concerns what the difference might be, if any, between "natural" nor- mativity and human normativity. Considering what has already been said about freedom and necessity as well as about nature and culture, it will be easy to see that a simple fact-value dualism is too easy for me.

38. See CR, 16.

39. See Hempel, ASE, 233.

40. In the sense of *objective* as discussed in chapter 5.

41. The fact that an ethical assertion cannot be analytically objective does not necessarily imply, however, that it cannot be ethically objective, i.e., ob- jective to our ethical experience.

42. It is precisely the necessary character, we might even say the determining character, of also the human relations of order (moral, religious, economic, social, jural, etc.) that makes a decision to ignore them or to replace them, or to deform them, necessarily destructive of reality. It is literally impossible (over time) to have human life that is unjust, immoral, etc.

43. This should not be dialectically read to mean: order is subject$_1$ to the sub- jective$_1$ will of humans. Rather, it means that order *requires* the coopera- tion of human subjectivity$_1$ in willing subjection$_1$.

44. Hermeneutical disciplines inquire into the individual meaning of subjec- tive$_1$ events. They interpret. Scientific disciplines inquire into the necessary relations evident in subjective$_1$ events. They explain.

45. Buytendijk's discussion of human physiology is a classic in this field.

46. Sometimes one may even get the impression that simply to say about oneself that one is a dualist is to court rejection in the scholarly marketplace. Armstrong (USR2, 58), Quinton (88-105 and 314-50), Rorty (PM, 17-127), Laszlo (SP, 143-63), Polanyi (throughout), Buytendijk (56-77), Jaki (BMC throughout), and many others all clearly reject at least all crude forms of mind-body dualism. But not all of them for that reason

accept a brain-mind identity theory or a crude materialism. Rejection of materialism or brain-mind identity no longer simply implies dualism, while rejection of dualism no longer simply implies physicalism. See Kripke (NN, 155). We are apparently on the verge of a general acceptance of more nuanced and subtle theories than crude dualism or crude monism. In my usage, *dualism* will never be used to name the fact of legitimate duality.

47. Most of volume 1 of Dooyeweerd (NC) is devoted to a discussion of this.

48. See Kripke, NN, 155.

49. See Quinton, 104, Rorty, PM, 38, and Wilfred Cantwell Smith, especially the concluding chapters of both books.

50. See Plantinga, BIG, 27.

51. A more extensive discussion of this problem can be found in Plantinga, GN, Clouser, RL, and Hart, DC.

52. See 4.4.1 and also my RC. The foundations of rational justification, if there are such foundations and if there is such justification, would in any case not themselves be rationally justifiable, lest rational justification turns out to be self-justification, a form of justification which seldom inspires trust. About the relation between rational belief and faith see W. Cantwell Smith's important *Faith and Belief*.

53. This is not the place to explain in detail my view that our rationality is essentially our ability to grasp order, in terms of structure, conceptually. In that way our rational view of the empirical universe is our conceptual view of the empirical universe from the vantage point of its order. So if rationality sees things as ordered, then what is beyond the grasp of rationality is: things as subjective$_1$ and individual, principles of order as themselves not subject$_1$ to order, and the origin of order as not subject$_1$ to order. At the same time, all of these can be *known*, since knowing is not limited to rationality, even though in all knowing the factor of rationality is always present. So even when these three cannot as such be grasped *in* a concept, the knowledge of them is not *without* concepts.

54. This does not imply that people thinking about God can dispense with logicality. It only implies that conclusions arrived at on the basis of abstract and formal reasoning alone are likely to miss the mark. God cannot be *defined*, cannot be grasped *within* a concept.

55. I am here following the tradition of Calvinism on this point. Besides John Calvin himself, that tradition is followed by theologians such as Karl Barth, Herman Bavinck, Gerrit Berkouwer, and Hendrikus Berkhof. (See Hart, van der Hoeven, and Wolterstorff.) In biblical teaching God never *must* anything.

56. The notion of omnipotence, except in the analogical language of faith, is a self-contradictory notion if viewed from a formal, purely logical point of view. Omnipotence would have to include the potency to accept limits on

one's omnipotence, one could say. But the whole point of such words as omnipotence is that they are "second order" words. They represent understandings that do not apply to themselves. Some philosophers have held that if God is to be omnipotent it would be necessary to at least accept logical limits for what God can or cannot do. Omnipotence would mean: not bound by nonlogical limits. But this notion is itself logically contradictory. If omnipotence is being without limit, then being logically limited is being limited and thus not being without limit. See Plantinga, GOM, 118. The way I see it, the notion omnipotence, if taken in a strictly formal logical sense, will lead to absurdities no matter how we view it, as soon as we take it to its logical consequences. If omnipotence means logically limited it cannot mean omnipotence. If omnipotence means absolutely without limit one would have to accept contradictory notions, which is also logically unacceptable. For me this implies that the notion of omnipotence cannot be taken to have formal conceptual meaning, but only confessional-conceptual meaning. Formal conclusions made in abstraction do not apply.

57. To logical creatures such as ourselves, it is possible to comprehend what is itself logical and it is also possible to see what it is for something to be illogical. But it is not possible to understand what might be meant by something to which the categories of logical comprehension do not normally apply. For there we not only cannot comprehend, but we can also not speak of it in terms of incomprehensibility. For what is incomprehensible somehow is still measured by rules of comprehension and then found wanting. But where such rules do not apply we get the sort of situation in which it is meaningless to, e.g., say of the number twenty-three that it does or does not have color. Our experience of God is first and foremost an experience of faith. And faith, though not irrational does transcend rationality. It is of the order of faith that it experiences what transcends experience. And this can itself only be understood in faith.

58. The logical mind would insist that we at least need to know whether it is at any time *true* that God is a person. And my response would be: if by truth we mean something conceptual or semantic in the line of correspondence theory, then it just is not true that God is a person. But if we take truth in the way of coherence, perspective, dependability, then in some contexts it is true that God is person. (Though it needs to be said immediately that our modern concept of a person is not by and large what Christian dogma intended to say with "person" before the nineteenth century. Consequently, there is never any appeal possible to ancient tradition in the church on this point.)

59. Of course, from the point of view of an *ultimate* commitment to rationality this would be very clear. If rationality is the ultimate reference point for all our experience, then laws of logic would have to apply without limit to everything. However, such a commitment is by no means obviously compatible with biblical revelation. And on the basis of argument

alone it would not be wise to accept the ultimacy of argument. In fact, such acceptance is possible only on the basis of an ultimate commitment to the ultimacy of argument; itself not being justifiable by argument. And I can see no clear reason why such commitment is more recommendable than the apparent inconsistencies with which a Christian *may* be confronted *from* that point of view if he or she is not committed *to* that point of view. It is, in that case, an open question whether these inconsistencies are real.

60. The supreme revelation is also the supreme paradox: God became human. Yet all the while humanity was created as God's image. The mystery of knowing God is the mystery of total submission, a mystery which can be known only in that submission. The fear to let go of the ultimacy of logical categories is Western, born of the worship of rationality. The dominance of this tradition is what has led to seeing faith as belief and belief as the acceptance of propositions, to see Christianity as a system of doctrine, and to see Christian truth as dogma.

61. *Knowing* is used here in the sense of note 53 above. Knowing "passes understanding," though it is not without understanding.

62. For those who require a more sustained argument on the matters of faith, belief, knowledge, and truth, I refer to W. Cantwell Smith's *Faith and Belief* as the most outstanding contemporary study of that problem in a theological context, but highly relevant for philosophy.

Notes to Appendix

1. The exposition of beliefs which follows is a clarification of Christian theistic beliefs. I simply assume the validity of being a Christian as well as being a Christian of the sort I am, a neo-evangelical (see Robert Booth Fowler and George Marsden) in the Calvinian tradition. I understand the characterization neo-evangelical to include the following features: (a) submission to the authority of Scripture without being an inerrancy fundamentalist; (b) acceptance of the importance of confessions, doctrines, and theology without accepting that Christian faith is intellectual assent to propositions or that it is a belief system (see Hendrikus Berkhof, Hans Küng, and Wilfred Cantwell Smith); (c) stressing the importance of living the Christian life in the biblical way of seeing religion as a way of life and therefore concerned with all dimensions of being human, indeed all dimensions of being in our world; (d) strong loyalty to the ecumenical spirit of contemporary Christianity, in submission to the guidance of the Holy Spirit. The wide spectrum of contemporary orientation in which (c) and (d) can be concretized may lead some to identify some of my views in this part as leftist, liberal, or progressive. I accept this and can identify with it in terms of contemporary labels. But in view of (a) and (b) I reject the labels. Those who do not share my perspective may not wish to read this part of the book, since it assumes a sympathetic openness to my views in the manner in which I expose them. It should also be recognized that I in no way pretend, even to myself, that the remarks which follow can lay claim to qualities of scholarship. At best I hope they articulate well what in fact my religious beliefs are on those issues of which I know that they have profoundly influenced my writing of the preceding chapters.

2. It is an experience similar to hanging a large poster or banner. While one person climbs a ladder to fasten a corner, another is needed to hold up the rest. It is too large for one person to concentrate merely on one section while neglecting the rest. The poster might become damaged or soiled. So it is necessary to get help when one person concentrates on one aspect of it. Only when the poster is hanging can both people step back and survey the whole. Similarly, the ontology I have been presenting can only be appreciated from a distance, and then only if we are sure it is securely

fastened. Now that I have hung the poster, I can step back and try to show *how* it is secured, i.e., show the help I had while hanging it.

3. See Alston, XL.

4. On the relation of commitment to theory, see Wolterstorff, RwR and Hart, RC.

5. Both Wolterstorff (UN, 299-300) and Armstrong (USR1, 126) have formulated very brief, consistent, and apparently complete worldview hypotheses. But they differ considerably. Obviously the theism of Wolterstorff and the atheism of Armstrong have had a great deal to do with that difference, since their work on universals (as a result of which they have formulated these hypotheses) by itself, given their mutual sympathies, will not suffice to explain the differences. Yet neither author explores the connection between the more basic assumptions of his theism and atheism and his stated worldview hypothesis.

6. See Wolterstorff (RwR, chapter 4), Chisholm, and Kolakowski.

7. See Alston, XK and Polanyi, PK, 59-62.

8. In terms of the viewpoint developed in this text, it is important to discover whether these beliefs are primarily pistic in their functional nature (though referring us retrocipatorily back to analytic functioning) or whether they are primarily conceptual in nature (though referring us anticipatingly to pistic functioning). See D.W. Hamlyn, 78-111 and Hart, RC.

9. Beliefs always have a component of facticity (*something* is conceived to be *the case*) and a component of assent, of acceptance. In the beliefs I here discuss the stress is on assent and not on comprehension.

10. This sort of devotion is found in Latin American worship of national security, South African dedication to racial purity, and North American allegiance to democracy and free enterprise.

11. This poses difficult problems for the Christian faith, in which a diversity of historical and contemporary positions have traditionally been viewed as the truth. But Christians who think this about their own positions can do so only from within these positions. And if one places oneself in the positions of Christians from other traditions and one attempts to view their loyalty to the Bible from within their tradition, they also appear to be very biblical. If one's view of *the* truth is that it can be articulated in a statement which is true and which implies that deviating statements are false, then one has a rationalistic view of truth. Yet we must articulate the truth and we can only be in a tradition when doing so. And from within our tradition our own articulation appears to be true.

Are we not then to subscribe to supraarbitrary, intersubjective criteria for articulating truth? Yes, I believe we must. But what are they? Not our traditions, for they are accepted as true according to or in response to such criteria. Traditions are not norms or criteria for judgment themselves, but our valued responses to norms. Within the Christian community this must perhaps even be admitted about centuries-old and widely accepted confessional statements, such as that of Nicea; though perhaps that may not do justice to what the Church believes about God's Spirit. At any rate, what are the criteria? Are they criteria for orthodoxy or for orthopraxis? If for both, does one have priority? Are they separable? Is the Bible the only ultimate norm? Is it right to say that the historic tradition of the communion of saints is not decisive and authoritative? What does this imply for the tradition which holds this? What does it imply for 2000 years of Roman Catholic tradition over against 450 years of Reformation tradition?

To recognize truth in other Christians, perhaps one must be persuaded in one's own heart that such others, whose position deviates from our own, have arrived at that position and are holding it in the sincere conviction that it is *according to the Scriptures*. Nothing else can be asked of any Christian position except that it be held as being truly according to the Scriptures. And if there truly be a communion of saints in the Spirit of all truth, then that Spirit will reveal to all of us in our hearts, according to the Scriptures, that the others are in fact holding their position according to the Scriptures. So holding one's position in truth is not just a matter of one's own sincere conviction, but also a matter of the supraarbitrary role of the Scriptures within the Christian community.

This does not make matters any easier. Every concrete position one takes, no matter what, will have consequences in this world that are biblically questionable, seriously so, from other biblical points of view. What counts for all Christians is this: Did we arrive at our position in and from faith? (See *Romans* 14.) Is that faith observable to the other faithful? One can ask no more. Nevertheless, many positions which must thus be acknowledged as being truly those of believers according to the Scriptures are deeply incompatible. However, no one can make a genuine contribution to a community except from within a tradition and with integrity from within that tradition. All that can be asked is that positions be relativized as traditions, that people make their contributions both loyal to themselves and open to others, in subjection to the Scriptures and the Spirit.

12. See Lakatos, 92.

13. *Ultimate* commitment to a (legitimate) *proximate* goal is destructive of such a goal. Ultimate commitment to national security leads to the devising of ways for global destruction. Ultimate commitment to economic growth leads to widespread economic stagnation.

14. See Polanyi, PK, 249-324.

15. See S. Körner, CF, for a brief analysis of the structure of categorial frameworks.

16. I believe that all philosophers, but among philosophers certainly ontologists, must be articulate and open about their ultimate assumptions. They ought to explore them, acknowledge them, and display them; not as

part of philosophy, but as necessary and closely related prolegomena. Many philosophers now do admit the presence and the efficacy of these assumptions. But few let us know what they are. But see Wolterstorff, UN, 299-300 and Armstrong, USR1, 127ff. I, at any rate, experience the ties between my ultimate philosophical categories and my ultimate assumptions to be so crucial and direct, that I would lack integrity in my own eyes if I did not declare myself on this point.

17. I have in mind the *Heidelberg Catechism*. See also Plantinga, RB and W.C. Smith.

18. Consequently, when I here explore my confessions as they precede my scholarship, they cannot also be part of my scholarship. And my exploration of them in this context cannot be a scholarly exploration. Which is not to say that a form of scholarly exploration of people's confessions is not possible or legitimate.

19. The links between one's commitment to God and a specific theory of science are, of course, seldom (perhaps never) direct or simple. Intervening linkages are confessions, theologies, worldviews, philosophies, scientific field paradigms, broad theoretical contexts, etc.

20. A thoughtful statement on the role of Christian belief in our culture is found in a letter of Eric Voegelin to T.J.J. Altizer. See Ellis Sandoz, 189-91.

21. What has been said in the transition at the end of chapter 7 about the impossibility of univocal speech and the applicability of concepts and propositions to the matters here raised remains my conviction here too. See again note 11 above.

22. To my mind the text here is inelegant and jarring. The term *God* just occurs too many times. Natural usage of pronouns is absent. But I find this unavoidable in the present context. Originally I had written *he, himself, his*, and similar terms. But now I find this usage too obviously sexist. And I am persuaded that overt efforts to eradicate sexist language are in order. I am equally persuaded that no alternate usage has become generally acceptable and that no alternate usage sounds elegant. So I purposely chose inelegance over sexist language. I apologize for the lack of elegance, but not for the choice.

23. As a word, *fixed* can mean static, but it does not need to mean static. I have used *steadfast* to avoid this problem.

24. In my view faith is one form of knowledge, while understanding is another. Belief is a form of faith.

25. "I am the Alpha and the Omega, the Beginning and the End" (*Revelation* 21:6).

26. If we tried, we would then not conclude that these would be God's order and thus we would not correctly understand them. Also, if we tried, we would still be getting at them from some other ultimate perspective.

27. This language is, of course, confessional. From a logical point of view such language might seem unnecessarily prejudicial; especially so if the logical point of view stems from a tradition of commitment to logicality. But the priority of beliefs of commitment over a logic of commitment should be kept in mind here. (See my RC.) Just as an analysis of any phenomenon (the state, a cell, numerical relations) does not logically prescribe what these realities must be like, so logic cannot prescribe what the realities of confessional beliefs must be like. Confessionally I arrive at the belief that a theory of God is impossible. And only in the context of such a belief do I analyze its nature.

28. "He fixed their bounds which cannot be passed" (*Psalm* 148:6).

29. See *Genesis* 1; *Leviticus* 26; *Deuteronomy* 6:4-9; 10:12 to 11:1; *Job* 38-41; *Psalm* 2, 8, 33, 47, 104, 115, 147, and 148; *Proverbs* 8:22-31; and *Isaiah* 40:12-26. Someone might initiate a philosophical theory with a central belief in the love of God. Because philosophy is theory and theory works with order, law, necessity, etc., sovereignty seems a more suitable starting point. But there is no a priori reason why love could not also be used. It is indeed possible that another core belief might produce a theory that displayed features very different from the one developed here.

30. See *Genesis* 1, *Proverbs* 8 and 9, and *John* 1. When the Bible speaks of "all things" as made by God, the *all* is a confessional ultimate. Nothing is to be excluded. *John* 1:3 is to be taken literally in this respect.

31. See *Genesis* 1:1-3 (to which reference is made in *John* 1:1-14 and in *Proverbs* 8:22-31); *Exodus* 31:1-5; and 35:30 to 36:1; *Numbers* 11:24-30; *Deuteronomy* 8:3; *Psalm* 19, 119, 147, and 148; *Joel* 2:27-29; *Amos* 8:11; *John* 1:33; 3:34; 4:24; 5:19 and 26-30; 14:6, 16-17, and 26; 15:10 and 26; 16:13-15; *II Corinthians* 3:17 and 18; *Colossians* 1:1-15; *Hebrews* 1:1 to 2:9; and *Revelation* 19:10. These verses are fundamental, so they are to be believed for their own witness and not on the basis of certain other, prior, established material. An understanding of creation in the Christian religion is important, especially in the light of future-oriented theologies such as the theology of W. Pannenberg. Creation in the Bible signifies that the world has a definite origin from which it moves toward the future. This origin has established a foundation for the world. Therefore order is not something toward which we slowly evolve but is in principle given from the beginning. However, evil has produced chaos. The world now in its movement toward redemption (*Romans* 8:22ff.) is again moving along to its *original* destiny from its original order (*John* 1:1-5 together with 14-17).

32. See *Proverbs* 8 and 9; *John* 1; *I John* 1; and *Hebrews* 1 and 2. Although I subscribe to trinitarian teachings (I do believe in God the Father, the Son, and the Holy Spirit), I do not believe that it is at all possible, even in the language of faith, to say in creedal propositions how we are to *conceive* of the *nature* of this relation. I do not believe the Bible tells us this, nor does it ever intend to do so. In my own thought the most felicitous formulation

appears to be that God is the Creator and Sustainer of the universe. This God is called Father in the Bible (though other things as well). It is this God whose Word was incarnate in the human being Jesus of Nazareth. He was truly human and therefore called Son of Humanity. He was truly human in full obedience to God and therefore called Son of God, being in the flesh the very will of God. The Holy Spirit is the Spirit of God and therefore also the Spirit of God's Word and therefore also the Spirit of Jesus. If the Church is the Body of Christ, then that Spirit is also the Spirit of the Church. And if we have our being as members of the Church, then that Spirit is also our Spirit. See *I Corinthians* 2:11-13; *I Peter* 4:6; and *II Peter* 1:4. See also *Matthew* 5:9; *Romans* 8:23; and *Galatians* 4:6-7.)

33. In creation (*Genesis* 1) and re-creation (*Acts* 2).

34. See *II Corinthians* 3:17 and *Revelation* 19:10.

35. See *Exodus* 35:30 to 36:1.

36. There are many uses of *word* and *Word* in the Bible. In all cases we have the core meaning of authoritative divine address to creation (a single person, a nation, the whole creation) whenever the word or Word is the word or Word of God. Whoever or whatever is addressed by God stands as ordered, i.e., is called to obedience. Being created by the Word is having one's being in being obedient to God's will. So confessionally speaking or ultimately speaking, all necessity, all order in the universe, is there as a consequence of creation's being subjected$_1$ to the Word of God. All that must be has its ground in God's declared will for creation. It is sometimes said, in a sense of what I take to be misplaced piety, that one must not denature the will of God to the laws of mathematics or physics. This problem is seen as especially acute when we see that Christ is the Word incarnate. However, if we say that God's Word orders creation, we understand that laws of mathematics and physics are founded in the Creator's will. That is why they are laws, necessities. God willed it so. Apart from that confession we cannot escape realism, i.e., the doctrine that God, too, is subject$_1$ to order. For then order is there apart from God. And the incarnation does then not mean that Christ is the realization of mathematical laws, but that in the complete submission of Christ to all God's will, all the laws of the universe are working towards redemption, as they originally were intended to be working towards all that was good. This does not lead to the conclusion that laws of logic and the second person of the Trinity are identical. But see Plantinga, GN, 140-46.

37. The Word is torah, i.e., directive. A word of the Lord points us in the direction of goodness. (See *Romans* 14:17.)

38. See *John* 4:24.

39. Again, see *Romans* 14:17.

40. In this way the mystery of relationship is the mystery of the coherence of reality in Christ (*Colossians* 1:15-20), the communion of creation through humanity in Christ with God.

41. See the section on the Bible, 8.1.5.

42. In *Proverbs* 8 wisdom may be both Word and Spirit. See also *John* 1:29-34. The treatment of the themes of this section (Word, Spirit, Jesus, creation) by Hendrikus Berkhof and Hans Küng's treatment of the Spirit strike me as particularly helpful.

43. See, e.g., *Hebrews* 1:1-6.

44. See *Genesis* 1 and 2 and 5-9, and *Jeremiah* 31:31-37.

45. See *Genesis* 5-9.

46. The New Testament term *Kingdom of God* or *Kingdom of Heaven* can fairly be said to be equivalent to the Old Testament term *covenant*. The latter, too, was originally the sovereign arrangement between a ruler and a people, whereby the ruler asked for submission in return for protection.

47. This does not entail that each creature will in fact be what it must of necessity be. This is the mystery of evil, of rebellion. Now, in all of creation, we find things are not what they must be. If things persist in time to deviate from their calling they disintegrate.

48. See *Deuteronomy* 6:5, *Isaiah* 28:27-29, and *Matthew* 22:37-40; also *I John* 2:4-11, 3:11-24, and 4:7 to 5:5.

49. See *Philippians* 2:5-11.

50. See *Isaiah* 52:13 to 53:12.

51. See *I Corinthians* 2:9-16.

52. See 8.1.6 and 8.2.3.

53. *Meaning* is used here as defined in chapter 4 (see 4.2.2).

54. See *Isaiah* 28:23-29. See also the church's doctrines of providence and of creation.

55. See *Acts* 17:22-31 and *I Corinthians* 15:28.

56. To speak of creation's being or essence as meaning is to express here that the essential reality of creation lies in its response to an order which needs to be spiritually met in its intent. It is for this reason as well that the developing direction of empirical existence has its foundation in being guided by human faith. Without human faith the world would not be able to be in touch with its destiny. And that destiny is included in the essential reality of what things are.

57. These senses of contingency include those that may be found in the more nihilistic expressions of existentialism.

58. See *Genesis* 1.

59. See *Genesis* 6, 8:20-22; *Isaiah* 57:16-19; and *Hosea* 11:9. God is determined to overcome evil. See also *Psalm* 33.

60. The Word Incarnate in Jesus Christ is subject to the will of God. There are many references to this in *John* (e.g., 5:19-31). But the Word Incarnate is also truth and life (*John* 14:6) and there is no sin in him (*I John* 3:5 and *II Corinthians* 5:21).

61. Only what is possible can relate to what is actual in a way that allows us to say of something that it could have been different. What we mean is that the possibility did not need to become actual as it did. But what is itself actual, of course, could only be what it is. It could not be or have been different. Whatever would be different would not be this, for which reason this could never be different. At the same time, all that is possible is necessarily possible only in the ways of the limits of possibility. It is possible to be human in many different ways. But these ways do not include crossing the Atlantic in three big steps.

62. Miracle is similar to mystery, in that it transcends our ability to explain it. In that sense individuality and subjectivity$_1$ are both miraculous and mysterious. This fact accounts for our inability to have a general concept of individuality and subjectivity$_1$. We can at best name them.

63. See note 11 above. The verdict reached by the Jerusalem synod described in *Acts* 15 would indicate that the early church was unusually flexible about tradition and that it certainly did not look upon Scripture as a timeless and infallible set of propositions, to be intellectually assented to as propositional truth. The Jewish church and the Greek church were each to go their own way, with few restrictions put on the Greek church. (Only two restrictions, one of which Paul strongly relativized in *Romans* 14.) But subsequent evidence would suggest that the Greek church soon hardened into that attitude from which it successfully freed itself in relation to legalistic Jewish Christians.

64. Typical of this attitude is the opening section in Lakatos, entitled "Science: Reason or Religion?" (91).

65. All ultimate beliefs are by definition religious beliefs. But to acknowledge that science is linked to such beliefs and to openly call them religious is still not very acceptable. Quoting, e.g., the writings of Stanley Jaki or Michael Polanyi is still something not easily done by "self-respecting" scholars.

66. All forms of rationalism have the unfortunate consequence that they declare all forms of faith to be irrational and unjustified unless rationally justified. This particular doctrine makes it impossible for a rationalist to see rationalism as a faith and as a commitment. Commitment to reason as ultimate excludes commitment from reason.

67. The Word is declared, revealed, proclaimed, made known, etc. Many terms can be used to refer to how the Word is appropriated by believers and addressed by God. The key notion is that it is clearly knowable and visible for believers and hidden for unbelievers. It takes faith to know it and see it. In faith it is evident. But nothing private is intended, nor anything mystical. As one finds the law of gravity from observing falling objects, so one knows the order of things from observing things in subjection$_1$ to that order. The subjection$_1$ is what is at stake here.

68. For the meaning of *objective* see 5.4.2. For a discussion of the Bible in

relation to truth and human subjectivity$_{1,2}$ see Baarda, *God with Us: On the Nature of the Authority of Scripture*, and the analyses of this report by the Synod of Delft of 1979 of the Reformed Churches in the Netherlands (GKN) in *RES Theological Forum* (see Weijland). See also the discussion of truth in the same *Forum*. The views of biblical authority here set forth are in line with the views expressed in *God with Us* and those on truth in line with the views expressed by P. Holtrop in the *Forum*.

69. See Olthuis, CH.

70. In *John* 5:39-47 Jesus teaches that the Scriptures, according to their own testimony, refer to the Word.

71. This characteristic of the Bible also guarantees the individual believer a protection from a tyrannical, traditionalist imposition of the church. See also *II Peter* 3:15, 16.

72. In *John* 5:39 Jesus rebukes people for believing in the Bible as itself a source of life. For a distinction between Word and Scripture see also *Jeremiah* 7:22-23 and *John* 10:35.

73. The entry into subjectivity$_1$ of the Word in the Scriptures requires that only in a subjective$_1$ relation to them does the Word become known in truth. This in turn involves our ability to become intersubjective$_1$ with the times and authors of the Bible. As a consequence, certain segments of Scripture may speak anew, freshly, differently, or for the first time in relation to the sort of subjectivity$_1$ characteristic of the reader and the times.

74. See *John* 5:19-31.

75. Here I do not mean to deny the teaching of the gospel that the truth will be brought to mind in the Church by the Spirit. (See *John* 14:15-17, 26; 15:26.)

76. See again *John* 5:39ff.

77. See note 11 above.

78. The Bible as book of the covenant enters, must enter, fully into the mystery of relationship.

79. Thus, when in Christ we can believe the Scriptures to open us to the Word, we can also re-enter into a reading of creation (created according to the Word, by the Word) that will uncover for us (reveal!) the directives intended by God to lead us to a life of shalom and to an existence of creation that is good. When in the Spirit of Christ we are led to understand the Word as revealed in creation and we can by the Spirit believe what we see to be according to the Scriptures, then we can have courage to follow the directives (torah) so discovered. I positively appreciate the human ability to be in touch with truth and justice even in our age, contrary to Adorno (in ND).

80. See *I Corinthians* 2 and *II Corinthians* 3.

81. The Bible's position in creation is extremely complex from the point of view of analysis, though simple from the point of view of faith. From the

point of view of analysis we have to remember its role as law for the believing subject₁ and as objective subject₁ for the believing subject₂. This is further complicated by the fact that the pistic mode of functioning plays such a peculiar role in creation.

82. See *I Corinthians* 7.

83. See the discussion with Holtrop in *RES Theological Forum*.

84. The outstanding example, of course, is Michael Polanyi's *Personal Knowledge*. The drive for radical departures from tradition, however, is present in the publications of others as well. See note 86 below.

85. See the relevant articles in G. Kittel's *Theological Dictionary of the New Testament*.

86. See Gadamer, E.J. Gibson, J.J. Gibson, Habermas, Hamlyn, Maslow, Piaget, Radnitzky, Rorty, and Smith.

87. See Kittel on *truth*. The Johannine literature in the New Testament and *Hosea* in the Old Testament are particularly significant.

88. By the rationality of knowledge I mean the human ability to grasp conceptually what is evident of the order of reality via the structures of empirical existence. All knowledge includes that element, some knowledge is legitimately characterized by that element (science). All knowledge, including science, also has many more dimensions than just the rational one.

89. See *I Corinthians* 2 and 12.

90. Body and spirit are not two entities. See Rorty, PM, 44, note.

91. See *Genesis* 2 and 6. Smith defines humans as creatures of faith or spirit.

92. All creatures are God's servants. Only the human creature bears authority in God's name. The qualification (in God's name) both deepens and limits human authority. Human authority is serving on God's behalf.

93. See *Genesis* 1.

94. See *Psalm* 115:16; *Genesis* 1:28; and *Psalm* 8.

95. People are not immortal in the Bible. But they can put on immortality. They are mortal. And the wages of sin is death. Evil has its own spiritual dynamic. It too directs. It leads to death and destruction, according to the same Word. See *Deuteronomy* 27 and 28, as an outworking of *Genesis* 2:15-17.

96. But see Laszlo (SP) and Bunge. For a study of the nature of such paradigms see Körner, CF. See also Toulmin, RC and Arthur Holmes, WV.

97. No articulated conceptual model is adequate in principle to catch what it tries to grasp. I believe this even applies to the preceding sentence. One has to be aware of this in all areas of our experience and culture. Confessional statements of churches, philosophical models, developmental models, all catch the truth for us in ways that speak to our contemporary

situation. They all help us address the problems we now wish to solve. Models that no longer address contemporary problems lose their truth character of being liberating and directive. I apply what I've just said to what I've just said. I apply it also to this entire study. See again note 11 above. At the same time we can't logicize what I've just said to mean: this is only now the case and therefore not true. Even if it is only now the case, then it still can be true as now articulated.

98. Any talk here of ground, basis, or foundation has no relation to the philosophical stance called foundationalism.

99. See Laszlo, SP, especially the Introduction and part 1.

100. A biblical view of time would be linear rather than cyclical. Modern theologians, such as W. Pannenberg, tend to be futuristic in their orientation to time; they look to the calling future as the real origin of creation.

101. See *John* 1:3.

102. See *Genesis* 1 and *Colossians* 1:15-20.

103. Contemporary scientists, weary of metaphysics in any case, do not see scientific statements as correct and unchangeable formulations of the essential order of things, but at most as approaches to that order.

104. As a result, I see problems in Wolterstorff's presentation of what he refers to as a structure of all that exists. He seems to display a different and, from my point of view, incoherent approach. He posits the kind/example structure as one that *holds* for all reality. "Hence another structure holding for all reality is the kind/example structure," says Wolterstorff (UN, 300). Here he seems to present what I have called the order-world correlation. But he treats it as an *order which holds* for both order and subjectivity$_1$. Furthermore, it also holds for God. As the supreme origin, God is drawn into order and subjectivity$_1$. Finally, the relation *between* order and subjectivity$_1$ is viewed as both a condition and a subjective$_1$ reality. In Wolterstorff's terms they are, respectively, *relation* and *relationship*. From an abstractly conceptual, formal, logical point of view this position may seem coherent. From the perspective of commitment-oriented beliefs concerning order and subjectivity$_1$, however, this logical point of view appears too autonomous. I believe it cannot do justice to what must be believed.

105. Such philosophical procedure is then rooted in a commitment to realities that remain unacknowledged though still at work.

106. See Rorty, PM, 330-42. Contrary to much current analysis of Rorty (and Kuhn, for that matter) I believe that both are justified in not wanting to be portrayed as complete relativists or subjectivists, because I think that in fact that is not what they are.

107. I refer once more to Smith's seminal work, *Faith and Belief*, which cannot be ignored by anyone who wishes to participate in the discussion of the relation between rationality and religion.

Glossary

THE TERMS GATHERED HERE are almost all used in both a novel and a technical sense in the book. Occasionally a term may be used non-technically and then have a different meaning, but that will be apparent from the context. The brief description of the terms in this part of the book is not meant to be either complete or precise. Almost all terms are discussed extensively in the text. Here they are listed as an aid to memory and as a preventive for confusion. It is not wise to use this glossary in order to become acquainted with a term for the first time. But it will be helpful to look up a term more than once after it has been properly discussed, since the unusual sense of their conceptual referents will not become familiar except through reacquaintance and usage. However, a more thorough acquaintance with some of the key terms and concepts will be gained from using the Table of Contents as a guide to places where these key matters are discussed. For this latter use, the Glossary cannot be substituted.

Act. A functional whole in which many functions are typically integrated so as to exhibit a recognized structure. "Lifting the receiver" would be one of the *functions* integrated into the *act* of "making a telephone call."

Aesthetic. See symbolic.

Analogical, analogy. The actual interrelation of functions is evident in the reference within functions of one modal kind to functions of another modal kind. Such interfunctional reference is called an analogy. Metaphors refer to analogies. They name the presence of one reality in another.

Analytic, logical, rational, conceptual. These terms will be used as synonyms. They will refer to functions of one kind or mode, viz., the human ability to understand, grasp things intellectually, know conceptually, comprehend, explain, account for things, make and classify distinctions, argue, reason, give reasons, state grounds, define, form concepts and categories, know the nature of things, and so on. They will refer not only to humans as they actually function in this capacity, but also to the rules, methods, canons, and formal procedures that must be observed. We infer, and in so doing we must observe the rules of inference. And when human beings do so function and observe the proper rules, they successfully come to understand all sorts of things in our world. These terms will also refer to our understandings (concepts, propositions, theories, systems, and so on), as well as to the capacity of things to be so understood. We understand things when we intellectually grasp what conditions hold for their existence. We can understand or explain things that way because their existence is determined by the conditions. Understanding itself is also subject to conditions. It can thus also be understood. Only the conditions for conceptual knowing or understanding are logical or analytic conditions.

Anticipation. In the actual interrelation of functions, there will be evidence of how functions of one kind or mode relate to functions of another kind or mode. Some functions support or found others, while some functions open up, develop, and qualify others. When a function of some kind typically reflects the fact that a function of another and higher modality qualifies or opens it up, that function is called an anticipation. It anticipates the higher function.

A priori. I will use this term largely in a pejorative sense, to refer to arguments about reality pursued in mostly formal logical fashion—pursued in the belief that following the rules of logic and formal inference alone is sufficient to correctly comprehend or know something and to arrive at correct conclusions. I therefore disagree with Armstrong's position that philosophical analysis is inevitably a priori. (See USR1, xv.) A priori will, consequently, be used as an adjective for knowing, reasoning, arguing, conceiving, understanding. The only possible positive use of a priori occurs in references to rules or standards as a priori, meaning that the rules hold or obtain *prior* to the realities to which they pertain. In other words, when a priori means that determination of validity requires standards which are "independent" of the "subjective" influence of what is being adjudicated, then a priori has an acceptable meaning. However, rationalistic overtones must be avoided here too, as well as the absolutism which sees the "a priori" rule as being completely independent from what it rules, rather than being a correlative of what it rules.

Aspect, dimension, element, phase. Not technical terms. Just words used to draw attention to or focus on a narrower section of some field of attention. The words may be used to refer to sides of the ordered world as well as of the world order, of functors as well as functions, and of relations.

Assumption. A concept or idea which plays a founding role in our knowing and which is usually not examined in that context in which it plays its founding role, though in other contexts it may well be examined.

Attribute, quality, property. I will never mean anything by these except what is characteristic of a concrete particular and is therefore itself concrete and particular. The red of my lips is an actual, concrete, visible, individual red. It is, as Wolterstorff would say, a *case* of redness. (See UN, 89.) I thus disagree with Armstrong on the point that all properties are universals. (See USR1, 83-86.) Universals do not fade, while the red of my sweater may. Properties as well as actions, states, assertibles, and relations are, therefore, always attributable to functors in virtue of the fact that the functor meets certain conditions. (See Wolterstorff, UN, 63-86.) The conditions for red as comprehended in a single concept have been understood as the universal redness. But the complex of universally obtaining conditions for a thing's being red are not a property. The *thing* will have the property. It will be red if it meets the conditions. And the red we see the thing having is a property. We attribute red to actual things alone. Redness is at best a name for the concept we form of what it is for a thing to be red, or a name for the complex of conditions (which holds universally) to be met for red to occur.

Bad. As the antithesis of good, *bad* indicates evil in a cosmic sense when used as a technical term. The good-bad distinction is not a characteristic of just some dimension of reality, but indicates whatever is present in the world as a result of human resistance to the order of things in their intended direction. Good-bad is not the same as moral-immoral. It is also just-unjust, frugal-wasteful, sensitive-insensitive, logical-illogical, rational-irrational, and whatever other pair of opposites can be put in that series. But whereas that series is a series of properties, functor opposites should also be included, such as human-inhuman. And relational opposites also come in for the good-bad or good-evil distinction, such as coherent-incoherent. But it is important that good and evil always have to do with disorder as well as misdirection.

Basing or **basic** direction or sequence of modal order. See founding.

Belief. Firmly held or accepted concept, proposition, definition, etc.

Biotic, organic. The name for functions of a specific mode or for that mode. Usually referred to as life or living. Biotic functions are typical of an organism and do not fully yield to physical explanations.

Body. When used technically in connection with human existence, the body is the whole human being seen from the perspective of a person's functional existence.

Categorial distinction. Distinction made in classifying kinds of categories. The distinction between high level and low level categories would be a categorial distinction. The difference between irreducible ultimates in the world would be a categorial distinction. It differs from what I refer to as the radical distinction. By radical distinction I mean a stated difference which includes reality about which we cannot successfully form conclusive concepts. Thus, the distinction world origin, world order, and ordered world is a radical distinction, which cannot be conclusively grasped in a concept.

Category, concept. When we intellectually grasp, conceptually know, understand, think of (all synonyms) the structure of something, the conditions which obtain to make that thing possible, the properties which anything of that kind must necessarily have to be that thing, then we have a concept of it. A concept intellectually grasps a definition, where what defines a thing is the conditions that delimit the thing's possibility. When we refer to a class of things as the class of things falling under a certain concept, we may refer to that as a category. When concepts are used to sort things we refer to them as categories.

Cause. A concrete and actual circumstance, state, event, or occurrence such that (1) another event, circumstance, state, or occurrence came about as its consequence, and (2) the consequence can be accounted for (explained or predicted) because it represents a necessary sequence according to a universal law, rule, or condition. Conditions do not cause. They condition or determine, i.e., they delimit possibility and call for necessity. Events as such also do not cause. They may occur serially and in touch with one another, yet not be causally related. Causes are the effectual presence of conditions in contiguous events.

Certitudinal. See pistic.

Circumstance. Refers to specific, actual, concrete situations and events. As a technical term it replaces *conditions* when that term is used to indicate prevailing actualities such as: it is snowing here and now. I then refer to present circumstances rather than present conditions. Circumstances are subjective₁ realities.

Class, set. The complete collection of all entities sharing at least one attribute. Though to be a class the entities in question must all meet at least one condition, they can be quite arbitrarily designated and need not represent a selection mechanism other than human choice. The class of all moving objects that are gray and have tails could include mice, elephants, and airplanes. There is no reason to think that this is a useful class or that the three sorts of objects mentioned have anything else in common just because they have these three features in common. Only subjective existents can be members of classes.

Cognition. See knowledge.

Coherence. We speak of a complexity or multiplicity as coherent when the elements of that complexity relate properly, i.e., when they belong to that complexity in continuity and interrelate in that complexity as the result of a rule that obtains. The interrelating complexity is one we know as fitting.

Commitment. An action, function, or attitude characterized by its certitudinal or pistical nature. In commitment we give ourselves to, accept, or surrender to whatever it is we are committed to. We will see through whatever we are committed to. It is a reliant, dedicated, firm relationship to something which, while we are so committed, we do not question.

Community. Evidence in the existence of functors that they are of the same kind, as a result of which they sustain special relationships to each other. Human society is a community, but so is a herd of horses, a stand of pines, and a galaxy.

Community specialization. In the human community, at least, there is much differentiation of functions and roles. As a result there arise special kinds of relationships, such as families, schools, businesses, and clubs. These are community specializations.

Concept. See category.

Conceptual. See analytic.

Condition, law, norm, rule, nomic reality, limit, determination, standard. Every term here refers to the same concept, viz., that of a reality determining what things essentially are, a reality setting the limits of what it is proper for something to be, making possible whatever is possible, making necessary whatever is necessary. That this reality, whatever it is, can be understood with the help of our concepts of law, rule, determination, and the like is a postulate which will be acceptable or rejectable according to whether it allows us to develop a satisfactory account of what we wish to account for. That there is such a reality I will hold to be an experienced given. Such conditionality I will hold to be an irreducible correlate of our empirical world. By this I mean that no condition is conditioned or that no condition is a subjective existent; that no subjective existent is a condition or that no subjective existent is without conditions. The analogy here is this. There is no traffic in a modern city that is exempt from the rules, no traffic that itself sets the rules, and no traffic rules that are subject to traffic rules. The observation that traffic rules may obey other rules is not to the point, for the support this observation presumably gives to the idea that conditions may have conditions is in fact absent. That idea flows from the virtually contentless argument that, all things being subject to conditions, and conditions being something, conditions must then also be subject to conditions. *Thing* and *something* here are virtually contentless; so is the argument formed with these words. Upon analysis, given the meaning of condition and subjective existence here adopted, the conclusion simply does not follow. Conditions cannot be said to exist, be true, or be necessary. They are only determinative for and of what exists, they universally hold for what they determine. They also determine what is true and necessary, without themselves being true or necessary, since what is true or necessary is determined. The term I will mostly use to indicate what I am setting forth here is *nomic condition*. I will seldom use condition-1 or condition-2. (See chapter 2, 2.1.) Conditions as providing boundaries of possibility I will call *limits*. *Law* will be used to indicate relations between conditions that provide for necessary connections in our world. (See Armstrong, USR2, 148ff.)

Configuration. A constant complexity of conjoint nomic conditions determining that certain properties and relations are necessarily always found together.

Constitutive or **primary** structure, order, sequence of functions or modes. The retrocipatory elements in a mode are the constitutive elements of it, i.e., they are those elements of functions without which functioning of that kind would be impossible. So in a mode the retrocipatory analogies or the analogies which refer to more basic or founding functions are primary or constitutive. It is the essential nature of a functional mode.

Contingent. Refers to the unique and unpredictable side of concrete reality in its complexity of subjective$_1$ relations. It has a positive meaning. Never refers to happenstance irrationality, brute facticity, or other similar ideas.

Core, original, nuclear nature or order of a mode. That principle of order which essentially determines functions of a certain mode as the irreducible kind they are, is the core nature or nuclear nature of that mode. All functions of that kind have an original reality in that mode, which means that a particular core nature determines what their reality is like. Since concretely all functions also refer to other modes, they have analogical reality besides their original reality.

Determination. See condition.

Developing or developmental direction of modal order. See qualifying.

Differentiation. The historical process whereby the actions of functors eventually acquire a degree of complication that calls for specialization, which results in the development of new structural kinds.

Dimension. See aspect.

Direction. When used technically this term indicates most fundamentally the movement of the universe towards a destiny. Order directs things to such a destiny, or is the path along which things move in the direction of their destiny. In this sense *direction* is a "spiritual" term which indicates the spiritual movement of empirical reality.

Direction or **sequence** of modal order. If we conceive of the modes of functioning as constituting a series in which the relative place of each mode is fixed, then we can go through the series from a to z or from z to a. This is the direction or sequence of modal order. Going from the most basic to the highest is the founding direction. Going from the highest to the lowest is the qualifying or developing direction. *Direction* is used technically here.

Diversity. Correlate of unity. Not the same as division. Indicates the complexity of aspects, elements, or phases found within a unified field of existence.

Division. The uncalled for splitting of what is intended to be a unity.

Dualism. An unwarranted theory about legitimate ontic dualities usually interpreted from the viewpoint of antithetical directional divisions in reality.

Economic. Name for a mode of functioning or for functions of that mode. It is the irreducibly original reality of that sort of functioning which is characterized by the priorization of human choices and decisions in the use of and care for the world in which we live.

Element. See aspect.

Empirical. Used to indicate the experienced reality of subjective existence. The empirical world is the world as subject to order.

Enkaptic. Indicates the functioning of wholes in the context of larger wholes without becoming parts. A whole that functions within the context of another whole is enkaptically interwoven into that other whole.

Energetic. Original or core reality of that mode of functioning which qualifies all physical entities.

Entity, thing, phenomenon. When used technically its meaning is very general, viz., indicating anything whatsoever that is empirically real. What is so indicated can be both a functor or a function and it can also be a relation. But nothing that is order will be called entity or thing, neither will it be called phenomenon.

Essence, nature. That configuration which determines what properties an existent must necessarily have in order to be the thing that it is.

Ethical, moral. Name for a functional mode characterized by relations of troth and loyalty among human beings.

Event. A functional structure in which many acts are integrated so as to belong together in one event. "The fall of the government" would be an *event* into which many *acts* (such as "making a telephone call") would be integrated.

Evil. Not a merely moral category. Indicates anything in the empirical world caught up in a direction toward a destiny not intended in the order of the world and consequently resisting the order of reality.

Existence. Not a property. Not a genuine predicate either. (See Armstrong, USR2, 9ff.) Just a basic term which indicates the reality of whatever is subject to conditions. Holding or obtaining is the reality of nomic conditions. Rules obtain, while what is subject to rules (say traffic) exists. Whatever does exist has properties, is in relation, occurs in time and space, and cannot exist unless it is directly material or related to what is material. Existence is always subjective existence, i.e., it is subject to conditions. What exists is always individual and unique. But what exists also shows that the nomic conditions to which it is subject hold for it universally. The evidence for this is that individual existents display order. They have structure and pattern. There is regularity in what existentially occurs. Existence will be referred to as our world, the ordered world, the space-time world, the actual-concrete world, the empirical world, actual circumstances, events and states, and the like. That existence is subjective is evident in the consideration that, whereas nomic conditions hold universally and determine without exception whatever they determine, the existents so determined can and do deviate. Not only are they individual and unique within their limits, but they also deviate from their limits. Whatever exists simply "stands out," i.e., ex-sists, is perceptibly out there.

Experience. Our active awareness of our place in this world, cumulatively expanding in ability to be in that world successfully, by relating to what is in our world through intended submission to its conditions. It is both passive and active, including sensation, motor activity, skills, symbolic practices, conceptual cognition, and so on.

Fact. A believed state of affairs.

Field. See pattern.

Formative, technical. Original nature of those kinds of functions characterized by the occurrence of method, skill, means and ends, tools, instruments.

Founding, supporting, basing or **basic** direction or sequence of modal order. That direction in viewing the irreversible sequence in the series of irreducible functional kinds or modes which starts from the lowest, or from that mode which is not based or founded on other modes.

Function. A term intended to be a common denominator for properties, actions, states, qualities, and so on. Whenever an independently acting entity, a relatively independent unit of action such as an atom, a planet, a plant, an animal, a human being does something, has a property, or is in a state, I will refer to that as a function of that entity. Functions are what a thing can be said to have or do. However, not all I can have (my piano) is a function of mine. Functions are always the functions of something. No function can function just on its own terms. Each function is always both an individual function and one of a kind. For the significance of a function's being both unique and one of a kind, see the comments under *functor* below. A function is always the function of a functor only. They are Wolterstorff's "cases." (See UN, 133.) A *founding function* serves as the *conditio sine qua non* for the existence of a typical functional whole such as an act. A *qualifying function* is that which integrates and organizes the typical structure of a functional whole as the type it is. It defines the type. An *x/y structure* forms the relationship between the qualifying and founding functions of a typical whole (read: x over y).

Functor. An existing entity which acts or functions without itself being a function. A functor has properties, but it is never a property itself. An actual functor is always one of a kind and is unique; it is an individually functioning unit of its kind. In being of a kind, however, a functor also exhibits structural features which are evidence of its being included in a typical order which limits its existence and makes it possible. As *one* of a *kind*, a functor is an individual member of an ontic community of other members of the same kind with which it exists in community and which guarantees its typical continuity as well as its individual identity. No functor is a bare particular, since each can have its own individual properties. No functor is a bundle of properties either. And no functors are without spatial or material functions. It is the functor that does the functioning, i.e., it is the functor which has the properties, engages in the actions, and is in a state. The functor bears the functions; it is what functions. See Kripke, NN, 52 and Loux, SA, 158 and 165.

Functor specialization. Designations of functors according to the special role they may play in a specific context. Thus a person (i.e., a functor) may be referred to as a father or a sister or a nurse or a salesman when the person functions in specified ways in a specified context.

General. Often when we try to discover the nature of things through a study of those things themselves, they give inconclusive clues as to what their nature is. We may try to formulate what we have found on the strength of a statistically favorable sample. Often what we then know is known not to be universally determinative for every individual of the kind we are examining. What we know is at best generally true. I will use general to indicate evidence we have of universality that is not exhaustive or conclusive. Generality characterizes the behavior of a majority sample of members of a class. Generality characterizes our knowledge when it is statistical. Generality is applicable to actual behavioral patterns of subjective existents rather than to the scope of conditions that hold universally.

Good. The antithetical opposite of evil. When used technically, *good* will refer to all that in its subjection to order also moves in the direction intended in that order. Thus, the good-evil distinction includes all functionally specific indications of antinormative and normative behavior.

Guiding. As used in "*guiding* function" this term indicates the ubiquitous functional presence of pistical functioning in all of empirical reality. Our human functions of faith are the directional functional foundation for all of empirical reality. All x/y structures are thus guided structures, which can symbolically be indicated as $\frac{G}{x/y}$.

Hold, obtain. The relation of nomic conditions to subjective existence is one of holding or obtaining for them universally. To hold or obtain in that way is the very reality of nomic conditions. In holding, they condition what is conditioned, namely, subjective existence.

Identity. A term used to refer to the fact that functors or functions can remain the same, that there is continuity to what they are in time. It is also used to indicate that two names or concepts may refer to the same thing. The man who robbed the corner grocery store yesterday is the same as the man who abandoned a yellow station wagon on the main street today. They are identical. The fact of identity is the fact of the continuity of nomic conditions to which the existent remains subject continuously.

Individuality, uniqueness. Not a property. We call a thing unique and individual in virtue of the fact that each subjective existent, each functor, relates to its conditions in its own way, as no other. It is not just that each functor has some properties or some combinations of properties that are unique. Individuality is the irreducible reality of subjective existence. No concept of what is individual is possible. Individuality is just a primitive predicate to which no nomic condition corresponds. The functor and functions and relations are irreducible as individuals, i.e., they are not individuated complexes of properties and relations. I reject the problem of individuation. (See Loux, SA, 140ff.; Armstrong, USR2, 64; and Quinton, 12ff.) A functor, though individual, is never individual throughout, however. The individual functor also bears the evidence of its subjection to nomic conditions in its being an orderly functor.

Integration. Any process which brings about the unity of a diversity of functions into a coherent whole or totality. This matter will be discussed especially in chapter 6.

Irreducible. Individuals or particulars all have their own identity. Each entity is itself, no entity is another. But all particular existences are of kinds. Kinds, too, have their own identity. But they can be viewed as being subsumed under a higher kind. Whenever something, together with other things, can be taken as belonging to a kind, we can speak of being able to reduce things to that kind. No apples are oranges. These are (mutually) irreducible. But oranges and apples are fruits. They can be taken as fruits and we have then reduced a variety of things, viz., fruits, to just one kind. The variety fathers, sisters, and aunts and the variety apples and oranges cannot be reduced to one kind. These five are of two kinds: family members and fruits. When there is no possibility of reduction at all we can speak of radically irreducible. In this study, order and existence are radically irreducible. Existence has two irreducible forms, viz., functors and functions. Functions come in a dozen or more irreducible kinds or modes, functors in four irreducible kinds or realms.

Jural, juridical. Name for that irreducible mode of functioning characterized by the human call to justice.

Kind, species, sort. The configuration of which we have a concept when we refer to *the* such-and-such. *The* lion is not a lion. It names a kind. And the kind presents to us the complex of conditions that are to be met if a properly formed lion is to exist. Typically nomic interrelationship of conditions as determining the structure of functors, functions, and relations. (See Wolterstorff, UN, 245.)

Kinematic. Irreducible mode of functioning characterizing the sort of phenomena we study in mechanics. Kinematic functions are functions of motion.

Kingdom. See realm.

Knowing. See knowledge.

Knowledge, knowing, cognition. Any human being will have experience. It is not possible for a human being to exist and not to have experience. But when we take responsibility for our experience, develop it, check it, control it, improve it, work at it, and in that way take responsibility for the way in which the world develops, then experience can be called knowledge. Consciously rooting experience in responsibility and making it inclusive of all our human functioning makes experience cognitive.

Law. See condition.

Life. This term is not used to name the typical existence of organic forms of reality. Life is opposed to death. But whatever cannot ever have lived can also not be called dead. For that reason the life-matter view of reality is a mistaken imposition of the good-evil distinction on the material-supramaterial distinction. Life as used in this book is whatever exists as good, death is whatever is or will be annihilated as evil.

Limit. See condition.

Logical. See analytic.

Love. Another word which, like *life* and *good*, says something about existence in its totality in a directional way. *Love* has to do with the quality of human subjectivity as a whole. To love is not some specific human action or attitude, but is the direction which all of human actions, attitudes, and relations take when integrated with the direction intended in the order of reality.

Meaning. A term used to refer to the dependent, referential, relative character of both world and world order. Reality that is thus dependent refers to an origin in which it originates and which fixes its being. The being of relative reality is meaning. It is what it means.

Member. Name for a functor seen in relation to the community to which it belongs. Functors are always individual members of kind communities.

Modality. See mode.

Modal order. The irreversible sequence of the irreducible modes of functioning in which the relative position of each mode is fixed as well as the configuration of functional relations within each mode as intramodal evidence of this sequence.

Mode, modality. An irreducible kind of functioning or one of the most inclusive or highest kinds of functioning. The reality of each mode is functionally original, though all have their origin relatively speaking in their being modes of functioning or subjectivity.

Moral. See ethical.

Nature. See essence.

Necessity. A mode of the relation between nomic conditions and existence. Only subjectively existential functions and relations can be necessary. They are necessary *as* determined by nomic conditions. It is necessary *that* cows have four legs. It is necessary *that* a particular piece of gold is yellow. It is necessary *that* actual people have the capacity to analyze. It is necessary *that* when four apples are taken out of a box of eight, only four are left. It is necessary *that* my younger female sibling is not identical with my mother. All these are equally necessary. There is physical, biological, psychological, logical, economic, and other necessity. Physical necessity requires that a person jumping from a plane will fall. Logical necessity requires that I not arrive at contradictory conclusions. As much constant configuration of nomic conditions there is, so much necessary existence there will be. What is necessary is not always unavoidable. No conditions are necessary. Necessity is not a mode of nomic reality. Nomic reality necessitates. It is not itself necessary. That "being a cow" requires "having four legs" is just so. (See Kripke, NN, 106ff.)

Nomic. See condition; also see order.

Nominalism. The view that subjective existence is all that is real. As a consequence, all genuinely supraarbitrary intersubjective or transsubjective standards for existence are denied.

Norm. See condition.

Nuclear. See core.

Numeric. Name for that functional mode which we know as discrete quantity. Numerical relations are relations of quantity in an original sense that can be enumerated.

Object. Not used for thing or entity. The meaning of *object* is limited to the subject$_2$-object relation, in which the object is always object for an actual or possible subject. More precisely, when two functors are so related that the relation is characterized by a functional level on which only one of the functors functions actively, the other functor functions objectively or as object on that level.

Obtain. See hold.

Opening direction. See qualifying.

Order, world order. The totality of all nomic conditions in their coherent interrelations.

Organic. See biotic.

Original. See core.

Part. Those elements in a coherently structured whole or unity without which the whole could not exist, which themselves could only exist within the whole, and whose reality is determined by their presence within the structure of the whole.

Particular. Only subjective existence can be particular. But all particular existence shows both individuality and evidence of being ordered. A particular is always individual, but never individual throughout, since each particular is of some kind. A particular is an individually existing member of some kind. Only a singular term can be used to name it. And a genuine singular term names only it. What are called abstract singular terms are not really singular terms. They can better be called abstract specific terms.

Pattern, structure, system, field, regularity. These terms are used to refer to the evidence that the world is ordered. Subjective, individual existence shows in its having structure that it is subjected to a nomic order. Whereas it is what I provisionally called conditions-1 that display order, it is what I provisionally called conditions-2 that display system, pattern, and structure. Communities, e.g., interrelate, as in ecological systems, cities, nations, and so forth. When communities of different kinds are interrelated in structured ways, what results is a system.

Phase. See aspect.

Phenomenon. See entity.

Physical. Name used for that realm of existence whose nature is qualified by its energy functions.

Pistic, certitudinal. Name for that kind of human functioning in which we acquire certainty through faith, or through committing ourselves.

Possible. Another mode of the relation between conditions and existence. It is possible for a human being to run a mile in less than four minutes. Some of the things that are possible have never happened or existed. But they are possible. What is and is not possible is determined or conditioned by the nomic order. Only what is possible and necessary is determined. What will in fact be is contingent, i.e., is due to individual existence. Possibility is the room there is for existence to be individual, to be subjective, to be free. Possibility lies within the limits of nomic conditions. Whether what is thinkable is also possible is to be determined by more than a priori reasoning. Possible is not the same as conceivable, and certainly not the same as imaginable.

Predicate. Whenever we logically attribute something to an existent we name with a singular term, the semantic form for the attribution is called predication. The terms we use for predicating are called predicate terms. They always name what we think is a nomic condition or what we conceive as such. The fact that the language has a certain predicate, however, is no guarantee that the nomic condition is real. And there are likely nomic conditions that we have never thought of or named. (See Armstrong, USR2, 9). There is no one-to-one correspondence between nomic conditions and predicates.

Primary structure or order of modes or functions. See constitutive.

Principle. If the order of nomic conditions can change, i.e., if there are conditions now which were not there once, and if there were some once which no longer are there, then what? How about the conditions for dinosaurs? I prefer to speak differently. I prefer to say that conditions neither come into being, nor pass out of being, nor even exist now. They hold or obtain. So conditions for dinosaurs no longer obtain, one might say. (See Armstrong, USR2, 9-10; Wolterstorff, UN, 221ff.; and Loux, SA, 92ff.) But whenever, if ever, I want to refer to conditions as invariable and continuous, a priori and constant (if they are that), then I will call them principles. So principles of order will be constant and invariable nomic conditions. Principles are pure postulates.

Property. See attribute.

Proposition. A polyadic nomic condition or conditioning relation grasped with more than one concept and grasped either just as polyadic conditions or in relation to particulars.

Psychic, sensitive. Mode of functioning characterized by a functor's ability to relate meaningfully to itself, other functors, and the environment; not by physically touching that other reality, but rather by feeling it.

Qualify. A function or group of functions qualifies a functor, a multifunctional act, an event, or a relation when those functions fundamentally direct the nature of all functioning in that act or event by their own original nature. Qualifying functions are determining boundary functions of acts or events. An event qualified by juridical functions will be a juridical event, e.g., a session of the high court.

Qualifying, developing, opening direction. When we look upon the irreversible series of modes from higher modes to lower ones— higher ones always typically qualifying, directing, or opening up lower ones—we speak of the qualifying direction of modal order.

Quality. See attribute.

Radical distinction. When I distinguish in reality between origin of order, order, and ordered world I cannot refer to that as a normal categorial distinction, since the realities named are not susceptible to normal definition or conceptualization. For that reason I call this a radical distinction. It is the ultimate distinction there is.

Rational. See analytic.

Realism. The view that universals exist. I reject that view, though I accept that reality is not exhausted in existing particulars.

Reality. Not a property. This term or name, which can be used as a predicate but which does not correspond to any nomic conditions, is just a term or name. It refers to nothing particular or nothing specific. It indicates that whatever we name as real must be accepted by us on its own terms. Material objects are real as material objects. Words are real as words. Conditions are real as conditions. There is not a specific thing, a particular existent, or a universal condition known as reality.

Realm, kingdom. Names for the most fundamentally irreducible communities or functors, such as mineral, vegetable, animal, and human realms.

Reduction. Used in the sense of trying to understand or explain something in terms of another thing. Thus, trying to understand life by fully explaining it in terms of molecular processes is trying to reduce life to physical processes. All science is reductive, in the sense that science tries to understand complexities in simpler terms, or to subsume complexities under single or less complex laws or principles. To understand what it is to be a cow, we need not understand all the members of the class, but we can try to understand the kind cow.

Regularity. See pattern.

Relation. A primitive term for which no clear meaning can be found, but which is almost always immediately understood in its use in context. The reality of relations is not fully located in the empirical world, and so it seems to break through the irreducibility of world order and ordered world. Relation is found between these and among all that is on either side. Whatever is related is connected, is in touch. Besides things related, there are also the relations between them. Relations, too, are both individual and one of a kind.

Relative. Both in the sense of "it all depends" and in the sense of "relational" this term refers to the fundamental reality of relationship. All things, all reality, origin of order and world, world order, and ordered world, functors and functions are all in relation. And this relational character of reality makes for relativity. But relativity does not make for lack of continuity or lack of foundations for reliance. Order has a stable core. God can be trusted.

Religious. The meaning of all reality is ultimately founded in, determined by, and originated from its origin. The presence of all reality before or in relation to that origin, consciously so in humanity, is what is meant by religion. It is the relation of all things, all functions, to the ultimate origin of reality.

Revelation. Most basically the term means nothing else than: something's becoming known. It also means this, in a straightforward sense, when it is used in a religious sense. In that latter sense revelation occurs as a result of one's commitment to, faith in, or ultimate acceptance of what is ultimate. Religious revelation is something's becoming known from the point of view of our ultimate commitment. It occurs in all human beings.

Rule. See condition.

Semantic. Term indicating the reality of a body of coherently organized symbols designed to convey conceptual meanings clearly to others with whom one shares that semantic body.

Sensitive. See psychic.

Sentence, statement, term, word. Semantic realities without Platonic overtones. There is no such thing as: "There exists the type sentence such-and-such as well as its tokens on a given occasion." Sentences only mean what a user means by them. And wise users will use communal conventions of the language. But nothing is guaranteed. All semantic devices in the first place are designed to refer to conceptual realities, with the notable exception of proper names. But in actual use, both words and sentences have the meaning which the user intends them to have in the context. Scholarly usage attempts to have more strictly univocal meanings and well-defined conventions. Words are then more likely to be called terms, i.e., the technical jargon designed to refer to hopefully clear and well-defined concepts. Sentences are then more likely to be called statements, i.e., semantic vehicles specifically crafted to present propositions as clearly as possible. Generally speaking, terms or words are defined as to their agreed reference and have the meaning they have in their use. The definition refers to the concept named by the word or term. The meaning refers to the wider function of the concept in its environment.

Sequence. See second definition of direction.

Set. See class.

Singular. Will be used only to designate that certain terms or words name only a particular or particulars, or refer only to a particular or particulars. The difference between a proper name and a singular term is just that a singular term can be used in another context as a universal term. Quantified terms are all singular terms, since they always refer to particulars, whether one, some, or all.

Social. A mode of human functionality typical of the conscious, skilled, intentionally developed actions which have no other purpose than to interrelate or associate.

Sort. See kind.

Soul. See spirit.

Spatial. Mode of functioning characterized by continuous extension, space.

Species. See kind.

Specific. Used as the correlate of particular, to designate one nomic condition rather than another. The term refers to the limitation of boundaries of possibility, which are specified by conditions.

Spirit, soul. Refers to any agent consciously participating in guiding the world to its destiny. Human beings are spirits. They do not *have*, but *are* spirits. As spirit a person is a bodily spirit. As body a person is a spiritual body.

Standard. See condition.

State of affairs. Could be used to mean either a specific order or a given structure. I will use it to designate specified structures. Specific orders are configurations.

Statement. See sentence.

Structure. See pattern.

Subject, subjective, subjectivity. One use of *subjective* will always have the meaning of being subject to conditions. This is the only use in the first four chapters. Any particular can always be referred to as a subject. Subjective will never mean: personal, arbitrary, mental, private, or the like. Subjective indicates existence of material objects in space and time (people, animals, plants, minerals) as well as their actions, functions and behaviors, and the relations between these. All these are what they are in subjection to order. The term also designates some existing entity as subject, to be distinguished from another as object. When that is done, I will distinguish subject$_1$ and subject$_2$ (from 5.4 onward).

Supporting direction or order. See founding.

Symbolic, aesthetic. Type of functoning characterized by its instrumental intent to refer to specific reality other than the symbol or the symboling.

System. See pattern.

Technical. See formative.

Term. See sentence.

Thing. See entity.

Time. Not the coordinate of space. Used to indicate the relation between world order and ordered world. The ordered world is in time and world order is a temporal order.

Totality. Any multiplicity with boundaries defined by structured coherence of internal relations.

Truth, validity. Both terms refer to the successful, intended, proper, expected, right relationship between subjective existence and the obtaining conditions. *Truth* and *validity* in my usage never refer only to statements or arguments. Anything in the world that measures up to its standards can be true and valid. Whatever is true conforms to its standards. But we can use specific terms to refer to specific kinds of relations. Thus, true or valid can be translated, depending on the context, as correct, right, just, sensitive, clear, etc.

Typical. Term indicating a nomic configuration. The interrelations among the broken pieces on the pavement resulting from the spill of a truckload of earthenware is not typical but random. Typical relations occur in the same way whenever they occur. *Typical* is a term for relations governed by law.

Ultimate. Primitive term. Foundation which itself has no ground but is the ground of all grounds. Accepted not on grounds but as ground.

For Christians God is ultimate. But human beings do attach themselves in faith to many other ultimates: humanity, love, science, reason, fate, matter, life, and so on.

Unique. See individuality.

Unity. Correlate of diversity. Indicates a totality structured to function as one unit.

Universal, universality. *A* universal, i.e., something to which the noun refers, will only be a term referring to the universality of a specific concept or condition. Universality refers to the scope with which some condition holds for subjective existence, i.e., the condition obtains without exception, it determines all possible existence of this kind. *Universal* simply means: no exceptions to the condition within its scope.

Validity. See truth.

Value. Not a term I use myself. As used by others I take it to refer to what I mean either by *good* or by *norm* or *standard*.

Whole. A unified totality whose diversity consists of parts, i.e., elements without which the whole could not exist, that themselves cannot exist outside of the whole, and that are defined by their presence as constitutive elements of the whole.

Word. See sentence.

World order. See order.

Bibliography

Aay, H. "A Re-examination: Geography—the Science of Space." *Monadnock* 46 (1971): 20-31.

Adorno, Theodor W.; Albert, Hans; Dahrendorf, Ralf; Habermas, Jürgen; Pilot, Harald; Popper, Karl R. *The Positivist Dispute in German Sociology.* Translated by G. Adey and D. Frisby. London: Heinemann Educational Books, 1976. (PD)

―――. *Negative Dialectics.* Translated by E.B. Ashton. A Continuum Book. New York: Seabury Press, 1979. (ND)

Alston, William P. "Meta-Ethics and Meta-Epistemology." In *Values and Morals,* edited by A.I. Goldman and J. Kim, pp. 275-97. Dordrecht: D. Reidel Publishing Co., 1978. (ME)

―――. "The Requirements for Christian Knowledge." 1978. Unpublished. (XK)

―――. "Christian Language Games." Paper from 2d Conference on Philosophy of Religion, Notre Dame, 1979. (XL)

―――. "Level Confusions in Epistemology." *Midwest Studies in Philosophy.* Vol. 5. 1980.

―――. "The Role of Reason in the Regulation of Belief." In *Rationality in the Calvinian Tradition,* edited by Hendrik Hart, Johan van der Hoeven, and Nicholas Wolterstorff. Lanham: University Press of America, 1983.

Anastasiou, H. "Faith, Knowledge and Science: A Systematic Exposition of the Thought of Michael Polanyi." Unpublished Master of Philosophy thesis, Institute of Christian Studies, Toronto, 1979.

Anderson, Alan Ross, ed. *Minds and Machines.* Englewood Cliffs: Prentice-Hall, 1964.

Apel, K.O. "Analytic philosophy of language and the 'Geisteswissenschaften.' " *Foundations of Language.* Suppl. Series, vol. 5. Dordrecht: D. Reidel Publishing Co., 1967.

Armstrong, D.M. *Nominalism and Realism: Universals and Scientific Realism.* Vol. 1. Cambridge: Cambridge University Press, 1978. (USR1)

_____. *A Theory of Universals: Universals and Scientific Realism.* Vol. 2. Cambridge: Cambridge University Press, 1978. (USR2)

Austin, J.L. *Sense and Sensibilia.* Oxford: Oxford University Press, 1970.

Ayer, A.J. *Language, Truth and Logic.* New York: Dover Publications, 1946. (LTL)

_____. *Logical Positivism.* New York: Macmillan, 1959.

_____. *The Central Question of Philosophy.* New York: Penguin Books, 1978. (CQ)

_____. *The Problem of Knowledge.* New York: Penguin Books, 1979. (PK)

Baarda, T., et al. *God with Us: On the Nature of the Authority of Scripture.* Grand Rapids: Reformed Ecumenical Synod, 1980.

Barfield, Owen. *Saving the Appearances: A Study in Idolatry.* New York: Harcourt, Brace & World, n.d.

Barth, Karl. *Fides quaerens intellectum: Anselms Beweis der Existenz Gottes im Zusammenhang seines theologischen Programms.* Zollikon: Evangelischer Verlag AG, 1958.

Bealer, George. *Quality and Concept.* Oxford: Clarendon Press, 1982.

Bergson, Henri. *L'Evolution créatrice.* 22d ed. Paris: Librairie Felix Alcan, 1920.

Berkhof, Hendrikus. *Christian Faith.* Grand Rapids: Wm. B. Eerdmans, 1979.

Berkouwer, Gerrit C. *Man, the Image of God.* Grand Rapids: Wm. B. Eerdmans, 1962.

Blondel, Maurice. *La Pensée.* Bibliothèque de philosophie contemporaine. Paris: Presses universitaires de France, 1948.

Bloomfield, L. "Linguistic Aspects of Science." *International Encyclopedia of Unified Science.* Vol. 1, no. 4. Chicago: University of Chicago Press, 1969.

Blum, A. *Theorizing.* London: Heinemann Educational Books, 1974.

Boer, J., ed. "Biblical Quotations on Justice, Stewardship and Economics." Institute for Christian Studies, Toronto, 1980. Mimeographed.

Botha, Elaine. "Religious Commitment and Scientific Beliefs, Alternative Approaches." King's College, Edmonton, 1981. Typewritten.

Bouwsma, O.K. *Towards a New Sensibility.* Lincoln: University of Nebraska Press, 1982.

Brouwer, John. "The Year of Jubilee: A Call for Liberation and Restoration." Institute for Christian Studies, Toronto, 1979. Mimeographed.

Brouwer, W. "Christian Commitment and Scientific Theories." Association for the Advancement of Christian Scholarship, Toronto, 1977. Mimeographed.

Bunge, Mario. *Treatise on Basic Philosophy.* Vol. 3, *Ontology I—The Furniture of the World.* Dordrecht: D. Reidel Publishing Co., 1977.

Butterfield, Herbert. *The Origins of Modern Science, 1300-1800.* Toronto: Clarke, Irwin & Co., 1968.

Buytendijk, F.J.J. *Prolegomena of an Anthropological Physiology.* Pittsburgh: Duquesne University Press, 1974.

Carnap, Rudolf. *The Logical Structure of the World.* Translated by R.A. George. Berkeley: University of California Press, 1969.

Casey, Edward S. *Imagining: A Phenomenological Study.* Bloomington: Indiana University Press, 1976.

Cassirer, Ernst. *The Philosophy of the Enlightenment.* Translated by F.C.A. Koelln and J.P. Pettegrove. Humanities Series. Boston: Beacon Press, 1962.

Chaplin, Jonathan P. "Dooyeweerd's Theory of Public Justice." Unpublished Master of Philosophy thesis, Institute for Christian Studies, Toronto, 1983.

Chisholm, R.M. *The Theory of Knowledge.* Foundations of Philosophy Series. Englewood Cliffs: Prentice-Hall, 1966.

Clouser, Roy A. "Religious Language: A New Look at an Old Problem." In *Rationality in the Calvinian Tradition*, edited by Hendrik Hart, Johan van der Hoeven, and Nicholas Wolterstorff, pp. 385-407. Lanham: University Press of America, 1983.

Copi, I.M. *Introduction to Logic.* 5th ed. New York: Macmillan, 1978.

———. *Symbolic Logic.* 5th ed. New York: Macmillan, 1979.

Coulson, C.A. *Science and Christian Belief.* Fontana Books. London: Collins Press, 1967.

Cramp, A.B. "Notes Towards a Christian Critique of Secular Economic Theory." Institute for Christian Studies, Toronto, 1975. Mimeographed.

———. "The Economic Systems." In *Justice in the International Economic Order*, pp. 139-66. Grand Rapids: Calvin College, 1980.

Davidson, Donald. "On the Very Idea of a Conceptual Scheme." *Proceedings of the American Philosophical Association* 17 (1973-74): 11.

De Graaff, Arnold H. "Anthropology and Psychology in Christian Perspective: Some Readings and Propositions." Institute for Christian Studies, Toronto, 1974. Mimeographed.

———. "Towards a New Anthropological Model." In *Hearing and Doing*, edited by John Kraay and Anthony Tol, pp. 97-118. Toronto: Wedge Publishing Foundation, 1979. (AM)

———. "Psychology: Sensitive Openness and Appropriate Reactions." *Bulletin of the Christian Association of Psychological Studies*, 1980. (SO)

_____. "Toward an Integral Model of Psychotherapy." *Bulletin of the Christian Association of Psychological Studies*, 1981.

_____, ed. "Views of Man and Psychology in Christian Perspective: Some Readings." Institute for Christian Studies, Toronto, 1977. Mimeographed.

De Graaff, Arnold H., and Olthuis, James H. "Models of Man in Theology and Psychology." Institute for Christian Studies, Toronto, 1978. Mimeographed. (MM)

_____, eds. "Toward a Biblical View of Man: Some Readings." Institute for Christian Studies, Toronto, 1978. Mimeographed.

De Jager-Seerveld, Tim. "Grene's Anti-reductionist Ontology. An Inquiry into the Foundations of Biology." Institute for Christian Studies, Toronto, 1982. Mimeographed.

_____. "Commitment and Meaning in Biology: Michael Polanyi's Critique of Reductionism." Unpublished Master of Philosophical Foundations Thesis, Institute for Christian Studies, Toronto, 1983.

Dewey, John. *Logic: The Theory of Inquiry.* New York: Henry Holt & Co., 1938. (L)

_____. "Theory of Valuation." *International Encyclopedia of Unified Science.* Vol. 2, no. 4. Chicago: University of Chicago Press, 1962.

Dewey, John, and Bentley, A.F. *Knowing and the Known.* Boston: Beacon Press, 1949.

_____. *A Philosophical Correspondence, 1932-1951.* New Brunswick: Rutgers University Press, 1964.

Diemer, J.H. *Nature and Miracle.* Toronto: Wedge Publishing Foundation, 1977.

Dijksterhuis, E.J. *The Mechanization of the World Picture.* Oxford: Clarendon Press, 1961.

Dooyeweerd, Herman. *A New Critique of Theoretical Thought.* 4 vols. Philadelphia: Presbyterian & Reformed Publishing Co., 1953-58. (NC)

_____. *In the Twilight of Western Thought: Studies in the Pretended Autonomy of Philosophic Thought.* Philadelphia: Presbyterian & Reformed Publishing Co., 1960. (TWT)

_____. *Roots of Western Culture: Pagan, Secular, and Christian Options.* Translated by John Kraay. Edited by Bernard Zylstra and Mark VanderVennen. Toronto: Wedge Publishing Foundation, 1979. (WC)

Dray, William H. *Philosophy of History.* Foundations of Philosophy Series. Englewood Cliffs: Prentice-Hall, 1964.

Dufrenne, M. *The Phenomenology of Aesthetic Experience.* Translated by E. Casey, A. Anderson, W. Domingo, and L. Jacobsen. Evanston: Northwestern University Press, 1973.

Echeverria, E.J. *Criticism and Commitment: Major Themes in Contemporary "Post-critical" Philosophy.* Amsterdam: Rodopi, 1981.

Eibl-Eibesfeldt, I. *Love and Hate: The Natural History of Behavior Patterns.* Translated by G. Strachan. New York: Schocken Books, 1974.

Ellul, Jacques. *Autopsie de la révolution.* Paris: Calmann-Levy, 1969.

———. *Le système technicien.* Paris: Calmann-Levy, 1977.

Faghfoury, Mostafa, ed. *Analytical Philosophy of Religion in Canada.* Ottawa: University of Ottawa Press, 1982.

Ferguson, T. "The Changing Economy of Knowledge and the Changing Politics of Philosophy of Science." *Telos* (1973): 124-37.

Fernhout, H. "Faith: Searching for the Core of the Cube," chapter two in Craig Dykstra, Sharon Parks and Barbara Wheeler, eds., *Faith Development and Ministry.* To be published by Religious Education Press (Birmingham, Alabama), 1985.

———. "Man, Faith, and Religion in Bavinck, Kuyper, and Dooyeweerd." Unpublished Master of Philosophy thesis, Institute for Christian Studies, Toronto, 1975.

———. "Man: The Image and Glory of God." In "Toward a Biblical View of Man: Some Readings," edited by Arnold H. De Graaff and James H. Olthuis, pp. 5-34. Institute for Christian Studies, Toronto, 1978. Mimeographed.

———. "On Habermas' Use of the Work of Cognitive-Developmental Theorists." Unpublished paper, 1982.

———. "The Relation of Religion or Faith to Morality According to Lawrence Kohlberg and James Fowler." M.A. thesis, University of Toronto, 1982. (FM)

Fernhout, H. and Boyd, Dwight. "Faith in Autonomy: Developments in Kohlberg's Thought on Religion and Morality." Forthcoming in the Winter issue of *Religious Education.*

Feyerabend, Paul K. *Against Method.* New York: Schocken Books, 1978.

Fowler, James W. *Stages of Faith.* San Francisco: Harper & Row, 1981.

Fowler, Robert Booth. *A New Engagement: Evangelical Political Thought, 1966-1976.* Grand Rapids: Wm. B. Eerdmans, 1982.

Fox, Sidney W.; Harada, Kaoru; Krampitz, Gottfried; Mueller, George. "The Chemical Origins of Cells." *C & EN* (June 1970): 80-94.

Free University. *Concern about Science: Proceedings of the Centennial Congress of the Free University of Amsterdam,* 1980.

Gadamer, Hans Georg. *Truth and Method.* New York: Seabury Press, 1975.

Gaffron, H. "Resistance to Knowledge." *Annual Review of Plant Physiology* 20 (1969). Reprint.

Gardiner, Patrick, ed. *Theories of History.* New York: Free Press, 1959.

_____, ed. *Philosophy of History*. London: Oxford University Press, 1974. (PH)

Gibson, E.J. *Principles of Perceptual Learning and Development*. New York: Appleton, Century & Crofts, 1969.

Gibson, J.J. *The Senses Considered as Perceptual Systems*. New York: Houghton Mifflin Co., 1966.

Giet, Nicholas F. *Wittgenstein and Phenomenology: A Comparative Study of the Later Wittgenstein, Husserl, Heidegger and Merleau Ponty*. Albany: State University of New York Press, 1981.

Goodman, D.C., ed. *Science and Religious Belief, 1600-1900: A Selection of Primary Sources*. Open University Press, 1973.

Goon, Carroll. "The Nature of Historical Explanation: An Analysis and Critique of the Hempel-Dray Debate." Institute for Christian Studies, Toronto, 1984. Mimeographed.

Gorovitz, Samuel, et al. *Philosophical Analysis: An Introduction to Its Language and Techniques*. 3d ed. New York: Random House, 1979.

Goudzwaard, B. "Economic Stewardship Versus Capitalist Religion: A Series of Seminar Lectures." Institute for Christian Studies, Toronto, 1972. Mimeographed.

Goudzwaard, B., and van Baars, J. "Norms for the International Economic Order." In *Justice in the International Economic Order*, pp. 223-53. Grand Rapids: Calvin College, 1980.

Grene, Marjorie. *The Knower and the Known*. Berkeley: University of California Press, 1974.

_____, ed. *Approaches to a Philosophical Biology*. New York: Basic Books, 1965, 1968.

_____, ed. *Interpretations of Life and Mind*. London: Routledge & Kegan Paul, 1971.

Habermas, Jürgen. *Knowledge and Human Interests*. Translated by J.J. Shapiro. Boston: Beacon Press, 1972.

Hamlyn, D.W. *The Theory of Knowledge*. London: Macmillan, 1976.

Hanson, N.R. *Patterns of Discovery*. Modern Introductions to Philosophy. Cambridge: Cambridge University Press, 1972.

Hart, Hendrik. "Can the Bible Be an Idol?" *Sola Fide* 17 (September 1964): 3-10.

_____. "Dewey's Logic: The Theory of Inquiry." *Philosophia Reformata* 30 (1965): 13-25.

_____. *Communal Certainty and Authorized Truth: An Examination of John Dewey's Philosophy of Verification*. Amsterdam: Swets & Zeitlinger, 1966. (CC)

_____. "The Democratic Way of Death." Toronto: CJL Foundation, 1967. Reprinted in *Christian Politics* (Indiana: Jubilee, 1976): 51-65. (DD)

_____. "Scientific Method." *Perspektief* 6 (March 1968): 128-46.

_____. "Calvinism as a Cosmoscope." In *Die Atoomeeu in U Lig*, pp. 52-61. Potchefstroom: UCHE, 1969. Reprinted in *International Reformed Bulletin* 13 (Spring 1970): 16-23.

_____. "Jerusalem and Athens." *Crux* 7, no. 3 (May 1970): 3-6.

_____. "Problems of Time: An Essay." In *The Idea of a Christian Philosophy*, pp. 30-42. Toronto: Wedge Publishing Foundation, 1973. (PT)

_____. "Anthropology: Some Questions and Remarks." In "Anthropology and Psychology in Christian Perspective: Some Readings and Propositions," edited by Arnold H. De Graaff. Reprint. Institute for Christian Studies, Toronto, 1974. Mimeographed.

_____. *The Challenge of Our Age*. Toronto: Wedge Publishing Foundation, 1974. (CA)

_____. "Theorizing between Boethius and Ockham." Written with students. Institute for Christian Studies, Toronto, 1974. Mimeographed.

_____. The Calvinist Tradition in Philosophy." *Perspektief* 15 (June 1976): 1-17.

_____. "The Idea of Christian Scholarship." *Christian Higher Education* (Potchefstroom: IAC, 1976): 69-97.

_____. "The Idea of an Inner Reformation of the Sciences." Institute for Christian Studies, Toronto, 1978. Mimeographed.

_____. "The Impasse of Rationality Today: A Precis." *Circular* (Clearing House of the ICRIHE) 9 (April 1978): 60-68.

_____. "Theses on Scripture." *Crux* 14, no. 1 (1978): 3-31.

_____. "On the Distinction between Creator and Creature." *Philosophia Reformata* 44 (1979): 183-93. (DC)

_____. "Struggle for a New Direction." In *Hearing and Doing*, edited by John Kraay and Anthony Tol, pp. 1-13. Toronto: Wedge Publishing Foundation, 1979. (ND)

_____. "Critical Reflections on Wolterstorff's *Reason within the Bounds of Religion*." Institute for Christian Studies, Toronto, 1980. Mimeographed. (WRR)

_____. "The Recognition of Science as Knowledge." Institute for Christian Studies, Toronto, 1980. Mimeographed.

_____. "Theory and Praxis: A Response." In *Justice in the International Economic Order*, pp. 99-103. Grand Rapids: Calvin College, 1980.

_____. "The Impasse of Rationality Today." In *Wetenschap, Wijsheid, Filosoferen*. Essays dedicated to Prof. Dr. Ir. Hendrik van Riessen. Edited by P. Blokhuis, et al. Assen: Van Gorcum, 1981.

______. "The Articulation of Belief: A Link between Rationality and Commitment." In *Rationality in the Calvinian Tradition*, edited by Hendrik Hart, Johan van der Hoeven, and Nicholas Wolterstorff. Lanham: University Press of America, 1983. Also in *Tydskrif vir christelike wetenskap* 19de Jaargang, 1ste-2de Kwaartaal, 1983. (RC)

______. "Commitment as a Foundation for Rational Belief." Proceedings of the 17th World Congress of Philosophy in Montreal, August 1983.

Hart, Hendrik, and Olthuis, James H. "Theses on Science and Revelation." Institute for Christian Studies, Toronto, 1978. Mimeographed.

Hart, Hendrik; van der Hoeven, Johan; and Wolterstorff, Nicholas; eds. *Rationality in the Calvinian Tradition*. Lanham: University Press of America, 1983.

Hasker, William. *Metaphysics: Constructing a World View*. Downers Grove: InterVarsity Press, 1983.

Hempel, C.G. *Aspects of Scientific Explanation*. New York: Free Press, 1965. (ASE)

______. *Philosophy of Natural Science*. Englewood Cliffs: Prentice-Hall, 1966. (PNS)

______. "Formulation and Formalization." In *The Structure of Scientific Theories*, edited by F. Suppe, pp. 244-53. Chicago: University of Illinois Press, 1974.

Hills, A. "A Philosophical Approach to Landscape Planning." *Landscape Planning* 1 (1974): 339-71.

Holmes, Arthur F. *Christian Philosophy in the Twentieth Century*. Grand Rapids: Baker Book House, 1969.

______. *Faith Seeks Understanding*. Grand Rapids: Wm. B. Eerdmans, 1971.

______. *Philosophy: A Christian Perspective*. Downers Grove: InterVarsity Press, 1975.

______. *All Truth Is God's Truth*. Grand Rapids: Wm. B. Eerdmans, 1977.

______. *Contours of a World View*. Grand Rapids: Wm. B. Eerdmans, 1983. (WV)

Holtrop, P.C. "Toward a Biblical Conception of Truth and a New Mood for Doing Reformed Theology." *RES Theological Forum* 5, no. 2 (June 1977).

Honderich, Ted, and Burnyeat, Myles, eds. *Philosophy as It Is*. New York: Penguin Books, 1979.

Hook, J. " 'Analytic' vs. 'Pluralist' Debate Splits Philosophical Association." *Chronicle of Higher Education* (January 12, 1981).

Hooykaas, R. *Religion and the Rise of Modern Science*. Grand Rapids: Wm. B. Eerdmans, 1972.

Horkheimer, Max. *Eclipse of Reason*. New York: Seabury Press, 1974.

House, Vanden. "Echeverria on 'Post-critical' Philosophy." *Anakainosis* 5, nos. 2 and 3 (December 1982—March 1983): 22ff.

Husserl, Edmund. *Formal and Transcendental Logic.* Translated by D. Cairns. The Hague: Martinus Nijhoff, 1969.

Jaki, Stanley. *Brain, Mind and Computers.* South Bend: Gateway Press, 1969. (BMC)

_____. *Science and Creation: From Eternal Cycles to an Oscillating Universe.* Edinburgh: Scottish Academic Press, 1974.

_____. *"Culture and Science." Two lectures delivered at Assumption University, Windsor, Canada on February 26 and 28, 1975.* Windsor: University of Windsor Press, 1975.

_____. *The Road of Science and the Ways to God.* Chicago: University of Chicago Press, 1978.

_____. *The Origin of Science and the Science of Its Origin.* South Bend: Regnery/Gateway Press, 1979.

_____. *From Angels through Apes to Man.* LaSalle, Ill.: Sherwood Sugden & Co., 1983.

Jaspers, Karl. *Der philosophische Glaube.* Hamburg: Fischer Bucherei, 1958.

_____. *Der philosophische Glaube angesichts der Offenbarung.* Munich: R. Piper & Co., 1963.

Jeeves, M.A. *The Scientific Enterprise and the Christian Faith.* Downers Grove: InterVarsity Press, 1971.

Joldersma, Clarence W. "Beliefs and the Scientific Enterprise: A Framework Model Based on Kuhn's Paradigms, Polanyi's Commitment Framework, and Radnitzky's Internal Steering Fields." M. Phil. thesis, Institute for Christian Studies, Toronto, 1982.

Kalsbeek, L. *Contours of a Christian Philosophy.* Toronto: Wedge Publishing Foundation, 1975.

Kant, Immanuel. *Critique of Pure Reason.* Translated by J.M.D. Meiklejohn. New York: P.F. Collier & Son, 1910.

Kerkut, G.A. *Implications of Evolution.* Elmsford, N.Y.: Pergamon Press, 1960.

Kierkegaard, Sören A. *Concluding Unscientific Postscript.* Translated by D. Swenson. Princeton: Princeton University Press, 1941.

Kittel, Gerhard, and Friedrich, Gerhard, eds. *Theological Dictionary of the New Testament.* Translated by G.W. Bromiley. 10 vols. Grand Rapids: Wm. B. Eerdmans, 1964-74.

Kline, Meredith. *Images of the Spirit.* Baker Biblical Monograph. Grand Rapids: Baker Book House, 1980.

Kneale, W., and Kneale, M. *The Development of Logic.* Oxford: Clarendon Press, 1964.

Köhler, W. *Gestalt Psychology.* A Mentor Book. New York: New American Library, 1947. (GP)

_____. *The Task of Gestalt Psychology.* Princeton: Princeton University Press, 1969.

Kolakowski, L. *The Alienation of Reason.* Translated by N. Guterman. Anchor Books. New York: Doubleday & Co., 1969.

Körner, Stephan. *Conceptual Thinking.* New York: Dover Publications, 1959. (CT)

_____. *Categorial Frameworks.* Oxford: Basil Blackwell, 1974. (CF)

Kraay, John, and Tol, Anthony, eds. *Hearing and Doing: Philosophical Essays Dedicated to H. Evan Runner.* Toronto: Wedge Publishing Foundation, 1979.

Kripke, S. *Naming and Necessity.* Cambridge: Harvard University Press, 1972. (NN)

_____. "Identity and Necessity." In *Philosophy as It Is,* edited by Ted Honderich and Myles Burnyeat. New York: Penguin Books, 1979.

Kuhn, Thomas S. "Logic of Discovery or Psychology of Research?" In *Criticism and the Growth of Knowledge,* edited by I. Lakatos and A. Musgrave, pp. 1-23. Cambridge: Cambridge University Press, 1974.

_____. "Reflections on My Critics." In *Criticism and the Growth of Knowledge,* edited by I. Lakatos and A. Musgrave, pp. 231-78. Cambridge: Cambridge University Press, 1974.

_____. "Second Thoughts on Paradigms." In *The Structure of Scientific Theories,* pp. 459-517. Chicago: University of Illinois, 1974.

_____. "The Structure of Scientific Revolutions." *International Encyclopedia of Unified Science.* Vol. 2, no. 2. Chicago: University of Chicago Press, 1975. (SSR)

Küng, Hans. *The Church.* Garden City, N.Y.: Doubleday, 1976.

_____. *On Being a Christian.* Garden City, N.Y.: Doubleday, 1976.

Lakatos, I., and Musgrave, A., eds. *Criticism and the Growth of Knowledge.* Cambridge: Cambridge University Press, 1970.

Langer, Susan K. *An Introduction to Symbolic Logic.* New York: Dover Publications, 1967.

Laszlo, Ervin. *Introduction to Systems Philosophy.* New York: Gordon & Breach, 1971. (SP)

_____. *A Strategy for the Future.* New York: George Braziller, 1974.

Leach, E.R. "We Scientists Have the Right to Play God." *Saturday Evening Post* (November 16, 1968).

Leith, T. H. "Bibliography on Science and Religion." York University, Toronto, 1967. Typewritten.

_____. "Bibliography." Atkinson College, Toronto, 1976. Mimeographed.

_____. "Bibliography on Science and Pseudo-Science." York University, Toronto, 1976. Mimeographed.

Loux, Michael J. *Universals and Particulars: Readings in Ontology.* Revised ed. Notre Dame: University of Notre Dame Press, 1970.

_____. *Substance and Attribute: A Study in Ontology.* Dordrecht: D. Reidel Publishing Co., 1978. (SA)

Lorenz, K., and Leyhausen, P. *Motivation of Human and Animal Behavior: An Ethological View.* New York: D. Van Nostrand Co., 1973.

McHugh, P. "On the Failure of Positivism." In *Understanding Everyday Life*, edited by J.D. Douglas, pp. 320-35. Chicago: Aldine Publishing Co., 1970.

McIntire, C.T. "The Ongoing Task of Christian Historiography." Institute for Christian Studies, Toronto, 1974.

_____, ed. *God, History, and Historians: An Anthology of Modern Christian Views of History.* New York: Oxford University Press, 1977.

_____, ed. *Herbert Butterfield: Writings on Christianity and History.* New York: Oxford University Press, 1979.

Mackay, Donald. *The Clockwork Image.* Downers Grove: InterVarsity Press, 1974.

Mackie, J.L. "A Conditional Analysis of the Concept of Causation." In *Philosophy as It Is*, edited by Ted Honderich and Myles Burnyeat, pp. 381-416. New York: Penguin Books, 1979.

_____. *The Cement of the Universe: A Study of Causation.* Oxford: Clarendon Press, 1980.

Mackloop, Fritz. *Knowledge and Knowledge Production.* Princeton: Princeton University Press, 1980.

Marcuse, Herbert. *One Dimensional Man.* Boston: Beacon Press, 1964.

Maritain, Jacques. *Existence and the Existent.* Translated by L. Galantiere and G.B. Phelan. Image Books. New York: Doubleday & Co., 1957.

Marsden, George. *Fundamentalism and American Culture: The Shaping of Twentieth Century Evangelicalism, 1870-1925.* New York: Oxford University Press, 1980.

Marshall, Paul. *Thine Is the Kingdom: A Biblical Approach to Government and Politics Today.* London: Marshall, Morgan and Scott, 1984.

Maslow, Abraham H. *The Psychology of Science.* Chicago: Henry Regnery Co., 1969.

Merleau-Ponty, M. *The Primacy of Perception.* Translated by A.B. Dallery, J.M. Edie, J. Wild, W. Cobb, C. Dallery, N. Metzel, and J. Flodstrom. Evanston: Northwestern University Press, 1964.

_____. *The Phenomenology of Perception.* Translated by C. Smith. London: Routledge & Kegan Paul, 1976.

Moore, J.A. *Science for Society: A Bibliography for the Commission on Science Education.* American Association for the Advancement of Science.

Mullins, N.C., and Mullins, C.J. *Theories and Theory Groups in Contemporary American Sociology.* New York: Harper & Row, 1973.

Naess, A. *The Pluralist and Possibilist Aspect of the Scientific Enterprise.* London: Allen & Unwin, 1972.

Nozick, Robert. *Philosophical Explanations.* Cambridge: Belknap Press of Harvard University Press, 1981.

Ogden, C.K., and Richards, I.A. *The Meaning of Meaning.* A Harvest Book. New York: Harcourt, Brace & World, 1923.

Olthuis, James H. "Values and Valuation: With Particular Attention to Ethical Thought in Twentieth Century Britain." *Philosophia Reformata* 32 (1967).

_____. *Facts, Values and Ethics: A Confrontation with Twentieth Century British Moral Philosophy, in particular G.E. Moore.* Assen: Van Gorcum, 1968; New York: Humanities Press, 1969. (FV)

_____. "The Reality of Social Structures." Institute for Christian Studies, Toronto, 1970. Mimeographed.

_____. "The Word of God and Science." Institute for Christian Studies, Toronto, 1970. Mimeographed.

_____. "The Word of God and Biblical Authority." Institute for Christian Studies, Toronto, 1973. Mimeographed.

_____. "Towards Reconstruction in Ethics: A Proposal." *RES Theological Bulletin* 2, no. 4 (December 1974). Grand Rapids: Reformed Ecumenical Synod.

_____. "God, Word and Creation: A Reply to Professor Frame." *Vanguard* (January-February 1975): 9-11.

_____. "Towards a Certitudinal Hermeneutic." In *Hearing and Doing,* edited by John Kraay and Anthony Tol, pp. 65-85. Toronto: Wedge Publishing Foundation, 1979. (CH)

_____. "Visions of Life and Ways of Life: The Nature of Religion." Institute for Christian Studies, Toronto, 1981. Mimeographed. (VL)

Peterson, M. *Evil and the Christian God.* Grand Rapids: Baker Book House, 1982.

Piaget, Jean. *Logic and Psychology.* Translated by Mays and Whitehead. Manchester: Manchester University Press, 1965.

_____. *The Place of the Sciences of Man in the System of Sciences.* New York: Harper & Row, 1970.

_____. *Psychology of Intelligence.* Translated by D.E. Berlyne. Totowa: Littlefield, Adams & Co., 1973.

_____. *Psychology and Epistemology.* Translated by A. Rosin. New York: Viking Press, 1974.

Plantinga, Alvin. *God and Other Minds.* Ithaca: Cornell University Press, 1967. (GOM)

_____. "Which Worlds Could God Have Created?" *Journal of Philosophy* 70 (November 1973): 539-52.

_____. *The Nature of Necessity.* Oxford: Clarendon Press, 1977. (NN)

_____. "De Essentia." *Grazer Philosophische Studien* 7/8 (1979): 101-21.

_____. "Is Belief in God Rational?" In *Rationality and Religious Belief,* edited by C.F. Delaney. Notre Dame: University of Notre Dame Press, 1979. (BIG)

_____. "The Probabilistic Argument from Evil." *Philosophical Studies* 35 (1979). Dordrecht: D. Reidel Publishing Co.

_____. "Is Belief in God Properly Basic?" *Nous* 15 (March 1981): 41-52. (BGB)

_____. "How To Be an Anti-realist." *Proceedings of the American Philosophical Association* (1983).

_____. "The Reformed Objection to Natural Theology." In *Rationality in the Calvinian Tradition,* edited by Hendrik Hart, Johan van der Hoeven, and Nicholas Wolterstorff. Lanham: University Press of America, 1983. Also in *Proceedings of the American Catholic Philosophical Association* 15 (1980): 49-62.

Plantinga, Alvin, and Wolterstorff, Nicholas, eds. *Faith and Rationality: Reason and Belief in God.* Notre Dame: Notre Dame University Press, 1983. (RB)

Polanyi, Michael. *Personal Knowledge: Towards a Post-critical Philosophy.* London: Routledge & Kegan Paul, 1958. (PK)

_____. "Life Transcending Physics and Chemistry." *Chemical and Engineering News* (1967): 54-66. (LT)

_____. *The Tacit Dimension.* Anchor Books. New York: Doubleday & Co., 1967.

_____. "Life's Irreducible Structures." *Science* 160 (1968): 1308-12. (LIS)

Popper, Karl. *Conjectures and Refutations: The Growth of Scientific Knowledge.* New York: Harper & Row, 1968. (CR)

_____. *The Logic of Scientific Discovery.* New York: Harper & Row, 1968.

_____. *The Poverty of Historicism.* London: Routledge & Kegan Paul, 1974.

_____. *Objective Knowledge: An Evolutionary Approach.* Oxford: Clarendon Press, 1979.

Putnam, Hilary. "The Corroboration of Theories." In *Philosophy as It Is,* edited by Ted Honderich and Myles Burnyeat, pp. 349-80. New York: Penguin Books, 1979.

_____. *Reason, Truth and History.* Cambridge: Cambridge University Press, 1981.

Quine, W.V. *Philosophy of Logic.* Foundations of Philosophy Series. Englewood Cliffs: Prentice-Hall, 1970. (PL)

_____. *From a Logical Point of View.* Cambridge: Harvard University Press, 1979. (LPV)

Quinton, Anthony. *The Nature of Things.* London: Routledge & Kegan Paul, 1973.

Radnitzky, Gerard. *Contemporary Schools of Metascience.* Chicago: Henry Regnery Co., 1973.

Ramsey, Ian. *Prospects for Metaphysics.* New York: Greenwood Press, 1969.

Rescher, Nicholas. *Methodological Pragmatism: A Systems-Theoretic Approach to the Theory of Knowledge.* Oxford: Basil Blackwell, 1977.

Rickert, Heinrich. *Der Gegenstand der Erkenntnis Einfuhrung in die transzendental Philosophie.* 3d ed. Tubingen: J.C.B. Mohr Verlag, 1915.

Ricoeur, Paul. *Main Trends in Philosophy.* New York: Holmes & Meier, 1979.

Ridderbos, Herman. *Paul: An Outline of His Theology.* Grand Rapids: Wm. B. Eerdmans, 1975.

Ridderbos, N.H. *Is There a Conflict between Genesis 1 and Natural Science?* Grand Rapids: Wm. B. Eerdmans, 1957.

Rorty, Richard. *Philosophy and the Mirror of Nature.* Princeton: Princeton University Press, 1979. (PM)

_____. *Consequences of Pragmatism.* Minneapolis: University of Minnesota Press, 1982.

Runner, H. Evan. *The Relation of the Bible to Learning.* 5th revised ed. St. Catharines, Ontario: Paideia Press, 1982.

Russell, Bertrand. *The Future of Science with a "Self-portrait" of the Author.* New York: Philosophical Library, 1959.

Russell, C.A., ed. *Science and Religious Belief: A Selection of Recent Historical Studies.* Open University Press, 1973.

Sacks, Sheldon, ed. *On Metaphor.* Chicago: University of Chicago Press, 1979.

Salmon, W. *Logic.* Englewood Cliffs: Prentice-Hall, 1973.

Sandoz, Ellis, ed. *Eric Voegelin's Thought: A Critical Appraisal.* Durham: Duke University Press, 1982.

Scheler, Max. *Man's Place in Nature.* Translated by H. Meyerhoff. New York: Noonday Press, 1962.

Schouls, P.A. *Man in Communication.* Toronto: Association for Reformed Scientific Studies, 1968. (MC)

_____. "Communication, Argumentation, and Presupposition in Philosophy." Institute for Christian Studies, Toronto, 1969. (CAP)

_____. *The Imposition of Method: A Study of Descartes and Locke.* Oxford: Clarendon Press, 1980.

Schuurman, E. *Reflections on the Technological Society.* Toronto: Wedge Publishing Foundation, 1977.

_____. "Technology in a Christian-Philosophical Perspective." Institute for Christian Studies, Toronto, 1979. Mimeographed.

Seerveld, Calvin G. "Modal Aesthetics: Preliminary Questions with an Opening Hypothesis." In *Hearing and Doing*, edited by John Kraay and Anthony Tol, pp. 263-94. Toronto: Wedge Publishing Foundation, 1979.

_____. *Rainbows for the Fallen World.* Toronto: Tuppence Press, 1980. (FW)

Sellars, Wilfred. *Science, Perception and Reality.* London: Routledge & Kegan Paul, 1967.

Shinn, R.L., and Albrecht, P. *Faith and Science in an Unjust World.* 2 vols. Geneva: World Council of Churches, 1980.

Sinnema, Don. "The Uniqueness of the Language of Faith." Institute for Christian Studies, Toronto, 1975. Mimeographed.

Smith, Wilfred Cantwell. *The Meaning and End of Religion.* San Francisco: Harper & Row, 1978.

_____. *Faith and Belief.* Princeton: Princeton University Press, 1979.

Spiegelberg, Herbert. *The Phenomenological Movement.* 2 vols. The Hague: Martinus Nijhoff, 1960.

Stafleu, M.D. "Individualiteit in de fysica." In *Reflexies*, edited by D.M. Bakker, et al., pp. 288-305. Amsterdam: Buyten & Schipperheijn, 1968. (IP)

_____. *Time and Again: A Systematic Analysis of the Foundations of Physics.* Toronto: Wedge Publishing Foundation, 1980. (TA)

_____. *Foundations of Physics: A Christian View.* Forthcoming. (FP)

Stebbing, L.S. *A Modern Introduction to Logic.* London: Methuen & Co., 1961.

Steiner, Rudolf. *Grundlinien einer Erkenntnistheorie der goetheschen Weltanschauung/Wahrheit und Wissenschaft.* Stuttgart: Freies Geistesleben Verlag, 1961.

Stent, Günther S. "That Was the Molecular Biology that Was." *Science* 160 (1968): 390-95.

Stevenson, Leslie. *Seven Theories of Human Nature.* New York: Oxford University Press, 1974.

Stout, Jeffrey. *Flight from Authority.* Notre Dame: Notre Dame University Press, 1981.

Strawson, P.F. *Introduction to Logical Theory*. London: Methuen & Co., 1967.

_____. *Meaning and Truth*. Oxford: Oxford University Press, 1970.

Suppe, F., ed. *The Structure of Scientific Theories*. Chicago: University of Illinois, 1974.

Swartz, N., and Bradley, R. *Possible Worlds: An Introduction to Logic and Its Philosophy*. Oxford: Basil Blackwell, 1979.

Tarski, A. "The Semantic Conception of Truth and the Foundations of Semantics." *Philosophy and Phenomenological Research* (1944): 341-76.

Tol, Anthony. "Counting, Number Concept and Numerosity." In *Hearing and Doing*, edited by John Kraay and Anthony Tol, pp. 295-332. Toronto: Wedge Publishing Foundation, 1979.

Torrence, T.F. *God and Rationality*. London: Oxford University Press, 1971.

_____. *Theological Science*. Oxford: Oxford University Press, 1978.

Toulmin, Stephen E. *The Philosophy of Science*. New York: Harper & Row, 1960. (PS)

_____. *Human Understanding*. Princeton: Princeton University Press, 1972.

_____. "Does the Distinction between Normal and Revolutionary Science Hold Water?" In *Criticism and the Growth of Knowledge*, edited by I. Lakatos and A. Musgrave, pp. 39-47. Cambridge: Cambridge University Press, 1974.

_____. "The Structure of Scientific Theories." In *The Structure of Scientific Theories*, edited by F. Suppe, pp. 600-14. Chicago: University of Illinois, 1974.

_____. *The Uses of Argument*. Cambridge: Cambridge University Press, 1974. (AR)

_____. *Knowing and Acting*. New York: Macmillan, 1976.

_____. *The Return to Cosmology: Post-modern Science and the Theology of Nature*. Berkeley: University of California Press, 1982. (RC)

Vander Goot, Henry, ed. *Life Is Religion: Essays in Honor of H. Evan Runner*. St. Catharines: Paideia Press, 1981.

Van der Hoeven, Johan. "Wetten en feiten. De 'Wijsbegeerte der wetsidee' temidden van hedendaagse bezinning op dit thema." In *Wetenschap, Wijsheid, Filosoferen*. Essays dedicated to Prof. Dr. Ir. Hendrik van Riessen. Edited by P. Blokhuis, et al. Assen: Van Gorcum, 1981.

Van der Vyver, J. "Norms for the International Economic Order: A Response." In *Justice in the International Economic Order*, pp. 254-67. Grand Rapids: Calvin College, 1980.

Van Eikema Hommes, H.J. *History of Legal Philosophy: A Survey*. Translation of *Hoofdlijnen van de geschiedenis der rechtsfilosofie*. Deventer: Kluwer, 1972.

Van Fraasen, B.C. *The Scientific Image.* Oxford: Clarendon Press, 1980.

Verburg, P.A. "Delosis and Clarity." In *Philosophy and Christianity. Philosophical essays dedicated to Prof. Dr. Herman Dooyeweerd.* Amsterdam: North Holland; Kampen: Kok, 1965.

Verhoog, H. *Science and the Social Responsibility of Natural Scientists.* Meppel: Krips Repro., 1980.

Voegelin, Eric. *Anamnesis.* South Bend: University of Notre Dame, 1978.

Wagner, F. *Die Wissenschaft und die gefahrdete Welt.* Munich: Beck'sche Verlagsbuchhandlung, 1969.

Walsh, Brian. "Futurity and Creation: Explorations in the Eschatological Theology of Wolfhart Pannenberg." Unpublished Master of Philosophy thesis, Institute for Christian Studies, Toronto, 1979.

Walsh, Brian, and Chaplin, Jon. "Dooyeweerd's Contribution to a Christian Philosophical Paradigm." *Crux* 19, no. 1 (March 1980).

Walsh, Brian, and Middleton, Richard. *Biblical Vision and Cultural Task: World-view Discernment in a Secular Age.* Downers Grove: Inter-Varsity, 1984.

Walsh, W.H. *Philosophy of History.* New York: Harper & Row, 1968.

Weijland, H. "Introduction." *RES Theological Forum* 9, nos. 3 and 4 (January 1982).

Whitehead, Alfred North. *Wissenschaft und moderne Welt.* Erkenntnis und Leben Series, vol. 3. Zurich: Morgarten Verlag, 1949.

_____. *The Interpretation of Science: Selected Essays.* Edited by A.H. Johnson. The Library of Liberal Arts. New York: Bobbs-Merrill Co., 1961.

_____. *A Philosopher Looks at Science.* New York: Philosophical Library, 1965.

Wittgenstein, Ludwig. *Tractatus Logico-Philosophicus.* Translated by C.K. Ogden. London: Routledge & Kegan Paul, 1978.

Wolfe, David L. *Epistemology: The Justification of Belief.* Downers Grove: InterVarsity Press, 1982.

Wolters, Albert. "Facing the Perplexing History of Philosophy." Institute for Christian Studies, Toronto, 1978.

Wolterstorff, Nicholas P. *On Universals.* Chicago: University of Chicago Press, 1970. (UN)

_____. "God Everlasting." In *God and the Good,* edited by C.J. Orlebeke and L.B. Smedes. Grand Rapids: Wm. B. Eerdmans, 1975. (GE)

_____. *Reason within the Bounds of Religion.* Grand Rapids: Wm. B. Eerdmans, 1976. (RwR)

_____. *Art in Action.* Grand Rapids: Wm. B. Eerdmans, 1980.

_____. "Theory and Commitment: II." In *Justice in the International Economic Order*, pp. 78-98. Grand Rapids: Calvin College, 1980.

_____. *Works and Worlds of Art*. Oxford: Oxford University Press, 1980.

_____. "Once Again, Creator/Creature." *Philosophia Reformata* 46, no. 1 (1981): 60. (CC)

_____. "Thomas Reid on Rationality." In *Rationality in the Calvinian Tradition*, edited by Hendrik Hart, Johan van der Hoeven, and Nicholas Wolterstorff. Lanham: University Press of America, 1983.

_____. *Until Justice and Peace Embrace*. Grand Rapids: Wm. B. Eerdmans, 1983.

Zigterman, K. "Normativity and Analysis." Institute for Christian Studies, Toronto, 1975. Typewritten.

_____. "Dooyeweerd's Theory of Individuality Structures." Unpublished Master of Philosophy thesis, Institute for Christian Studies, Toronto, 1977. (DTS)

Zuidema, S.U. *Communication and Confrontation: A Philosophical Appraisal and Critique of Modern Society and Contemporary Thought*. Assen: Van Gorcum; Kampen: Kok, 1972.

Zuidervaart, Lambert. "Kant's Critique of Beauty and Taste: Explorations into a Philosophical Aesthetics." Unpublished Master of Philosophy thesis, Institute for Christian Studies, Toronto, 1977.

_____. *Refractions: Truth in Adorno's Aesthetic Theory*. Unpublished doctoral dissertation, 1981.